ISBN 978-1-5281-1685-5
PIBN 10906327

1 MONTH OF
FREE
READING

at
www.ForgottenBooks.com

Ward 2—Precinct 1

CITY OF BOSTON

LIST OF RESIDENTS
20 YEARS OF AGE AND OVER

(NON-CITIZENS INDICATED BY ASTERISK)
(FEMALES INDICATED BY DAGGER)

AS OF

JANUARY 1, 1944

THOMAS F. SULLIVAN, *Chairman*
FREDERIC E. DOWLING, *Secretary*
WILLIAM A. MOTLEY, Jr.
FRANCIS B. McKINNEY
EVERETT R. PROUT

Listing Board.

CITY OF BOSTON PRINTING DEPARTMENT

Page.	Letter.	FULL NAME.	Residence, Jan. 1, 1944.	Occupation.	Supposed Age.	Reported Residence, Jan. 1, 1943. Street and Number.

Adams Street

A	Lally Mary E—†	20	matron	70	here
B	Ott Mary A—†	20	housewife	59	49 Monum't av
C	Ott William A	20	U S C G	48	49 "
D	Murphy Bridget E—†	20	housekeeper	76	here
E	Murphy John A	20	laborer	71	"
F	Murphy Mary A—†	20	boxmaker	68	"
G	Murphy Mortimer H	20	retired	74	
H	Murphy Nora J—†	20	housekeeper	63	"
K	Donoghue Bridie—†	26	ropemaker	30	Belmont
L	Hartigan Anna F—†	26	housewife	52	here
M	Hartigan Helen F—†	26	stenographer	30	"
N	Hartigan John E	26	U S A	22	"
O	Hartigan Patrick J	26	janitor	56	"
P	McBrearty Sarah—†	26	waitress	55	18 Prospect
R	Meade David	28	retired	81	here
S	Meade Kathleen B—†	28	stenographer	36	"
T	Meade Marion E—†	28	"	38	"
U	Meade Nina—†	28	housewife	74	"
V	Meade Robert E	28	U S A	34	
W	Meade William L	28	"	32	"
X	Lavery Anna G—†	32	bookbinder	58	"
Y	Morley Anna G—†	32	operator	51	"
Z	Morley Cecelia L—†	32	bookbinder	58	"

2

A	Morley Mary G—†	32	"	59	
B	Morley William H	32	laborer	57	
C	Morley Winifred A—†	32	housekeeper	55	"
D	Neville Bessie V—†	34	housewife	69	"
E	Neville John	34	retired	73	
F	Neville John E	34	letter carrier	29	"
G	McMinn Charles W	34	retired	69	
H	McMinn Charles W, jr	34	stock receiver	30	"
K	McMinn Elizabeth J—†	34	housewife	69	"
L	Carmody Leo	36	laborer	46	
M	English Addie—†	36	housewife	75	"
N	Mahoney Helen V—†	36	typist	40	6 Prospect
O	Mulrooney Thomas F	36	electrician	70	Wilmington
P	Nicolai Eleanor—†	36	housewife	40	here
R	Nicolai Mario	36	printer	47	"
S	Shaw Jeremiah C	36	salesman	67	"

Page.	Letter.	Full Name.	Residence, Jan. 1, 1944.	Occupation.	Supposed Age.	Reported Residence, Jan. 1, 1943. Street and Number.

Adams Street—Continued

	T	Stevens William	36	electrician	48	here
	U	Nelson Frances E—†	38	housewife	47	Maine
	V	Nelson Henry J	38	machinist	48	"
	W	O'Connell Edward	38	seaman	20	"
	X	O'Connell Harold R	38	U S A	24	"
	Y	Murphy Alice—†	38	housewife	66	38 Mt Vernon
	Z	Murphy Cornelius	38	longshoreman	41	38 "
3						
	A	Murphy John	38	"	74	38 '
	B	Murphy John	38		46	38 '

Call Street

	C	Frasca Armando	16	barber	54	here
	D	Frasca Joseph N	16	machinist	28	"
	E	Frasca Josephine—†	16	housewife	51	"
	H*	Higby Alice I—†	20	housekeeper	57	"
	K	McDonald Edward	20	laborer	52	
	L	Duffy Hugh V	20	longshoreman	28	"
	M	Duffy Irene A—†	20	housewife	26	"

Call Street Place

| | N | Tricomi Joseph R | 2 | laborer | 26 | here |
| | O | Tricomi Josephine K—† | 2 | housewife | 28 | " |

4   Chelsea Street

	D	Maglio Louis	12	merchant	58	here
	E	Maglio Nuncia—†	12	housewife	57	"
	F	Gezzio Christina—†	12	"	26	"
	G	Maglio Phyllis—†	12	bookkeeper	31	"
	P	Fiore Stanley	16	merchant	69	"
	R*	Connolly Peter	16	retired	63	
	U	Corcoran William J	18	salesman	45	"
	V	Lutch Samuel	18	cook	45	"
	Z	Lofsted Maurice A	20	electrician	63	11 Harvard
5						
	C	McLaughlin Margaret—†	22	housewife	60	here
	D	McLaughlin William	22	fireman	61	"
	E	Buchannan Ida—†	22	housewife	60	"

Page.	Letter.	FULL NAME.	Residence, Jan. 1, 1944.	Occupation.	Supposed Age.	Reported Residence, Jan. 1, 1943. Street and Number.

Chelsea Street—Continued

	w	Norling Sarah—†	35	cleaner	60	52 Tremont
	x	Cummings James F	35	longshoreman	46	here
	y	Heuston Joseph T	35	"	47	"
	z	Heuston Lillian M—†	35	waitress	20	"
6						
	A	Heuston Mason J	35	longshoreman	23	"
	B	Heuston William F	35	"	53	"
	c	Nadeau Eva M—†	35	housewife	49	"
	D	Nadeau Louis P	35	U S A	20	"
	E	Nadeau Mathias D	35	bartender	50	"
	s	Ahtio Aino—†	44	housewife	62	"
	T	Ahtio Julius	44	machinist	63	"
	U	Haggerty Dorothy—†	44	waitress	33	"
	v	Haggerty William	44	longshoreman	31	"
	w	McDonald Anthony	44	repairman.	47	"
	x	McDonald Margaret—†	44	housewife	42	"
	Y	Giles Frederick	46	pipefitter	61	"
	z	Matte Marie—†	46	welder	22	24 Harvard sq
7						
	A	Cummins John M	46	laborer	35	here
	B	Driscoll John M	46	longshoreman	48	34 Soley
	c	Laidler Henry J	46	"	38	here
	D	Laidler Susan—†	46	housewife	39	"
	F	Beaulieu Horace	48	plumber	40	"
	G	Beaulieu Robert	48	electrician	29	"
	H	Chapman Fannie B—†	48	housewife	59	"
	K	Chapman John E	48	retired	64	"
	L	Dagle Renard	48	electrician	36	Lowell
	M	Lisle George D	48	repairman	41	Mississippi
	N	Lursier Peter	48	laborer	30	Fitchburg
	o	Manard Adolph	48	retired	77	here
	P	Winoski Sadie—†	48	waitress	34	"
8						
	c	Gearin Alice—†	67	housewife	34	"
	D	Gearin Patrick	67	U S N	40	
	E	Langan Annie E—†	67	housewife	56	"
	F	Langan John	67	U S N	21	"
	G	Langan Thomas J	67	longshoreman	56	"
	K	Hess Frank	67	laborer	53	"
	L	Hess Rita—†	67	housewife	43	"
	M	Curran Elizabeth G—†	67	"	34	

Chelsea Street—Continued

N	Fitzgerald David F	67	longshoreman	54	here
O	Fitzgerald Edward	67	electrician	24	"
P	Fitzgerald Eleanor—†	67	at home	21	"
R	Fitzgerald George	67	U S A	25	
S	Fitzgerald Laura—†	67	housewife	48	"
X	Donahue Christopher	81	longshoreman	60	84 Chelsea
Y	Dyer Edward M	81	U S A	23	90 Henley
Z	Dyer Francis	81	"	20	90 "

9

A	*McGee Mary—†	81	housewife	51	90 "
B	Wilson Bernard	81	welder	52	here
C	Feist Florence—†	83	housewife	39	4 Ferrin
D	Avgouleas Kiracos	83	cook	48	here
E	Avgouleas Marie—†	83	manager	43	"
F	Wiltse Evelyn—†	83	housewife	24	"
G	Wiltse Kenneth	83	electrician	25	"
H	Wiltse Ruby—†	83	painter	50	Iowa
K	Marchese Agnes—†	85	housewife	30	here
L	Marchese Charles	85	cutter	32	"
M	Passalaqua John B	85	baker	59	"
N	Passalaqua Lea—†	85	housewife	59	"
O	Hurley Agnes—†	85	laundress	49	"
P	Hurley Henry	85	U S N	22	
R	Crogan Gertrude M—†	87	housewife	61	"
S	Crogan Mary B—†	87	clerk	65	"
T	Greenwood Leo J	87	"	59	
U	Greenwood Margaret L—†	87	housewife	63	"
V	Hardcastle William J	87	retired	66	Revere
W	Mullen Ellen C—†	87	housewife	42	"
X	Farley Catherine A—†	89	"	68	here
Y	Farley Hugh	89	retired	67	"
Z	Duggan Jeremiah	89	policeman	47	"

10

A	Duggan Margaret—†	89	electrician	34	31 Hereford
B	Sullivan Mary S—†	89	housekeeper	62	here
C	O'Neill Frederick J	89	cable splicer	60	"
D	O'Neill Iva A—†	89	at home	51	"
F	Doherty Catherine—† rear	89	waitress	60	"
G	*McLaughlin Mary—† "	89	at home	75	"
H	Early James	91	laborer	50	"
K	McArdle Isabella—†	91	at home	64	"

Page.	Letter.	FULL NAME.	Residence, Jan. 1, 1944.	Occupation.	Supposed Age.	Reported Residence, Jan. 1, 1943. Street and Number.

Chelsea Street—Continued

	L	Leahy Ellen—†	91	stenographer	25	here
	M	Leahy James J	91	retired	59	"
	N	Leahy Nellie—†	91	housewife	60	"
	O	Fehliman Roy	92	electrician	54	60 Magnolia
	P	Foley Helen—†	92	housewife	58	here
	R	*Kehoe John	92	shipper	50	"
	S	Kelly Charles J	92	U S A	32	"
	T	Lufkin Frank	92	pipefitter	52	New Jersey
	U	Sullivan Ellen—†	92	at home	62	104 Main

Chestnut Street

| | Y | Gearin Grace E—† | 9 | housewife | 41 | here |
| | Z | Gearin Mark V | 9 | chauffeur | 43 | " |

11

		Fitzpatrick John	11	longshoreman	57	"
	A	Geswell Mary E—†	11	housewife	53	"
	C	Geswell Walter J	11	clerk	55	
	D	Hogan James F	11	longshoreman	44	"
	E	Landers Michael	11	laborer	56	
	F	McGrath Joseph	11	longshoreman	42	"
	G	O'Brien Jeremiah A	11	chauffeur	47	"
	H	Dwyer Alice B—†	13	housewife	46	"
	K	Dwyer Edward	13	sorter	50	
	L	McSweeney Dennis F	13	towerman	75	"
	N	Mahoney Charles	14	bartender	50	"
	O	Anderson Anna J—†	15	housewife	31	"
	P	Anderson Raymond	15	machinist	34	"
	R	Doran Joseph F	15	retired	74	
	S	Doran Lilly B—†	15	housewife	69	"
	T	Doran Sarah J—†	15	housekeeper	79	"
	U	*Fowler Thomas	16	longshoreman	40	"
	V	Halliwell Joseph	16	engineer	40	"
	W	Kinsley William	16	retired	71	
	X	Mahoney Hannah—†	16	housekeeper	65	"
	Y	McCarthy Anna F—†	16	bookkeeper	35	"
	Z	O'Connor Dennis	16	retired	73	"

12

	A	Parvin Albert	16	machinist	54	"
	B	Crowley William	17	electrician	56	Maine
	C	Madden Anna P—†	17	housewife	34	here

6

·Chestnut Street—Continued

D	Madden Edward H	17	welder	33	here
E	Murphy Luke	17	longshoreman	48	5 Mt Vernon
F	Roach James	17	machinist	55	here
G	Wilton Virginia—†	17	metalworker	25	24 Harvard
H	Booth Edwin	18	carpenter	35	Lawrence
K	Conway James	18	machinist	30	here
L	Hiller Margaret—†	18	housewife	54	"
M	Hiller Martin	18	shipfitter	56	"
N	Monahan Richard H	18	electrician	59	Harborville
O	Curry John	19	engineer	37	Honolulu
P	Dick Annie—†	19	housewife	71	50 Monum'nt sq
R	Dick John	19	clerk	51	50 "
S	Dick William	19	U S N	37	50 "
T	Harrington Margaret—†	19	clerk	37	50 '
U	Harrington Nelson	19	guard	50	50 "
V	Landry Mary—†·	19	assembler	27	Peabody
W	McGonagle Philip	19	shipfitter	38	here
X	Milo Edward	19	rigger	28	New York
Y	*Brunetta Frank	20	retired	75	here
Z	*Brunetta Mary—†	20	housewife	66	"

13

A	Brunetta Frederick	20	laborer	34	
B	Brunetta Salomea—†	20	housewife	30	"
C	Welch Catherine J—†	20	packer	50	
D	Welch Daniel F	20	longshoreman	48	"
E	Welch Marion J—†	20	housewife	42	"
F	Burke Sylvester	21	laborer	43	
G	Cantillon William	21	retired	69	
H	Decker Otis	21	boilermaker	64	"
K	Dolphin Nartin	21	shipfitter	63	Still River
L	Gannon James	21	driller	43	here
M	Giles David	21	laborer	31	468 Mass av
N	Hagan Daniel A	21	shipfitter	57	30 Concord
O	Kent Jeremiah	21	freighthandler	47	here
P	Manning Jennie—†	21	housewife	62	"
R	Manning Timothy	21	horseshoer	64	"
S	McCarthy Hannah—†	21	waitress	45	"
T	O'Malley Michael	21	calker	27	74 Fenway
U	Powers John	21	retired	83	here
V	Shepard Alexander	21	machinist	67	Lexington

Chestnut Street—Continued

w	Tisbert William J	21	coremaker	43	Andover
x	Toland John	21	laborer	56	here

14   City Square

M	Baker Roland H	32	laborer	61	here
N	Beightler William L	32	U S N	25	"
O	Biggs Randall A	32	"	33	"
P	Braley Harry E	32	"	22	N Hampshire
R	Brooks Woodrow J	32	"	21	Rhode Island
S	Brown Daniel W	32	seaman	33	Gallup's Island
T	Connolly Benjamin T	32	U S N	31	here
U	Cox Leon F	32	U S C G	21	Kansas
W	Crateau Ernest	32	U S N	26	Maine
V	Crepeau Raymond J	32	seaman	21	here
X	Depro Robert M	32	U S N	25	"
Y	Dick Harold R	32	"	27	Rhode Island
Z	Dopper Norman F	32	U S C G	23	here

15

A	Dow Gordon A	32	U S N	32	Maryland
B	Ellis Julius E	32	"	24	Maine
C	Ellis Stanley L	32	"	24	481 Summer
E	Falk Daniel S	32		21	Minnesota
D	Falk Louis F	32	"	35	New York
F	Fisher Harold C	32	U S C G	27	here
G	Fratlo Paul J	32	"	21	Maryland
H	Fugett James A	32	"	27	here
K	Garnic Harry	32	"	20	Gloucester
L	Germano Edward A	32	U S N	20	New York
M	Gilbert William M	32	fireman	50	N Hampshire
N	Greeley Joseph F	32	U S C G	31	27 Wood
O	Grenshaw William H	32	U S N	37	here
P	Gunn Raymond	32	machinist	46	"
R	Guthridge Boyce	32	U S C G	20	520 Boylston
S	Hare Robert C	32	seaman	29	New Jersey
T	Hawkes Benjamin	32	"	24	New York
U	Haywood George F	32	U S C G	28	"
V	Heitmeyer Ralph	32	"	30	"
W	Henrickson Stanley	32	U S N	23	here
X	Hodgen Isaac	32	retired	64	"
Y	Hogan James M	32	U S N	43	Rhode Island

8

City Square—Continued

z	Ingraham David	32	U S N	20	Squantum
16						
A	Johnson Gerald W	32	U S C G	27	Gloucester
B	Jolliffe Benton W	32	U S N	21	here
C	Kappel Theodore	32	"	22	"
D	Kelley Joseph J	32	"	51	Leeds
E	Kingsley George G	32		29	New York
F	Krenicki William	32	"	23	New Jersey
G	Leavitt Leon N	32	"	60	N Hampshire
H	Lee Cecil D	32	fireman	40	here
K	Longo Victor J	32	seaman	23	Rhode Island
L	Lundberg Richard M	32	U S N	23	California
M	Mackeit Melvin F	32	U S C G	28	Maryland
N	Massar Joseph	32	"	22	here
O	McGerr Robert J	32	U S N	21	Illinois
P	McGovern Burton J	32	"	32	Holyoke
R	McGrath Donald M	32	U S C G	22	Gloucester
S	McGuigan James A	32	"	22	New Jersey
T	Merrill George A	32	U S N	39	here
U	Mitchell Paul C	32	"	30	New York
V	Norford Nelson K	32	"	25	here
W	O'Neill Thomas J	32	U S C G	22	New York
X	O'Toole Owen M	32	U S N	24	here
Y	Phipps Lawrence	32	"	38	Florida
Z	Potuchek William	32	seaman	31	New York
17						
A	Powers Ralph E	32	U S N	52	here
B	Price Prince A	32	U S C G	25	Pennsylvania
C	Raffe Erwin R	32	U S N	24	here
D	Robbins Arthur N	32	"	30	Taunton
E	Roche Harold T	32	"	23	Illinois
F	Rowe David M	32	"	22	here
G	Schubert William G	32	U S C G	23	New York
H	Smith Kenneth	32	U S N	35	Virginia
K	Stackowicz Frank	32	seaman	21	New York
M	Stec Tadeusz	32	"	21	"
L	Stephenson George	32	U S N	49	here
N	Tannock Raymond	32	"	23	Rhode Island
O	Thornton John P	32	"	20	271 Dartmouth
P	Tucker F Maynard	32	U S A	23	here
R	Turner George W	32	U S C G	45	Florida

City Square—Continued

	Letter	Full Name	Res.	Occupation	Age	Reported Residence
	s	Turner John E	32	U S N	23	Ohio
	t	Vicare Michael J	32	"	39	Woods Hole
	u	Williams Dock J	32	"	20	Rhode Island
	v	Wilson William A	32		63	Maine
	w	Winchell James C	32		28	New York
	x	Worobeskey Meyer	32		26	here

Common Street

	Letter	Full Name	Res.	Occupation	Age	Reported Residence
	z	Jennett John J	1	watchman	50	here
18						
	a	Jennett Mary A—†	1	housekeeper	48	"
	b	Foley Alice G—†	2	housewife	36	"
	c	Foley Jeremiah F	2	longshoreman	41	"
	d	McLaughlin Daniel A	2	clerk	54	
	e	McLaughlin James E	2	"	52	
	g	McLaughlin Katherine—†	10	supervisor	39	"
	k	Bradley Bridget E—†	12	housekeeper	79	26 Cross
	l	Fitzpatrick Catherine T—†	12	"	73	here
	m	Morrissey Annie M—†	14	shipper	29	42 Mt Vernon
	n	Morrissey Mary—†	14	housekeeper	65	42 "
	o	Morrissey Mary F—†	14	attendant	31	42 "
	p	Bunker Hercules R	14	ropemaker	39	461 Main
	r	Bunker James	14	U S N	37	461 "
	s	Bunker John	14	laborer	27	461 "
	t	Obery Pimelia—†	14	housekeeper	66	461 "
	u	Grant Philip A	16	clerk	44	here
	v	Logue Charles	16	retired	76	"
	w	Logue Helen C—†	16	teacher	36	"
	x	Logue Patrick J	16	drawtender	43	"
	y	Logue Sarah M—†	16	teacher	37	"
	z	Cahill James J	22	ropemaker	56	"
19						
	a	Cahill Julia A—†	22	housewife	56	"
	b	Cahill Katherine F—†	22	typist	21	
	c	Lee Yee	26	laundryworker	63	"
	d	Cure Henry	27	U S N	50	
	e	Cure Mary C—†	27	housewife	49	"
	f	Nitzsche Albert O	27	metalworker	46	"
	g	Nitzsche Vernetta G—†	27	housewife	51	"
	h	Wagner Marion F—†	27	saleswoman	45	Pennsylvania
	k	Brisson Agnes M—†	27	nurse	22	here

Common Street—Continued

	L	Brisson Victoria—†	27	housewife	52	here
	M	Brisson William A	27	oiler	51	"

Ellwood Street

	N	Cooke Albert H	5	U S N	40	here
	O	Cooke Marion F—†	5	housewife	35	"
	P	Passalaqua Beatrice—†	5	"	46	"
	R	Passalaqua John	5	barber	53	
	S	Passalaqua Joseph	5	longshoreman	25	"
	T	Passalaqua Michael	5	clerk	28	
	U	Fleming Alice V—†	5	housewife	23	"
	V	Fleming John F	5	U S A	25	
	W	Peterson John I	5	stevedore	52	"
	X	Fisher Catherine M—†	rear 6	inspector	22	"
	Y	Fisher Charles C	" 6	laborer	33	
	Z	Fisher Francis E	" 6	U S A	32	

20

	A	Fisher Margaret A—†	" 6	housewife	59	"
	B	Fisher Peter J	" 6	laborer	35	
	C	Fisher William H	" 6	U S A	26	"
	D	Buchino Frank X	7	laborer	31	10 McNulty ct
	E	Buchino Mabel—†	7	housewife	28	10 "
	F	Conroy Edward F	7	longshoreman	30	here
	G	Conroy Mary—†	7	housewife	24	"
	H	Brennan Dorothy A—†	7	"	36	"
	K	Brennan Robert G	7	stevedore	31	"
	L	*Curran Edmund	11	retired	70	
	M	Curran Edward C	11	U S N	22	
	N	Curran Mary—†	11	housewife	60	"
	O	Curran Mary—†	11	welder	20	"
	P	Garceau Eleanor M—†	11	housewife	52	41 Baldwin
	R	Garceau John	11	laborer	57	41 "
	S	Sullivan Dennis J	11	fireman	56	here
	T	Sullivan Margaret T—†	11	housewife	49	"
	U	Clifford Catherine M—†	11	"	30	"
	V	Clifford Charles A	11	longshoreman	48	"
	W	Hingston Frank R	11	U S A	20	
	X	Hingston Jennie C—†	11	housewife	48	"
	Y	Hingston William J	11	U S A	22	"
	Z	Goodwin Inez M—†	11	housewife	42	14 Franklin

21

Ellwood Street—Continued

A	Goodwin Ralph A	11	tilesetter	47	14 Franklin
B	O'Connor James E	17	rigger	34	here
C	FitzGibbons Edna M—†	17	housewife	37	17 Mt Vernon
D	FitzGibbons William J	17	clerk	37	17 "
E	Simpson Eleanor P—†	19	housewife	31	here
F	Simpson Robert C	19	chauffeur	41	"
G	Peckham John L	20	painter	50	128 Glenville av
H	Peckham Mary C—†	20	housewife	43	128 "
L	Dolan Margaret G—†	20	at home	67	here
M	Keeley Mary C—†	20	"	70	"

Foss Street

N	Ysebart Lillian L—†	2	housewife	45	here
O	Ysebart Louis	2	laborer	47	"
P	*Roche Mary E—†	2	housewife	46	99 Henley
R	*Roche William E	2	longshoreman	52	99 "

Gray Street

Z	O'Connor Agnes M—†	17	at home	21	here

22

A	O'Connor Patrick H	17	foreman	49	"

Harvard Place

D	Boni Henry	1	laborer	35	here
E	Burns Mary—†	1	housewife	40	11 Monum'nt av
F	Danielson Axel	1	machinist	65	here
G	Doherty John C	1	janitor	38	"
H	Donahue Arthur	1	retired	70	"
K	Drohan Ralph	1	laborer	40	Lawrence
L	Greenfield Mary—†	1	at home	80	here
M	Patton Thomas	1	retired	65	N Hampshire
N	Robertson Raymond J	1	mechanic	50	Worcester
O	Snodgrass Robert	1	laborer	50	here
P	Anctil Charlotte—†	2	housewife	39	18 Harvard
R	Anctil Odilon	2	plumber	40	18 "
S	Labbe Aime	2	welder	31	N Hampshire
T	Murphy Alvina—†	2	"	34	14 Monum'nt sq

Harvard Place—Continued

u	Murphy Henry	2	electrician	45	14 Monum'nt sq
v	Pickford Pauline—†	2	clerk	22	N Hampshire
w	Stearns Marion—†	2	saleswoman	20	18 Harvard
x	Allen Leo	3	chauffeur	40	36 "
y	Devlin Margaret—†	3	clerk	36	Ireland
z	Devlin Sarah R—†	3	housewife	65	here

23

a	Mansfield George	3	clerk	64	"
b	McKinnon Hugh	3	"	40	16 Devens
c	Morley John	3	loftsman	52	here
d	Riley Henry	3	retired	70	"
e	Rush John	3	laborer	52	"
f	Shredd John	3	chauffeur	45	8 Wash'n
g	Welden Charles	3	laborer	49	here
h	Adato Estalato	4	"	45	Ayer
k	Howard Robert	4	metalworker	51	N Hampshire
l	Hutchinson Walter	4	tinworker	62	"
m	Kent Henry W	4	chipper	48	403 Main
n	Mailhot Zado	4	shipfitter	46	18 Harvard
o	McDevitt Andrew	4	"	44	here
p	McDevitt Catherine—†	4	housewife	43	"
r	McGoldrick Thomas	4	mechanic	52	"

Harvard Square

s	Delahunt Priscilla—†	25	housewife	29	here
t	Mathison William M	25	carpenter	47	"
u	Cunningham James J	27	clerk	26	"
v	McGinty Francis E	27	electrician	29	"
w	McGinty Mary M—†	27	housewife	29	"

Harvard Street

x	Brausard Emil A—†	7	burner	21	Chicopee Falls
y	Coughlin Dennis L	7	drawtender	59	32 City sq
z	Enos Catherine—†	7	housewife	62	here

24

a	Enos Manuel J	7	clerk	57	
b	Falvey Arthur T	7	printer	48	"
c	Farren Bernard J	7	clerk	51	"
d	Flanagan Thomas	7	retired	58	8 Wash'n

Page.	Letter.	FULL NAME.	Residence, Jan. 1, 1944.	Occupation.	Supposed Age.	Reported Residence, Jan. 1, 1943. Street and Number.

Harvard Street—Continued

	E	Kordes John P	7	longshoreman	49	here
	G	McDermott John J	7	retired	65	"
	H	*Novack Joseph	7	laborer	47	Everett
	F	Redford William E	7	millwright	61	"
	K	Donovan David A	9	molder	48	here
	L	Ebsary Katherine V—†	9	housewife	51	"
	M	Ebsary Richard E	9	carpenter	62	"
	N	Gallant Prosper J	9	"	65	
	O	McNulty Sarah—†	9	at home	86	"
	P	Nauha Sanfrid L	9	welder	48	Weymouth
	R	Carney Rose—†	11	housewife	48	here
	S	Fagen Leo	11	carpenter	30	"
	T	Foley Patrick	11	operator	64	81 Melville av
	U	Gould William	11	mechanic	70	N Hampshire
	V	Lemeaux William	11	actor	53	here
	W	Reed Mary E—†	11	housewife	22	Rhode Island
	X	Reed Walter	11	U S N	26	"
	Y	Regan Peter L	11	laborer	21	Oak Bluffs
	Z	Rice Benjamin	11	mechanic	35	here

25

	A	Rice John S	11	policeman	49	"
	B	Walker Louis R	11	clerk	25	Pennsylvania
	C	Workman Harry M	11	U S N	59	N Hampshire
	D	Lynch Catherine—†	13	housewife	43	here
	E	Lynch James	13	bartender	45	"
	F	Lynch Robert	13	U S A	22	"
	G	McNamara Annie—†	13	housewife	63	"
	H	McNamara Mary—†	13	clerk	32	
	K	Harkins Annie—†	13	housewife	63	"
	L	Harkins Annie—†	13	bookkeeper	35	"
	M	Harkins Catherine—†	13	collector	26	"
	N	Harkins Margaret—†	13	designer	23	"
	O	Harkins William	13	U S A	22	"
	P	Hurley Mary—†	13	housewife	32	Medford
	R	Hurley Michael	13	U S N	36	"
	S	McElroy Frank	13	mechanic	32	here
	T	Starrett John	13	laborer	28	"
	U	Gill Hannah—†	15	housewife	25	"
	V	Gill John	15	chauffeur	48	"
	W	Doherty Ellen—†	15	housewife	65	"
	X	Doherty William	15	laborer	62	

14

Page.	Letter.	FULL NAME.	Residence, Jan. 1, 1944.	Occupation.	Supposed Age.	Reported Residence, Jan. 1, 1943. Street and Number.

Harvard Street—Continued

Y	Harkins James	15	laborer	49	15 Cordis
Z	Harkins Susan—†	15	housewife	48	15 "
26						
A	Klemin Emil	16	mechanic	38	New York
B	Lehan Julia—†	16	housewife	49	here
C	Litchfield Eugene	16	clerk	32	"
D	Litchfield Nora—†	16	housewife	30	"
E	McGuire Lloyd	16	electrician	48	"
F	Steffens Raymond	16	"	36	
G	Tetlow Allen	16	U S N	65	
H	Tetlow Winnie—†	16	housewife	46	"
K	Wrathall Donald	16	machinist	36	"
L	Bautista Roberta—†	17	housewife	21	"
M	Bautista Tetam	17	U S N	31	"
N	Eisner Virginia—†	17	defense wkr	33	2 Wash'n
O	Foster Catherine M—†	17	housewife	64	2 "
P	Goddard Hubert E	17	carpenter	43	here
R	Tackaberry Robert	17	retired	60	8 Wash'n
S	Brown Charles L	18	metalworker	51	Somerville
T	Mills Virginia—†	18	clerk	22	Tennessee
U	Sanborn Cornelius R	18	carpenter	58	N Hampshire
V	Sanborn Lillian M—†	18	housewife	44	"
W	Stapleton Dorothy—†	18	stitcher	30	Tennessee
X	McColgan Edward	19	U S A	28	here
Y	McColgan Frances—†	19	teacher	41	"
Z	McColgan George	19	retired	75	"
27						
A	McColgan Margaret M—†	19	secretary	38	"
B	McColgan Mary—†	19	housewife	64	"
C	Hunt Mary—†	19	nurse	31	
D	Gargan John	19	engineer	57	"
E	Gargan Nora—†	19	housewife	55	"
F	Altoulla Frank	20	clerk	51	Chelsea
G	Amato Joseph	20	mechanic	25	New York
H	Griffin John	20	laborer	40	here
K	Griffin Rose—†	20	housekeeper	76	"
L	Heath Clyde S	20	carpenter	54	Vermont
M	Hinds Jerome J	20	U S N	35	Quincy
N	Spidel Emily—†	20	housewife	35	New York
O	Dignan Anna—†	21	"	52	here
P	Gaton John	21	laborer	40	98 Wash'n

Page.	Letter.	FULL NAME.	Residence, Jan. 1, 1944.	Occupation.	Supposed Age.	Reported Residence, Jan. 1, 1943. Street and Number.

Harvard Street—Continued

R	Kanolos George	21	chef	58	Watertown
S	Anderson Harry	22	mechanic	52	N Hampshire
T	Corrigan Jeremiah	22	laborer	42	here
U	Covent Thomas	22	chauffeur	24	Somerville
V	Curran Laurence	22	retired	76	here
W	Palmer John B	22	chauffeur	53	N Hampshire
X	Doherty Daniel J	23	laborer	38	here
Y	Doherty Mary—†	23	housewife	34	"
Z	Doherty Sarah—†	23	"	65	"
	28				
A	O'Connell Ellen—†	23	merchant	34	"
B	O'Connell Thomas	23	U S N	30	
C	Brennan Edward J	23	U S A	23	
D	Brennan Mary—†	23	housewife	52	"
E	Brennan Mary T—†	23	cashier	26	
F	Brennan Philip	23	laborer	53	"
G	Drews Anna A—†	24	housewife	43	5 Monument
H	Enderline Ruth—†	24	machinist	24	Malden
K	Frankland Owen J	24	rigger	59	18 Chestnut
L	Halpin Frank A	24	electrician	69	Chelsea
M	Marchant Albert J	24	mechanic	59	Taunton
N	Michaud Alphonse E	24	metalworker	57	N Hampshire
O	Muenchen Alice—†	24	housewife	24	Illinois
P	Muenchen Henry	24	U S N	31	"
R	Osborne Faust R	24	"	36	Panama
S	Osborne Frank	24	"	36	"
T	Osborne Julia C—†	24	housewife	33	California
U	Osborne Rita—†	24	"	32	"
V	LaCascia Calogero	28	longshoreman	58	here
W	LaCascia Peter	28	mechanic	30	"
X	LaCascia Philip	28	"	22	"
Y	LaCascia Rosaly—†	28	housewife	50	"
Z	Ferrante Giovanni	28	freighthandler	54	"
	29				
A	Ferrante Joseph	28	mechanic	20	"
B	LaCascia Mary A—†	28	at home	93	"
C	Lombardo John	28	laborer	60	
D	Moro Anthony	28	carpenter	43	"
E	Moro Millie—†	28	dressmaker	39	"
F	Lane Bernard J	30	bookkeeper	58	"
G	Lane Mary E—†	30	housekeeper	69	"

Harvard Street—Continued

H	Lane Sarah B—†	30	at home	60	here
K	Connolly Michael	32	laborer	54	"
L	Doherty Patrick	32	fireman	60	"
	Doyle John J	32	boilermaker	39	"
	Grant Daniel	32	chauffeur	44	"
M	Kelley Ellen—†	32	housewife	61	"
R	Kirby John	32	U S N	36	Alabama
O	Morceau Catherine J—†	32	clerk	37	here
S	Morceau Patrick	32	fireman	42	"

Henley Street

T	Foster Doris H—†	1	secretary	22	here
U	Foster George A	1	salesman	49	"
V	Foster Helena M—†	1	housewife	49	"
X	Mistretta Josephine—†	27	"	57	
Y	Mistretta Rose—†	27	clerk	28	
	30				
C	Baudanza Frances—†	37	housewife	29	"
D	Baudanza Joseph	37	laborer	28	"
E	Lombardo Anthony	37	pipebender	56	"
F	Lombardo Antoinette—†	37	housewife	47	"
G	Lombardo Michael	37	U S N	22	
H	Guinasso Clara D—†	39	housewife	24	"
K	Guinasso William L	39	salesman	34	"
L	Gustaferro Anna—†	39	housewife	30	"
M	Gustaferro Samuel	39	shoeworker	33	"
N	Leyman Isabelle—†	39	housekeeper	53	"
O	Sullivan Alba—†	39	housewife	41	"
P	Mirisola Eleanor—†	44	packer	24	"
R	Mirisola John	44	carpenter	28	"
S	Mirisola Salvatore	44	retired	62	
T	*Mirisola Salvatrice—†	44	housewife	59	"
U	Weber Mary—†	44	operator	40	621 Tremont
V	Kelleher Maud A—†	44	cook	60	here
W	Judge Harriet W—†	44	housekeeper	57	"
X	Cerra Anthony	48	laborer	58	"
Y	*Cerra Frances—†	48	housewife	48	"
Z	Cerra Salvatore	48	U S A	24	
	31				
C	Shine Ellen—†	60	housewife	59	"

2—1

Henley Street—Continued

D	Shine James	60	retired	68	here
E	Conley Edward J	60	lawyer	37	"
F	Conley Nora—†	60	housekeeper	75	"
G	Harrington Mary—†	60	"	68	"
H	Reardon Mary—†	60	clerk	60	
K	Hamano Kinzo	62	U S A	25	
L	*Hamano Yoneno—†	62	housewife	55	"
M	*Rikitake Gengo	62	cook	52	
N	Yamasaki Tokitchi	62	retired	64	
O	Holland Rita—†	68	housewife	37	"
P	Maher John J	68	retired	68	"
S	Bacigalupo Thomas	70	laborer	65	"
T	Doherty Julia J—†	70	housewife	59	"
U	Doherty Raymond E	70	laborer	22	
V	Harris Myles E	70	U S A	24	
W	McInnis Daniel	70	spotter	36	
X	McInnis Mary—†	70	housewife	29	"

32

C	Brennan John J	82	seaman	24	
D	Brennan Joseph F	82	U S A	29	
E	Brennan Josephine E—†.	82	housewife	52	"
F	Brennan Robert F	82	retired	52	
G	Brennan Thomas F	82	U S A	21	
M	Doherty Catherine—†	86	housewife	44	"
N	Doherty Joseph '	86	U S N	56	
O	Murphy Catherine—†	86	housekeeper	66	"
P	Murphy Johanna—†	86	clerk	27	"
R	Murphy Walter	86	machinist	30	"
S	Costa Carmelo	88	welder	53	
T	Costa Peter N	88	U S A	21	
U	Costa Rose—†	88	housewife	44	"
V	Landry Abraham	88	painter	51	
W	Landry Bertha—†	88	housewife	43	"
X	Fisher Christopher J	88A	cleanser	30	23 Austin
Y	Fisher Mary H—†	88A	housewife	29	23 "
Z	McLaughlin Annie L—†	89	housekeeper	56	here

33

A	McLaughlin Frederick J	89	laborer	49	
B	McLaughlin Mary L—†	89	housewife	52	"
C	McLaughlin William O	89	laborer	58	
E	Gearin Francis	89	"	35	"

Henley Street—Continued

F	Hughes Mary—†	89	housewife	37	here
G	Hughes Stephen	89	electrician	40	"
H	Juliano Mary H—†	90	housekeeper	53	51 Lawrence
L	Johnson Frederick A	90A	laborer	30	here
M	Johnson Mary F—†	90A	housewife	26	"
P	Trainor Archibald	91	boilermaker	27	"
R	Trainor Martha—†	91	housekeeper	22	"
S	Slattery Ellen M—†	93	housewife	44	"
T	Slattery James	93	U S N	21	
U	*Slattery John J	93	operator	59	"
V	Slattery Mary C—†	93	boxmaker	26	"
W	Sherman Beatrice—†	93	housewife	36	N Adams
X	Sherman Harry	93	rigger	43	"
Y	Connor Marietta—†	93	packer	44	here
Z	Corcoran Anna M—†	93	clerk	20	"
	34				
A	Corcoran Catherine—†	93	housewife	64	"
B	Corcoran Patrick	93	retired	70	

Hudson Street

E	Brucciani Joseph	7	restaurateur	43	99 Bartlett
D	Grant Harry L	7	retired	56	here
F	Schultheis Florence K—†	8	housekeeper	33	Florida
G	Schultheis William	8	guard	48	"
K	Dellarocco Joseph	11	dishwasher	45	here
L	Dellarocco Massimino	11	retired	68	"
M	Maguire James P	11	laborer	31	22 Union
N	Maguire Josephine G—†	11	at home	25	22 "
O	Moore Patrick	11	longshoreman	55	here
P	Colantuoni Alfred	11	porter	31	"
R	Colantuoni Charles	11	clerk	37	"
S	Colantuoni Grace—†	11	at home	39	"
T	Colantuoni Mary—†	11	"	·64	
U	Colantuoni Sabino	11	laborer	66	"
X	Fournier Frank	14	"	35	Lowell
Y	Higgins John J	14	clerk	38	80 Warren
Z	Higgins Mary F—†	14	at home	38	80 "
	35				
B	Padanon Clara—†	15	"	36	32 Chestnut
C	Padanon Flaviano	15	U S N	43	32 "

Page.	Letter.	FULL NAME.	Residence, Jan. 1, 1944.	Occupation.	Supposed Age.	Reported Residence, Jan. 1, 1943. Street and Number.

Hudson Street—Continued

E	Algeri Antonio	15	laborer	45	44 Chestnut
G	Bouche Pearl M—†	18	at home	22	here
H	Bouche William	18	chauffeur	29	"

Jenner Street

L	Weddle Doris—†	4	housewife	35	24 Wash'n
N	Burokas Ruth—†	4	"	34	20 Park
O	Burokas William J	4	U S N	47	20 "
R	Andrews Etta—†	4	housewife	68	24 Wash'n
S	Andrews Walter W	4	laborer	37	24 "
T	White Dorothy E—†	4	housekeeper	23	here
U	White Jennie—†	4	at home	68	"

Joiner Street

X	Green Cyril M	6	laborer	45	Danvers
Y	Wilkinson James	6	laundry wkr	52	here
Z	Flynn Caroline E—†	6	tel instructor	46	"
	36				
A	Crawford John W	7	defense wkr	47	"
B	Johnson Joseph S	7	retired	75	
C	Johnson Lena M—†	7	housekeeper	61	"
D	Little Mark	7	defense wkr	59	"
E	Manning Timothy B	7	longshoreman	33	"
F	Snow William C	7	retired	78	
G	*Devanser Anthony	9	"	58	
H	Sheehan Patrick J	9	"	73	"
K	Kocincki Emily—†	9	at home	33	11 Park
L	O'Keefe Catherine T—†	11	housewife	58	here
M	O'Keefe John T	11	longshoreman	30	"
N	Langford Horace W	11	machinist	35	"
O	Langford Josephine—†	11	defense wkr	31	"
P	Sullivan Mary A—†	22	at home	68	"
R	DeArmon Francis H	22	U S N	50	
S	DeArmon Mary C—†	22	at home	46	"
T	Walsh Emma G—†	24	"	45	
U	Walsh Mary F—†	24	housewife	47	"
V	Closson Jennie—†	24	waitress	52	"
W	McCarron Rose A—†	24	at home	67	"
X	*McKenney Charles	24	retired	68	

20

Joiner Street—Continued

z	*Bergeron Elmira—†	26	millhand	72	here
	37				
A	Stage Stella I—†	26	waitress	52	"
B	Adamczyk Grace L—†	26	"	40	Brookline
C	Irgens Anna M—†	26	at home	59	here
D	Irgens Laurence W	26	merchant	59	"
E	*Currie Jennie—†	28	waitress	68	"
F	Barton Ellen C—†	28	at home	63	"
G	*Barton Hamilton T	28	longshoreman	62	"
H	Comeau Andrew J	28	U S A	22	
K	Comeau Joseph A	28	U S N	45	
L	Comeau Mary—†·	28	housewife	46	"
M	Williams William C	30	retired	75	"
N	Chace Albert H	30	fireman	68	
O	Chace Mary A—†	30	housewife	65	"
P	Goldthwaite Minnie—†	30	at home	71	"
R	Dziezic Anthony F	32	cook	46	
S	*Perrotte Antonetta—†	32	at home	54	"
T	Perrotte Concetta—†	32	stitcher	29	"
U	Perrotte Eleanor—†	32	houseworker	23	"
V	Perrotte Jeffrey	32	builder	27	
W	*Perrotte Raphael	32	laborer	64	
X	Harkins Mary A—†	37	housewife	63	"
Y	Rattigan Annie—† ·	37	"	65	
Z	Rattigan Patrick	37	retired	68	
	38				
A	*Rattigan Annie T—†	39	at home	72	"
B	*Rattigan Julia—†	39	"	70	"
C	Sexen John	39	houseman	56	"
D	Sexen Mary—†	39	domestic	60	"

Main Street

F	Donnini Mary C—†	20	housekeeper	63	here
G	Donnini Vincent	20	pharmacist	68	"
H	Donnini Vincent R	20	cigarmaker	61	"
K	DeSilva Joseph	20	U S A	28	
L	DeSilva Joseph P	20	retired	78	
M	DeSilva Mary R—†	20	housewife	65	"
N	Demming Cora—†	22	matron	38	44 Main
O	Feeney John	22	longshoreman	33	14 Union

Main Street—Continued

P	Feeney Peter	22	longshoreman	35	14 Union
R	Greatorex Mary—†	22	housewife	37	here
S	Greatorex Robert	22	riveter	43	"
T	Greatorex Thomas E	22	chauffeur	38	"
U	McDermott John	22	longshoreman	65	7 Harvard
V	Medice Harriet—†	22	hostess	28	Georgia

39

E	Scribner Marie A—†	32	housewife	33	here
F	Scribner William	32	electrician	33	"
G	*Chin Edwin	32	laundryman	40	"
H	Chin Mary—†	32	housewife	36	"
P	Hughes Joseph F	47	sole sorter	52	"
R	Hughes Mary L—†	47	housewife	93	"
S	Nelson Mary H—†	47	"	58	
T	Stone Jane G—†	47	physician	70	"
W	Donovan John R	51	U S N	24	"
X	Donovan Lillian A—†	51	at home	46	"
Y	Donovan Lillian R—†	51	stenographer	21	"
Z	Donovan Peter A	51	engineer	49	"

40

A	Donovan Peter A, jr	51	U S A	27	"
B	Harrington Marcella M—†	51	at home	24	"
C	O'Neil James	51	chauffeur	34	"
D	O'Neil Margaret—†	51	housewife	65	"
E	O'Neil William J	51	repairman	64	"

Monument Avenue

V	McFeeley Anna—†	7	at home	26	here
W	McFeeley Beatrice —†	7	housewife	52	"
X	McFeeley John P	7	U S A	30	"
Y	McFeeley Patrick	7	laborer	53	
Z	McGuire Ellen—†	7	housewife	33	"

41

A	McGuire John	7	laborer	36	"
B	Green Annie—†	7	housewife	49	"
C	Green Freda C—†	7	at home	21	"
D	Green George	7	merchant	48	"
E	Doherty Katherine—†	9	clerk	38	
F	Warren Emma F—†	9	at home	84	"
G	Drinkwater Harriet M—†	9	stenographer	69	"

Monument Avenue—Continued

H	Vairy Mary—†	11	candymaker	39	here
K	Burke Jennie—†	11	housekeeper	55	"
L	Burke John	11	chauffeur	52	"
M	Seward Marie—†	11	housewife	23	30 Pearl
N	Seward William F	11	clerk	28	16 Lincoln

Park Street

P	Framzosa Frank R	11	tailor	21	16 Call
R	Framzosa Grace—†	11	housewife	46	16 "
S	Framzosa Michael	11	barber	66	16 "
T	Moccia Felix A	11	U S N	27	44 Henley
U	Moccia Josephine—†	11	housewife	29	44 "
V	Cerra Antoinette—†	11	tailor	22	48 "
W	Cerra Frank W	11	chauffeur	21	48 "
X	Hurlihy Mary—†	13	cleaner	48	here
Y	Alves Catherine—†	13	housekeeper	65	"
Z	Fitzpatrick Mary H—†	13	housewife	45	"
	42				
B	Doak Mary M—†	14A	"	35	488 Main
C	Doak Vernon M	14A	repairman	45	23 Lincoln
D	Page Mary T—†	14A	inspector	38	Cambridge
E	Cain Catherine L—†	14A	housewife	24	Pennsylvania
F	Cain James E	14A	U S N	42	"
G	Sullivan Andrew F	14A	laborer	48	here
H	Sullivan Nora F—†	14A	housewife	50	"
M	Conlan Margaret—†	16A	housekeeper	65	25 Lincoln
N	Wilson Charles F	16A	laborer	45	here
O	Wilson Lillian C—†	16A	housewife	35	"
P	Fish Margaret—†	16A	housekeeper	52	"
S	McDonald Sarah J—†	18A	"	73	"
T	Martin John J	18A	operator	53	"
U	Martin John T	18A	electrician	21	"
V	Martin Mary E—†	18A	housewife	47	"
W	Doherty Catherine—†	18A	factoryhand	45	"
X	Doherty James E	18A	laborer	25	
Y	Foley Margaret—†	18A	welder	34	
	43				
A	Johnson Earl L	19	machinist	38	"
B	McVean William J	19	retired	67	"
C	Middleton George	19	driller	47	"

Park Street—Continued

D	Murphy Catherine C—†	19	housekeeper	56	here
E	Murphy Josephine E—†	19	saleswoman	54	"
F	McCreevan Esther L—†	20	housewife	34	"
G	Hickman Cynthia T—†	20	"	20	
H	Lilienthal Evelyn F—†	20	waitress	29	"
K	Lilienthal Lester F	20	U S A	27	
L	Lilienthal Mary E—†	20	clerk	52	
M	Foley Catherine M—†	20	finisher	43	"
N	Foley John J	20	laborer	38	
P	Gallagher Thomas J	22	steamfitter	51	"
R	Kinney Cornelius F	22	laborer	43	
S	Kinney James J	22	painter	37	
T	Kinney John J	22	laborer	35	
U	Kinney Mary M—†	22	housewife	73	"
W	Canney Daniel	23	watchman	57	"
X	Corcoran Morris	23	retired	90	
Y	Hoffman Adolph	23	tinsmith	60	"
Z	McLaughlin Catherine—†	23	housekeeper	62	"
	44				
A	Piper Lee	23	shipfitter	57	"
B	Piper Margaret—†	23	housewife	58	"
E	LaMonica Josephine—†	35	"	50	
F	LaMonica Stephen	35	watchman	55	"
G	LaMonica Grace—†	35	packer	24	
H	LaMonica Josephine—†	35	factoryhand	21	"
L	*Doenges Elli—†	40	housewife	36	"
M	Doenges Gerhard	40	baker	39	
N	Eugley Arthur L	40	laborer	41	
O	Fitzgerald Henry N	40	lineman	57	"
P	Peroni Joseph	40	plumber	35	New York
R	Lyons John	40	clerk	45	Lowell
U	McLaughlin Mary A—†	44	housewife	85	here
V	McLaughlin William J	44	clerk	58	"
X	Buttimer Catherine—†	44A	housekeeper	35	"
Y	Buttimer Mary J—†	44A	housewife	65	"
Z	Buttimer Maurice F	44A	laborer	63	"
	45				
	Brown John	44A	retired	71	
	Brown Julia T—†	44A	housewife	79	"
	Ferrera John	47	machinist	57	"
	Ferrera Rose—†	47	housewife	55	"

Park Street—Continued

	Letter	Full Name	Res.	Occupation	Age	Reported Residence
	G	McLaughlin Agnes—†	48	housewife	63	here
	H	McLaughlin John F	48	blacksmith	39	"
	K	McLaughlin Neil	48	retired	68	"
	M	Arnold Estelle V—†	49	housekeeper	53	"
	N	Perry Ethel V—†	49	waitress	41	"
	P	Argenzio Theresa—†	51	factoryhand	42	"
	R	Brock Edward	51	clerk	40	
	S	Dillon John O	51	drawtender	57	"
	T	Dillon Mary E—†	51	examiner	50	"
	U	Malone John D	52	retired	70	
	V	Kennedy Mary—†	52	housekeeper	60	"
	W	Madden Winifred F—† rear	52	"	70	"
	X	Bowdren Frances J—† "	52	"	56	
	Y	Bowdren James J "	52	clerk	59	"
	Z	Mistretta Catherine—†	55	housewife	21	6A Atherton
46						
	A	Mistretta Marie M—†	55	"	32	here
	Γ	Mistretta Philip	55	electrician	26	27 Henley
	C	Alessi Albert M	55	U S A	35	here
	D	Lane Rose L—†	55	housekeeper	62	Somerville
	E	Riley Michael J	55	U S A	36	here
	F	Scanlan Francis J	55	"	35	Somerville

Putnam Street

	Letter	Full Name	Res.	Occupation	Age	Reported Residence
	G	Foley Marie E—†	5	housewife	26	here
	H	Foley Walter F	5	clerk	33	"
	K	Riorden Margaret—†	5	packer	40	"
	L	Curran Nicholas	8	U S A	35	
	M	Galvin Bridget—†	8	housewife	74	"
	N	Galvin Thomas	8	retired	71	
	O	Dunne Alfred J	10	electrician	25	"
	P	Dunne Catherine I—†	10	housewife	56	"
	R	Dunne James G	10	electrician	25	"
	S	Dunne John C	10	laborer	35	
	T	Dunne John T	10	carpenter	57	"
	U	Dunne Mary C—†	10	nurse	29	
	V	Dunne Thomas J	10	U S A	37	
	W	Orne Elizabeth A—†	12	housewife	75	"
	X	Orne Frederick J	12	retired	72	
	Y	McCarthy Elizabeth F—†	12	housewife	51	"

Page.	Letter.	FULL NAME.	Residence, Jan. 1, 1944.	Occupation.	Supposed Age.	Reported Residence, Jan. 1, 1943. Street and Number.

Putnam Street—Continued

	z	McCarthy Patrick J	12	bartender	51	here
47						
	A	McCarthy Thomas J	12	laborer	22	
	B	McCarthy William J	12	U S A	20	"
	C	Fournier Anna—†	14	housewife	60	"
	D	Fournier John M	14	supt	59	
	E	Fournier Kenneth J	14	electrician	26	"
	F	Fournier Stanton J	14	U S N	21	
	G	Jordan Ellen V—†	14	operator	31	"
	H	Stevens Rachel E—†	14	at home	70	"
	K	Duffy George T	18	U S A	22	"
	L	*Duffy Margaret—†	18	housewife	59	"
	M	Farren Patrick	18	retired	68	
	N	Raso Margaret M—†	18	clerk	31	
	P	Leary Mary E—†	19	packer	53	
	R	Quinn Alice T—†	19	clerk	23	

Rutherford Avenue

	s	Peters Catherine—†	8	housewife	45	here
	T	Peters Thomas W	8	machinist	46	"
	U	Blaisdell Ellen—†	8	housewife	66	"
	V	Blaisdell James B	8	awnings	70	"
	X	Toscano Antoinetta—†	10	housewife	29	"
	Y	Toscano Raymond	10	merchant	24	"
	z	Moccia Eugene	10	U S N	22	"
48						
	A	Moccia Mary J—†	10	housewife	49	"
	B	Moccia Salvatore	10	laborer	51	
	C	Iacone Marietta—†	10	housewife	26	"
	D	Iacone William	10	U S N	31	
	E	Faulkner George	12	clerk	32	
	F	Faulkner Grace—†	12	housewife	33	"
	G	Manning Joseph	12	chauffeur	37	"
	H	Cellat Antoinette—†	12	housekeeper	61	"
	K	Cellat Charlotte—†	12	student	20	"
	L	Cellat Ovid	12	messenger	32	"
	M	Gatto Joseph	12	chauffeur	53	101 Rutherford av
	N	Gatto Margaret—†	12	housewife	37	101 "
	P	Doherty Annie—†	17	"	67	here
	R	Doherty Eugene	17	shipfitter	32	"

Rutherford Avenue—Continued

s	Doherty John	17	retired	70	here
T	Doherty Philip F	17	laborer	29	"
U	Regan Ellen—†	17	housewife	55	"
V	Regan James P	17	clerk	28	
W	Regan John	17	waiter	24	
X	Regan Patrick	17	laborer	65	
Y	Tognarelli Emma—†	17	housewife	60	"
Z	Tognarelli Oscar	17	bartender	60	"
	49				
A	Tognarelli Flavia—†	17	housewife	45	"
B	*Tognarelli Romano	17	agent	52	
C	Tognarelli Velma—†	17	packer	23	··
E	Hayes William A	33	seaman	23	
F	Lucy Florence—†	33	housewife	44	"
G	Lucy Timothy F	33	longshoreman	45	"
H	Woosley Anna—†	33	housewife	21	"
K	Regan Bernard	33	longshoreman	41	"
L	Regan Bridget T—†	33	housewife	37	"
M	Monahan Mary—†	33	"	45	
N	Gethen Ellen—†	55	"	54	··
O	Gethen George	55	chauffeur	52	".
P	Toomey Catherine—†	55	bookkeeper	65	66 Wash'n
R	Toomey Thomas	55	retired	70	66 "
S	Ellison Ernest W	55	U S M C	24	here
T	Manning Alice—†	55	housewife	50	"
U	Manning John P	55	chauffeur	49	"
V	Courchesne Eva—†	57	housewife	33	"
W	Courchesne Leopold	57	machinist	36	"
X	Devlin Rose—†	57	at home	75	"
Y	Ledford Francis	57	laborer	21	
Z	Ledford Mary J—†	57	clerk	43	"
	50				
A	Ledford Rose—†	57	"	22	
B	Dolan Henry C	57	retired	49	
C	Dolan William P	57	painter	58	
D	Ryder Mary A—†	57	housewife	69	"

Stetson Court

G	Ranieri Joseph P	1	retired	73	here
H	Dubois Joseph A	2	boilermaker	52	"

Stetson Court—Continued

K	O'Neil Fred	2	laborer	39	here
L	*O'Neil Nellie—†	2	housewife	84	"
M	Bergen Catherine—†	2	housekeeper	28	"
N	Bergen Helen—†	2	factoryhand	30	"
O	Myers Mary—†	3	housewife	65	"
P	Connolly Hannah—†	3	cleaner	61	20 Ellwood
R	Fitzgerald Beatrice A—†	3	housewife	64	40 Park

Wall's Place

W	Mulhern Lillian—†	2	clerk	64	here
X	Bistany Maron	2	machinist	65	6 Gray
Y	Dantuony Felix	2	laborer	57	6 "
Z	Henry Anne A—†	3	housewife	40	here

51   Wapping Street

H	Matte Henry L	12	U S N	55	here
K	Matte Marie A—†	12	at home	48	"
M	Frasca John	19A	merchant	53	"

52   Warren Street

E	Whalen Alice M—†	44	housewife	58	2 Cordis
F	Whalen Thomas	44	watchman	66	2 "
G	Jones Annie—†	rear 44	at home	80	here
H	Collins Margaret—†	46	"	82	"
K	O'Brien Nora—†	46	housewife	75	"
P	Carney Dennis	58	laborer	64	12 Monument
R	Carney Francis J	58	U S A	31	12 "
S	Carney Frederick J	58	laborer	22	12 "
T	Carney George J	58	"	27	12 '
U	Carney Helen R—†	58	housekeeper	33	12 "
V	Carney Margaret—†	58	housewife	49	12 "
W	Leahy Margaret H—†	58	at home	72	here
X	Leahy Nora F—†	58	"	73	"

Washington Street

Z	Appels Anna—†	2	housewife	36	here

Page.	Letter.	FULL NAME.	Residence, Jan. 1, 1944.	Occupation.	Supposed Age.	Reported Residence, Jan. 1, 1943. Street and Number.

53
Washington Street—Continued

A	Appels Felix	2	U S N	39	here
B	Schaffer Joseph	2	electrician	59	"
C	Schaffer Mary—†	2	housewife	43	Lynn
D	Lewis James	6	clerk	26	here
E	Wiles Anna M—†	6	housewife	77	"
F	Wiles George E	6	clerk	47	"
G	Wiles Marguerite A—†	6	teacher	34	"
K	Davis James	10	retired	66	"
L	Duffy Thomas	10	mechanic	42	Scotland
M	Hines George	10	U S N	63	here
N	King Joseph F	10	retired	32	"
O	Lewis Michael D	10	laborer	64	"
P	McDonald Frank	10	retired	73	
R	Norton Henry	10	sorter	46	
S	O'Brien James J	10	laborer	33	
T	Radley William D	10	retired	64	
U	Stone Jasper	10	jeweler	72	
V	Scannell Alice—†	12	brazier	37	
W	Scannell Louise—†	12	operator	38	"
Y	McCaffrey Irene—†	12	housewife	35	"
X	McCaffrey James	12	laborer	28	
Z	Heuston William	12	"	52	

54

A	Noyes Frances—†	12	waitress	36	"

Washington Terrace

D	Scannell Annie—†	1	housewife	75	63 Tremont
E	Scannell John J	1	U S A	33	63 "
F	Scannell William	1	laborer	40	63 "
G	Heuston Anna—†	1	housewife	23	here
H	Heuston William	1	U S A.	26	"
K	Holetz Patricia—†	1	housewife	28	14A Park
L	Prevost Helen—†	1	stitcher	23	Cambridge

Winthrop Street

U	O'Sullivan Mary E—†	3	at home	66	here
W	Robinson Julia—†	5	housewife	68	"
X	Delay Helen—†	5	packer	60	"

29

Page.	Letter.	Full Name.	Residence, Jan. 1, 1944.	Occupation.	Supposed Age.	Reported Residence, Jan. 1, 1943. Street and Number.

Winthrop Street—Continued

y	Leest Jennie—†	5	housekeeper	62	here
	55				
a	Colbert Leo O	7	U S N	62	50 Monum'nt sq
b	Colbert Rose C—†	7	housewife	63	50 "
e	McGonigle Bridget—†	8	"	68	Somerville
f	Buckley Anna—†	8	operator	25	here
g	Buckley Caroline—†	8	saleswoman	28	"
h	Buckley Ellen—†	8	housewife	66	"
k	Buckley Helen—†	8	operator	21	"
l	Buckley Irene—†	8	clerk	31	
m	Crowley Dennis J	9	retired	69	
n	McCarthy Elizabeth G—†	9	at home	50	"
o	Pentes Ernest	9	riveter	45	
r	Gallagher Owen J	10	B F D	56	
s	Boyce Mary—†	10	housewife	80	"
t	Cashin Ethel R—†	14	"	45	
u	Cashin William J	14	undertaker	45	"
x	Vining Francis E	29	chipper	33	"
y	Vining Sarah L—†	29	housewife	33	"
z	Pierce Daniel F	29	clerk	64	
	56				
a	Pierce Grace E—†	29	housewife	64	"
b	Pierce Joseph G	29	U S A	35	
c	Sullivan Helen M—†	29	at home	47	"
d	Doherty John	29	retired	73	
e	Lynch Theresa T—†	29	machinist	26	"
f	Lynch Thomas	29	merchant	66	"
g	Fahey Agnes M—†	31	housewife	50	10½ Hancock
h	Fahey Alice—†	31	laundress	27	10½ "
k	Fahey James	31	longshoreman	54	10½ "
l	Fahey Mary A—†	31	laundress	29	10½ "
m	Fahey Mildred—†	31	clerk	22	10½ "
n	O'Brien Eleanor—†	31	housewife	36	here
o	O'Brien William H	31	longshoreman	39	"
p	Fitzpatrick Elizabeth M-†	31	housewife	39	"
r	Powers Anna—†	33	packer	30	48 Harvard
s	*Fleming Ellen T—†	33	at home	75	here
t	Malpin Maria J—†	33	waitress	60	"
v	Bradley Mary—†	35	housewife	72	"
w	Monagle Mary—†	35	at home	60	"
x	Gasper Hilary A	35	policeman	52	66 Lyndhurst

Winthrop Street—Continued

Y	Stover Joseph B	35	U S C G	38	here
z	Stover Margaret M—†	35	housewife	35	"
57						
A	Bradley Daniel P	35	meter reader	37	"
B	Bradley Mary A—†	35	housewife	38	"
c	Murphy Elizabeth B—†	37	"	69	
D	Murphy Richard F	37	retired	69	
E	Porter Sarah V—†	37	at home	66	"

10

2
1

3

12

4

5

14

6

15

7

16

8

Ward 2–Precinct 2

CITY OF BOSTON

LIST OF RESIDENTS
20 YEARS OF AGE AND OVER

(NON-CITIZENS INDICATED BY ASTERISK)
(FEMALES INDICATED BY DAGGER)

AS OF

JANUARY 1, 1944

THOMAS F. SULLIVAN, *Chairman*
FREDERIC E. DOWLING, *Secretary*
WILLIAM A. MOTLEY, JR.
FRANCIS B. McKINNEY
EVERETT R. PROUT

Listing Board.

CITY OF BOSTON ⬡ PRINTING DEPARTMENT

200

Chelsea Street

B	Broderick Ida—†	145	housewife	30	149 Chelsea
C	Broderick Lawrence	145	U S A	29	149 "
D	Chretien Joseph	145	retired	59	here
E	Chretien Leah—†	145	housewife	55	"
F	Moody Bella—†	145	"	26	"
G	Moody Robert J	145	U S A	30	Medford
H	Kehoe Bessie—†	146	housewife	49	here
K	Chiampa Rita—†	146	"	28	Florida
L	Sullivan Anna—†	146	"	52	166 Chelsea
M	Sullivan John B	146	U S N	20	166 "
N	Sullivan John L	146	watchman	60	166 "
O	McGlinchy Sarah—†	146	metalworker	49	here
P	Haggerty Charles	147	laborer	36	"
R	Haggerty Mabel—†	147	housewife	32	"
S	Millard John	147	laborer	41	Maine
T	Millard Mildred—†	147	housewife	40	"
U	Bilodeau Alice—†	147	weaver	45	here
V	Bilodeau Thomas	147	student	21	"
W	Finneran Annie—†	147	housekeeper	54	"
X	McDermott Andrew P	148	U S N	23	41 Decatur
Y	McDermott Bertha—†	148	housewife	20	41 "
Z	Cardello Margaret—†	148	"	51	here

201

A	Cardello Theresa—†	148	operator	23	"
B*	Juliana Mary—†	148	at home	81	"
C	Manwoth Susan—†	149	housewife	52	95 Decatur
D	Bowles Winifred—†	149	at home	73	here
E	Crowell John	149	janitor	57	"
G	McLaughlin Joseph	151	laborer	35	"
H	White Theresa—†	151	housewife	46	"
K	Desmond Elizabeth—†	151	"	50	
L	Desmond Helen—†	151	operator	25	"
M	Desmond Humphrey F	151	U S A	20	
N	Desmond Humphrey J	151	clerk	52	
O	Desmond John	151	U S A	21	
P	Desmond William T	151	clerk	23	
R	Jaccocio Ellen—†	152	bookbinder	43	"
S	Power Helen—†	152	maid	40	
T	Power Maurice	152	longshoreman	41	"
U	Blattner Charles R	152	painter	48	

Chelsea Street—Continued

v	Blattner Helen C—†	152	housewife	42	here
w	Bratten James	152	longshoreman	55	"
x	Sullivan James C	153	riveter	46	154 Chelsea
y	Sullivan Mary A—†	153	housewife	44	154 "
z	Riggs Martha—†	153	"	28	80 Warren
	202				
a	Riggs Russell	153	U S N	28	80 "
b	Duggan Edward J	153	laborer	38	here
c	Duggan Johanna J—†	153	housewife	37	"
d	Gallagher John	153	watchman	65	"
f	Beleca Catherine—†	154	at home	24	34 Anderson
g	Curtin Anne C—†	154	"	53	34 "
h	Curtin Timothy T	154	U S N	21	34 "
k	Curtin Alice—†	154	housewife	21	here
l	Curtin John J	154	guard	26	"
o	McKinney Catherine —†	157	at home	75	"
p	McKinney Patrick J	157	longshoreman	47	"
s	Kelleher Joseph M	158	ropemaker	30	"
t	Kelleher Julia—†	158	housewife	63	"
u	Mitchell Catherine—†	158	"	38	
v	Mitchell Daniel P	158	nickelplater	40	"
x	Fitzgerald James A	159	U S A	23	
y	Fitzgerald John F	159	longshoreman	20	"
z	Fitzgerald Mary B—†	159	housewife	55	"
	203				
a	Smith Genevieve—†	159	at home	65	"
b	O'Malley Thomas	161	laborer	38	"
c	Cotter Mary—†	161	housewife	22	94 Bartlett
d	Cotter Walter J	161	U S N	25	94 "
e	Cole James	161	laborer	50	1 Foster ct
f	Cole Lillian—†	161	housewife	38	1 "
g	Murray Charles E	162	mechanic	33	here
h	Murray Henrietta—†	162	housewife	33	"
k	Foster Grace C—†	162	nurse	35	"
l	Foster Mary E—†	162	housewife	66	"
m	Swales Avis—†	163	"	28	
n	Swales George W	163	longshoreman	28	"
o	Clifford Ann—†	163	welder	21	
p	Clifford Elizabeth—†	163	shipper	41	
r	Haggerty Doris—†	163	housewife	22	"
s	Kenny Abbie—†	163	at home	75	"

Chelsea Street—Continued

T	Desimone Catherine—†	163	housewife	45	here
U	Faulkner Helen—†	163	at home	48	"
V	Faulkner Morris	163	factoryhand	26	"
204					
D	Donnelly Albert J	166	bartender	34	"
E	Donnelly Mary L—†	166	housewife	28	"
F	Crowell Nina—†	166	"	30	
G	Crowell Roland	166	longshoreman	35	"
K	*Coughlin Bridget—†	167	housewife	72	"
L	Coughlin Catherine—†	167	waitress	38	"
M	Coughlin James	167	checker	44	"
N	Coughlin Timothy	167	retired	76	
O	*Elwood Bridget—†	167	housewife	66	"
P	*Elwood Michael	167	retired	67	
R	Carroll Bernadette E—†	168	clerk	20	
S	Carroll Helen F—†	168	housewife	50	"
T	Carroll John J	168	filer	52	
U	Carroll Joseph F	168	U S A	21	
V	Finn John R	168	pressman	47	"
W	Finn Mary E—†	168	housewife	48	"
X	Fuller William	168	guard	22	
Y	Swift Margaret E—†	169	at home	69	"
205					
B	Carter Nellie—†	170	"	74	
C	McCarthy Eugene	170	clerk	29	
D	McCarthy Margaret—†	170	housewife	56	"
E	Lane Mary—†	170	"	44	
F	Gibbons Patrick	171	retired	80	
G	Pierce Gertrude—†	171	electrician	43	"
H	Pierce Gertrude—†	171	factoryhand	21	"
K	Walsh Helen—†	171	housewife	21	"
L	Walsh Jeremiah	171	longshoreman	32	"
M	Haggerty Doris—†	172	housewife	22	"
N	Haggerty Jackson	172	U S N	32	"
O	Tallent Charles	172	laborer	27	Everett
R	Tallent Johanna—†	172	housewife	27	"
P	Holland Anna L—†	172	"	74	here
S	Morrissey Flora E—†	173	"	42	"
T	Morrissey Marie M—†	173	stenographer	21	"
U	Morrissey Thomas J	173	inspector	42	"

Chelsea Street—Continued

v	Tagney Maurice D	173	retired	70	here
x	Cummings Catherine—†	174	housewife	40	"
y	Cummings James	174	laborer	42	"
z	Dacey Catherine—†	174	teacher	28	..
	206				
a	Dacey Ellen J—†	174	housewife	65	"
b	Dacey James F	174	clerk	62	"
c	Dacey James F, jr	174	shipper	30	"
d	Hassett Catherine E—†	174	at home	70	"
e	Hassett Margaret L—†	174	operator	60	"
f	O'Hare Margaret J—†	175	"	67	
g	McCarthy Isabelle—†	176	housewife	45	"
h	McCarthy John R	176	inspector	43	"
k	McCarthy Frank A	176	clerk	47	
l	Driscoll Eugene C	177	retired	71	
m	Driscoll Julia—†	177	housewife	68	"
n	Shumway Catherine—†	178	"	25	Shrewsbury
o	Shumway Harold	178	shipfitter	39	"
p	Gibbons Bernard	178	retired	72	here
r	Gibbons Cornelius B	178	laborer	43	"
s	Gibbons Michael J	178	retired	45	"
t	Gibbons James A	178	fireman	40	
u	Gibbons Julia F—†	178	housewife	40	"
v	Gustus Marion—†	179	"	83	
w	Gustus Olga M—†	179	weaver	50	
x	Rogers Catherine A—†	179	housewife	50	"
y	Rogers Frank B	179	drawtender	60	"
	207				
c	Wells William A	181	retired	84	2 Hillside pl
d	Chickering Annie—†	181	at home	54	10 Mystic pl
e	Chickering Jennie—†	181	buttonmaker	32	10 "
f	Proctor John	181	U S N	21	Somerville
g	Proctor Marguerite—†	181	waitress	23	"
h	Proctor Mary—†	181	housewife	56	"
k	Proctor Pearl—†	181	at home	24	"
l	Mitchell Catherine—†	182	housewife	25	here
m	Mitchell Edward	182	U S A	31	"
n	Kelly Irene M—†	182	at home	20	"
o	Kelly John E	182	U S A	28	"
p	Kelly Roger F	182	B F D	56	

Page.	Letter.	FULL NAME.	Residence, Jan. 1, 1944.	Occupation.	Supposed Age.	Reported Residence, Jan. 1, 1943. Street and Number.

Chelsea Street—Continued

	R	Cronin Bessie—†	183	waitress	50	here
	s	Cronin Ruth—†	183	stenographer	22	"
	u	Foster Florence L—†	184	housewife	62	"

Corey Street

	v	Papasodero Mary—†	9	housewife	23	here
	w	Papasodero Michele	9	smelter	28	"
	x	Butler Hyacinth—†	9	housewife	22	9 Samuel Morse way
	y	Butler William R	9	manager	24	here
	z	McClearn Charlotta—†	9	housewife	32	"

208

	A	McClearn Patrick	9	freighthandler	38	"
	B	Scott William S −	9	assembler	38	59 St Rose
	c	Killilea Michalena—†	9	housewife	29	here
	D	Killilea Thomas J	9	motorman	35	"
	E	Liedtke Isabelle—†	9	housewife	31	"
	F	Liedtke Oscar A	9	fireman	44	..
	G	Sault Edna—†	9	at home	33	"
	H	*Gawlinski Beatrice—†	9	"	55	
	K	Novello Tino	9	chauffeur	31	"
	L	Novello Viola—†	9	housewife	28	"
	M	Digiacomo Helen E—†	9	"	27	42 Tufts
	N	Digiacomo John F	9	metalworker	34	42 "
	o	Boure Edward M	9	agent	43	here
	P	Boure Mildred L—†	9	housewife	39	"
	R	Thomas Ann—†	9	saleswoman	22	"
	s	Thomas Mary—†	9	at home	48	"
	T	*Guy Bridget—†	17	"	74	
	u	Shea Annie—†	17	"	73	
	v	Keane Annie—†	17	housewife	41	"
	w	Keane Edward J	17	laborer	53	
	x	Doherty Daniel J	17	longshoreman	28	"
	y	Doherty Jennie N—†	17	housewife	26	"
	z	Beck Margaret—†	17	at home	41	"

209

	A	Brown Chester F	17	U S N	27	Somerville
	B	Brown Evelyn V—†	17	housewife	24	"
	c	*Cassidy Catherine—†	17	"	33	65 Bunker Hill
	D	Cassidy William L	17	supt	37	65 "
	E	Crowley Dorothy B—†	17	housewife	38	here

6

Corey Street—Continued

F	Crowley Timothy E	17	laborer	39	here
G	Holloway James W	17	chauffeur	24	"
H	Holloway Mildred—†	17	housewife	22	"
K	Kalb Joseph H	17	laborer	38	"
L	Kalb Mary—†	17	housewife	35	"
M	Duffy Edward C	17	pipefitter	40	"
N	Duffy Mary—†	17	housewife	31	"
O	O'Neil Mary C—†	17	at home	39	"
P	Bragen Helen—†	17	mechanic	39	Revere
R	Bragen Nathan	17	U S N	37	"
S	Heenan Daniel J	25	chauffeur	32	here
T	Heenan Mary—†	25	housewife	26	"
U	Tracey John G	25	pipefitter	30	"
V	Tracey Mary C—†	25	housewife	29	"
W	Woods John F	25	electrician	36	"
X	Woods Madeleine C—†	25	housewife	35	"
Y	Griffin William J	25	chef	53	
Z	Hill Christina—†	25	at home	51	"
	210				
A	Sullivan Elizabeth—†	25	defense wkr	33	"
B	Sullivan Phillip F	25	U S A	38	
C	Whelan Julia—†	25	at home	62	"
D	Conawan Joseph P	25	laborer	47	"
E	Conawan Katherine—†	25	housewife	37	"
F	Murphy Elizabeth—†	25	"	21	
G	Murphy George	25	laborer	26	
H	McLaughlin Georgia—†	25	housewife	27	"
K	McLaughlin James S	25	operator	26	"
L	Gognon Germaine—†	25	housewife	33	38 High
M	Gognon Roland	25	U S A	29	38 "
N	Gognon Gladys—†	25	welder	27	Grafton
O	St Jean Raymond E	25	laborer	39	here
P	St Jean Viola—†	25	housewife	38	"
R	Doherty Eugene	25	janitor	58	53 Tremont
S	Earle Louis B	33	retired	73	here
T	Earle Lucy B—†	33	at home	74	"
U	*Galipien Alice C—†	33	housewife	37	89 Polk
V	Galipien Wilfred L	33	U S A	36	89 "
W	Alexander Joseph M, jr	33	electrician	24	11 Hecla
X	Alexander Natalie J—†	33	housewife	23	11 "
Y	Kavanagh Alice I—†	33	"	32	here

Corey Street—Continued

z	Kavanagh Charles P	33	waiter	34	here
	211				
A	Poelaert Elizabeth C—†	33	housewife	60	"
B	Poelaert Oscar	33	cigarmaker	60	"
c	Sullivan Catherine—†	33	housewife	34	"
D	Sullivan Cornelius	33	laborer	35	"
E	McAnulty Grace K—†	33	factoryhand	45	383 Bunker Hill
F	McAnulty Margaret M—†	33	housewife	50	383 "
G	O'Brien Harold J	33	machinist	37	here
H	O'Brien Mary A—†	33	housewife	38	"
K	Curran Anna V—†	33	defense wkr	31	27 Faulkner
L	Curran James P	33	U S A	32	27 "
N	Walsh Louise C—†	33	defense wkr	39	here
o	Smith Frances M—†	33	housewife	33	"
P	Smith Walter E	33	U S N	40	"
R	Manning John W	41	printer	56	
s	Manning Mary M—†	41	housewife	52	"
T	Beaton Agnes M—†	41	matron	38	107 Russell
U	Corcoran Mary—†	41	housewife	34	here
V	Corcoran Timothy D	41	laborer	38	"
W	Coleman Annie J—†	41	housewife	60	"
X	Coleman Charles A	41	U S A	27	
Y	Coleman Mary G—†	41	defense wkr	29	"
z	Ryan Joseph W	41	longshoreman	39	7 Marion
	212				
A	Ryan Theresa A—†	41	housewife	33	7 "
B	Curran Hazel B—†	41	"	29	here
c	Curran Ralph M	41	treasurer	30	"
E	Burke Ruth M—†	41	operator	49	"
F	Quinlan Gertrude C—†	41	factoryhand	44	"
G	Kinney Ella J—†	41	housewife	26	"
H	Kinney Robert F	41	U S M C	28	"
K	Clark Mary E—†	41	at home	52	58 W Canton
L	Clark Richard L	41	U S A	27	58 "
M	Parker Albert R	41	painter	31	58 "
N	Parker Eileen—†	41	housewife	28	58 "
o	Gill Hugh J	41	driller	43	66 Medford
P	Gill Mary C—†	41	housewife	34	66 "
R	Bennett Emma M—†	41	"	21	42 Guild
s	Bennett Robert E	41	welder	33	283 Cabot
T	Leason Joseph A	49	rigger	52	Melrose

Corey Street—Continued

u	Leason Marie E—†	49	at home	21	Melrose
v	Doherty Grace E—†	49	housewife	41	here
w	Doherty John J	49	chauffeur	50	"
x	Gosnell George J	49	retired	78	"
y	Gosnell Mary F—†	49	at home	77	"
z	Walls Charles T	49	U S A	38	
	213					
a	Walls Eileen M—†	49	housewife	38	"
b	Emerson Charles	49	defense wkr	28	"
c	Emerson Mary—†	49	housewife	25	"
d	Bartlett Frederick W	49	laborer	50	
e	Bartlett Myra—†	49	housewife	42	"
g	Connolly Helen L—†	49	"	42	"
h	Sutherland Mary M—†	49	"	31	Nantasket
k	Sutherland Ray F	49	electrician	38	"
m	Healy Frank L	49	solicitor	39	Somerville
n	Healy Mary C—†	49	housewife	39	"
o	Mason Mary—†	49	"	37	here
p	Mason Robert V	49	pipefitter	47	"
r	Bozzdlo Beatrice A—†	49	housewife	33	"
s	Bozzdlo Henry J	49	bartender	38	"

Decatur Street

t	McGrath Rita—†	21	housewife	24	here
u	Murphy Gertrude D—†	21	matron	54	"
v	Pierro Rocco	21	laborer	66	"
w	Holubowich Adolph J	23	operator	29	"
x	Holubowich Mary J—†	23	housewife	26	"
y	Mitchell Josephine G—†	23	"	40	
z	Mitchell William F	23	plater	39	
	214					
b	Monagle Bernard J	25	watchman	52	"
c	Monagle Catherine A—†	25	housewife	42	"
d	Monagle Rose A—†	25	seamstress	55	"
f	McGonigle Celia A—†	27	at home	63	"
g	McGonigle James J	27	laborer	68	
k	Cullen Francis D	29	"	43	
l	Cullen James A	29	longshoreman	41	"
m	Cullen Thomas J	29	fireman	42	
n	Byrnes Margaret F—†	29	housewife	66	"

9

Decatur Street—Continued

o	O'Hara Mary—†	29	defense wkr	43	here
p	McDonald Sarah—†	31	at home	65	8 Ferrin
r	Perry Manuel	31	laborer	50	131 Chelsea
s	Perry Phoebe—†	31	housewife	50	131 "
t	Shandon Elizabeth—†	31	at home	78	here
u	Shandon Mary A—†	31	"	68	"
v	Haney Elizabeth—†	33	clerk	45	"
w	McMenamie Alice F—†	33	"	52	"
x	McMenamie Catherine—†	33	at home	80	"
y	McMenamie Mary L—†	33	milliner	49	"
z	McLaughlin Bridget—†	35	housewife	53	"

215

a	McLaughlin Francis J	35	engineer	55	"
b	Bockelman Mary E—†	35	clerk	56	
c	Brennan Francis—†	37	housewife	47	"
d	Brennan Joseph M	37	operator	47	"
e	McGonigle Henry J	37	U S A	29	
f	Barry Eileen—†	37	clerk	24	"
g	Barry John J	37	"	30	
h	Barry Mary C—†	37	housewife	60	"
l	McLaughlin Annie B—†	39	at home	59	"
m	McLaughlin Ellen A—†	39	housewife	70	"
o	Boyle Rose E—†	41	"	45	"
p	Doherty Aloysius	41	U S A	23	25 Albion pl
r	Doherty Rose—†	41	at home	23	here
s	McDermott Andrew P	41	U S N	23	"
t	McDermott Bertha M—†	41	at home	20	"
u	Foley Eleanor M—†	43	prob'n officer	58	"
v	Sullivan Elizabeth V—†	43	clerk	56	"
w	Sullivan John F	43	surveyor	57	"
x	Kenney Eugene	47	U S N	30	
y	Kenney Mildred—†	47	housewife	28	"
z	Rae Ellen A—†	47	"	42	

216

a	Rae William F	47	metalworker	21	"
b	McLaughlin Henry J	49	polisher	66	"
c	McLaughlin Mary E—†	49	housewife	65	"
d	Bailey Sarah T—†	49	at home	74	"
e	Bailey Walter A	49	retired	62	
f	Callahan James P	50	"	37	"
g	Callahan Mary E—†	50	housewife	39	"

Decatur Street—Continued

H	O'Neil George A	50	laborer	33	here
K	O'Neil Gertrude R—†	50	housewife	31	"
L	Smith Anastasia—†	50	at home	32	"
M	Fitzgerald Margaret—†	50	"	43	"
N	Mulholland John	50	retired	77	"
O	Mulholland Nellie L—†	50	at home	77	"
P	O'Donnell Helen—†	50	housewife	38	"
R	O'Donnell John	50	laborer	36	"
S	Grady Elinore—†	50	at home	33	"
T	Duffy Daniel J	50	teacher	38	
U	Duffy Helen B—†	50	housewife	34	"
V	McLaughlin Agnes U—†	50	"	38	
W	McLaughlin William	50	painter	35	"
X	Cronin Andrew F	50	trackman	31	49 Calumet
Y	Hickey Anna N—†	50	housewife	35	here
Z	Hickey Cornelius F	50	machinist	37	"

217

A	Gray Anna R—†	50	at home	38	"
B	Cahill Catherine E—†	50	housewife	35	"
C	Cahill Stephen J	50	baker	36	
E	Bronk Susan E—†	51	matron	54	"
F	McDermott John J	51	clerk	60	"
G	McDermott Mary A—†	51	housewife	64	"
H	McIntosh John	53	seaman	55	"
K	Green Elizabeth—†	53	librarian	30	Winthrop
L	Dillon Mary A—†	55	clerk	59	here
M	Dillon William F	55	"	61	"
N	Hughes Albert O	55	executive	49	"
O	Hughes Mary M—†	55	housewife	82	"
P	Xavier Lillian F—†	55	at home	73	"
R	O'Connor Charles W	57	storekeeper	51	161 Chelsea
S	O'Connor Mary E—†	57	housewife	50	161 "
T	Reddy Elizabeth M—†	57	secretary	37	here
U	Reddy Mary E—†	57	housewife	65	"
V	Church Lillian M—†	57	operator	37	"
W	*Chrostouski Malvina—†	58	housewife	37	N Hampshire
X	Chrostouski Stanley	58	pipefitter	37	"
Y	Murphy Daniel F	58	clerk	48	99 Alexander
Z	Murphy Mary—†	58	housewife	31	here

218

A	McCormack Margaret—†	58	"	30	

Decatur Street—Continued

		FULL NAME	Residence	Occupation	Age	Reported Residence
B		McCormack Robert F	58	trackman	32	here
C		Murphy John	58	printer	36	"
D		Murphy Mary—†	58	at home	65	"
E		Matson Mary—†	58	"	36	"
F		Pugliese Mildred F—†	58	housewife	22	9 Samuel Morse way
G		Pugliese Robert R	58	laborer	22	9 "
H		Kelly Bridget—†	58	housewife	37	here
K		Kelly Patrick	58	janitor	42	"
L		Harris Helen—†	58	at home	24	"
M		Wood Helen A—†	58	housewife	48	"
N		Wood Violet E—†	58	clerk	20	
O		McLaughlin Florence C—†	58	housewife	43	"
P		McLaughlin Michael H	58	storekeeper	42	"
R		Powers Francis	58	operator	36	"
S		Powers Mary—†	58	housewife	36	"
T		Davis James	58	chauffeur	52	"
U		Davis Nellie—†	58	housewife	47	"
V		McDermott Elizabeth—†	59	"	76	
W		McDermott William	59	laborer	50	
X		Grace John J	59	electrician	52	"
Y		Grace Joseph F	59	U S N	21	
Z		Grace Sarah A—†	59	housewife	52	"
		219				
A		Welch Richard L	59	clerk	39	
B		O'Reilly Katherine—†	59	packer	62	
C		Sullivan Helen—†	59	grader	40	"
E		Hines Alice E—†	63	housewife	60	"
F		Hines Andrew	63	watchman	70	"
G		Feeney Dorothy C—†	63	packer	21	..
H		Feeney John J	63	electrician	25	"
K		Feeney Mary T—†	63	housewife	50	"
L		Farren Anna E—†	65	at home	71	"
M		Farren Katherine F—†	65	housekeeper	69	"
N		Farren Anna—†	65	clerk	32	"
O		Farren Elizabeth—†	65	housewife	58	"
P		Farren Frances—†	65	clerk	30	
R		Farren John T	65	U S A	34	
S		Farren Joseph E	65	laborer	27	
T		Cochrane Dorothy—†	66	at home	20	"
U		Seabrook Charles	66	U S N	35	Florida
V		Seabrook Grace—†	66	housewife	33	"

Page.	Letter.	FULL NAME.	Residence, Jan. 1, 1944.	Occupation.	Supposed Age.	Reported Residence, Jan. 1, 1943. Street and Number.

Decatur Street—Continued

w	Avedian Alice—†	66	housewife	33	Haverhill
x	Avedian John	66	"	40	"
y	Donohue Mary—†	66	"	23	here
z	Donohue Thomas	66	brazier	24	"

220

a	Murray Dorothy J—†	66	housewife	58	478 Shawmut av
b	Murray James H	66	pipecoverer	61	478 "
c	Murray James H, jr	66	U S A	20	478 "
d	Spinney Harold W	66	laborer	41	here
e	Spinney Helen B—†	66	housewife	38	"
f	Breen Alice R—†	66	"	29	"
g	Breen Leo J	66	operator	31	"
h	Yaroschuck Anna—†	66	housewife	27	"
k	Yaroschuck Michael	66	baker	30	"
l	Walters Frederick G	66	laborer	37	Lynn
m	Walters Margaret—†	66	housewife	35	"
n	Salter George C	66	guard	37	here
o	Salter Rebecca C—†	66	housewife	30	"
p	Schwartz Carl M	66	U S N	29	170 Chelsea
r	Schwartz Madelaine—†	66	housewife	27	170 "
s	Tiernan Agnes—†	66	at home	34	here
t	Crowell Stuart E	67	ropemaker	43	"
u	McGonagle Patrick W	67	laborer	64	"
v	McGonagle William P	67	retired	68	
w	Brady John F	69	"	77	
x	Dunn Margaret—†	69	packer	62	
y	McDonald Rose—†	69	housewife	62	"
z	McDonald William	69	U S N	28	

221

a	Eldridge Mildred—†	71	housewife	40	25 Myrtle
b	Lyman Annie—†	71	at home	77	25 "
c	McCabe Cornelius	71	longshoreman	30	here
d	McCabe Margaret—†	71	housewife	27	"
e	O'Brien Eleanor—†	71	waitress	23	"
f	O'Brien John	71	U S N	20	
g	Toohig John E	71	fireman	49	"
h	Duggan Anna R—†	73	housewife	56	"
k	Duggan Grace R—†	73	secretary	22	"
l	Duggan James L	73	retired	70	
m	Duggan James L, jr	73	U S N	27	
n	Higgins Gertrude M—†	73	clerk	59	

Decatur Street—Continued

o	Daly Elizabeth R—†	74	housewife	24	here	
p	Daly John J	74	U S A	25	"	
s	Walsh Margaret J—†	74	housewife	38	"	
t	Walsh Richard F	74	shipfitter	41	"	
u	Connors Mary—†	74	at home	59	"	
v	Flanagan Charlotte—†	74	"	32	21 Ditson	
w	O'Connor Anna V—†	74	housewife	26	here	
x	O'Connor Francis E	74	clerk	30	"	
y	Sheehan Helen—†	74	housewife	42	"	
z	Sheehan William	74	laborer	41		

222

a	Barry George F	74	welder	29		
b	Boodey Delia—†	74	at home	52	"	
c	Crouse Charles R	74	shipbuilder	64	119 Lexington	
d	Crouse Ellen E—†	74	housewife	66	here	
e	O'Neil Margaret—†	74	at home	43	"	
f	Murphy Frances—†	74	"	26	"	
g	Murphy Ralph	74	clerk	55		
h	Torpey Mary E—†	74	at home	43	"	
k	O'Neill Arthur V	74	U S A	25	102 Poplar	
l	O'Neill Lena C—†	74	housewife	24	102 "	
m	Green Josephine—†	75	at home	75	here	
n	Driscoll Catherine—†	75	housewife	71	"	
o	Driscoll John F	75	laborer	34	"	
p	Driscoll Katherine E—†	75	operator	36	"	
r	Buckley Harry	75	longshoreman	60	"	
s	Buckley John P	75	U S A	29		
t	Buckley Lucy—†	75	housewife	60	"	
u	Hollenberg Stella—†	77	"	49	33 Green	
v	Hollenberg William	77	chauffeur	60	33 "	
w	McLaughlin Margaret A—†	77	at home	54	here	
x	McLaughlin Mary I—†	77	bookbinder	57	"	
y	Crowley Daniel J	77	laborer	40	"	
z	Crowley Edward	77	longshoreman	50	"	

223

a	McCarthy Daniel	79	"	24		
b	McCarthy Mary—†	79	housewife	22	"	
c	Vaughan Catherine A—†	79	"	76	"	
d	Vaughan Daniel J	79	retired	76	"	
f	Smith Catherine M—†	81	housewife	60	"	
g	Smith Catherine M—†	81	packer	22		

Decatur Street—Continued

H	*Flynn Frederick E	81	longshoreman	51	here	
K	*Flynn John	81	"	56	"	
M	White Elizabeth—†	82	at home	72	"	.
N	White Francis R	82	retired	88		
O	King Carl P	82	butcher	42	"	
P	King Daisy M—†	82	housewife	36	"	
R	Dowd Mary M—†	82	at home	57	"	
S	Riley George F	82	longshoreman	34	, "	
T	Riley Mabel F—†	82	saleswoman	26	"	
U	McGee Anna J—†	82	at home	43	"	
V	*Rupe Clara M—†	82	"	25		
W	Beasley Hannah V—†	82	housewife	37	"	
X	Beasley Jeremiah J	82	operator	44	"	
Y	Sweeney John	82	retired	67		
Z	Tansey Mary E—†	82	at home	31	"	

224

A	Kelly Agnes—†	82	clerk	45	23 Bowdoin	
B	Kelly Cornelius	82	freighthandler	52	23 "	
C	Dunican Joseph T	82	retired	60	here	
D	Dunican Mary J—†	82	at home	66	"	
E	Gorham Dorothy R—†	82	housewife	36	"	.
F	Gorham Thomas F	82	maintenance	43	"	
G	Carey Della J—†	82	at home	43	"	
H	Liotta Eleanor M—†	82	housewife	27	"	
K	Liotta Michael	82	B F D	30		
L	Williams Edna—†	83	windowdresser	20	"	
M	Williams Harold	83	chauffeur	40	"	
N	Brown Anne K—†	83	saleswoman	43	"	
O	Brown John C	83	clerk	60		
P	Brown Mary A—†	83	at home	83	"	
R	Brown William F	83	clerk	58	117 Warren	
S	Thoms Elizabeth—†	83	housewife	67	here	
T	Thoms Fred	83	retired	68	"	
U	Thoms Watson	83	orderly	32	"	
V	Gormley Julia L—†	85	at home	57	"	
W	Gormley Mamie—†	85	storekeeper	65	"	
X	Donovan Elsie—†	85	housewife	25	"	
Y	Donovan John D	85	longshoreman	34	"	
Z	McGlee Ora—†	90	housewife	27	Lawrence	

225

A	McGlee Earl	90	welder	27		

3

4

5

Decatur Street—Continued

B	Chase Carl	90	U S A	26	here
C	Chase Ethel M—†	90	housewife	27	"
D	DeViller Anna—†	90	"	39	"
E	DeViller Joseph	90	shipbuilder	42	"
F	MacIsaac Neil	90	oiler	33	10 Tufts
G	Scully Joseph L	90	clerk	25	here
H	Scully Lillian—†	90	housewife	27	"
K	Brennan Frederick L	90	foreman	43	"
L	Brennan Kathryn M—†	90	housewife	41	"
M	Sheehan Esther G—†	90	"	38	
N	Sheehan Michael E	90	insulator	42	"
O	White Catherine J—†	90	at home	74	"
P	White William J	90	cook	49	"
R	Dambriso Mary C—†	90	at home	22	198 St Botolph
S	Spinney George A	90	welder	24	10 Jeffries
T	Spinney Vincenza—†	90	housewife	21	10 "
U	Cannata George W	90	barber	44	here
V	Cannata Marion J—†	90	housewife	39	"
X	Pinkos Anna R—†	98	"	31	Virginia
Y	Pinkos Stanislaus J	98	U S N	27	"
Z	Cocco Silvio	98	kitchenman	52	74 Decatur
	226				
A	Cocco Tina—†	98	at home	29	74 "
B	Buonopane Anthony L	98	waiter	27	here
C	Buonopane Lena A—†	98	housewife	22	"
D	Sullivan Mary L—†	98	at home	56	"
E	Tolan Susan E—†	98	"	68	"
F	Waterson Mary E—†	98	"	64	"
G	Egan Francis G	98	clerk	60	90 Decatur
H	Egan Nettie W—†	98	housewife	55	90 "
K	Sklover Ann—†	98	at home	37	here
L	Toomey Cecelia F—†	98	"	42	"
N	Berry Louise N—†	98	housewife	36	N Hampshire
O	Berry Ralph G	98	toolmaker	37	"
R	Pendlebury Burt L	98	salesman	45	here
S	Pendlebury Dorothy M–†	98	housewife	31	"
U	Gerrier Helen L—†	103	inspector	28	"
V	Gerrier Loretta—†	103	welder	21	
W	Gerrier Nora—†	103	housewife	52	"
X	King Anna J—†	105	packer	39	

Decatur Street—Continued

	Y	King George W	105	laborer	33	here
	z	King John J	105	longshoreman	47	"

227   Medford Street

	E	Doherty Frances—†	12	housewife	54	here
	F	Doherty Grace—†	12	shipfitter	20	"
	G	Doherty Helen F—†	12	clerk	20	"
	H	Doherty John	12	U S M C	23	"
	K	Doherty Philip J	12	laborer	55	"
	L	McCarthy Charles J	14	U S A	35	"
	N	Lyst Margaret—†	34	housewife	47	Florida
	O	Cherryngton Ida—†	34	"	73	here
	P	Cherryngton James	34	retired	68	"
	R	Gregore Joseph	34	chauffeur	29	183 Webster
	s	Gregore Mary—†	34	housewife	28	183 "
	T	Murphy Elizabeth—†	34	"	37	here
	U	Murphy James	34	printer	37	"
	V	Brennan Margaret—†	34	clerk	24	"
	W	Brennan Mary—†	34	housewife	74	"
	X	Doherty Mary F—†	34	"	32	
	Y	Doherty Patrick J	34	clerk	39	
	z	Wiemert Anna G—†	34	housewife	42	"
		228				
	A	Wiemert Lawrence J	34	laborer	46	"
	B	Hauglin Joseph E	34	U S A	40	1031 Saratoga
	C	Hauglin Joseph E, jr	34	"	20	1031 "
	D	Hauglin Marion—†	34	housewife	38	1031 "
	E	Hatch Mary—†	34	"	65	here
	F	Parrino Dorothy—†	34	"	20	"
	G	Parrino Salvatore	34	mechanic	24	"
	L	Toner Arthur	50	metalworker	32	"
	M	Toner Dorothy—†	50	housewife	30	"
	N	Donovan Helen E—†	50	"	35	
	O	Donovan James W	50	clerk	42	
	P	Peyton Fred	50	repairman	37	"
	R	Peyton Mary—†	50	housewife	37	"
	s	Donovan Neil A	50	agent	44	
	T	Donovan Pearl A—†	50	housewife	53	"
	U	McNelley Beatrice—†	50	"	30	

Medford Street—Continued

v	McNelley Edward	50	laborer	33	here	
w	Ryle Elizabeth—†	50	housewife	38	"	
x	Ryle John J	50	chauffeur	44	"	
y	Ryle Thomas F	50	U S A	20		
z	Cowan Joseph R	50	messenger	31	"	
	229					
a	Cowan Sarah M—†	50	housewife	29	"	
b	Shea Margaret—†	50	"	32	"	
c	Shea Patrick	50	laborer	33	"	
d	DeAngelis Carmine	50	ropemaker	34	"	
e	DeAngelis Mabel—†	50	housewife	34	"	
f	Driscoll Catherine—†	58	"	26		
g	Driscoll Cornelius	58	chauffeur	31	"	
h	Lock Frederick J	58	machinist	32	"	
l	McCrevan Catherine—†	58	housewife	48	9 Monum'nt so	
m	McCrevan John	58	laborer	59	9 "	
n	McCrevan William J	58	U S N	22	9 "	
o	Doucette Helen F—†	58	housewife	35	N Hampshire	
p	Doucette Rodney	58	fireman	38	"	
r	Portanova Donato	58	rigger	26	Cambridge	
s	Portanova Mary—†	58	housewife	27	"	
r	Taylor Dorothy—†	66	"	31	541 Tremont	
u	Taylor Joseph T	66	U S N	38	541 "	
v	MacDonald Ivy M—†	66	housewife	36	here	
w	MacDonald John C	66	inspector	41	"	
x	Dinsmore Agnes—†	66	housewife	39	"	
y	Dinsmore Robert	66	retired	46		
z	Bean Harry E	66	papercutter	33	"	
	230					
a	Bean Mary L—†	66	housewife	31	"	
b	Clifford Bridget—†	66	"	47		
c	Clifford Dennis	66	laborer	48		
d	Barry Catherine T—†	66	housewife	41	"	
e	Barry Joseph	66	laborer	39		
f	McCarthy Gertrude H—†	66	housewife	36	"	
g	McCarthy Joseph W	66	chauffeur	37	"	
h	Fidler Edward J	66	electrician	30	"	
k	Fidler Esther J—†	66	housewife	28	"	
l	Cahill Marie E—†	66	"	37		
m	Cahill Thomas L	66	clerk	38		
n	Comeau Emily E—†	66	saleswoman	40	"	

18

o	Arpin Bridget F—†	74	matron	65	here
p	Cadigan Margaret—†	74	housewife	72	"
r	Cadigan William	74	retired	49	"
s	Boudreau Henry J	74	U S N	37	"
t	Boudreau Jennie—†	74	housewife	40	"
u	Driscoll Helen—†	74	"	26	172 Bunker Hill
v	Kennedy Homer	74	fireman	27	48 Hereford
w	Kennedy Verna—†	74	housewife	22	48 "
x	Tobin Rose A—†	74	"	27	here
y	Tobin Thomas W	74	bookkeeper	30	"
z	Merry Mary M—†	74	housewife	64	"
	231				
a	Merry Thomas F	74	laborer	64	"
b	Carroll Anthony J	74	clerk	66	
c	Carroll Mary E—†	74	housewife	64	"
d	Gibbons Daniel	74	laborer	39	"
e	Gibbons Mary—†	74	housewife	38	"

Moulton Street

f	Goodman Charles J	17	chauffeur	38	here
g	Goodman Honora—†	17	housewife	36	"
h	Anthony Joseph A	17	shipper	28	"
k	Anthony Sarah E—†	17	housewife	27	"
l	Doherty Bridget—†	17	maid	60	
m	Toland James	17	cook	65	
n	Toland Sarah—†	17	maid	59	"
o	Anthony Kenneth W	17	baker	54	
p	Turinsky Maximilian	17	welder	35	
r	Turinsky Rose E—†	17	housewife	32	"
s	Mullen Elizabeth A—†	17	"	32	
t	Mullen Frank J	17	baker	43	
u	Morss David B	21	retired	78	
v	Tibbetts Mildred E—†	21	packer	43	
w	O'Connell Helen G—†	21	housewife	54	"
x	O'Connell John J	21	U S N	34	
y	O'Connell William F	21	"	33	"
z	Sheehan Agnes G—†	21	typist	35	11 Elmwood
	232				
a	Sheehan Mary E—†	21	housewife	67	11 "
b	Lane Dorothy C—†	21	operator	48	here

Moulton Street—Continued

C	Montgomery Georgianna A—†	21	housewife	67	here
D	Dunn Bridget—†	21	examiner	41	"
E	*Joyce Bernard	21	welder	25	"
F	*Joyce Bridget M—†	21	housewife	64	"
G	*Joyce Patrick J	21	retired	64	
H	Ryan Irene E—†	23	housewife	34	"
K	Ryan Joseph F	23	craneman	40	"
L	Ryan Mary A—†	23	housewife	69	"

O'Brien Court

M	Murphy Alice—†	26	housewife	37	58 Decatur
N	Murphy John	26	printer	35	58 "
O	Considine James P	26	longshoreman	32	here
P	Considine Marion—†	26	housewife	28	"
R	Pennachio Margaret—†	26	"	31	"
S	Pennachio Vincent J	26	printer	35	"
T	Krajewski Charlotte—†	26	housewife	34	Wisconsin
U	Krajewski Frank	26	molder	35	"
V	Donlin Mary—†	26	housewife	37	here
W	Donlin Michael F	26	janitor	40	"
X	Cummings Josephine—†	26	housewife	26	Somerville
Y	Cummings Waldo	26	shipfitter	26	"
Z	Kossiver Florence—†	34	housewife	29	Pennsylvania
	233				
A	Kossiver Jack	34	machinist	31	"
B	Rousseau Ernest J	34	laborer	33	here
C	Buchpert Edwin H	34	electrician	25	22 Cross
D	Buchpert Marion W—†	34	housewife	23	22 "
E	Santos Manuel A	34	laborer	35	here
F	Santos Sarah—†	34	housewife	37	"
G	Ryan Clara—†	34	"	28	"
H	Ryan John J	34	electrician	36	"
K	Dolan Mary—†	34	housewife	33	"
L	Gill Cecelia—†	34	secretary	31	"
M	Johnson Ellen V—†	50	housewife	23	"
N	Johnson Walter H	50	U S M C	27	"
O	Cataldo Lewis, jr	50	seaman	27	
P	Cataldo Mary A—†	50	housewife	22	"
R	Harrington Jeremiah J	50	rigger	29	
S	Harrington June—†	50	housewife	26	"

O'Brien Court—Continued

T	Addy Ella F—†	50	housewife	24	Hawaii
U	Addy William	50	machinist	30	"
V	McLaughlin Agnes—†	50	ropemaker	42	101 Rutherford av
W	McLaughlin Michael	50	retired	73	101 "
X	Taylor Dawn—†	50	housewife	21	here
Y	Smith Anna—†	58	"	27	"
Z	Smith William H	58	laborer	28	"

234

A	Seretta Anthony	58	carpenter	29	"
B	Seretta Louise—†	58	housewife	31	"
C	Harris Anna—†	58	"	25	
D	Harris George W, jr	58	electrician	27	"
E	McCann Leah—†	58	housewife	26	"
F	McCann Vincent	58	longshoreman	28	"
H	Drinkwater Alma—†	58	housewife	30	"
G	Drinkwater Charles	58	laborer	31	"
K	O'Neil John E	58	pipefitter	26	Medford
L	O'Neil Margaret—†	58	housewife	27	"
M	Shackelford John	66	guard	33	here
N	Shackelford Margaret—†	66	housewife	27	"
O	Russo Agatino	66	machinist	38	" .
P	Russo Florence—†	66	housewife	32	"
R	Lonergan Anna M—†	66	"	40	
S	Lonergan Frederick L	66	rigger	43	
T	Rock Frances L—†	66	housewife	33	"
U	Rock Richard J	66	leatherworker	33	"
V	Doherty Daniel	66	chipper	33	"
W	Doherty Mary—†	66	housewife	30	"
X	Florentino Arthur	66	operator	36	"
Y	Florentino Helen—†	66	housewife	34	"

235   Samuel Morse Way

A	Winters Charles F	9	laborer	31	here
B	Winters Mary T—†	9	housewife	27	"
C	O'Neil James	9	longshoreman	31	"
D	O'Neil Rita—†	9	housewife	22	"
E	Langan James L	9	longshoreman	25	"
F	Langan Margaret J—†	9	housewife	25	"
G	Mahoney Mary—†	9	at home	50	"
H	Kenney Frank H	9	laborer	27	

Samuel Morse Way—Continued

K	Kenney Marie E—†	9	housewife	27	here
L	Robbins Florence B—†	9	"	40	"
M	Robbins Milford A	9	timekeeper	37	"
N	Corbett Bernard F, jr	9	rigger	27	"
O	Corbett Elizabeth A—†	9	housewife	27	"
R	Cefalo Albert C	9	plumber	27	47 Lawrence
S	Cefalo Dorothy R—†	9	housewife	20	27 Austin
T	Warwick Jane E—†	9	"	37	here
U	Warwick William	9	bartender	37	"
V	Petruzielo Gerardo R	25	chauffeur	40	26 Tufts
W	Petruzielo Gertrude L—†	25	housewife	34	26 "
X	Glidden Carl H	25	driller	27	N Hampshire
Y	Glidden Dorothy K—†	25	housewife	25	"
Z	Marburger George H	25	die sinker	26	Cambridge
	236				
A	Marburger Lucille—†	25	housewife	22	"
B	Curran Catherine G—†	25	"	34	here
C	Curran Patrick	25	clerk	36	"
D	Bouba Anna—†	25	operator	28	"
E	Bouba Joseph	25	mechanic	35	"
F	Mitchell David W, jr	25	electrician	22	12 Wapping
G	Mitchell Elaine B—†	25	housewife	23	Illinois
H	Mitchell Lillian—†	25	student	25	here
K	Bowie Clyde A	25	operator	54	"
L	Bowie Emma C—†	25	housewife	54	"
M	Lipps Hugo O	25	retired	68	2 St James
N	Lipps Lillian F—†	25	housewife	58	2 "

Starr King Court

O	Gillen Elizabeth A—†	1	housewife	38	here
P	Gillen George E	1	carcleaner	42	"
R	Griffin John J	1	laborer	39	"
S	Griffin Margaret C—†	1	housewife	35	"
T	Finn Mildred A—†	1	"	46	
U	Finn William P	1	welder	49	
V	Buckley Alice C—†	1	housewife	37	"
W	Buckley Robert F	1	longshoreman	38	"
X	Maggelet Frank	1	clerk	33	
Y	Maggelet Grace—†	1	waitress	29	"
Z	Maloney Margaret M—†	1	housewife	45	"

237
Starr King Court—Continued

A	Maloney Patrick J	1	clerk	50	here
B	Adams Isabelle—†	9	housewife	42	"
C	Adams John H	9	longshoreman	46	"
D	Daley Anna—†	9	housewife	39	"
E	Daley Charles	9	coppersmith	38	"
F	White Kathleen M—†	9	housewife	46	"
G	White Robert E	9	operator	22	"
H	White Thomas E	9	laborer	52	
K	Cassidy Anna—†	9	housewife	47	"
L	Cassidy Charles J	9	hotelworker	44	"
M	Regan Margaret H—†	9	housewife	40	"
N	Regan Martin J	9	longshoreman	40	"
O	Tierney Francis V	9	janitor	44	
P	Tierney Mary E—†	9	housewife	40	"
R	O'Brien Catherine M—†	9	laborer	40	
S	Sances Catherine A—†	9	housewife	32	"
T	Sances Nicholas J	9	shipfitter	34	"
U	McCarthy Mary C—†	9	housewife	40	"
V	McCarthy Thomas H	9	machinist	39	"
W	Regan Anna M—†	25	at home	34	"
X	Regan Frances—†	25	housewife	68	"
Y	Regan John M	25	retired	79	
Z	Sullivan Timothy J	25	chauffeur	34	"
	238				
A	Sullivan Zoe—†	25	housewife	29	"
B	DeLorey Agnes—†	25	"	29	
C	DeLorey Lawrence M	25	brakeman	32	"
D	Whitney Agnes—†	25	at home	63	"
E	Hurley Evelyn—†	25	housewife	28	Quincy
F	Hurley Paul	25	machinist	37	"
G	Scaro John F	25	barber	37	here
H	Scaro Mary V—†	25	housewife	28	"
K	Magaldi Fredrick A	25	laborer	30	"
L	Magaldi Rose A—†	25	housewife	28	"
M	Allen Aaron	33	retired	90	Saugus
N	Nicoll Louise—†	33	clerk	45	Medford
O	Nicoll Maynard	33	seaman	23	"
P	Robinson Hazel C—†	33	housewife	31	Wash'n D C
R	Robinson Sidney S	33	U S N.	31	"
S	Moriarty Irene T—†	33	housewife	32	here

Starr King Court—Continued

T	Moriarty John J	33	laborer	32	here
U	Gooby John E	33	longshoreman	27	34 Sumner
V	Kelly Robert C	33	U S N	22	34 "
W	Sullo Johanna A—†	33	housewife	50	34 "
X	Raneri Leo A	33	calker	30	here
Y	Raneri Mary C—†	33	housewife	25	"
Z	Sheerin Nellie—†	33	"	50	"

239

A	Sheerin William	33	laborer	61	
B	Sheehan Margaret E—†	41	housewife	28	"
C	Sheehan Walter D	41	U S N	27	
D	Mahoney Bridget—†	41	housewife	39	"
E	Mahoney William	41	freighthandler	49	"
F	Regan John J	41	U S N	35	6 Harrison pk
G	Regan Thelma V—†	41	housewife	32	6 "
H	Stanley Mary A—†	41	"	26	here
K	Stanley Walter V	41	machinist	26	"
L	Burns Claire J—†	41	clerk	40	341 Bunker Hill
M	Schnebbe Regina—†	41	"	35	341 "
N	Long Ethel L—†	41	housewife	31	94 Forbes
O	Long Francis E	41	shipfitter	31	94 "
P	Berry Ann C—†	49	housewife	27	25 Dennis
R	Berry Hollis M	49	U S N	26	25 "
S	Maglio Helen E—†	49	housewife	31	65 St Alphonsus
T	Maglio James V	49	U S N	38	65 "
U	Manning Janet—†	49	housewife	30	Virginia
V	Manning William	49	plumber	35	"
W	Brown Dorothy M—†	49	housewife	27	here
X	Brown James	49	longshoreman	29	"
Y	Rooney Catherine T—†	49	housewife	33	"
Z	Rooney William J	49	clerk	31	

240

A	McKillop Ethel M—†	49	housewife	29	"
B	McKillop John E	49	chauffeur	28	"

Vine Street

C	DiGrezio Anthony	3	U S A	29	here
D	DiGrezio Gennaro	3	shoemaker	60	"
E	DiGrezio George	3	electrician	21	"
F	DiGrezio Lena A—†	3	housewife	24	"

Walford Way

G	Doherty Ellen R—†	9	welder	33	here
H	Doherty John J	9	printer	33	"
K	Leary Helen—†	9	nurse	63	"
L	Fuller Gladys A—†	9	housewife	33	N Hampshire
M	Fuller Henry E	9	brazier	29	"
N	Willan Eva—†	9	housewife	25	here
O	Willan Peter F	9	metalworker	27	"
P	Beauchamp Lucien W	9	laborer	40	"
R	Beauchamp Nancy K—†	9	housewife	31	"
S	Gooby Edward A	9	U S N	23	..
T	Gooby Mary W—†	9	housewife	59	"
U	Reilly Catherine R—†	9	"	36	
V	Reilly John A	9	U S N	42	"
W	Beadle Clyde E	9	boilermaker	46	26 Tremont
X	Beadle Gladys L—†	9	housewife	44	26 "
Y	Waterman Lorene D—†	9	clerk	22	26 "
Z	Tognarelli Marie—†	9	housewife	27	here

241

A	Tognarelli Vincent R	9	operator	27	"
B	Mayo Blanche M—†	9	painter	22	19 Concord
C	Thibodeau Ann F—†	9	housewife	30	19 "
D	Thibodeau George T	9	rigger	38	19 "
E	Fitzgerald Ann F—†	10	housewife	38	26 O'Brien ct
F	Fitzgerald Chester W	10	guard	35	26 "
G	Hurley Catherine F—†	10	at home	64	here
H	Lucas Catherine L—†	10	housekeeper	68	"
K	Kelly Francis W	10	laborer	55	Somerville
L	Kelly Marjorie—†	10	housewife	44	"
M	Crann Elizabeth—†	10	"	45	here
N	Crann James	10	operator	55	"
O	Daly Josephine—†	10	"	37	New York
P	Daly Mary K—†	10	at home	73	Maine
R	Shea Catherine—†	10	"	78	here
S	Shea Catherine—†	10	cashier	37	"
T	Hurley Elizabeth N—†	10	housewife	38	"
U	Hurley Michael J	10	policeman	39	"
V	Long Annie M—†	10	housewife	29	22 Monum'nt sq
W	Long Benjamin W	10	U S N	39	22 "
X	Leary Amelia—†	10	housewife	25	here
Y	Leary Thomas F	10	floorman	31	"
Z	McCullough Eugene T	25	driller	32	"

2—2

25

242
Walford Way—Continued

A	McCullough Mary C—†	25	housewife	30	here
B	Spada Frank	25	retired	73	"
C	Spada Vincenza—†	25	housewife	65	"
D	Green Albertina H—†	25	"	44	
E	Green William J	25	rigger	45	
F	Graham James F	25	machinist	32	"
G	Graham Madeleine C—†	25	housewife	32	"
H	Quackenbush Gladys—†	25	"	21	New York
K	Quackenbush Walter	25	U S N	21	"
L	Tinkham Ralph E	25	painter	53	here
M	Tinkham Viola—†	25	housewife	50	"
N	Abbott Eleanor B—†	25	"	31	"
O	Abbott John B	25	clerk	34	"
R	Yancoskie Francis	25	U S C G	31	"
S	Yancoskie Ruth—†	25	housewife	24	"
T	Rupp Anna S—†	26	"	34	715 Walk Hill
U	Rupp William J	26	pipefitter	36	715 "
V	Cole Benjamin G	26	fireman	55	here
W	Cole Mary J—†	26	housewife	61	"
X	McCarthy Catherine R—†	26	"	39	"
Y	McCarthy Thomas J	26	laborer	42	"
Z	Nadolina Fred A	26	seaman	39	Lynn

243

A	Nelson Catherine S—†	26	housewife	47	Everett
B	Nelson William M	26	brazier	48	"
C	Kenne George C	26	U S C G	35	here
D	Kenne Marion A—†	26	housewife	30	"
E	Sullivan Lorraine D—†	26	"	35	"
F	Sullivan William H	26	foreman	41	"
G	Sturtevant Elsie M—†	26	housewife	34	Cambridge
H	Sturtevant Kenneth M	26	executive	36	"
K	Boyd Grace—†	26	clerk	30	here
L	Boyd Mary—†	26	waitress	55	"
M	Hermann Virginia T—†	26	housewife	20	"
N	Waters Mary A—†	26	"	44	
O	Waters Thomas J	26	electrician	43	"

10

11

3

12

4

1

5

14

6

15

7

16

8

d 2–Precinct 3

ITY OF BOSTON

F RESIDENTS
S OF AGE AND OVER

ENS INDICATED BY ASTERISK)
ES INDICATED BY DAGGER)

AS OF

U   1, 1944

THOMAS F. SULLIVAN, *Chairman*
FREDERIC E. DOWLING, *Secretary*
WILLIAM A. MOTLEY, JR.
FRANCIS B. McKINNEY
EVERETT R. PROUT

Listing Board.

OSTON ⬥ PRINTING DEPARTMENT

10
11
12
4
13
5
1
6
1
7
8

300
Bunker Hill Street

	Letter	Full Name	Residence	Occupation	Age	Reported Residence
	w	Lupo Leonora—†	21	housekeeper	76	here
	x	Danahy Patrick F	21	brakeman	20	283 Main
	y	Malone Catherine R—†	21	housewife	52	283 "
	z	Malone Joseph F	21	laborer	36	283 "

301

	Letter	Full Name	Residence	Occupation	Age	Reported Residence
	a	Byam Sarah—†	22	at home	69	here
	b	Doherty Mary A—†	22	"	65	"
	c	Donahoe Ellen—†	22	"	70	"
	d	Thompson Elizabeth—†	22	"	70	"
	e	McGinnis Edward M	23	retired	65	
	f	Kirk Catherine A—†	23	housewife	33	"
	g	Kirk William N	23	painter	35	"
	h	Lefford George E	23	U S N	50	52 Tremont
	k	Toner John L	24	ropemaker	46	here
	l	Toner Rose E—†	24	housewife	40	"
	m	Gemellaro Basil	25	shipfitter	25	37 Henley
	n	Gemellaro Katherine—†	25	housewife	24	37 "
	o	Calabresi Frank	25	shoeworker	38	85 Ferrin
	p	Calabresi Rose—†	25	housewife	30	85 "
	r	Coffey Mary J—†	26	forewoman	22	here
	s	Ryan Mary F—†	26	housewife	42	"
	t	Ryan Patrick	26	attendant	42	"
	v	Donoghue Bernard C	28	innkeeper	60	"
	w	Laffey John	28	retired	70	

302

	Letter	Full Name	Residence	Occupation	Age	Reported Residence
	b	McMahon Elizabeth J—†	31	housewife	56	"
	c	McMahon Francis A	31	U S N	31	
	d	McMahon Helen V—†	31	operator	28	"
	e	Kehoe Elizabeth—†	31	at home	74	"
	g	*Ramsey Phoebe—†	32	housewife	59	15 Decatur
	h	Ramsey Walter	32	chipper	30	15 "
	m	Horrigan Ellen E—†	34A	housewife	70	here
	n	Sullivan Daniel	34A	watchman	64	"
	p	Kelly Claudia B—†	35	stenographer	23	"
	r	Kelly Grace P—†	35	"	26	"
	s	Kelly Joseph D	35	mortician	59	"
	t	Nice Margaret—†	36	cook	55	
	u	Delli Veneri Margaret M—†	36	housewife	49	"
	v	Delli Veneri Vincent E	36	statistician	47	"

Page.	Letter.	FULL NAME.	Residence, Jan. 1, 1944.	Occupation.	Supposed Age.	Reported Residence, Jan. 1, 1943. Street and Number.

Bunker Hill Street—Continued

	w	*Yee Gin Ning	38	laundryman	29	here
	z	Barry Barbara—†	40½	housewife	50	"
303						
	A	Barry Patrick F	40½	fireman	54	..
	B	Murphy Anna V—†	42A	housekeeper	60	"
	E	Donati Eda—†	46	shoeworker	22	"
	F	Donati Marie—†	46	housewife	40	"
	G	Donati Vittorio	46	cook	50	
	H	Ercolini Frank	46	innkeeper	56	"
	K	*Pelosi Eleanor—†	46	housewife	57	"
	L	Pelosi Joseph	46	retired	67	

Chelsea Street

	O	Cronin Kathleen M—†	112	inspector	43	here
	P	Cronin Michael	112	retired	77	"
	R	King Helen T—†	112	boxmaker	40	"
	S	King John W	112	supt	34	·
	T	King Mark J	112	investigator	29	"
	U	King Mary F—†	112	forewoman	42	"
	V	King Mary M—†	112	housewife	68	"
	W	King Thomas J	112	clerk	38	
	Y	Stafford Florence—†	128	housewife	37	"
	Z	Stafford Walter M	128	guard	45	..
304						
	A	Lyons Catherine—†	128	housewife	34	"
	B	Lyons Catherine B—†	128	"	58	
	C	Pinder Margaret—†	128	welder	28	
	F	Eatherton Elizabeth—†	130	housewife	53	"
	G	Eatherton Francis	130	U S A	26	"
	H	Eatherton Joseph	130	packer	28	
	K	Eatherton Philip	130	seaman	· 26	"
	L	Foster Helen—†	130	housewife	23	"
	M	Foster Raymond	130	U S N	25	
	N	McCaffrey James E	130	laborer	61	
	O	McCaffrey Katherine—†	130	clerk	34	
	P	McCaffrey Martin	130	U S A	20	
	R	McCaffrey Mary—†	130	operator	29	"
	T	Giangrieco Nicola	136	laborer	50	"
	U	Hogan Mary E—†	136	stitcher	45	"

Chelsea Street—Continued

v	Hogan Peter	136	pipefitter	46	here
w	Tarquini Emilio L	136	welder	31	"
x	Tarquini Josephine M—†	136	housewife	28	"
y	Fields Anna V—†	137	"	37	10 Mystic pl
z	Stella Marie—†	137	"	31	here

305

a	Stella William	137	laborer	39	
b	Connolly Delia J—†	137	cleaner	56	
d	Alleruzzo Antonio	138	barber	60	
e	Alleruzzo Pasqualino	138	retired	48	
f	Alleruzzo Peter	138	machinist	57	"
k	*Alleruzzo Mary—†	139	at home	82	"

Corey Street

m	Howell Jean P—†	40	housewife	25	here
n	Howell Luke	40	longshoreman	29	"
o	Burke Bernard F	40	retired	32	36 Harold
p	Burke Mary—†	40	housewife	62	36 "
r	Burke Michael	40	rigger	62	36 "
s	O'Neil Charles W	40	chauffeur	39	here
t	O'Neil Emma G—†	40	housewife	33	"
u	Keenan Anna—†	40	"	40	"
v	Keenan John	40	collector	50	"
w	Peterson Charles	40	U S N	40	"
x	Peterson Emily M—†	40	housewife	39	"
y	Hurley Alice M—†	40	"	32	"
z	Hurley Joseph P	40	chauffeur	34	"

306

a	LaPlante Catherine E—†	48	housewife	24	"
b	LaPlante Francis L	48	pipefitter	27	"
c	Hastings Ann J—†	48	housewife	34	"
d	Hastings Leonard T	48	clerk	38	
e	Griffin Laura—†	48	housewife	23	"
f	Woods Helen—†	48	clerk	45	
g	Woods Helen—†	48	packer	21	"
h	Boyden Anna N—†	48	housewife	24	Medford
k	Boyden James R	48	chauffeur	26	"
l	Taylor Helen V—†	48	clerk	31	here

Corey Street—Continued

	M	Long Ernest C	48	U S N	31	here
	N	Long Rita M—†	48	housewife	28	"

Decatur Street

	s	Shay Nora—†	7	housewife	65	here
	T	Olenick William	7	shipper	41	"
	U	Daly Agnes E—†	7	operator	51	"
	V	Daly Helena G—†	7	"	52	
	W	Fitzpatrick Mary C—†	7	clerk	36	"
	X	Dyer Theresa—†	9	housewife	60	"
	Y	Egan Emily J—†	9	housekeeper	43	"
307						
	A	Kelly Frederick	10	U S A	21	"
	B	Kelly Lemuel	10	pipefitter	48	"
	c*	Kelly Margaret—†	10	housewife	31	"
	D	Capuano James	10	laborer	33	"
	E	Capuano Trina—†	10	housewife	29	"
	F	Tambuzza Celia—†	10	stitcher	21	"
	G	Tambuzza Jennie—†	10	housewife	41	"
	H	Tambuzza Joseph	10	laborer	53	"
	K	Hanson Etta J—†	11	housewife	70	"
	L	Houghton Cornelius	11	laborer	69	"
	M	Houghton Elizabeth—†	11	housewife	69	"
	N	Doherty Sarah—†	11	maid	65	"
	R	Collins Herbert J	13	laborer	43	"
	s	Dinsmoor Florence E—†	13	housewife	66	"
	T	McLaughlin Annie—†	13	"	58	
	U	McLaughlin Eugene	13	laborer	58	"
	V	Marston Susan—†	13	housewife	77	"
	W	Wilson Arthur L	15	shipfitter	52	N Hampshire
	X	Wilson Hilda D—†	15	housewife	53	"

308   Edgeworth Street

	D	Hamilton Edward L	4	shipfitter	57	here
	E	Wilson John L	4	chauffeur	27	"
	F	Wilson Marion—†	4	at home	21	"
	H	Leonard Elizabeth M—†	6	"	55	"

Edgeworth Street—Continued

	K	Leonard John J	6	clerk	26	here
	L	Leonard William	6	longshoreman	54	"

Ferrin Street

	N	Daggett Leona—†	4	operator	50	here
	O	Toomey Florence E—†	4	housewife	25	"
	P	Toomey Joseph P	4	clerk	25	"
	R	Caiander Axel	10	retired	77	
	S	Gaines Susan—†	10	at home	72	"
	T	Kennedy Christopher B	10	seaman	44	New Jersey
	U	White Lulalene—†	10	housewife	50	here
	Y	Brannigan Harvey	12	U S N	22	"
	Z	McCarthy Charles H	12	electrician	32	"
309						
	A	McCarthy James F	12	retired	71	
	B	McCarthy James J	12	U S N	31	
	C	McCarthy Mary E—†	12	clerk	25	
	D	McCarthy Nora J—†	12	housewife	68	"
	E	McCarthy Vincent F	12	letter carrier	29	"
	F	Brice William	14	chauffeur	58	14 Pearl
	G	Craig Joseph	16	laborer	58	38 Mead
	L	Cardinale Angelo A	22	dishwasher	64	here
	M*DeCristoforo Michelena-†	22	at home	72	"
	R	DeAngelo Emma—†	24	housewife	36	"
	S	DeAngelo Peter	24	plasterer	42	"
	T	English Mariano	26	retired	60	
	U*Jesso Grace—†	26	housewife	39	"
	V	Jesso Michael	26	presser	45	
	W*Apice Antoinette D—†	26	housewife	29	"
	X	Apice Generoso D	26	cutter	26	
	Y*McDermott Delia A—†	28	at home	51	"
	Z	Devlin Bernard E	29	laborer	23	
310						
	A	Devlin Dorothy M—†	29	housewife	25	"
	B	Pollock Ethel B—†	29	"	40	
	C	Pollock Robert H	29	machinist	43	"
	D	Donohue Frances—†	29	at home	65	"
	E	Lamb Mary—†	30	"	68	
	F	Hamilton Edward P	32	retired	84	
	G	Hamilton Esther V—†	32	at home	31	"

Age.	Letter.	FULL NAME.	Residence, Jan. 1, 1944.	Occupation.	Supposed Age.	Reported Residence, Jan. 1, 1943. Street and Number.

Ferrin Street—Continued

	H	Glavin Richard	32	laborer	45	here
	K	Stapleton Martin	32	"	40	"
	L	Cottingham Frances J—†	32	at home	22	"
	M	Cottingham John W	32	machinist	59	"
	N	Cottingham Robert N	32	U S A	24	
	O	Cottingham Sarah—†	32	housewife	58	"
	P	McIntosh Bessie—†	32	at home	59	"
	R	Butler John J	33	laborer	53	"
	T	Tampkins Josephine—†	33	housewife	31	"
	U	Tompkins Raymond C	33	chauffeur	30	"
	V	Gilmore Arthur H	35	U S A	34	
	W	Gilmore Rose E—†	35	housewife	61	"
	X	Gilmore Samuel W	35	laborer	33	"
	Y	Leseuer John F	35	"	56	147 Chelsea
	Z	Leseuer Mary—†	35	housewife	54	147 "
		311				
	A	Lailer Mary E—†	35	at home	28	here
	B	O'Brien Isabella C—†	38	housewife	36	"
	C	O'Brien Joseph J	38	metalworker	37	"
	E	Sullivan Marie G—†	40	housewife	49	"
	F	Sullivan William F	40	storekeeper	56	"

McNulty Court

	H	Perry Louis P	1	machinist	33	127 Brighton
	K	Perry Ruth A—†	1	housewife	26	127 "
	L	Cataldo Lena R—†	1	"	21	here
	M	Cataldo Philip J	1	U S A	23	"
	N	Power John J	1	laborer	68	Belmont
	O	Power Mary O—†	1	housewife	49	"
	P	Moran Bridget—†	1	nurse	29	here
	R	Shea Abbie—†	1	housewife	61	"
	S	O'Driscoll John	1	U S A	20	"
	T	Perreault Catherine—†	1	housewife	23	"
	U	Perreault Lucian	1	U S A	26	
	V	Walsh Alice H—†	9	housewife	24	"
	W	Walsh Redmond C	9	freighthandler	25	"
	X	Martin Eileen—†	9	housewife	32	"
	Y	Martin John	9	chauffeur	37	"
	Z	Hartnett Helen—†	9	housewife	34	Alabama

312

McNulty Court—Continued

A	Sullivan Daniel F	9	sorter	58	here
B	Sullivan Melvina—†	9	housewife	55	"
C	Allegra Dominic J	9	plumber	28	"
D	Allegra Margaret—†	9	housewife	28	"
E	Rumney Ann R—†	9	"	34	
F	Rumney Robert C	9	chemist	30	"
G	Mantineo Pearl—†	9	housewife	28	"
H	Mantineo Ralph	9	U S N	31	
K	Woods Dorothy E—†	17	housewife	39	"
L	Woods John S	17	U S A	42	
M	Crowley James F	17	chauffeur	23	"
N	Crowley Olive V—†	17	housewife	21	"
O	Gass Joseph W	17	chauffeur	22	98 Walford way
P	Gass Louise—†	17	housewife	25	98 "
R	Murphy George F	17	chauffeur	35	here
S	Murphy Mary D—†	17	housewife	29	"
T	Fiore Alphonso	17	checker	36	"
U	Fiore Catherine T—†	17	housewife	30	"
V	Nardone Frances—†	17	"	30	"
W	Nardone Joseph	17	U S N	31	

Medford Street

Y	Cousens Charles A	90	attendant	33	here
Z	Cousens Laura J—†	90	housewife	31	"

313

A	Kerrigan Joseph N	90	electrician	28	Connecticut
B	Kerrigan Naomi—†	90	housewife	25	"
C	Teal Annabella—†	90	"	36	30 Staniford
D	Teal Arthur	90	guard	44	30 "
E	Farrell Helen—†	90	housewife	34	here
F	Farrell James H	90	laborer	32	"
G	Kelly Bridget—†	90	housewife	53	"
H	Kelly Charles A	90	salesman	48	"
K	Pelton Andrew R	90	U S N	27	Fall River
L	Pelton Mildred R—†	90	housewife	25	"
M	Rutledge Gertrude—†	90	clerk	46	Tewksbury
N	Rutledge Robert J	90	operator	48	"
O	Dowling John	90	retired	73	` here
P	Dowling Margaret M—†	90	housewife	62	"

8

Medford Street—Continued

R	McGah Mary S—†	90	clerk	28	here
S	Moore Helen—†	98	housewife	59	"
T	McGowan Helen—†	98	"	57	"
U	McGowan John J	98	retired	70	"
V	Mason Anna—†	98	housewife	55	"
W	Mason William	98	chauffeur	55	"
Y	McCarthy Eugene	98	attendant	50	"
Z	McCarthy Mildred—†	98	housewife	49	"

314

A	Connolly John F	98	baker	51	
B	Connolly Mary A—†	98	housewife	37	"
C	Tyrrell James J	98	attendant	38	"
D	Tyrrell Pauline—†	98	housewife	29	"
E	Monahan Mary—†	98	"	56	"
F	Masterson Anna M—†	98	"	37	
G	Masterson Thomas J	98	rigger	42	

Moulton Street

M	Kelley Catherine C—†	9A	housewife	51	here
N	Kelley Francis A	9A	U S N	28	"
O	Kelley Stephen J	9A	clerk	54	"
P	Kelley William J	9A	U S A	33	
R	Flaherty Rita V—†	9A	secretary	28	"
S	Holm Herbert B	9A	retired	66	
U	Harris Helen M—†	11	housewife	21	"
V	Lupo Emma M—†	11	"	47	
W	Lupo Joseph J	11	printer	55	
X	McCarthy Henry F	11	storekeeper	48	"
Y	Doherty Arthur J	11	seaman	22	"
Z	Doherty Elizabeth M—†	11	marker	44	"

315

A	Doherty John A	11	machinist	54	"
B	Doherty Joseph E	11	laborer	28	

O'Reilly Way

C	Maxon Robert	1	retired	67	here
D	Connors John J	1	chauffeur	26	14½ Mt Vernon
E	Connors Patrick J	1	retired	58	14½ "
F	Roche Thomas H	1	chauffeur	41	here

O'Reilly Way—Continued

G	Corella Joseph T	1	pipefitter	51	Somerville
H	Corella Louise M—†	1	housewife	51	Lowell
K	Dailly Helen—†	1	"	32	here
L	Dailly John B	1	U S N	32	"
M	Santarpio Henry M	1	chauffeur	35	"
N	Santarpio Stella—†	1	housewife	32	"
O	Osusky Mary—†	1	"	53	
P	Osusky Paul	1	boilermaker	57	"
R	Pederson Edward M	1	broommaker	41	"
S	Pederson Mary M—†	1	housewife	40	"
T	Keating Henry	1	machinist	36	"
U	Keating Lillian—†	1	housewife	29	"
V	Coughlin Mary L—†	9	"	37	
W	Coughlin William H	9	welder	40	
X	Raftery John T	9	chauffeur	27	"
Y	Raftery Rita—†	9	housewife	25	"
Z	Smith Isabel—†	9	"	21	118 Medford

316

A	Smith William E	9	meter reader	22	118 "
B	Malcolmson James M	9	pipefitter	47	here
C	Malcolmson Mary—†	9	housewife	43	"
D	McClellan Gilford	9	retired	42	"
E	McClellan Martha—†	9	clerk	44	
F	Sheehan Helen V—†	9	housewife	23	"
G	Sheehan John H	9	mechanic	25	"
H	Ballou Louise M—†	9	housewife	42	"
K	Ballou Thomas J	9	maintenance	44	."
L	Leonard Agnes B—†	9	clerk	39	"
M	Leonard Gladys—†	9	"	36	
N	Hennessey Arthur J	9	machinist	36	"
O	Hennessey Catherine—†	9	housewife	40	"

Prospect Avenue

P	Donovan Arthur B	1	bartender	48	here
R	Donovan Mary B—†	1	housewife	34	"
S	Lento Mary R—†	1	"	43	48 Henley
T*	Connolly Abbie—†	1	"	46	here
U	Connolly Martin	1	longshoreman	47	"
V	Gould Bridget F—†	2	housewife	41	"
W	Gould John F	2	U S N	21	

Prospect Avenue—Continued

x	Gould Thomas J	2	longshoreman	51	here
y	Bowman Stella—†	2	inspector	29	"
z	Giuffre Anna—†	2	clerk	25	"
	317				
a	Giuffre Caterina—†	2	housewife	52	"
b	Giuffre Nunzio	2	laborer	23	"
c	Normandie Earl	2	U S A	30	New York
d	Normandie Lena—†	2	stenographer	24	here
e	Feehy Daniel J	2	machinist	62	"
f	*Feehy Mary A—†	2	housewife	55	"
g	Feehy Mary E—†	2	clerk	22	"
h	Currier Margaret C—†	3	housewife	33	23 Elm
k	Currier William H	3	laborer	23	23 "
m	McDonald John F	3	boilermaker	42	52½ Wash'n
o	*Connolly Bridget—†	4	housewife	48	here
p	Connolly Mark	4	longshoreman	46	"
r	Sullivan Mary T—†	4	stenographer	20	"
s	Lynch Margaret M—†	4	housewife	23	28 Clifford
t	Manning Catherine—†	4	"	51	here
u	Manning Catherine F—†	4	operator	25	"
v	Manning Dennis	4	janitor	56	"
w	Manning Mary A—†	4	clerk	22	

Prospect Street

x	Burns Mabel H—†	3	housewife	32	here
y	Burns William E	3	watchman	33	"
z	Smith James	3	U S A	25	"
	318				
a	Smith Pauline—†	3	supervisor	40	"
b	Mizokami Ellen M—†	3	housewife	47	"
c	Mizokami Sado	3	retired	59	
d	Gonnella Catherine—†	3A	housewife	38	"
e	Gonnella John J	3A	bartender	44	"
f	Deery John J	3A	pipefitter	41	"
g	Deery Joseph P	3A	chauffeur	39	"
h	Deery Margaret—†	3A	housewife	68	"
k	Burns George N	3A	seaman	22	"
l	Burns John T	3A	letter carrier	30	"
m	Burns Katherine—†	3A	housewife	53	"
n	DeAngelis Aldagesa—†	5	clerk	20	

Prospect Street—Continued

o	*DeAngelis Concetta—†	5	housewife	50	here	
p	DeAngelis Michael A	5	laborer	56	"	
r	Zeeman Chester B	5	U S N	25 .	"	
s	Zeeman Rose M—†	5	housewife	24	"	
t	Kenney Ralph E	5	shipper	24		
u	Paz Ethel I—†	5	housewife	26	"	
v	Paz Faustino B	5	ropemaker	51	"	
w	Pierce Rita F—†	5	housewife	29	70 Russell	
x	Pierce William F	5	longshoreman	30	70 "	
y	Whitney Arthur L	7	chipper	44	42 Pleasant	
z	Whitney Fanny B—†	7	housewife	41	42 "	

319

a	Donovan Mary—†	7	housekeeper	66	here	
b	Cuddihy James M	7	salesman	20	"	
c	Cuddihy Thomas J	7	U S A	22	"	
d	Rizzo Edmund J	7	electrician	31	"	
e	Rizzo Mary M—†	7	housewife	31	"	
f	Shea Bridget M—†	9	"	48	"	
g	Shea Patrick F	9	builder	50	"	
h	LaTerz Catherine T—†	9	operator	21	Somerville	
k	LaTerz Michael F	9	U S N	26	"	
l	Rumley Helen L—†	9	operator	25	here	
m	Rumley Mary—†	9	housewife	54	"	
n	Rumley Thomas F	9	laborer	56	"	
o	Rumley Thomas J	9	U S N	23	"	
p	*McLaughlin Charles E	9	baker	53	33 Winthrop	
r	*McLaughlin Florence A—†	9	housewife	46	33 "	
s	Young Andrew L	11	shipwright	49	here	
t	Young Dorothy G—†	11	housewife	47	"	
u	Hogan Elizabeth J—†	11	"	55	"	
v	Hogan George T	11	clerk	27	"	
w	Morris Irene E—†	11	bookkeeper	34	"	
x	Bishop Elizabeth A—†	11	housewife	33	" .	
y	Bishop Robert W	11	U S N	42		
z	McInnis Ellen T—†	11	at home	70	"	

320

a	McInnis Francis P	11	rigger	29	"	
b	McInnis John A	11	watchman	70	"	
c	Savage Frances M—†	15	operator	24	"	
d	Savage Frank	15	fireman	51	"	
e	Savage Jennie C—†	15	housewife	50	"	

Prospect Street—Continued

F	Savage Ruth M—†	15	stenographer	21	here
G	Morrissey Edward W	15	U S N	28	"
H	Morrissey Gertrude A—†	15	teacher	29	"
K	Morrissey Helen N—†	15	stenographer	20	"
L	Morrissey Johanna—†	15	housewife	57	"
M	Morrissey Thomas	15	laborer	70	"
N	Morrissey Thomas E	15	U S A	35	"
O	Morrissey Frances L—†	15	operator	50	"
P	Cotter Alice G—†	17	housewife	43	"
R	Cotter John F	17	chauffeur	45	"
S	Cotter Nelson T	17	U S N	20	"
T	Vessella Angelo A	17	riveter	29	
U	Vessella Leonora—†	17	housewife	37	"
V	Morrissey Joan—†	17	"	71	
W	Morrissey Richard B	17	longshoreman	65	"
X	Leahy Henry E—†	19	shipfitter	48	"
Y	Leahy Josephine A—†	19	housewife	54	"
Z	Anadore Charles E	19	U S A	30	"
	321				
A	Anadore Francis J	19	shipfitter	28	"
B	Anadore John J	19	clerk	64	
C	Anadore Mary B—†	19	stenographer	33	"
D	Anadore Sarah H—†	19	housewife	62	"
E	Greene Daniel	19	retired	72	
F	Greene Mary A—†	19	clerk	60	
G	Hanley Margaret—†	19	waitress	30	"
H	Toomey John E	21	clerk	34	"
K	Toomey John J	21	retired	72	"
L	Toomey Mary—†	21	housewife	62	"
M	VonHartenstein Harriet-†	21	"	71	"
N	VonHartenstein Siegfried	21	retired	71	
O	Barry Margaret A—†	21	housewife	72	"
P	Barry Margaret M—†	21	secretary	32	"
R	Murphy Bridget A—†	21	housewife	54	"
S	Murphy John J	21	clerk	59	
T	Havey Robert W	23	U S N	23	
U	Havey Rosemarie—†	23	housewife	23	"
V	Maisey Ann C—†	23	clerk	20	
W	Maisey Margaret M—†	23	housewife	48	"
X	Maisey William A	23	ironworker	56	"
Y	Maisey William A	23	U S N	25	"

Page.	Letter.	FULL NAME.	Residence, Jan. 1, 1944.	Occupation.	Supposed Age.	Reported Residence, Jan. 1, 1943. Street and Number.

322

Prospect Street—Continued

A	Giannelli Anna—†	27	bookkeeper	34	here
B	Giannelli Christina—†	27	clerk	22	"
C	Giannelli Fidele	27	retired	67	"
D	Giannelli John	27	technician	27	"
E	Giannelli Joseph	27	fireman	31	"
F	Curry Mary E—†	29	housewife	31	"
G	Curry Stephen C	29	plumber	39	"
H	Gillespie Catherine T—†	31	housewife	54	"
K	Gillespie Margaret—†	31	clerk	21	
L	Shannon Anna M—†	31	"	32	
M	Moffitt Julia—†	31	housewife	60	"
N	Sweeney Catherine B—†	31	"	30	
O	Sweeney Edward F	31	investigator	38	"

Tremont Street

Y	Kelley David E	50	pipefitter	37	19 Hall
Z	Kelley Mary J—†	50	housewife	29	19 "

323

A	Doherty Helen V—†	50	housekeeper	51	here
B	McCarthy Mary—†	50	housewife	65	"
C*	Hjorth Gehard	52	painter	50	"
D	Hjorth Theresa—†	52	housewife	50	"
E	Vogelhuber Nora—†	52	"	45	
H	Morehart Sarah F—†	53	clerk	31	
K	Scannell Daniel J	53	laborer	53	
L	Scannell David	53	"	48	
M	Quinn Doris I—†	53	housewife	27	"
N	Quinn Joseph F	53	welder	31	
O	Byrnes Robert	54	laborer	56	
P	Murphy Agnes—†	54	housewife	60	"
R	Murphy Michael J	54	operator	60	"
S	Mullen James F	55	salesman	55	"
T	Mullen Michael J	55	painter	60	
V	McMahon Bridget—†	55	housewife	75	"
W	Brunetta Jennie—†	56	"	25	
X	Brunetta John	56	watchman	31	"
Y	Gallagher Rose—†	56	candymaker	40	"
Z	Pelosi Elizabeth—†	56	housewife	43	"

Page.	Letter.	Full Name.	Residence, Jan. 1, 1944.	Occupation.	Supposed Age.	Reported Residence, Jan. 1, 1943. Street and Number.

324
Tremont Street—Continued

A	*Pelosi Joseph	56	cobbler	47	here	
B	Courtney Winfield	57	draftsman	23	"	
C	Roche Walter	57	retired	51	"	
D	Carrigan Helen—†	57	seamstress	50	"	
E	O'Meara John	57	supervisor	45	"	
F	O'Meara Mary—†	57	dressmaker	50	"	
G	Bumstead George	57	shipfitter	41	"	
H	Bumstead Mary—†	57	clerk	48		
K	Bumstead Robert	57	foreman	52	"	
M	Donovan Catherine—†	58	housewife	35	"	
N	Donovan William	58	laborer	38	"	
O	Brett Dorothy—†	58	housewife	28	77 School	
P	Brett John F	58	laborer	30	77 "	
S	O'Neil John P	60	"	34	170 Medford	
T	O'Neil Mary R—†	60	housewife	29	170 "	
U	Smith George H	60	U S N	39	here	
V	Smith Mary A—†	60	painter	39	"	
W	Devlin Albert C	61	laborer	40	"	
X	Devlin Frances A—†	61	forewoman	42	"	
Y	Devlin Julia—†	61	housewife	67	" .	
Z	Doucette Alice—†	61	"	44		

325

A	Doucette Leon	61	dairyman	46	"	
B	Doucette Rita—†	61	factoryhand	22	"	
C	McCarthy Margaret—†	61	housekeeper	49	"	
D	Sullivan Elizabeth—†	61	clerk	35	"	
E	Sullivan John	61	U S N	39		
F	Sloane Catherine—†	62	housewife	49	"	
H	Mealey Agnes—†	63	cashier	55		
K	McCarthy Anna J—†	63	assembler	24	"	
L	McCarthy John F	63	U S A	27	"	
M	McCarthy John J	63	checker	56	"	
N	McCarthy Mary M—†	63	housewife	52	"	
S	O'Donnell Mary J—†	65	"	66		
T	O'Donnell William F	65	retired	69		
U	Daly John T	65	laborer	65		
V	Daly Nora J—†	65	housewife	56	"	
W	O'Rourke Catherine A—†	65	clerk	21	"	
X	Roche John J	65	laborer	60	"	

15

Tremont Street—Continued

Y	Roche Mary F—†	65	housewife	48	here
z	Roche Mary F—†	65	student	21	"
326					
A	Grennell Frederick	66	boilermaker	52	"
B	Hannafin Anna F—†	66	housewife	62	"
c	Hannafin John F	66	U S N	26	"
D	Lordan Dennis	66	laborer	41	2 Prospect
E	*Lambert Mary—†	67	domestic	59	here
F	Davis Frank	67	chauffeur	50	"
G	Davis Marie—†	67	housewife	44	"
H	Sullivan Mary—†	67	"	60	
K	Fallon Annie—†	68	"	67	
L	Fallon Everett J	68	retired	73	
M	Gaffney Catherine—†	68	at home	72	"
N	Butler Irene—†	68	pipefitter	36	"
o	Butler Walter	68	chauffeur	39	"
P	Quinn Alice—†	69	housekeeper	23	2 Foss
R	Quinn Patricia A—†	69	WAVE	20	here
s	Quinn Stephen	69	laborer	53	2 Foss
T	Lavoie Louis	69	boilermaker	33	N Hampshire
U	Lavoie Pauline—†	69	housewife	29	"
v	Devlin Harold F	69	shipfitter	30	here
w	Devlin Mary—†	69	housewife	28	"
x	Brennan Evelyn—†	70	tel operator	30	Uxbridge
Y	Brennan Lawrence	70	electrician	35	"
z	Morandi Ella—†	72	housewife	50	here
327					
A	Morandi Richard	72	steamfitter	50	"
B	Taylor Mildred—†	72	waitress	32	"
c	Brophy Florence—†	72	housewife	35	"
D	Brophy Harold	72	boilermaker	35	"
E	Weil Antionette—†	74	housewife	27	"
F	Weil George	74	rigger	38	
G	*Pennachio Joseph	74	retired	72	
H	Pennachio Pasquale	74	U S A	28	
K	*Pennachio Theresa—†	74	housewife	68	"
L	Coviello John A	74	chipper	27	"
M	Coviello Madeline—†	74	housewife	26	"
N	Thompson Anna—†	76	"	39	12 Medford
o	Thompson Mary—†	76	"	76	12 "
P	LaPointe Phebia	76	laborer	48	1A Pleasant

Page.	Letter.	Full Name.	Residence, Jan. 1, 1944.	Occupation.	Supposed Age.	Reported Residence, Jan. 1, 1943. Street and Number.

Tremont Street—Continued

R	La Pointe Yvonne—†	76	housewife	42	1A Pleasant
s	*Houghton Catherine—†	76	waitress	34	here
T	*Houghton Mary—†	76	housewife	39	"
U	*Houghton Phillip	76	laborer	36	"
v	Murphy James J	78	policeman	50	"
w	Sullivan Mary F—†	78	housewife	43	"
x	Sullivan Patrick	78	laborer	45	"
Y	Whitney Francis C	80	fireman	43	85 Tremont
z	Whitney Mary E—†	80	housewife	30	85 "

328

A	Matson Emma—†	80	"	63	here
B	Matson Sumner F	80	laborer	22	"
c	Pratt Ruth J—†	80	housewife	26	"
D	Stingel Clara—†	80	"	30	92 Bunker Hill
E	Stingel George	80	laborer	40	92 "
F	Shaw James F	84	"	61	76 Tremont
G	Sinnott Charles E	84	"	37	56 Bartlett
H	Sinnott Joseph P	84	"	39	56 "
K	Sinnott Mary H—†	84	housewife	33	56 "
L	Duato Margaret A—†	84	housekeeper	46	65 Ferrin
M	Blake Charles H	86	electrician	33	here
N	Brown Gertrude—†	86	housewife	56	Holden
o	Brown Hazel—†	86	"	23	24 Haviland
P	Wilson Catherine—†	86	"	66	here
R	Wilson Harold	86	rubberworker	22	"
T	Cain Frances A—†	90	housewife	31	"
U	Cain Gerald T	90	seaman	33	
v	*Ramsey Frederick	90	laborer	33	"
w	*Ramsey Mary—†	90	housewife	61	"
x	Jannone Nellie—†	90	"	34	
Y	Jannone Samuel	90	laborer	47	

329   Tufts Street

c	Reidy Kathleen—†	10	housewife	31	58 Medford
D	Reidy Patrick	10	clerk	30	58 "
E	McNeil Charles J	10	chauffeur	50	here
F	McNeil Margaret B—†	10	housewife	41	"
G	Piraino Angela—†	10	"	34	"
H	Piraino Anthony	10	clerk	35	"
K	Clarke James	10	watchman	63	"

2—3   17

Page.	Letter.	FULL NAME.	Residence, Jan. 1, 1944.	Occupation.	Supposed Age.	Reported Residence, Jan. 1, 1943. Street and Number.

Tufts Street—Continued

L	McLellan Raymond	10	painter	38	here
M	McLellan Rose—†	10	housewife	36	"
N	DeVoss Lillian—†	10	"	32	"
O	De Voss Richard	10	carpenter	32	"
P	Mortimer Mary—†	10	housewife	26	74 Decatur
R	Mortimer Walter C	10	operator	29	74 "
S	Coakley Honora M—†	13	teacher	40	Haverhill
T	Coleman Mary E—†	13	"	40	Lynn
U	Corkum Margaret M—†	13	"	29	here
V	Cox Rose A—†	13	cook	35	"
W	Creutz Rose T—†	13	teacher	24	"
X	Cutler Edith C—†	13	"	55	
Y	Donnellan Cecelia—†	13	"	27	
Z	Kelley Margaret M—†	13	"	40	"

330

A	Kelly Eleanor M—†	13	"	36	Cambridge
B	Kenney Eleanor A—†	13	"	26	here
C	McCann Helen—†	13	"	45	Marlboro
D	O'Connor Margaret M—†	13	"	49	here
E	O'Mara Mary C—†	13	"	68	"
F	Parker Mary—†	13	"	56	"
G	Doucot Catherine—†	18	housewife	36	"
H	Doucot Charles M	18	U S N	36	"
K	Helfrich Christine—†	18	housewife	39	Lawrence
L	Helfrich John	18	mechanic	40	"
M	Pagliaro Catherine A—†	18	housewife	42	here
N	Pagliaro Louis	18	repairman	39	"
O	Dalton Hazel—†	18	housewife	33	"
P	Dalton William J	18	longshoreman	38	"
R	Guarente Joseph E	18	chauffeur	30	33 Corey
S	Guarente Ruth A—†	18	housewife	30	33 "
T	Cormier Adeline—†	18	clerk	30	here
U	Cormier Florence—†	18	housewife	60	"
W	Reddington Helen—†	26	"	34	"
X	Reddington James	26	stockman	37	"
Y	Gallant Mary—†	26	housewife	45	117 St Alphonsus
Z	Beven Allen E	26	warehouse	31	here

331

A	Beven Hattie—†	26	housewife	28	"
B	Costa Isabel—†	26	"	27	
C	Costa Joseph	26	manager	37	"

18

Tufts Street—Continued

D	Hazelton Mary F—†	26	housewife	27	here
E	Hazelton William C	26	electrician	29	"
F	Kelly James	26	manager	26	"
G	Kelly Regina—†	26	housewife	22	"
H	Clark Helen—†	45	"	24	..
K	Clark Thomas H	45	receiver	29	"
L	Mosher Bernard	45	metalworker	45	"
M	Mosher Mary—†	45	housewife	43	"
N	Toland Anne—†	45	"	28	
O	Toland Clarence D	45	repairman	28	"
P	Toland George	45	U S N	31	
R	Toland Mary—†	45	housewife	30	"
S	Long Anna H—†	45	"	30	"
T	Long Joseph F	45	engineer	49	Pepperell
U	Millard Dorothy M—†	45	shipfitter	37	here
V	Aymond Bronis	53	welder	38	140 O'Callaghan way
W	Guiggio Josephine—†	53	housewife	29	here
X	Smith Gertrude—†	53	"	34	"
Y	Smith John	53	manager	33	"
Z	McGaffigan Catherine—†	53	housewife	46	"

332

A	McGaffigan Joseph	53	clerk	20	
B	Clark Ruth—†	53	housewife	29	"
C	Clark Verdun	53	U S M C	26	"
D	Mahoney Maurice J	53	electrician	27	"
E	Mahoney Norma K—†	53	housewife	25	"

Vine Street

F	Murray Francis	12	chauffeur	28	here
G	Murray James J	12	manager	51	"
H	Murray Joseph P	12	chauffeur	20	"
K	Murray Sarah E—†	12	housekeeper	49	"
L	Murray William	12	U S N	24	"
O	Jackson Ellen F—†	22	operator	27	"
P	Jackson Mary C—†	22	housewife	53	"
R	Clance Helen M—†	22	housekeeper	67	"
S	Lee Henry W	22	clerk	44	"
T	Campbell Edward J	49	clergyman	60	"
U	Evers Henry J	49	"	47	
V	Foley Catherine—†	49	domestic	39	"

Page.	Letter.	FULL NAME.	Residence, Jan. 1, 1944.	Occupation.	Supposed Age.	Reported Residence, Jan. 1, 1943. Street and Number.

Vine Street—Continued

w	Laverty Anthony P	49	clergyman	47	here
x	MacIntosh Martina—†	49	domestic	59	Dover
y	*McGrath Annie—†	49	"	57	here

Walford Way

z	Pilkington Hannah C—†	49	matron	38	Revere
	333				
A	Cronin John W	49	ironworker	31	here
B	Cronin Lucille G—†	49	housewife	29	"
c	Benoit Henry J	49	U S N	28	"
D	Benoit Mary G—†	49	housewife	29	"
E	Chrisholm Helen—†	49	clerk	42	"
F	Mazzo Joseph D	49	brazier	28	45 Hooker
G	Mazzo Mary J—†	49	housewife	28	45 "
H	Barreda Elizabeth A—†	49	"	50	here
K	Barreda Manuel E	49	waiter	34	"
L	Clausen Alice B—†	49	housewife	50	N Hampshire
M	Flomand Vivian—†	49	"	27	"
N	Clark Margaret E—†	49	"	29	here
o	Morrissey John J	49	salesman	37	"
P	Morrissey Mary A—†	49	housewife	33	"
R	Belliveau Charles A—†	50	electrician	40	"
s	Belliveau Donelda—†	50	housewife	44	"
T	Travis James F	50	machinist	55	"
U	Travis James F	50	U S A	20	"
v	Travis Rita M—†	50	housewife	47	"
w	Flaherty Anna E—†	50	"	35	99 Decatur
x	Flaherty William M	50	chauffeur	36	99 "
Y	Tolan Annie—†	50	housewife	78	99 "
z	Gosnell George J	50	retired	72	here
	334				
A	Strout Edward	50	U S N	28	
B	Strout Eileen—†	50	housewife	27	"
c	Harrington Christine—†	50	houseworker	39	"
D	Katowski Iola L—†	50	housewife	32	S Carolina
E	Keane John	50	janitor	45	49 Polk
F	Keane Mary—†	50	housewife	37	49 "
G	Mahady Frederick	50	builder	33	here
H	Mahady Helen—†	50	housewife	31	"
K	*White Frederick	50	retired	63	"

Walford Way—Continued

L	Cullen Margaret M—†	50	housewife	41	here
M	Cullen Patrick J	50	electrician	43	"
N	DeBeaucourt Margaret—†	50	housewife	32	"
O	Goggin Mary—†	57	"	38	30 Bunker Hill
P	Goggin Maurice P	57	clerk	39	30 "
R	Fraser Glenna E—†	57	housewife	56	here
S	Fraser William J	57	retired	68	"
T	Connolly Catherine—†	57	clerk	63	"
U	Connolly Catherine—†	57	at home	48	"
V	Wallace Frederick E	57	rigger	35	
¹V	Wallace Mary G—†	57	housewife	35	"
X	Wojczyk Edward N	57	metalworker	23	61 Exeter
W	Wojczyk Ethel J—†	57	housewife	23	61 "
Y	McNamara Agnes F—†	57	"	49	here
Z	McNamara Frank	57	rigger	65	"
	335				
A	Rounds Carl W	57	guard	50	
B	Rounds Florence M—†	57	housewife	37	"
D	Jacobson Arthur C	57	clerk	36	13 Chestnut
E	Jacobson Rebecca F—†	57	housewife	31	7 Peabody
F	Clifford Edmund F	58	chipper	39	here
G	Clifford Margaret M—†	58	housewife	37	"
H	Parrin Edward A	58	clerk	25	"
K	Parrin Elizabeth W—†	58	waitress	52	"
L	St Peter Gertrude A—†	58	housewife	22	"
M	Crory Frieda—†	58	"	28	
N	Crory Philip E	58	painter	31	··
O	Mazzone Catherine—†	58	waitress	37	"
P	Doherty Bernard	58	longshoreman	43	9 Walford way
R	Doherty Mary C—†	58	housewife	32	9 "
S	Cahill Edward J	58	engineer	41	here
T	Cahill June T—†	58	housewife	29	"
U	*Blake Anna M—†	58	"	36	"
V	Blake John J	58	laborer	36	
W	MacDonald Anthony F	74	machinist	34	"
X	MacDonald Muriel F—†	74	housewife	29	"
Y	Crooks Charlotte G—†	74	"	56	75 W Eagle
Z	Crooks Robert A	74	U S A	22	75 "
	336				
A	Crooks Woodrow E	74	"	26	75 "
B	Carbonello Henry M	74	musician	21	2 Sherman

Page.	Letter.	FULL NAME.	Residence, Jan. 1, 1944.	Occupation.	Supposed Age.	Reported Residence, Jan. 1, 1943. Street and Number.

Walford Way—Continued

	c	Joyce Agnes T—†	74	housewife	36	here
	D	Joyce John W	74	attendant	45	"
	E	Brown Louise—†	74	clerk	24	"
	F	Brown Ronald	74	welder	29	
	G	Olson Gertrude—†	74	clerk	38	"
	H	Dole Anna M—†	74	housewife	37	335 Faneuil
	K	Dole Warren F	74	electrician	45	335 "
	L	Teixeira Joan R—†	74	housewife	24	here
	M	Teixeira Joseph C	74	foreman	30	"
	N	Brown Louise—†	74	clerk	25	Milford
	O	Brown Ronald	74	chipper	27	"
	P	Boyington Doris E—†	82	housewife	25	Revere
	R	Boyington Lincoln E	82	machinist	24	"
	S	Driscoll Antoinette—†	82	housewife	26	36 Prospect
	T	Driscoll Henry M	82	pipefitter	32	36 "
	U	Jarasitis Francis W	82	operator	30	10 McNulty ct
	V	Jarasitis Vera M—†	82	housewife	30	10 "
	W	Burley Charles H	82	laborer	61	21 Prescott
	X	Burley Elwin W	82	metalworker	24	21 "
	Y	Allwood Arthur F	82	steamfitter	24	30 Mead
	Z	Allwood Dorothy F—†	82	housewife	21	30 "
		337				
	A	Mains Charles L	82	checker	32	here
	B	Mains Irene P—†	82	housewife	34	"
	C	Deehan Mary—†	82	at home	63	"
	D	Deehan Mary—†	82	clerk	26	"
	E	Peroni Thomas	82	rigger	34	Wilmington
	F	Curley Francis A	82	"	40	Palmer
	G	Curley Margaret M—†	82	housewife	40	"

Ward 2-Precinct 4

CITY OF BOSTON

LIST OF RESIDENTS
20 YEARS OF AGE AND OVER

(NON-CITIZENS INDICATED BY ASTERISK)
(FEMALES INDICATED BY DAGGER)

AS OF

JANUARY 1, 1944

THOMAS F. SULLIVAN, *Chairman*
FREDERIC E. DOWLING, *Secretary*
WILLIAM A. MOTLEY, Jr.
FRANCIS B. McKINNEY
EVERETT R. PROUT

Listing Board.

400
Bunker Hill Street

	Letter	Full Name	Residence	Occupation	Age	Reported Residence
	c	Pauley Edward	65	machinist	32	here
	d	Pauley Ethel—†	65	housewife	41	"
	e	Kiley Bernard	65	guard	35	Taunton
	f	Kiley Bertha—†	65	housewife	58	"
	g	Breen Gerald	65	shipper	39	here
	h	Breen Mary—†	65	housewife	30	"
	k	Monroe Arthur	65	machinist	39	66 Wash'n
	l	Monroe Dorothy—†	65	stenographer	39	66 "
	m	Warren Grace B—†	65	housewife	26	113 Bunker Hil
	n	Warren John	65	shipper	28	113 "
	o	Lawrence Emily—†	65	housewife	76	77 Marion
	p	Lawrence Louise V—†	65	dressmaker	52	77 "
	r	Domino Hazel—†	65	housewife	24	Vermont
	s	Domino Leon	65	painter	26	"
	t	Houlihan Catherine—†	65	housewife	61	here
	u	Houlihan George P	65	dentist	61	"
	v	Carroll Catherine—†	65	housewife	62	"
	w	Carroll Jeremiah	65	watchman	65	"
	x	Morrison Laura—†	65	clerk	25	
	y	Morrison Marion M—†	65	housewife	55	"
	z	Daley Francis	65	driller	31	Lynn

401

	Letter	Full Name	Residence	Occupation	Age	Reported Residence
	a	*Daley Kathleen—†	65	nurse	32	"
	d	Sheehan Christina—†	68	housewife	31	here
	e	Sheehan Daniel	68	laborer	41	"
	f	Gorey Elizabeth—†	68	tel operator	38	"
	g	McBrine Jane—†	68	housewife	69	"
	h	Davis Anna F—†	70	"	36	
	k	Davis Mark F	70	laborer	37	"
	l	Semple Andrew	72	U S N	46	
	m	McMackin Bernard S	72	mortician	77	"
	n	McMackin Charles B	72	inspector	44	"
	o	McMackin Theresa P—†	72	housekeeper	28	"
	p	King Fred	73	U S A	36	Holyoke
	r	King Rose—†	73	clerk	36	"
	s	Kuyava Eileen—†	73	housewife	32	26 N Anderso
	t	Kuyava George	73	sandblaster	38	26 "
	u	Wolf Ada—†	73	housewife	26	66 Decatur
	v	Wolf Louis	73	clerk	35	66 "
	w	Gagnon Agnes—†	73	operator	24	17 Albion pl

2

Page.	Letter.	FULL NAME.	Residence, Jan. 1, 1944.	Occupation.	Supposed Age.	Reported Residence, Jan. 1, 1943. Street and Number.

Bunker Hill Street—Continued

x	Lynch Charles	73	bartender	52	17 Albion pl
y	Lynch Helen—†	73	housewife	50	17 "
z	Lynch William	73	U S N	21	17 "

402

B	McGah Helen—†	73	housewife	34	12 Common
c	O'Neil Margaret—†	73	"	73	12 "
D	Porter James	74	fireman	68	here
E	Porter Sarah M—†	74	housewife	65	"
F	Turcotte Esther—†	74	domestic	50	"
G	McLaughlin Elizabeth—†	76	housewife	69	"
H	McLaughlin Patrick J	76	seaman	36	
K	Lavellee Helen—†	76	manager	36	"
M	Twohig Grace J—†	78	housewife	40	1 Coral pl
N	Twohig Joseph S	78	shipfitter	41	1 "
P	Griffin Bridget—†	81	housewife	36	Somerville
R	Griffin Thomas	81	shipper	39	"
s	Dizoglio Beatrice—†	81	housewife	36	here
T	Dizoglio Joseph A	81	painter	39	"
U	Gibbons James J	81	shipfitter	26	"
v	Gibbons Mary—†	81	housewife	26	"
w	Tripp Margaret P—†	81	clerk	50	
x	Sherman Anna—†	81	housewife	46	"
Y	Sherman William	81	U S M C	27	"
z	Sherman William	81	brazier	48	

403

A	Blais Agnes—†	81	housewife	39	"
B	Blais Carl	81	bellboy	35	
c	Sherman Anna—†	81	at home	47	"
D	Sherman William J	81	clerk	48	
E	Kennealy Annie—†	81	housewife	66	"
F	Kennealy Catherine—†	81	at home	27	"
G	Collins Patrick A	81	laborer	38	
H	Collins Theresa H—†	81	housewife	35	"
K	Durham Jeanette—†	81	"	35	"
L	Durham John	81	carpenter	37	"
M	Murphy Bridget T—†	81	housewife	47	"
N	Murphy Michael J	81	laborer	58	
O	McNevin Dorothy—†	81	housewife	34	"
P	McNevin Joseph A	81	bellboy	34	"
R	Sweeney James F	82	U S A	37	
s	Sweeney Margaret F—†	82	housewife	35	"

Bunker Hill Street—Continued

T	O'Neil Margaret M—†	84	at home	71	here
U	Otto Arthur	84	U S A	38	"
V	Furey Dora—†	84	housewife	68	"
W	Furey Patrick H	84	retired	65	
X	Hurley William E	84	clerk	52	
Y	Cavanaugh James J	84	U S A	23	
Z	Hayes Irene—†	84	housewife	48	"
	404				
A	Hayes John J	84	laborer	48	
B	Noonan Margaret G—†	84	housewife	24	"
C	Fitzgerald Helen V—†	86	"	51	
D	Fitzgerald James P	86	defense wkr	64	"
E	Healey Wilfred J	86	U S A	23	
F	Naughton Catherine E—†	86	supervisor	48	"
G	Naughton Charles W	86	plumber	45	"
H	Naughton John J	86	clerk	42	"
K	Naughton Thomas F	86	laborer	47	
L	Delander Anna V—†	86	packer	39	
M	Delander George F	86	boilermaker	36	"
N	Delander Joseph	86	seaman	42	"
¹N	Delander Margaret—†	86	housewife	69	"
O	Delauder Mary—†	86	stenographer	38	"
P	Duggan Irene—†	88	housewife	29	"
R	Duggan James	88	warehouse	40	22 Concord
S	Ashland Harry R	88	laborer	65	here
T	Chase Alfred F	88	stevedore	26	"
U	Chase Edward P	88	U S N	22	"
V	Chase Frederick	88	"	21	"
W	Chase Sadie L—†	88	housekeeper	61	"
X	Harrington John	88	stevedore	61	"
Y	Harrington Josephine—†	88	housewife	50	"
Z	Terencio Flamina—†	89	"	34	8 Napier pk
	405				
A	Terencio Vincent	89	pipefitter	39	8 "
B	Trembly Joseph	89	welder	64	Connecticut
C*	Trembly Rosetta—†	89	housewife	64	"
D	Donovan Frederick	89	laborer	31	here
E	Donovan Mary—†	89	housewife	26	"
F	Farren Bridget—†	89	"	67	"
G	Farren Dennis	89	laborer	57	
H	Graves Anna—†	89	housewife	20	"

Page.	Letter.	Full Name.	Residence, Jan. 1, 1944.	Occupation.	Supposed Age.	Reported Residence, Jan. 1, 1943. Street and Number.

Bunker Hill Street—Continued

	K	Graves Robert	89	U S N	25	here
	L	Hill Margaret A—†	89	at home	72	"
	M	Hill Mary—†	89	"	75	"
	N	Hablitz Charles	89	clerk	40	
	O	Hablitz Mary—†	89	housewife·	40	"
	P	Powers Elizabeth—†	89	"	23	
	R	Powers Francis J	89	U S N	31	"
	S	Vanstry Gladys—†	89	housewife	23	17 Carney ct
	T	Vanstry Philip	89	clerk	26	17 "
	U	Cook Adeline—†	89	cashier	54	here
	V	Cook John D	89	clerk	25	"
	W	Smith Irene V—†	89	housewife	26	"
	X	Smith Thomas L	89	clerk	29	"
	Y	McKenna Josephine—†	89	housewife	67	"
	Z	McKenna Patrick F	89	janitor	83	
406						
	A	Mulcahy George E	90	laborer	52	
	B	Mulcahy Rose—†	90	housewife	49	"
	C	Munz Annie M—†	90	"	74	"
	D	Kimball John E	90	guard	33	"
	E	Kimball Mary A—†	90	housewife	65	"
	F	Kimball William F	90	U S A	35	
	G	Walsh Nellie—†	92	housekeeper	72	"
	H	Kennedy Grace—†	92	housewife	32	"
	K	Kennedy William	92	shipwright	32	"
	M	Carrington Anna—†	94	housewife	50	"
	N	Carrington Lynn O	94	machinist	50	"
	O	Butts Victoria—†	94	defense wkr	26	New York
	P	Zugibe Anna—†	94	housewife	49	"
	R	Dewey Margaret—†	94	"	29	here
	S	Reardon Annie M—†	96	"	65	"
	T	Reardon Robert J	96	U S N	28	"
	U	Toland John I	96	laborer	69	
	V	Toland Patrick F	96	retired	85	"
	W	McGonagle Patrick J	96	U S A	41	"
	X	McGonagle Susan—†	96	housewife	71	"
	Y	Sheridan Catherine E—†	96	"	38	"
	Z	Sheridan Joseph	96	janitor	45	"
407						
		McInnis John P	97	guard	48	"
	B	McInnis Margaret—†	97	housewife	31	"

Bunker Hill Street—Continued

c	Lyons Emily C—†	97	housewife	30	here	
D	Lyons Joseph	97	clerk	37	"	
E	McDonough John	97	laborer	27	"	
F	McDonough Josephine—†	97	housewife	28	"	
G	Sands Mary—†	97	clerk	32		
H	Sands Mary—†	97	housewife	68	"	
K	Sands Stephen	97	retired	68		
L	Mirabile Catherine—†	97	laundress	52	"	
M	Mirabile Clara—†	97	saleswoman	24	"	
N	Mirabile Theodore	97	U S A	21	"	
O	Flammini Anthony	97	laborer	21		
P	Flammini Lillian—†	97	housewife	21	"	
S	Lynch Catherine—†	105	"	27		
T	Lynch Edward	105	molder	29		
U	Hooper Marie—†	105	housewife	52	"	
V	Hooper Walter J	105	clerk	53		
W	Higgins Ethel T—†	105	housewife	29	"	
X	Higgins James	105	shipper	29	"	
Y	McLaughlin Clara—†	105	housewife	55	"	
Z	McLaughlin William P	105	freighthandler	30	"	

408

A	Carroll Elizabeth V—†	105	housewife	42	22 School	
B	Carroll James J	105	U S N	21	22 "	
C	Flemming Ellen—†	105	housewife	63	here	
D	Flemming Joseph W	105	U S A	38	"	
E	Flemming Mary V—†	105	demonstrator	35	"	
F	Sullivan Edith F—†	105	housewife	29	"	
G	Sullivan Edward J	105	fireman	31		
H	Davidson Edgar	105	retired	72	"	
K	Davidson Elizabeth—†	105	housewife	83	"	
L	McDonough Anthony J	105	bartender	44	"	
M	McDonough Catherine A—†	105	housewife	42	"	
N	Moriarty Bridie—†	105	clerk	33		
O	Moriarty Margaret—†	105	"	29		
P	O'Brien Imogene—†	105	defense wkr	46	"	

Ferrin Street

U	Derocher Frances L—†	59	housekeeper	66	here	
V	Costin Martin	59	guard	45	61 Ferrin	
W	Costin Mary—†	59	housewife	45	61 "	

Ferrin Street—Continued

x	Tallent Frank	59	foreman	61	here
y	Tallent Vesta—†	59	housewife	58	"
	409				
a	Brennen Bernard J	61	U S A	21	75 Ferrin
b	Brennen Bessie—†	61	housewife	52	75 "
c	Brennen James A	61	laborer	58	75 "
d	Flateau Frank J	61	chauffeur	38	here
e	Flateau Mary A—†	61	housewife	40	"
g	Dupont Loretta—†	63	welder	23	"
h	Dupont Ralph	63	stitcher	47	"
k	Dupont Romeo	63	U S N	21	
l	Dupont Yvonne—†	63	housewife	43	"
m	Meehan Daniel J	63	laborer	50	
n	Goncalves Cizaltinea—†	63.	stitcher	38	"
o	Goncalves Joseph	63	fireman	38	
p*	Maderios Frank	63	cleaner	83	
r*	Pinho Manuel P	63	fireman	34	"
s	Kelley Ethel—†	64	housewife	50	"
t	Kelley Nicholas	64	plumber	49	"
v	Butler Anna—†	65	housewife	48	"
w	Butler Gertrude—†	65	electrician	20	"
x	Butler Joseph	65	U S A	24	
y	Cassidy Lillian—†	65	housekeeper	26	"
z	Geagan Annie A—†	65	housewife	52	"
	410				
a	Geagan Eileen V—†	65	seamstress	20	"
b	Geagan John	65	laborer	22	"
c	Geagan Mary—†	65	electrician	28	"
d	Geagan Michael J	65	stevedore	62	"
e	Agcaoile Antonio A	66	U S C G	25	"
f*	Agcaoile Mabel—†	66	housewife	22	"
g*	Rios Adilia—†	66	"	43	
h	Rios Sebastian	66	ropemaker	57	"
k*	Rios Weber	66	rubberworker	21	"
l	Furey Elizabeth—†	67	stenographer	21	"
m	Furey Mary—†	67	housewife	71	"
n	Walsh Margaret—†	67	housekeeper	25	"
o	Aspell Bernard F	67	stevedore	58	"
p	Aspell Edward F	67	"	24	
r	Aspell Katherine —†	67	housewife	52	"
s	Aspell Kathleen—†	67	clerk	20	

Ferrin Street—Continued

t	Whooley Margaret T—†	67	metalworker	22	here
u	*Smyth Mary—†	67	housewife	39	"
v	Smyth William	67	clerk	42	"
w	Beaton Catherine—†	68	housewife	52	"
x	Beaton James A	68	retired	69	
y	St Angelo Augustus L	70	machinist	50	"
z	St Angelo Sadie A—†	70	housewife	48	"

411

b	Hall Mary A—†	75	at home	78	"
c	Kimball Alfred H	75	U S A	25	
d	Kimball Ida M—†	75	housekeeper	54	"
e	Sproul Andrew	75	operator	59	"
f	Sproul Andrew V	75	U S N	23	
g	Sproul Elizabeth—†	75	housewife	50	"
h	Rooney Frederick A	76	retired	66	
k	Rooney Frederick J	76	plumber	39	"
l	Devlin Albert C	78	ironworker	46	"
m	Devlin Margaret A—†	78	housewife	41	"
n	MacNeill Silas	83	carpenter	66	"
o	McCarthy Catherine—†	83	housewife	67	"
p	McCarthy Jeremiah F	83	fireman	35	"
r	McCarthy Mary A—†	83	clerk	39	
s	McCarthy Patrick	83	laborer	65	
t	O'Donovan Margaret—†	83	at home	80	"
u	DeCastro Bernard P	85	U S A	21	
v	DeCastro Bessie F—†	85	housewife	49	"
w	DeCastro Jose R	85	chef	49	
x	DeCastro Joseph V	85	U S N	24	"
y	Donavan Mary A—†	85	shipfitter	38	137 High
z	Young Elinor E—†	85	housewife	36	137 "

412

a	Young John T	85	boilermaker	37	137 "
b	Salvo Charles D	85	barber	59	here
c	Salvo Mary—†	85	housewife	39	"
e	Murphy Marguerite F—†	93	clerk	49	"
f	Murphy Mary—†	93	"	52	

Jackson Street

h	Raftelle Christina—†	2	housewife	39	here
k	Raftelle Costas	2	manager	58	"

Jackson Street—Continued

L	Raftelle William	2	student	20	here
M	Amann Helen V—†	2	housekeeper	31	"
N	Amann Julia—†	2	housewife	67	"
O	Moore William H	2	rigger	63	
P	Judge John	3	laborer	54	
R	Judge Thelma—†	3	housewife	28	"
S	Judge William F	3	operator	33	"
T	Kelly Bridget—†	5	housewife	54	"
U	Kelly James	5	U S A	24	
V	Kelly John	5	stevedore	56	"
W	Kelly Mary—†	5	stenographer	21	"
X	Kelly Patrick	5	U S A	29	
Y	Harrington Annie F—†	5	housewife	56	"
Z	Harrington Henry L.	5	stevedore	59	"

413

A	Sheridan Elizabeth V—†	5	housekeeper	54	"
B	Murphy Jeanette M—†	7	housewife	40	"
C	Murphy Timothy J	7	chauffeur	40	"
D	O'Neil George	7	U S C G	44	"
E	O'Neil Mary F—†	7	housewife	42	"
F	Buckley Margaret A—†	9	"	65	
G	Buckley Stephen F	9	laborer	65	
H	Davin Mary—†	9	grinder	32	
K	Davin Richard	9	chauffeur	32 .	"

Lexington Street

L	Peters Alma S—†	3	matron	49	here
M	Woodman Elizabeth K—†	3	at home	78	"
N	Woodman William H	3	blacksmith	51	"
O	Austin Leslie	5	proprietor	30	"
P	Kilduff Annie—†	5	housewife	64	"
R	Kilduff Frank T	5	musician	42	"
S	Moynihan George F	5	electrician	38	"
T	Moynihan Ruth—†	5	housewife	33	"
U	Batchelder Webster	7	welder	35	Vermont
V	Campbell Francis A	7	U S N	27	here
W	Campbell James J	7	stevedore	25	"
X	Campbell Margaret—†	7	housewife	49	"
Y	Campbell Margaret W—†	7	clerk	21	"
Z	McLaughlin Neil	7	laborer	52	"

414
Lexington Street—Continued

A	Walsh Sally A—†	7	housewife	23	here
B	Lane Margaret A—†	9	at home	80	"
C	Chase Francis J	9	stevedore	35	"
D	Chase Rose M—†	9	housewife	32	"
E	Smith John L	9	shipfitter	45	"
F	Smith Louise C—†	9	housewife	41	"
G	Clarke Margaret T—†	11	domestic	38	"
H	Clarke Mary—†	11	"	49	
K	Martin Hannah E—†	11	housewife	58	"
L	Martin Patrick J	11	plumber	70	"
M	*Troy Julia E—†	13	housewife	34	"
N	Troy Nicholas F	13	fishcutter	41	"
O	Kelly John T	13	pipefitter	46	"
P	Kelly Rose H—†	13	housewife	43	"
R	Toland Ellen—†	13	at home	70	"
S	Toland Theresa G—†	13	"	35	
W	Ahearn Alfred V	17	U S A	28	
X	Ahearn Ellen—†	17	matron	62	
Y	Ahearn John J	17	U S A	31	

415   Madison Avenue

A	McAuley Adelaide A—†	1	bookkeeper	52	here
B	McAuley Ella E—†	1	at home	60	"
C	McAuley Georgina M—†	1	"	57	"
D	Goggin Harriet—†	2	housewife	39	"
E	Goggin John	2	laborer	42	
F	Daniels Cecelia—†	3	housewife	32	"
G	McGuire Catherine—†	3	"	51	
H	McGuire William	3	laborer	24	
K	Nearen Cecelia—†	3	housewife	76	"
L	Nearen William	3	retired	77	
M	Fick Alfred A	6	guard	52	
N	Fick Dorothy E—†	6	waitress	24	"
O	Fick Jennie V—†	6	housewife	49	"

McNulty Court

P	Hydock Anna—†	10	housewife	38	here
R	Hydock Stanley R	10	manager	39	. "

McNulty Court—Continued

	s	Taylor Edith C—†	10	stitcher	41	80 Moreland
	t	Taylor Karl M	10	manager	42	80 "
	u	Maloney Joseph W	10	U S N	29	33 O'Reilly way
	v	Maloney Sarah E—†	10	housewife	25	33 "
	w	Woods Agnes E—†	10	"	33	58 Medford
	x	Woods Thomas R	10	cashier	33	58 "
	y	Dowd Albert T	10	packer	30	here
	z	Dowd Mary E—†	10	housewife	28	"
416						
	a	Thompson Eugenie E—†	10	"	27	34 Hall
	b	Thompson Leland R	10	U S N	32	34 "
	c	McNamee Ellen A—†	18	housewife	38	here
	d	McNamee Henry J	18	machinist	44	"
	e	Flaherty Joseph M	18	clerk	29	"
	f	Flaherty Rita J—†	18	housewife	28	"
	g	Feeney John A	18	U S N	21	25 Samuel Morse way
	h	Feeney Mary C—†	18	housewife	20	25 "
	k	Dennis Esther—†	18	"	66	here
	l	Dennis John F	18	retired	68	"
	m	Spain Joseph	18	"	65	"
	n	Olsen Joseph M	18	electrician	29	"
	o	Olsen Ruth E—†	18	housewife	32	"
	r	Fone Rita M—†	33	"	22	
	s	Fone Robert E	33	U S N	24	
	t	Lamond John L	33	machinist	27	"
	u	Lamond Mary E—†	33	housewife	25	"
	v	McDonald James	33	musician	34	"
	w	McDonald Lee—†	33	housewife	32	"
	x	Zibrofski Edward F	33	bartender	23	"
	y	Zibrofski Gertrude E—†	33	housewife	23	"
	z	Clements Fra S	33	guard	34	25 Walford way
417nk						
	a	Clements Mildred L—†	33	housewife	32	25 "
	b	Smith Florence A—†	33	"	38	here
	c	Smith Harry D	33	U S N	34	"
	d	McDonald Charles	34	supt	33	"
	e	McDonald Rita—†	34	housewife	23	"
	f	Sweeney Louise M—†	34	"	38	364 Main
	g	Nicholas Anne E—†	34	"	23	here
	h	Nicholas James J	34	laborer	23	"
	k	Murphy Cornelius J	34	"	35	"

11

Page.	Letter.	FULL NAME.	Residence, Jan. 1, 1944.	Occupation.	Supposed Age.	Reported Residence, Jan. 1, 1943. Street and Number.

McNulty Court—Continued

L	Murphy Mary—†	34	housewife	33	here
M	Francis Dorothy C—†	34	"	26	"
N	Francis Victor I	34	chipper	30	"
O	Hughes Matthew J	34	U S N	34	"
P	Hughes Ruth E—†	34	housewife	30	"
R	Taylor Madeline—†	41	"	30	
S	Taylor Walter	41	U S N	31	"
T	Little Hazen L	41	rigger	27	16 Monum'nt sq
U	Little Virginia—†	41	housewife	25	16 "
V	Guarente Louis J	41	chauffeur	22	90 Decatur
W	Guarente Michelina—†	41	housewife	20	90 "
X	Quinn Helen—†	41	clerk	38	here
Y	Poole Florence E—†	41	housewife	24	"
Z	Poole Samuel H	41	millwright	28	"
	418				
A	Bevens Mary J—†	41	clerk	43	"
B	King Irene—†	42	housewife	26	64 Wash'n
C	King John A	42	mechanic	32	64 "
D	DelDatto Elizabeth—†	42	housewife	25	here
E	DelDatto John J	42	pipecoverer	25	"
F	Parshley Frank G	42	watchman	57	"
G	Parshley Maude E—†	42	housewife	52	"
H	King Anna—†	42	"	25	
K	King John F	42	operator	29	"
L	Albert Florence L—†	42	housewife	27	"
M	Albert Morris R	42	U S N	26	"
N	Clark Catherine—†	42	housewife	27	"
O	Clark John F	42	printer	33	"

Medford Street

P	Cullen Harold F	110	fireman	32	here
R	Cullen Jeanette M—†	110	housewife	27	"
S	Grady Mary L—†	110	stenographer	34	"
T	Mullen Catherine—†	110	housewife	74	"
U	Mullen John C	110	retired	78	
V	Curran Elizabeth M—†	110	housewife	32	"
W	Curran Francis W	110	agent	33	"
X	Murphy Bridget—†	110	matron	58	"
Y	Murphy James F	110	laborer	22	
Z	Brandon Annie—†	110	housewife	62	"

419
Medford Street—Continued

A	Brandon Leonard G	110	retired	78	here
B	Colby James	110	stevedore	34	"
C	Colby Rose D—†	110	housewife	28	"
E	Ciozzo Dante	110	mechanic	25	Saugus
F	Ciozzo Mary—†	110	housewife	20	"
G	Carriere Flora M—†	118	"	72	here
H	Carriere Joseph J	118	retired	69	"
K	Farrell Annie V—†	118	at home	70	"
L	Higgins Daniel J	118	retired	75	"
M	Leary Hollis J	118	B F D	31	41 McNulty ct
N	Leary Rita C—†	118	housewife	27	41 "
O	McCarthy Joseph F	118	inspector	32	1301 Com av
P	McCarthy Roberta M—†	118	housewife	26	360 Park
R	Krause Violet F—†	118	housekeeper	42	here
S	McCarthy Margaret—†	118	at home	80	"
T	Kent Helen—†	118	housewife	29	58 Medford
U	Kent Henry T	118	fireman	32	58 "
V	Commerford Charles W	118	U S N	23	Canada
X	Coyman Johanna C—†	118	housewife	32	here
Y	O'Leary James A	118	waiter	31	Somerville
Z	Palmer Elizabeth—†	138	housewife	28	here

420

A	Palmer Harry	138	machinist	29	"
B	Dyer John	138	retired	72	
C	Dyer Mary—†	138	at home	72	"
D	Bough Annette—†	138	clerk	33	
E	Cummings Arthur J	138	electrician	32	"
F	Cummings Ellen M—†	138	cleaner	38	
H	Ellis Mary L—†	138	at home	66	"
K	O'Leary Anna L—†	138	operator	27	"
L	Black Francis R	138	brazier	37	Lowell
M	Black Grace E—†	138	housewife	42	"
N	Rolinson Florence—†	138	"	69	here
O	Rolinson Frank A	138	retired	72	"
P	Brickley Mary—†	138	clerk	56	"
R	Elliott Eva—†	146	"	48	Brockton
S	Yanco Ruth C—†	146	"	22	"
T	LeBlanc Catherine—†	146	housewife	39	here
U	Rosen Eleanor I—†	146	"	30	"
V	Rosen William J	146	operator	30	"

Medford Street—Continued

w	Rosen Harry P	146	mechanic	53	here
x	Rosen Lena—†	146	housewife	47	"
y	Rich Elizabeth J—†	146	"	69	"
z	Rich William C	146	retired	71	

421

a	Sheehan Francis J	146	U S N	40	Cambridge
b	*Sheehan Wanda M—†	146	housewife	25	"
c	Tucker Benjamin F	146	retired	71	here
d	Tucker Katherine M—†	146	housewife	55	"
e	Sullivan Ellen V—†	146	at home	81	"
f	Sullivan Gertrude I—†	146	"	48	"
g	*Carroll Julia A—†	146	housewife	34	90 Decatur
h	Carroll Patrick G	146	chauffeur	40	90 "

Monument Square

k	Burnham Beatrice—†	15	housewife	54	here
l	Burnham George	15	shipfitter	52	"
m	Curran William	15	shoemaker	45	Plymouth
n	Delaney Anthony	15	seaman	42	Everett
o	Fitzpatrick William	15	machinist	30	Billerica
p	Harnois Raymond	15	"	50	32 City sq
r	Karabin Martha—†	15	housewife	21	Pennsylvania
s	Karabin Nick	15	U S A	24	"
t	Little Margaret—†	15	housewife	56	here
u	Matson Samuel T	15	painter	48	Fitchburg
v	Olsen Eli	15	machinist	50	Gloucester
w	Olsen Mary—†	15	housewife	48	"
x	Petrin Laurient	15	shipfitter	28	N Hampshire
y	Rees Harry	15	machinist	46	Gardner
z	Rees Josephine—†	15	housewife	46	"

422

a	White Tobert	15	radios	32	32 City sq
b	Woods John	15	shipfitter	40	Fitchburg
c	Dumas Dorothea—†	16	housewife	20	92 High
d	Dumas George R	16	electrician	21	92 "
e	Shay Florence—†	16	clerk	56	here
f	Shay Leo	16	shipwright	54	"
g	Shay Thomas L	16	U S A	22	"
h	Terrell Margaret E—†	16	housewife	34	"
k	Terrell Robert F	16	inspector	33	"

Monument Square—Continued

L	Neville Edward	16	longshoreman	51	here
M	Neville Nicholas	16	student	23	"
N	Neville Rose A—†	16	housewife	56	"
O	Hidler Walter E	17	plumber	49	Newfoundland
P	Johnson Harry D	17	U S A	24	here
R	Morgan Mary—†	17	housewife	54	"
S	Chandler Albert	18	carpenter	55	Northampton
T	Dacey Frank	18	salesman	44	here
U	Dacey Helen F—†	18	housewife	36	"
V	Hinkley Ernest	18	electrician	52	"
W	Howell Luke	18	stevedore	28	40 Corey
X	Long John	18	"	26	here
Y	Lorenza William	18	metalworker	50	N Bedford
Z	McNeil Ray	18	foreman	42	here
	423				
A	Parker Arthur	18	waiter	55	N Hampshire
B	Toffe Francis	18	sailmaker	60	here
C	Morrow Margaret V—†	19	at home	58	"
D	Murphy Nicholas S	19	salesman	63	19 Cook
E	Gallagher Jane B—†	20	at home	29	here
F	Gallagher Theresa B—†	20	"	45	" .
G	Basiliere Amy—†	21	factoryhand	35	"
H	Basiliere George	21	electrician	40	"
K	Bilodeau Helen—†	21	housewife	30	N Hampshire
L	Bilodeau Raymond	21	boilermaker	30	"
M	Campbell Alice—†	21	housewife	55	New York
N	Campbell John	21	pipefitter	55	"
O	Gillis Frank	21	seaman	28	Rhode Island
P	Gomes John	21	"	22	"
R	Richardson Herbert	21	boilermaker	50	N Hampshire
S	Richardson Mabel—†	21	housewife	40	"
T	Sinclair Alice—†	21	"	63	170 Medford
U	Waitkus Alice—†	21	clerk	30	170 "
V	Boynton Clyde J	22	retired	59	Texas
W	Boynton Ellen—†	22	factoryhand	62	"
X	Carley William	22	guard	61	here
Y	Gagne Irene—†	22	housewife	24	Worcester
Z	Gagne Romeo	22	boilermaker	35	"
	424				
A	Gallivan William	22	machinist	59	here
B	Green Anna—†	22	housewife	40	Brockton

Monument Square—Continued

c	Green Walter	22	stevedore	44	Brockton
D	Ingraham Irving	22	calker	48	Pittsfield
E	Johnson John	22	carpenter	59	Gloucester
F	Malinberg Carl	22	rigger	38	Worcester
G	Schraffenberger Margaret—†	22	housewife	38	here
H	Schraffenberger Winslow	22	chauffeur	43	"
K	Mahan Mary—†	23	housewife	64	"
L	Morris Earl W	23	milkman	37	"
M	Morris Elden	23	retired	82	
N	Morris Evelyn E—†	23	housewife	37	"
O	Fowler Agnes M—†	23	at home	26	"
P	McHugh Edward F	23	electrician	24	"
R	McHugh Festus T	23	stevedore	65	"
S	McHugh John A	23	U S N	22	
T	McHugh Mary E—†	23	clerk	32	
U	McHugh Mary L—†	23	housewife	61	"
V	McHugh William J	23	U S A	31	"
W	LeClaire David	23	U S N	38	6 Tremont
X	LeClaire Rose—†	23	housewife	39	6 "
Y	Powers Edward J	24	B F D	46	here
Z	Powers Edward J, jr	24	welder	21	"
	425				
A	Powers Helen F—†	24	secretary	22	"
B	Powers Julia A—†	24	housewife	46	"
C	Mahoney Helen—†	24	"	48	
D	Mahoney James	24	chauffeur	49	"
E	Mahoney William M	24	U S C G	23	"
F	Baldwin Dorothy C—†	24	housewife	24	13 Adams
G	Baldwin John E	24	retired	53	here
H	Baldwin John E	24	warehouse	27	13 Adams
K	Baldwin Rose M—†	24	housewife	53	here
L	Doherty Rose M—†	24	at home	30	"
M	Castor Mary A—†	24	housewife	22	"
N	Herlihy Daniel J	24	manager	57	"
O	Herlihy Joseph F	24	seaman	22	
P	Herlihy Margaret J—†	24	housewife	52	"
R	Doyle John	25	tailor	57	
S	Doyle Mary—†	25	housewife	55	"
T	Horgan Anna—†	25	"	58	
U	Hogran John F	25	retired	58	
V	McKay Elizabeth—†	25	housewife	73	"

Page.	Letter.	FULL NAME.	Residence, Jan. 1, 1944.	Occupation.	Supposed Age.	Reported Residence, Jan. 1, 1943. Street and Number.

Monument Square—Continued

	W	McTiernan John	25	shipper	44	here
	X	McManus Edward F	25	U S A	28	"
	Y	McManus Patrick A	25	foreman	60	"
	Z	McManus Richard F	25	U S A	31	
426						
	A	Leonard John	26	mechanic	24	"
	B	Leonard Virginia—†	26	housewife	22	"
	C	Moynihan Dorothy—†	26	"	35	
	D	Moynihan Humphrey	26	laborer	35	"
	E	Marcella Albert	26	welder	25	
	F	Marcella Alice—†	26	housewife	24	"
	G	Callahan John	26	repairman	23	16 Trenton
	H	Callahan Richard P	26	U S N	20	16 "
	K	Murphy Catherine—†	26	housewife	33	16 "
	L	Murphy John J	26	U S A	28	16 "
	M	Davison Elizabeth J—†	27	housewife	74	here
	N	Davison Thomas W	27	clergyman	73	"
	O	Hyson Marion L—†	27	nurse	45	"
	P	Carter Mary V—†	28	housewife	39	"
	R	Carter William G	28	operator	48	"
	S	Carter William G, jr	28	U S N	20	"
	T	Griffiths Ambrose J	28	fisherman	30	"
	U	Griffiths Dorothy H—†	28	housewife	25	"
	V	Doyle Arthur L	28	tel worker	28	"
	W	Doyle Mary R—†	28	housewife	27	"
	X	Riley Louise M—†	28	"	28	11 Concord
	Y	Riley Thomas J	28	welder	28	20 Oak Sq av

O'Meara Court

	Z	Murray Richard A	9	electrician	26	41 O'Reilly way
427						
	A	Murray Ruth E—†	9	housewife	21	41 "
	B	Finnegan Florence—†	9	clerk	35	here
	C	Nolan Rose—†	9	at home	73	"
	¹C	Robertson Mary H—†	9	housewife	38	Maine
	D	Robertson Ralph T	9	draftsman	37	"
	E	Buckley Elizabeth A—†	9	housewife	29	81 Polk
	F	Buckley George L	9	clerk	36	81 "
	G	Scollins Lillian E—†	9	at home	27	77 Knoll
	H	Yeretsky Josephine H—†	9	housewife	61	80 Gardner

2—4   17

	Residence, Jan. 1, 1944.	Occupation.	Supposed Age.	Reported Residence, Jan. 1, 1943. Street and Number.

O'Meara Court—Continued

K	Yeretsky Myer E	9	clerk	75	80 Gardner
L	Samms Grace A—†	17	housewife	35	here
M	Samms William H	17	foreman	36	"
N	Gurksnis Alexander	17	painter	34	"
O	Gurksnis Sophia—†	17	housewife	30	"
P	Will Margaret—†	17	at home	35	"
R	O'Halloran Evelyn M—†	17	housewife	27	"
S	O'Halloran Thomas V	17	electrician	27	"
T	Benson Blanche L—†	17	housewife	28	97 Walford wa
U	Benson Walter S	17	checker	31	97 "
V	Wells Irma E—†	17	housewife	41	here
W	Wells John L	17	laborer	37	"
X	Kennedy Dorothy—†	33	housewife	25	"
Y	Kennedy Edward J	33	laborer	29	
Z	Kennedy Josephine A—†	33	housewife	32	"

428

A	Kennedy Martin T	33	pipefitter	34	"
B	Anglin Dorothy M—†	33	housewife	27	"
C	Anglin Paul H	33	operator	28	"
D	Donnellan Madeline—†	33	housewife	33	"
E	Donnellan William A	33	operator	37	"
F	Niethold Elizabeth—†	33	housewife	25	"
G	Niethold Robert W	33	chauffeur	32	"
H	Donovan Elizabeth M—†	33	housewife	27	"
K	Donovan Paul F	33	salesman	30	"
L	Allen Milton	41	chauffeur	25	"
M	Allen Ruth—†	41	housewife	22	"
N	Chappelle Anna M—†	41	"	29	
O	Chappelle Edward W	41	guard	29	"
P	McDonald Charles L	41	brakeman	41	Cambridge
R	McDonald Ruth M—†	41	housewife	40	"
S	Pomeroy Marshall J	41	pipefitter	37	here
T	Pomeroy Mary F—†	41	housewife	34	"
U	Smith Catherine C—†	41	"	24	27 Blue Hill av
V	Smith Robert J	41	U S A	27	27 "
W	Murphy Helen—†	41	housewife	27	here
X	Murphy Mark	41	U S A	31	"

O'Reilly Way

Y	Woods Ellen—†	33	housewife	63	24 Concord
Z	Woods Thomas F	33	freighthandler	62	24 "

429
O'Reilly Way—Continued

A	Bellino Carmen C	33	driller	25	here
B	Bellino Mary—†	33	housewife	24	"
C	Fitzgerald Anna C—†	33	"	44	New York
D	Fitzgerald Barrett H	33	U S N	44	"
E	Haggerty Frank	33	chauffeur	39	Milford
F	Haggerty Martha—†	33	housewife	38	"
G	Moore Margaret J—†	33	"	70	here
H	O'Neil Annie E—†	33	"	64	"
K	Doyle Francis J	33	assembler	39	"
L	Doyle Madeline A—†	33	housewife	39	"
M	Field Carmella F—†	33	"	57	10 McNulty ct
N	Krovesky Edward J	33	shipfitter	26	Southbridge
O	Krovesky Irene—†	33	housewife	21	"
P	Sullivan Helen—†	33	"	40	Medford
R	Sullivan Richard J	33	pipefitter	43	"
S	Ryan Frances C—†	41	housewife	31	here
T	Ryan Raymond F	41	brazier	45	"
V	McCabe Marie C—†	41	clerk	24	236 Lake
W	McCabe Mary E—†	41	housewife	57	236 "
X	Flaherty Mary W—†	41	"	36	97B H
Y	Flaherty Peter T	41	welder	35	97B "
Z	Belmonte Dorothy M—†	41	housewife	23	here

430

A	Belmonte Thomas J	41	clerk	27	
B	Trifari Almerinda—†	41	housewife	76	"
C	Trifari Joseph	41	retired	66	"
E	O'Doherty Evelyn—†	41	housewife	29	Malden
F	O'Doherty John	41	welder	31	"
G	Curtis Elizabeth—†	41	housewife	36	here
H	Curtis Henry T	41	welder	37	"

Tremont Street

K	Oullette Joseph E	2	boilermaker	46	here
L	Crowley Daniel	2	electrician	40	"
M	Crowley Nellie—†	2	housewife	66	"
N	Francis Helen—†	2	housekeeper	57	"
O	Francis Margaret G—†	2	stenographer	23	"
P	McGovern Margaret E—†	4	packer	45	
R	McGovern Mary A—†	4	housewife	71	"
S	McGovern Mary C—†	4	operator	47	"

19

Tremont Street—Continued

T	McGovern Patrick E	4	U S N	43	here
U	Woods Michael	4	retired	61	"
V	Sears Isaiah	6	clergyman	29	"
W	Sears Ruth G—†	6	housewife	30	"
X	Coleman Marion B—†	8	"	43	
Y	Coleman Maurice E	8	supervisor	45	"
Z	Keating Paul A	8	clerk	53	"
	431				
A	Steele Henry E	8	"	52	
B	Steele Mary J—†	8	secretary	53	"
C	Burns John	10	U S A	25	
D	Burns Susan—†	10	housewife	23	"
E	Barry Catherine—†	10	"	51	
F	Barry John A	10	laborer	52	"
G	Bowen Matthew	10	"	58	
H	Daniels Paul L	10	operator	33	"
K	Munns Kathleen V—†	10	secretary	23	"
L	Munns Mary—†	10	housewife	57	"
M	Denehy Timothy	12	bartender	45	"
N	Lang Frank	12	laborer	55	31 Winthrop
O	Lang Nora A—†	12	housewife	46	here
P	Lang William E	12	shipper	52	"
R	McCarthy John F	12	guard	52	"
S	Sawyer Margaret D—†	16	teacher	53	
T	Mellen Joseph E	18	clerk	32	
U	Mellen Margaret M—†	18	housewife	61	"
V	Mellen Rose V—†	18	at home	59	"
W	Keefe Elizabeth—†	20	housewife	82	"
X	Keefe Helen—†	20	supervisor	41	"
Y	Keefe Johanna—†	20	housekeeper	52	"
Z	Keefe Margaret—†	20	clerk	48	"
	432				
A	Byrne Mary—†	22	housewife	41	"
B	Byrne Thomas	22	bartender	45	"
C	Irving Mary J—†	22	housewife	60	"
D	Irving Muriel E—†	22	electrician	30	"
E	Irving Ronald P	22	"	60	"
F	Simpson Florence C—†	26	housewife	51	Salem
G	Simpson John T	26	toolmaker	53	"
H	Murphy Julia B—†	26	housewife	55	here
K	Murphy Mary E—†	26	"	65	"
L	Martineau Gideon	26	machinist	48	N Hampshire

Tremont Street—Continued

M	Martineau Louise—†	26	housewife	40	N Hampshire
N	Keeley Helen—†	28	"	26	here
O	Keeley Margaret T—†	28	"	70	"
P	Fitzgerald Ellen J—†	28	attendant	57	"
R	Herlihy Daniel J	28	shipfitter	29	"
S	Herlihy Grace C—†	28	housewife	21	"
T	Pilicy George J	28	U S A	29	"
U	Pilicy George J	28	engineer	57	"
V	Pilicy Grace C—†	28	housewife	52	"
W	Green Catherine F—†	30	"	59	
X	McNamara Helen—†	30	clerk	20	
Y	McNamara Julia—†	30	housewife	70	"
Z	McNamara William F	30	U S N	41	

433

A	McNamara Winifred—†	30	housewife	37	"
B	Dunn Elizabeth—†	30	"	65	
C	Lowney Rose C—†	30	"	22	
D	Lowney William D	30	electrician	26	"
E	Dobie Francis E	32	U S A	31	"
F	Dobie Paul V	32	"	20	
G	Dobie Samuel J	32	clerk	54	"
H	Dobie Samuel J, jr	32	"	25	"
K	Dobie Walter J	32	U S A	24	"
L	Irvin John	32	"	23	
M	Irvin Ruth—†	32	housewife	22	"
N	Brennan Anna L—†	32	operator	21	"
O	Cunniff Anna T—†	32	housewife	56	"
P	Cunniff James A	32	guard	56	"
R	Rout Clinton	32	watchman	70	"
S	Hughes Catherine A—†	34	housewife	32	"
T	Hughes William F	34	letter carrier	37	"
U	Houghton Cornelius	34	laborer	42	"
V	Kerns Agnes—†	34	housewife	48	"
W	Kerns Peter W	34	U S N	21	
X	Ianetta Lawrence	34	laborer	40	"
Y	Ianetta Marion—†	34	housewife	36	"

434　Tufts Street

A	Paige Priscilla—†	42	clerk	44	N. Hampshire
B	Frizzell Elizabeth—†	42	housewife	60	Ohio
C	Frizzell James	42	retired	77	"

Tufts Street—Continued

D	Booth Gertrude—†	42	housewife	30	here
E	Booth John	42	machinist	30	"
F	Elmore Helena—†	42	housewife	66	"
G	Carey Gertrude—†	42	"	36	
H	Carey John	42	chauffeur	36	"
K	Skidmore Alfred	42	pipefitter	33	"
L	Skidmore Alice—†	42	housewife	27	"
M	Zawacki John	42	machinist	43	"
N	Zawacki Mary—†	42	"	34	".
O	Wallace Joseph A	50	painter	31	43 Crescent
P	Wallace Marjorie T—†	50	housewife	29	43 "
R	Polikoff Celia—†	50	"	31	here
S	Polikoff Samuel	50	chauffeur	32	"
T	Dumont Guy S	50	fireman	31	305 Shawmut av
U	Dumont Nora—†	50	housewife	35	305 "
V	Foley Francis L	50	foreman	27	here
W	Foley Mary—†	50	housewife	26	"
X	McNeil James A	50	fireman	29	"
Y	McNeil Mildred E—†	50	housewife	·25	"
Z	Anderson Clara M—†	50	"	41	16 Polk

435   Walford Way

A	Shalvarjian Hartchik—†	73	housewife	51	here
B	Flynn Elizabeth—†	73	"	79	"
C	Curtis Elizabeth—†	73	"	31	"
D	Curtis Walter L	73	chauffeur	33	"
E	Nardinez Christina—†	73	housewife	42	"
F	Nardinez Maria—†	73	packer	39	
G	McIntyre Gabriel	73	retired	77	
H	McIntyre Mary A—†	73	housewife	73	"
K	McLaughlin John B	73	meatcutter	51	"
L	McLaughlin Marie—†	73	housewife	44	"
M	Foster Albert B	73	laborer	65	9 Walford way
N	Foster Annie M—†	73	housewife	68	9 "
O	La Porta Anthony	73	clerk	26	7 Baldwin pl
P	La Porta Florence—†	73	housewife	24	3 Margaret
R	McTurnan Edward	73	watchman	36	here
S	McTurnan Mary C—†	73	housewife	35	"
T	O'Donnell Mary—†	81	"	36	"

Page.	Letter.	FULL NAME.	Residence, Jan. 1, 1944.	Occupation.	Supposed Age.	Reported Residence, Jan. 1, 1943. Street and Number.

Walford Way—Continued

	U	Fitzpatrick Catherine M—†	81	housewife	63	here
	V	Fitzpatrick James H	81	operator	62	"
	W	Walsh Anna L—†	81	housewife	62	"
	X	Walsh Thomas F	81	brakeman	63	"
	Y	O'Brien Anna M—†	81	housewife	29	"
	Z	O'Brien John A	81	laborer	36	"
436						
	A	Smith Beatrice—†	81	housewife	24	79 Chambers
	B	Smith Otis	81	rigger	26	79 "
	C	Beck Florence—†	81	saleswoman	42	here
	D	Beck Raymond L, jr	81	U S A	22	"
	E	Simard Alfred	81	shipfitter	30	26 Grady ct
	F	Simard Helen—†	81	housewife	29	26 "
	G	Sizemore Emma—†	81	"	36	here
	H	Sizemore Harold	81	shipfitter	35	"
	K	Thoburn Elliot W	81	"	42	Belmont
	L	Thoburn Winifred V—†	81	housewife	36	"
	O	Nowosadko Emily—†	97	"	23	Webster
	P	Nowosadko Stanley	97	welder	23	Dudley
	R	Fahy Marion—†	97	housewife	47	here
	S	Fahy William	97	porter	55	"
	T	Walker Frederick	97	welder	29	"
	U	Walker Marie—†	97	housewife	26	"
	V	Maffie Alphonse	97	pipefitter	27	"
	W	Maffie Marcelle—†	97	housewife	25	"
	X	Johnson Albert C	97	baker	36	
	Y	Johnson Helen A—†	97	housewife	32	"
	Z	Ouilette Hazel M—†	97	clerk	42	59 St Rose
437						
	A	Kelley Bernice J—†	97	housewife	25	here
	B	Kelley Willard T, jr	97	shipfitter	27	"
	C	Downs Helen—†	97	housewife	32	63 Allen
	D	Downs James	97	rigger	33	63 "
	E	Cowles Catherine—†	98	housewife	38	18 O'Meara ct
	F	Cowles George N	98	clerk	38	18 "
	G	Walsh Dorothy—†	98	housewife	26	38 Prospect
	H	Walsh John F	98	U S A	31	38 "
	K	Feeney Edward	98	laborer	39	here
	L	Feeney Sheila—†	98	housewife	38	"
	M	McDonough Bridget—†	98	"	42	"

Walford Way—Continued

	N	McDonough Michael	98	laborer	52	here
	o	Robbins Frederick S	98	musician	55	"
	P	Robbins Jennie A—†	98	housewife	54	"
	R	Callahan Arthur J	98	electrician	22	17 Chestnut
	s	Callahan Virginia—†	98	housewife	21	17 "
	T	Vogel Jean—†	98	"	26	here
	U	Vogel Louis	98	counterman	30	"
	v	Akerly Daniel	98	welder	27	"
	w	Akerly Dorothy—†	98	housewife	31	"
	x	Shannon Louise—†	98	"	27	"
	Y	Shannon Thomas J	98	inspector	29	"
	z	Sheehy Elinore—†	105	housewife	32	"
438						
	A	Sheehy Francis W	105	clerk	36	
	B	Almeda Alfred	105	brakeman	46	"
	c	Almeda Ruth—†	105	housewife	53	"
	D	Grace Grace E	105	"	28	
	E	Grace John J, jr	105	electrician	26	"
	F	Connolly James J	105	meatcutter	47	"
	G	Connolly Mary T—†	105	housewife	38	"
	H	McNealy Catherine—†	105	"	66	
	K	Collins Cecelia F—†	105	"	66	
	L	Collins Edmund W	105	clerk	43	"
	M	Coughlin Malachi	105	inspector	27	10 O'Meara ct
	N	Coughlin Margaret—†	105	housewife	26	10 "
	o	Stanton Frank	105	stevedore	54	41 O'Reilly way
	P	Foley Mary L—†	105	housewife	26	here
	R	Foley Thomas J	105	policeman	27	"
	s	Myles Anna L—†	105	waitress	52	"
	T	Rogers Ellen—†	106	housekeeper	65	"
	U	Glinski Antoinette—†	106	housewife	26	"
	v	Glinski Leo	106	welder	25	
	w	Page Beatrice—†	106	housewife	35	"
	x	Page Herbert L	106	riveter	42	"
	Y	Turner Albert	106	caretaker	24	46 Mystic
	z	Turner Louise—†	106	housewife	23	46 "
439						
	A	Healy Margaret—†	106	"	60	41 Corey
	B	Sullivan Margaret R—†	106	clerk	26	41 "
	c	Foley Alice—†	106	housewife	32	42 McNulty ct
	D	Foley Joseph	106	electrician	32	42 "

Full Name.	Residence, Jan. 1, 1944.	Occupation.	Supposed Age.	Reported Residence, Jan. 1, 1943. Street and Number.

Walford Way—Continued

E	Dawgiallo Edward	106	machinist	27	here
F	Dawgiallo Joan—†	106	housewife	28	"
G	Walsh Doris D—†	106	"	31	56 Clarendon
H	Walsh James B	106	U S A	27	56 "
K	Walsh John F	106	assembler	38	56 "
L	Richman Abraham H	106	clerk	45	here
M	Richman Rose—†	106	housewife	42	"

Ward 2–Precinct 5

CITY OF BOSTON

LIST OF RESIDENTS
20 YEARS OF AGE AND OVER

(NON-CITIZENS INDICATED BY ASTERISK)
(FEMALES INDICATED BY DAGGER)

AS OF

JANUARY 1, 1944

THOMAS F. SULLIVAN, *Chairman*
FREDERIC E. DOWLING, *Secretary*
WILLIAM A. MOTLEY, Jr.
FRANCIS B. McKINNEY
EVERETT R. PROUT

Listing Board.

CITY OF BOSTON ⬦ PRINTING DEPARTMENT

10

11

12

1

6

1

7

1

8

500
Bartlett Street

A	Hafey Celia A—†	1	housewife	35	here
B	Hafey William F	1	chauffeur	39	"
C	Glazer Anna—†	1	housewife	52	"
D	Glazer Harry	1	U S A	22	"
¹D	Glazer Hyman	1	welder	20	
E	Glazer Morris	1	storekeeper	53	"
F	Glazer Rubin	1	U S A	30	"
¹F	Lucas Edward J	1	laborer	21	
G	Lucas Lydia G—†	1	housewife	43	"
H	Lucas William J	1	chauffeur	46	"
K	Prince Elizabeth R—†	3	housewife	43	"
L	Prince James	3	U S N	20	
M	Prince William	3	seaman	22	"
N	McDonald Stephen	3	laborer	50	30 Mystic
O	McDonald Theresa B—†	3	housewife	48	30 "
P	Severie George V	3	U S C G	26	1565 River
R	Severie Marion—†	3	housewife	22	here
S	Thompson Catherine M—†	3	clerk	31	"
T	Thompson Dora—†	3	housewife	25	Cambridge
U	Thompson Frederick L	3	U S N	21	here
V	Thompson Joseph F	3	"	30	"
W	Thompson Julia—†	3	housewife	59	"
X	Thompson Monica—†	3	packer	24	
Y	Forman Leo	9	storekeeper	46	"
Z	Daly Frederick J	11	U S A	29	"

501

A	Daly John J	11	bookbinder	60	"
B	Daly Virginia G—†	11	housewife	53	"
C	Daly Walter L	11	U S A	27	
D	Ford Alice G—†	1	saleswoman	50	"
E	Ford James	1	retired	53	
G	Nice Mary C—†	1	housewife	34	"
H	Nice William J	1	packer	37	
K	Stuart Eva—†	13	clerk	38	

Bunker Hill Street

L	Lamb Elizabeth—†	113	clerk	25	Somerville
M	Lamb Margaret—†	113	at home	50	"
N	Riley Frances—†	113	housewife	27	here

2

Bunker Hill Street—Continued

o	Riley Joseph	113	shipfitter	26	here	
P	Polley David L	113	U S N	37	"	
R	Polley Helene B—†	113	housewife	34	"	
s	Feeney Thomas	113	retired	69		
T	Feeney Winifred G—†	113	housewife	71	"	
U	Brennen Robert J	113	welder	25	"	
V	Brennen Ruth E—†	113	housewife	25	"	
W	Crowley Bridget A—†	113	"	73		
X	Crowley Cornelius J	113	retired	73		
Y	Happeny Eileen—†	113	housewife	33	"	
Z	Happeny Thomas	113	timekeeper	35	"	
	502					
A	Bradbury Ethel L—†	113	housewife	25	31 Bartlett	
B	Bradbury Ewart	113	electrician	25	31 "	
C	Connolly James H	113	laborer	34	here	
D	Connolly Melvina—†	113	housewife	29	"	
E	O'Donnell Mary—†	113	"	63	"	
F	Wagner Cecelia—†	113	waitress	36	"	
G	Wagner Mary P—†	113	housewife	57	"	
H	Slattery Julia—†	113	"	65	56 Everett	
K	Slattery Mathew	113	retired	70	56 "	
N	McInness Daniel B	121	laborer	70	288 Marginal	
O	McInness Edith L—†	121	stenographer	37	288 "	
P	McInness Ellen—†	121	housewife	56	288 "	
R	Fowler Catherine—†	121	"	24	Malden	
s	Fowler Edward	121	foreman	29	"	
T	Jones Evelyn B—†	121	housewife	35	here	
U	Jones John	121	metalworker	44	"	
V	Meema Joseph	121	machinist	40	"	
W	Meema Susan—†	121	housewife	48	"	
X	Smith Anna M—†	121	"	23	81 Bunker Hill	
Y	Smith James	121	plumber	25	81 "	
Z	Curwin Margaret—†	121	housewife	48	here	
	503					
A	Solari Dorothy M—†	121	clerk	20		
B	Solari Margaret—†	121	"	27		
F	McDevitt Dorothy M—†	128	stenographer	23	"	
G	McDevitt John J	128	U S N	27		
H	McDevitt Mary—†	128	housewife	46	"	
K	Leary Helen G—†	128	clerk	69	"	
L	Riviccio Joseph	129	"	21	36 W Newton	

3

Page.	Letter.	FULL NAME.	Residence, Jan. 1, 1944.	Occupation.	Supposed Age.	Reported Residence, Jan. 1, 1943. Street and Number.

Bunker Hill Street—Continued

	M	Riviccio Josephine—†	129	housewife	41	36 W Newton
	N	Cole Frank D	129	clerk	57	here
	O	Morgan Alice M—†	129	housewife	55	"
	P	Morgan John G	129	guard	56	"
	R	Hafner Melvena—†	129	housewife	53	Somerville
	S	Hafner William A	129	laborer	53	"
	T	Davin Jeannette V—†	129	housewife	28	here
	U	Kenney John P	129	laborer	45	"
	V	Kenney Mary E—†	129	housewife	70	"
	W	Redmond Anne—†	129	"	28	
	X	Redmond Herbert	129	machinist	34	"
	Y	Hurley Edwin	129	U S N	30	
	Z	Hurley Mary—†	129	housewife	55	"
504						
	A	Graney Edith M—†	129	"	33	"
	B	Graney William J	129	foreman	37	"
	C	Sewell Julia—†	129	housewife	26	"
	D	Sewell Philip C	129	shipper	28	"
	E	Casey Leo	129	metalworker	34	"
	F	Casey Mary—†	129	housewife	27	"
	G	Dwyer Mary—†	129	"	46	
	H	Dwyer Michael F	129	rigger	43	"
	K	Toomey Anna M—†	129	housewife	29	39 Auburn
	L	Toomey John J	129	clerk	32	39 "
	M	Feeney Helen A—†	130	housewife	50	here
	N	Feeney Phillip S	130	realtor	58	"
	P	Berren Rose—†	132	housewife	58	"
	R	Lively Ruth—†	132	"	35	
	¹R	O'Hara William F	132	retired	67	"
	T	Doherty Catherine—†	137	housewife	40	98 Decatur
	U	Doherty William	137	chauffeur	42	98 "
	V	Rosetta Deborah V—†	137	housewife	62	Somerville
	W	Rosetta Evelyn V—†	137	operator	38	"
	X	Nickson Frank A	137	printer	47	25 Corey
	Y	Nickson Margaret—†	137	housewife	41	25 "
	Z	Ross Helen A—†	137	"	43	New Bedford
505						
	A	Ross Truman W	137	shipper	45	"
	B	Riley Joseph E	137	winder	45	73 Polk
	C	Riley Philomena—†	137	housewife	36	73 "
	D	Maxwell Albert G	137	chauffeur	49	Everett

Page.	Letter.	FULL NAME.	Residence, Jan. 1, 1944.	Occupation.	Supposed Age.	Reported Residence, Jan. 1, 1943. Street and Number.

Bunker Hill Street—Continued

	E	Maxwell Alice M—†	137	housewife	38	Everett
	F	Jones Alice—†	137	"	28	41 O'Meara ct
	G	Jones Maurice D	137	laborer	34	41 "
	H	Dolan Ellen M—†	137	housewife	52	Somerville
	K	Dolan James	137	laborer	22	"
	L	Dolan John A	137	U S A	27	"
	M	Hutchinson Agnes—†	137	housewife	36	57 Walford way
	N	Hutchinson James	137	chauffeur	36	57 "
	O	Chretien Lillian—†	137	housewife	25	Fall River
	P	Chretien Lucien	137	machinist	22	"
	R	Collins Catherine—†	137	housewife	33	58 O'Brien ct
	S	Collins John F	137	laborer	54	58 "
	T	Fowler John	137	"	50	Florida
	U	Fowler Nettie—†	137	housewife	45	here
	X	Donavon John M	144	laborer	38	"
	Y	Donavon Mary A—†	144	housekeeper	27	"
	Z	Scavoni Mary—†	144	housewife	48	"
506						
	A	Scavoni Matteo	144	laborer	55	"
	C	Tobin Florence—†	145	housewife	26	Stoneham
	D	Porter Ewart	145	shipfitter	36	Rhode Island
	E	Porter Lillian—†	145	housewife	37	"
	F	McCarthy Evelyn M—†	145	"	45	Somerville
	G	McCarthy Michael J	145	storekeeper	51	"
	H	Mahoney Beatrice—†	145	housewife	22	Medford
	K	Mahoney William	145	machinist	34	"
	L	Rogers Helen—†	145	housewife	47	Revere
	M	Nelson James	145	machinist	31	Lawrence
	N	Nelson Ruth—†	145	housewife	26	"
	O	Anderson Harry G	146	laborer	53	here
	R	Reynolds Glynn	148	U S A	38	Pennsylvania
	S	Reynolds Isabel—†	148	housewife	35	"
	T	Keane Elizabeth—†	148	"	59	46 Tufts
	U	Devlin Bernard	150	retired	73	here
	V	Devlin John	150	U S A	20	"
	W	Devlin Mary—†	150	packer	34	"
	X	Devlin Rose—†	150	housewife	54	"
	Y	Christmas Bertram	152	operator	40	"
	Z	Christmas Cynthia—†	152	housewife	36	"
507						
	A	Wike Arlene—†	153	"	25	15 Monum'nt sq

5

Bunker Hill Street—Continued

B	Wike Walter	153	machinist	27	15 Monum'nt sq
C	Burke Anna—†	153	housewife	27	85 Monument
D	Burke Francis	153	brazier	33	85 "
E	Thompson Grace E—†	153	housewife	62	Malden
F	Thompson William I	153	electrician	64	"
G	Cobb Alice—†	153	housewife	29	Vermont
H	Cobb Howard	153	electrician	31	"
K	Corriveau Rene	153	laborer	28	Salem
L	Corriveau Theresa—†	153	housewife	23	"
M	Grady Mary E—†	153	"	43	61 Monument
N	Grady Robert	153	shipfitter	43	61 "
O	Alouosius Bernard	153	electrician	26	Vermont
P	Alouosius Estelle—†	153	housewife	26	"
R	Halley George	153	metalworker	27	Medford
S	Halley Letitia—†	153	at home	25	"
T	Rose Cedric A	153	bartender	48	Hudson
U	Rose Sandra—†	153	housewife	43	"
V	Coveney Emilia—†	153	"	28	25 Polk
W	Coveney George E	153	U S N	33	25 "
X	Cagle Irene—†	153	electrician	26	Reading
Y	Cline Edith—†	153	housewife	29	Kansas
Z	Cline Joseph	153	U S N	29	"

508

E*	Olsen Jennie—†	rear 166	housewife	76	here
F	Olsen Tillie—†	" 166	factoryhand	34	"
H	Lynch John	168	retired	45	"
K	Lynch Mary—†	168	housewife	45	"
L	Keigney Eleanor—†	rear 168	"	28	3 Payson pl
M	Keigney Thomas	" 168	laborer	31	3 "
N	Morrissey Gertrude R—†	170	housewife	38	20 Trenton
O	Morrissey John W	170	clerk	38	20 "
P	Smiton Margaret—†	170	housewife	58	here
R	Smiton Steward	170	foundryman	59	"

Carney Court

S	Keating Mary A—†	9	housewife	66	Somerville
T	Keating Mary I—†	9	clerk	26	"
U	Keating Thomas J	9	chipper	66	"
V	Buckley Arthur L	9	tinsmith	47	here
W	Buckley Bernard P	9	U S N	20	"

Page.	Letter.	Full Name.	Residence, Jan. 1, 1944.	Occupation.	Supposed Age.	Reported Residence, Jan. 1, 1943. Street and Number.

Carney Court—Continued

	x	Buckley Helen M—†	9	housewife	42	here
	y	McLaughlin John	9	laborer	38	"
	z*	McLaughlin Mary J—†	9	housewife	37	"
509						
	a	Maraghy John L	9	clerk	36	"
	b	Maraghy Mary E—†	9	housewife	74	"
	c	Carideo Carmello T	9	U S N	24	Lynn
	d	Carideo Stella A—†	9	housewife	23	"
	e	Knehr George W	9	U S N	25	138 Medford
	f	Knehr Mary—†	9	housewife	21	138 "
	g	Murphy George	9	machinist	41	here
	h	Murphy Marion—†	9	housewife	35	"
	k	Short Fred A	9	musician	58	"
	l	Short Nellie F—†	9	housewife	60	"
	m	O'Neil Cornelius	9	shipper	27	2 Carney ct
	n	O'Neil Natalia—†	9	housewife	25	2 "
	o	Ready Eda—†	9	"	47	here
	p	Fox Edward	9	shipfitter	39	"
	r	Fox Margaret—†	9	housewife	35	"
	s	Fisher Dorothy M—†	9	"	20	Medford
	t	Fisher George P	9	U S A	29	New York
	u	McCabe Catherine R—†	17	supervisor	42	here
	v	McCabe Joseph	17	U S A	38	28 Concord
	w	McCabe Mary T—†	17	housewife	63	28 "
	x	Sullivan Edward C	17	clerk	35	here
	y	Sullivan Mary—†	17	housewife	43	"
	z	Marco John W	17	chauffeur	36	"
510						
	a	Marco Virginia—†	17	housewife	35	"
	b	Campbell Mary P—†	17	"	26	14 Parker Hill av
	c	Campbell William T	17	rectifier	29	14 "
	d	Russell Isabel—†	17	bookkeeper	55	here
	e	Russell John	17	mattressmaker	65	"
	f	Brown Alice G—†	17	housewife	37	"
	g	Brown Francis A	17	checker	38	"
	h	Gately Mary—†	17	housewife	32	"
	k	Gately Peter T	17	baggageman	33	"
	l	Norris James J	17	draftsman	40	431 Bunker Hill
	m	Norris Mary B—†	17	saleswoman	41	431 "
	n	DiFrummolo Joseph	17	laborer	28	17 Tileston
	o	DiFrummolo Lillian—†	17	presser	22	140 Dudley

7

Carney Court—Continued

P	Griffin Jane—†	17	housewife	36	18 Carney ct
R	Griffin John	17	trackman	41	18 "
S	Durant Francis J	17	salesman	37	here
T	Durant Gladys—†	17	housewife	34	"
U	James Mary J—†	17	waitress	30	"
V	Mahoney Dennis	17	retired	68	"
W	Bennett John	25	electrician	24	"
X	Bennett Louise—†	25	housewife	26	"
Y	Barry Myrtle—†	25	"	29	17 Ballou av
Z	Barry Raymond	25	fireman	30	17 "

511

A	Reed Adelbert B	25	supervisor	62	Medford
C	Reed Maurice L	25	joiner	38	32 Colonial av
B	Reed Olive H—†	25	housewife	31	32 "
D	Hoke Marion—†	25	"	27	here
E	Hoke Neil C	25	U S N	28	"
F	Russell Helen—†	25	housewife	35	"
G	Russell Stanley	25	chauffeur	35	"
H	Deatte Gerald	25	retired	70	"
K	Deatte Hannah—†	25	housewife	73	"
L	Matthews Bernice—†	25	"	34	
M	Matthews George C	25	attendant	38	"
N	Matthews William H	25	retired	70	
O	Hanrahan Alice—†	25	housewife	23	"
P	Hanrahan James	25	electrician	23	"
R	Tucker Albert	25	welder	25	
S	Tucker Alice—†	25	housewife	24	"
T	Sylvian Napolean	25	U S N	28	Rhode Island
U	McCarthy Jeannette A—†	25	housewife	27	here
V	McCarthy John A	25	clerk	35	"
W	Broakhorst Issac	25	retired	68	"
X	Broakhorst Julia—†	25	housewife	66	"
Y	Sullivan Anna G—†	33	"	47	
Z	Sullivan Geraldine—†	33	attendant	20	"

512

A	Coyne Velma—†	33	waitress	31	"
B	Rand Mary—†	33	housewife	60	"
C	Rand Victor	33	laborer	61	
D	Feeney Catherine—†	33	housewife	35	"
E	Feeney Harold G	33	laborer	34	

Page.	Letter.	FULL NAME.	Residence, Jan. 1, 1944.	Occupation.	Supposed Age.	Reported Residence, Jan. 1, 1943. Street and Number.

Carney Court—Continued

	F	Doherty Elizabeth—†	33	housewife	29	here
	G	Meaney Patrick	33	laborer	49	"
	H	Meaney Theresa—†	33	houseworker	38	"
	K	O'Donnell Charles V	33	pipefitter	52	Worcester
	L	O'Donnell Marie—†	33	housewife	53	"
	M	Muise Frank P	41	retired	73	301 Harvard
	N*	Muise Jane—†	41	housewife	72	301 "
	O	Robbins Earl	41	packer	32	here
	P	Robbins Eva—†	41	housewife	32	"
	R	Reynolds Esther R—†	41	"	61	"
	S	Reynolds Laurence J	41	pipefitter	58	"
	T	MacKillop Donald	41	operator	30	25 Queensberry
	U	MacKillop Veronica—†	41	housewife	28	25 "
	V	Samms Cecile—†	41	"	53	344 Chelsea
	W	Samms James	41	fishcutter	51	344 "
	X	Moynihan Anna M—†	41	packer	37	here
	Y	Moynihan Edward L	41	machinist	43	"
	Z	Reynolds Margaret—†	41	housewife	75	"
		513				
	A	VonBergen Edwin	41	electrician	53	25 Queensberry
	B	VonBergen Mary—†	41	housewife	51	25 "
	C	Eastman Gertrude—†	41	"	40	8 Weld av
	D	Eastman William	41	U S A	34	8 "
	E	Fistori Bridget—†	41	housewife	23	22 Albion pl
	F	Fistori Melvin	41	U S A	25	22 "
	G*	Webb Marion—†	41	housewife	33	here
	H	Webb William	41	rigger	35	"
	K	Shirr Anna F—†	41	housewife	69	"
	L	Shirr Thomas P	41	retired	71	"
	M	Lloyd Arthur	41	U S A	21	"
	N	Pelton Catherine T—†	41	housewife	45	"

Concord Avenue

	O	Bourne George	4	U S N	34	here
	P	Bourne Lavina—†	4	clerk	31	"
	R	Farrell Elizabeth F—†	4	housewife	61	"
	S	Farrell John	4	retired	61	"
	T	Hannaford Florence L—†	5	housewife	60	Stoneham
	U	Hannaford Herbert C	5	painter	27	"

Page.	Letter.	FULL NAME.	Residence, Jan. 1, 1944.	Occupation.	Supposed Age.	Reported Residence, Jan. 1, 1943. Street and Number.

Concord Street

	x	Cronin Gerald	2	painter	32	here
	y	Cronin Hannah—†	2	housewife	75	"
	z	Cronin Henry	2	checker	39	"
		514				
	A	Benson Frances M—†	2	housewife	23	Vermont
	B	Benson Gerald H	2	electrician	33	"
	C	Callahan Frank	2	rigger	55	here
	D	Callahan Sarah—†	2	housewife	54	"
	E	Walsh Mary—†	2	bookkeeper	53	"
	F	Lee Harold F	4	repairman	38	"
	G	Lee Mary F—†	4	housewife	34	"
	H	O'Brien Annie F—†	4	"	52	"
	K	O'Brien Edward T	4	longshoreman	27	10 Monument
	L	O'Brien Mary E—†	4	housewife	27	10 "
	M	Sullivan Joseph D	4	clerk	55	here
	N	Blue Dorothea A—†	4	librarian	39	26 St Andrew rd
	O	Blue Irene A—†	4	housewife	62	26 "
	P	Tebbetts Edgar W	4	electrician	43	26 "
	R	Trainor Harriet M—†	6	housewife	41	here
	S	Trainor John O	6	rigger	43	"
	T	Walker Charles M	6	policeman	45	"
	U	Walker Charles M, jr	6	U S N	20	
	V	Mickewiez Agnes R—†	8	supervisor	35	"
	X	Mickewiez Stanislaus	8	plumber	61	"
	W	Mickewiez Theresa M—†	8	housewife	57	"
	Y	McDonald Averill C—†	10	"	45	
	z	McDonald George F	10	U S A	21	..
		515				
	A	McDonald John H	10	chauffeur	46	"
	B	McDonald John H, jr	10	"	24	
	C	Bretemps Gertrude E—†	11	operator	35	"
	D	Hafey Dorothy M—†	11	stenographer	24	"
	E	Hafey Edmund L	11	engraver	39	"
	F	Hafey Gerald J	11	clerk	32	
	G	Hafey Michael J	11	"	32	
	H	Roche Edmund J	11	porter	55	
	K	Roche James J	11	teamster	55	"
	L	Roche Marguerite M—†	11	housekeeper	46	"
	M	Lenane Mary—†	14	boxmaker	28	"
	N	Lenane Michael	14	U S A	24	

Page.	Letter.	FULL NAME.	Residence, Jan. 1, 1944.	Occupation.	Supposed Age.	Reported Residence, Jan. 1, 1943. Street and Number.

Concord Street—Continued

o	Raffi Joseph C	14	U S A	28	here
p	Raffi Julia—†	14	operator	29	"
r	Harkins Anna—†	15	"	34	"
s	Harkins Margaret—†	15	"	28	"
t	Murphy Bessie—†	16	housewife	76	"
u	Michaels Charles J	16	painter	57	
v	Michaels Margaret—†	16	housewife	43	"
w	Golden Catherine F—†	17	at home	69	"
x	Golden Francis J	17	retired	71	"
y	Greene Emma N—†	18	housewife	52	"
z	Greene Fred L	18	photographer	28	"

516

a	Greene Percy F	18	watchman	59	"
b	Greene Raymond J	18	U S N	25	
c	Greene William J	18	"	22	"
d	Cavanaugh Bridget—†	18	housewife	64	122 Bartlett
e	Cavanaugh Michael	18	retired	69	122 "
f	Brandon Bridget E—†	18	housewife	61	here
g	Brandon Paul F	18	letter carrier	26	"
h	Morey Ruth V—†	19	housewife	29	23 Mt Vernon
k	Morey William F	19	engineer	35	23 "
l	Callahan Catherine B—†	20	housekeeper	21	here
m*	Callahan Daniel J	20	mechanic	45	"
n	Callahan Lillian R—†	20	housewife	43	"
o	Campbell Margaret—†	21	operator	37	"
p	Evans Richard	22	clerk	21	
r	Evans Sadie—†	22	housewife	48	"
s	Langille Dorothy C—†	22	"	40	
t	Bradley Neil	22	laborer	65	
u	Brennan Cecilia—†	22	housewife	55	"
v	Linton Arthur	23	retired	82	
w	Shea Elizabeth—†	23	clerk	53	
x	Toomey Edward F	23	ironworker	55	"
y	Toomey Lela—†	23	housewife	51	"

517

a	McCarthy Dennis	24B	U S A	32	20 Cook
c	Sullivan John J	24B	"	26	20 "
b	Sullivan Mary R—†	24B	housewife	49	20 "
d	Woods Edward J	24B	laborer	27	here
e	Woods Ellen—†	24B	housewife	63	"

11

Page.	Letter.	Full Name.	Residence, Jan. 1, 1944.	Occupation.	Supposed Age.	Reported Residence, Jan. 1, 1943. Street and Number.

Concord Street —Continued

F	Woods Thomas F	24B	laborer	62	here
G	Halleran Christopher A	25	"	50	3 Harvard pl
H	Halleran Margaret A—†	25	housewife	49	3 "
K	Norton William	25	laborer	53	here
L	O'Brien Joseph P	25	U S A	26	"
M	O'Brien Mary O—†	25	clerk	21	"
N	Hilt Hannah—†	25	housekeeper	21	Pennsylvania
O	Devlin James	26A	engineer	55	here
P	Devlin James T	26A	U S N	23	"
R	Devlin Mary E—†	26A	housewife	44	"
S	Devlin Mary P—†	26A	operator	20	"
T	Sloane Mary E—†	26A	housewife	65	"
U	Bemis Harry	28	shipfitter	38	Framingham
V	Stevens James	28	U S N	32	Lynn
W	Stevens Margaret—†	28	housewife	28	"
X	Neary Catherine F—†	28	operator	22	here
Y	Neary Gregory G	28	laborer	56	"
Z	Neary James G	28	U S A	26	"
	518				
A	Neary Pauline V—†	28	housewife	54	"
B	Santos Julia—†	28	"	67	
C	Santos Tony	28	barber	67	
D	Smith Millard L	30	U S N	29	
E	Smith Vivian—†	30	housewife	30	"
F	Downey Bridget—†	30	"	56	32 Haverhill
G	Downey Kathleen—†	30	operator	29	32 "
K	McAvoy Catherine—†	32	housewife	67	here
L	McAvoy John J	32	bartender	46	"
M	McAvoy Joseph	32	longshoreman	35	"
N	McAvoy Laurence J	32	clerk	33	
O	Williams Ethel P—†	34	housewife	46	"
P	Williams William E	34	operator	50	"
R	Williams William T	34	U S A	21	
S	Orvosh Paul	34	U S N	30	
T	Orvosh Ruth—†	34	housewife	26	"
U	Byrne Mary L—†	36	"	32	
V	Byrne Thomas D	36	longshoreman	42	"
W	Murphy Francis J	36	U S A	28	
X	Murphy John H	36	chauffeur	53	"
Y	Murphy John H, jr	36	U S A	33	
Z	Murphy Mary L—†	36	housewife	52	"

12

519

Jefferson Avenue

E	Noonan Catherine—†	25	housekeeper	74	here
F	Doherty John D	25	U S A	20	"
G	Doherty Julia F—†	25	housewife	42	"
H	Hayes Alice T—†	30	packer	23	
K	Hayes Catherine T—†	30	housewife	52	"

Lexington Avenue

L	Dillon James	3	painter	25	here
M	Dillon Margaret B—†	3	housewife	34	"
N	Dillon William G	3	rigger	34	"
O	Dinn William F	3	clerk	32	
P	Buckley Elizabeth A—†	5	housewife	32	"
R	Buckley James P	5	electrician	39	"
S	O'Halloran Annie—†	7	housewife	54	"
T	O'Halloran John	7	longshoreman	55	"
U	O'Halloran John T	7	U S A	24	
V	O'Halloran Mary C—†	7	clerk	21	"
W	O'Halloran William J	7	U S N	23	
X	Gallagher Edward T	8	U S A	20	
Y	Gallagher George J	8	laborer	47	
Z	Gallagher Helen—†	8	housewife	47	"

520

A	Graham Herbert	8	teamster	62	"
B	Pilcher Arthur P	10	B F D	35	
C	Pilcher John J	10	retired	73	
D	Caldwell Mary E—†	12	housekeeper	77	"
E	Laprise Margaret C—†	12	at home	44	"
F	Murphy Anna—†	14	housewife	46	"
G	Murphy John J	14	engineer	48	"
H*	Morrissey Theresa—†	19	housewife	38	161 Chelsea
K	Walsh Nicholas	19	U S A	36	here

Lexington Street

L	Anderson James F	2	retired	65	here
M	Boushell Catherine R—†	2	housewife	45	"
N	Boushell Catherine R—†	2	clerk	22	"
O	Boushell James L	2	ropemaker	46	"
P	Beaton Annie J—†	4	housewife	69	"

Lexington Street—Continued

R	Beaton Edward V	4	chauffeur	37	here
s	Beaton Francis A	4	U S A	33	"
T	Mangeri Nunzio	4	barber	45	"
U	Moynihan Jeremiah	4	longshoreman	64	"
v	*Salmon Thomas L	4	laborer	45	
w	Sullivan John	4	operator	50	"
x	Battos Mary E—†	6	at home	58	"
Y	Calabro Anthony	6	U S N	36	
z	Calabro Mary A—†	6	housewife	32	"

521

A	Everett Cecelia E—†	6	at home	60	"
B	Everett Claire P—†	6	stenographer	21	"
c	Everett John F	6	U S N	25	"
D	Everett Mildred E—†	6	stenographer	35	"
E	Banks Miriam—†	8	housewife	38	"
F	Banks Morris	8	lawyer	49	
K	Maguire Daniel J	12	driller	46	
L	Maguire Frances G—†	12	housewife	42	"
M	Maguire Frances G—†	12	operator	23	"
N	McGonagle Louise M—†	12	clerk	22	
o	McGonagle Mary E—†	12	at home	45	"
P	Anderson Leo	14	rigger	50	
R	Doherty Dennis	14	laborer	48	"
s	Hagerty William	14	retired	71	
T	Kelly Ellen A—†	14	at home	70	"
U	Long Harry	14	driller	65	"
v	O'Donnell Bertha E—†	16	inspector	49	"
w	O'Donnell Helen L—†	16	at home	37	"
x	O'Donnell Hugh J	16	shipfitter	45	"
Y	Croall James E	18	"	20	
z	Croall John F	18	U S N	25	

522

A	Croall John M	18	operator	55	"
B	*Croall Margaret B—†	18	housewife	57	"
c	Croall Patrick J	18	U S N	26	
D	Croall Sarah V—†	18	typist	22	
E	Croall Thomas J	18	U S A	24	
F	Reardon Catherine—†	20	at home	21	"
G	Reardon Julia A—†	20	housewife	60	"
H	Reardon Robert	20	operator	69	"
K	*Walsh Thomas	20	longshoreman	33	"

Lexington Street—Continued

L	Dacey Bartholomew	22	retired	70	here
M	Dacey Catherine—†	22	housewife	70	"
N	Dacey Joseph F	22	laborer	32	"
O	Gravelle Joseph N	22½	machinist	64	"
P	Gravelle Mary E—†	22½	housewife	60	"
R	McGowan Daniel W	24	foreman	54	"
S	McGowan Daniel W, jr	24	U S A	22	
T	McGowan Margaret—†	24	tel operator	21	"
U	Anthony Mary—†	24	candymaker	48	"
V	Anthony William J	24	salesman	50	"

Medford Street

W	*Loughrey Bridget—†	162	housewife	44	here
X	Loughrey Patrick	162	laborer	47	"
Y	Jones Margaret E—†	162	driller	39	145 N
Z	Hayden Margaret B—†	162	housewife	52	6 Joiner
	523					
A	Hayden Thomas P	162	retired	53	6 "
B	Porter James	162	chauffeur	34	42 O'Meara ct
C	Porter Winifred C—†	162	housewife	31	42 "
D	LaPorta Inez—†	162	"	28	here
E	LaPorta Michael	162	salesman	30	"
F	Flannigan Helen—†	162	housewife	49	"
G	Manning Doris—†	162	operator	26	"
H	Kennedy James	162	welder	22	"
K	Kennedy John	162	U S A	20	
L	Kennedy Margaret—†	162	housewife	40	"
N	Coughlin Charles	162	retired	70	
O	Coughlin Mary—†	162	housewife	62	"
R	Boyce Mary E—†	170	"	56	37 Mallet
S	Fortin Bertha S—†	170	"	31	here
T	Fortin John W	170	engineer	42	"
U	Mack Margaret—†	170	clerk	42	"
V	Monagle Mary—†	170	operator	21	11 Trenton
W	Monagle Sarah—†	170	housewife	39	11 "
X	Sullivan Catherine—†	170	"	42	21 Russell
Y	McInnis Helen—†	170	"	20	18 Franklin
Z	McInnis Joseph	170	U S N	20	18 "
	524					
A	Groves Mary J—†	170	bookkeeper	29	here

15

Medford Street—Continued

	B	Groves Mary N—†	170	housewife	65	here
	C	Giguere Albert M	170	boilermaker	38	"
	D	Giguere Helen M—†	170	housewife	33	"

Monument Square

	E	Herlihy Ann E—†	29	housewife	29	here
	F	Herlihy William J	29	policeman	30	"
	G	Russell Agnes M—†	29	housewife	46	"
	H	Russell Dorothy C—†	29	clerk	24	
	K	Russell Walter J	29	"	23	
	L	Russell Walter R	29	policeman	54	"
	M	Russell Warren F	29	U S A	21	
	N	Carey Gertrude—†	29	operator	33	"
	O	Carey Josephine—†	29	housewife	56	"
	P	Carey Thomas	29	U S A	26	
	R	Carey William	29	U S N	24	"

Monument Street

	S	Carrier Andrew	5	sign painter	70	here
	T	Carrier Mary F—†	5	housewife	58	"
	U	Flemming Ellen—†	5	"	23	43 Chestnut
	V	Flemming William	5	shipfitter	29	43 "
	W	McIlvaine William	5	chipper	22	3 Adams
	X	Little Harry	5	longshoreman	35	here
	Y	Little Mary—†	5	housewife	32	"
	Z	Ryan Edward T	6	U S N	23	"
		525				
	A	Ryan James M	6	U S A	20	"
	B	Ryan Melinda J—†	6	housewife	53	"
	C	Ryan Thomas E	6	engineer	58	"
	D	Rogan Rose—†	6	matron	61	
	E	McDonald Edith—†	7	clerk	33	
	F	Connolly Bridget—†	7	housewife	60	"
	G	Connolly Michael	7	laborer	58	
	H	Vidito Florence—†	7	clerk	25	
	K	Heelin John	rear 7	operator	25	"
	L	Heelin Mary—†	7	housewife	23	"
	M	Harkins Mary A—†	8	"	73	
	N	Casey John	8	shipper	55	

16

Monument Street—Continued

o	Casey Mary A—†	8	housewife	50	here
p	Fears Irene—†	8	"	30	"
r	Fears Roger	8	welder	35	"
s	Brunetta Anthony	9	operator	39	"
t	Brunetta Rose—†	9	housewife	43	"
u	Calabrase Antoinetta—†	9	houseworker	69	"
v	Donahue Dennis L	9	janitor	66	"
w	Donahue Edward L	9	chipper	28	"
x	Donahue Elizabeth V—†	9	housewife	27	"
y	Mahoney Elizabeth V—†	9	janitor	57	..
z	Cook Annie J—†	9	at home	65	"

526

a	Dutil Elsa—†	10	housewife	20	22 Monum'nt sq
b	Dutil Roger	10	shipfitter	29	22 "
c	Harkins Mary—†	10	at home	88	here
d	O'Neil Francis	11	rigger	25	"
e	O'Neil Mary E—†	11	housewife	58	"
f	O'Neil Rita—†	11	clerk	23	
g	O'Neil Thomas	11	laborer	21	"
k	Aspell Olive—†	13	operator	25	Somerville
l	Bradley Bernice—†	13	housewife	40	here
m	Dunn Helen L—†	13	waitress	47	"
n	Dunn Mary B—†	13	cook	78	"
o	Feeney Edward F	13	pipefitter	28	"
p	Feeney Helen C—†	13	clerk	29	
r	Feeney Theresa M—†	13	housewife	55	"
t	Peterson Dorothy—† rear	13	"	40	13 Monument
u	Peterson Gustav "	13	mechanic	50	13 "
v	Chase Mary—†	14	housekeeper	70	here
w	Connors Bartholomew	14	policeman	29	"
x	Connors Daniel	14	bridgetender	72	"
y	Connors Daniel L	14	metalworker	39	"
z	Connors Hannah—†	14	housewife	74	"

527

a	Hinckley Charles	14	machinist	52	"
b	Hinckley Lillian—†	14	housewife	43	"
c	Russell Edward	15	chipper	34	N Hampshire
d	Russell Marion—†	15	housewife	33	"
e	Richards James	15	sailmaker	81	here
f	Richards Raymond J	15	U S A	23	"
g	Darcy Joseph S	15	retired	79	"

Monument Street—Continued

		FULL NAME	Res.	Occupation	Age	Reported Residence
	H	Heenan Winifred—†	15	houseworker	30	here
	K	Kirrane Mary—†	16	housewife	42	97 Walford way
	L	Kirrane Patrick	16	painter	42	97 "
	M	Seeley Catherine—†	16	typist	28	here
	N	Burbank Frederick	17	embalmer	50	"
	O	Kulbaci Stanley	17	welder	25	"
	P	McDevitt Mary—†	17	housewife	31	"
	R	McDevitt Michael	17	laborer	32	
	S	Butchart Elizabeth—†	19	clerk	29	
	T	Butchart Samuel	19	shipper	54	··
	U	Butchart Sarah—†	19	housewife	48	"
	V	Clinton Bridget—†	19	"	55	
	W	Clinton Thomas	19	janitor	57	"
	X	*Allen Hazel—†	20	waitress	36	22 Monument
	Y	*Cain Annie—†	20	housewife	54	22 "
	Z	Gibbons Bernard	21	laborer	50	here
528						
	A	Gibbons Helen—†	21	housewife	48	"
	C	Kelley John J	23	U S N	22	
	D	Kelley Margaret—†	23	housewife	39	"
	E	Kelley William H	23	laborer	40	
	F	Richards Evelyn—†	24	waitress	36	"
	G	Cass Elizabeth J—†	24	housewife	60	"
	H	Leary Arthur S	24	laborer	63	"
	K	Carey Mabel—†	24	housekeeper	30	84 Tremont
	L	Reed Chester	24	welder	49	Malden
	M	Conway Helen—†	26	clerk	52	here
	N	Mullaly Alice—†	26	matron	51	"
	O	Watts Daniel	26	laborer	58	"
	P	Hall Ida M—†	26	attendant	30	"
	R	Hall Laura M—†	26	at home	45	"
	S	Hall Lewis A	26	blacksmith	48	"
	T	Carney Catherine—†	26	housewife	39	"
	U	Carney James E	26	policeman	42	"
	V	Casey Mary—†	28	at home	75	"
	W	Duncliff Frances A—†	28	"	43	
	X	Duncliff Mary A—†	28	housewife	73	"
	Y	Duncliff Mary A—†	28	clerk	44	
	Z	Duncliff Richard	28	shipfitter	49	"
529						
	A	Duncliff William	28	clerk	42	

Letter.	FULL NAME.	Residence, Jan. 1, 1944.	Occupation.	Supposed Age.	Reported Residence, Jan. 1, 1943. Street and Number.

Monument Street—Continued

Letter.	FULL NAME.	Residence, Jan. 1, 1944.	Occupation.	Supposed Age.	Reported Residence, Jan. 1, 1943. Street and Number.
B	Bowden Eva—†	28	clerk	44	here
C	Hennessey Lena—†	28	housewife	20	"
D	Hennessey William	28	cooper	22	"
E	Scalli Evelyn—†	32	housewife	31	"
F	Scalli Salvatore	32	storekeeper	33	"
G	Brennan James P	32	retired	64	
H	Farley Catherine C—†	32	housewife	49	"
K	Farley Helen G—†	32	operator	21	"
L	Farley John W	32	U S N	23	
M	Farley William F	32	B F D	52	
N	Farley William J	32	U S A	26	
O	Jacques William E	32	U S N	42	"
P	Paquette Gustave	50	laborer	63	Brockton
R	Evers Alice—†	50	housewife	33	98 Decatur
S	Evers Thomas	50	metalworker	34	98 "
T	Bradley Hugh	50	melter	28	73 Codman pk
U	Bradley Rita—†	50	housewife	27	73 "
W	Porter Frances B—†	50	"	32	here
X	Porter James F	50	clerk	31	"
Y	McGonagle Edward F	50	U S A	20	"
Z	Walsh Edward F	50	laborer	41	"
	530				
A	Walsh Mary—†	50	housewife	41	"
B	Dowd Frances—†	50	at home	57	38 St Martin
C	Dowd Frances—†	50	stenographer	26	38 "
D	Dowd Leo	50	U S N	21	38 "
E	Doe Kenneth	50	clerk	20	here
F	Doe Margaret—†	50	housewife	23	"
G	Finnegan Robert	50	laborer	28	21 Elm
H	Finnegan Sally—†	50	housewife	25	21 "
K	Whalen James	50	chauffeur	55	here
L	Whalen Mabel—†	50	housewife	50	"
M	Whalen Rita—†	50	defense wkr	22	"
N	Sheridan Catherine—†	50	housewife	34	"
O	Sheridan Francis	50	operator	39	"
P	Henneberry Francis	50	pipefitter	29	110 Medford
R	Monagle Dennis	50	driller	22	110 "
S	Monagle Margaret—†	50	housewife	31	110 "
T	Cayon Grace—†	53	"	27	here
U	Cayon Mario	53	laborer	26	"
V	Manning Jennie—†	53	housewife	34	"

19

Monument Street—Continued

w	Manning John	53	operator	36	here
x	Pappas Mary—†	53	housewife	27	"
y	Pappas Peter	53	laborer	27	"
z	Aubrey Annie—†	53	housewife	42	"
	531				
A	Aubrey Edward R	53	guard	47	
B	Juby Harold	53	baker	39	"
C	Juby Marion—†	53	housewife	37	"
D	Tuttle Charles	53	U S A	25	
E	O'Connell John	53	machinist	37	"
F	O'Connell Margaret—·†	53	housewife	36	"
G	Grandison John J	58	retired	79	
H	Roehnig Abbie G—†	58	housewife	74	"
K	Roehnig Frederick E	58	retired	·76	
L	Young Emma F—†	58	housewife	63	"
M	Young Joseph H	58	merchant	66	"
N	Young Mildred—†	58	packer	33	
O	McGoff Michael H	58	accountant	43	"
P	Young Ellen M—†	58	housewife	41	"
R	Pierce Margaret—†	58	"	52·	"
S	McCarthy John J	58	laborer	35	
T	McCarthy Lucy—†	58	housewife	36	"
U	O'Connor Arthur L	58	machinist	31	"
V	O'Connor Eileen—†	58	housewife	26	"
W	Reynolds John T	58	janitor	45	
X	Reynolds Ruth—·†	58	housewife	39	"
Y	Malone Anna—†	58	"	23	20 Park
z	Flemming Joseph	58	machinist	30	here
	532				
A	Flemming Rose—†	58	housewife	28	"
C	McGee Edith G—†	58	"	35	41 O'Reilly w
D	McGee Francis	58	chauffeur	36	41 "
E	Hayes Cornelius J	58	cooper	38	here
F	Hayes Eileen—†	58	at home	36	"
G	Longo Mary J—†	61	housewife	25	65 O'Reilly w
H	Longo Raymond E	61	electrician	28	65 "
K	King Elmer M	61	repairman	35	here
L	King Sadie—†	61	housewife	39	"
M	Burke Dorothy—†	61	"	26	"
N	Burke Francis	61	electrician	25	"
O	O'Neil Joseph F	61	"	27	

Page.	Letter.	FULL NAME.	Residence, Jan. 1, 1944.	Occupation.	Supposed Age.	Reported Residence, Jan. 1, 1943. Street and Number.

Monument Street—Continued

	P	O'Neil Mildred L—†	61	housewife	23	here
	R	McCall Eliza—†	61	at home	67	"
	S	Stacey Earl	61	U S A	23	"
	T	Stacey Marjorie—†	61	housewife	22	"
	U	Kelley Josephine—†	61	"	32	
	W	Goldberg Ann—†	76	"	32	
	X	Goldberg Myer	76	shipfitter	29	"
	Y	Manning Michael J	76	investigator	31	"
	V	Manning Nellie—†	76	housewife	30	"
	Z	Brennan James	76	laborer	65	
533						
	A	Brennan Margaret—†	76	housewife	49	"
	B	Dalton Germaine—†	76	"	37	336 Medford
	C	Dalton Hubert	76	salesman	40	336 "
	E	Walsh Richard	76	watchman	35	65 Polk
	F	Walsh Rose—†	76	at home	33	65 "
	G	Coleman Elizabeth—†	76	housewife	35	here
	H	Coleman Francis	76	clerk	38	"
	K	Galvin Clara—†	76	housewife	23	"
	L	Galvin Robert F	76	shipfitter	27	"
	M	MacKinnon Doris—†	76	clerk	29	
	N	MacKinnon Helen—†	76	saleswoman	63	"
	O	Angelos Agnes—†	76	clerk	30	
	P	Freeman Ellen—†	76	at home	68	"
	R	Stewart Fred A	76	U S A	49	
	S	Stewart Margaret M—†	76	cook	49	
	T	Brown Alice—†	76	housewife	30	"
	U	Brown William L	76	manager	35	"
	V	Regan Leo	77	laborer	32	"
	W	Regan Marion—†	77	housewife	27	"
	X	Brady Edward J	77	clerk	34	
	Y	Brady Helen V—†	77	housewife	57	"
	Z	Brady Mary K—†	77	"	29	
534						
	A	Anderson Marion—†	77	"	23	12 Marion
	B	Anderson William	77	supervisor	31	12 "
	C	Budreau Eleanor—†	77	housewife	24	here
	D	Budreau Harold	77	fishcutter	30	"
	E	Ahern Anna M—†	77	housewife	33	"
	F	Ahern James H	77	painter	33	
	G	Carmody Anna E—†	77	housewife	43	"

Monument Street—Continued

H	Fidler Anna—†	84	housewife	24	here
K	Fidler Jacob	84	machinist	25	"
L	Murphy Julia—†	84	operator	36	"
M	O'Toole Dorothy—†	84	housewife	24	"
N	O'Toole Thomas F	84	policeman	30	"
O	DellOrfano Marie—†	84	housewife	25	"
P	DellOrfano Orlando	84	driller	27	"
R	Beukema Donald R	84	U S N	44	Virginia
S	Beukema Mildred—†	84	housewife	44	"
T	Merritt Ann—†	84	"	20	here
U	Merritt Robert	84	chipper	24	"
V	Colwell Louise—†	85	housewife	30	"
W	Zani Julio	85	letter carrier	34	"
X	Zani Margaret—†	85	housewife	31	"
Y	McGregor Barbara M—†	85	"	29	156 Lamartine
Z	McGregor David	85	molder	34	156 "
	535				
A	Chase Rita E—†	85	housewife	29	here
B	Chase William	85	laborer	31	"
C	Banks Margaret—†	85	housewife	36	"
D	Banks Thomas	85	checker	33	"
E	Thompson David	85	clerk	50	
F	Thompson Mary A—†	85	housewife	40	"
G	Connell Alfred	92	laborer	47	
H	Connell Mary B—†	92	housewife	43	"
K	O'Connor Clara—†	92	"	57	24 Kimball
L	O'Connor John	92	laborer	59	24 "
M	Pelcher Eleanor—†	92	housewife	30	here
N	Pelcher Thomas	92	pressman	31	"
O	Crowley Rose—†	92	nurse	66	"
P	Stone Linda—†	92	"	72	
R	Silva Albert	92	machinist	38	"
S	Silva Mildred—†	92	housewife	36	"
T	McSween Mary—†	92	at home	74	"
U	Walsh Anastasia—†	92	"	72	
V	Sharkey Mary V—†	92	housewife	45	"
W	Sharkey Peter J	92	laborer	48	
X	Lannon Annie—†	92	housewife	79	"
Y	Lannon John J	92	retired	81	
Z	Lyons Anastasia—†	92	housewife	26	"

Page.	Letter.	FULL NAME.	Residence, Jan. 1, 1944.	Occupation.	Supposed Age.	Reported Residence, Jan. 1, 1943. Street and Number.

536
Monument Street—Continued

A	Lyons James	92	longshoreman	30	here
B	Fitzgerald Margaret—†	92	housewife	31	Tewksbury
C	Fitzgerald Patrick	92	clerk	47	"
D	Thomas Agnes F—†	92	housewife	36	here
E	Thomas Matthew	92	welder	37	"
F	Kenty Helen—†	92	housewife	32	7 Ellwood
G	Kenty Russell	92	rigger	36	7 "

O'Meara Court

H	Chase Dorothy M—†	10	housewife	23	65 Bunker Hill
K	Chase James A	10	laborer	24	65 "
L	Scalli Anthony	10	U S A	29	here
M	Scalli Elizabeth—†	10	housewife	29	"
N	Babcock Ernest H	10	mechanic	29	"
O	Babcock Mary—†	10	housewife	27	"
P	Martell Mary—†	10	"	46	"
R	Gaines Mary K—†	10	"	62	33 O'Reilly way
S	Smith Mary E—†	10	"	26	33 "
T	Smith Warren E	10	U S N	27	33 "
U	Gardiner Anna V—†	10	housewife	24	here
V	Gardiner Arthur J	10	clerk	30	"
W	Crilley Joseph V	18	bartender	38	"
X	Crilley Mary E—†	18	housewife	32	"
Y	Leahy Ella M—†	18	"	35	
Z	Leahy Walter P	18	electrician	42	"

537

A	Holland Edith—†	18	housewife	23	Somerville
B	Holland John	18	electrician	29	"
C	Capraro Florence—†	18	housewife	35	here
D	Capraro Vito	18	chauffeur	35	"
E	Durr Dorothy L—†	18	housewife	20	73 Walford way
F	Durr John E	18	welder	23	73 "
G	Osofsky David H	18	chauffeur	41	here
H	Osofsky Nellie—†	18	housewife	38	"
K	Buck Frederick J	34	chauffeur	27	"
L	Buck Grace M—†	34	housewife	26	"
M	Roach Harry	34	laborer	56	"
N	Roach Sarah—†	34	housewife	55	"

Page.	Letter.	FULL NAME.	Residence, Jan. 1, 1944.	Occupation.	Supposed Age.	Reported Residence, Jan. 1, 1943. Street and Number.

O'Meara Court—Continued

o	Kitchin Dorothy M—†	34	housewife	29	here
p	Kitchin John E	34	brakeman	30	"
r	Malone Bernard	34	laborer	30	"
s	Malone Elizabeth—†	34	housewife	29	"
t	Mitchell Frances—†	34	"	26	"
u	Mitchell Joseph A	34	packer	32	"
v	White Irene—†	34	housewife	22	10 Walford way
w	White Peter	34	welder	30	10 "
x	Dabrowski Alice—†	42	housewife	24	here
y	Dabrowski Thaddeus	42	repairman	27	"
z	Hennelly Joseph P	42	clerk	30	Somerville
	538				
a	Hennelly Mary—†	42	housewife	22	"
b	McGrath Joseph	42	U S N	32	here
c	Noonan Mary—†	42	housewife	30	"
d	Toomey Edward F	42	laborer	27	9 Walford way
e	Toomey Rita—†	42	housewife	24	9 "
f	McGrath James B	42	laborer	31	162 Medford
g	McGrath Rita A—†	42	housewife	27	162 "
h	Egan Ann C—†	42	"	22	50 Monument
k	Egan Walter J	42	laborer	27	50 "

O'Reilly Way

l	Upperstrom Carl F	65	molder	59	106 St Stephen
m	Upperstrom Rosella—†	65	housewife	58	106 "
n	Kozak Joseph J	65	electrician	34	here
o	Kozak Sophie M—†	65	housewife	30	"
p	Gormley Joseph	65	laborer	40	"
r	Gormley Muriel—†	65	housewife	32	"
s	Burger Frederick P	65	repairman	62	"
t	Burger Mary E—†	65	housewife	59	"
u	Smith James J	65	U S N	31	1850 Com av
v	Smith Marion—†	65	housewife	30	1850 "
w	Biggins Alice R—†	65	"	35	here
x	Biggins Luke	65	chauffeur	40	"
y	Taylor George S	65	retired	73	"
z	Taylor Margaret J—†	65	housewife	55	"
	539				
b	Sullivan Dorothy—†	65	"	26	
c	Sullivan John	65	mechanic	31	"

O'Reilly Way—Continued

D	Carey Anna—†	73	housewife	31	here
E	Carey James R	73	chauffeur	31	"
F	Quinn Della B—†	73	at home	67	"
G	Bartlett Bertha—†	73	housewife	49	"
H	Bartlett Henry F	73	operator	53	"
K	Cronshaw John J	73	rigger	54	51 Claybourne
L	Cronshaw Mary E—†	73	housewife	54	51 "
M	Halloran Catherine—†	73	"	35	here
N	Halloran Festus	73	laborer	40	"
O	Lagorio Victoria E—†	73	housewife	40	"
P	Conway John H	73	U S A	30	23 Mystic
R	Conway Nora—†	73	housewife	64	23 "
S	Hope Charlotte E—†	73	"	31	here
T	Hope Joseph P	73	chauffeur	37	"
U	Scott Charles L	73	U S A	27	"
V	Scott Charlotte F—†	73	housewife	27	"
W	Richardson Helen M—†	73	"	24	"
X	Richardson John J	73	laundryman	25	"

Trenton Street

Y	Devlin Bernard	1	laborer	52	here
Z	Devlin Catherine—†	1	housewife	50	"
	540				
A	Devlin John C	1	longshoreman	22	"
B	Devlin Phillip J	1	U S A	27	
C	Trider Rose H—†	3	housewife	38	"
D	Trider Walter E	3	chauffeur	38	"
E	Rose Gertrude E—†	5	at home	35	1 Oak
F	Turner Mabel E—†	5	auditor	61	here
G	Badger Alphonso M	5	retired	72	"
H	Badger Minnie E—†	5	housewife	72	"
K	Copithorn Alfred W	7	U S N	34	102 Pearl
L	Copithorn Alice G—†	7	housewife	24	44 Polk
M	Garcelon Eugene	7	baker	56	here
N	Garcelon Eva H—†	7	housewife	33	"
P	Dwyer Margaret—†	9	"	70	"
R	Robinson Helen M—†	9	"	35	W Boxford
S	Robinson Samuel H	9	seaman	37	"
T	Keane Margaret M—†	9	clerk	22	here
U	Woods Harold A	9	U S N	20	"

Trenton Street—Continued

v	Woods John E	9	longshoreman	51	here
w	Woods Joseph P	9	U S A	26	"
x	Woods Nora M—†	9	housewife	55	"
y	Woods Thomas W	9	longshoreman	28	"
z	Woods William P	9	U S A	23	
	541				
a	Doherty Mary A—†	11	at home	61	"
b	*Monagle Mary A—†	11	waitress	24	3 Mystic pl
c	Doherty Josephine V—†	11	housewife	59	here
d	Doherty Katherine—†	11	stenographer	20	"
e	Doherty Patrick J	11	laborer	52	"
f	Doherty Walter E	11	U S N	21	"
g	Woods Edward J	13	melter	27	24 Concord
h	Woods Grace V—†	13	housewife	23	23 High
k	Whelton Helen J—†	13	messenger	20	here
l	Whelton Margaret M—†	13	housewife	56	"
m	Whelton Mary T—†	13	operator	26	"
n	Whelton Michael J	13	foreman	65	"
o	O'Hare Anna T—†	15	housekeeper	63	"
p	O'Hare Mildred L—†	15	cleaner	37	"
r	McBride John J	15	operator	53	"
s	McBride Mary A—†	15	housekeeper	47	"
t	McBride William J	15	clerk	48	"
u	McBride William J, jr	15	U S A	24	"
v	McCormack Estelle—†	17	housewife	70	195 Bunker Hil
w	Moynihan Ethel D—†	17	messenger	22	here
x	Moynihan John J	17	chauffeur	48	"
y	Moynihan Mary E—†	17	housewife	48	"
z	Toomey John J	19	clerk	30	
	542				
a	Toomey Mary T—†	19	housekeeper	70	"
b	Toomey Theresa M—†	19	at home	28	"
c	Mausell Frances L—†	19	housewife	47	"
d	Mausell Samuel F	19	clerk	47	
e	Carver Elizabeth J—†	19	housewife	52	"
f	Carver Joseph A	19	U S A	25	
g	Carver William J	19	guard	55	
h	McDermott Catherine E-†	21	stenographer	30	"
k	McDermott Francis J	21	reporter	39	"
l	McDermott Henry A	21	U S A	42	
m	Sullivan Catherine F—†	21	housewife	36	"

Trenton Street—Continued

N	Sullivan Leo X	21	chauffeur	39	here
o	Sullivan Cornelius J	23	B F D	50	"
P	Sullivan Edith A—†	23	student	20	"
R	Sullivan Edith G—†	23	housewife	40	"
s	Gillogly Elizabeth M—†	23	secretary	48	"
T	Mullen James J	25	chauffeur	27	40 Allston
U	Mullen John M	25	U S A	25	40 "
v	Mullen Mary E—†	25	stitcher	57	40 "
w	Mullen Thomas	25	U S A	22	40 "
x	Morrissey Joseph E	25	operator	29	here
Y	Morrissey Margaret—†	25	housewife	68	"
z	Morrissey Margaret M—†	25	clerk	39	"

543

A	Castor Charles H	25	foreman	65	"
B	Castor Charles H, jr	25	U S N	30	
c	Castor Mary J—†	25	housewife	61	"
D	Marquis Joseph M	27	foreman	28	"
E	Marquis Margaret—†	27	at home	21	"
G	Howell Leo W	27	checker	38	"
F	Howell Stella A—†	27	housewife	36	"
H	O'Hara Joseph J	27	machinist	25	"
K	O'Hara Louise E—†	27	clerk	28	

Walford Way

L	Santiago Catherine—†	121	housewife	23	here
M	Santiago Raphael	121	welder	24	"
N	Casey Alice—†	121	waitress	21	177 Rutherford av
o	Casey Thomas F, jr	121	U S N	21	Somerville
P	McQuade John F	121	machinist	50	177 Rutherford av
R	McQuade John W	121	electrician	25	Honolulu
s	*Gillis Josephine—†	121	housewife	28	here
T	Gillis Robert Q	121	shipfitter	31	"
U	Davide Adeline—†	121	housewife	29	"
v	Davide Luciano	121	operator	28	"
w	Wright Ella—†	121	housewife	28	"
x	Wright Stanley	121	U S N	25	"
Y	Collins Edith—†	121	factoryhand	28	"
z	Collins John A	121	U S N	30	"

544

A	Coughlin Mabel—†	121	housewife	38	"

Page.	Letter.	FULL NAME.	Residence, Jan. 1, 1944.	Occupation.	Supposed Age.	Reported Residence, Jan. 1, 1943. Street and Number.

Walford Way—Continued

B	Coughlin Walter	121	mechanic	43	here
C	O'Gara Eugene	121`	U S A	29	"
D	O'Gara Jennie—†	121	housewife	59	"
E	O'Gara John J	121	U S A	31	
F	O'Gara Thomas	121	"	23	
G	Juliano Catherine—†	121	housewife	40	"
H	Juliano Guy	121	foreman	40	"
K	Boghosian Helen L—†	122	housewife	32	"
L	Boghosian Sarkis	122	manager	35	"
M	LeBrun Dorothy—†	122	housewife	24	Newton
N	LeBrun Verdun F	122	U S M C	25	"
O	Wyse James M	122	U S A	26	here
P	Wyse Marguerite—†	122	housewife	61	"
R	Wyse Michael	122	seaman	67	"
S	Gallagher Raymond	122	U S N	41	
T	Gallagher Ruth—†	122	houswife	36	"
U	Lannon Madeline—†	122	U S M C	23	"
V	Lannon Mary—†	122	housewife	55	"
W	Parente Marie E—†	122	"	52	Fairhaven
X	Parente Manuel R	122	boatbuilder	50	"
Y	Devine Mary H—†	122	housewife	56	here
Z	Hakala Catherine—†	122	"	34	Cambridge
	545				
A	Hakala Emil A	122	ropemaker	33	"
B	Williams Catherine—†	122	housewife	55	here
C	Williams Francis	122	manager	60	"
D	McGrath Emma F—†	129	housewife	40	"
E	McGrath James C	129	laborer	50	
F	Spader May B—† i	129	housewife	60	"
G	Spader Samuel	129	retired	61	
H	Lividoti Eileen—†	129	housewife	20	"
K	Lividoti Thomas F	129	metalworker	23	"
L	Shean Francis A	129	machinist	33	"
M	Shean Mary J—†	129	housewife	30	"
N	Jones Annie—†	129	operator	48	"
O	Leonard Agnes E—†	129	housewife	46	"
P	Leonard Ruth A—†	129	bookkeeper	23	"
R	Doherty Edward	129	laborer	50	"
S	Doherty Margaret—†	129	housewife	43	"
T	Cody Lena—†	129	matron	52	191 Cambridge
U	Curry Elizabeth A—†	129	tel operator	49	429 Brookline av

Page.	Letter.	FULL NAME.	Residence, Jan. 1, 1944.	Occupation.	Supposed Age.	Reported Residence, Jan. 1, 1943. Street and Number.

Walford Way—Continued

v	Ferracane Louis	129	U S A	25	Somerville
w	Ferracane Margaret—†	129	housewife	23	"
x	Metzger Annie T—†	130	"	66	here
y	Weymouth Irene T—†	130	clerk	40	"
z	Graham Annie—†	130	housewife	51	21 Moulton

546

A	Graham John J	130	watchman	58	21 "
B	Graham John J, jr	130	U S N	26	21 "
c	Rodden Catherine A—†	130	at home	80	here
D	Rodden Joseph F·	130	retired	73	"
E	Rodden Mary E—†	130	at home	78	"
F	Rodden Theresa F—†	130	"	75	"
G	McCarthy John E	130	welder	23	41 Cedar
H	McCarthy Margaret E—†130		housewife	26	41 "
K	Rose Manuel	130	repairman	25	here
L	Rose Rita P—†	130	housewife	26	"
M	Stanley Mildred M—†	130	"	41	"
N	Stanley William H	130	rigger	40	"
O	Buckley Madeline—†	130	housewife	21	Malden
P	Buckley William	130	machinist	23	63 Etna
R	Vinet Horatio	130	clerk	42	Medford
S	Vinet Mary—†	130	housewife	33	"
T	Ascolese Joseph	130	metalworker	34	here
U	Ascolese Rose—†	130	housewife	29	"

Ward 2–Precinct 6

CITY OF BOSTON

LIST OF RESIDENTS
20 YEARS OF AGE AND OVER

(NON-CITIZENS INDICATED BY ASTERISK)
(FEMALES INDICATED BY DAGGER)

AS OF

JANUARY 1, 1944

THOMAS F. SULLIVAN, *Chairman*
FREDERIC E. DOWLING, *Secretary*
WILLIAM A. MOTLEY, JR.
FRANCIS B. McKINNEY
EVERETT R. PROUT

Listing Board.

CITY OF BOSTON PRINTING DEPARTMENT

600
Adams Street

A	Sweeney Catherine A—†	1	housekeeper	83	here
B	Sweeney Leo E	1	U S A	28	"
C	Sweeney Margaret M—†	1	housekeeper	54	"
D	Sweeney Marguerite F—†	1	social worker	27	"
E	Chadderton Laurence	2	waiter	36	
F	Cote David	2	shipfitter	26	"
G	Kelly Bridget—†	2	housewife	71	"
H	Kelly Daniel	2	retired	73	
K	Kelly John D	2	U S A	27	
L	Looney Daniel	2	laborer	66	
M	O'Connor William F	2	watchman	69	"
N	St Jean George	2	machinist	46	"
O	Wallace John	2	bartender	61	"
P	Williamson Roy B	2	electrician	40	43 Chestnut
R	Murphy Margaret M—†	3	housekeeper	70	here
S	Honohan Henry	3	U S A	21	"
T	McCarthy Hannah—†	3	housekeeper	66	"
U	McIlvaine Mary A—†	3	housewife	51	"
V	McIlvaine Mary G—†	3	waitress	25	"
W	McIlvaine William T	3	quartermaster	61	"
X	Cast Margaret J—†	3	housekeeper	34	"
Y	Warner George	3	retired	75	"
Z	Warner Richard J	3	U S A	25	

601

A	Driscoll John	4	foreman	48	"
B	Gleason Ellen—†	4	cook	40	
C	Jordan Bridget—†	4	housewife	57	"
D	Jordan Thomas	4	U S A	30	"
E	Jordan Veronica—†	4	clerk	32	
F	O'Brien Mary—†	4	"	31	
G	O'Leary Elizabeth—†	4	"	20	
H	O'Leary Daniel	4	"	57	
K	Paff George	4	blacksmith	42	"
L	Aubin Alfred J	5	molder	55	Worcester
M	Bathgat Peter	5	"	28	"
N	Callahan Edward	5	messenger	73	here
O	Campbell Mary—†	5	welder	28	New Bedford
¹O	Carroll Francis	5	U S A	21	here
²O	Carroll Helen M—†	5	clerk	24	"
P	Carroll Julia—†	5	housekeeper	53	"

2

Adams Street—Continued

	Letter.	FULL NAME.	Residence Jan. 1, 1944.	Occupation.	Supposed Age.	Reported Residence, Jan. 1, 1943. Street and Number.
	R	*Carroll Patrick J	5	retired	58	here
	S	Gorman George E	5	ropemaker	30	Dracut
	T	Keating Jeremiah	5	engraver	52	here
	U	O'Driscoll James	5	painter	51	"
	V	O'Leary Cornelius	5	guard	56	24 Oak
	W	Sullivan Agnes T—†	6	housewife	60	here
	X	Sullivan Charles R	6	U S A	32	"
	Y	Sullivan Frederick R	6	"	37	"
	Z	Sullivan Joseph M	6	supt	62	··
		602				
	B	Hermanson Catherine—†	8	housewife	48	"
	C	Hermanson Edgar D	8	foreman	54	"
	D	*Callahan Floretta—†	8	housewife	46	"
	E	*Callahan Francis L	8	woodworker	48	"
	F	*Callahan Rita L—†	8	stenographer	23	"
	G	Carney Elizabeth G—†	8	tel operator	58	"
	H	Carney George A	8	retired	75	17 Greenville
	K	Carney James J	8	"	73	here
	L	Carney Margaret T—†	8	housekeeper	60	"
	M	Fitzgibbons John	8	laborer	34	"
	N	Hafner Andrew W	8	U S A	23	
	O	Hafner Mary L—†	8	housekeeper	43	"
	P	Brown Margaret E—†	9	housewife	45	"
	R	Brown William F	9	laborer	21	··
	S	Hingston Mary V—†	9	housewife	24	"
	T	Crotty Madeline—†	9	"	26	·:
	U	Crotty Thomas	9	longshoreman	26	"
	V	O'Connor Rita—†	9	housewife	25	"
	W	Lehan Ellen K—†	10	housekeeper	58	"
	X	Lehan Rose M—†	10	packer	50	"
	Y	Cannon Alice A—†	11	SPAR	24	
	Z	Cannon Austin L	11	planner	63	"
		603				
	A	Cannon Katherine C—†	11	supervisor	34	"
	B	Cannon Marguerite L—†	11	stenographer	30	"
	C	Cannon Mary L—†	11	housewife	60	"
	D	Cannon Mary L—†	11	WAVE	32	
	E	Cannon Phyllis C—†	11	clerk	20	
	F	Cannon Virginia C—†	11	housekeeper	26	"
	G	Tansey Mary A—†	12	"	68	··
	L	Linehan Gertrude N—†	13	laundrywkr	37	"

Adams Street—Continued

M	Linehan Helene L—†	13	manager	41	here
N	Linehan Jeremiah J	13	U S A	44	"
O	Linehan Margaret—†	13	housekeeper	68	"
P	Gaffney Anna E—†	13·	packer	40	"
R	Haley John	13	mechanic	62	"
S	McCormack John	25	retired	57	
T	Murray Alice—†	25	housewife	34	"
U	Murray Hugh	25	manager	43	"
V	Supple Richard	25	laborer	44	"
W	Supple William	25	repairman	43	"
X	Donovan Ellen J—†	27	housekeeper	42	"
Y	Donovan Frank L	27	proprietor	51	"
Z	Donovan Robert T	27	B F D	41	"
	604				
A	Ahearn Catherine—†	29	housewife	25	"
B	Ahearn Edwin J	29	policeman	28	"
D	Caggiano Charles	29	attorney	50	"
E	Caggiano Madeline—†	29	housewife	40	"
F	McCormack Alice—†	29	housekeeper	77	"

Chelsea Street

K	Connolly Dorothy—†	106	metalworker	24	46 Mt Vernon
L	Sheehan Elizabeth C—†	106	housewife	52	46 "
N	Sheehan John	106	coppersmith	54	46 "
M	Sheehan Ruth A—†	106	housekeeper	21	46 "
O	Lombard Gertrude I—†	106	housewife	50	here
P	Lombard John B	106	dentist	51	"
R	*Aspell Mary—†	106	housekeeper	48	"
S	Zinkowski Samuel	106	painter	36	"
T	Geary Anna—†	106	housekeeper	65	"
U	Creed Margaret J—†	106	"	65	"
V	Moore James C	106	U S A	35	
W	O'Leary Michael J	106	freighthandler	30	"
X	Fitzgerald Margaret—†	106	clerk	23	
Y	Murphy David	106	metalworker	53	"
Z	Murphy Margaret—†	106	housekeeper	55	"
	605				
A	*Murphy Nora—†	106	"	54	
B	Jones Mary H—†	106	housewife	47	"
C	Jones Stanley	106	U S N	42	

Chestnut Street

F	Goodnoh Edmond	22	storekeeper	72	here
G	Goodnoh Rose—†	22	at home	46	"
H	Ryan Catherine—†	22	"	52	"
K	Ryan Louise—†	22	"	50	
L	Donovan Lilia—†	28	"	70	
O	Lynch James	28	longshoreman	58	"
M	Miller Mary A—†	28	at home	38	"
N	Powers William	28	clerk	25	41 Chestnut
P	Weldon Joseph	28	longshoreman	47	here
R	Quinn Mary—†	30	at home	45	"
S	Nation Mary—†	30	"	36	"
T	Puzo Angelo	30	retired	67	
U	Puzo Catherine—†	30	at home	63	"
V	Carmody Doris—†	30	"	21	Chelsea
W	Carmody George	30	shipfitter	43	"
X	Finn Anna—†	32	clerk	28	34 Bartlett
Y	Finn Margaret—†	32	at home	26	34 "
Z	Gookin Frank	32	shipfitter	50	here

606

A	Gorovan Thomas	32	"	63	33 Rutherford av
B	Kafton Stephen	32	machinist	27	here
c*	Moriarty Nellie—†	32	at home	42	Cambridge
D	Walsh Anna—†	32	"	33	here
E	Walsh James	32	laborer	39	"
F*	Campino Joseph	34	retired	68	"
G*	Campino Louisa—†	34	housewife	59	"
H	Campino Peter	34	U S A	25	
K	Campino Mary—†	34	at home	23	"
M	Downey John J	40	shipfitter	45	"
N	Harrison Delores—†	40	at home	34	"
O	Keefe Josephine—†	40	"	38	"
P	Mahan Dorothy—†	40	"	38	50 Monum'nt av
R	Mellino Joseph L	40	retired	68	here
S	Richards Norma—†	40	at home	21	"
T	Buckley Charles P	41	U S A	22	"
U	Buckley Edith G—†	41	at home	47	"
V	Buckley John F	41	U S A	20	
W	Buckley Mary L—†	41	bookkeeper	24	"
X	Fogarty Ellen C—†	42	housewife	48	"
Y	Fogarty Joseph J	42	clerk	52	
Z	Foley Thomas T	42	longshoreman	51	"

5

607
Chestnut Street—Continued

	A	Carpenter Clyde D	42	U S N	40	here
	B	Carpenter Olive—†	42	housewife	39	"
	C	Maher Lillian—†	42	"	41	"
	D	Maher Robert A	42	policeman	42	"
	E	Gallagher Charles H	43	boilermaker	60	"
	F	Gallagher Eugene	43	machinist	30	"
	G	Hersey Frederick	43	"	59	
	H	Savage George	43	"	47	
	K	Steine Gerald	43	baggageman	34	"
	L	Marino Mary—†	44	housewife	42	"
	M	Marino Vincent	44	clerk	47	
	P	Caron Louis M	45	U S A	23	
	R	Caron Margaret J—†	45	housewife	23	"
	S	O'Connell Catherine E—†	45	clerk	23	
	T	O'Connell Edward F	45	U S A	21	
	U	O'Connell Mary A—†	45	housewife	54	"
	V	O'Connell Mary A—†	45	at home	24	"
	W	O'Connell Samuel J	45	laborer	65	
	Z	Lambert Helena C—†	46	housewife	61	"
	X	O'Brien Eleanor K—†	46	"	28	
	Y	O'Brien Francis W	46	U S A	29	

608

	A	Lambert John F	46	retired	69	
	B	Lambert John F, jr	46	U S A	27	"
	C	Lambert Mary A—†	46	at home	30	"
	D	Anderson Anna E—†	47	housewife	45	"
	E	Anderson Nils	47	retired	54	
	F	Curry Catherine M—†	47	at home	38	"
	G	Curry Frances R—†	47	clerk	34	
	H	Curry Mary E—†	47	housewife	70	"
	K	Curry William E	47	retired	73	
	L	Curry William E	47	U S A	32	
	M	Griffin Helen F—†	47	at home	75	"
	N	Buckley John P	48	attorney	54	"
	O	Buckley Mary A—†	48	at home	46	"
	P	Buckley William J	48	clerk	45	
	R	Morrissey Helen C—†	49	housewife	28	"
	S	Morrissey Thomas F	49	chauffeur	29	"
	T	Meehan John F	49	retired	55	"
	U	Meehan Lena M—†	49	housewife	45	"

6

Chestnut Street—Continued

	Letter	FULL NAME	Residence Jan. 1, 1944	Occupation	Supposed Age	Street and Number
	v	Brines John F	50	rigger	34	here
	w	Brines Mary F—†	50	at home	59	"
	x	Burnes Mary—†	50	packer	59	6 Prospect
	y	Pierce Martin E	51	B F D	22	here
	z	Pierce Mary E—†	51	housewife	22	"
609						
	a	Lombard Elizabeth V—†	51	"	53	
	b	Lombard Janet V—†	51	welder	21	"
	c	Lombard Richard F	51	chauffeur	52	"
	d	Lombard Thomas B	51	retired	82	
	e	Lombard Thomas F	51	U S N	22	
	f	McCormick James	51	retired	70	
	g	Sweeney Mary—†	51	bookkeeper	55	"
	h	DeCristoforo Julia—†	54	at home	67	"
	k	DeCristoforo Lillian—†	54	bookkeeper	21	"
	l	DeCristoforo Louisa—†	54	clerk	24	..
	m	DeCristoforo Nicholas	54	laborer	58	
	n	DeCristoforo Frank N	54	chauffeur	30	"
	o	DeCristoforo Lena—†	54	at home	29	"
	p	Prizio Catherine C—†	54	housewife	32	"
	r	Prizio Frank C	54	shipfitter	34	"
	s	Corbett Mary J—†	55	housewife	72	"
	t	Corbett William J	55	retired	75	"
	u	Brown George E	55	policeman	48	"
	v	Brown Sarah M—†	55	housewife	48	"
	w	Corbett Joseph A	55	collector	37	"
	x	Wilson Ellen W—†	58	clerk	45	
	y	Wilson George W, jr	58	laborer	43	
	z	Fleming John F	59	fisherman	40	"
610						
	a	Fleming Margaret F—†	59	housewife	39	"
	b	Aaron Dorothy P—†	59	stenographer	24	"
	c	Aaron Lillian M—†	59	housewife	67	"
	d	Aaron Lillian M—†	59	operator	29	"
	e	Aaron Robert F	59	U S M C	20	"
	f	Aaron Solomon E	59	retired	73	"
	g	Aaron Walter R	59	clerk	35	
	h	Peterson Harold J	60	"	47	
	k	Peterson Kathleen—†	60	housewife	41	"
	l	Falvey Augusta M—†	63	executive	40	"
	m	Falvey Mary C—†	63	teacher	45	"

Chestnut Street—Continued

N	Falvey Patrick	63	retired	78	here
O	Garwitz Bernice—†	64	housewife	31	"
P	Garwitz Lawrence D	64	machinist	33	"
R	Kane Patrick F	64	retired	74	
S	Beaton Mary C—†	64	secretary	36	"
T	Carney Winifred M—†	64	at home	55	"
U	Donoghue Daniel	64	retired	77	
V	Donoghue John L	64	social worker	49	"
W	Doherty Daniel T	64	U S A	32	
X	Doherty Rita—†	64	clerk	27	
Y	Lambert Frederick F	64	secretary	62	"
Z	McCarthy Abbie L—†	65	housewife	61	"
	611				
A	McCarthy Henry J	65	retired	71	"
B	Leonard Catherine J—†	65	operator	21	"
C	Leonard Katherine J—†	65	at home	57	"
D	Fitzpatrick Catherine A-†	65	housewife	73	"
E	Fitzpatrick John H	65	retired	84	
F	Fitzpatrick Veronica C—†	65	manager	31	"
G	Barrett Margaret A—†	66	housewife	68	"
H	Barrett MargaretM—†	66	operator	33	"
K	Barrett Mildred A—†	66	bookkeeper	26	"
L	Barrett Peter J	66	retired	78	"
M	Barrett Robert J	66	U S A	30	
N	Carney Daniel	66	longshoreman	53	"
O	Carney John G	66	U S N	25	
P	Fitzgerald David T	66	U S A	30	
R	Fitzgerald Jane F—†	66	at home	28	"
S	Lombard Catherine A—†	66	"	22	
T	Lombard John P	66	U S N	22	"
U	Hennessey Helen F—†	66	at home	39	37 Pearl
V	McKenna Catherine I—†	66	housewife	42	here
W	McKenna James	66	engineer	42	"
X	Reynolds Helen M—†	66	millhand	42	"
Y	Gill Joseph A	66	agent	34	
Z	Gill Mary A—†	66	housewife	32	"
	612				
A	Dalton Peter	67	longshoreman	54	"
B	Deckrow Oscar	67	pipefitter	51	"
C	Hoar Grace—†	67	housewife	31	"

Chestnut Street—Continued

D	Hoar Thomas A	67	U S N	39	here
E	Jones George J	67	welder	23	Springfield
F	McLaughlin Leslie P	67	"	37	Chelsea

Monument Court

G	Burke Margaret—†	12	housewife	36	here
K	Churchill Alfred	12	laborer	45	"
L	Churchill Frances—†	12	housewife	40	"
M	Papineau Blanche—†	14	"	53	"
N	Ryan George	14	laborer	24	"
O	Ryan Joseph R	14	U S N	27	
P	Ryan Thomas	14	U S A	21	
R	Bagley Thomas P	28	foreman	68	"
S	Carr Elizabeth L—†	28	at home	39	"
T	Carr Emily M—†	28	cleaner	38	"
U	Carr John B	28	B F D	54	
V	Carr William F	28	laborer	51	"
W	Smith Mary L—†	28	ropemaker	50	"

Monument Square

X	Allchin Frederick J	1	clergyman	65	here
Y	Bailey Edward C	1	"	41	"
Z	Connell Catherine M—†	1	housekeeper	69	"
	613				
A	Farrell Ralph W	1	clergyman	49	"
B	Flanagan William J	1	"	34	"
C	McLaughlin Francis A	1	"	42	
D	Brown Clara B—†	2	teacher	51	"
E	Brown Marie—†	2	"	23	
F	Curran Margaret—†	2	"	48	
G	Dooley Margaret M—†	2	"	34	
H	D'Orazio Theresa A—†	2	"	28	
K	Egan Catherine H—†	2	"	59	"
L	Fitzgerald Julia M—†	2	"	22	Framingham
M	Galvin Mary E—†	2	"	26	here
N	Ivers Mary A—†	2		25	"
O	Manning Margaret—†	2	"	24	Framingham
P	McCarthy Mary—†	2	"	37	Somerville

7

Page	Letter	FULL NAME.	Residence, Jan. 1, 1944.	Occupation.	Supposed Age.	Reported Residence, Jan. 1, 1943. Street and Number.

Monument Square—Continued

	R	McCarthy Phoebe G—†	2	teacher	44	here
	s	McCool Regina M—†	2	"	31	"
	T	McCormack Mary B—†	2	"	46	"
	U	McGovern Anna F—†	2	"	53	..
	v	McNulty Alice R—†	2	"	34	
	w	Michaud Frances A—†	2	"	34	
	x	O'Connor Gertrude E—†	2	"	22	
	y	Richardson Olive E—†	2	"	35	
	z	Tobin Irene—†	2	"	33	

614

	A	Quigley Gerard J	4	U S N	26	
	B	Quigley Margaret G—†	4	housewife	53	"
	c	Quigley William S	4	physician	55	"
	E	Caldwell Margaret—†	6	housewife	34	"
	F	Caldwell William	6	blacksmith	39	"
	G	Estcourt George	6	electrician	22	"
	H	Cooney Annie—†	6	housewife	68	"
	K	Cooney James F	6	driller	33	
	L	Cooney Mary—†	6	housewife	30	"
	M	Patry Edna M—†	6	"	60	
	N	Patry Joseph L	6	laborer	60	
	o	Craddick Margaret E—†	7	clerk	71	
	P	Kane Margaret M—†	7	teacher	33	..
	R	Burns Cathleen—†	7	tel operator	26	"
	s	Burns Helen—†	7	clerk	22	
	T	Burns Mary—†	7	"	50	
	U	Kelly Eileen—†	8	housewife	23	"
	v	Kelly Lester A, jr	8	chauffeur	24	"
	w	Holbert Joseph	8	"	47	
	x	Holbert May—†	8	housewife	47	"
	y	Brogan Gertrude M—†	8	clerk	42	
	z	Brogan Mary—†	8	"	47	

615

	A	Glynn Mary—†	8	at home	83	"
	B	Gates Albert S—†	8	shipfitter	55	"
	c	Gates Lelia M—†	8	housewife	49	"
	D	Harrington Catherine—†	9	"	53	
	E	Harrington Catherine J—†	9	clerk	25	
	F	Harrington Frank A	9	inspector	28	"
	G	Harrington William T	9	coppersmith	23	"
	H	Peffer Harold R	9	laborer	30	

Monument Square—Continued

K	Peffer Mary L—†	9	housewife	26	here
L	Murphy Francis X	9	U S A	30	"
M	Murphy Mary F—†	9	housewife	60	"
N	Murphy Mary T—†	9	clerk	24	
O	Murphy Paul J	9	U S A	26	
P	Murphy Timothy F	9	supervisor	62	"
R	McDermott Annie L—†	9	at home	70	"
S	McDermott Elizabeth G-†	9	housewife	66	"
T	McDermott John J	9	guard	44	
U	McDermott Mary E—†	9	stenographer	25	"
V	McDermott Mary J—†	9	binder	68	"
W	Blute James F	9	mechanic	39	69 Baldwin
X	Blute Mary—†	9	housewife	38	69 "
Y	Sullivan Florence T—†	9	operator	32	69 "
Z	Sullivan Timothy B	9	U S A	30	69 '
	616				
A	Trudeau Joseph	9A	shipfitter	57	here
B	Trudeau Mary—†	9A	housewife	59	"
C	O'Connell Margaret—†	9A	"	50	2 Pearl
D	O'Connell Mary—†	9A	clerk	22	2 "
E	O'Brien Mary—†	9A	housewife	25	20 Devens
F	O'Brien Vincent F—†	9A	laborer	28	20 "
H	Sullivan John J	10	U S N	25	here
K	Sullivan Margaret—†	10	housewife	24	"
L	Crowley Gerald J	10	clerk	36	"
M	Crowley Mary A—†	10	housewife	33	"
N	Irving Clyde M—†	10	"	49	"
O	Irving George E	10	clerk	52	
P	Schulze Eric	10	electrician	39	"
R	Schulze Mary—†	10	housewife	31	"
S	Morris Augustine J	11	repairman	34	"
T	Morris Frances M—†	11	housewife	28	"
U	Brophy Florence C—†	11	clerk	20	
V	Brophy Florence I—†	11	housewife	51	"
W	Brophy James B	11	compositor	56	"
X	Moisan Emma A—†	11	secretary	38	"
Y	Moisan Helen E—†	11	clerk	36	"
Z	Moisan Lucy M—†	11	teacher	32	"
	617				
A	Moisan Margaret M—†	11	at home	66	"
B	Moisan Patricia K—†	11	nurse	30	New York

7

1'

Monument Square—Continued

c	Picardi Florencia—†	11	housewife	59	here
d	Picardi Joseph	11	U S M C	22	"
e	Murphy Catherine D—†	12	housewife	52	"
f	Murphy Charles H	12	organist	70	"
g	Barnes Bert A	13	shipfitter	56	"
h	Corbett Joseph	13	longshoreman	65	"
¹h	Fuller Charles J	13	laborer	21	Plymouth
k	Herrick Johanna E—†	13	at home	80	here
l	Keating Edward B	13	longshoreman	44	"
m	Keating Mary—†	13	housewife	47	"
n	Lent Albert H	13	U S N	40	New York
o	Lent Anne—†	13	housewife	27	"
p	Lial Josephine—†	13	at home	72	35 Breed
r	McFee Robert	13	clerk	47	here
s	O'Leary Jeremiah	13	longshoreman	34	"
¹s	Peukert Bernard R	13	U S N	25	New York
t	Peukert Wilma—†	13	housewife	24	"
u	Grath Catherine—†	14	"	65	Missouri
v	McDonough Alice M—†	14	"	35	Everett
w	McDonough John H	14	laborer	40	"
x	Payne Anna E—†	14	housewife	40	Missouri
y	Payne Fred R	14	laborer	50	"
z	Rich Flora—†	14	housewife	28	Lynn

618

a	Rich Herbert	14	U S N	28	"
b	Slaney Adele—†	14	at home	70	here
c	Slaney Robert W	14	bartender	41	"
d	Sprouse Jessie E—†	14	housewife	26	Missouri
e	Sprouse John W	14	U S N	33	"
f	Tolar Margaret D—†	14	housewife	30	here
g	Tolar Reece	14	U S N	29	"
h	Turnbough James R	14	laborer	64	"
k	Warren George E	14	"	44	
l	Barry Charles J	48	clerk	26	
m	Barry Mary B—†	48	housewife	53	"
n	Barry Mary I—†	48	secretary	29	"
o	Behenna Margaret M—†	48	tel operator	35	"
p	Brady Delia—†	48	housewife	54	"
r	Brady James	48	retired	56	
s	Brady Mary E—†	48	nurse	24	
t	Casey Anna J—†	48	stenographer	38	"

Monument Square—Continued

U	Flanagan Catherine M—†	48	housewife	58	here
V	Flanagan Daniel J	48	inspector	69	"
W	Flanagan James F	48	U S N	24	"
X	Swanson Dennis J	49	custodian	65	"
Y	Swanson Ellen M—†	49	housewife	63	"
Z	Swanson Samuel A	49	U S A	42	
	619				
A	Kilty Catherine H—†	49	housewife	74	"
B	Kilty William P	49	retired	71	
C	Murphy Joseph	49	"	51	
D	Murphy Mary—†	49	stenographer	46	"
E	Buckley John	49	clerk	40	26 Cordis
F	Buckley Therese—†	49	housewife	31	Somerville
G	Flanagan John F	50	clerk	62	here
H	Flanagan Mary E—†	50	"	56	"
K	Ilsley Edwin D	50	U S N	28	8 Glade av
L	Ilsley Mary J—†	50	at home	26	8 "
M	Watson Catherine J—†	50	clerk	45	here
N	Halley Ellen—†	50	housewife	63	"
O	Halley Ellen H—†	50	stenographer	29	"
P	Halley Michael	50	foreman	37	"
R	Brock James J	50	contractor	68	33 Cordis
S	Factor Anne L—†	50	clerk	39	33 "
T	Hynes Edward B	50	instructor	63	33 "
U	Monihan Dorothy—†	50	nurse	25	33 '
V	Pope Samuel J	50	B F D	48	33 "
W	Pope Josephine—†	50	stenographer	33	33 "
X	Mahon Joseph E	50	clerk	43	here
Y	Perkins Mildred—†	50	housewife	39	"
Z	Perkins William J	50	accountant	48	"
	620				
A	McGlinchey Caroline V–†	50	nurse	46	"
B	McGlinchey Charles F	50	guard	45	
C	McGlinchey Edward F	50	B F D	57	
D	McGlinchey Joseph	50	clerk	48	
E	McGlinchey William A	50	"	59	"
F	Breman Henry T, jr	50	U S N	23	
G	Breman Mary J—†	50	housewife	57	"
H	Breman Paul J	50	shipfitter	21	"
K	Sadler Alice C—†	50	cleaner	50	"
L	Pattee Alice—†	50	housewife	70	"

7

8

13

Page.	Letter.	FULL NAME.	Residence, Jan. 1, 1944.	Occupation.	Supposed Age.	Reported Residence, Jan. 1, 1943. Street and Number.

Monument Square—Continued

	M	Pattee John E	50	clerk	54	here
	N	Baker Mary T—†	50	at home	55	"
	o	Murphy Anna F—†	50	housewife	60	"
	P	Murphy Robert J	50	clerk	22	

Mount Vernon Avenue

	s	Falvey Helen M—†	1	at home	71	here
	T	Falvey Julia A—†	1	"	69	"
	u	Aughwan Patrick	2	laborer	47	"
	v	Aughwan William	2	"	38	
	w	Iula Anna—†	2	housewife	31	"
	x	Iula Elizabeth—†	2	clerk	20	
	y	Iula Vito	2	boilermaker	24	"
	z	Griffin Ellen—†	4	housewife	64	"
		621				
	A	Griffin George	4	clerk	64	
	B	Doherty Patrick	4	retired	74	
	c	Doherty Sarah—†	4	housewife	78	"
	D	McElaney Mary—†	4	clerk	20	
	E	McElaney Michael	4	"	57	
	F	McElaney Rita—†	4	"	26	
	G	Cerella George	6	U S N	21	
	H	Cerella John A	6	laborer	70	
	K	Cerella Lillian—†	6	operator	24	"
	L	Cerella Marie—†	6	cook	36	
	M	Cerella Marie—†	6	housewife	60	"
	N	DeRosay Mary—†	6	housekeeper	62	"
	o	Horsfall Joseph H	6	rigger	52	"

Mount Vernon Street

	P	Logue Julia B—†	1	housewife	53	here
	R	Logue Mary—†	1	machinist	25	"
	s	Logue Ruth—†	1	shipfitter	20	"
	T	Logue Thomas	1	U S A	29	
	u	Garceau George A	2	chauffeur	23	"
	v	Garceau Mary A—†	2	housewife	22	"
	w	Halvey Marguerite—†	2	clerk	27	

Mount Vernon Street—Continued

x	Halvey Mary—†	2	packer	48	here
y	*Kelly Margaret O—†	2	at home	79	"
z	McCarthy Joseph P	2½	chauffeur	40	"
	622				
a	Kirby Alfred F	2½	machinist	27	"
b	Kirby Emily A—†	2½	housewife	24	"
d	Gaetjens Ruth—†	3	"	20	Pennsylvania
e	Gaetjens William	3	U S N	25	Connecticut
f	Wallis Clarence A	3	"	36	Panama
g	Wallis Marie—†	3	housewife	28	Pennsylvania
h	Smith Loretta A—†	4	operator	38	here
k	Smith Thomas E	4	retired	78	"
l	Smith William A	4	clerk	51	"
m	Doherty James	5	oiler	45	
n	Donaghey Celia—†	5	housewife	35	"
o	Donaghey William C	5	laborer	33	"
p	Hilferty James	5	"	45	"
r	Burr Marion—†	7	cashier	34	"
s	Conway Helen—†	7	housewife	39	"
t	Conway Timothy J	7	chipper	43	"
u	Morton Cecilia—†	7	bookbinder	51	"
v	Tipping Francis	8	retired	51	23 Monum'nt sq
w	Tipping Mary—†	8	housewife	50	23 "
x	Houghton Barbara E—†	8	"	26	23 "
y	Houghton Eugene D	8	U S A	26	23 "
z	Fortunati Arthur	9	laborer	41	here
	623				
a	Fortunati Mary—†	9	housewife	38	"
b	*Gallerani Louise—†	9	at home	66	"
c	Ghisellini Dorothy—†	9	student	20	"
d	Ghisellini Louis	9	laborer	56	"
e	Ghisellini Theresa—†	9	housewife	52	"
f	Thompson Charles J	10	drawtender	67	"
g	Thompson Charlotte J—†	10	saleswoman	25	"
h	Thompson Margaret W—†	10	housewife	63	"
k	Thompson Margarita J—†	10	secretary	25	"
l	Thompson Winifred A—†	10	teacher	31	"
m	Tassinari Joseph	11	carpenter	37	"
n	Tassinari Thresa—†	11	houswife	34	"
o	*Tassinari Agata—†	11	"	65	
p	Tassinari Fred	11	sexton	72	

15

7

8

Mount Vernon Street—Continued

R	Tassinari Virginia—†	11	stitcher	29	here
S	Dolan Alice M—†	12	housekeeper	78	"
T	Dolan Anne E—†	12	domestic	63	"
U	Dolan Katherine V—†	12	"	59	
W	Brennan Dorothy A—†	12	housewife	31	"
X	Brennan Neil P	12	longshoreman	32	"
Y	Tierney Alice R—† °	13	clerk	35	
Z	Tierney Catherine L—†	13	secretary	40	"

624

A	Cooney Alice G—†	14	housewife	59	".
B	Cooney Alice G—†	14	operator	36	"
C	Cooney Frederick L	14	U S N	28	
D	Cooney John M	14	"	39	
E	Cooney Michael S	14	printer	68	
F	Cooney Robert S	14	U S N	32	
G	O'Neil Mary J—†	14	at home	81	"
H	Carey Edward J	14½	supervisor	54	29 Mt Vernon
K	Carey Mary E—†	14½	housewife	54	29 "
L	O'Neil Frederick L	14½	technician	52	here
M	O'Neil Mary A—†	14½	housewife	84	"
N	Sullivan Richard C	14½	checker	58	"
O	Hayden Bridget A—†	14½	at home	75	"
P	Amann Anna M—†	15	housewife	44	"
R	Amann John A	15	U S N	43	
S	*Roska Victoria E—†	15	at home	76	"
T	Gunning Catherine M—†	15	"	65	
U	McElaney Allen T	16	machinist	30	"
V	McElaney Joseph P	16	pipefitter	28	"
W	McElaney Nellie—†	16	housewife	64	"
X	Kulicke Etta B—†	16	"	57	
Y	*Kulicke Otto K	16	laborer	59	
Z	Campbell Frederick	17	chauffeur	35	"

625

A	Campbell Ida—†	17	housewife	31	"
B	Doherty Eugene	17	electrician	53	8 Chestnut
C	Doherty Joseph	17	laborer	26	8 "
D	Doherty Margaret—†	17	housewife	55	8 "
E	Doherty William	17	seaman	29	8 "
F	Hansen Margaret—†	17	housewife	22	27 Russell
G	Morrison Harriet—†	17	"	36	here
H	Morrison Harry	17	machinist	38	"
K	McCabe John J	18	fireman	33	"

Letter.	Full Name.	Residence, Jan. 1, 1944.	Occupation.	Supposed Age.	Reported Residence, Jan. 1, 1943. Street and Number.

Mount Vernon Street—Continued

Letter.	Full Name.	Residence, Jan. 1, 1944.	Occupation.	Supposed Age.	Reported Residence
L	McCabe Leona F—†	18	housewife	31	here
M	Gunning John	18	U S A	22	"
N	Gunning John	18	freighthandler	53	"
O	Gunning Margaret—†	18	housewife	52	"
P	Gunning Mary—†	18	clerk	21	
R	Doherty Annie—†	19	housewife	75	"
S	Doherty Francis	19	laborer	20	
T	Doherty Michael	19	"	50	
U	McGaffigan John A	20	retired	69	
V	McGaffigan Theresa A—†	20	housewife	60	"
W	McGaffigan Catherine—†	20	at home	60	"
X	McGaffigan Mary V—†	20	"	50	"
Y	Casey Blanche G—†	20	housewife	50	"
Z	Casey James S	20	steamfitter	59	"
	626				
A	McCabe Margaret M—†	21	housewife	27	"
B	McCabe William P	21	planer	31	
C	Lynch Mary A—†	21	at home	68	"
D	McCabe Jennie G—†	21	housewife	67	"
E	McCabe Mary R—†	21	stenographer	33	"
F	Cunningham Maurice	22	watchman	58	"
G	Hennessey Mary A—†	22	housewife	69	"
H	Méconis Margaret M—†	22	"	24	
K	Morrissey James F	22	U S N	21	
L	Morrissey Mary—†	22	housewife	52	"
M	Morrissey Maurice D	22	laborer	54	
N	Stafford Anna M—†	22	housewife	40	"
O	Stafford Martin D	22	chauffeur	48	"
P	Harrigan John	23	retired	69	
R	Morey Edward	23	clerk	40	
S	Morey Mary—†	23	housewife	64	"
U	Wilkins Lester W	24	machinist	32	"
V	Wilkins Rita A—†	24	housewife	33	"
W	Hayes Bridget—†	25	"	58	
X	Hayes Edward	25	carpenter	67	"
Y	Hayes Edward J	25	U S A	23	
Z	Hayes Joseph M	25	machinist	21	"
	627				
A	Long Katherine F—†	25	housewife	57	"
B	Long William	25	laborer	60	"
C	Morrison Katherine V—†	26	housewife	24	"

2—6   17

Mount Vernon Street—Continued

D	Morrison Malcolm J	26	shipper	28	here	
E	Doherty Elizabeth R—†	26	housekeeper	59	"	
F	Doherty Phillip P	26	retired	66	"	
G	Doherty Sarah A—†	26	at home	57	"	
H	McLaughlin Beatrice—†	26	housewife	37	"	
K	McLaughlin Owen	26	laborer	45		
L	Sullivan Josephine—†	27	saleswoman	53	"	
M	Toomey Alexander F	27	U S A	20		
N	Toomey Annie T—†	27	housewife	49	"	
O	Toomey David	27	B F D	62		
P	Toomey John A	27	U S A	22		
R	Bur. e Mary B—†	28	clerk	51		
S	Lee Mary A—†	28	retired	86	"	
T	Matson Bertha—†	29	housewife	26	W Virginia	
U	Matson James	29	welder	27	"	
V	Dwyer John F	29	policeman	34	here	
W	Young Elinor M—†	29	housewife	31	"	
X	Young Joseph S	29	policeman	31	"	
Y	McCaig James A	30	cashier	71		
Z	McCaig Louise B—†	30	housewife	64	"	
	628					
A	Cargill Catherine—†	30	housekeeper	65	"	
B	Cargill Frederick	30	guard	53	"	
D	Mooney Annie—†	31	housewife	57	"	
E	Mooney Loretta—†	31	clerk	22		
F	Mooney Sylvester J	31	laborer	59		
G	Mooney Sylvester J, jr	31	rigger	28		
H	Sullivan Arthur	31	pipefitter	47	"	
K	Sullivan Ida M—†	31	housewife	45	"	
L	Carney Daniel J	31½	U S A	24	Georgia	
M	Carney Dorothy E—†	31½	clerk	23	here	
N	Carney Hannah M—†	31½	housewife	57	"	
O	Carney William L	31½	clerk	27	"	
P	Coyne Anna E—†	33	housewife	43	"	
R	Coyne Edward J	33	installer	53	"	
S	Doherty John J	33	retired	83		
T	Moran David J	33	B F D	47		
U	Moran David, jr	33	U S A	24		
V	Moran Gerard A	33	student	22		
W	Moran Joseph A	33	U S N	20		
X	Moran Paul X	33	investigator	21	"	

Page.	Letter.	Full Name.	Residence, Jan. 1, 1944.	Occupation.	Supposed Age.	Reported Residence, Jan. 1, 1943. Street and Number.

Mount Vernon Street—Continued

	Y	Moran Susan C—†	33	housewife	42	here
	z	Finan Harold J	35	policeman	49	"
629						
	A	Finan Helen U—†	35	housewife	51	"
	B	Finn Annie G—†	35	"	59	
	c	Finn Gertrude M—†	35	teacher	40	"
	D	Finn Thomas F	35	retired	69	"
	E	*Howard Anna—†	36	housekeeper	60	"
	F	Howard Ellen J—†	36	operator	27	"
	G	*Koeneik Peter	36	laborer	59	"
	H	Downey John E	36	U S A	20	
	K	Downey John M	36	clerk	64	
	L	Downey Nora T—†	36	housewife	54	"
	M	Harrington Cornelius	36	freighthandler	55	"
	N	Leary John F	36	U S A	39	
	o	Moriarty Timothy F	36	rigger	24	
	P	Nichols Edmund J	36	welder	38	
	R	Nichols Mary C—†	36	housewife	38	"
	s	Colantuoni Lena—†	37	"	59	
	T	Colantuoni Sylvester	37	laborer	61	"
	U	Doherty Mary—†	37	housewife	70	"
	v	Driscoll John J	37	clerk	43	
	w	Driscoll Mildred A—†	37	housewife	43	"
	x	White Charles A	38	chauffeur	23	41 Baldwin
	Y	White Margaret G—†	38	housewife	20	41 "
	z	Linehan Grace—†	38	clerk	32	here
630						
	A	Linehan Jeremiah F	38	laborer	38	"
	B	Linehan John	38	U S A	35	
	c	Linehan Mary—†	38	housewife	69	"
	D	Curtin David	38	U S N	21	
	E	Curtin Eileen—†	38	typist	23	"
	F	Curtin Hannah—†	38	housewife	60	"
	G	*Curtin Jeremiah J	38	longshoreman	65	"
	H	Farren Bernard J, jr	39	janitor	38	112 Academy Hill rd
	K	O'Neil Dennis W	39	watchman	69	here
	L	O'Neil Mary A—†	39	housewife	61	"
	M	Bruce Albert	39	machinist	40	"
	N	Bruce Catherine—†	39	housewife	33	"
	o	Crawford George	39	U S N	37	
	P	Crawford Mary E—†	39	at home	74	"

Mount Vernon Street—Continued

R	Crawford Mary J—†	39	housewife	36	here
s	O'Neil Catherine J—†	39	housekeeper	72	"
T	Hagstrom Charles	40	boilermaker	45	"
U	Hagstrom Margaret—†	40	housewife	43	"
V	Graham William	40	watchman	58	"
W	Noseworthy Alice F—†	40	housewife	27	"
X	Noseworthy Thomas F	40	carpenter	25	"
Y	Barron Michael	40	meter reader	50	"
Z	Barron Miriam E—†	40	housewife	52	"

631

A	Hickey Mary F—†	40		76	
B	Dwyer Julia—†	41	"	44	
C	Dwyer Timothy	41	riveter	44	"
D	Denbro Madeline—†	41	housewife	36	"
E	McCreven Catherine—†	41	"	60	
F	McCreven Cornelius	41	U S N	27	
G	McCreven George	41	U S A	29	
H	McCreven John	41	"	30	
K	Sullivan Bridget T—†	42	housewife	65	"
L	Sullivan John	42	electrician	64	"
M	Kelliher Helen—†	42	secretary	38	29 Adams
N	Kelliher John	42	rigger	36	29 "
O	Daniels Alma—†	42	housewife	46	here
P	Daniels William M	42	fireman	45	"
R	McLaughlin Annie M—†	43	housewife	54	"
S	McLaughlin Francis X	43	U S N	23	
T	McLaughlin Michael J	43	B F D	56	
U	Rose Mary—†	43	clerk	21	
V	Riordan Helena—†	44	stenographer	36	"
W	Riordan John T	44	retired	71	"
X	Riordan Julia—†	44	stenographer	34	"
Y	Norton Agnes M—†	45	housewife	41	"
Z	Norton John J	45	shipfitter	44	"

632

A	Norton Mary R—†	45	typist	21	"
B	Wilson Priscilla—†	46	housewife	32	19 Tremont
C	Wilson Robert S	46	U S C G	34	19 "
D	Young Alexander	46	U S A	38	Maine
E	Harte Bernard	48	laborer	65	here
F	Harte Eleanor L—†	48	stenographer	30	"
G	Harte Margaret L—†	48	"	27	"

Mount Vernon Street—Continued

H	Toomey Katherine—†	48	housewife	28	here
K	Caffrey James T	48	engineer	67	"
L	Caffrey Julia A—†	48	housewife	67	"
M	Sullivan Cornelius J	48	retired	63	"
N	Sullivan Edwina M—†	48	housewife	51	"
O	Sullivan Frank J	48	retired	58	"
P	Cadogan Agnes B—†	50	secretary	26	Pennsylvania
R	Leonard John F	50	retired	49	here
S	Leonard Joseph H	50	clerk	22	"
T	O'Brien Fred A	50	salesman	32	"
U	O'Brien Mary B—†	50	housewife	32	"
Z	Johnson Charles	52	U S A	35	"
¹Z	Johnson Mary K—†	52	stenographer	38	"
V	Keegan Catherine G—†	52	housewife	68	"
W	Keegan Frances R—†	52	stenographer	32	"
X	Keegan Paul X	52	metallurgist	25	"
Y	Keegan Rose M—†	52	stenographer	35	"

633   Prospect Street

B	Fidler Anna M—†	6	housewife	50	5 Prospect
C	Fidler Edward M	6	drawtender	55	5 "
D	Fidler Francis J	6	U S N	25	5 "
E	Fidler Joseph G	6	"	23	5 "
F	Lewis William H	6	drawtender	55	5 "
G	Fitzpatrick Anna E—†	6	saleswoman	50	here
H	Fitzpatrick Helen F—†	6	housewife	42	"
K	Fitzpatrick Mary E—†	6	accountant	23	"
L	Fitzpatrick Rose M—†	6	saleswoman	38	"
M	Fitzpatrick Thomas F	6	attorney	54	"
N	Fitzpatrick Thomas F, jr	6	electrician	20	"
O	Kearns Josephine M—†	6	housewife	28	21 Monum'nt av
P	Kearns William	6	salesman	27	21 "
R	Geary Gladys G—†	8	housewife	50	here
S	Geary Philip J	8	laborer	50	"
T	Brady Arthur J	8	U S N	25	"
U	Brady George F	8	B F D	55	
V	Brady Joseph A	8	U S A	31	"
W	Brady Mary J—†	8	housewife	54	"
X	Brady Mildred A—†	8	"	24	
Y	Brady Richard J	8	U S N	25	"

7

Prospect Street—Continued

z	Lynch Irene—†	8	housewife	32	here	
634						
A	Lynch James A	8	engineer	56	"	
B	Lynch Mary F—†	8	housewife	52	"	
C	Lynch Robert J	8	machinist	33	"	
D	Madray Harry A	.8	U S A	30		
E	Carroll Daniel A	10	"	38		
F	Carroll Mary J—†	10	operator	29	"	
G	*Carroll Mary L—†	10	housewife	59	. "	
H	Carroll Theresa—†	10	waitress	20	"	
K	Collins Elizabeth—†	10	bookkeeper	42	."	
L	Collins John F	10	chauffeur	68	"	
M	Pollack Philip	10	grocer	37	"	
N	Pollack Theresa M—†	10	housewife	32	"	
O	Ducey Anna V—†	10	" .	54		
P	Ducey Frank M	10	clerk	58		
R	Ducey John	10	"	27		
S	Mealey Mary A—†	12	housewife	75	"	
T	Buckley Margaret E—†	12	"	51		
U	Buckley Timothy S	12	B F D	50		
V	Buckley Walter J	12	U S A	20	"	
W	Callahan John J	14	operator	57	67 Dorchester	
X	McNeil Wilfred A	14	meat packer	48	30 Spring	
Y	Hurley Bernard F	14	U S A	22	here	
z	Hurley Jeremiah J	14	longshoreman	58	"	
635						
A	Hurley Mary B—†	14	waitress	49	"	
B	Gowe Jeanette C—†	16	housewife	26	"	
C	Gowe Richard J	16	longshoreman	30	"	
E	Ahearn Helen M—†	16	housewife	24	28 Monument	
F	Ahearn William F	16	longshoreman	31	28 "	
G	Duggan Patrick	18	retired	65	here	
H	Duggan Richard	18	cook	42	"	
K	Donahue Donald D	18	U S M C	20	"	
L	Donahue Laurence D	18	U S N	47	"	
M	Donahue Theresa E—†	18	housewife	48	"	
N	Moschillo Charles A	18	shipper	50	29 Ferrin	
O	Moschillo Marion L—†	18	operator	37	29 "	
P	Riley James J	20	longshoreman	46	18 School	
R	Riley Loretta L—†	20	housewife	36	18 "	
S	Kennedy James	20	retired	53	here	

Page.	Letter.	Full Name.	Residence, Jan. 1, 1944.	Occupation.	Supposed Age.	Reported Residence, Jan. 1, 1943. Street and Number.

Prospect Street—Continued

	T	Kennedy John T	20	clerk	21	here
	U	Kennedy Theresa—†	20	housewife	50	"
	V	Fidalgo Frederick	20	chauffeur	29	151 Chelsea
	W	Fidalgo Madeline—†	20	housewife	26	151 "
	X	McCallion John	22	fireman	41	here
	Y	McCallion Rose—†	22	housewife	37	"
	Z	Kelly Cornelius	22	blacksmith	52	"
636						
	A	*Kelly Julia C—†	22	housewife	35	"
	B	Kelly Neal	22	retired	72	
	C	Fitzgerald Edward J	22	storekeeper	43	"
	D	Fitzgerald Frances L—†	22	housewife	40	"
	E	Brady Daniel A	24	electrician	51	"
	F	Lang Carl H	24	coppersmith	28	"
	G	Meek Mary—†	24	housewife	63	"
	K	Mullen Annie A—†	24	"	74	73 Walford way
	L	Mullen Patrick	24	fireman	75	73 "
	H	O'Neill Cornelius	24	retired	69	50 Prospect
	M	Briand Anna—†	26	housewife	31	here
	N	Briand Henry J	26	shipfitter	36	"
	O	McDonough Grace I—†	26	nurse	40	261 Bunker Hill
	P	McDonough John F	26	laborer	45	261 "
	R	Foley Edward J	26	chauffeur	32	38 High
	S	Foley Elizabeth F—†	26	housewife	25	38 "
	T	Myers Mary B—†	26	clerk	52	38 "
	U	Leonard Katherine—†	28	teacher	48	here
	V	Sullivan Jeremiah G	30	U S N	35	"
	W	Sullivan Ruth R—†	30	secretary	33	"
	X	Sullivan Catherine A—†	30	housewife	69	"
	Y	Sullivan John L	30	clerk	45	"
	Z	Bastie Mary—†	30	housewife	28	W Virginia
637						
	A	Bastie William L	30	U S N	30	"
	B	Trott Oscar E	30	mechanic	58	Maine
	C	Stack Ann M—†	32	housewife	22	here
	D	Stack George P	32	U S N	25	"
	E	Houghton Joseph A	32	U S A	32	"
	F	Houghton Joseph F	32	timekeeper	59	"
	G	Jewell George E	32	rigger	28	..
	H	McCauley Aline M—†	32	housewife	32	"
	K	McCauley John J	32	fireman	33	"

7

23

Page	Letter	Full Name.	Residence, Jan. 1, 1944.	Occupation.	Supposed Age.	Reported Residence, Jan. 1, 1943. Street and Number.

Prospect Street—Continued

	Letter	Full Name.	Residence	Occupation.	Age	Reported Residence
	L	Lowney Isabel C—†	32	housewife	46	here
	M	Lowney John J	32	U S C G	46	"
	N	Lowney Robert J	32	machinist	20	"
	O	Lowney William B	32	U S C G	21	"
	P	Blewett Honora—†	34	housekeeper	83	"
	R	Blewett Honora E—†	34	operator	40	"
	S	Blewett Timothy B	34	laborer	46	
	T	Dennis Helen D—†	34	operator	43	"
	U	Bergstrom Carl G	34	U S C G	22	"
	V	Bergstrom Margaret C—†	34	clerk	22	
	W	Whiting John H	34	supervisor	47	"
	X	Whiting Margaret G—†	34	housewife	48	"
	Z	Fitzpatrick Agnes J—†	36	secretary	32	"
		638				
	A	Fitzpatrick Francis J	36	operator	24	"
	B	Fitzpatrick Hannah—†	36	at home	60	"
	D	Ward Anna M—†	38	operator	39	"
	E	Ward Annie—†	38	housewife	70	"
	F	Ward Francis H	38	laborer	26	
	G	Ward George J	38	clerk	38	
	H	Ward Mary—†	38	packer	40	
	L	Curry Edward	42	laborer	35	
	M	Curry Mary—†	42	at home	78	"

Soley Street

	Letter	Full Name.	Residence	Occupation.	Age	Reported Residence
	N	McAdams Anna G—†	21	storekeeper	42	here
	P	Harrison Bridget—†	27	housewife	65	"
	R	Harrison John	27	laborer	70	"
	T	Flynn Alice M—†	29	saleswoman	25	"
	U	Flynn Bridget M—†	29	housewife	52	"
	V	Flynn Robert W	29	longshoreman	52	"
	W	Flynn Ruth C—†	29	operator	27	"
	X	Lyons Catherine A—†	31	housewife	73	"
	Y	Lyons Hugh T	31	retired	80	
	Z	Baker Ruth—†	31	clerk	38	
		639				
	A	Counihan John E	31	shipper	68	
	B	McCarthy Catherine T—†	31	housekeeper	63	"
	C	Ross Elizabeth—†	33	at home	27	6 Chestnut
	D	Ross Sarah—†	33	"	52	6 "

24

Page.	Letter.	Full Name.	Residence, Jan. 1, 1944.	Occupation.	Supposed Age.	Reported Residence, Jan. 1, 1943. Street and Number.

Soley Street—Continued

	Letter	Full Name	Res.	Occupation	Age	Reported Residence
	E	Ross William	33	laborer	22	6 Chestnut
	F	Chisenhall Eileen—†	33	housewife	44	6 "
	G	Chisenhall Fornie	33	U S N	48	6 "
	H	Regan Ellen—†	33	at home	83	6 "
	K	O'Neil Eileen—†	35	teacher	30	here
	L	O'Neil Joseph G	35	manager	34	"
	M	O'Neil Julia A—†	35	housewife	70	"
	N	O'Neil Patrick	35	clerk	71	
	O	Kelley Mary M—†	35	housewife	70	"
	P	O'Neil James J	35	salesman	44	"
	R	Smith Margaret—†	35	housewife	72	"
	S	Smith Mary M—†	35	clerk	31	
	T	Smith Patrick	35	retired	69	
	W	Egan Catherine—†	39	housewife	64	"
	X	Egan Marion—†	39	clerk	34	
	Y	Murphy Bridget—†	39	housewife	71	"
	Z	Murphy Daniel J	39	ropemaker	42	"
640						
	A	Murphy Margaret R—†	39	packer	27	
	B	Murphy Michael	39	retired	76	
	E	Cook Earl	41	U S A	32	"
	C	Cook Margaret—†	41	clerk	28	
	D	Ryan Anna—†	41	cleaner	51	
	F	Ryan Leo A	41	U S N	26	
	G	Abbott Catherine A—†	41	housewife	42	"
	H	Abbott James	41	shipfitter	41	"
	K	Kelly Florence—†	43	housewife	40	"
	L	Kelly Vincent	43	clerk	47	
	M	*Connolly Bridget—†	43	housewife	57	"
	N	Connolly Francis	43	U S A	22	"
	O	*Connolly Mark	43	laborer	58	"
	P	Connolly Mark	43	U S N	24	
	R	*Bradley Celia—†	43	housewife	47	"
	S	Bradley Patrick J	43	laborer	49	"
	T	Lang Madeline G—†	45	housewife	41	"
	U	Lang Walter E	45	compositor	47	"
	V	Gillen George T	45	foreman	37	"
	W	Gillen Mary L—†	45	housewife	38	"
	X	Peterson Mary L—†	45	at home	72	5 Concord pl
	Y	Bragdon Cecelia—†	47	operator	34	here
	Z	Bragdon Irving	47	U S A	38	"

641

Soley Street—Continued

A	Teabo Cora—†	47	operator	24	here
B	Teabo George	47	clerk	55	"
C	Walsh Julia J—†	47	at home	66	"
D	*Doherty Catherine—†	49	housewife	43	"
E	Doherty Hugh	49	laborer	47	
F	Healey Fred	49	clerk	54	
G	Healey Helen G—†	49	housewife	52	"
H	Corniello John	51	machinist	23	"
K	Corniello Margaret—†	51	housewife	21	"
L	Guilfoyle Charles	51	U S A	28	
M	Guilfoyle John	51	clerk	38	

Tremont Street

N	Fieldsond Chester	1	driller	43	Lawrence
O	Fieldsond Emelia—†	1	housewife	40	"
P	Doherty Mary—†	1	"	41	here
R	Doherty Patrick	1	longshoreman	45	"
S	Fournier Mary—†	1	at home	68	"
T	O'Leary Dennis	rear 1	meatcutter	49	"
U	O'Leary Mary—†	" 1	housewife	56	"
V	Dillon Robert E	3	laborer	65	
W	Fernald Susan R—†	3	housekeeper	80	"
X	Ingram Merton F	3	inspector	43	Gardner
Y	Leary John J	3	laborer	60	here
Z	Orf George	3	welder	37	Vermont

642

A	Patience John J	3	metalworker	51	Rockport
B	Simonds James B	3	laborer	65	Peabody
C	Taylor John T	3	retired	73	Reading
D	Welsh Blanche B—†	13	housewife	52	here
E	Welsh Harold B	13	porter	59	"
F	Ward Catherine—†	13	waitress	33	"
G	Ward Russell	13	U S A	35	
H	Fitzpatrick Annie—†	13	saleswoman	53	"
K	Fitzpatrick Josephine—†	13	candyworker	55	"
L	Murray Henrietta—†	15	housewife	23	18 Decatur
M	Murray James P	15	bartender	24	18 "
N	Murray Margaret F—†	15	housewife	55	here

26

Page.	Letter.	FULL NAME.	Residence, Jan. 1, 1944.	Occupation.	Supposed Age.	Reported Residence, Jan. 1, 1943. Street and Number.

Tremont Street—Continued

o	Murray Margaret T—†	15	operator	22	here
p	Murray Patrick S	15	clerk	59	"
r	McCabe John J	15	laborer	52	"
s	McCabe Joseph F	15	clerk	47	
t	McCabe Margaret A—†	15	"	36	"
u	Casey Patrick J	17	blacksmith	39	Somerville
v	Casey Theresa M—†	17	housewife	37	"
w	Harrington Annie—†	17	"	65	here
x	Harrington Mary F—†	17	operator	30	"
y	Harrington Michael	17	longshoreman	60	"
z	Beals Helen—†	17	housewife	22	18 School
	643				
a	Evers James M	17	U S A	31	18 '
b	Evers John	17	longshoreman	30	18 "
c	Evers Margaret E—†	17	housewife	51	18 "
d	Evers Thomas J	17	foreman	57	18 "
e	Rogers Dorothy—†	19	housewife	35	here
f	Lester Christopher	19	electrician	34	20 Walker av
g	McCart Jennie—†	19	housewife	62	20 "
h	Eaton Elena—†	21	"	31	46 High
k	Eaton Ralph J	21	supervisor	27	46 "
l	Flynn Marie—†	21	tel operator	22	here
m	Flynn Marie—†	21	housewife	46	"
n	Flynn William	21	salesman	46	"

Wallace Court

o	Cronin John J	1	retired	66	here
p	Cronin Margaret B—†	1	housewife	60	"
r	Doyle Dorothy E—†	1	"	34	"
s	Doyle Francis R	1	clerk	43	
t	Baker Anna M—†	2	operator	27	"
u	Guthrie George C	2	rigger	36	
v	Guthrie Ruth E—†	2	housewife	34	"
w	Cotter Ellen N—†	3	"	65	
x	Cotter Helen R—†	3	teacher	24	"
y	Cotter John F	3	U S A	38	
z	Cotter Marion A—†	3	teacher	41	"
	644				
b	Whelan Edward L	4	electrician	31	"
c	Whelan Kathleen M—†	4	housewife	28	"

Wallace Court—Continued

D	Maher Andrew	4	longshoreman	56	here
E	Maher Annie—†	4	housewife	54	"
F	Maher William F	4	U S A	22	"
G	Donoghue Florence R—†	4	housewife	38	"
H	Donoghue Walter A	4	calker	42	..
L	Doherty Joseph M	5	longshoreman	39	"
M	Doherty Loretta K—†	5	housewife	34	"
P	Bryan Ellen E—†	7	teacher	41	
R	Bryan James H	7	manager	65	"
S	Bryan Mary E—†	7	at home	58	"
T	Bryan William T	7	clerk	63	
U	McLaughlin Joseph F	8	"	53	
V	McLaughlin Marion L—†	8	housewife	42	"
W	Spence Elizabeth H—†	8	broker	50	

Winthrop Street

X	Browne Alice V—†	30	attendant	59	here
Y	Browne Mary E—†	30	auditor	24	"
	645				
A	Reycroft Arthur D	32	druggist	71	"
B	Torkey Mary B—†	32	housekeeper	72	"
C	Belcher Amelia—†	32	housewife	44	"
D	Belcher Joseph	32	rigger	34	..
E	Lawlor Elizabeth C—†	34	dressmaker	62	"
F	Lawlor Harriet—†	34	housekeeper	72	"
G	Gorman Eugene J	34	policeman	32	"
H	Gorman Mary A—†	34	storekeeper	39	"
K	Crowley Richard F	34	policeman	36	"
L	Crowley Rose M—†	34	housewife	36	"
M	Broderick Mary A—†	36	stenographer	42	"
N	Burns Anna T—†	36	teacher	32	"
O	Burns Carrie E—†	36	housekeeper	49	"
P	McDonough William P	36	teacher	52	..
R	Carr Catherine D—†	38	stenographer	51	"
S	Carr Isabel R—†	38	teacher	45	.:
T	Dooley Charlotte M—†	38	manager	53	"
U	O'Hara Anna F—†	38	at home	53	"
V	O'Hara John J	38	U S N	24	
W	Riordan Abigail H—†	40	teacher	38	"

Page.	Letter.	Full Name.	Residence, Jan. 1, 1944.	Occupation.	Supposed Age.	Reported Residence, Jan. 1, 1943. Street and Number.

Winthrop Street—Continued

x	Riordan Anna G—†	40	teacher	42	here
y	Riordan Charles A	40	U S N	33	"
z	Riordan Margaret—†	40	at home	73	"
	646					
a	Riordan Margaret M—†	40	teacher	34	
b	Buckley Jeremiah J	42	clerk	45	
c	Hally Eleanor J—†	42	operator	32	"
d	Hally Julia F—†	42	housewife	68	"
e	Hally Marion F—†	42	teacher	35	"
f	O'Neill Helen M—†	42	housewife	43	57 Town
g	O'Neill John H	42	manager	48	35 Soley
h	Hurley Helen V—†	44	clerk	44	here
k	Hurley Mary A—†	44	housewife	68	"
l	Lee Helen V—†	44	stenographer	26	"
m	Lee Mary A—†	44	housewife	46	"
o	Lee Robert L	44	U S A	25	"
p	Lee Robert L	44	investigator	46	"
n	Lee Thomas E	44	U S N	21	"
r	Eden Mary—†	56	housewife	60	"
s	Eden Thomas C	56	laborer	50	
t	Regan Mary—†	56	housewife	70	"
u	Regan Stephen M	56	retired	74	
v	Regan William M	56	"	85	"
w	Harper Harry L	58	mechanic	42	"
x	Harper Helen—†	58	clerk	41	
y	Mullaly Bridget T—†	58	manager	32	"
z	Mullaly Margaret M—†	58	supervisor	36	"
	647					
a	Mullaly Mary—†	58	housekeeper	77	"
b	Fitzpatrick Gertrude V—†	58	teacher	65	"
c	Connolly Cornelius	60	clerk	37	
d	Connolly Marguerite E—†	60	housewife	35	"
e	Maguire Annie—†	60	"	53	
f	Maguire John F	60	U S A	21	
g	Maguire Joseph A	60	U S N	26	
h	Maguire Thomas F	60	pipefitter	54	"
k	Maguire Thomas P	60	U S A	27	
l	Gilfoyle Francis P	60	clerk	40	"
m	Gilfoyle Winifred J—†	60	housewife	39	"
n	Clarke Mary J—†	63	at home	77	"
o	Clarke Robert J	63	U S N	34	"

29

Winthrop Street—Continued

p	Mahoney Margaret M—†	63	housekeeper	75	here
r	Phalan Edna F—†	63	stenographer	22	"
s	Phalan Paul E	63	U S A	25	41 Whitfield
t	Sheehan Elizabeth V—†	63	housewife	49	here
u	Sheehan Joséph M	63	supervisor	52	"
v	Blood Elizabeth M—†	65	housewife	42	11 Gray
w	Blood Wiley M •	65	boilermaker	46	11 "
x	Sullivan Patrick C	65	foreman	44	11 "
y	Cullen Bridget—†	65	housewife	30	15 "
z	Parcell Mary M—†	65	clerk	33	15 '

648

c	McAuliffe Hazel S—†	67	housewife	34	here
d	McAuliffe John F	67	attorney	40	"
e	Gouldhart Catherine—†	67	clerk	57	"
f	Gallagher Thomas W	70	laborer	53	
g	Hawkins Charles C	70	porter	59	
h	Hawkins Mary E—†	70	housewife	54	"
k	Hayes Edward J	70	U S A	37	
l	Hurley Bartholomew	70	retired	76	
m	Terrell Mary M—†	70	housewife	33	"
n	White Elizabeth—†	70	at home	83	"
o	Teaffe Elizabeth—†	72	housewife	65	"
p	Teaffe Joseph P	72	electrician	65	"
r	Riley John H	72	printer	76	
s	Riley Margaret J—†	72	housewife	76	"
t	Callahan Eileen E—†	72	clerk	26	
u	Callahan Joseph L	72	electrician	31	"
v	Callahan Timothy P	72	B F D	56	

Ward 2–Precinct 7

CITY OF BOSTON

LIST OF RESIDENTS
20 YEARS OF AGE AND OVER

(NON-CITIZENS INDICATED BY ASTERISK)
(FEMALES INDICATED BY DAGGER)

AS OF

JANUARY 1, 1944

THOMAS F. SULLIVAN, *Chairman*
FREDERIC E. DOWLING, *Secretary*
WILLIAM A. MOTLEY, JR.
FRANCIS B. McKINNEY
EVERETT R. PROUT

Listing Board

CITY OF BOSTON PRINTING DEPARTMENT

Page.	Letter.	Full Name.	Residence, Jan. 1, 1944.	Occupation.	Supposed Age.	Reported Residence, Jan. 1, 1943. Street and Number.

700

Boyle Street

	A	Doherty Mary—†	4	housewife	50	here
	B	Doherty William	4	fireman	47	"
	c	Kinsley John	4	chauffeur	49	"
	D	Godding Robert	6	U S M C	20	40 Russell

Church Court

	E	Oliver Robert W	7	retired	88	here
	F	Beaven Fannie E—†	7	housewife	61	"
	G	Beaven John E	7	guard	61	"
	H	Lee Ella M—†	7	housewife	48	"
	K	Lee James M.	7	shipfitter	52	"

Cordis Street

	L	Carney Kathleen—†	1	clerk	36	here
	M	Carney Margaret—†	1	housewife	76	"
	N	Carney Margaret—†	1	engraver	39	"
	O	Carney Mildred—†	1	supt	33	
	P	Joyce Anna G—†	1	housewife	63	"
	R	Joyce John J	1	retired	68	
	S	Williams Elizabeth—†	1	housewife	54	"
	T	Williams Julia C—†	1	secretary	31	"
	U	Williams Richard P	1	operator	64	"
	V	Haley Mary E—†	2	housewife	76	20 Cedar
	W	Haley Michael J	2	retired	82	20 "
	X	Carbone Mabel—†	2	housewife	57	here
	Y	Downes Bridget A—†	2	at home	80	"
	Z	Reynolds Marguerite J—†	2	housewife	47	39 Pleasant

701

	A	Reynolds Thomas E	2	letter carrier	51	39 "
	B	Collins Margaret—†	3	housekeeper	65	here
	c	DeBlois Louis	3	contractor	55	Clinton
	D*	Gilson Alston E	3	clerk	60	here
	E	Leary Peter O	3	longshoreman	67	"
	F	Montgomery Hugh	3	clerk	50	"
	G	Russell Robert	3	laborer	54	38 Harvard
	H	Torres Joseph	3	electrician	43	New Bedford
	K	Towle Eileen R—†	4	packer	21	here
	L	Towle Helen G—†	4	attendant	57	"

2

Cordis Street—Continued

	Letter	Full Name	Res.	Occupation	Age	Reported Residence
	M	Towle Marguerite M—†	4	saleswoman	24	here
	N	Keating Frank J	4	policeman	35	"
	O	Keating Mary—†	4	housewife	73	"
	P	Driscoll Jessie L—†	4	"	41	46 Chelsea
	R	Driscoll William R	4	boilermaker	43	46 "
	S	Cole Arthur O	5	retired	51	here
	T	Cole Arthur O, jr	5	U S A	25	"
	U	Cole Mary E—†	5	housewife	48	"
	V	Cole Mary E—†	5	clerk	23	
	W	Cole William F	5	U S A	21	..
	X	Robinson Joseph F	5	"	30	
	Y	McDonough John S	6	longshoreman	46	"
	Z	McDonough Lucy—†	6	housewife	79	"

702

	Letter	Full Name	Res.	Occupation	Age	Reported Residence
	A	*Miller Catherine—†	6	housekeeper	76	"
	B	*Miller Harry A	6	printer	67	"
	C	*Scott Reginald S	6	janitor	52	"
	D	Lenius Edward C	6	boilermaker	42	" '
	E	Lenius Zoe J—†	6	housewife	40	"
	G	*Marshon Charles H	8	carpenter	71	"
	H	*Marshon Sarah A—†	8	housewife	69	"
	K	Plante Bertha A—†	8	at home	41	"
	L	Davis Emory	8	salesman	58	"
	M	Davis Emory J	8	U S N	21	
	N	Davis Jennie F—†	8	housewife	48	"
	O	Dyer George B	8	U S N	21	Cambridge
	P	George Adam	8	"	60	here
	R	George Frederick A	8	manager	26	"
	S	George Myrtle—†	8	housewife	59	"
	T	Bradley Joseph A	9	operator	35	"
	U	Coughlin Nellie—†	9	stenographer	55	"
	V	Crilly Matilda—†	9	housewife	63	"
	W	Russo Alfred	9	welder	38	Medford
	X	Saulnier Ralph J	9	riveter	28	Ipswich
	Y	Simpson William	9	laborer	39	12 Austin
	Z	Starr Charlotte—†	9	operator	53	here

703

	Letter	Full Name	Res.	Occupation	Age	Reported Residence
	A	Heggarty Grace L—†	11	housewife	36	"
	B	Heggarty Joseph J	11	electrician	42	"
	C	O'Brien Anne L—†	12	nurse	29	"
	D	O'Brien Jennie W—†	12	housewife	62	"

Cordis Street—Continued

E	Wall Catherine N—†	12	cook	64	here
F	Robinson Richard	12	watchman	57	"
G	Lincoln Florence A—†	12	realtor	61	"
H	Greatorex Frank W	13	chauffeur	35	36 Sullivan
K	Greatorex Helen A—†	13	housewife	33	36 "
L	King Cecilia T—†	13	secretary	21	here
M	King John	13	laborer	52	"
N	King Mary E—†	13	housewife	52	"
O	King Mary E—†	13	operator	22	"
P	Bradshaw Ann A—†	13	housewife	46	"
R	Bradshaw Charles J	13	longshoreman	52	"
S	Pratt Margaret M—†	13	machinist	23	Maine
T	Hall Frances G—†	14	housewife	49	42 Soley
U	Hall Frank J	14	painter	48	42 "
V	*Ribeiro Filomena S—†	14	at home	96	here
W	Rose Arminda R—†	14	timekeeper	64	"
X	Rose Joseph L	14	retired	70	"
Y	Murphy Bridget A—†	14	housewife	65	"
Z	Murphy Timothy J	14	laborer	62	
	704				
A	Thompson Ellen T	14	at home	72	"
B	Andrews George T	15	U S N	37	Quincy
C	Andrews Lillian E—†	15	housewife	35	"
D	Burns John J	15	clerk	65	here
E	Burns Julia M—†	15	housewife	59	"
F	*Brennan Michael	15	laborer	61	"
G	Crowley Annie J—†	15	housekeeper	59	"
H	Kearney Patrick	15	laborer	40	"
K	Crowley Cornelius	16	retired	67	
L	McInerney Katherine T—†	16	attendant	68	"
M	Sweeney Leo F	16	deckhand	46	"
N	Van Annan Margaret—†	16	at home	66	"
P	Hunt Sarah E—†	17	housewife	72	"
R	A'Hearn Mary A—†	17	"	27	"
S	A'Hearn Timothy S	17	metalworker	31	"
T	Doherty Neil F	17	retired	87	
U	St Germaine Margaret M—†	17	housewife	39	"
V	Moore Louise—†	18	housekeeper	51	"
W	Roy Caroline—†	18	at home	80	"
X	Roy Emma S—†	18	manager	50	"
Y	Connolly Martin T	20	retired	60	

Cordis Street—Continued

z	Saunders Alice F—†	20	housewife	31	25 Monument av
705					
A	Saunders Robert J	20	operator	29	25 "
B	Burns Charles	21	U S A	25	here
C	Burns Dorothy J—†	21	at home	35	"
D	Burns Frances G—†	21	housewife	67	"
E	Burns Frank J	21	clerk	39	
F	Gillette Helen H—†	21	bacteriologist	47	"
G	Glidden Alva B—†	22	teacher	48	"
H	Glidden Berton A	22	salesman	75	"
K	Glidden Edythe R—†	22	housewife	62	"
L	Glidden Samuel J	22	retired	79	Melrose
M	Strangman Emily G—†	22	housewife	51	"
N	Strangman Warren A	22	engineer	48	"
O	Kenefick Johanna A—†	23	housewife	81	here
P	Doherty Mary J—†	23	bookbinder	56	"
S	Hall Daniel E	26	laborer	54	"
T	Hall Mary E—†	26	housewife	52	12 Thompson
U	Sullivan Catherine—†	26	housekeeper	67	here
V	Sullivan Charles R	26	electrician	25	"
W	Sullivan Joseph D	26	U S A	28	"
X	Kenney Elizabeth A—†	26	at home	67	"
Y	Shea Frances—†	27	housewife	48	"
Z	Shea James	27	laborer	25	"
706					
A	Shea Kieran O	27	bartender	35	"
B	Doherty Alice G—†	28	housewife	46	"
C	Doherty Arthur J	28	warehouse	25	"
D	Doherty Stephen J	28	"	49	
E	Lincoln Alfred V	28	retired	69	
F	Lincoln Harry L	28	welder	44	"
G	Doherty Gladys M—†	28	housewife	56	"
H	Doherty Katherine T—†	28	clerk	22	
K	Doherty Margaret I—†	28	operator	25	"
L	Doherty Patrick J	28	clerk	67	"
M	Barry Decklan F	29	shipper	62	"
N	Barry Mary M—†	29	housewife	60	"
O	McHugh Joseph A	29	clerk	52	
P	McHugh Mary T—†	29	at home	73	"
R	McHugh Winifred G—†	29	housewife	66	"
V	Quozzo Carroll	29	U S C G	35	102 Bennington

Page.	Letter.	FULL NAME.	Residence, Jan. 1, 1944.	Occupation.	Supposed Age.	Reported Residence, Jan. 1, 1943. Street and Number.

Cordis Street—Continued

	s	Regan Susan—†	29	housewife	76	here
	t	Regan Theresa—†	29	"	36	"
	u	Sullivan Catherine—†	29	forewoman	40	"
	w	Burns Joseph H	32	proba'n officer	42	"
	x	Burns Mary F—†	32	housewife	36	"
	y	Doherty Clement G	33	clerk	41	80 Bunker Hill
	z	Doherty Emma J—†	33	housewife	39	80 "
707						
	a	Doherty John	33	laborer	46	80 '
	b	Doherty Joseph D	33	bartender	52	80 "
	c	Doherty Rita B—†	33	clerk	21	80 '

Cordis Street Avenue

	f	Keger Alexis—†	5	housewife	26	here
	g	Long Katherine—†	5	"	47	"
	h	Long Peter	5	U S A	23	"
	k	Martin Phyllis—†	5	housewife	22	"
	l	Kelly Margaret—†	5	"	23	"
	m	Leonard Celia—†	5	"	50	
	n	Leonard James F	5	U S A	20	
	o	Leonard Neil	5	laborer	54	
	p	Hayes John F	5	"	53	
	r	Hayes Joseph F	5	U S C G	21	"
	s	Hayes Mary L—†	5	housewife	48	"

Dexter Row

	t	Leen Cecelia V—†	2	at home	67	here
	u	Leen Theresa E—†	2	housekeeper	55	"
	v	Wiles Daniel A	3	undertaker	37	"
	w	Wiles Marion F—†	3	housewife	33	"
	x	Alongi Alfonso	4	laborer	41	2 Frothingham
	y	Alongi Arlene L—†	4	housewife	26	2 "
	z	Cremens Daniel A	4	U S A	35	here
708						
	a	Cremens Rita M—†	4	clerk	24	
	b	Peck Mary A—†	4	housewife	67	"
	c	Peck Stanley A	4	watchman	72	"

Page.	Letter.	Full Name.	Residence, Jan. 1, 1944.	Occupation.	Supposed Age.	Reported Residence, Jan. 1, 1943. Street and Number.

Green Street

	G	Boyle Helen—†	16	housewife	39	here
	H	Boyle John J	16	shipfitter	42	"
	K	Caffrey Anna—†	16	at home	67	"
	M	Williams Bernard A	17	physician	40	"
	N	Williams Ida F—†	17	housewife	38	"
	O	McNamara George	17	custodian	42	"
	P	McNamara Gertrude—†	17	housewife	42	"

High Street

	R	Gillooly Alice M—†	24	stenographer	32	here
	S	Gillooly John J	24	machinist	62	"
	T	Gillooly Mary—†	24	housewife	62	"
	U	McCaffrey Catherine L—†	24	"	42	
	V	McCaffrey John J	24	collector	46	"
	W	Collins Laurence N	24	U S N	20	"
	X	Collins Maude—†	24	housewife	47	"
	Y	Howard Avery B	26	retired	75	
	Z	Howard Mabel J—†	26	housewife	62	"
709						
	A	Brassil Margaret—†	28	"	28	"
	B	Brassil Thomas	28	printer	35	"
	C	Donahue Francis	28	ropemaker	44	"
	D	Finneran Anna—†	28	packer	45	
	E	Mayhood John	28	welder	45	
	F	McCarthy Anna—†	28	cook	45	
	G	O'Shea Ellen—†	28	at home	53	"
	H	Sinnott Florence—†	28	housewife	24	"
	K	Sinnott Francis	28	welder	26	"
	L	O'Connell Agnes L—†	30	housewife	37	"
	M	O'Connell William J	30	supt	41	"
	N	Stafford Agnes—†	30	secretary	25	"
	O	Stafford Daisy—†	30	operator	50	"
	P	Stafford Warren	30	engineer	52	"
	R	Stafford Warren, jr	30	U S A	22	
	S	M'Carthy Charles B	30	ropemaker	47	"
	T	McCarthy Nora T—†	30	housewife	40	"
	U	Brown Elizabeth—†	32	at home	65	"
	V	Scott Catherine—†	34	saleswoman	72	"
	W	Williams Mary—†	34	housewife	72	"
	X	Breen Mary E—†	36	housekeeper	69	"

Page.	Letter.	FULL NAME.	Residence, Jan. 1, 1944.	Occupation.	Supposed Age.	Reported Residence, Jan. 1, 1943. Street and Number.

High Street—Continued

	Y	McCarron Cassandra—†	36	housewife	48	here
	z	McCarthy Jeremiah J	36	clerk	53	N Hampshire
710						
	A	Boyle Isabel—†	38	housewife	54	81 Chelsea
	B	Boyle Thomas J	38	machinist	57	81 "
	C	Gregoire Hedwidge—†	38	housewife	53	here
	D	Gregoire Joseph A	38	shipfitter	61	"
	E	McCutcheon Frank M	38	retired	88	"
	F	Monk Kate—†	38	housewife	45	"
	G	Monk Wallace M	38	clerk	48	"
	K	Castaldini Angelo	46	retired	73	
	L	Castaldini Catherine—†	46	clerk	36	"
	M	Castaldini Frances—†	46	"	29	
	N	Castaldini James	46	U S A	24	
	O	Castaldini Josephine—†	46	nurse	26	
	P	Castaldini Rose—†	46	housewife	68	"
	R	Castaldini Theresa—†	46	organist	40	"
	S	Harrington Arthur B	46	attorney	69	"
	T	Harrington Elizabeth—†	46	housewife	69	"
	U	Burke Catherine—†	46	"	63	9A Elm
	V	Burke Catherine—†	46	typist	20	9A "
	W	Burke William	46	painter	64	9A "
	X	Burke William, jr	46	laborer	26	9A "
	z	Lynch Agnes M—†	50	housewife	40	here
711						
	A	Lynch John L	50	laborer	42	
	B	Potter Cecelia M—†	52	housewife	65	"
	C	Potter Edward J	52	roofer	66	
	D	Potter Edward J, jr	52	shipfitter	39	"
	E	Ryan Albina F—†	52	housewife	38	"
	F	Ryan Edward J	52	laborer	44	
	G	Loftus Arthur F	52	clerk	34	
	H	Loftus Martin J	52	bartender	52	"
	K	Loftus William B	52	clerk	38	
	L	Roberto Joseph F	52	machinist	43	"
	M	Roberto Margaret R—†	52	housewife	46	"
	N	Pierce Mary A—†	54	"	39	21 Cross
	O	Pierce William J	54	letter carrier	41	21 "
	P	Foley Anna J—†	54	stenographer	22	here
	R	Foley Helen T—†	54	secretary	25	"

High Street—Continued

s	Foley Jeremiah F	54	U S A	31	here
t	Foley Julia A—†	54	housewife	55	"
u	Foley Patrick J	54	collector	60	"
v	Heffernan Leo F	54	U S N	26	
w	Heffernan Margaret K—†	54	housewife	26	"
x	Maher Frederick R	54	U S A	30	
y	Maher Mary A—†	54	operator	29	"
z	Gilmore Helen A—†	56	housewife	68	"

712

a	Gilmore Helen C—†	56	clerk	38	
b	Gilmore John F	56	attorney	46	"
c	Gilmore Mary V—†	56	bookkeeper	39	"
d	Gill Daniel	56	court officer	51	"
e	Gill Margaret F—†	56	housewife	51	"
f	Coleman Rose R—†	56	operator	38	"
g	Hannon Marie K—†	56	tel operator	44	"
h	McKenna James F	56	retired	73	
k	McKenna Mary C—†	56	housewife	72	"

Main Street

m	McCreavan Patrick	75	longshoreman	37	45 Main
n	Quinn Celia—†	75	housewife	40	45 "
o	Quinn John J	75	longshoreman	42	45 "
p	Watts Beatrice A—†	75	housekeeper	47	here
r	Watts William	75	brakeman	63	"
s	Edwards Fannie—†	75	housekeeper	65	"
t	Soule Nora V—†	75	sorter	38	"
v	Corkery Catherine—†	79	housewife	81	Westford
w	Corkery Maurice	79	painter	78	"
x	Fidelis William	79	barber	52	here
y	Houlihan Timothy	79	longshoreman	43	"
z	Kilduff Christopher	79	porter	49	"

713

d	Biagiotti Joseph	87	storekeeper	46	"
e	Jones John	89	retired	75	

714

c	Sylvester Annabelle—†	137	housewife	48	"
d	Sylvester Warren	137	welder	48	
e	Towne Marie—†	137	housewife	20	"

Monument Avenue

o	Donahue Christina E—†	14	housewife	45	here
p	Donahue Frank M	14	mortician	46	"
r	Barstow John N	15	laborer	53	"
s	Barstow Mary U—†	15	housewife	61	"
t	Doherty Walter P	15	watchman	52	"
u	Harkins Daniel J	15	curator	53	
v	Harkins Loretta A—†	15	housewife	45	"
w	Carey Daniel A	17	clerk	40	1 Tremont
x	Carey Mary A—†	17	housewife	33	1 "
y	McCallum Joseph	17	pipefitter	52	here
z	Reardon John	17	chauffeur	54	"

715

a	Breslin Florence T—†	19	student	27	"
b	Breslin John G	19	physician	57	"
c	Breslin Mae E—†	19	housewife	56	"
d	Kearns Theresa—†	19	matron	56	17 Monum'nt av
e	Kearns Frank J	21	supt	60	here
f	Kearns Josephine M—†	21	housewife	27	"
g	Kearns Mary E—†	21	WAVE	21	"
h	Kearns Thomas P	21	U S N	26	
k	Kearns William E	21	salesman	28	"
l	Kearns Zita C—†	21	housewife	51	"
m	Alves Gilbert	22	guard	36	
n	Corey Charles	22	retired	73	"
o	Foley Maurice	22	B F D	61	32 City sq
p	Haney Patrick	22	laborer	51	2 Tremont
r	Harkins James	22	"	60	here
s	Matthews Edward W	22	clerk	57	"
t	Matthews Lena G—†	22	housewife	57	"
u	Maynard Roswell	22	painter	63	
v	Miller Frank	22	laborer	57	
w	Reardon Frank D	22	clerk	42	
x	Rivers Hector	22	molder	55	
y	Sweeney James J	22	retired	77	
z	Richardson Florence E—†	23	housewife	67	"

716

a	Cotter Theresa M—†	24	teacher	48	..
b	Hurley Josephine A—†	24	"	46	
c	Hurley Katherine E—†·	24	"	48	"
d	McCarron Eileen F—†	25	housewife	40	14 Common
e	McCarron John J	25	retired	75	14 "

Monument Avenue—Continued

F	McCarron John J, jr	25	shipper	43	14 Common
G	*McConalogue Bridget—†	25	at home	67	54 Elmwood
H	*McConalogue Catherine-†	25	"	65	54 "
K	Fardy Catherine—†	26	charwoman	50	here
L	Lynch Mary T—†	26	seamstress	65	"
M	McLaughlin Joseph A	26	shipfitter	62	"
N	McLaughlin Mary E—†	26	housekeeper	67	"
O	Fitzgerald Delia S—†	27	at home	63	"
P	Foley David	27	retired	57	
S	Gardner Dorothea M—†	28	teacher	29	
T	Hurley Thomas F	28	laborer	50	
U	McNamara Elizabeth—†	29	clerk	51	
V	Pekar Catherine—†	29	housewife	28	"
W	Pekar Stephen J	29	shipfitter	33	"
X	Callaghan Adeline F—†	30	assessor	34	"
Y	Callaghan Mildred M—†	30	clerk	38	
Z	Callaghan Thomas J	30	retired	71	

717

A	Haynes Eleanore F—†	30	secretary	36	"
B	Kirk Bernard F	31	foreman	37	"
C	Kirk Gertrude M—†	31	housewife	33	"
D	Mahoney Mary G—†	31	at home	75	"
E	Golden Richard J	32	electrician	35	"
F	Rose Catherine L—†	32	housewife	36	"
G	Rose Richard H	32	agent	39	
H	Rogan Eleanor—†	33	housewife	63	"
K	Rogan John F	33	proofreader	66	"
L	Rogan Katherine S—†	33	librarian	61	"
M	Wiley John J	34	shipfitter	26	"
N	Wiley Margaret M—†	34	housewife	25	"
O	Hallahan Francis T	34	laborer	57	"
P	Hallahan James H	34	U S A	22	
R	Hallahan Jennie A—†	34	housewife	47	"
S	McCarthy Mary A—†	35	at home	68	393 Bunker Hill
T	Roche Elizabeth—†	35	bookkeeper	55	here
U	George Clifford E	36	longshoreman	39	"
V	George Louise B—†	36	housewife	51	"
W	Shaw Albert	36	pipefitter	54	Billerica
X	Smith Eleanor	36	welder	30	Swampscott
Y	Burns Frank	37	attorney	37	here
Z	Burns Josephine—†	37	housewife	50	"

718
Monument Avenue—Continued

A	McCarthy William J	37	policeman	47	here
B	Barry Mary E—†	38	at home	71	"
C	Maloney Eloise—†	38	teacher	30	"
D	Maloney Mary M—†	38	housewife	68	"
E	Allen-Jeremiah	39	laborer	51	"
F	Allen Mary—†	39	housewife	54	"
G	Donovan Michael T	40	operator	55·	"
H	Saunders Daniel	41	retired	76	
K	Foster Bernice—†	43	nurse	49	"
L	Lane Susie E—†	43	at home	77	"
M	Mitchell Forest	43	retired	74	"
N	Phinney Edith—†	43	housewife	45	"
O	Phinney Frederick F	43	clerk	45	
P	Seeckts Albert	43	retired	74	"
R	Dugan Barbara J—†	44	clerk	30	
S	Dugan Bernard V	44	inspector	62	"
T	Dugan Mary A—†	44	housewife	58	"
U	Schlough Arthur	44	electrician	48	"
V	Schlough Laura—†	44	housewife	48	"
W	Doherty James	45	laborer	64	"
X	Doherty William	45	engineer	54	"
Y	Mayer Shirley—†	45	at home	25	"
Z	O'Reilly Dennis C	45	U S A	24	"

719

A	O'Reilly Rita A—†	45	housewife	22	"
B	Tims Claire V—†	45	"	23	
C	Tims Hugh L	45	electrician	24	"
D	Tims June—†	45	welder	21	
	Tims Robert E	45	supervisor	48	"
F	Tims Stella—†	45	housewife	46	"
G	Coughlin Carrie—†	46	matron	61	
H	Coughlin Joseph J	46	U S N	41	"
K	Coughlin Mary A—†	46	housewife	40	25 Bellevue
L	Hildreth Maude—†	46	maid	59	here
M	Garrity Francis M	46	lineman	38	16 Cobden
N	Garrity Mary C—†	46	clerk	35	26 Cordis
O	Sheehe Katherine A—†	46	housewife	34	here
P	Sheehe William H	46	embalmer	36	"
R	Manning Margaret A—†	47	housekeeper	68	"
S	McCarthy Elizabeth G—†	47	dressmaker	58	"

Page.	Letter.	FULL NAME.	Residence, Jan. 1, 1944.	Occupation.	Supposed Age.	Reported Residence Jan. 1, 1943. Street and Number.

Monument Avenue—Continued

	T	McCarthy John J	47	retired	70	here
	U	McCarthy Mary E—†	47	at home	66	"
	V	Bergen Frank E	48	welder	43	"
	W	Bowen George	48	retired	81	"
	X	Greaves Frederick L	48	proprietor	65	"
	Y	Haggerty William	48	clerk	50	"
	Z	Patterson Carl H	48	seaman	36	"

720

	A	Patterson Herbert J	48	retired	62	
	B	Patterson Olive B—†	48	housewife	59	"
	C	Galvin Ella M—†	49	"	35	
	D	Galvin William J	49	manager	39	"
	E	McCarthy Mary C—†	49	at home	43	"
	F	Murphy Agnes M—†	50	housekeeper	53	"
	G	Connelly Elizabeth A—†	51	housewife	73	"
	H	Connelly Lillian M—†	51	teacher	36	
	K	Connelly Mary R—†	51	nurse	29	
	L	Orlandella George	52	lrborer	46	
	M	Orlandella Joseph	52	bartender	58	"
	N	Orlandella Mary—†	52	stitcher	53	"
	O	Rotondi Joseph	52	U S A	25	
	P	Rotondi Rose—†	52	housewife	24	"
	R	Stigliani Antonio M	52	glazier	49	
	S	Stigliani Margaret—†	52	housewife	51	"
	T	Duffy James J	53	salesman	33	"
	U	Duffy Ruth—†	53	wireworker	21	"
	V	Duffy Winifred L—†	53	housewife	31	"
	W	Duggan John	53	driller	45	"
	X	Kelley Clara—†	53	stitcher	36	Maine
	Y	Kelley Woodie	53	ironworker	41	"
	Z	Canney Edward F	54	watchman	51	here

721

	A	Carswell Alexis—†	54	housewife	62	"
	B	Carswell James B	54	electrician	71	"
	C	Gorman Carroll W	54	salesman	40	"
	D	Gorman Mary T—†	54	housewife	46	"
	E	Griffin Anna—†	54	waitress	21	17 Pleasant
	F	Townsend Jeanette F—†	54	housewife	59	here
	G	Townsend Joseph E	54	salesman	64	"
	H	Barrett John F	56	machinist	48	Springfield
	K	Chartier Edward J	56	shipfitter	54	here

13

Monument Avenue—Continued

L	Crowley Mary—†	56	housewife	52	here
M	Crowley Michael	56	shipfitter	53	"
N	Regan Agnes A—†	56	at home	56	"
O	Stevens Mary E—†	56	"	70	
P	Taylor Charles	56	retired	80	
R	Allen John J	57	foreman	41	"
S	Flanagan Katherine M–†	57	housewife	43	"
T	Flanagan Mary J—†	57	clerk	45	
U	Linehan Francis J	57	guard	37	"
V	Rourke Albert	57	B F D	47	New York
W	Merello Joseph A	57	painter	64	here
X	Minahan Edna M—†	57	operator	39	"
Y	Murphy Josephine A—†	57	at home	65	"
Z	Murtha James E	57	toolmaker	50	"

722

A	Nolan John J	57	clerk	50	
B	Shortell John R	57	toolmaker	50	"
C	Beattie Dorothy L—†	57	housewife	20	"
D	Beattie Thomas B—†	57	U S A	21	
E	Sutton John B	57	longshoreman	51	"
F	Sutton John B, jr	57	U S A	23	
G	Sutton Josephine G—†	57	housewife	46	"
H	Brousseau William	58	shipfitter	46	"
K	Comtois Valmore H	58	driller	48	Williamsett
L	Dalton Thomas F	58	metalworker	41	N Hampshire
M	Livermore Ralph H	58	"	52	"
N	McGovern James E	58	clerk	54	here
O	O'Brien Martin J	58	bartender	52	"
P	Shlosser Thomas A	58	machinist	26	"
R	Valade Alfred	58	painter	27	N Hampshire
S	Valade Yvette P—†	58	winder	25	"
T	Martin Alice A—†	59	housewife	47	here
U	Martin John J	59	inspector	51	"
V	Doherty Edward J	59	U S A	28	"
W	Doherty John F	59	policeman	26	"
X	Doherty Rebecca F—†	59	housewife	60	"
Y	Doherty Walter G	59	U S A	24	
Z	Boisvert David	59	foundryman	56	"

723

A	Boisvert Emma C—†	59	housewife	57	"
B	Donnelly Jane E—†	60	"	34	

14

Monument Avenue—Continued

c	Lee Jennie E—†	60	at home	69	here
d	Smith Charles F	60	clerk	45	"
e	Smith Mary R—†	60	"	27	"
f	Smith Ralph A	60	manager	51	"
g	Smith Ralph T	60	U S A	25	"
h	Smith Sarah T—†	60	housewife	48	"
k	Toland Elizabeth—†	61	"	34	17 Elmira
l	Toland George	61	policeman	35	17 "
m	Mitchell Mary C—†	61	at home	75	here
n	Edwards May G—†	61	social worker	58	"
o	Whitcomb William E	61	optometrist	69	"
p	Murphy Elizabeth B—†	65	clerk	53	"
r	Murphy Patrick J	65	guard	64	"
s	Doherty Joseph P	67	metalworker	34	"
t	Doherty Mary K—†	67	housewife	31	"
u	Thomas Emma C—†	67	"	46	
v	Thomas John H	67	engineer	52	"

Monument Square

w	Quigley Elizabeth M—†	37	teacher	40	here
x	Sheehan Esther M—†	37	"	42	"
y	Considine Catherine—†	38	clerk	28	"
z	VonBulson Arthur R	38	publisher	71	"
	724				
a	VonBulson Carrie F—†	38	housewife	62	"
b	Kane Daniel J	39	lawyer	42	
c	Kane Mary F—†	39	housewife	37	"
d	O'Kane James L	39	U S A	34	Medford
e	O'Kane Kathleen —†	39	clerk	23	"
f	Cassidy Walter D	40	longshoreman	46	68 Russell
g	Healey Ellen V—†	40	housewife	46	here
h	Healey George J	40	seaman	21	"
k	Healey George P	40	chauffeur	46	"
l	Sullivan John	40	retired	69	
m	Cuttler Walcott	41	clergyman	51	"
n	Macey Arthur F	41	auditor	60	"
o	Macey Lula A—†	41	housewife	58	"
p	Mason Florence—†	41	teacher	60	"
r	Fleming Josephine F—†	45	housewife	46	"
s	Fleming Richard H	45	B F D	46	"

Monument Square—Continued

T	Thomas Esther M—†	46	clerk	51	here	
U	Davis Agnes M—†	46	"	29	"	
V	Davis Bridget—†	46	housewife	62	"	
W	Davis Harold P	46	U S N	34		
X	Davis Mark	46	rigger	62	"	
Y	Breen Kenneth H	47	awnings	29	16 Devens	
Z	Breen William H	47	"	21	16 "	

725

A	Breen William H	47		57	16 '	

Perry Place

B	Smith Emma A—†	1	housewife	67	here	
C	Dockherty Florence—†	1	"	69	" .	

Pleasant Street

D	Connolly John J	1	chauffeur	40	10 Pleasant	
E	Connolly Margaret—†	1	housewife	40	10 "	
F	Page Ida—†	1	"	33	here	
G	Page Ralph M	1	painter	37	"	
H	Sweeney Leon	1½	electrician	39	34 Harvard	
L	Norftill Catherine—†	3	housewife	45	here	
M	Norftill Lawrence	3	grinder	38	"	
N	Clark Helen F—†	3	housewife	33	12 Franklin	
O	Clark John F	3	pipefitter	37	12 "	
P	Puccetti Frank	5	longshoreman	50	here	
R	Powers James	5	carpenter	34	Waltham	
S	Powers Jean—†	5	housewife	35	here	
V	Rock Elizabeth—†	11	at home	65	Somerville	
W	Fowler Elizabeth A—†	11	housewife	60	here	
X	Fowler William	11	painter	60	"	
Y	McCarthy William	11	chauffeur	41	"	
Z	*Fong Chin—†	18	housewife	53	"	

726

A	Fong Edward L	18	agent	24		
B	Fong Jennie L—†	18	clerk	23		
C	*Fong Lee	18	laundryman	65	"	
E	Fee Ethel F—†	20	clerk	28		
F	Fee George	20	freighthandler	57	"	
G	Fee Margaret M—†	20	housewife	59	"	

16

Pleasant Street—Continued

D	Fee Margaret T—†	20	operator	26	here
H	Merrill Catherine—†	20	matron	60	"
K	Sexton Agnes E—†	22	housewife	33	"
L	Sexton John L	22	baker	36	"
M	McGuire Annie—†	23	housewife	50	"
N	McGuire John J	23	U S N	22	
O	McGuire John J	23	watchman	67	"
P	Duffy Margaret—†	24	housewife	74	"
R	McDermott Lillian—†	24	candymaker	62	"
S	Powers Gertrude—†	24	housewife	64	"
T	Powers Michael B	24	retired	70	
V	Awalt Bruce	25	chauffeur	30	"
U	Awalt Jean—†	25	housewife	25	"
W	Creedon Dennis	25	laborer	63	"
X	Moore Charles B	25	"	52	25 Park
Y	Chevalier Agnes—†	25	housewife	35	here
Z	Chevalier Odell	25	mechanic	31	"
	727				
A	Greenlaw Margaret—†	26	housewife	57	"
B	Greenlaw Percy E	26	shipfitter	57	"
C	Heuston Joseph W	26	laborer	27	16 Prospect
D	Heuston Rita—†·	26	housewife	26	16 "
E	Bates Alejo	26	painter	45	here
F	Bates Germaine—†	26	housewife	37	"
G	Brown Bernard	27	electrician	34	"
H	Brown Gertrude—†	27	housewife	33	"
K	O'Donnell Cornelius T	27	janitor	42	"
L	O'Donnell Mary—†	27	housewife	33	"
M	Warren Ellen—†	27	"	55	
N	Warren Helen—†	27	clerk	25	
O	Warren John	27	packer	57	
P	McLaughlin Catherine—†	28	housewife	67	"
R	McLaughlin John J	28	U S N	26	
S	McLaughlin Margaret—†	28	operator	35	"
T	Lourenco Custadio	28	machinist	39	55 Park
U	Lourenco Ella—†	28	housewife	34	55 " ·
V	Rocco Mary—†	28	packer	31	55 "
W	Hagerty Alice—†	28	at home	79	here
X	Tierney Agnes—†	28	domestic	58	"
Y	Tierney Elizabeth F—†	28	housewife	30	"
Z	Tierney Walter F	28	guard	31	

2—7   17

728

Pleasant Street—Continued

A	O'Donnell James H	29	clerk	56	here
B	O'Donnell Rose—†	29	housewife	53	"
D	Sullivan Catherine—†	29	"	65	"
E	Holt Garrett	31	longshoreman	63	"
F	Holt Martha—†	31	typist	24	
G	O'Hara Annie E—†	31	housewife	78	"
H	O'Hara Elizabeth C—†	31	clerk	58	
K	*Herlihy Corneluis	31	longshoreman	60	"
L	Herlihy George	31	U S A	33	
M	*Herlihy Mary—†	31	housewife	55	"
O	Smith Mary—†	32	at home	71	57 Walker
P	Peterson Nelson	33	attendant	70	here
R	*Mangan Catherine—†	33	housewife	71	"
S	Mangan Catherine M—†	33	clerk	39	"
T	Mangan James M	33	orderly	38	"
U	Doherty John	33	longshoreman	42	"
V	Steward Anna—†	33	housewife	45	"
X	Thorpe Edward P	34	chauffeur	51	24 Frothingham av
Y	Winters Patrick J	34	laborer	55	24 "
Z	Kelly Carl	36	inspector	49	here

729

A	Kelly John J	36	U S A	22	"
B	Kelly Laura—†	36	housewife	44	"
C	Kelly Marguerite—†	36	operator	23	"
D	Doherty Bernard	38	U S A	20	
E	Doherty John	38	"	25	
F	Doherty Joseph	38	laborer	52	
G	White Edward	38	longshoreman	50	"
H	White Edward	38	U S A	26	
K	White John	38	"	20	
L	White Mabel—†	38	housewife	46	"
M	Gillis Anna—†	39	clerk	48	
N	Gillis John	39	molder	49	
O	Shea John D	39	B F D	42	
P	McLaughlin Adeline—†	39	housewife	44	"
R	McLaughlin Bernard C	39	letter carrier	47	"
S	Powers Thomas F	39	clerk	47	
T	Chase Guy P	39	counterman	70	"
U	Kelly Evelyn—†	39	housewife	32	"
V	Kelton Alberta—†	39	"	64	

18

Page.	Letter.	FULL NAME.	Residence, Jan. 1, 1944.	Occupation.	Supposed Age.	Reported Residence, Jan. 1, 1943. Street and Number.

Pleasant Street—Continued

w	Hoppe Evelyn—†	40	housewife	33	here
x	Hoppe Joseph	40	grinder	58	"
y	Russell Charles	40	foreman	50	"
z	Russell Elizabeth—†	40	housewife	45	"
	730				
a	Russell George	40	shipfitter	20	"
b	Doherty Bernard	40	mechanic	42	"
c	Doherty Helen C—†	40	housewife	42	"
d	Kelly Ellen—†	40	at home	72	"
e	White Margaret—†	41	housewife	25	93 High
f	White Thomas	41	clerk	25	93 "
g	Delli Veneri Alfred	41	meter reader	40	here
h	Delli Veneri Concetta—†	41	housewife	72	"
k	Delli Veneri Rose—†	41	cashier	37	"
l	Flynn Elizabeth—†	41	housewife	52	"
m	Gilmore George	41	electrician	27	"
n	Gilmore Lillian—†	41	housewife	25	"
o	Walker Mae—†	42	"	45	Somerville
p	Shackford Alice—†	42	housekeeper	66	21 Salem
r	Shackford Alice R—†	42	waitress	35	21 "
s	Shackford Charles A	42	U S A	21	21 "
t	Shackford Herbert	42	papercutter	47	21 "
u	Walker Arthur	42	laborer	47	Somerville
v	Ring Catherine—†	42	clerk	38	"
w	Sullivan Joseph	43	laborer	30	here
x	McLaughlin John	43	machinist	37	"
y	McLaughlin Mary—†	43	housewife	38	"
z	McGrath Mary—†	44	bookkeeper	33	"
	731				
a	Murphy Jeremiah P	44	inspector	29	"
b	Murphy Julia—†	44	housewife	64	"
c	Hollis James L	44A	U S A	26	
d	Hollis Oliver	44A	machinist	57	"
e	Doherty Susan—†	44A	housewife	38	81½ Warren
f	Doherty Timothy	44A	agent	40	81½ "
g	Daley Harry	45	laborer	42	here
h	Upton Emily—†	45	housewife	30	"
k	Upton Joseph	45	U S N	31	"
m	Sullivan Anna M—†	46	housewife	43	"
n	Sullivan John	46	chauffeur	56	"
o	Sullivan John	46	U S N	33	Maine

Pleasant Street—Continued

P	Sullivan Violette J—†	46	housewife	30	Medford
R	Grace James	46A	retired	69	here
S	Grace James P	46A	U S A	32	"
T	Grace Mary—†	46A	housewife	69	"
U	Grace William E	46A	clerk	54	"
V	Neville Dorothy W—†	46A	proofreader	25	"
W	Neville Frederick	46A	clerk	30	
X	Neville James L	46A	retired	71	
Y	Neville Louise M—†	46A	proofreader	33	"
Z	Neville Robert	46A	U S A	22	"

732

A	Fitzgibbons James L	47	"	22	
B	Fitzgibbons Joseph T	47	rigger	53	
C	Fitzgibbons Mary E—†	47	housewife	52	"
D	*Houghton Rose—†	48	"	37	15 Monument
E	*Houghton William	48	laborer	39	15 "
F	McLaughlin Margaret—†	48	housewife	74	here
G	McLaughlin Michael	48	cook	53	"
H	*Quirk Dennis	48	laborer	46	"
K	Quirk Marjorie—†	48	housewife	41	"
L	Fitzgibbons Charlotte M-†	49	"	56	
M	Fitzgibbons William H	49	U S A	25	
N	Fitzgibbons William H	49	cooper	63	"
O	Carroll Charles	50	clerk	47	22 School
P	Jay Robert C	50	electrician	42	here
R	Jay Virginia M—†	50	housewife	42	"
S	Connolly Frank	50	clerk	52	"
T	McDonough Agnes R—†	50	operator	46	"
U	McDonough Mary—†	50	housewife	73	"
V	Doherty Hugh	50	mechanic	53	"
W	Doherty John	50	"	59	
X	Doherty Margaret—†	50	housewife	49	"
Y	Donaghey James	50	clerk	51	
Z	McCarthy Dorothy—†	51	housewife	43	"

733

A	McCarthy William J	51	packer	22	"
B	Candelora Doris A—†	51	housewife	20	Revere
C	Candelora Leonard J	51	U S A	21	"
D	Stewart Dorothy A—†	51	saleswoman	28	here
E	Stewart George J	51	laborer	26	"
F	Donaghy Patrick	52	"	45	"

Pleasant Street—Continued

G	Donaghy Rose—†	52	housewife	39	here
H	*Canny Mary—†	52	"	41	"
K	*Canny Patrick	52	laborer	42	"
L	Corbett John	52	U S N	28	
M	Corbett Mary—†	52	housewife	54	"
N	Corbett Mary M—†	52	U S M C	21	"
O	Corbett William	52	U S A	24	..
P	Maraghy William	52	"	28	
R	*McLaughlin Celia—†	58	housewife	70	"
S	McLaughlin Charles	58	shipper	37	"
T	Leonard John	60	laborer	59	"
U	Leonard Mary B—†	60	operator	23	"
V	Fabiano Pauline—†	60	teacher	23	8 Mill
W	Smith Bertha M—†	60	clerk	25	8 "
X	Smith George	60	U S A	24	8 "
Y	Smith John W	60	fireman	29	8 "
Z	Smith John W	60	chauffeur	53	8 "

734   Pleasant Street Court

A	Trevette Henry	1	mechanic	47	here
B	Whitney Georgetta—†	1	at home	72	"
C	Fellows Georgiana—†	2	"	78	"
D	Green Mary—†	2	housewife	21	"
E	Green William T	2	U S N	23	
F	Cormier Harry E	3	realtor	74	"
G	Cormier Lillian M—†	3	housewife	58	"
H	Swift William	4	retired	72	
K	Farren Matthew	4	"	78	"
L	Farren Ruth A—†	4	housewife	51	18 Sullivan
M	Farren William J	4	laborer	43	18 "
N	Clancy James J	5	manager	51	here
O	Doherty Bernard	5	laborer	42	"
P	Doherty Rose—†	5	housewife	38	"

Soley Street

R	Adams Peter T	6	foreman	34	here
S	Dole Francis A	6	U S N	54	"
T	Dole Lillian C—†	6	housewife	45	"
U	Prior Agnes—†	·6	domestic	34	"

Page.	Letter.	FULL NAME.	Residence, Jan. 1, 1944.	Occupation.	Supposed Age.	Reported Residence, Jan. 1, 1943. Street and Number.

Soley Street—Continued

v	Drummey Katherine F—†	8	housekeeper	66	here
w	Galvin George V	8	storekeeper	46	"
x	McCarthy Helen—†	10	housewife	45	"
y	McCarthy John J	10	B F D	23	
z	McCarthy Mary—†	10	clerk	20	
	735				
a	Duffy Anne—†	20	housekeeper	80	"
b	Duffy John J	20	collector	42	"
c	Grattan Henry M	20	U S M C	37	"
d	Grattan Madeline—†	20	housewife	38	"
e	Garvin Dorothy M—†	22	clerk	23	
f	Garvin James A	22	U S A	36	
g	Garvin Margaret A—†	22	housekeeper	77	"
h	Garvin Timothy J	22	chauffeur	51	"
k	Donavan Elizabeth—†	24	storekeeper	38	39 Monument av
l	Donavan Timothy	24	porter	44	39 "
n	Doherty Catherine—†	26	housekeeper	56	here
o	Gilman Mary F—†	26	at home	80	"
p	Gilman Sarah E—†	26	"	82	"
r	Hilton Theresa—†	26	housekeeper	34	"
s	Houghton John P	26	plumber	32	"
t	Carroll Thomas	28	checker	63	"
u	Connors Gertrude—†	28	boxmaker	43	"
v	McLaughlin Elizabeth—†	28	housewife	53	"
w	McLaughlin Rose A—†	28	at home	85	"
x	McNamara Michael J	28	investigator	42	"
y	Murray Henry W	28	bartender	43	"
z	Shepard Loretta—†	28	nurse	54	
	736				
c	Roman Evelyn—†	32	housewife	26	"
d	Roman Peter	32.	chauffeur	31	"
e	Roche Catherine M—†	32	housewife	20	34 Monument av
f	Roche John F	32	longshoreman	23	90 Henley
g	Potter Catherine G—†	32	housewife	37	41 Eden
h	Potter David M	32	U S N	44	41 "
k	Porter Eleanor—†	34	packer	30	here
l	Porter John	34	mechanic	32	"
m	Porter Margaret—†	34	housekeeper	58	"
n	Jones Robert	34	laborer	62	"
p	Mitchell David H	36	motorman	56	"
r	Mitchell Jane L—†	36	housekeeper	68	"

22

Soley Street—Continued

s	Mitchell Mary A—†	36	at home	70	here
T	Neylon Margaret—†	36	housewife	55	"
U	Neylon Patrick	36	policeman	55	"
V	Donovan Catherine—†	36	seamstress	54	"
W	Donovan Mary—†	36	cleaner	58	"
X	Fitzpatrick John J	40	custodian	62	37 Mead
Y	Hayes Dennis J	40	oiler	53	here
Z	Hayes Margaret J—†	40	housewife	50	"
	737				
A	Hayes Margaret M—†	40	clerk	20	"
B	Hennessey Eulalia—†	42	housewife	40	"
C	Hennessey John L	42	steamfitter	38	"
E	Matthews Mary E—†	48	clerk	56	"
F	Matthews Robert C	48	engineer	57	"
G	Miles Mary D—†	48	housekeeper	50	"
H	O'Connell Daniel	50	retired	82	
L	O'Connell Francis	50	longshoreman	32	"
L	O'Connell Mary—†	50	housewife	66	"
O	Wallace Anna—†	54	stenographer	20	"
P	*Wallace Hannah—†	54	housewife	50	"
R	Wallace James	54	U S A	21	
S	*Wallace Jeremiah	54	longshoreman	53	"
T	Wallace Jeremiah, jr	54	U S A	23	
U	Wallace Julia—†	54	clerk	27	
V	Hennessey Catherine—†	58	housekeeper	75	"
W	Hennessey William J	58	U S A	33	"
X	Crotty Arthur F	58	stevedore	42	"
Y	Crotty Margaret M—†	58	housewife	42	"
Z	Herman Annie R—†	60	housekeeper	25	"
	738				
A	Herman Gladys H—†	60	housewife	53	"
B	Herman John O	60	U S A	23	
C	Herman Joseph C	60	engineer	53	"
D	Herman Natalie C—†	60	clerk	26	
E	Herman Richard J	60	U S A	21	

Thompson Street

G	Halloran Elizabeth—†	1	clerk	20	here
H	Halloran Margaret—†	1	housewife	51	"
K	Halloran Martin	1	laborer	53	"

Page.	Letter.	FULL NAME.	Residence, Jan. I, 1944.	Occupation.	Supposed Age.	Reported Residence, Jan. 1, 1943. Street and Number.

Thompson Street—Continued

	L	Halloran Martin	1	U S A	21	here
	M	McGonagle Ann—†	2	typist	21	"
	N	*McGonagle Helen—†	2	housewife	40	"
	O	*McGonagle Patrick	2	laborer	48	
	P	MacKillop Laura J—†	2	housekeeper	77	"
	R	Narcotta Bartholomew	2	laborer	50	"
	S	Carroll Marguerite V—†	9	secretary	38	"
	T	Carroll Thomas H	9	painter	42	"
	U	Bosari Alfonsina—†	12	housewife	43	"
	V	Bosari Beatrice A—†	12	clerk	24	"
	W	Bosari Nando	12	shipper	44	"
	X	Oertel Arthur C	12	machinist	36	Haverhill
	Y	Oertel Frances—†	12	housewife	34	"
	Z	Lucas Catherine—†	12	"	33	here
	739					
	A	Lucas Edward F	12	boilermaker	43	"

Warren Street

	C	Bernier Edward L	59	electrician	36	here
	D	Burgue Adrian	59	painter	42	N Hampshire
	E	Donovan James J	59	retired	67	here
	G	Donovan Frederick B	59	U S A	31	"
	F	Felch Evelyn E—†	59	housewife	41	"
	H	Felch Lauren E	59	electrician	42	"
	K	Green James M	59	"	39	Florida
	L	Haley Henry B	59	shipfitter	56	20 Common
	M	Kileen Edward	59	U S N	44	New York
	N	Kileen Mary—†	59	waitress	41	"
	O	Leary Michael	59	laborer	51	here
	P	McNamara Richard L	59	carpenter	37	Andover
	R	Minnehan Thomas F	59	machinist	34	Somerville
	S	Mogren Ralph	59	metalworker	37	here
	T	Powers Phillip	59	retired	74	"
	U	Shaughnessey John	59	salesman	41	"
	V	Adams Annie G—†	72	at home	63	"
	W	Guinee John H	72	retired	70	
	X	Guinee Margaret E—†	72	dietitian	68	"
	Y	Guinee Michael C	72	furrier	75	
	Z	Cooney Robert A	74	shipfitter	51	"

740

Warren Street—Continued

A	Cooney Theresa M—†	74	housewife	36	here
B	Conley John J	76	freighthandler	23	46 Polk
C	Wiswell Mary F—†	76	housewife	28	80 Russell
D	Wiswell Russell D	76	metalworker	33	80 "
E	Maloney James E	rear 76	chauffeur	23	here
F	Pike George H	" 76	U S N	24	"
G	Pike Mary L—†	" 76	housewife	25	"
H	Kerrissey Theresa—†.	77	at home	77	"
K	McGeohan Annie—†	77	"	49	"
L	Gallagher Mildred P—†	78	housewife	22	12 Sheafe
M	Thorpe Ethel M—†	78	"	50	24 Frothlngham av
N	Lapete Elmer M	78	maintenance	34	here
O	*Lapete Lillian V—†	78	housewife	38	"
P	*Doherty John	79	retired	73	3 Seminary
R	Gilpin Joseph	79	"	73	43 Harvard
S	Hale John	79	"	60	here
T	Hale Mary E—†	79	housewife	55	"
U	McCarthy Daniel	79	garageman	55	200 Main
V	Meyers Alexander J	79	freighthandler	62	52 Tremont
W	Sullivan Agnes—†	79	housekeeper	53	here
X	Sennett Ernest A	80	retired	73	496 Main
Z	Barber Dorcas M—†	81	waitress	45	here

741

A	Barber Marie F—†	81	at home	63	"
B	Walsh Dorothy R—†	81	inspector	25	"
C	Walsh James F	81	retired	72	
D	Walsh Mary M—†	81	housewife	67	"
E	Tucker Adeline T—†	81½	"	42	
F	Tucker John B	81½	metalworker	43	"
G	Farrell Noraine—†	81½	packer	35	"
H	Madden John P	81½	retired	60	
K	Madden Mary E—†	81½	housewife	63	"
L	Buckley Joseph	84	plumber	53	31 Monument av
M	Callahan Richard	84	longshoreman	47	64 Chestnut
N	Forsyth Arthur	84	machinist	50	Lexington
O	Hamilton John	84	longshoreman	53	59 Warren
P	Hampton James	84	rigger	55	here
R	Holland Michael	84	retired	65	"
S	Leary Jeremiah	84	freighthandler	59	"
T	Mann George	84	laborer	34	"

2—7   25

Warren Street—Continued

Page.	Letter.	Full Name	Residence Jan. 1, 1944	Occupation	Supposed Age	Reported Residence Jan. 1, 1943. Street and Number
	U	Powers Joseph A	84	retired	57	here
	V	Rowley Mary—†	84	housewife	49	"
	W	Rowley William J	84	carpenter	59	"
	X	Hart Jeannette—†	85	housewife	65	"
	Y	Pike Oscar T	85	painter	48	
	Z	Carey Hannah—†	85	housewife	68	"
742						
	A	Cummings Edward M	86	U S A	25	
	B	Cummings John J	86	U S N	23	
	C	Cummings Margaret—†	86	housewife	60	"
	D	Cummings Nicholas	86	laborer	55	"
	E	Buckley Delia W—†	88	housewife	63	6 Wall
	F	Buckley Thomas A	88	retired	61	6 "
	H	Nicolosi Jeannette—†	88	housewife	30	here
	P	Cass Anna T—†	98	"	26	"
	R	Green James E	98	U S A	27	"
	S	Green Rita M—†	98	housewife	30	"
	T	Ryan Annie—†	98	"	66	
	U	Ryan Patrick J	98	retired	69	
	W	Dorgan Catherine—†	101	housewife	47	"
	X	Dorgan William R	101	laborer	52	
	Y	Murphy James	101	bartender	45	"
	Z	Murphy Patrick	101	guard	43	
743						
	A	Kelly Frank C	101	freighthandler	55	"
	B	Kelly Josephine—†	101	housewife	55	"
	C	McLaughlin James D	101	clerk	30	
	D	Buckley Josephine L—†	101	housewife	46	"
	F	Griffiths Thomas	103	fisherman	30	"
	G	Griffiths Violet M—†	103	housewife	59	"
	H	Louder Dorothy M—†	103	"	23	
	K	McNeil Edward M	103	U S A	22	
	L	McNeil Margaret A—†	103	cleaner	44	
	M	Stack Mary A—†	103	at home	75	"
	P	Picardi Frederick	103	merchant	61	"
	N*	Picardi Lena—†	103	housewife	53	"
	O	Picardi Patrick	103	U S A	22	"
	R	Kinsman Clara E—†	107	housewife	30	492 Medford
	S	Kinsman Eldridge M	107	packer	32	492 "
	T	Tochterman Grace M—†	107	housewife	40	here
	U	Tochterman James H	107	laborer	50	"

Warren Street—Continued

v	Reade Alice M—†	109	housewife	60	here
w	Reade Vincent D	109	mortician	65	"
x	Sheehe Bertha L—†	109	receptionist	59	"

Wood Street

z	Greeley Charles	27	operator	28	here
	744				
A	Greeley Joseph	27	bartender	29	"
B	Greeley Martha A—†	27	housewife	60	"

8

Ward 2–Precinct 8

CITY OF BOSTON

LIST OF RESIDENTS
20 YEARS OF AGE AND OVER

(NON-CITIZENS INDICATED BY ASTERISK)
(FEMALES INDICATED BY DAGGER)

AS OF

JANUARY 1, 1944

THOMAS F. SULLIVAN, *Chairman*
FREDERIC E. DOWLING, *Secretary*
WILLIAM A. MOTLEY, JR.
FRANCIS B. McKINNEY
EVERETT R. PROUT

Listing Board.

CITY OF BOSTON PRINTING DEPARTMENT

Page.	Letter.	FULL NAME.	Residence, Jan. 1, 1944.	Occupation.	Supposed Age.	Reported Residence Jan. 1, 1943. Street and Number.

800

Austin Street

	c	Morrasse Ernest	2	carpenter	38	Lawrence
	d	Morrasse Mary—†	2	housewife	59	"
	e	Andrea Manuel	2	laborer	50	here
	f	Andrea Mary—†	2	housewife	49	"
	g	Coughlin Cecilia F—†	8	"	42	"
	h	Coughlin Daniel J	8	postal clerk	45	"
	k	Bradley Catherine T—†	8	waitress	40	"
	l	Bradley Harold V	8	U S A	32	
	m	Fitzgerald John A	8	chauffeur	34	"
	n	Fitzgerald Ruth—†	8	housewife	27	"
	o	Nigro Josephine—†	10	operator	34	"
	p	Nigro Phyllis—†	10	teacher	43	
	r	Nigro Christopher	10	machinist	34	"
	s	Nigro Mary—†	10	housewife	33	"
	t	Nigro Virginia—†	10	bookkeeper	37	"
	u	Sheehan Helen M—†	12	operator	56	"
	v	Trotter Alexander J	12	U S A	26	
	w	Trotter Mary A—†	12	housekeeper	65	"
	x	Gugliotte Thomas D	12	carpenter	68	"
	y	Reidy Catherine P—†	·12	housewife	29	"
	z	Reidy William J	12	electrician	29	"

801

	b	O'Donnell Annie—†	12	housewife	48	35 Lawrence
	a	O'Donnell Peter	12	laborer	44	35 "
	c	Dennehy Charles	14	U S A	23	here
	d	Dennehy Sadie—†	14	typist	45	"
	e	Cutlip Bertha F—†	14	housewife	40	"
	f	Cutlip Harold E	14	laborer	42	
	g	Frasier Katherine—†	14	clerk	28	
	h	Frasier Mary—†	14	laundress	50	"
	k	Cody Hazel—†	16	housekeeper	22	15 Lexington
	l	Cody Joseph M	16	U S A	22	15 "
	m	Dockharty Mary E—†	16	housewife	45	15 "
	n	Dockharty William W	16	laborer	50	15 "
	o	Burke Annie E—†	16	at home	70	here
	p	Wedick Frank L	16	shipper	68	"
	r	Wedick Minnie—†	16	housewife	69	"
	u	Fallon Patrick	16	retired	87	
	s	Flanigan James	16	laborer	50	
	t	Flanigan Mary—†	16	housewife	85	"

Austin Street—Continued

w	Kelley Joseph H	30	electrician	51	here
x	Kelley Pauline A—†	30	housewife	53	"
y	Maglio Blanche M—†	32	"	27	"
z	Maglio Ralph	32	clerk	32	56 Wrentham

802

a	Nigro Albert R	32	U S A	20	here
b	Nigro Frank P	32	laborer	58	"
c	Nigro Vincent J	32	"	29	Medford
d	Nigro Helen—†	34	housewife	28	here
e	Nigro Joseph W	34	electrician	31	"
f	Connolly Bridget—†	34	housewife	38	"
g	Connolly John J	34	laborer	40	
h	Doherty Patrick	34	watchman	49	"
k	Doherty Sarah—†	34	housewife	45	"
o	Collins Dennis J	38	retired	76	
p	Scanlon Ellen—†	38	housewife	47	"
r	Scanlon Rose F—†	38	"	35	
s	Scanlon Thomas F	38	laborer	36	
u	McCarthy Catherine—†	40	housewife	70	"
v	Glagan Catherine V—†	40	"	38	99 Wash'n
w	McCarthy Margaret—†	40	"	65	here
x	Paddon George	42	painter	68	"
y	Sayre Mary E—†	42	housewife	60	"
z	Kelley Agnes M—†	42	"	24	10 Chapman

803

a	Kelley Joseph	42	sorter	21	10 "
b	Harrington Catherine—†	42	housewife	36	here
c	Pollock Ada—†	44	"	67	2 Gray
d	Pollock Ada—†	44	clerk	33	2 "
e	Madden John	44	laborer	47	here
f	Winters Eva V—†	44	housewife	37	"
g	Winters John D	44	teamster	41	"

Central Place

m	Macdonald Isabelle—†	1	housewife	26	Malden
n	O'Brien William J	1	retired	71	here
o	Ryan Grace E—†	1	housekeeper	58	"
r	Brown Gerald	3	U S A	40	"
s	Thayer Frank	3	starter	45	

3

Page.	Letter.	FULL NAME.	Residence, Jan. 1, 1944.	Occupation.	Supposed Age.	Reported Residence, Jan. 1, 1943. Street and Number.

Central Place—Continued

T	Corcoran John	3	longshoreman	37	9 Forster's ct
U	Corcoran Marion—†	3	housewife	26	9 "

Devens Street

V	Sullivan Cecelia—†	9	at home	62	here
W	Gaudette Inez M—†	9	"	67	"
X	Gaudette Peter.	9	retired	65	"
Y	Cox Bessie—†	9	at home	66	"
Z	Cox Mary—†	9	stitcher	59	"
	804				
A	Bayton Lillian—†	11	at home	32	"
B	Burns Catherine I—†	14	stenographer	31	"
C	Burns Helen F—†	14	teacher	26	"
D	Burns Mary—†	14	at home	61	"
E	Burns Michael	14	freighthandler	62	"
F	O'Brien Patrick J	14	watchman	62	"
G	Murphy Eileen—†	15	at home	36	"
H	Murphy John	15	laborer	41	"
K	Fitzgerald Joseph L	16	clerk	48	57 Wash'n
L	Fitzgerald Mary K—†	16	at home	48	Arlington
M	Daley Cornelius	16	longshoreman	47	here
N	Daley Ellen M—†	16	at home	47	"
O	McKinnon Alice—†	16	"	44	"
P	McKinnon Eleanor—†	16	"	22	
R	McLaughlin Eugene E	17	chauffeur	33	"
S	McLaughlin Mary—†	17	at home	31	"
T	Bowdren Catherine—†	18	"	70	
U	Bowdren Ella—†	18	clerk	30	
V	Bowdren Patrick B	18	retired	70	
W	Bowdren Thomas	18	U S A	34	
X	Stevenson Elizabeth—†	18	at home	72	"
Y	Stevenson Fred A	18	retired	70	
Z	Stevenson Harold F	18	shipfitter	44	"
	805				
A	Connolly Joseph E	18	U S A	25	
B	Connolly Martin W	18	policeman	53	"
C	Connolly Mary M—†	18	at home	46	"
D	Allwood John L	19	laborer	22	41 Austin
E	Allwood Frances T—†	19	at home	21	41 "
F	McLaughlin Catherine—†	19	"	39	here

Devens Street—Continued

	Letter	Full Name	Res.	Occupation	Age	Reported Residence
	G	Burke Loretta—†	19	packer	32	here
	H	Burke Mary—†	19	at home	71	"
	K	McEnany Helen M—†	23	"	62	"
	L	McEnany Thomas A	23	retired	68	
	M	Dufour Peter E	23	laborer	45	
	N	Dufour Yvonne—†	23	at home	36	"
	O	Driscoll Honora—†	23	"	72	"
	P	Ross Archie	23	welder	55	Lancaster
	R	Norton Cecelia—†	23	at home	48	here
	S	Norton Robert E	23	seaman	47	"

Devens Street Place

	Letter	Full Name	Res.	Occupation	Age	Reported Residence
	U	Sullivan John J	4	laborer	56	here
	V	Sullivan John J, jr	4	U S A	26	"
	W	Sullivan Mary T—†	4	at home	52	"
	X	Sullivan Patrick F	4	U S A	25	
	Y	Sullivan Thomas J	4	U S N	21	
	Z	Keegan Mary T—†	4	at home	23	"
		806				
	A	Keegan Richard M	4	U S A	25	

Forster's Court

	Letter	Full Name	Res.	Occupation	Age	Reported Residence
	C	Wixon Lidia M—†	1	packer	26	here
	D	Wixon Rose M—†	1	housekeeper	52	5 Union ct
	F	Dwyer Mary—†	2	at home	67	here
	G	Enos Mary P—†	2	"	80	5 Union ct
	H	Leger Hector	9	carpenter	51	here
	M	Glines Josephine—†	10	housekeeper	67	"

Harvard Square

	Letter	Full Name	Res.	Occupation	Age	Reported Residence
	N	Melanson John C	37	U S A	23	here
	O	Melanson Joseph A	37	"	25	"
	P	Melanson Joseph A	37	chauffeur	50	"
	R	Melanson Mary—†	37	clerk	21	
	S	Melanson Mary E—†	37	housewife	51	"

5

Page.	Letter.	FULL NAME.	Residence, Jan. 1, 1944.	Occupation.	Supposed Age.	Reported Residence, Jan. 1, 1943. Street and Number.

Harvard Square—Continued

	u	*Dardarian Annie—†	37	housewife	57	here
	v	Dardarian Richard	37	barber	56	"
	w	Gallagher Ethel C—†·	39	housekeeper	51	"

807   Harvard Street

	A	Burnside Robert	36	laborer	49	713 Tremont
	B	Dever Catherine—†	36	housekeeper	50	42 Harvard
	C	Parker Julia C—†	36	at home	66	6 Monument sq
	D	Brodeley Patrick E	38	longshoreman	45	Somerville
	E	Carey Mary—†	38	at home	68	here
	F	Judge Richard H	38	clerk	49	Chelsea
	G	McDevitt Alice—†	38	at home	62	here
	H	McDevitt Mary—†	38	housekeeper	76	"
	K	O'Connell Maurice	38	carpenter	47	"
	L	Welch Jeremiah	38	retired	57	27 Cross
	M	White Benjamin N	38	laborer	47	15 Harvard
	N	Doherty Daniel	42	longshoreman	56	here
	O	Goodwin Thomas	42	clerk	37	Malden
	P	Lucas Joseph E	42	welder	36	Watertown
	R	McGaffigan John	42	longshoreman	37	here
	S	McGaffigan Mary E—†	42	housewife	37	"
	T	McGaffigan Susan—†	42	at home	70	"
	U	Thompson Andrew	42	retired	66	6 Lawnwood pl
	V	White John ·	42	"	68	here
	W	Burns Catherine—†	44	housewife	48	"
	X	Burns John J	44	rigger	49	"
	Y	Carney Ellen—†	44	clerk	50	
	Z	Carney John J	44	rigger	49	
		808				
	F	Blunt William	44	mechanic	50	"
	A	Crimlish Daniel	44	laborer	60	
	B	Fallon James	44	retired	75	
	C	Horgan Michael	44	longshoreman	55	"
	D	Orsini Dominick	44	pipefitter	30	Springfield
	E	Sullivan Daniel	44	retired	84	here
	G	Dillon Thomas	46	laborer	50	"
	H	Kenny John J	46	retired	75	"
	K	McCabe James	46	laborer	42	
	L	McCarthy Charles	46	retired	75	
	M	Meaney Patrick	46	laborer	40	

6

Harvard Street—Continued

n	O'Neil Bridie—†	46	housewife	36	here
o	O'Neil Charles P	46	mechanic	44	"
p	Smith Mildred—†	46	housewife	23	New York
r	Smith Ralph R	46	U S N	40	"
s	Winslow Oscar	46	laborer	40	here
t	Corcoran Eileen J—†	48	waitress	34	8 Pompeii
u	Harrington Anna—†	48	clerk	35	here
v	Latorella Fred	48	mechanic	50	"
w	Marino Andrew	48	bartender	46	"
x	Adams Jessie—†	50	clerk	44	
y	Peavey Frederick J	50	U S A	25	
z	Tucker Alfred	50	janitor	36	

809

a	Tucker Alice—†	50	housekeeper	72	"
b	McKeigue Kathleen—†	50A	clerk	44	"
c	McKeigue Mary—†	50A	"	37	
d	McCarthy Charles J	52	U S N	28	
e	McCarthy Elizabeth A—†	52	at home	56	"
f	Kyle Francis X	54	U S A	22	
g	Kyle Joseph E	54	bridgetender	49	"
h	Kyle Joseph E, jr	54	U S N	23	
k	Kyle Katherine A—†	54	housewife	46	"
m	Griffin John A	58	laborer	51	
n	Griffin Lillian R—†	58	housewife	46	"
o	Driscoll Catherine F—†	58	"	66	
p	Driscoll Michael F	58	laborer	65	
r	Murray Catherine T—†	58	typist	27	"
s	Murray Catherine V—†	58	housewife	52	"
t	Murray Mary G—†	58	typist	22	"
u	Murray Thomas J	58	longshoreman	52	"
w	Doherty John J	60	rigger	28	
x	Doherty Mary E—†	60	housewife	26	"
y	McGaffigan Patrick J	60	clerk	22	
z	Carey Katherine—†	60	stitcher	57	"

810

a	Carey Thomas	60	plumber	48	"

Henley Street

c	Cadigan Catherine M—†	6	housekeeper	40	here
d	Gill Katherine E—†	6	at home	68	"

Page.	Letter.	FULL NAME.	Residence, Jan. 1, 1944.	Occupation.	Supposed Age.	Reported Residence, Jan. 1, 1943. Street and Number.

Henley Street—Continued

| | E | Kenney Eugenia F—† | 6 | housekeeper | 61 | here |
| | F | Kenney Roland D | 6 | longshoreman | 42 | " |

Lawrence Street

	G	Humphrey Beatrice—†	7	houseworker	33	here
	H	Lyman Frances P—†	7	housewife	52	"
	K	Lyman Frederick	7	plumber	55	"
	L	Hurley James J	7	laborer	66	"
	M	Fahey Nellie—†	8	housewife	73	"
	N	McDonough Bridget—†	8	clerk	55	9 Lawrence
	O	Barringer Eleanor—†	9	cashier	27	here
	P	Parker Eleanor—†	9	saleswoman	50	"
	R	Parker John	9	U S A	25	"
	S	Smith Harold E	9	guard	45	
	T	Boudreau Bernice—†	9	WAC	33	
	U	Boudreau Charles V	9	ironworker	61	"
	V	Boudreau Ruth—†	9	housewife	61	"
	W	Boudreau Ruth—†	9	WAC	23	"
	X	Coyne Sadie—†	9	housewife	47	44 Austin
	Y	Tiernan Mary—†	9	clerk	22	here
	Z	Tiernan William	9	U S A	20	"

811

	A	Gorrell Lillian N—†	10	housewife	34	"
	¹A	Gorrell Robert E	10	chauffeur	35	"
	B	Malone Honora A—†	10	maid	45	
	E	Sacco Angelo	16	welder	23	
	F*	Sacco Annette—†	16	housewife	53	"
	G	Sacco Carmella—†	16	defense wkr	28	"
	H	Sacco Contetto—†	16	waitress	25	"
	K	Sacco Teresa—†	16	bookkeeper	20	"
	L	Sacco Thomas	16	carpenter	54	"
	M	Lowell Mary E—†	18	housewife	68	93 Decatur
	N	Knudsen Ellen—†	18	textileworker	24	here
	O	Knudsen Helen—†	18	housewife	49	"
	P	Knudsen Johanna—†	18	waitress	21	"
	R	Connell Mary—†	18	housewife	67	"
	S	Graney Ethel—†	20	"	45	
	T	Graney Lawrence	20	machinist	51	"
	U	Ahern Daniel	20	U S A	29	
	V	Ahern Michael	20	laborer	66	

8

Lawrence Street—Continued

w	Ahern Nellie—†	20	housewife	64	here
x	Ahern Timothy	20	U S A	31	"
y	Hayes Frederick J	20	newsdealer	33	"
z	Hayes Joseph J	20	manager	27	"
	812				
a	Hayes Margaret—†	20	housewife	66	"
b	Hayes Margaret P—†	20	factoryhand	29	"
c	Hayes Mary L—†	20	chauffeur	24	"
d	Hayes Michael A	20	laborer	62	

Lynde Street

e	Ross Catherine M—†	1	at home	57	here
f	Gello Angelo	1	laborer	27	"
g	Gello Katherine M—†	1	at home	27	"
h	Walsh Mary A—†	1	"	67	"
l	Stillman George	3	retired	76	
m	Stillman Maude F—†	3	at home	69	"
r	Ghiradelli Andrew	35	seaman	21	
s	Ghiradelli Emma—†	35	at home	46	"
t	Ghiradelli John	35	retired	66	"
w	Sullivan Anna M—†	43	at home	41	"
x	Sullivan Daniel	43	manager	40	"
y	Coveney Annie—†	43	at home	72	"
z	Keane Dennis	65	mechanic	53	"

813   Main Street

¹e	Clancy Grace M—†	44½	housewife	50	here
k	DeJesus Domingo	54	U S N	46	"
l	DeJesus Ernestine—†	54	housewife	36	"
m	Hart Anna—†	54	housekeeper	82	"
n	Madeira Anna—†	54	at home	22	"
o	Mahoney William	54	U S A	25	
	814				
c	Barker Mildred—†	92	housewife	34	"
d	Barker William	92	foreman	36	"
e	Coffey Katherine—†	92	housewife	70	"
g	Brouillard Anna—†	98	"	43	6 School
h	Brouillard Arthur	98	fireman	56	6 "
k	Santerre Loretta—†	98	operator	21	6 "

9

Main Street—Continued

L	Kane Paul	98	laborer	21	37 Mystic
M	Vesey Delia—†	98	housewife	53	here
N	Vesey John	′98	laborer	21	"
O	Vesey Thomas	98	riveter	51	"
P	Alves Ella S—†	98	operator	34	3 Pleasant
R	Alves Frank G	98	machinist	37	3 "
S	Butler Bessie—†	98	housekeeper	55	3 "
T	Scanlon Anna—†	98½	housewife	27	here
U	Scanlon Gerald	98½	boilermaker	32	"
Y	Burke Martin J	104	operator	29	48 Walker
Z	Burke Mildred M—†	104	housewife	23	48 "
	815				
B	Sullivan Edward G	104	chipper	29	here
C	Sullivan Evelyn B—†	104	housewife	28	"
D	Walles Evelyn D—†	104½	"	26	327 Main
E	Walles James E	104½	laborer	27	327 "
F	Gustus Albert F	104½	warehouse	43	319 "
G	Lyons Henry W	104½	foreman	20	319 "
H	Lyons Mary L—†	104½	housekeeper	44	319 "
K	Blaikie Howard W	104½	foreman	44	48 Walker
L	Blaikie Howard W	104½	U S N	22	48 "
M	Blaikie Ida A—†	104½	housekeeper	43	48 "
O	Nigro Alfred	108	electrician	23	here
P	Nigro Joseph ·	108	shipper	40	"
R	Nigro Lucy—†	108	housekeeper	69	"
S	Nigro Phyllis—†	108	at home	33	"
T	Nigro Rita—†	108	packer	27	
U	Kelly Katherine—†	108	waitress	21	"
V	Nelson Catherine A—†	108	rigger	52	
W	Nelson John C	108	"	54	
X	Nigro Benjamin A	108	metalworker	44	"
Y	Nigro Josephine—†	108	housewife	41	"
Z	Cotter William J	112	laborer	28	
	816				
A	Kelly Lillian F—†	112	housekeeper	55	"
B	Mitza Joseph	112	rigger	39	..
C	Walsh Ellen—†	112	at home	68	"
D	Hickey Catherine—†	114	cleaner	47	
F	Lydon Margaret M—†	114	housewife	67	"
E	Lydon Philip J	114	clerk	67	"
G	Lynch John J	114	laborer	65	116 Main

Main Street—Continued

H	Lynch Margaret—†	114	housewife	37	116 Main
K	Mahoney Daniel	114	retired	71	here
L	Mahoney Joseph	114	longshoreman	35	Medford
M	Woods Arthur	114	barber	50	N Hampshire
T	DeCoste Edward	132A	chauffeur	31	here
U	DeCoste Mary—†	132A	housewife	55	"
V	DeCoste Norman	132A	watchman	33	"
W	DeCoste Peter	132A	carpenter	72	"

817

A	Finelli Angelina E—†	136½	housewife	34	"
B	Finelli Joseph A	136½	fruit	49	
C	Saccardo Annie—†	138	housewife	51	"
D	Saccardo Biagio	138	barber	60	"
E	Saccardo Ernest	138	U S A	22	
F	Fathering Gertrude—†	138	clerk	54	
G	Lepore Charles A	138	truckman	54	"
H	Lepore Charles A	138	storekeeper	28	"
K	Lepore Harriett J—†	138	housewife	54	"
N	Henry Edward E	142	storekeeper	49	"
M	Henry Robert B	142	clerk	56	"
O	Henry Tamsey S—†	142	housekeeper	54	"
P	McLaughlin Bernard J	144	seaman	21	"
R	McLaughlin Charles P	144	U S A	29	
S	McLaughlin Edward J	144	seaman	26	"

Prescott Street

U	Casey Jennie C—†	1	at home	64	here
V	Casey Joseph H	1	retired	62	"
W	Smith Edmond	1	checker	57	57 Chapman
X	Crowley James H	3	clerk	43	98½ Main
Y	Crowley James H, jr	3	U S A	22	98½ "
Z	Crowley John J	3	retired	78	98½ "

818

A	Crowley John J	3	electrician	21	98½ "
B	Crowley Margaret M—†	3	at home	40	98½ "
C	Gillespie Daniel P	3	U S N	22	here
D	Gillespie John J	3	"	25	"
E	Gillespie Margaret M—†	3	waitress	23	"
F	Gillespie Rose A—†	3	at home	59	"
G	Kirby Catherine—†	3	"	53	"

11

Prescott Street—Continued

H	Kirby Edward J	3	longshoreman	59	here
K	Healy Christine M—†	5	stenographer	25	"
L	Healy Josephine P—†	5	bookkeeper	24	"
M	Healy Katherine T—†	5	at home	54	"
N	Healy Margaret T—†	5	clerk	33	"
O	Healy Patrick F	5	watchman	65	"
S	Fahey Agnes V—†	7	at home	42	"
T	Fahey Catherine A—†	7	"	67	
P	Gallagher Thomas F	7	retired	71	
R	Gallagher Thomas L	7	U S A	37	"
U	Morse Chester E	21	conductor	60	14A Hudson
V	Morse Mary J—†	21	at home	52	14A "
W	Woolsey Dorothy M—†	21	"	27	14A "
X	Mahoney Arthur J	21	freighthandler	22	here
Y	Mahoney Dorothy F—†	21	packer	20	"
Z	Mahoney Gertrude F—†	21	at home	54	"
	819				
A	Lazzare Filippo	21	laborer	45	
B	Gallagher Gertrude C—†	23	clerk	45	
C	Gallagher Herbert J	23	fireman	41	..
D	Gallagher Joseph F	23	U S N	43	
E	Gallagher Joseph H	23	retired	74	
F	Hynes Lucy —†	23	matron	55	

Rutherford Avenue

O	Freestone Bridget V—†	101	housewife	54	5 Wash'n sq
P	Freestone Joseph	101	longshoreman	34	5 "
R	Freestone Robert W	101	U S A	22	5 "
S	Freestone Stanley W	101	"	20	5 "
T	Helbert Alice B—†	101	housewife	38	8 Hudson
U	Helbert John F	101	freighthandler	58	8 "
V	Hickey Catherine M—†	101	maid	53	here
W	Kupper Mary A—†	101	at home	51	"
X	Kupper Patrick F	101	operator	29	"
Y	Murphy Hannah—†	103	housewife	51	"
Z	Murphy John J	103	U S A	25	
	820				
A	Devlin James D	103	janitor	59	
B	Devlin James G	103	U S N	22	

Rutherford Avenue—Continued

c	*Devlin Theresa—†	103	housewife	58	here
d	*Doherty Annie—†	103	at home	70	"
e	Fearen Elizabeth—†	103	housekeeper	72	"
f	Graham Malcolm H	103	cook	66	"
g	Hurley Daniel F	104	U S N	29	"
h	Hurley Mary F—†	104	housewife	29	"
k	McLaughlin Catherine—†	104	"	49	"
l	McLaughlin Catherine A—†	104	at home	25	"
m	McLaughlin James	104	meatcutter	54	"
n	McLaughlin James J	104	U S A	27	"
o	McLaughlin William S	104	electrician	21	"
p	Sullivan Julia—†	105	housewife	71	"
r	Green Elizabeth—†	105	"	49	11 Park
s	Green William J	105	laborer	58	11 "
t	Green William J, jr	105	U S A	25	11 "
u	Belmont Antonina—†	105	housewife	30	here
v	Belmont Dionisio	105	coppersmith	40	"
w	Lively Arthur E	107	mechanic	48	"
x	*Lively Margaret E—†	107	housewife	47	"
y	O'Neill Delia F—†	107	"	33	
z	O'Neill John J	107	shipper	36	"
	821				
a	Parrino Angela—†	107	at home	26	"
b	*Parrino Carmella—†	107	housewife	49	"
c	Parrino Joseph	107	fruit	54	"
f	O'Brien Marie—†	116	housewife	36	"
g	Quinn John W	116	laborer	20	"
h	Doherty Catherine—†	116	housewife	36	"
k	Doherty Cornelius	116	foreman	43	"
l	West Oscar	116	longshoreman	56	"
m	Hayes Stephen	117	U S N	39	"
n	Murphy Julia A—†	117	housekeeper	51	"
o	Murphy Julia P—†	117	nurse	21	"
p	Murphy Mary J—†	117	WAVE	24	"

Seminary Street

t	Crowe Joseph M	1	clerk	34	9A Monum'nt sq
u	Crowe Mary C—†	1	housewife	29	9A "
v	Better Mary—†	1	houseworker	65	Somerville

13

9

Seminary Street—Continued

w	Magner Gerard J	1	clerk	20	here
x	Magner Margaret M—†	1	housewife	63	"
y	Magner Patrick J	1	policeman	65	"
z	Magner Robert D	1	welder	26	
	822				
a	McPherson Catherine F–† r	2	housewife	73	"
b	McPherson William M	" 2	electrician	66	"
c	Maher Frances M—†	" 2	housewife	39	"
d	Maher Leo F	" 2	mechanic	40	"
f	Guyette Joseph W	3	painter	46	322 Main
g	Tucker Grace—†	3	housekeeper	37	322 "
h	Coleman Mary A—†	8	housewife	53	here
k	Coleman Mary K—†	8	clerk	21	"
l	Coleman Patrick J	8	foreman	56	"
m	Coleman Patrick J	8	clerk	22	
n	Connolly Sheila—†	8	"	29	
o	Connolly William V	8	U S A	26	
p	Harkins Eleanor T—†	10	nurse	21	
r	Harkins John J	10	laborer	64	
s	Harkins Joseph W	10	U S N	25	
t	Harkins Nettie G—†	10	housewife	58	"
u	Harkins Vincent P	10	U S M C	20	"
v	Connolly Elizabeth—†	12	housewife	59	"
w	Connolly Joseph	12	U S A	28	
x	*Connolly Patrick	12	laborer	60	
y	Guittar Helen—†	12	housewife	23	"
z	Sanborn Charles	12	U S A	22	
	823				
a	Sanborn Mary—†	12	riveter	23	
b	Lagorio Ella—†	12	housewife	49	"
c	Lagorio John	12	cable installer	57	"
d	*Crowell Harry S	14	retired	74	
e	Foley John W	16	mason	55	
f	Foley Joseph A	16	shipper	38	
g	Foley Mary A	16	housewife	77	"
h	Foley Michael S	16	steamfitter	40	"
k	Ford Harriet—†	18	housewife	26	42 O'Meara ct
l	Ford Walter	18	trainman	25	42 "
m	McDonald Gordon	18	U S M C	24	here
n	McDonald Ida—†	18	clerk	50	"
o	McDonald Vernon	18	U S A	22	"

14

Union Street

R	Quinn Cecelia G—†	9	housekeeper	55	here	
S	Kiley Ellen—†	9	"	60	"	
T	Zink George	11	laborer	50	"	
U	Zink Effie C—†	11	housewife	33	"	
V	Hohn Catherine A—†	11	"	43		
W	Hohn Joseph	11	chauffeur	50	"	
X	Doherty Anastasia H—†	11	operator	30	"	
Y	Doherty Ellen V—†	11	cleaner	56	"	
Z	Doherty John D	11	U S A	31		

824

A	Parker Alfred T	11	laborer	28	Maine	
B	Parker Mary A—†	11	housewife	28	here	
C	Crowley James	13	laborer	41	"	
D	Dorman Ralph E	13	"	69	"	
E	Emmons Frances E—†	13	housekeeper	81	"	
F	Stone George H	13	retired	74		
G	*Flaherty Anna—†	15	housewife	43	"	
H	Flaherty Joseph	15	laborer	43		
K	Harmon Lily M—†	15	housewife	33	"	
L	Harmon Silas M	15	U S N	43		
M	Strong Ella D—†	15	at home	21	"	
N	Bell Catherine M—†	15½	"	73		
O	Pitts Elizabeth F—†	16	housewife	50	"	
P	Pitts Harvard J	16	foreman	53	"	
R	Driscoll Bridget—†	16	at home	68	"	
S	O'Malley Ellen—†	16	housewife	66	"	
T	O'Malley Martin	16	retired	75		
U	Hamilton Ellen—†	16	housewife	54	"	
V	Hamilton James	16	U S A	24		
W	Donaghey Fanny—† rear	16	housewife	46	"	
X	*Donaghey Hugh "	16	laborer	50		
Y	Canny Dennis "	16	"	45	"	
Z	Canny Mary—† "	16	housewife	43	"	

825

A	Doherty Cornelius "	16	laborer	48		
B	Friel Bernard "	16	U S A	37		
C	Friel John "	16	freighthandler	50	"	
D	Friel Margaret—† "	16	housewife	42	"	
F	Balharry Bridget—†	17	at home	65	"	
G	Smith Robert W	17	laborer	30	Concord	
L	Stimpson Helen M—†	17	housewife	32	here	

15

Page.	Letter.	Full Name.	Residence, Jan. 1, 1944.	Occupation.	Supposed Age.	Reported Residence, Jan. 1, 1943. Street and Number.

Union Street—Continued

	H	Stimpson Roscoe J	17	operator	44	here
	K	Stimpson Roscoe J, jr	17	U S A	23	"
	N	Durant Catherine M—†	18	WAVE	20	"
	O	Durant ·Edward C	18	welder	22	
	P	Durant Margaret E—†	18	operator	26	"
	R	*Durant Marie A—†	18	housewife	58	"
	S	Forrest Mary C—†	18	collector	35	"
	T	Forrest Matthew J	18	U S A	34	
	U	Forrest Patrick J	18	retired	70	
	V	Callahan Katherine A—†	19	housewife	30	"
	W	Callahan Timothy T	19	stevedore.	28	"
	X	Lemist Willard D	19	clerk	45	"
	Y	McCreven Patrick J	19	seaman	26	41 Mt Vernon
	Z	Upton Blanche M—†	20	waitress	50	here
		826				
	A	Upton Herbert H	20	electrotyper	51	"
	C	Wallace Kathryn A—†	20	housewife	28	"
	D	Wallace Thomas E	20	U S A	32	52 Tremont
	E	Chadwick Charles	21	author	59	here
	F	Chadwick Grace S—†	21	housewife	39	"
	G	Russell William D	22	clerk	40	"
	H	Doherty Michael O	22	U S N	22	"
	K	Doherty William	22	laborer	60	"
	L	Bird Rose M—†	22	housewife	42	"
	M	Bird Thomas G	22	laborer	60	
	N	Marcella Dora G—†	22½	housewife	30	"
	O	Marcella Thomas D	22½	longshoreman	35	"
	P	Coleman Irene A—†	22½	housewife	20	104½ Main
	R	Coleman John D	22½	stitcher	29	8 Seminary
	S	Hennessey Johanna—†	22½	housewife	48	here
	T	Hennessey John F	22½	U S N	21	"
	U	MacMillan Anna L—†	23	housewife	29	Medford
	V	MacMillan Robert J	23	U S N	26	"
	W	Spooner John B	23	seaman	50	here
	X	Spooner Naomi M—†	23	housewife	54	"
	Y	Spooner Roscoe O	23	U S A	21	"
	Z	Prewitt Benjamin	23	seaman	29	"
		827				
	A	Prewitt Ruth E—†	23	housewife	24	"
	B	Randall Mary J—†	25	"	29	
	C	*Walsh Helen—†	25	"	36	

Page.	Letter.	FULL NAME.	Residence, Jan. 1, 1944.	Occupation.	Supposed Age.	Reported Residence, Jan. 1, 1943. Street and Number.

Union Street—Continued

D	Walsh Thomas	25	clerk	39	here
E*	McGonagle Helen—†	25	housewife	36	42 Pleasant
F	McGonagle John	25	laborer	39	42 "
G	Monagle Bridget—†	25	housewife	38	here
H	Monagle Robert	25	laborer	38	"
K	Wilson Louise H—†	26	housewife	47	"
L	Wilson William F	26	janitor	48	"
M	Purdon Philip E	26	paperhanger	71	"
N	Sharp Alonzo L	26	laborer	68	"
O	Sharp Ellen B—†	26	housewife	66	"
S	Hayes Bartholomew	29	bartender	54	"
T	Butterworth Catherine M—†	29	housewife	41	"
U	Butterworth Walter C	29	pipefitter	41	"
V	Lawrence Charles E	30	rigger	53	"
W*	O'Neil Jeremiah	30	laborer	60	30 Lynde
X	Walsh Mary E—†	30	housekeeper	27	here
Y	Sweeney Katherine R—†	31	housewife	60	"
Z	Sweeney Richard F	31	custodian	60	"
	828				
A	Barry Joseph J	31	janitor	64	..
B	Barry Joseph R	31	electrician	31	"
C	Barry Sadie M—†	31	housewife	66	"
D	Denning Henry	31	clerk	66	
E	Denning Nora T—†	31	housewife	63	"
F	Greene Margaret T—†	31	clerk	54	
G	Doherty Anna M—†	35	nurse	28	
H	Doherty Edward	35	retired	70	
K	Doherty Joseph E	35	laborer	39	"
L	Doherty Letitia—†	35	housewife	72	"
M	Doherty Letitia E—†	35	clerk	35	..
N	Doherty Mary C—†	35	operator	37	"
O	Fitzgerald Mary—†	37	housewife	56	"
P	Fitzgerald Maurice F	37	U S A	24	
R	Fitzgerald William F	37	laborer	59	"
S	Fitzgerald William P	37	U S A	21	
T	DeCoste Gordon E.	37	chauffeur	34	"
U	DeCoste Grace E—†	37	housewife	24	"
V	Bingham Charles E	37	cook	49	
W	Bingham Georgette B—†	37	housewife	40	"
X	Shanahan Catherine—†	39	"	66	"
Y	Shanahan Michael E	39	porter	68	

2—8   17

Page.	Letter.	Full Name.	Residence, Jan. 1, 1944.	Occupation.	Supposed Age.	Reported Residence, Jan. 1, 1943. Street and Number.

Union Street—Continued

	z	Toland John J	39	laborer	56	here
829						
	A	Toland Rose A—†	39	housewife	51	"
	B	Doherty Michael	39	welder	39	"
	C	Doherty Sarah—†	39	housewife	37	34 W Cedar

Washington Place

	D	Tuttle Mary C—†	1	housewife	27	25 Austin
	E	Tuttle Wendell P	1	laborer	32	25 "

Washington Square

	G	Carroll John J	2	retired	56	here
	H	Carroll Mary A—†	2	housewife	58	"
	K	Carroll Mary B—†	2	clerk	21	"
	L	Carroll Thomas L	2	U S A	35	
	M	Gregory Eleanor—†	3	housewife	40	"
	N	Gregory Walter H	3	metalworker	45	"
	O	Stone Gretchen H—†	3	storekeeper	35	"
	P	Kocincki Rita—†	4	housewife	26	"
	R	Kocincki Stanley	4	rigger	41	"
	S	Muse Flora—†	5	housewife	42	20 Lincoln
	T	Muse Joseph H	5	laborer	54	20 "
	U	Carroll Henrietta A—†	5	matron	43	32 Pleasant
	V	Carroll Madeline A—†	5	clerk	21	32 "
	W	Carroll Patrick J	5	plumber	57	32 "
	X	Wear Alice—†	5	housewife	22	here
	Y	Wear Charles E	5	inspector	23	"
	Z	Donaghy Henry	6	clerk	51	"
830						
	A	Gilman Mary E—†	6	waitress	49	"
	B	Hanley John J	6	clerk	54	
	C	Haggerty Agnes—†	7	"	23	
	D	Haggerty Annie—†	7	housewife	60	"
	E	Haggerty Frances—†	7	packer	20	
	F	Haggerty John	7	laborer	62	
	G	Haggerty John J	7	"	32	"
	H	Carey Leo	8	pressman	30	23 Union
	K	Carey Mary—†	8	housewife	28	23 "
	L	Lowney Anna—†	8	clerk	24	here

Washington Square—Continued

M	Lowney Frances M—†	8	housewife	54	here
N	Lowney Margaret—†	8	clerk	22	"
O	Whitney Grace—†	9	housewife	40	"
P	Whitney Walter	9	shipfitter	51	"

Washington Street

R	Haggerty Bernard D	5	laborer	28	here
S	Haggerty Margaret L—†	5	housewife	28	"
T	Hogan Madeline—†	5	"	29	"
U	Hogan Richard	5	agent	29	"
V	McGuire Francis	5	boilermaker	29	"
W	McGuire Mary—†	5	housewife	27	"
X	Boyce Barbara—†	5	"	23	Maine
Y	Boyce Lester	5	laborer	23	"
Z	McLaughlin Bridget—†	11	housekeeper	60	here
	831				
A	Newman Margaret T—†	11	housewife	64	"
B	Toomey Margaret—†	11	at home	78	15 Harvard
C	Ross Mabel—†	24	housewife	59	here
D	Sigmund Mildred—†	24	"	32	"
M	Dennehy Cornelius E	26	metalworker	41	"
N	Dennehy Nora—†	26	housewife	65	"
O	Coot Jennie—†	26	domestic	63	"
P	Crawford Arthur W	27	retired	68	
R	Crawford Catherine H—†	27	housewife	43	"
S	Crawford John M	27	attorney	63	"
T	Crawford Walter D	27	custodian	48	"
U	Crawford Walter D, jr	27	U S N	21	
V	Hayes Mary—†	28	housewife	55	"
W	Hayes Peter	28	laborer	55	
X	Kelly Dennis D	28	watchman	69	"
Y	Kelly Eleanor J—†	28	houseworker	30	"
Z	Kelly Ellen M—†	28	housewife	63	"
	832				
A	Kelly Veronica—†	28	stenographer	24	"
B	Northrup Edward	28	shipfitter	57	83 Chelsea
C	Northrup Myrtle B—†	28	housewife	58	83 "
D	Brennan John	29	engineer	64	here
E	Fitzgerald Catherine R—†	29	housewife	29	"
F	Fitzgerald James B	29	U S N	34	"

Washington Street—Continued

G	Lehan Bridget—†	29	housewife	50	here
H	Lehan Dennis	29	laborer	60	"
K	Downey Anthony	30	watchman	69	12 Rutherford av
L	Downey Hannah—†	30	housewife	56	12 "
M	Downey John	30	U S N	28	12 "
N	Downey Joseph	30	U S A	23	12 "
O	Burns Daniel J	30	laborer	50	here
P	Burns James E	30	repairman	30	"
R	Burns Margaret M—†	30	housewife	49	"
S	Burns Thomas A	30	laborer	52	
T	Pokaski Catherine T—†	30	waitress	26	"
U	Pokaski Joseph M	30	U S A	34	44 Emerald
W	O'Leary Arthur	31	laborer	44	here
X	O'Leary Sarah—†	31	housewife	47	"
Y	Considine Leo	31	U S A	30	"
Z	Donovan James	31	bartender	54	"

833

A	Donovan John	31	U S A	20	"
B	Donovan Margaret—†	31	housewife	50	"
C	Donovan Mary—†	31	clerk	22	"
D	Dempsey Mary—†	32	"	43	24 Wash'n
E	Doherty Anna—†	32½	bookkeeper	42	here
F	Gillespie Bridget—†	32½	cleaner	59	"
G	Gandolfo James	33	laborer	52	"
H	Gandolfo Marie—†	33	housewife	42	"
K	Beraldi Salvatore	33	machinist	22	"
L	Beraldi Santos—†	33	housewife	21	"
M	Graham Nora—†	34	"	51	
N	Graham William J	34	freighthandler	56	"
O	Graham William T	34	U S A	20	"
P	Manning Margaret M—†	34	at home	50	"
T	Irozzi Hazel—†	35	housewife	31	"
U	Irozzi Louise—†	35	operator	35	"
V	Dower Thomas	36	casketmaker	56	"
W	Kelly Mary E—†	36	housewife	58	"
X	Kelly Patrick J	36	weigher	61	"
Y	McCarthy Edward F	36	salesman	34	"
Z	McCarthy Johanna J—†	36	housewife	68	"

834

A	McCarthy Patrick	36	retired	78	
B	McGonagle James	36	operator	35	"

Washington Street—Continued

c	Kelley Margaret C—†	37	floorwoman	68	here
d	Kelley Thomas F	37	retired	63	"
e	Monahan Julia A—†	37	at home	59	"
f	Doherty Edward M	39	inspector	51	"
g	Doherty Edward M, jr	39	U S A	21	
h	Farrell Edmund D	39	U S C G	38	"
k	Farrell Helen F—†	39	housewife	38	"
l	McLaughlin George	39	retired	66	"
m	Scafida John	40	chauffeur	54	Revere
n	Fariner Bernadette—†	40	housewife	22	here
o	Fariner Norman H	40	U S A	26	"
p	Vallee Catherine L—†	40	housewife	39	"
r	Vallee Fredrick M	40	chipper	43	..
s	Melli Joseph	41	canvasmaker	54	"
t	*Melli Mary—†	41	housewife	51	"
u	Diggins John J	41	guard	49	
v	Diggins John R	41	U S A	24	
w	Diggins Mary A—†	41	housewife	46	"
x	Diggins Mary E—†	41	packer	22	
y	Lynch Dorothy—†	41	housewife	26	"
z	Manning Catherine M—†	41	"	30	
	835				
a	Manning William E	41	chauffeur	36	"
b	Scafidi Alfio	42	U S A	25	Wilmington
c	Scafidi Frank	42	chauffeur	57	"
d	Scafidi Mary—†	42	housewife	54	"
e	*Santry Bridget—†	42	"	46	here
f	*Santry John	42	laborer	47	"
g	Friel Ruth—†	42	stenographer	20	"
h	Friel William	42	laborer	46	"
k	*Novello Rocco	43	"	57	
l	*Serrania Angelina—†	43	housewife	63	"
m	Ricciadi Anthony	43	machinist	23	"
n	*Ricciadi Elvira—†	43	housewife	44	"
o	*Ricciadi Paul	43	fruit	48	
p	Stone Brenford	43	metalworker	42	"
r	Stone Catherine—†	43	housewife	32	"
s	Mahoney Margaret—†	44	at home	67	10 Lincoln
t	Childs Ernest W	44	packer	28	here
u	Childs Harold E	44	"	33	"
v	Childs Marie—†	44	housewife	68	"

Washington Street—Continued

w	Childs William J	44	retired	76	here
x	Boyle Winifred C—†	46	housewife	71	"
y	McDonough Patrick J	46	operator	68	"
z	McDonough William F	46	lawyer	62	

836

A	Devlin John	48	longshoreman	40	"
B	McColgan Bridget—†	48	packer	50	"
c*	McColgan Mary—†	48	housekeeper	75	"
D	Bestony Fred	50	assembler	42	"
E	Robinson Muriel—†	50	hairdresser	37	"
F	Sheppard Gertrude—†	50	maid	68	
G	DeDombrosia Lillian—†	50½	bookkeeper	22	"
H	DeDombrosia Michael	50½	shoemaker	51	"
K	DeDombrosia Rose—†	50½	housewife	44	"
M	Stuart Ethel—†	51	operator	20	Stoneham
N	Wear Charles J	51	supervisor	44	here
o	Wear Grace—†	51	housewife	40	"
P	Crowne John F	52	foreman	55	"
R	Crowne Theresa C—†	52	housewife	49	"
s	Crowne Thomas E	52	U S A	22	
T	Crowne Thomas J	52	chauffeur	48	"
U	Donovan Rita M—†	52	clerk	24	
v	Nagle Catherine—†	52½	matron	55	
w	Nagle Marie—†	52½	stenographer	23	"
x	Nagle William P	52½	U S N	20	"
y	O'Brien Ellen—†	52½	housekeeper	59	"
z	Sheehan Elizabeth—†	52½	housewife	28	"

837

A	Sheehan John	52½	physician	30	11 Decatur
c	Bench John	53	guard	50	here
D	Kirk Mary—†	53	clerk	47	"
E	Morrisson Catherine—†	53	laborer	46	"
F	Ryan Hugh	53	welder	30	
G	Frost James	54	laborer	21	
H	Frost Mary—†	54	housewife	21	"
K	McLaughlin Margaret—†	54	"	54	
L	McLaughlin William	54	U S C G	22	"
M	Senenchuck Fanny—†	56	housewife	27	"
N	Senenchuck William	56	shipwright	30	"
o*	Rullan Gabriel	56	cook	50	42 Chestnut
p*	Rullan Grace—†	56	housewife	45	42 "

Washington Street—Continued

Page.	Letter.	FULL NAME.	Residence, Jan. 1, 1944.	Occupation.	Supposed Age.	Reported Residence, Jan. 1, 1943. Street and Number.
	R	Farren Charles	57	laborer	43	here
	S	Farren Mary E—†	57	housewife	53	"
	T	Fitzgerald Nicolas	57	laborer	51	"
	U	McEleney Ellen—†	57	housewife	60	"
	V	McEleney Mary K—†	57	clerk	20	
	W	McEleney Neil	57	laborer	57	"
	Y	O'Donnell Annie—†	59	housewife	41	"
	Z	O'Donnell Joseph	59	checker	39	"
838						
	A	O'Donnell Mary—†	59	clerk	28	
	B	O'Donnell Michael	59	U S N	24	
	C	O'Donnell Rose—†	59	bookkeeper	25	"
	D	Hendreckson Alfred	59½	laborer	39	"
	E	Hendreckson Anna—†	59½	housewife	40	"
	F	Devlin Edward	60	longshoreman	41	"
	G	Devlin Mary—†	60	housewife	36	"
	K	Sammara Anthony	60	contractor	49	"
	L	Sammara Carmilla—†	60	housewife	49	"
	M	Callahan Mary E—†	62	"	61	1 Arrow
	N	Callahan Peter J	62	laborer	33	1 "
	O	Fopiano Frank S	62	chauffeur	57	here
	P	Fopiano Helen V—†	62	housewife	42	"
	R	Fopiano May L—†	62	clerk	20	"
	T	Malcolm Lloyd W	64	operator	27	Everett
	U	Malcolm Marguerite T—†	64	housewife	26	"
	V	Fiorentino Amelia—†	64	packer	26	here
	W	Fiorentino Anthony A	64	fireman	50	"
	X	Fiorentino Mary—†	64	housewife	49	"
	Y	Fiorentino Rose—†	64	clerk	21	
839						
	C	Fitzpatrick Thomas	67	teamster	55	Malden
	D	Harrington Arthur	67	machinist	54	here
	E	Harrington Margaret—†	67	at home	80	"
	F	Mahoney John	67	laborer	66	"
	G	Reardon Kate—†	67	at home	75	"
	H	Stuart Annie—†	67	"	55	
	K	Haynes Louise—†	72	operator	48	"
	L	Stevens Joseph	72	clerk	58	
	M	Doherty Isabell—†	72	housekeeper	63	"
	N	Feeney James	72	retired	70	"
	O	Sullivan Annie—†	72	at home	75	12 Sackville

Page.	Letter.	FULL NAME.	Residence, Jan. 1, 1944.	Occupation.	Supposed Age.	Reported Residence, Jan. 1, 1943. Street and Number.

Washington Street—Continued

P	Sullivan Annie F—†	72	housewife	57	here
R	Sullivan Eugene F	72	pipefitter	54	"
s	Carney Margaret T—†	72	housewife	65	"
T	Carney William E	72	prob'n officer	65	"
U	Donohue Daniel	74	U S A	38	"
V	Donohue Mary—†	74	housewife	35	"
w	Friel William	74	longshoreman	36	"
x	McCarthy Henry J	74	retired	70	"
Y	McLaughlin John	74	laborer	36	"
z	Purcell William	74	retired	66	

840

A	*Doyle Margaret—†	76	housekeeper	52	"
B	Doyle Rita A—†	76	secretary	26	"
c	Henry Vaughan	76	mechanic	20	"
D	McGrane Frank	76	retired	68	
E	Murphy Dennis	76	bridgetender	45	"
F	Clark Thomas	78	welder	40	76 Wash'n
G	Goggin Anna E—†	78	housewife	38	here
H	Goggin Frank A	78	millwright	48'	"
K	Smith Harry K	78	engineer	60	"
L	Frager Charles	80	grinder	31	21 Harvard
M	Higgin Edward F	80	printer	60	New York
N	O'Connor Catherine—†	80	housewife	79	here
o	O'Connor Harold	80	laborer	38	122 Heath
P	*Stuart Louis	80	watchman	59	here
R	Butter John J	82	laborer	60	"
s	Cushing Albert	82	welder	55	"
T	Frachetti Louis	82	painter	35	"
U	O'Donnell Patrick	82	laborer	42	
V	O'Donnell Sarah—†	82	housewife	42	"
w	Quigley Mary J—†	82	waitress	35	"
x	Clougherty Bridget—†	84	housewife	73	"
Y	*O'Donnell Ellen J—†	84	at home	67	"
z	Harrington Daniel F	84	chauffeur	34	"

841

A	Maguire Alice—†	84	housekeeper	31	"
B	Maguire Margaret—†	84	clerk	29	"
c	Maguire Thomas	84	U S A	27	
D	McCaffrey Abbie—†	85	housewife	53	"
E	McCaffrey Ellen F—†	85	clerk	55	
F	McCaffrey Patrick J	85	laborer	50	

Washington Street—Continued

G	Coughlin Helen L—†	85	housewife	51	16 Austin
H	Coughlin Timothy J	85	laborer	59	16 "
K	Cassidy Alice L—†	85	clerk	45	here
M	Hartigan Margaret—†	86	housewife	29	Quincy
L	Hartigan Patrick	86	U S N	29	"
N	McNicholas Nellie—†	86	housewife	55	here
O	McNicholas Thomas J	86	laborer	55	"
P	Crowley James J	87	retired	67	2 Harvard pl
R	Horrigan Anna M—†	87	packer	32	here
S	Horrigan Catherine—†	87	stenographer	24	"
T	Horrigan Helen C—†	87	"	34	"
U	Horrigan Helen M—†	87	housewife	54	"
V	Horrigan Michael	87	laborer	58	"
W	Horrigan Rita—†	87	packer	22	"
X	Horrigan Thomas	87	U S N	20	"
Y	Binneau Daniel	88	rigger	52	"
Z	Chad George	88	electrician	35	Panama

842

A	*Monagle Catherine—†	88	housewife	41	here
B	Monagle Patrick	88	machinist	39	"
C	Mooney William	88	retired	64	"
D	Galvin Mary—†	90	housewife	72	"
E	Hurley John J	90	U S A	28	
F	Hurley Margaret T—†	90	operator	30	"
G	O'Connell Margaret T—†	90	housewife	50	"
H	Barry James J	91	retired	75	"
K	Barry Theresa—†	91	housekeeper	62	"
L	McGowan Charles	91	rigger	51	
M	McGowan James F	91	U S C G	25	"
N	McGowan Winifred B—†	91	housewife	51	"
O	McGowan Winifred B—†	91	clerk	25	"
P	Parmenter Fred M	91	U S N	27	"
R	Parmenter Muriel A—†	91	housewife	27	"
S	Bruno Albert C	92	guard	40	
T	Bruno Frances—†	92	housewife	68	"
U	Bruno James	92	U S A	37	
V	Bruno Leo	92	guard	35	
W	McGarry Catherine A—†	92	housewife	70	"
X	Brennan Alice G—†	93	housekeeper	49	"
Y	Murphy Annie E—†	93	"	59	"
Z	Clougherty John E	94	fireman	32	"

2—8   25

843
Washington Street—Continued

A	Clougherty Anna M—†	94	housewife	33	here
B	Doherty Annie—†	94	housekeeper	74	"
C	Maraghy Joseph E	94	boxmaker	39	"
D	Maraghy Mary E—†	94	at home	64	"
E	Conaghan Daniel	96	fireman	33	New Bedford
F	Daley Jane E—†	96	housekeeper	56	here
G	Daley John	96	laborer	67	"
H	Stack Helen M—†	96	operator	20	"
K	Dennehy Joseph	96	freighthandler	45	"
L	Leonard Timothy	96	laborer	65	
M	Reynolds John	96	welder	37	
N	Sullivan Edward	96	laborer	36	

10

11

12

13

14

15

16

9 17

Ward 2–Precinct 9

CITY OF BOSTON

LIST OF RESIDENTS
20 YEARS OF AGE AND OVER

(NON-CITIZENS INDICATED BY ASTERISK)
(FEMALES INDICATED BY DAGGER)

AS OF

JANUARY 1, 1944

THOMAS F. SULLIVAN, *Chairman*
FREDERIC E. DOWLING, *Secretary*
WILLIAM A. MOTLEY, JR.
FRANCIS B. McKINNEY
EVERETT R. PROUT

Listing Board.

CITY OF BOSTON PRINTING DEPARTMENT

900

Austin Street

c	Wong Que	11	laundryman	62	here
D*	Wong Chin Shee—†	11	housewife	46	"
E	Wong Charles L	11	machinist	20	"
F	Wong L You	11	U S A	36	"
K	Smith Nora—†	23	housewife	40	141 Rutherford av
L	Smith Angus T	23	painter	40	141 "
M	Burnham Melvin	25	shipfitter	24	4 Salem St av
N	Canty Bertha E—†	25	housewife	67	4 "
O	Canty Martin W	25	carcleaner	64	4 "
R	Hayes Daniel F	27	riveter	26	20 Wall
S	Hayes Marion C—†	27	housewife	25	20 "
T	Iveson Florence—†	29	operator	20	here
U	Iveson Jessie K—†	29	housewife	68	"
W	Brennan Bernard J	29	U S A	21	"
X	Brennan Mary—†	29	housewife	55	"
Y	Brennan Patrick B	29	warehouse	65	"
¹Y	Scott Helen M—†	31	housewife	34	"
Z	Scott Henry C	31	machinist	40	"

901

A	Serio Adele T—†	31	saleswoman	27	"
B	Serio Concetta—†	31	housewife	28	"
C	Serio Francisco	31	retired	64	
D	Serio Humbert M	31	tailor	22	
E	Serio Joseph	31	U S A	32	
F	Serio Louis A	31	tailor	29	
G	Serio Vincent E	31	"	25	"
L	Rizzotto Guy	35	driller	27	16 Summer
M	Golling Charles R	35	guard	35	here
N	Golling Eleanor—†	35	housewife	36	"
O	McDonald Beatrice—†	35	maid	38	Maine
P	Conca Anna—†	37	housewife	44	here
R	Conca Anthony	37	machinist	44	"
S	McSweeney Daniel F	37	retired	74	"
T	McSweeney Daniel F, jr	37	U S N	33	
U	McSweeney Margaret—†	37	housewife	32	"
W	Crowley John F	39	electrician	28	44 Cranston
X	Freeman Alice F—†	39	housewife	65	42 Wash'n
Y	Freeman Edmund E	39	U S A	30	42 "
Z	Freeman Joseph E	39	cook	65	42 "

Page.	Letter.	Full Name.	Residence, Jan. 1, 1944.	Occupation.	Supposed Age.	Reported Residence, Jan. 1, 1943, Street and Number.

1

902
Austin Street—Continued

A	Holland Arthur F	39	chauffeur	34	5 Wash'n sq
B	Holland Frances—†	39	housewife	22	5 "
c	Hosford Evelyn—†	41	"	26	here
D	Hosford Walter	41	chauffeur	35	"
F	Hickey Catherine—†	41	housewife	21	"
G	Hickey William J	41	U S A	21	"
H	McGaffigan Alice—†	41	operator	50	"
K	Kelly James	43	laborer	54	"
L	Kelly John	43	U S N	22	
M	Kelly Marcella—†	43	housewife	42	"
N	Kelly Edward	43	laborer	55	"
o	Kelly Mary—†	43	housewife	49	"
P	Kelly Philip P	43	U S N	21	"
R	Toomey John G	45	U S A	38	"
s	Toomey Thomas F	45	operator	45	"
T	Ahern Helen T—†	45	housewife	47	"
U	Ahern John P	45	U S A	20	"
V	Ahern Sylvester P	45	manager	47	"
W	Toomey James F	45	welder	41	
X	Mercurio Kathryn A—†	47	defense wkr	39	"
Y	Hosford James	47	U S N	27	
Z	Hosford Nellie—†	47	housewife	74	"

903

B	Allwood Grace L—†	49	operator	20	"
¹B	Allwood John J	49	metalworker	44	"
c	Allwood Mary G—†	49	housewife	43	"
F	McCarthy Mary—†	51	"	66	"
M	Cahill David	71	retired	83	
N	Cahill Mary—†	71	housewife	75	"
o	Morrison Richard	71	U S A	21	
P	Rudd Richard G	71	retired	78	"
s	Murphy Ellen—†	73	housewife	64	"
T	Murphy James E	73	laborer	63	"
U	Murphy Margaret L—†	73	teacher	31	"
V	Finlayson Gertrude E—†	73	housewife	26	"
W	Finlayson Robert A	73	machinist	33	Somerville
X	Hurley Louise B—†	73	clerk	28	here
Y	Harrington Blanche M—†	75	housewife	47	"
Z	Harrington George H	75	storekeeper	50	"

904

Austin Street—Continued

A	McKenzie Charles	75	electrician	54	here
B	McKenzie Katherine—†	75	housewife	52	"
C	Brennan Catherine—†	75	"	57	"
¹C	Brennan James	75	watchman	74	"
D	Brennan Mark	75	shoeworker	53	"
E	Ferretti Margaret—†	89	housewife	30	25 Favre
F	Graves Frank W	89	warden	61	here
G	Graves Mary C—†	89	housewife	49	"

Benedict Street

H	Munden Charles A	1	longshoreman	33	here
K	Munden Mary G—†	1	housewife	35	"
L	Castranova Antoinette—†	9	forewoman	30	"
M	*Castranova Francesca—†	9	housewife	54	"
N	Castranova Joseph J	9	U S A	20	
O	Castranova Salvatore J	9	"	24	
P	Carbonello Aida—†	9	housewife	34	"
R	Carbonello Joseph	9	custodian	41	"
S	Cimino Joseph	9	policeman	24	"
T	Cimino Rita T—†	9	clerk	22	"

Chapman Street

U	Campbell William H	7	longshoreman	49	here
V	McLaughlin Anna V—†	7	housewife	23	"
W	McLaughlin James F	7	longshoreman	24	"
X	Gravelli Charles J	7	chauffeur	39	14 Chapman
Y	Gravelli Maude G—†	7	housewife	46	14 "
Z	McGahan Catherine—†	8	"	68	here

905

A	McGahan Daniel	8	electrician	37	"
B	Noonan Patrick J	8	checker	65	
C	*Outerbridge Harrison	8	mechanic	32	"
D	Outerbridge Mary—†	8	housewife	32	"
E	Findlay Mary L—†	9	"	25	17 Chapman
F	Findlay Reginald H	9	laborer	31	17 "
G	Keddie Edward F	9	electrician	31	here
¹G	Keddie Lena H—†	9	housewife	29	"
H	Foley Edwin H	10	fireman	23	"

K	Foley John T	10	canvasworker	60	here
L	Foley Margaret H—†	10	housewife	58	"
M	Shea Jeremiah	10	seaman	59	"
N	Stimpson Bertha—†	10	cleanser	61	"
O	Stimpson Robert	10	chauffeur	27	"
P	Burk Alice E—†	11	housewife	70	"
R	Burk Daniel J	11	retired	76	
S	Carlton Catherine—†	11	pipecoverer	54	"
V	Smart Mary T—†	15	housewife	63	16A Park
W	*Cahill Patrick	15	retired	73	here
X	*Rooney Daniel	15	"	68	"
Y	Rooney Daniel, jr	15	laborer	29	"
	906				
B	Gallagher Alexandria C—†	16	housewife	41	"
C	Gallagher Sarah—†	16	defense wkr	44	"
D	Gallagher William J	16	ropemaker	41	"
F	Devlin Catherine J—†	17	tel operator	21	"
G	Devlin Sarah—†	17	cook	53	
H	Simpson Katheleen V—†	18	housewife	35	"
K	Simpson William F	18	chauffeur	38	8 School
L	Allwood Lucy—†	18	housewife	59	here
M	Allwood Robert E	18	laborer	28	"
N	Allwood Thomas W	18	U S N	29	"
P	Fitzpatrick Peter A	19	laborer	52	16 Miller
R	Smith Arthur G	19	freighthandler	63	16 "
S	Smith Ruth L—†	19	housewife	49	16 "
T	Morris Francis	19	U S N	32	9 Chapman
U	Morris Sarah P—†	19	housewife	28	9 "
W	Kane Mary—†	41	toymaker	21	here
X	Mullin Mary—†	41	housewife	50	"
Y	Morin Mary F—†	41	"	66	"
	907				
B	Page Andrew M	43	mechanic	48	"
C	Page Mildred D—†	43	housewife	39	"
D	Hoskins Ernest W	43	chauffeur	40	"
F	Bradley Isabel M—†	43	housewife	64	"
E	Kennedy Frank S	43	painter	46	"
K	Seymour Marion—†	45	cook	38	"
L	Scully Mary A—†	45	housewife	62	1262 Dor av
M	Thorn Albert C	45	laborer	59	1262 "
R	Conway Mary E—†	61	housewife	64	here

Chapman Street—Continued

s	Prendergast James A	61	U S A	33	here
T	Prendergast John E	61	guard	65	"
U	Prendergast John E	61	student	35	"
W	Burns George W	66	U S M C	21	"
x	Burns Sarah L—†	66	housewife	37	"
Y	Higgins William J	66	policeman	65	"
z	Smith James J	66	U S A	23	

908

A	Smith Lillian F—†	66	housewife	39	"
B	Campbell Agnes M—†	66	"	29	
c	Campbell William J	66	machinist	30	"
D	O'Connell Francis J	66	welder	25	
¹D	O'Connell Mary A—†	66	housewife	54	"

Dunstable Street

E	Walles Catherine—†	1	housewife	58	327 Main
F	Walles William	1	laborer	20	327 "
G	Wharff Clifford	1	"	40	327 "
H	Wharff Gertrude—†	1	housewife	31	327 "
P	DiMasi Mary—†	44	hairdresser	35	here
R	DiMasi Pasqualina—†	44	housewife	58	"
s	DiMasi Philomena—†	44	seamstress	27	"

Frothingham Avenue

U	Hitchcock Edward	1	foreman	43	here
V	Hitchcock Eleanor—†	1	housewife	24	"
W	Cain Nellie M—†	1	"	71	"
Y	Callahan Emma—†	3	"	47	
z	Callahan Margaret—†	3	seamstress	21	"

909

A	Callahan Timothy J	3	retired	49	
B	Lang Helen—†	5	stenographer	20	"
c	Lang Ida—†	5	housewife	48	"
D	Lang John	5	fishcutter	59	"

Hathon Square

F	Healy Irene—†	5	at home	20	here
G	Healy Jeremiah	5	blacksmith	55	"

Hathon Square—Continued

H	Healy Mary—†	5	clerk	27	here
K	Hines James	5	longshoreman	32	"
¹K	Hines Obelina—†	5	housewife	32	"
L	Powers Mary E—†	5	"	64	"
M	Powers Maurice	5	retired	65	"
N	Hughes Annie M—†	5½	housewife	64	86 Wash'n
O	Hughes James J	5½	clerk	31	86 "
P	Hughes Michael W	5½	retired	73	86 "
R	Ivey James J	5½	electrician	27	19 Park
S	Francey Caleb A	5½	pedler	74	here
T	Francey Julia—†	5½	housewife	49	"
U	Houlihan Lucy—†	6	"	45	"
V	Houlihan Rose—†	6	leatherworker	23	"
W	Selig Eleanor—†	6	packer	21	"
X	Selig Harriet—†	6	housewife	41	"
Y	Selig Virginia—†	6	clerk	20	
Z	Selig William	6	longshoreman	42	"

910

A	McDonald Angus	7	clerk	40	
B	Ratchford James	7	electrician	39	"
C	Ratchford Vivian—†	7	housewife	32	"
D	Cole George	7	carpenter	44	Vermont
E	Cole Margaret—†	7	housewife	43	"
F	Ashe Richard	8	pedler	51	here
G	*Hurley Catherine—†	8	housekeeper	61	"

High Street

H	Bell Burgess	58	U S N	37	Oklahoma
K	Bell Dorothy—†	58	housewife	23	"
L	Brown Bessie—†	58	"	51	here
M	Brown Harry	58	manager	52	"
N	Byerly Juliet—†	58	machinist	44	"
O	Byerly Louis	58	laborer	45	"
P	Davis Gertrude—†	58	housewife	63	"
R	Davis Wilbur	58	machinist	60	"
S	Feihert Lester	58	boilermaker	50	"
T	Feihert Nellie—†	58	housewife	46	"
U	Hickox Ata—†	58	"	30	Virginia
V	Hickox John	58	U S N	31	"

Page.	Letter.	FULL NAME.	Residence, Jan. 1, 1944.	Occupation.	Supposed Age.	Reported Residence, Jan. 1, 1943. Street and Number.

High Street—Continued

	w	Mulvey Henry	58	mechanic	54	47 Monum'nt sq
	x	Mulvey Isabelle—†	58	housewife	53	47 "
	y	Pigeon Helen—†	58	"	44	New Bedford
	z	Pigeon Walter	58	laborer	48	"
911						
	A	Slane Edward J	58	manager	59	here
	B	Santos Blandina—†	66	housewife	68	"
	c	Santos Joseph L	66	ropemaker	52	"
	D	Connors John J	66	electrician	34	"
	E	Hourihan Mary—†	66	housewife	30	"
	F	Hourihan William J	66	coppersmith	32	"
	G	Myers Ellen—†	66	housewife	36	"
	H	Kirk Helen M—†	68	"	42	
	K	Kirk James F	68	electrician	43	"
	L	Collins Helen G—†	68	housewife	33	"
	M	Collins James J	68	lineman	41	"
	N	Collins Joseph	68	seaman	21	
	P	Delory Sarah G—†	70	housewife	45	"
	R	Lawless Catherine J—†	70	"	51	
	s	Lawless Catherine M—†	70	typist	24	
	T	Lawless Joseph F	70	policeman	53	"
	U	Aaron Edward A	70	teacher	38	
	V	Blagdon Joseph M	70	physician	55	"
	w	Monahan Frank	70	clerk	75	
	x	Monahan Frank, jr	70	U S N	42	
	Y	Monahan Helen—†	70	stenographer	30	"
	z	Monahan Joseph	70	U S A	38	..
912						
	A	Campbell Clara—†	72	housewife	25	58 High
	B	Campbell Ray	72	U S A	25	58 "
	c	Cummings John	72	laborer	40	here
	D	Cummings Joseph	72	"	37	"
	E	Cummings Margaret—†	72	housewife	38	"
	F	Isabelle Claude J	72	steamfitter	40	"
	G	Isabelle Florence—†	72	housewife	48	"
	H	Kruper Eva—†	72	"	25	
	K	Kruper John	72	U S A	27	"
	L	Mitchell Alfred	72	"	35	Florida
	M	Mitchell Frances—†	72	secretary	36	"
	N	Piper Helen—†	72	housewife	42	12 Park

8

o	Piper John	72	laborer	42	14 Monum'ntav
p	Piper Leo W	72	"	50	12 Park
r	Piper Mary—†	72	housewife	38	14 Monum'ntav
t	Skrzesniuski Frederick	72	U S A	32	here
s	Skrzesniuski Helen—†	72	housewife	29	"
u	Fields Alice E—†	74	"	40	10 Salem
v	Fields Walter S	74	steamfitter	42	10 "
w	Coe Calvin	76	teamster	75	here
x	Coe Ellsworth W	76	U S A	26	"
y	Coe Herbert K	76	stockman	39	"
z*	Coe Theresa—†	76	housewife	60	"

913

a	Coe Walter L	76	packer	41	
b	Kaczenski Thomas J	76	blacksmith	53	"
c	Mosher Frederick E	76	retired	68	"
d	Wardwell Walter	76	shipwright	50	"
e	Keegan Dora T—†	80	housewife	50	"
f	Keegan Mary—†	80	clerk	22	
g	O'Leary Cecelia—†	80	stitcher	47	"
h	McCabe Anne—†	80	matron	40	"
k	McCabe Frank	80	laborer	42	" .
l	Gillen George	82	retired	65	
m	Gillen Helen—†	82	housewife	65	"
n	Gillen Rose—†	82	clerk	36	
o	McDonald Pauline—†	82	bookkeeper	38	"
p	Frost Beatrice A—†	84	domestic	49	"
r	Ramsey Ada—†	84	housewife	75	"
s	Ramsey Alice—†	84	clerk	47	
t	Ramsey Forrest	84	"	47	"
u	Keating John	86	laborer	25	15 Lincoln
v	Keating Miriam E—†	86	housewife	26	15 "
w	McLaughlin Agnes M—†	86	"	73	here
x	O'Brien Margaret—†	86	"	50	"
y	O'Brien Patrick	86	laborer	52	"
z	Doherty Anna—†	88	housewife	34	"

914

a	Doherty Thomas	88	longshoreman	37	"
b	Doherty Charles	88	laborer	60	"
c	Doherty Grace—†	88	housewife	55	"
d	Doherty Theresa—†	88	typist	22	

9

Page.	Letter.	FULL NAME.	Residence, Jan. 1, 1944.	Occupation.	Supposed Age.	Reported Residence, Jan. 1, 1943. Street and Number.

High Street—Continued

E	Higgins Edward T	90	laborer	63	here
F	Higgins Rose H—†	90	housewife	67	"
G	Chase Julia—†	90	"	26	"
H	Corcoran Annie—†	90	"	50	
K	Corcoran Michael	90	laborer	60	
L	Corcoran Timothy	90	U S A	24	
M	Fraser Joseph L	92	laborer	58	
N	Fraser Mary A—†	92	housewife	51	"
O	McLaughlin Catherine F-†	92	packer	38	114 High
P	McLaughlin James	92	teamster	37	114 "
R	McLaughlin Rose E—†	92	housewife	70	here
S	Duke Hazel—†	92	"	20	Montana
T	Duke Willard	92	U S N	23	"
U	Sharkey Maxine—†	92	housewife	20	34 Monum'nt sq
V	Sharkey Ray	92	U S N	34	34 "
W	Cataldi Helen—†	94	housewife	21	here
X	O'Neil Harriett M—†	94	"	45	"
Y	O'Neil James F	94	laborer	46	"
Z	Manning James	94	"	54	
	915				
A	Manning James	94	U S A	22	
B	Manning John F	94	"	25	
C	Manning Joseph	94	"	23	
D	Manning Mary—†	94	clerk	20	
E	Manning Nora—†	94	housewife	57	"
F	Pailley Helen—†	96	"	25	
G	Pailley Norman	96	laborer	30	
H	Crowley Joseph	96	"	50	"
K	Dever Mary—†	96	housewife	57	"
L	Donovan Joseph	96	laborer	47	
M	Hutchinson Edna—†	98	housewife	37	"
N	Hutchinson James A	98	carpenter	38	"
O	Irving Alice—†	98	housewife	76	"
P	Irving Belle S—†	98	secretary	45	"
R	Irving Russell H	98	clerk	49	"
S	Irving William D	98	retired	75	
T	McNamara Catherine—†	100	housewife	71	"
U	McNamara Catherine—†	100	chemist	38	"
V	McNamara John	100	longshoreman	40	"
W	Roche Patrick	100	janitor	72	Burlington

Homestead Place

z	Johnson Frank R	5	inspector	20	here
	916				
A	Johnson Helen—†	5	housewife	52	"
B	Johnson Helen—†	5	dressmaker	22	"
C	Craffam Goldie B—†	5A	housewife	41	"
D	Doyle Augustus	5A	retired	73	
E	Hurd Abbie A—†	5A	at home	75	"
F	Keigney Helen F—†	5A	housewife	33	"
G	Keigney John F	5A	laborer	33	"
H	Baird Annie B—†	7	housewife	80	Malden
K	Baird Seth C	7	laborer	67	"
L	Ault Frederick W	7	operator	57	here
M	Ault Margaret J—†	7	housewife	46	"
N	Emerald Emelia—†	7A	"	66	56 School

Johnson Avenue

O	Plunkett John E	8	retired	59	18 Frothingham av
P	Plunkett Margaret T—†	8	housewife	49	18 "
R	Powell Harold J	8	laborer	43	18 "
S	McLaughlin Ellen—†	8	housewife	58	here
T	McLaughlin Francis P	8	U S A	29	"
U	McLaughlin Joseph M	8	shipfitter	26	"
V	McLaughlin Mary E—†	8	at home	24	"
W	McLaughlin Patrick J	8	laborer	64	"
X	Wallace Albert A	8	"	37	96 Bartlett
Y	Wallace Ethel L—†	8	housewife	38	96 "
z	Lutton Ernest	10	janitor	42	here
	917				
A	Spaulding Mary J—†	10	housewife	27	Malden
B	Spaulding Walter J	10	clerk	29	"
C	Doherty Madge—†	10	housewife	35	here
D	Doherty Patrick	10	laborer	36	"
E	Letellier Emma R—†	12	housewife	46	"
F	Letellier Francis J	12	U S N	24	"
G	Letellier Joseph T	12	trackman	49	"
H	Letellier Joseph T, jr	12	shipfitter	27	"
K	Letellier Rita R—†	12	saleswoman	24	"
L	Lyons Gertrude F—†	12	housewife	67	"

11

Johnson Avenue—Continued

	M	Abbott Grace—†	12	housewife	70	here
	N	Stone Frances—†	12	inspector	35	"

Lawnwood Place

	O	Brennan Daniel J	1	retired	72	Michigan
	P	Brown Hannah J—†	1	housewife	74	here
	R	Brown James	1	retired	73	"
	S	Childs Dorothy—†	1	secretary	34	"
	T	Childs George L	1	U S A	35	Natick
	U	Kelly Edwin	1	retired	76	34 Harvard
	V	McLaughlin Joseph	1	freighthandler	33	Everett
	W	Murray Cornelius	1	"	38	Texas
	X	Manley Patrick	2	retired	76	here
	Y	Manley Rita P—†	2	at home	27	"
	Z	Mulkern Mary J—†	2	housewife	35	195 Cornell
		918				
	A	Manley Edward J	2	foreman	40	here
	B	Manley William P	2	mechanic	42	"
	C	Chiampa Edward J	3	U S A	29	"
	D	Chiampa Flora R—†	3	housewife	61	"
	E	Chiampa Florence T—†	3	factoryhand	27	"
	F	Chiampa Gertrude—†	3	housewife	28	"
	G	Chiampa Joseph	3	cook	37	
	H	Chiampa Louise—†	3	factoryhand	33	"
	K	Chiampa Mary A—†	3	"	42	
	L	*Chiampa Pasquale	3	retired	62	
	M	King Alice—†	3A	factoryhand	35	"
	N	Monahan James J	3A	pipefitter	56	"
	O	Monahan Rhoda E—†	3A	housewife	50	"
	P	Kosak Frances—†	3A	saleswoman	21	"
	R	Kosak Gertrude—†	3A	housewife	50	"
	S	Kosak Louis	3A	presser	52	
	T	Davis Julia C—†	3A	housewife	33	"
	U	Davis Wynn C	3A	inspector	44	"
	V	Hutchings Mildred—†	3A	forewoman	45	43 Fabyan
	W	Galvin Florence C—†	4	housewife	43	here
	X	Galvin Francis J	4	U S A	21	"
	Y	Galvin Maurice F	4	chauffeur	42	"
	Z	Long Peter	4	cabinetmaker	60	"

919

Lawnwood Place—Continued

A	McKendry Daniel V	5	painter	56	here
B	McKendry Leo F	5	clerk	45	"
C	McKendry Mary E—†	5	housekeeper	62	"
D	Sullivan Elizabeth M—†	5	"	66	"
E	Cavanagh John P	6	carpenter	49	Rhode Island
F	Cavanagh Mary I—†	6	housewife	43	here
G	Cavanagh Walter J	6	longshoreman	21	"
H	Cavanagh Walter S	6	carpenter	47	"
K	Drummond James	6	rigger	57	
L	Sargent George B	6	laborer	56	"
M	Sweeney Joseph	6	restaurateur	61	"
N	Tucker James	6	longshoreman	65	"
O	Kelly Agnes—†	7	housewife	39	"
P	Kelly Daniel W	7	chauffeur	48	"
R	Fidler Arthur E	8	laborer	29	
S	Fidler Edward L	8	U S A	25	
T	Fidler James R	8	retired	68	
U	Fidler James R, jr	8	painter	37	"
V	Fidler Raymond F	8	U S A	27	"
W	Fidler Robert H	8	"	30	
X	Fidler Susan—†	8	housewife	61	"
Z	Wager George F	8	chauffeur	38	"
Y	Wager Marion—†	8	housewife	39	"

920

A	Birt Charles	9	retired	66	"
B	Collins Michael J	9	"	71	71 Main
C	Gillis William	9	shipfitter	47	here
D	*Kehoe Augustine	9	laborer	66	"
E	*Kehoe Margaret—†	9	housewife	49	"
F	O'Keefe John E	9	retired	77	"
G	Shuman George W	9	laborer	53	
H	Fraser William A	10	salesman	57	"
K	McClean George C	10	U S A	22	"
L	McClean Henry P	10	warehouse	68	"
M	McClean Josephine E—†	10	housewife	63	"
N	McClean Josephine P—†	10	at home	24	"
O	McClean William R	10	U S A	28	
P	Ruiz Evelyn K—†	10	at home	34	"
R	Black John	11	clerk	60	"
S	Hansen Albert J	11	U S N	21	"

13

Page.	Letter.	FULL NAME.	Residence, Jan. 1, 1944.	Occupation.	Supposed Age.	Reported Residence, Jan. 1, 1943. Street and Number.

Lawnwood Place—Continued

T	Hansen Lundal	11	longshoreman	54	here
U	Hansen Mary—†	11	housewife	57	"
V	Hansen William J	11	U S A	22	"
W	McPhee Lawrence	11	watchman	54	"
X	Tobin Mary—†	11	housewife	30	"
Y	Degnan William J	12	electrician	52	"
Z	Fisher Francis X	12	U S N	28	Somerville

921

A	Fisher Margaret—†	12	waitress	22	"
B	Goodall Robert L	12	U S N	24	Fitchburg
C	Goodall Virginia D—†	12	cashier	22	"
D	Harvey Loren L	12	welder	30	"
E	Harvey Phyllis M—†	12	packer	28	"
G	Mansfield Frieda K—†	12	housewife	67	here
F	Ford Katherine T—†	14	"	62	"
H	Ford William T	14	salesman	69	"
K	Heckley Freeman	15	painter	42	2 Franklin
L	Heckley George W	15	"	43	2 "
M	Heckley Gertrude—†	15	housewife	40	2 "
N	Heckley John	15	U S N	20	2 "
O	Masters William	15	retired	70	2 "

Lawrence Avenue

P	Roberts Madison	2	shipfitter	48	Lowell
R	Barnum Jean—†	2	housewife	35	here
S	Barnum Reese	2	operator	40	"
T	McQuade George	2	seaman	25	"
U	McQuade Susan—†	2	housewife	22	"

Lawrence Street

V	Doherty Albert A	23	U S A	31	here
W	Doherty Cornelius F	23	mechanic	40	"
X	Doherty James R	23	laborer	33	"
Y	Doherty Mary E—†	23	housewife	63	"
Z	Doherty Mary E—†	23	clerk	22	

922

A	Moran Leo	25	retired	78	
B	Rogers Charlotte F—†	25	housewife	65	"
C	Rogers James J	25	stevedore	58	"

14

Lawrence Street—Continued

F	Godfrey Estelle M—†	27	milliner	20	here	
G	Godfrey Lillian—†	27	housewife	43	"	
H	Godfrey Walter M	27	chipper	45	"	
L	Auld Ellen E—†	34	housewife	53	"	
M	Auld Eugene R	34	U S A	20		
N	Auld Francis	34	freighthandler	30	"	
O	Auld George	34	U S A	28		
P	Auld Mary E—†	34	housekeeper	23	"	
R	Auld Robert E	34	laborer	62	"	
S	Connors Francis E	34	"	53	"	
T	Needham Bridget A—†	34	housekeeper	59	"	
U	Smith James D	34	operator	37	"	
V	Smith Helen M—†	34	housekeeper	36	"	
W	Godfrey Beatrice C—†	34	cook	53	"	
X	Chiampa Patrick W	35	electrician	24	3 Lawnwood pl	
Y	Chiampa Virginia—†	35	housewife	22	8 "	
Z	Downey Julia—†	35	cashier	20	Somerville	
	923					
A	Ruiz Dorothy—†	35	housewife	23	16 Franklin	
B	Ruiz Edward	35	U S A	24	16 "	
C	Novello Margaret—†	35	housewife	28	16 Lawrence	
D	Novello Rosario	35	fireman	32	16 "	
E	McCarthy Catherine H—†	39	cashier	44	here	
F	McCarthy Cornelius F	39	shipfitter	42	"	
G	McCarthy Margaret F—†	39	housekeeper	29	"	
H	McCarthy Mary J—†	39	"	38	"	
M	Murphy James E	43	foreman	40	"	
N	Murphy Margaret—†	43	housewife	38	"	
O	O'Brien Catherine V—†	45	"	32		
P	O'Brien Gerald T	45	chauffeur	34	"	
R	Cefalo John	47	laborer	57		
S	Cefalo Mary—†	47	candyworker	20	"	
T	*Cefalo Stella—†	47	housewife	51	"	
U	Rowe Josephine G—†	49	"	68		
V	Rowe Nicholas J	49	retired	67		
W	Murphy Josephine G—†	49	housewife	32	"	
X	Murphy Leo J	49	freighthandler	43	"	
Y	Tortella Charles	49	clerk	68		
Z	Tortella Della—†	49	housewife	66	"	
	924					
B	Powers Josephine—†	51	"	58		

15

Page.	Letter.	FULL NAME.	Residence, Jan. 1, 1944.	Occupation.	Supposed Age.	Reported Residence, Jan. 1, 1943. Street and Number.

Lawrence Street—Continued

c	Green Aidan J	61	longshoreman	46	here
D	Green Elizabeth M—†	61	housewife	48	"
E	Davis Edward	63	retired	84	"
F	Dunn George P	63	florist	60	
G	O'Neil Mary F—†	65	housewife	34	"
H	O'Neil Matthew A	65	longshoreman	37	"
N	Kelsey Bertha—†	71	housewife	53	345 Main
O	Kelsey Francis	71	laborer	22	345 "
P	Kelsey Thomas	71	chauffeur	25	345 "
R	McLennan Dorothy—†	71	canvasmaker	28	345 "
S	McLennan Joseph	71	laborer	28	345 "
T	Howard Pearl A—†	71	housewife	28	45 Chapman
U	Howard Robert	71	chauffeur	31	45 "
V	Sweeney Agnes A—†	71	restaurateur	62	here
W	Sweeney Catherine E—†	71	housekeeper	69	"
X	Sweeney Charles E	71	packer	59	"
Y	Kelley Catherine—†	73	housewife	33	"
Z	Kelley William C	73	painter	34	"

925

A	Young Mary E—†	73	electrician	37	"
B	Young Orick D	73	U S N	40	
D	Gillespie Edward G	75	fireman	57	"
E	Gillespie George T	75	retired	80	
F	Gillespie William F	75	fireman	56	..

Lynde Avenue

L	Anini Antonio	6	retired	61	here
N	Love Henry S	6	painter	58	"

Main Street

U	*Bushard Lucy—†	160	at home	64	here
V	*Bushard Uldric	160	retired	65	"
W	Ringer Albert T	160	longshoreman	41	"
X	Ringer Mary—†	160	housewife	43	"
Y	Hawkins Mary—†	160	"	45	
Z	Hawkins William	160	laborer	45	

926

B	O'Leary Margaret—†	166	cook	37	
C	Connolly Francis	166	U S A	21	

16

D	Connolly Gertrude—†	166	baker	25	here
E	Connolly Joseph M	166	U S A	24	"
F	Connolly Mary G—†	166	housewife	57	"
G	Connolly Michael F	166	retired	61	
H	Connolly Mary F—†	166	packer	30	
O	Morrison Malcom	174	retired	70	
P	Proulx Florence—†	174	housewife	57	"
R	Proulx Joseph	174	carpenter	58	"
S	Proulx Rita J—†	174	clerk	22	
T	Proulx Wilfred J	174	U S A	24	
W	Devlin Margaret—†	188	housewife	35	"
X	Devlin Michael	188	laborer	48	"
Y	Tipton Anna—†	188	welder	20	19 Chapman
Z	Tipton Catherine—†	188	housewife	45	19 "
	927				
A	Tipton William	188	chauffeur	44	19 "
K	Ruiz Eleanor—†	191	at home	49	here
L	Ruiz Fernando	191	shipfitter	65	"
M	Masavy Donato B	191	packer	52	"
R	*McGowan Catherine—†	198	housewife	67	"
S	*McGowan John	198	retired	74	"
T	O'Hare Catherine—†	198	stenographer	34	"
U	O'Hare Edward	198	supervisor	34	"
V	McGowan Catherine F—†	200	housewife	50	"
W	McGowan James E	200	retired	73	
X	Godsell Annie—†	200	housewife	64	"
Y	Godsell John E	200	laborer	50	"
Z	Laudato Gaetano J	200	fireman	26	"
	928				
A	Laudato Margaret J—†	200	housewife	24	"
F	Benetto Joseph	206	longshoreman	60	349 Main
G	Collins John	206	laborer	63	79 Warren
H	Dickerson Edward	206	retired	65	here
K	Esterbrook Theodore	206	laborer	40	19 Perkins
L	Homes George	206	retired	70	here
M	Mahoney Michael	206	longshoreman	52	"
N	McFacy James	206	chauffeur	55	23 Green
O	McGrath Michael	206	laborer	54	here
P	McNamara Charles	206	retired	70	"
R	O'Connor Daniel	206	longshoreman	41	"
S	Raftell Charles	206	storekeeper	52	"

2—9   17

Page.	Letter.	FULL NAME.	Residence, Jan. 1, 1944.	Occupation.	Supposed Age.	Reported Residence, Jan. 1, 1943. Street and Number.

Main Street—Continued

T	Reardon John	206	retired	64	here
U	Scanlon John	206	longshoreman	63	"
V	Burns Michael	208	laborer	62	"
W	Burns William	208	longshoreman	41	"
X	*Carlson Gerda—†	208	housewife	59	"
Y	*Carlson Malcolm	208	manager	63	"
Z	Casey John	208	laborer	63	

929

A	Coady John.	208	"	67	..
¹A	Corcoran Robert	208	machinist	55	"
B	Gill John	208	retired	65	"
C	Graham Archibald	208	plumber	65	22 Harvard
D	Kelly Patrick	208	laborer	62	here
E	Kinsella John	208	retired	75	"
F	Murphy Michael	208	"	66	8 Salem St av
G	Webb Alexander	208	fireman	50	here
H	Higgins William	209	laborer	25	Somerville
K	Keeley Florence—†	209	clerk	22	here
L	McNeill Mary A—†	209	at home	87	"
M	Walsh James J	209	longshoreman	35	Somerville
N	Walsh John	209	"	38	"
O	Walsh Julia—†	209	housewife	60	"
P	Walsh Timothy J	209	chauffeur	21	"
R	Walsh William	209	longshoreman	25	"
S	Dwyer Patrick	210	laborer	52	here
T	Kelly John	210	retired	67	"
U	Kelly Sarah J—†	210	housewife	69	"
W	*Byrne Mildred—†	212A	"	35	Canada
X	Manson Grace L—†	213	"	43	here
Y	Manson Peter M	213	chauffeur	43	"

930

C	Faye James	217	longshoreman	58	"
D	Faye Margaret—†	217	housewife·	56	"
E	Faye Margaret V—†	217	clerk	26	
F	McInnis Anna F—†	217	housewife	39	"
G	McInnis John P	217	driller	41	
Z	Peters Arthur M	255	clerk	40	

931

A	Peters Jennie E—†	255	housewife	38	"
B	Murphy Anna M—†	255	"	53	
C	Murphy Frank J	255	laborer	60	

D	Lauretano Carmella—†	256	housewife	64	16 Call
E	Lauretano Frank	256	barber	37	16 "
F	Lauretano Vincent	256	shoemaker	66	16 "
G	Gilgum Joseph A	256	U S A	21	here
H	Gilgum Mary E—†	256	housewife	55	"
K	Gilgum Thomas	256	laborer	51	"
L	Gilgum Thomas, jr	256	U S A	23	
M	Eidelman Annie—†	257	housewife	62	"
N	Eidelman Louis	257	retired	67	
O	Eidelman Dora J—†	257	housewife	51	"
P	Eidelman Nathan	257	broker	56	
R	Benham Walter E	258	longshoreman	29	"
S	Brodie George F	258	chemist	59	58 Sullivan
T	Coffey Daniel J	258	laborer	45	here
U	Crowley Timothy	258	retired	80	"
V	Farmer Leo F	258	machinist	49	"
W	Henker Elizabeth—†	258	housewife	55	189 Main
X	Henker Emil	258	storekeeper	55	here
Y	Kwasnieski Joseph	258	laborer	30	Deerfield
Z	Lacey Patrick	258	"	29	New Bedford
	932				
A	McNeil Joseph	258	machinist	56	here
B	Moore Walter P	258	shipfitter	42	"
C	Mullowney Michael E	258	carpenter	58	"
D	O'Leary Michael	258	rigger	39	
E	O'Neil William D	258	electrician	42	"
F	Rafferty George W	258	watchman	63	"
G	Regan Ralph	258	chauffeur	42	Somerville
H	Semerino Basil	258	laborer	30	Pittsfield
K	Sullivan William J	258	pipefitter	51	390 Main
L	Walsh George J	258	longshoreman	44	here
M	Wininger George F	258	laborer	42	"
R	Crogan Evelyn M—†	261A	housewife	23	"
S	Crogan Francis	261A	chauffeur	53	"
T	Bromfield Margaret—†	261A	housewife	65	"
U	Littlefield Fred H	261A	chauffeur	65	"
V	Gordon David	263	U S A	27	
W	Gordon Edward T	263	student	20	"
X	Gordon Jennie—†	263	housewife	58	"
Y	Gordon Nathan A	263	U S A	33	
Z	Gordon Samuel	263	storekeeper	54	"

Page.	Letter.	FULL NAME.	Residence, Jan. 1, 1944.	Occupation.	Supposed Age.	Reported Residence, Jan. 1, 1943. Street and Number.

933
Main Street—Continued

A		Faldetta Charles	263	barber	64	here
B		Faldetta Theresa—†	263	housewife	54	"
D		Madden Catherine—†	267	at home	81	"
E		Madden Ellen—†	267	"	75	
F		Phalen John J	267	retired	63	

Miller Street

T		Gaynor Mary—†	4	housewife	64	41 Lawrence
U		Carrigan Mary—†	9	"	62	here
V		Covell Arthur	9	shipper	60	"
W		Moscaritolo Ferna—†	9	defense wkr	30	N·Hampshire
X		Moscaritolo Louis	9	chipper	31	"
Y		Harrington Alice—†	10	housewife	36	here
Z		Harrington John	10	laborer	37	"

934

A		Gallant Adeline—†	11	housekeeper	65	17 Trenton
B		Rogers Annie V—†	11	housewife	45	here
C		Rogers Dorothy—†	11	typist	21	"
D		Rogers Frederick	11	chauffeur	46	"
F		Brack Frederick A	13	U S A	30	
G		Brack Louise E—†	13	operator	27	"
H		Brack Margaret M—†	13	matron	50	
K		Brack Samuel C	13	attendant	24	"
L		Doocey Dorothy—†	13	"	23	Long Island
N		Loveless Burton	15	clerk	32	here
O		Loveless Catherine—†	15	matron	55	"
P		Loveless Dorothy—†	15	housewife	31	"
R		Loveless Edwin	15	chauffeur	31	"
S		Cushing Lottie G—†	16	housewife	77	"
T		Smith Charles	16	chauffeur	30	3310 Wash'n
U		Smith Edmund	16	machinist	30	3310 "
V		Smith Edwin	16	laborer	66	3310 "
W		Smith Ella—†	16	housewife	26	3310 "
X		Harris Katherine—†	18	"	65	here
Y		Harris Richard	18	laborer	68	"

935

A		Harris Richard	18	U S A	33	
B		Harris Thomas	18	"	34	
C		Lynch James J	18	longshoreman	45	"

Miller Street—Continued

D	Lynch Mary—†	18	housewife	40	here
E	Gould Annie G—†	20	"	64	"
F	Gould Joseph L	20	teamster	62	"

Phipps Street

G	Alpert Eva—†	1	housewife	49	here
H	Alpert Ralph	1	U S N	29	"
K	Estudila Felix	1	"	40	"
L	Estudila Florence—†	1	housewife	34	"
M	Green Philip	1	shipper	55	"
N	Smith Charles	1	rigger	30	Uxbridge
O	Smith Ethel—†	1	housewife	29	"
P	Ahern Arlene—†	3	"	43	here
R	Ahern Philip	3	electrician	47	"
S	Colby Henry	7	laborer	30	"
T	Colby Susie—†	7	housewife	69	"
U	Hatcher Alan	7	laborer	46	47 Sullivan
V	White Eva—†	7	packer	40	here
W	Blaikie John	12	U S C G	38	"
X	Blaikie Mary—†	12	saleswoman	30	"
Y	Langille Fred F	12	mechanic	31	384 Main
Z	Langille Mary A—†	12	housewife	30	Brookline

936   Rutherford Avenue

G	Boucher Catherine M—†	175	housewife	43	here
H	Parrino Manuele	175	shoeworker	49	"
K	*Parrino Lorretta—†	175	housewife	43	"
L	Ott Annie—†	175	at home	66	"
M	Ott Frederick	175	longshoreman	60	"
N	Dowd Anna E—†	177	housewife	32	"
O	Venezia James A	177	shoe worker	28	"
P	Venezia Josephine—†	177	housewife	26	"
R	Wilson Ada A—†	177	at home	53	"
T	Maloney Nora—†	190	housewife	68	"
U	Maloney Patrick F	190	retired	74	
V	O'Hearn Catherine F—†	190	housewife	29	"
W	O'Hearn Edward J	190	chauffeur	32	"
X	Coughig Elizabeth—†	194	housekeeper	64	"
Y	Doyle Corabell—†	194	housewife	40	"

Rutherford Avenue—Continued

	z	Doyle John F	194	laborer	45	here
937						
	B	Vance Mildred I—†	214	housewife	47	"
	c	Vance Perley S	214	guard	47	"
	D	Nolan Ann J—†	216	at home	65	"
	E	Kelley Edwin	218	student	20	"
	F	Kelley Helen—†	218	housewife	45	"
	G	Kelley John D	218	guard	47	
	H	Kelley John D, jr	218	U S N	21	"
	K	McKenna Timothy A	218	clerk	73	Somerville

938　　Salem Street

	c	McDonald Frank	1	pressman	40	here
	D	McDonald Mary—†	1	housewife	33	"
	E	Scadding Elizabeth—†	1	student	24	58 School
	F	Scadding James	1	mechanic	20	58 "
	G	Scadding John	1	U S N	50	58 "
	H	Scadding John	1	"	24	58 '
	K	Scadding Joseph	1	U S A	22	58 '
	L	Scadding Julia—†	1	housewife	52	58 "
	M	*Donovan Elva—†	1	"	40	here
	N	*Robles Cardina—†	5	"	53	"
	o	Robles Emilio	5	fireman	60	"
	P	Robles Erminia—†	5	clerk	23	
	R	Robles Mary—†	5	stitcher	25	"
	s	Preston Jennie L—†	7	housewife	54	"
	T	Bux Anna A—†	9	stenographer	21	"
	u	Bux Mary C—†	9	housewife	50	"
	v	Bux Michael A	9	mechanic	59	"
	w	Bux Modest P	9	U S N	30	
	x	Bux Vincent	9	rigger	36	
	y	Austin Edward A	11	foreman	44	"
	z	Austin Margaret—†	11	housewife	30	"
939						
	A	Lent Arthur	11	driller	54	
	B	Lent Arthur R	11	U S A	26	
	c	Lent Edith F—†	11	clerk	20	
	D	Lent Florence—†	11	housewife	50	"
	E	Ryder Mabel A—†	11	housekeeper	56	"
	F	O'Donnell James H	13	chauffeur	44	"

Page.	Letter.	FULL NAME.	Residence, Jan. 1, 1944.	Occupation.	Supposed Age.	Reported Residence, Jan. 1, 1943. Street and Number.

Salem Street—Continued

G	O'Donnell Jane—†	13	housewife	73	here
H	O'Donnell Joseph N	13	policeman	42	"
K	O'Donnell Mary A—†	13	housewife	39	"
N	Kelly Thomas	17	longshoreman	20	244 Bunker Hill
O	Zaccone Antonio	17	laborer	57	here
P	Zaccone Catherine—†	17	housewife	54	"
R	Zaccone Josephine—†	17	clerk	24	"
S	Zaccone Rose C—†	17	secretary	22	"
T	Nagle Nora—†	17	housewife	46	"
U	Howard Barbara L—†	19	operator	20	"
V	Howard Catherine—†	19	"	25	
W	Howard Irene—†	19	housewife	48	"
X	Howard John	19	pipefitter	51	"
Y	Howard John R	19	U S A	27	
Z	Howard Victor A	19	fireman	24	"
	940				
A	Howard Walter E	19	U S A	23	
B	Howard William F	19	"	25	"
C	Gillen Joseph P	21	electrician	35	"
G	Gillen Mary G—†	21	housewife	33	"
F	McCarthy Frank	21	laborer	50	"
G	Mazloumian Mardiros	25	"	54	
H	*Mazloumian Zarouhi—†	25	housewife	46	"

School Street

K	Walsh Mary—†	1	housewife	51	here
L	Walsh Thomas	1	U S N	24	"
M	Walsh William	1	laborer	53	"
N	Tompkins Adeline—†	1	at home	68	"
O	Tompkins Catherine—†	1	housewife	23	"
P	Tompkins Donald	1	stevedore	34	"
S	Mitchell Henrietta—†	3	housewife	43	212A Main
T	Mitchell Joseph F	3	rigger	44	212A "
U	Mitchell Paul F	3	U S N	20	212A "
V	Killilea Elizabeth—†	5	housekeeper	66	27 Lawrence
W	Robertson Rovina—†	5	sorter	37	27 "
X	Shea William	5	laborer	40	here
Z	Oxenham Annie—†	5	housekeeper	60	"
	941				
A	Millard Isaac	5	laborer	40	"

School Street—Continued

c	Shea Edith—†	6	housewife	52	17 Oak
d	Shea Patrick	6	laborer	54	17 "
e	Simpson Edward	8	chauffeur	35	here
f	Simpson Juanita—†	8	housewife	35	"
g	Smith Albert	8	longshoreman	47	"
h	Smith Florence J—†	8	housewife	22	"
k	Smith Mary T—†	8	"	47	
l	Smith Robert E	8	laborer	21	
n	Araya Paul R	10	baker	57	"
o	Mellen Arthur E	10	U S A	32	"
p	Mellen Margaret—†	10	housewife	68	"
r	Harrington James	12	laborer	70	"
s	McDermott Lillian—†	12	waitress	31	"
t	McDermott Walter	12	U S N	40	
u	Murphy Alice—†	12	saleswoman	40	"
v	Murphy Bridget—†	12	housewife	70	"
w	Wesley Albert L	12	guard	59	411 Main
y	French Charles W	14	finisher	74	here
z	French Joseph A	14	retired	76	"

942

a	French Mary E—†	14	housewife	67	"
b	Campbell Annie—†	14	"	48	
c	Campbell William	14	laborer	27	
d	Corbin Maud—†	16	boxmaker	43	"
e	Corbin William J	16	pipecoverer	43	"
f	Pendergast Joseph	16	retired	80	
g	Waldron Anthony J	16	salesman	58	"
h	Waldron Mary—†	16	housewife	62	"
k	Wylie Clara L—†	16	"	80	
l	Wylie George E	16	plumber	41	"
m	Wylie Hazel E—†	16	saleswoman	40	"
n	Wylie Kenneth G	16	mechanic	40	"
o	Cass William	18	engraver	67	"
p	Fayer Evelyn—†	18	housewife	83	43 Pearl
r	Curry Laura J—†	18	"	45	here
s	Curry William B	18	brakeman	44	"
u	Moore Ida—†	20	housewife	46	"
v	Moore William O	20	steelworker	53	"
¹v	Burns John	20	retired	81	
w	Melvin Frank	22	"	65	

24

School Street—Continued

X	Scott Elizabeth—†	22	housewife	56	here
Y	Scott George L	22	machinist	26	"

943   Washington Street

D	Lanagan Edward J	104	clerk	61	here
E	Lanagan Francis W	104	warden	59	"
F	Lanagan Nora M—†	104	housewife	59	"

Wood Street

G	Mulhern Anna M—†	2	at home	33	here
H	Mulhern John J	2	seaman	38	"
K	Wilson Elizabeth—†	2	clerk	25	"
L	Wilson Ellen—†	2	housewife	48	"
M	Wilson Mary—†	2	clerk	22	"
N	Doherty Catherine—†	2	housewife	46	24 Frothingham av
O	Doherty Hugh	2	longshoreman	47	24 "
P	Gannon Eunice—†	2	clerk	20	24 "
R	Queenan Julia—†	2	housewife	45	24 "
S	Doherty James J	6	chauffeur	41	here
T	Doherty Margaret—†	6	housewife	35	"
U	Driscoll Ellen—†	6	housekeeper	72	"
V	Driscoll Gertrude—†	6	housewife	40	"
W	Driscoll William	6	longshoreman	32	"
X	Finn James J	6	"	50	
Y	Finn Mary E—†	6	housewife	31	"
	944				
A	Wiggin Ruth—†	12		53	
B	Holland Catherine—†	12	"	68	
C	O'Brien Catherine C—†	12	"	28	
D	O'Brien Timothy	12	retired	69	
E	Bloom John	14	storekeeper	59	"
F	Bloom Lena—†	14	housewife	43	"
G	Harrington Agnes L—†	14	teacher	48	"
H	Harrington Mary T—†	14	at home	60	"
K	Harrington William A	14	U S A	38	

10

11

12

13

14

15

16

17

Ward 2–Precinct 10

CITY OF BOSTON

LIST OF RESIDENTS
20 YEARS OF AGE AND OVER

(NON-CITIZENS INDICATED BY ASTERISK)
(FEMALES INDICATED BY DAGGER)

AS OF

JANUARY 1, 1944

THOMAS F. SULLIVAN, *Chairman*
FREDERIC E. DOWLING, *Secretary*
WILLIAM A. MOTLEY, JR.
FRANCIS B. McKINNEY
EVERETT R. PROUT

Listing Board.

Page.	Letter.	FULL NAME.	Residence, Jan. 1, 1944.	Occupation.	Supposed Age.	Reported Residence, Jan. 1, 1943. Street and Number.

1000
Bartlett Street

	D	Tynan Joseph A	8	cook	37	here
	E	Tynan Marjorie—†	8	housewife	29	"
	F	Penchuck Harry V	8	storekeeper	62	"
	G	Batchelder Adeline—†	8	housewife	36	76 Monument
	H	Batchelder Walter	8	welder	37	76 "
	K	Manash George	10	storekeeper	48	here
	L	*Manash Mary—†	10	housewife	40	"
	M	Cody Catherine—†	17	houseworker	70	"
	N	Jones Francis A—†	17	housewife	73	"
	O	Jones Joseph C	17	laborer	30	
	P	Jones Mary E—†	17	bookkeeper	36	"
	R	Arslanian George	18	shoeworker	54	"
	S	*Boyajian Anna—†	18	housekeeper	75	"
	T	Kasparian Araxy—†	18	housewife	49	"
	U	Kasparian George	18	printer	49	
	V	Ralls Alice A—†	19	stenographer	33	"
	W	Ralls Annie—†	19	housewife	69	"
	X	Ralls Gertrude A—†	19	secretary	35	"
	Y	Ralls James	19	retired	69	"
	Z	Ralls Margaret M—†	19	stenographer	31	"

1001

	A	Grace John W	20	laborer	46	
	B	*Grace Vera—†	20	housewife	39	"
	C	Nihan Annie T—†	21	housekeeper	61	"
	D	O'Hare Florence F—†	21	housewife	54	"
	E	O'Hare William G	21	executive	54	"
	F	O'Hare William G, jr	21	U S A	27	
	G	Doherty Cecelia F—†	23	clerk	48	
		Doherty Daniel F	23	starter	47	"
		Bagdigian Elsie—†	29	housewife	45	"
	K	Bagdigian Nishan	29	storekeeper	49	"
	M	Bagdigian Elizabeth—†	29	clerk	24	"
	N	Wadman Alice—†	31	housewife	48	63 Bartlett
	O	Wadman Lucille—†	31	shoeworker	20	63 "
	P	Edwards Mary E—†	33	housewife	35	here
	R	Edwards Robert W	33	inspector	35	"
	S	Lowrie Bessie C—†	34	housewife	56	20 Cedar
	T	Lowrie Walter M	34	engineer	56	20 "
	U	Emery Thomas A	34	laborer	51	here
	V	Emery Yvonne A—†	34	housewife	53	"

Bartlett Street—Continued

w	Thompson Ida L—†	34	housewife	74	here
x	Granlee Gayle	35	U S N	27	"
y	Granlee Margaret—†	35	housewife	28	"
z	Baker Mary E—†	35	housekeeper	67	"

1002

a	McDonald Annie—†	35	housewife	69	"
b	McDonald Frank A	35	retired	73	"
c	McDonald Fred F	35	lineman	38	"
d	Finn Emily G—†	36	boxmaker	66	"
e	Finn Emma J—†	36	at home	66	"
f	Finn James J	36	drawtender	61	"
g	Finn Margaret J—†	36	teller	52	
h	Finn Mary B—†	36	housekeeper	69	"
k	Finn Mary E—†	36	boxmaker	62	"
l	*McColgan Elizabeth—†	37	housewife	71	"
m	*McColgan Henry	37	polisher	68	"
n	Burke Edward J	37	timekeeper	33	"
o	Burke Helen R—†	37	operator	31	"
p	Harty James R	37	U S A	35	
r	Harty John	37	watchman	73	"
s	Harty Margaret—†	37	housewife	70	"
t	Harty Thomas	37	seaman	29	"
u	Robinson James T	38	clerk	44	
v	Robinson Veronica M—†	38	housewife	43	"
w	Seaton Dorothy—†	39	clerk	43	49 Elm
x	Welsh Mary J—†	39	at home	83	here
y	Welsh Mary L	39	clerk	55	"
z	Welsh Teresa E—†	39	"	53	"

1003

a	Fisher Alice R—†	39	"	22	35 Bartlett
b	Fisher Esther F—†	39	housewife	44	35 "
c	Fisher Francis E	39	clerk	50	35 "
d	Keane Ellen T—†	40	housewife	56	here
e	Keane James	40	fireman	66	"
f	Keane James, jr	40	U S A	22	"
g	Keane William	40	"	29	
h	Rocco Catherine—†	40	housewife	26	"
k	Rocco Paul	40	U S A	23	
l	Mordaunt Margaret V—†	41	housewife	63	"
m	Callahan Elizabeth—†	41	"	72	
n	Quigg Jane P—†	41	clerk	25	

3

Bartlett Street—Continued

o	Quigg Jane W—†	41	housewife	60	here
p	Quigg John F	41	U S A	29	"
r	Quigg William H	41	U S N	20	"
s	Riley Sally Q—†	41	secretary	23	"

Bunker Hill Street

t	Johnson Mary—†	172	electrician	23	63 Bartlett
u	Johnson William F	172	U S N	28	63 "
v	Webb Sarah E—†	172	tel operator	37	here
w	Mullen Abbie—†	172	housewife	47	"
x	Mullen Ann E—†	172	operator	21	"
y	Mullen Barbara—†	172	"	24	
z	Mullen Joseph	172	laborer	27	
	1004				
a	Mullen Patrick	172	"	48	
b	McCann John	174	chipper	45	
c	McDonnell Katherine—†	174	at home	50	"
f	Flavin Delia—†	174	housewife	68	"
g	Flavin John	174	engineer	72	"
d	Rowe Agnes T—†	174	housewife	30	"
e	Rowe Paul E	174	agent	29	
h	Westover Albert S	176	engineer	57	"
l	Sharp Edmund S	188	fireman	21	
m	Sharp James	188	laborer	41	"
n	Sharp Mildred F—†	188	ropemaker	43	"
o	Sharp Stephen L	188	fireman	45	"
p	Dewey Anna M—†	188	housewife	59	"
r	Dewey Frank F	188	U S A	39	
s	Dewey Herbert E	188	U S N	33	
t	Dewey John A	188	retired	71	
u	Dewey Mae—†	188	waitress	32	"
v	White Eva—†	204	housewife	69	"
w	Zarzecki Genevieve—†	204	domestic	28	"
x	Zarzecki Vincent	204	U S A	35	
y	Norton Mary—†	204	stenographer	48	"
z	Russell Arthur J	206	steamfitter	40	"
	1005				
a	Russell Louise M—†	206	housewife	37	"
b	Russell Rose—†	206	"	69	

Bunker Hill Street—Continued

c	Murphy Anne M—†	206	domestic	46	52 Baldwin
d	Fleming Mary A—†	206	packer	69	here

Cedar Street

e	French Leroy	5	riveter	40	here
f	French Marie—†	5	housewife	32	"
g	Francini Eliva—†	5	saleswoman	30	"
h	Francini Lovico	5	storekeeper	58	"
k	Francini Mary—†	5	housewife	54	"
l	Francini Victor	5	U S A	25	
m	Schnapper Eli	5	storekeeper	45	"
n	*Schnapper Ethel—†	5	housewife	43	"
o	Ahearn Joseph B	6	U S A	26	370 Main
p	Ahearn Olivia—†	6	saleswoman	24	22 Oak
r	Rossetti Carmella—†	6	housewife	57	22 "
s	Rossetti Gilda—†	6	librarian	32	22 "
t	Rossetti Jennie—†	6	clerk	27	22 "
u	Rossetti Olga—†	6	WAVE	30	22 "
v	Rossetti Philip	6	barber	66	22 "
w	Clinton John	7	operator	35	here
x	Clinton Mary—†	7	housewife	35	"
	1006				
a	Patterson Annie—†	8	"	58	
b	Patterson Earl	8	U S A	21	"
c	Patterson Helen E—†	8	housewife	28	Medford
d	Patterson John	8	meatcutter	63	here
e	Patterson John S	8	U S A	27	Medford
f	Patterson Lyman	8	instructor	24	"
g	Patterson Norman	8	welder	32	"
h	Lacy Edward	9	U S N	25	12 Pearl
k	Lacy Pauline—†	9	electrician	21	12 "
l	*Piantadosi Rose—†	9	housewife	38	here
m	Wright Howard	9	electrician	27	"
n	Wright Muriel—†	9	housewife	20	"
o	Kelly John W	10	U S N	28	
p	Kelly Josephine T—†	10	housewife	55	"
r	Kelly Rita B—†	10	typist	24	"
s	Kelly Timothy J	10	detective	59	"
t	O'Brien Mary E—†	12	housewife	44	"
u	O'Brien Patrick J	12	driller	44	

1

Page.	Letter.	FULL NAME.	Residence, Jan. 1, 1944.	Occupation.	Supposed Age.	Reported Residence, Jan. 1, 1943. Street and Number.

Cedar Street—Continued

	v	Hurley Mary L—†	14	operator	55	here
	w	Hurley Stephen E	14	wireworker	54	"
	x	Hurley William	14	clerk	51	"
	y	*Yaras Emelia—†	15	housewife	55	"
	z	Yaras Joseph	15	U S A	23	
1007						
	a	Lynch Dorothy E—†	15	clerk	37	
	b	Lynch Elizabeth J—†	15	at home	75	"
	c	Lynch Honora—†	15	binder	72	
	d	Harrington John J	16	clerk	45	"
	e	Leonard Annie M—†	16	at home	79	"
	f	Guarino Adeline—†	18	housewife	61	"
	g	Guarino Ernest	18	manager	35	"
	h	Guarino Louise—†	18	housewife	34	"
	k	Scelza Carmini	18	electrician	25	New York
	l	Scelza Concetta—†	18	housewife	21	"
	m	Foley Mary A—†	18	"	64	here
	n	Foley Mary F—†	18	clerk	40	"
	o	Hartwell Maude R—†	20	housewife	50	"
	p	Hartwell Thomas J	20	chipper	50	"
	r	Murphy Ellen E—†	20	housewife	43	3 Seminary
	s	Murphy Eugene H	20	U S N	24	3 "
	t	Murphy Thomas J	20	"	21	3 "
	u	Callahan Ann M—†	20	secretary	22	3 "
	v	Callahan Timothy B, jr	20	U S C G	28	3 "
	w	Apanell Anthony	22	welder	30	Hadley
	x	Apanell Louise—†	22	housewife	28	"
	y	Mullen James J	22	clerk	55	here
	z	Mullen Marguerite J—†	22	housewife	48	"
1008						
	a	Andrews Catherine J—†	26	"	60	
	b	Anderson Cornelius A	26	U S N	57	
	c	Clear Elizabeth G—†	26	at home	66	"

Cross Street

	f	Burns Anna—†	4	waitress	50	11 Queensberry
	g	Coffey Flora—†	4	tel operator	40	Somerville
	h	Corriveau Joseph	4	welder	46	"
	k	Corriveau Marie J—†	4	housewife	44	"
	l	Kolodzicj Walter	4	U S N	23	New York

6

Cross Street—Continued

M	Marineau Arthur J	4	shipfitter	39	58 High
N	Marineau Bernadette M—†	4	housewife	32	58 "
o	Hannon Helen—†	5	tel operator	47	here
P	Hannon John T	5	longshoreman	42	"
R	Hannon Margaret—†	5	at home	40	"
s	Hannon William F	5	longshoreman	44	"
T	Fidler Arthur G	6	baker	62	"
U	Fidler Margaret L—†	6	housewife	50	"
V	Maddock Catherine—†	7	buyer	58	
W	Maddock Edmund	7	U S A	31	"
X	Casey James E	9	"	35	Everett
Y	Casey Winifred L—†	9	housewife	33	here
Z	Wrenn Edward B	9	retired	68	"
	1009				
A	Wrenn James A	9	welder	38	
B	Wrenn Mary A—†	9	housewife	64	"
C	Wrenn Mary B—†	9	typist	35	"
F	Brennan Charles W	10	clerk	31	
G	Brennan William H	10	retired	74	
D	Canney Nellie L—†	10	housewife	68	"
E	Canney Edward J	10	U S A	34	
H	Gibbons Daniel J	11	shipper	50	"
K	Gibbons Elizabeth—†	11	housewife	49	"
L	Gibbons Mary—†	11	at home	76	"
M	Merrigan Mary A—†	11	housewife	46	"
N	Haas Emma—†	12	at home	82	10 Winthrop
O	Elwell Grace M—†	12	"	53	here
P	Gunn Georginna—†	12	"	79	"
R	Canarie Mary E—†	13	nurse	51	47 Monument sq
S	Curzon Frances C—†	13	housewife	53	47 "
T	McCormack James P	13	bookkeeper	33	New York
U	McCormack Thomas M	13	laborer	29	here
V	O'Connor Hilda M—†	13	housewife	44	"
W	South John V	13	pipefitter	34	"
X	South Pearl N—†	13	housewife	30	"
Y	Chandler Belle T—†	14	at home	85	"
Z	Chandler Percy A	14	designer	60	"
	1010				
A	Adams Grace H—†	14	at home	72	"
B	Fitzgerald Thomas	15	retired	73	
C	Griffin Annie—†	15	at home	80	"

Cross Street—Continued

D	Archer Edwin	17	bookkeeper	46	31 Mead
E	Raymond Windsor	17	clerk	60	here
F	Howes Laura N—†	19	at home	58	"
G	Tucker Cora S—†	19	"	81	"
H	Kellett Elizabeth M—†	21	housekeeper	38	"
K	Mullen Agnes F—†	21	housewife	66	"
L	Mullen Alice L—†	21	clerk	33	
M	Mullen Joseph L	21	storekeeper	66	"
N	Mateer Ella P—†	22	matron	60	Somerville
O	VanWart Archie W	22	U S N	38	here
P	VanWart Frank S	22	clerk	65	"
R	VanWart Margaret—†	22	housewife	65	"
T	Mullen Catherine L—†	23	tel operator	46	"
U	Robinson Frederick A	23	supervisor	51	"
V	Robinson Frederick A, jr	23	U S N	21	
W	Robinson Mary A—†	23	housewife	55	"
X	McGrath Sarah A—†	26	at home	73	"
Y	Bower Sarah—†	26	"	69	6 Holden row
Z	Swett Iona C—†	26	housewife	35	here
	1011				
A	Swett Joseph B	26	letter carrier	46	46 High
B	Brasill Natalie J—†	27	housewife	26	here
C	Little Muriel A—†	27	metalworker	30	"
D	McKeage Alexander	27	laborer	51	38 Harvard
E	Dugan John L	28	retired	53	here
F	Dugan Joseph S	28	letter carrier	48	"
G	Dugan Mary T—†	28	cleaner	56	"
H	Dugan Paul F	28	laborer	50	
L	Sullivan Alexander H	29	boilermaker	38	"
M	Sullivan Camille L—†	29	housewife	34	"
N	*Doran Nellie—†	30	"	42	
O	*Doran Patrick	30	plumber	45	"
P	Boyle Arthur P	30	U S A	20	
R	Boyle Hannah M—†	30	housewife	52	"
S	Boyle James M	30	U S A	21	
T	*Boyle Patrick	30	retired	54	
V	McManus Joseph	32	laborer	32	
X	McMaster Alexander A	34	electrician	53	"
Y	McMaster Beatrice M—†	34	housewife	53	"
Z	McMaster Evelyn F—†	34	operator	30	"

1012

Cross Street—Continued

A	Field Helen C—†	36	clerk	39	here
B	Field Mary E—†	36	matron	65	"

Cross Street Court

D	Trott Joseph H	1	laborer	54	9 Chappie
E	Trott Josephine M—†	1	housewife	31	9 "
G	Crehan Ruth T—†	3	clerk	25	here
H	Travers Anne B—†	3	housewife	33	"
K	Travers Joseph L	3	agent	33	"

Elm Street

L	McConalogue Eunice—†	7	at home	60	here
M	Shea Catherine A—†	7	"	53	"
N	Shea Ralph R	7	welder	29	"
P	Welsh Alice—†	9A	housewife	37	"
R	Welsh Charles	9A	chauffeur	39	"
S	Crowley Helen M—†	9A	clerk	26	11 Sumner
T	Smith Kenneth P	9A	U S N	42	11 "
U	*Smith Nellie M—†	9A	housewife	45	11 "
V	Doyle Francis T	9A	U S N	25	25 Sullivan
W	Doyle John F	9A	clerk	30	25 "
X	Doyle John J	9A	retired	65	25 "
Y	Doyle Joseph P	9A	coppersmith	27	25 "
Z	Doyle Nora M—†	9A	housewife	50	25 "
	1013				
A	Doyle William T	9A	electrician	28	25 "
C	McCusker Helen—†	17	housewife	60	here
D	McCusker Peter	17	retired	80	"
E	McIntosh Anna M—†	17	collector	58	"
F	McIntosh William F	17	electrician	68	"
G	Landry Lionel A	17	clerk	28	Franklin
H	Landry Mary R—†	17	housewife	29	"
K	Fullerton Annie—†	19	"	56	21 Elm
L	Fullerton Edward	19	chauffeur	58	21 "
M	Fullerton Ellen—†	19	clerk	26	21 "
N	Fullerton John	19	electrician	22	21 "
O	Fullerton Sarah—†	19	clerk	25	21 '

Elm Street—Continued

P	Barnes Helen M—†	19	forewoman	52	here
R	Lynch John W	21	U S N	24	68 High
S	Lynch Joseph L—†	21	longshoreman	51	68 "
T	Lynch Mary E—†	21	housewife	47	68 "
U	Marazzi Mary C—†	21	"	27	68 "
V	Marazzi Reno L	21	cook	27	68 "
W	Duprey Clayton A	23	shipfitter	49	Vermont
X	Duprey Margaret J—†	23	housewife	53	"

1014

A	Woods Earl	25	clerk	40	here
B	Woods Maude—†	25	housewife	61	"
C	Woods Warren	25	laborer	64	"
E	Doherty Elizabeth—†	25	at home	70	41 Austin
F	Dennett Grace M—†	25	"	72	170 Bunker Hill
G	Keezer Ida—†	25	"	59	here
H	Porter Margaret—†	25	"	76	35 Bartlett
K	Griffiths Blanche—†	25	operator	56	here
L	Casey Annie E—†	29	housewife	73	"
M	Casey Joseph H	29	machinist	70	"
N	Carroll Margaret F—†	29	clerk	27	
O	Carroll Margaret M—†	29	housewife	62	"
P	Carroll William J	29	laborer	67	
R	Reed Victoria—†	33	housewife	42	"
S	Reed William E	33	shipfitter	42	"
T	Therien Albina—†	33	housewife	79	"
U	Therien Salvina T—†	33	packer	51	
V	Therein Simeon	33	retired	76	
W	Shanahan Francis H	35	clerk	28	
X	Shanahan Margaret—†	35	cleaner	64	
Y	Shanahan Mary E—†	35	housewife	27	"
Z	McCue Catherine T—†	49	"	25	

1015

A	McCue Francis P	49	electrician	27	"
B	Buchanan Mina—†	49	at home	75	Everett
C	Buchanan Oswald P	49	retired	74	"
D	Orpin Isabella B—†	49	housewife	43	39 Bartlett
E	Orpin James F	49	B F D	43	39 "
F	Cohen Margaret R—†	51	at home	66	here
G	Donovan Catherine T—†	51	clerk	50	"
H	Donovan Elizabeth V—†	51	bookkeeper	56	"
K	Donovan M Louise—†	51	at home	45	"

Elm Street—Continued

L	Donovan Mary A—†	51	clerk	52	here
M	*Campbell Charles E	53	insulator	69	"
N	*Campbell Susie H—†	53	housewife	71	"
O	Duddy Agnes—†	53	operator	61	"
P	McGuirk Catherine—†	53	at home	76	"
R	McGuirk William R	53	retired	76	
S	Sweeney John J	55	laborer	62	"
T	Sweeney Maude E—†	55	housewife	58	"
U	Flannagan Catherine—†	55	clerk	23	
V	Miles Jennie M—†	55	housewife	45	"
W	Miles William H	55	policeman	47	"
X	Flaherty Delia—†	55	housekeeper	65	"
Y	Flaherty Frank J	55	clerk	42	"
Z	Tague Helen C—†	57	stenographer	27	"

1016

A	Tague Louise J—†	57	at home	37	"
B	Tague Mary L—†	57	"	67	"
C	Tague Dorothy H—†	57	"	28	Somerville
D	Tague John B	57	engineer	31	"
E	Askew Elsie V—†	59	housewife	52	here
F	Askew Henry R	59	pipefitter	67	"
G	MacDonald Alice—†	59	housewife	37	"
H	MacDonald Harry A	59	clerk	43	
K	Kelly Dorothy J—†	59	domestic	24	"
L	Kelly William	59	U S A	26	10 Jackson
M	Morrison Charles A	59	U S N	20	here
N	Morrison Elizabeth—†	59	housewife	57	"
O	Blankenburg Mary—†	61	"	73	32 Russell
P	Sharp Francis C	61	painter	21	32 "
R	Sharp Frank L	61	"	43	32 "
S	Walsh Alice M—†	61	housewife	40	here
T	Walsh Patrick J	61	letter carrier	49	"
V	Kearney Annie—†	61	at home	75	"
U	Kearney Annie E—†	61	"	45	
W	Kearney Frances W—†	61	stenographer	42	"
X	Kearney George H	61	U S A	36	"
Y	Kearney Mary A—†	61	cashier	50	"
Z	Kearney William	61	retired	75	

1017

A	Kearney William A	61	operator	44	"
B	Kripp Dorothy H—†	63	housewife	26	40 Soley

11

Page.	Letter.	FULL NAME.	Residence, Jan. 1, 1944.	Occupation.	Supposed Age.	Reported Residence, Jan. 1, 1943. Street and Number.

Elm Street—Continued

	c	Kripp Walter D	63	B F D	30	40 Soley
	D	Maguire Jennie T—†	63	housewife	40	here
	E	Maguire Joseph D	63	U S A	22	"
	F	Maguire Mary A—†	63	clerk	21	"
	H	Power Mary—†	67	housewife	40	"
	K	Power William	67	laborer	46	"
	L	Troy Catherine—†	67	at home	77	"
	M	Beatty Edward	69	retired	50	
	N	Olson George B	69	laborer	37	
	o	Olson Mary J—†	69	housewife	33	"
	P	*Smith Emma J—†	69	"	60	
	R	Smith Viola—†	69	clerk	24	
	s	Hurley Elizabeth F—†	71	housewife	51	"
	T	Hurley Gerald P	71	machinist	22	"
	U	Hurley Leo J	71	laborer	20	
	v	Hurley Margaret J—†	71	at home	21	"
	w	Hurley Michael J	71	longshoreman	55	"
	x	McGowan Mary E—†	71	housewife	24	"
	Y	McGowan Philip V	71	U S N	26	
	z	Doolin Catherine—†	73	housewife	53	"

1018

	A	Doolin John J	73	longshoreman	54	"
	B	Sullivan John E	73	U S A	26	
	c	Sullivan William J	73	U S N	21	

Green Street

	D	Scalli Elizabeth A—†	23	tel operator	25	236 Kelton
	E	Scalli Joseph H	23	U S A	27	236 "
	F	Gill Bridget—†	23	housewife	35	here
	G	Gill Patrick	23	pipefitter	45	"
	H	Martin Harold J	25	policeman	48	"
	K	Martin Lillian—†	25	housewife	34	"
	L	Callahan Cornelius	25	clerk	40	
	M	Dennehy Annie M—†	25	housewife	50	"
	N	Dennehy Dennis	25	clerk	50	
	o	Tipping Mary—†	25	housewife	21	"
	P	Fitzgerald John F	26	retired	79	16 Monument
	R	Jeffers Thomas F	26	machinist	34	here
	s	Moody Myron	26	manager	35	"
	T	Quinn John T	26	laborer	56	2 N Mead

12

Green Street—Continued

U Smith Blanid H—†	26	housewife	55	here
V Smith William H	26	clerk	60	"
W Duffy Catherine—†	27	typist	25	"
X Duffy Elizabeth—†	27	stenographer	22	"
Y Duffy John	27	bartender	59	"
1019				
A Galvin Bridget—†	28	housewife	70	"
B Galvin Eleanor H—†	28	"	36	"
C Galvin Michael J	28	U S A	37	"
D Galvin Thomas F	28	U S N	34	49 Monum'nt av
E Reagan Ellen E—†	28	housewife	41	here
F Reagan John F	28	estimator	41	"
G Hegarty Jeremiah	29	clerk	25	"
H Hegarty Maria—†	29	cleaner	49	"
K Hegarty Mary—†	29	clerk	23	
L Harrington Catherine—†	29	"	24	
M Harrington Jeremiah	29	laborer	59	"
N Harrington Margaret—†	29	housewife	59	"
O Crowley Helen T—†	30	"	48	
P Crowley Joseph	30	U S A	23	
R Brennan Sarah—†	31	at home	83	"
S Brennan William	31	roofer	43	
T Collins James J	31	mechanic	22	"
U Keating Elizabeth M—†	31	housewife	52	"
V Keating George	31	salesman	50	"
W Murphy Cecelia C—†	32	housewife	43	"
X Murphy Florence V—†	32	"	47	
Y Murphy Florence V—†	32	at home	25	"
Z Murphy John F	32	realtor	33	
1020				
A Murphy Joseph E	32	agent	43	
B Hassett Elizabeth—†	33	housewife	53	"
C Hassett Joseph	33	baker	53	"
D Shea Mary T—†	33	housewife	72	"
E Casey Mary E—†	34	clerk	64	
F Lynch Charles A	34	retired	72	
G *Martin Catherine A—†	34	housewife	78	"
H Martin Patrick J	34	operator	58	"
K Durgin Ellen F—†	35	at home	67	"
L Regan Catherine A—†	35	"	50	
M Regan Catherine E—†	35	clerk	24	

13

Page.	Letter.	FULL NAME.	Residence, Jan. 1, 1944.	Occupation.	Supposed Age.	Reported Residence, Jan. 1, 1943. Street and Number.

Green Street—Continued

o	Regan Jeremiah E	35	U S A	23	here
n	Regan Jeremiah S	35	boilermaker	51	"
p	Regan Joseph F	35	U S N	20	"
r	O'Brien Dorothy M—†	36	housewife	47	"
s	O'Brien Thomas J	36	shipfitter	49	"
t	Finn Catherine F—†	37	housewife	59	"
u	Finn John J	37	U S N	37	67 Winthrop
v	Finn John R	37	accountant	62	here
w	Finn Louise A—†	37	housewife	35	67 Winthrop
x	Finn Mary C—†	37	teacher	29	here
y	Nover Grace I—†	37	housewife	54	"
z	Nover Joseph W	37	U S N	21	"
	1021				
a	Nover Otto C	37	foreman	52	"
b	Hyde Nora—†	39	housewife	65	"
c	O'Brien Emily—†	39	typist	24	
d	O'Brien Emily F—†	39	housewife	54	"
e	O'Brien Michael	39	roofer	63	"
f	Termas Dorothy—†	39	housewife	24	California
g	Termas William	39	U S N	29	"
h	Finn Catherine F—†	40	housewife	57	here
k	Finn Joseph P	40	clerk	56	"
l	Finn Joseph W	40	stenographer	30	"
m	Finn Marion L—†	40	clerk	23	
n	Finn Robert J	40	U S A	21	
o	Finn William H	40	clerk	28	
p	Day James J	41	retired	80	
r	Day Nora M—†	41	housewife	75	"
s	Ferretti Leo J	42	inspector	52	"
t	Ferretti Leonard F	42	U S N	21	
u	Ferretti Mary E—†	42	housewife	52	"
v	Lee Ellen A—†	43	"	29	46 Monum'nt av
w	Lee Robert B	43	policeman	32	46 "
x	McTiernan Mary E—†	43	housewife	70	here
y	McTiernan Thomas	43	retired	77	"
z	McTiernan Thomas J	43	U S N	32	"
	1022				
a	Twomey Hugh	44	longshoreman	48	"
b	Twomey John	44	rigger	40	New York
c	Twomey Julia—†	44	housewife	41	here
d	Cameron Arthur	45	chauffeur	26	"

Green Street—Continued

	Name		Occupation	Age	Residence
E	Cameron Bertha—†	45	housewife	24	here
F	Cameron Charles W	45	laborer	39	"
G	Renfro Louis C	45	cashier	70	"
H	Rosetto Mary—†	46	housekeeper	69	"
K	Loring Henry J	48	metalworker	49	"
L	Loring John P	48	U S A	23	"
M	Loring Rose G—†	48	housewife	51	"
N	McCarthy John P	48	retired	53	"
O	Brown Alice S—†	48	housewife	29	"
P	Brown David A	48	chauffeur	31	"
R	Twomey James	50	clerk	34	
S	Twomey Nora—†	50	housewife	78	"
T	Barrett Charles R	50	blacksmith	28	"
U	Barrett Mary R—†	50	housewife	28	"
V	Batchelder Mary—†	50	at home	67	64 Green
W	McCormack Patrick H	50	U S N	21	here
X	Suckiel Anna—†	52	housewife	47	"
Y	Suckiel Anna—†	52	clerk	27	"
Z	Suckiel Jennie—†	52	housewife	21	106 Chestnut av
	1023				
A	Suckiel Julia—†	52	"	22	here ·
B	Suckiel Michael	52	repairman	55	"
C	Suckiel Michael	52	seaman	20	"
D	Suckiel Stanley	52	U S A	25	"
E	Suckiel Walter	52	U S N	24	106 Chestnut av
F	Seymour Lavinia B—†	53	at home	84	here
G	Seymour Mary G—†	53	bookkeeper	58	"
H	Hunt Louis E	53	shoecutter	70	"
K	Goodwin Emma L—†	54	housewife	50	"
L	Goodwin John A	54	cooper	60	
N	Walsh Francis J	55	retired	74	"
O	Walsh Mary J—†	55	housewife	72	"
P	LaTerz Helen R—†	56	clerk	24	
R	LaTerz Kathleen M—†	56	operator	25	"
S	LaTerz Margaret M—†	56	housewife	54	"
T	Gill Neil J	56	machinist	38	"
U	Gill Ruth E—†	56	housewife	38	"
V	Drane Ethel G—†	57	"	53	
W	Drane James E	57	laborer	55	"
X	Mahoney Francis J	57	decorator	39	"
Y	Mahoney James	57	cleaner	42	"

15

z	Troy Mary J—†	57	housewife	38	here
	1024				
A	Troy Thomas A	57	U S C G	40	"
B	Cavanaugh Edith L—†	61	housewife	63	14 Chapman
C	Cavanaugh Joseph A	61	laborer	65	14 "
D	McDonnell Edward S	61	shipfitter	53	here
E	McDonnell Mary—†	61	housewife	79	"
F	Capen Frank E	63	rigger	59	"
G	Farmer Florence—†	63	housekeeper	32	"
H	Edwards George G	63	painter	69	"
K	Sabean Irene—†	63	housewife	65	"
L	McCloud John	63	laborer	31	
M	McCloud Julia—†	63	operator	38	"
N	McCloud Mary—†	63	"	62	"
O	Butler Josephine—†	64	at home	60	53 Elm
P	Murray Dennis M	64	laborer	53	here
R	Redman Agnes—†	65	domestic	43	"
S	Redman Edward S	65	repairman	49	"
T	Thayer Eleanor—†	65	clerk	31	
U	Fortin Angelo	65	salesman	26	"
V	Morey John J	65	"	36	"
W	Morey Sarah—†	65	housewife	31	"
X	Williams Frances E—†	66	"	38	23 High
Y	Williams Vernon W	66	retired	41	23 "
	1025				
A	Moore Charles R	67	rigger	28	here
B	Moore Eileen M—†	67	housewife	29	"
C	Harrington Anastasia—†	67	"	54	"
D	Harrington Anna M—†	67	electrician	21	"
E	Harrington James L	67	U S N	31	"
F	Harrington James P	67	carpenter	65	"
G	Harrington Joseph D	67	U S N	20	
H	Harrington Thomas	67	carpenter	27	"
K	Harrington William G	67	U S A	26	
M	O'Connell John F	68	boxmaker	51	"
N	O'Connell Laurel S—†	68	housewife	54	"
L	Sullivan Elizabeth—†	68	boxmaker	32	"
O	Murphy Dorothy T—†	68	housewife	28	"
P	Murphy Eugene	68	longshoreman	30	"
R	Farley Catherine E—†	70	housewife	68	"
S	Peters Mary E—†	70	"	37	

Green Street—Continued

T	Peters Richard J	70	operator	42	here
U	Brennan Charles J	71	guard	52	"
V	Geysen Frank T	71	policeman	35	"
W	Geysen Winifred—†	71	housewife	32	"
X	Cullinane Joanna—†	73	clerk	35	
Y	Cullinane Mary E—†	73	packer	38	"
Z	Mahoney Christine—†	73	housewife	46	"
	1026				
A	Mahoney James	73	laborer	49	
B	Mahoney Mary—†	73	secretary	21	"
C	Sharp Alice M—†	74	housewife	45	"
D	Sharp Edmund J	74	fireman	46	
E	Sharp Irene M—†	74	teacher	22	
F	Hitchman Arthur E.	75	retired	36	"
G	Hitchman Mary B—†	75	housewife	34	"
H	Hickey Agnes G—†	75	tel operator	23	"
K	Hickey Margaret L—†	75	housewife	62	"
L	Hickey Patrick J	75	laborer	69	
M	Hickey Patrick J, jr	75	U S A	25	
N	Hickey Thomas J	75	U S N	20	
O	Murphy Julia—†	76	housewife	61	"
P	Murphy Patrick	76	laborer	71	
R	Monagle Charles	77	"	48	
S	Monagle Fannie—†	77	housewife	49	"
T	Houghton James	77	ironworker	45	"
U	Houghton Margaret —†	77	housewife	45	"
V	Hall Bridget M—†	78	"	34	"
W	Hall Thomas P	78	longshoreman	41	"
X	Shea Margaret—†	79	operator	45	"
Y	Mahon Edward L	80	engineer	47	"
Z	Mahon Margaret—†	80	housewife	37	"
	1027				
A	Perkins Fred L	81	watchman	66	"
B	Perkins James J	81	U S A	32	
C	Perkins John H	81	"	24	
D	Perkins Rita E—†	81	bookkeeper	22	"
E	Irons James F	82	retired	71	
F	Irons Mary A—†	82	housewife	66	"
G	Soutter Maude S—†	83	at home	63	"
H	Mahoney James J	83	U S A	24	"
K	Mahoney James T	83	letter carrier	48	"

Green Street—Continued

L	Mahoney Nellie G—†	83	housewife	48	here
M	McGowan Frank B	83	clerk	62	"
N	Walden Alice A—†	83	"	41	"
O	Walden Catherine—†	83	at home	53	"
P	Walden Edward A	83	policeman	45	"
R	Burke Helen—†	84	house	37	104 Elm
S	Burke John J	84	caretaker	32	104 "
T	Kelleher Alice—†	84	housewife	32	here
U	Kelleher Daniel	84	shipfitter	33	"
W	Robinson Lillian M—†	86	housewife	30	"
X	Robinson Stanley W	86	chauffeur	35	"
Y	Coleman Lillian—†	88	at home	60	"
Z	Kent Bridget M—†	88	housewife	50	"
	1028				
A	Kent Daniel F	88	U S C G	21	"
B	Kent Michael J	88	longshoreman	50	"
C	Orpen Irene—†	89	housewife	26	"
D	Orpen Richard	89	laborer	29	
E	McManus Dorothy—†	89	saleswoman	30	"
F	McManus Elizabeth—†	89	housewife	53	"
G	McManus John H	89	electrician	29	"
H	McManus Margaret F—†	89	waitress	22	"
K	McManus William H	89	piano tuner	50	"
L	Hagerty Mary—†	90	housewife	70	"
M	Coleman Catherine—†	90	"	73	..
N	Ballam Elizabeth—†	91	at home	69	"
O	Burnett Ethel M—†	91	housewife	43	"
P	Burnett Henry W	91	laborer	53	"
R	Burnett William C	91	U S A	20	
S	Sullivan Catherine—†	91	housewife	61	"
T	Sullivan Eleanor—†	91	painter	27	
U	Sullivan Frank T	91	retired	70	
V	Sullivan Harold	91	laborer	24	"
W	Flynn John R	92	retired	85	"
X	Gustus Arthur M	92	teacher	22	
Y	Gustus Helen R—†	92	housewife	49	"
Z	Gustus John A	92	custodian	56	"
	1029				
A	Gustus Warren J	92	U S N	21	
B	Charles John J	94	shipper	42	
C	Charles Leonora P—†	94	housewife	26	"

Green Street—Continued

D	Donovan Frances L—†	94	stitcher	33	here
E	Donovan Francis P	94	rigger	57	"
F	Donovan Margaret V—†	94	housewife	54	"

Hancock Street

G	Smith John E	3	U S N	44	Stoneham
H	Smith May—†	3	housewife	43	"
K	Sullivan Daniel J	4	clerk	27	here
L	Sullivan Eugene J	4	retired	74	"
M	Sullivan Margaret—†	4	housewife	68	"
N	Scannell Annie M—†	5	"	67	
O	Scannell James A	5	U S A	21	
P	Scannell Joseph	5	"	26	"
R	Scannell Michael D	5	U S C G	39	"
S	Scannell Rita M—†	5	tel operator	25	"
T	Brandenberg Mary—†	6	housewife	77	"
U	Carney Edward T	6	U S N	24	
V	Carney Helen F—†	6	housewife	44	"
W	Boyland Christopher J	7	porter	62	
X	Boyland Mary E—†	7	housewife	54	" .
Y	Barclay Mary B—†	8	clerk	26	"
Z	Linnane Ellen T—†	8	housewife	52	"
	1030				
A	Linnane Frank B	8	carpenter	52	"
B	Linnane Joseph M	8	U S A	24	
C	Linnane Rita F—†	8	packer	23	
D	Neary Helen T—†	8	electrician	20	"
E	Mitchell Irene E—†	9	housewife	51	"
F	Mitchell Theodore	9	painter	63	
G	O'Brien Charles W	9½	clerk	44	"
H	O'Brien Marion B—†	9½	housewife	39	"
K	O'Brien Mark	9½	painter	46	
L	O'Brien Mary —†	9½	at home	78	"
M	Lynch Eugene F	9½	laborer	44	"
N	Lynch Eugene F, jr	9½	welder	22	"
O	Lynch Helen G—†	9½	housewife	43	"
P	Lynch William J	9½	U S N	20	"
R	Nye Fernard	10	laborer	33	50 Chappie
U	Nye Florence—†	10	housewife	34	50 "
S	Morrissey Mary B—†	10	"	35	here

Page.	Letter.	FULL NAME.	Residence, Jan. 1, 1944.	Occupation.	Supposed Age.	Reported Residence, Jan. 1, 1943. Street and Number.

Hancock Street—Continued

	T	Morrissey Michael	10	retired	44	here
	v	Coyle Charles	10	electrician	23	"
	w	Coyle Joseph L	10	U S A	25	"
	x	Coyle William J	10	"	20	
	y	Sindoris John	10½	shipfitter	27	"
	z	Sindoris Mary—†	10½	housewife	26	"

1031

	A	Harvey Clifford	10½	laborer	50	26 Pleasant
	B	Robinson Laura—†	10½	housekeeper	71	26 "
	c	Girard Harriet—†	10½	operator	28	10 St Martin
	D	*Peters George J	10½	pressman	33	here
	E	Peters Laura H—†	10½	housewife	33	"
	F	Poland Vera L—†	11	"	27.	Haverhill
	G	Poland Warren H	11	laborer	30	"

High Street

	H	Buckley Francis X	19	shipper	31	here
	K	Buckley Johanna—†	19	housewife	41	"
	L	Dower George A	19	driller	62	"
	M	Dower William A	19	welder	24	"
	N	Kearney Mary—†	19	housewife	65	"
	o	Mullins Mary T—†	19	at home	39	"
	P	Childs Arthur F	23	operator	43	"
	R	McLeod Marjorie—†	23	housewife	57	"
	s	Donovan Catherine M—†	23	"	28	
	T	Donovan Edward F	23	stevedore	30	"
	U	Harkins Edward J	23	U S A	22	
	v	Harkins Grace I—†	23	housewife	56	"
	w	Harkins Hugh F	23	laborer	56	
	x	McGonagle May—†	27	at home	72	"
	Y	Harkins Edward	27	laborer	57	
	z	Harkins Elizabeth—†	27	housekeeper	60	"

1032

	A	Kane Harry J	27	watchman	60	45 Allston
	B	Martin Walter	27	laborer	65	here
	c	McCormack William F	27	"	31	Somerville
	D	Moore Edward	27	"	62	here
	E	Porter Anna—†	27	clerk	45	"
	F	O'Connell Elizabeth A—†	29	"	28	"
	G	O'Connell Joanna R—†	29	housewife	70	"

20

H	O'Connell Katherine F—†	29	teacher	30	here
K	O'Connell Margaret M—†	29	"	32	"
L	Maguire Alice M—†	31	housewife	29	"
M	Maguire Helen G—†	31	secretary	25	"
N	Maguire John J	31	teller	39	
O	Maguire Katherine E—†	31	secretary	33	"
P	Maguire Margaret M—†	31	teacher	27	"
R	Pilicy Francis X	33	foreman	27	"
S	Pilicy Mary G—†	33	housewife	27	"
T	Meikle Annie T—†	33	"	73	
U	Meikle Archibald T	33	teller	46	"
V	Mosher Frederick E, jr	33	electrician	40	"
W	Mosher Virginia P—†	33	housewife	26	"
Y	Roach Catherine E—†	35	"	64	
Z	Roach Claire A—†	35	teacher	34	"

1033

A	Roach Thomas F	35	retired	69	
C	Goff Catherine J—†	37	housewife	70	"
B	Goff Michael J	37	retired	76	
D	Mosher Doris E—†	39	secretary	42	"
E	Mosher Florence M—†	39	housewife	63	"
F	Goodfellow Hugh J	39	retired	64	"
G	Goodfellow Margaret G—†	39	housewife	63	"
H	Murray Elizabeth—†	39	"	77	
K	Murray Helen B—†	39	operator	49	"
L	Murray Mary—†	39	packer	43	"
M	Greene Anne G—†	39	housewife	32	"
N	Greene John J	39	embalmer	35	"
O	Breck May E—†	41	clerk	30	Arlington
P	Riley Dorothy M—†	41	secretary	25	here
R	Riley John J	41	electrician	53	"
S	Riley Margaret J—†	41	housewife	49	"
T	Doherty John P	41	attorney	37	"
U	Doherty Margaret C—†	41	housewife	32	"
V	Douglas Mary E—†	41	"	42	"
W	Douglas Patrick	41	engineer	53	"
X	Monagle James A	41	U S N	32	
Y	Doherty Catherine—†	41	housewife	69	"
Z	Doherty Mary I—†	41	clerk	44	

1034

A	Doherty Thomas	41	manager	43	"

Page.	Letter.	FULL NAME.	Residence, Jan. 1, 1944.	Occupation.	Supposed Age.	Reported Residence, Jan. 1, 1943. Street and Number.

High Street—Continued

	B	Lynch Elinor S—†	41	housewife	45	here
	C	Lynch Matthew P	41	manager	45	"
	D	Lynch Robert F	41	U S M C	23	"
	E	McSherry Annie—†	43	at home	82	"
	F	Murphy Alice—†	43	housewife	45	"
	G	Murphy Patrick	43	B F D	50	
	H	McLaughlin Nellie—†	43	housewife	27	"
	K	McLaughlin William A	43	B F D	28	
	L	Wall Catherine J—†	45	housewife	32	"
	M	Wall John R	45	painter	37	''
	N	Walsh Bertha V—†	45	housewife	60	"
	O	Walsh Leon S	45	clerk	53	
	P	Brennan Charles F	45	foreman	41	"
	R	Brennan Elinor K—†	45	housewife	37	"
	S	Buckes Oscar E	47	retired	68	
	T	Dennehy John F	47	longshoreman	48	"
	U	Wilkins Anna G—†	47	housewife	48	"
	V	Wilkins Henry T	47	U S A	25	"
	W	Wilkins Margaret F—†	47	clerk	20	
	X	Wilkins William J	47	policeman	48	"
	Z	Lyons Frederick L	51	physician	58	"
		1035				
	A	Lyons Marie—†	51	housewife	53	"
	B	Healey Mary R—†	53	clerk	21	
	C	Stewart Catherine M—†	53	housewife	42	"
	D	Stewart Hance N	53	salesman	40	"
	E	Curran John J	53	machinist	60	"
	F	Curran John J, jr	53	U S N	22	
	G	Curran Mary E—†	53	housewife	51	"
	H	Mahoney John D	55	plumber	42	"
	K	Mahoney Julia—†	55	housewife	41	"
	L	McDevitt Agnes D—†	55	"	36	
	M	McDevitt James P	55	social worker	35	"
	N	Monahan William J	57	mechanic	42	"
	O	Monahan Winifred F—†	57	housewife	42	"
	P	Florian Dorothy F—†	57	clerk	31	
	R	Florian Kingsley S	57	U S A	36	
	S	Griffin Frances C—†	57	housewife	50	"
	T	Griffin Thomas J	57	embalmer	58	"
	U	Priest Helen K—†	57	housewife	36	"
	V	Priest Lucien C	57	electrician	44	"

w	Priest Lucien J	57	retired	78	here
x	Barrett Helen M—†	59	housewife	39	"
y	Barrett John F	59	engraver	39	"
z	Colbert Marie S—†	59	housewife	53	"
	1036				
A	Colbert Sylvester B	59	court officer	56	"
B	Hart Julia A—†	59	clerk	38	"
c	Carver John J	59	electrician	33	"
D	Carver Mary E—†	59	housewife	26	"
E	Kelley Thomas L	59	inspector	55	"
G	Iverson Lillian E—†	61	at home	45	"
F	Robinson Ida J—†	61	"	79	"
H	Grandison Alice—†	65	housewife	63	"
K	Grandison Wilfred G	65	physician	65	"
L	Mylosky Alex	69	machinist	40	"
M	Mylosky Eva—†	69	housewife	36	"

Howard Place

N	Harrington Catherine M-†	2	housewife	57	here
o	Harrington John	2	longshoreman	60	"
P	Harrington John A	2	"	28	"
T	Noonan Joseph	3	electrician	33	"
u	Noonan Mary—†	3	housewife	30	"
v	Lundy Edward J	4	laborer	43	Kentucky
w	Lundy James J	4	"	58	here
x	Ross Emily E—†	4	housewife	33	"
y	Ross Neil D	4	machinist	38	"

Laurel Street

z	Sullivan Charles S	1	judge	68	here
	1037				
A	Sullivan Charles S, jr	1	U S N	41	"
B	Sullivan Mary L—†	1	housewife	68	"
c	Coughlin Daniel F	2	clerk	42	
D	Coughlin Minnie A—†	2	housewife	60	"
E	Coughlin Thomas G	2	U S N	40	
F	Coughlin Thomas J	2	retired	70	

Page.	Letter.	FULL NAME.	Residence, Jan. 1, 1944.	Occupation.	Supposed Age.	Reported Residence, Jan. 1, 1943. Street and Number.

Lincoln Place

	G	Brow Ella—†	2	housewife	44	here
	H	Derderian Mary—†	2	"	66	"
	K	Tracey Winifred—†	2	"	53	"
	N	Bengtson Florence S—†	3	"	29	
	O	Bengtson Roy G	3	chipper	31	"
	P	Dyer Edward E	3	machinist	33	Worcester
	R	Dyer Helen M—†	3	cleaner	27	"

Monument Square

	T	Columbie Edgar	31	welder	42	here
	U	Doucette Albert J	31	pipefitter	44	"
	V	Doucette Lydia W—†	31	housewife	31	N Hampshire
	W	Frutchey Leslie	31	U S A	28	Pennsylvania
	X	Frutchey Verna—†	31	housewife	22	"
	Y	Gray Louis N	31	shipwright	37	9 Ridgemont
	Z	McGuirk Arthur H	31	engineer	53	here
1038						
	A	McGuirk John J	31	yardmaster	60	"
	B	Robinson Thomas	31	electrician	38	"
	C	Shinney George W	31	U S N	33	
	D	Shinney Mary L—†	31	housewife	51	"
	E	Shinney William J	31	student	22	"
	F	Tyrrell Helen E—†	31	factoryhand	40	"
	G	Crockett Helen S—†	32	housewife	46	"
	H	Crockett Leon W	32	physician	50	"
	K	Stafford Adelaide—†	32	at home	86	"
	L	Crowe Catherine—†	33	printer	30	
	M	Crowe Margaret K—†	33	domestic	64	"
	N	Crowe Mary—†	33	typist	29	
	O	Crowe Michael	33	retired	68	
	P	Wall Dorothy L—†	33	clerk	33	
	R	Wall Florence J—†	33	housewife	60	"
	S	Wall George	33	painter	62	
	T	Wall Harold F	33	laborer	34	
	U	Wall Lester R	33	U S A	29	
	V	Brennan Catherine—†	33	housewife	67	"
	W	Brennan Catherine A—†	33	packer	30	
	X	Ferrick Helen—†	33	cook	45	
	Y	Gilmartin Bernard	33	clerk	40	
	Z	Gilmartin Margaret—†	33	operator	50	"

24

A	Gilmartin Mary A—†	33	operator	56	here
B	McGah David J	34	U S N	36	"
C	McGah Viola E—†	34	housewife	34	"
D	Browne Anna W—†	34	"	50	
E	Maginis Theresa—†	34	bookkeeper	47	"
F	Brown Alice—†	34	factory hand	40	"
G	McGinnis Eva—†	34	matron	43	"
H	McGinnis Frank	34	printer	50	
K	Fitzgerald Catherine M–†	34A	housewife	64	"
L	Fitzgerald John J	34A	U S A	26	
M	McGee John	34A	plumber	49	"
N	Tizani Annello	34A	electrician	38	"
O	Crowley Helen—†	34A	housewife	34	29 Mt Vernon
P	Crowley Thomas	34A	laborer	35	29 "
R	Howell Alice M—†	34A	clerk	28	29 "
S	Howell Annie—†	34A	housewife	65	29 "
T	O'Neill James W	34A	chauffeur	42	here
U	O'Neill Ruth E—†	34A	housewife	42	"
V	Parsons Harold L	34A	U S M C	21	"
W	Winter Frederick	35	U S A	21	
X	Winter George T	35	jeweler	53	"
Y	Winter Mary L—†	35	housewife	53	"
Z	Jankowski Josephine—†	35	operator	44	"

A	Lynch Catherine—†	35	housewife	73	"
B	Lynch John	35	laborer	70	"
C	Lynch Margaret—†	35	packer	31	"
D	Tennihan Anna E—†	35	housewife	38	"
E	Tennihan Myles J	35	foreman	43	"
F	Abate Elizabeth—†	36	housewife	65	"
G	Abate Frank	36	operator	68	"
H	Abate Louis	36	shipper	26	"
K	Reffi Anna—†	36	housewife	40	"
L	Reffi Manlio	36	printer	46	"
M	Schmidt Carl H	36	agent	53	"
N	*Schmidt Elfrieda—†	36	housewife	44	"
O	Conway Frank E	36	painter	37	"
P	*Conway John F	36	retired	73	
R	*Conway Julia R—†	36	housewife	67	"
S	Thorne Alice—†	36	typist	24	

Page.	Letter.	FULL NAME.	Residence, Jan. 1, 1944.	Occupation.	Supposed Age.	Reported Residence, Jan. 1, 1943. Street and Number.

Monument Square—Continued

	T	Thorne Charles	36	U S A	31	here
	U	Thorne Margaret—†	36	housewife	58	"
	V	Thorne Willard	36	meatcutter	60	"

Payson Place

	X	Collins Claire M—†	3	clerk	21	here
	Y	Collins George J	3	"	24	"
	Z	Collins Timothy J	3	"	55	"
1041						
	A	Collins Walter J	3	"	22	
	B	Collins Winifred E—†	3	housewife	57	"
	¹B	Connors Joseph H	4	teacher	59	1 Prospect av
	C	Sweeney John	4	attendant	35	here
	F	Kelly Sarah A—†	4	housewife	34	"
	G	Kelly William F	4	U S A	34	"
	D	Lambert Edna E—†	4	housewife	22	Connecticut
	E	Lambert Louis I	4	seaman	29	"
	H	Barron John J	5	laborer	58	here
	K	Connelly Francis H	5	U S N	21	"
	L	Connelly Leona M—†	5	housewife	44	"
	M	Connelly William J	5	laborer	49	

Trenton Street

	N	Carr Hugh	2	fireman	61	here
	O	Carr Katherine—†	2	housekeeper	51	"
	P	Doherty Daniel	2	U S A	24	"
	R	Doherty Ellen—†	2	housewife	60	"
	S	Doherty George A	2	U S A	27	
	T	Doherty John F	2	"	31	
	U	Salamone Anna—†	2	housewife	33	"
	V	Salamone Armand	2	U S N	32	
	W	Lynch Bella—†	2	at home	75	"
	X	McCarron Susan—†	4	housekeeper	68	25 Decatur
	Y	Abbott Annie M—†	4	operator	39	here
	Z	Abbott Elizabeth—†	4	housewife	64	"
1042						
	A	Abbott Joseph L	4	U S A	29	
	B	Abbott Thomas J	4	longshoreman	66	"

26

c	*McLaughlin Fannie—†	4	housekeeper	67	108 Baldwin
D	McLaughlin Margaret—†	4	"	87	108 "
E	Monagle Mary L—†	4	"	66	35 Winthrop
F	McGrann Anna—†	6	housewife	55	here
G	McGrann James J	6	manager	50	"
H	Goodhue Catherine—†	6	housewife	50	"
K	Goodhue Paul H	6	sorter	52	
L	Steele Mary—†	8	housewife	22	"
M	Steele John P	8	U S A	23	"
N	McClafferty Anna T—†	8	tel operator	28	"
O	McClafferty Grace M—†	8	secretary	38	"
P	McClafferty Helen R—†	8	clerk	30	"
R	McClafferty James F	8	"	34	
S	McClafferty John O	8	retired	68	
T	McClafferty Margaret E—†	8	clerk	41	
U	McClafferty Margaret T–†	8	housewife	67	"
V	Hanlon David J	10	machinist	27	7 Mystic
W	Hanlon Marie L—†	10	housewife	24	7 "
X	Coady Cecelia G—†	10	operator	32	here
Y	Coady Dennis	10	laborer	64	"
Z	Coady Mary E—†	10	housewife	30	"
	1043				
A	Coady Thomas J	10	checker	34	"
B	Brennan Florence I—†	12	housewife	31	"
C	Brennan James L	12	carpenter	37	"
D	Poore Francis J	12	manager	43	"
E	*Poore Margaret—†	12	housewife	40	"
G	Madden Helen J—†	14	"	28	
H	Madden William F	14	U S N	32	
K	Martine Elizabeth A—†	14	housewife	62	"
L	Martine Frederick J	14	U S A	21	
M	Scannell Bridget A—†	14	housewife	64	"
N	Scannell Edward	14	laborer	34	"
O	Scannell Paul D	14	U S A	28	"
T	Moriarty Anna J—†	18	housewife	36	"
U	Moriarty Joseph A	18	U S A	37	
V	Halley Francis X	18	"	34	
W	Halley Margaret T—†	18	housewife	46	"
X	Halley Maurice	18	machinist	47	"
Y	Halley Michael	18	retired	67	"
Z	Halley Mildred M—†	18	clerk	24	"

1044
Trenton Street—Continued

A	Halley William P	18	rigger	45	here
B	Halley William P, jr	18	U S N	23	"
C	Howell Mary—†	20	housewife	31	Everett
D	Howell Patrick G	20	fireman	35	"
E	Powers Edward J	20	electrician	35	here
F	Powers Mary A—†	20	housewife	35	"
G	Curran George H	22	shipfitter	42	"
H	Curran Mary C—†	22	housewife	42	"
K	Carr Elizabeth—†	22	"	64	
L	Carr John P	22	accountant	35	"
M	Carr Julia A—†	22	housewife	35	"
N	Scire Elizabeth—†	24	"	45	
O	Scire Frank	24	laborer	51	
P	Farlardeau Frank	24	machinist	63	"
R	Farlardeau Maud—†	24	housewife	63	"
S	Walsh Mabel E—†	24	"	55	
T	Walsh Mabel E—†	24	decorator	29	"
U	Walsh Madeline E—†	24	clerk	29	
V	Walsh William H	24	painter	51	

11

12

13

14

15

16

17

Ward 2–Precinct 11

CITY OF BOSTON

LIST OF RESIDENTS
20 YEARS OF AGE AND OVER

(NON-CITIZENS INDICATED BY ASTERISK)
(FEMALES INDICATED BY DAGGER)

AS OF

JANUARY 1, 1944

THOMAS F. SULLIVAN, *Chairman*
FREDERIC E. DOWLING, *Secretary*
WILLIAM A. MOTLEY, JR.
FRANCIS B. McKINNEY
EVERETT R. PROUT

Listing Board.

CITY OF BOSTON PRINTING DEPARTMENT

12

13

14

15

1(

1

1100
Bunker Hill Street

A	Brown Lawrence	161	brazier	28	Chelsea
B	Brown Mary—†	161	housewife	23	"
c	Dunn Arthur	161	foreman	35	Somerville
D	Dunn Helen A—†	161	housewife	30	"
E	O'Connell James	161	chauffeur	36	50 Tufts
F	O'Connell Mary—†	161	housewife	35	50 "
G	Ryan Marjorie—†	161	"	36	15 Monuments
H	Ryan Robert	161	plumber	29	15 "
K	Hannon Gertrude M—†	161	housewife	34	Somerville
L	Hannon William E	161	painter	42	"
M	Nolan Frank	161	shipper	25	Clinton
N	Nolan Mary—†	161	housewife	25	"
O	Stover Alice L—†	161	"	31	84 Monument
P	Stover Daniel	161	metalworker	36	84 "
R	Levasseur Alphonse	161	"	49	Lowell
s	Levasseur Helen T—†	161	housewife	39	"
T	Fay Helen—†	161	"	26	Vermont
U	Fay John	161	laborer	30	"
w	Higgins Frederick D	161	machinist	47	New Bedford
v	Higgins Frederick D, jr	161	U S A	21	"
X	Higgins Lillian M—†	161	housewife	45	"
z	Haney Helen C—†	161	"	30	18 Tufts
Y	Haney Joseph	161	machinist	32	18 "

1101

A	McDonald Regina—†	161	housewife	30	Malden
B	McDonald William	161	electrician	29	"
c	Kearn Dolores—†	169	housewife	26	Montana
D	Kearn Gerald	169	tinsmith	24	"
E	Gregory Bernard	169	operator	25	Pittsfield
F	Gregory Marjorie—†	169	housewife	25	"
G	Mazzocca Anthony	169	electrician	30	Somerville
H	Mazzocca Jessie—†	169	housewife	24	"
K	Rose Harry J	169	U S N	37	New Jersey
L	Rose Vera—†	169	housewife	31	"
M	Pickett Eleanor L—†	169	"	26	Somerville
N	Pickett Thomas F, jr	169	electrician	26	"
O	King Helen—†	169	housewife	31	"
P	King Robert	169	melter	32	
R	Larkin Harriett C—†	177	housewife	53	"
s	Larkin James A	177	laborer	66	"
T	Flanagan Ellen—†	177	housewife	36	65 Polk

Page.	Letter.	FULL NAME.	Residence, Jan. 1, 1944.	Occupation.	Supposed Age.	Reported Residence, Jan. 1, 1943. Street and Number.

Bunker Hill Street—Continued

	U	Flanagan Patrick	177	retired	39	65 Polk
	V	Wardman Harold	177	laborer	23	20 Green
	W	Wardman Helen—†	177	housewife	20	Somerville
	X	Adams Ruth—†	177	welder	25	Lee
	Y	Adams Venton	177	laborer	29	"
	Z	Hizney John	177	radio operator	27	Somerville
1102						
	A	Hizney Ruth—†	177	clerk	21	"
	B	Serino Albert	177	welder	26	33 Starr King ct
	C	Serino Mary—†	177	housewife	24	33 "
	D	Ekdahl Elroy	177	welder	28	N Hampshire
	E	Ekdahl Ethel—†	177	housewife	27	"
	F	Ryan Clara J—†	177	"	60	Lowell
	G	Ryan Edward J	177	shipwright	60	"
	K	Melanson Agnes—†	177	housewife	31	49 Starr King ct
	L	Melanson Joseph	177	laborer	39	49 "
	N	Watson John H	177	storekeeper	41	Wash'n D C
	O	Watson Mary D—†	177	clerk	33	"
	P	Beaudin Dorothy—†	195	housewife	25	58 Sullivan
	R	Beaudin Frederick I	195	storekeeper	43	58 "
	S	Lambert Mary—†	195	housewife	61	65 School
	T	McCormack Charles	195	oil dealer	23	278 Bunker Hill
	U	McCormack Lillian—†	195	housewife	24	278 "
	V	McCormack William	195	plumber	30	278 "
	W	Burke Alice—†	197	cakefroster	61	117 Elm
	X	Burke Eleanor M—†	197	laundress	24	117 "
	Y	Lynch Joseph T	197	letter carrier	36	Somerville
	Z	Lynch Margaret L—†	197	housewife	30	"
1103						
	B	Morrissey John	207	B F D	53	here
	C	Morrissey John, jr	207	teller	28	"
	D	Morrissey Mary—†	207	housewife	52	"
	E	Woodworth Ernest F	209	painter	67	"
	F	Woodworth Mary—†	209	housewife	63	"
	G	Lepito Bartholomew	209	U S N	51	
	H	Lepito Lillian—†	209	housewife	45	"
	N	Der Sem	219	laundryman	46	"

Carney Court

	T	Hardy Catherine—†	2	housewife	21	here
	U	Hardy Robert	2	chauffeur	21	"

3

Carney Court—Continued

Page.	Letter.	Full Name.	Residence, Jan. 1, 1944.	Occupation.	Supposed Age.	Reported Residence, Jan. 1, 1943. Street and Number.
	v	Mason Mary E—†	2	housewife	53	here
	w	Mason William F	2	rigger	53	"
	x	Hornsey Ivy M—†	2	housewife	55	15·Gloucester
	y	Hornsey John W	2	painter	59	15 "
	z	Murphy Margaret E—†	2	housewife	35	here
1104						
	a	Murphy Thomas F	2	painter	40	"
	b	*O'Connor Bridget—†	2	housewife	34	"
	c	O'Connor Patrick	2	waiter	32	
	d	Lannon Mary—†	2	housewife	46	"
	e	D'Amore Americo	2	coppersmith	25	32 Allen
	f	D'Amore Leona—†	2	housewife	24	32 "
	g	Charlebois Anna—†	2	"	27	here
	h	Charlebois Lawrence	2	stockman	31	"
	k	Noyes Harry F	2	clerk	35	17 Carney ct
	l	Noyes June B—†	2	housewife	23	17 "
	m	Roach James M	2	checker	40	here
	n	Roach Margaret P—†	2	housewife	33	"
	o	Arenberg Bernice—†	2	"	27	"
	p	Arenberg Isaac	2	clerk	30	"
	r	Griffin Agnes—†	2	housewife	41	"
	s	Griffin Andrew T	2	cleaner	42	
	t	Dempsey Helen T—†	10	housewife	31	"
	u	Dempsey John R	10	janitor	36	
	v	Ciambelli Henry	10	storekeeper	37	"
	w	Ciambelli Mary—†	10	housewife	36	"
	x	Cunningham Florence—†	10	"	27	
	y	Cunningham John J	10	U S N	32	
	z	Sodler James C	10	brakeman	30	"
1105						
	a	Sodler Mary—†	10	housewife	33	"
	b	Ellsworth John	10	operator	33	"
	c	Ellsworth Mildred—†	10	housewife	35	"
	d	O'Rourke Mary C—†	10	matron	40	14 Cordis
	e	Walsh William	10	retired	70	14 "
	f	Heafey Alice—†	18	housewife	27	here
	g	Heafey Daniel J	18	instructor	29	"
	h	Connor Catherine A—†	18	housewife	54	"
	k	Connor Mary A—†	18	secretary	30	"
	l	Conley Joseph J	18	longshoreman	36	"
	m	Conley Teresa J—†	18	housewife	31	"

Carney Court—Continued

N Fisher Bessie L—†	18	housewife	59	here
O Fisher Louella A—†	18	stenographer	23	"
P Magner Mary G—†	18	housewife	28	"
R Magner Thomas L	18	U S N	28	
S Bellaria Joseph	18	rigger	25	
T Bellaria Wanda—†	18	housewife	26	"
U Anastasio Joseph	18	barber	43	9 Carney ct
V Anastasio Julia M—†	18	housewife	38	9 "
w*Sartini James	18	chef	53	here
X Sartini Orestina—†	18	housewife	70	"
Y MacDonald Eugene	18	machinist	37	129 W Newton
Z MacDonald Thelma—†	18	housewife	37	129 "
1106				
A Dorsey Elizabeth—†	18	"	24	Lawrence
B Dorsey William A	18	welder	22	Haverhill
C Hanley Elsie—†	18	housewife	28	here
D Hanley Joseph	18	electrician	29	"
E Satcher Arlessia—†	18	housewife	51	Chatham
F Satcher Samuel L	18	rigger	45	"

Elm Street

G Raftell Demitra—†	78	housewife	45	here
H Raftell James	78	storekeeper	59	"
K Raftell William	78	U S C G	21	"
L Carr Anna A—†	79	housewife	50	"
M Carr Frank H	79	manager	49	"
N Carr Frank H, jr	79	U S A	23	
O Carr Mary E—†	79	student	20	"
P Carr William J	79	U S N	24	..
R Friel Joseph A	79	policeman	27	"
S Keville John	79	U S A	21	"
T Kerrissey George	80	laborer	55	9 Pleasant
U Mason Sarah—†	80	saleswoman	26	9 "
V Moores Mary—†	80	housewife	23	76 Monument
W Moores Tobias	80	chauffeur	23	76 "
X Mahoney Anna E—†	81	housewife	70	here
Y Mahoney Cornelius	81	retired	81	"
Z Mahoney Cornelius G	81	pipefitter	31	"
1107				
A Condon Eva M—†	81	saleswoman	66	"

Elm Street—Continued

B	Hanlon Agnes A—†	82	housewife	35	here
C	Hanlon John J	82	merchant	38	"
D	McGah Catherine E—†	83	bookkeeper	38	"
E	McGah David J	83	retired	63	''
F	McGah Edward J	83	U S A	25	
G	McGah Mary W—†	83	housewife	63	"
H	McGah Mary W—†	83	secretary	32	"
K	McGah Robert W	83	letter carrier	29	"
L	Currie Joseph A	84	chauffeur	45	"
M	Currie Margaret I—†	84	housekeeper	47	"
N	Cody Albert	85	U S N	45	''
O	Cody Anna—†	85	housewife	42	"
R	Coates John J	85	millhand	50	"
P	Coates John J, jr	85	U S A	20	
S	Coates Margaret A—†	85	housewife	54	"
T	Kelly Catherine—†	85	domestic	51	"
U	Kelly Thomas	85	laborer	49	
V	McLaughlin Catherine R–†	85	operator	21	"
W	McLaughlin Patrick	85	longshoreman	54	"
X	McLaughlin Patrick J	85	electrician	24	"
Y	McLaughlin Rose—†	85	housewife	53	"
Z	Birmingham Eleanor M—†	86	operator	24	"

1108

A	Birmingham John J	86	U S A	20	
B	Birmingham Mary W—†	86	housewife	44	"
C	Birmingham Thomas F	86	registrar	47	"
D	Birmingham Winifred M–†	86	supervisor	26	"
E	Cunningham Anne V—†	87	at home	54	"
F	Cunningham Mary J—†	87	bookkeeper	56	"
G	McGonagle Mary F—†	87	housewife	35	"
H	McGonagle Patrick J	87	drawtender	40	"
K	Kelly Grace E—†	88	housewife	30	"
L	Kelly Owen F	88	printer	31	
M	Grace Ellen M—†	89	at home	74	"
N	Grace Helen M—†	89	bookkeeper	39	"
O	Grace Thomas J	89	retired	75	"
P	Babine Mary—†	90	housewife	24	177 Col av
R	Bouchard Shirley—†	90	welder	21	New York
S	Campbell Christine—†	90	housewife	52	9 Concord av
T	Campbell Edith—†	90	clerk	21	9 "
U	Campbell Harvey	90	U S A	27	9 "

v	Campbell Joseph	90	janitor	53	9 Concord av
w	Campbell Roderick	90	U S A	30	9 "
x	O'Connell Margaret—†	90	housewife	24	17 Haverhill
y	Zugibe Benjamin	90	janitor	69	9 Concord av

1109

a	McLaughlin Francis J	92	clerk	36	here
b	McLaughlin Hugh R	92	U S A	30	"
c	McLaughlin John J	92	"	31	"
d	McLaughlin Rose A—†	92	housewife	63	"
e	Stevens Joseph E	92	clerk	34	..
f	Stevens Rosalie J—†	92	housewife	32	"
g	Walsh Hannah—†	94	"	78	
h	Walsh Julia—†	94	laundress	44	"
k	Walsh Redmond	94	laborer	72	"
l	Guilfoyle Eileen—†	96	housewife	28	184 Bunker Hill
m	Guilfoyle William R	96	longshoreman	28	25 Savin Hill av
n	Hyland George B	96	inspector	45	here
o	Hyland Mary—†	96	housewife	82	"
p	Collins Mildred V—†	96	"	40	"
r	Collins P William	96	laborer	42	..
s	O'Leary Anna M—†	98	housewife	52	"
t	O'Leary Daniel J	98	laborer	54	..
u	O'Leary Daniel F	98	U S N	29	"
v	O'Leary Joseph J	98	"	23	"
w	O'Leary John L	98	"	20	
x	Duffy Alicia F—†	99	at home	50	"
y	Duffy Charles F	99	retired	86	
z	Duffy Grace A—†	99	clerk	55	

1110

a	*Emery Alice—†	100	housewife	63	Somerville
b	*Emery Oliver	100	watchman	67	"
c	Flannagan Daniel J	100	fireman	31	5 Mystic
d	Flannagan Doris S—†	100	housewife	24	5 "
e	Sullivan Francis J	101	U S A	24	here
f	Sullivan James J	101	laborer	27	"
g	Sullivan Mary—†	101	housewife	50	"
h	Sullivan Timothy F	101	U S C G	21	"
k	Sullivan Timothy J	101	longshoreman	58	"
n	O'Neil Jennie—†	103	housewife	42	"
o	O'Neil Timothy J	103	freighthandler	42	"
s	McKinnon John W	104	longshoreman	37	"

Page.	Letter.	FULL NAME.	Residence, Jan. 1, 1944.	Occupation.	Supposed Age.	Reported Residence, Jan. 1, 1943. Street and Number.

Elm Street—Continued

T	McKinnon Julia T—†	104	housewife	40	here
U	Dunn Helen C—†	105	tel operator	20	"
V	Dunn Helen M—†	105	housewife	45	"
W	Dunn Mary M—†	105	bookkeeper	22	"
X	Dunn Thomas F	105	laborer	51	"
Y	Crowley Cornelius	106	clerk	36	
Z	Crowley Ellen F—†	106	housewife	69	"

1111

A	Crowley Helen T—†	106	housekeeper	28	"
B	Crowley John J	106	retired	70	"
C	Driscoll Agnes E—†	108	housewife	66	"
E	O'Brien Margaret G—†	110	at home	65	"
F	Raymond Grace M—†	110	housewife	50	"
G	Raymond Nicholas J	110	laundryman	50	"
H	Sullivan Francis E	112	electrician	43	"
K	Sullivan Mary C—†	112	housewife	40	"
L	Gallagher Albert A	113	ropemaker	39	"
M	Gallagher Edward J	113	laborer	56	
N	Gallagher Jeremiah P	113	U S A	35	
O	Conlon Joseph	114	electrician	38	"
P	Conlon Mary—†	114	housewife	35	"
R	Curran Martha—†	114	"	71	
S	Curran Maurice A	114	U S A	35	
T	Curran Maurice J	114	retired	69	
U	Doran Daniel J	115	"	63	
V	Holmes Margaret M—†	115	stenographer	21	"
W	Holmes Margaret M—†	115	housewife	51	"
X	Holmes Thomas C	115	chauffeur	51	"
Y	Reidy Emily—†	116	housewife	45	"
Z	Reidy John C	116	retired	54	

1112

A	Nolan Helen M—†	117	housewife	32	53 Chapman
B	Nolan Richard D	117	longshoreman	37	53 "
C	Costa Bartholomew C	118	rigger	30	here
D	Costa Margaret M—†	118	housewife	53	"
E	Costa Walter J	118	U S N	22	"
F	Kaliniak Elmer ·	119	U S M C	23	"
G	Kaliniak Lillian—†	119	housewife	24	"
H	Moore Mary E—†	119	"	46	
K	Moore William J	119	longshoreman	47	"
L	O'Donnell Catherine F—†	120	housewife	63	"

8

M	O'Donnell Josephine—†	120	clerk	22	here
N	Lewis Mary E—†	122	housekeeper	70	"
P	Cotter Mary —†	125	secretary	49	"
R	Cotter Richard	125	clerk	51	..
S	Toomey Ellen—†	125	housewife	68	"
T	Toomey Helen—†	125	clerk	42	
U	Toomey Thomas	125	laborer	71	"
V	*Lucash Mary—†	126	housewife	57	"
W	Nichols Catherine—†	126	waitress	32	"
X	Howell Julia—†	130	housewife	45	"
Y	Howell Louis J	130	U S A	25	
Z	Howell Robert S	130	U S N	22	

1113

A	Howell William	130	longshoreman	54	"
B	Burton Elizabeth A—†	130	housewife	37	"
C	Burton John J	130	chauffeur	36	"

Medford Street

F	Kuczyruk Sylvester	254	laborer	59	here
G	Marlinska Christie	254	"	32	"
H	*Marlinska Stella—†	254	housewife	51	"
K	*Vitito Mary—†	254	housekeeper	66	22 Mystic
L	Sokel Doris—†	256	housewife	28	64 Sullivan
M	Sokel Fred	256	U S A	30	64 "
N	Schuman Lewis	256	"	31	here
O	Schuman Rose—†	256	housewife	28	"
P	*Dogaluck Charles	256	laborer	50	"
R	Dowling Hazel A—†	260	housewife	34	25 Sullivan
S	Dowling Thomas H	260	chauffeur	38	25 "
T	Dennehy Daniel	286	manager	50	here
U	Dennehy Jane—†	286	housewife	50	"

Mystic Street

X	Fitzgerald Catherine M—†	1	housewife	46	here
Y	Fitzgerald James Y	1	U S N	22	"
Z	Brennan Jeremiah F	1	clerk	36	"

1114

A	Brennan Jeremiah J	1	stevedore	62	"
B	Brennan Mary A—†	1	U S M C	30	"

Mystic Street—Continued

c	Brennan Mary J—†	1	housekeeper	60	here
d	Brennan Nora J—†	1	secretary	32	"
e	Brennan William J	1	U S N	29	"
g	Mullen Catherine M—†	3	housewife	49	"
h	Mullen William J	3	clerk	55	
k	Mullen William J, jr	3	welder	23	"
l	Desmond Francis	3	U S A	27	66 Decatur
m	Desmond John	3	baker	27	46 Polk
n	Marsdon Mary—†	3	housewife	38	66 Decatur
o	Marsdon Vincent	3	longshoreman	36	66 "
p	Cauley Margaret—†	4	at home	78	here
r	Crowley Dennis F	4	supervisor	40	"
s	Crowley Nellie E—†	4	housewife	39	"
t	Broderick Mary—†	5	"	68	62 Tremont
u	Hudson Francis E	5	U S N	24	here
v	Hudson Isabelle—†	5	packer	53	"
w	Hudson James H	5	laborer	65	"
x	Scannell Edward M	5	foreman	53	"
y	Scannell Mary—†	5	housewife	47	"
z	Shea Daniel	6	merchant	43	"

1115

a	Shea Mary C—†	6	housewife	37	"
b	Tegan Elizabeth A—†	6	"	70	
c	Tegan George C	6	fireman	40	
d	McKittrick Harold	7	clerk	44	
e	McKittrick Margaret M—†	7	housewife	39	"
f	Hanlon Annie T—†	7	"	66	
g	Hanlon Arthur F	7	U S N	27	
h	Hanlon David	7	retired	73	
k	Stack Alice—†	8	housewife	60	"
l	Stack James P	8	U S A	33	"
m	Stack Patrick J	8	laborer	69	"
n	McManus Francis T	8	boilermaker	45	"
o	McManus Gladys E—†	8	housewife	45	"
p	Sawyer John H	9	mortician	32	"
r	Sawyer Mary M—†	9	housewife	31	"
s	Quigley Margaret M—†	9	operator	36	"
t	Quigley Veronica—†	9	tel operator	33	"
u	Quigley William F	9	retired	73	
v	Coughlin Margaret E—†	10	at home	87	"
w	Strout Henry M	10	agent	56	

x	Strout Henry V	10	U S A	20	here
y	Strout Marguerite V—†	10	investigator	56	"
z	Henchey Christina A—†	11	clerk	54	"
	1116				
a	Henchey James F	11	retired	85	
b	Henchey Mary M—†	11	secretary	54	"
c	McCann Phyrne M—†·	11	"	57	"
d	Howard John J	12	boilermaker	36	"
e	Howard Margaret L—†	12	housewife	36	"
f	McCully Arthur	12	rigger	56	
g	McCloud Elizabeth—†	12	housewife	58	"
h	Wilson Harry L	12	brakeman	65	"
k	Dukeshire Anna T—†	12	housewife	30	5 Sheafe
l	Dukeshire William B	12	chauffeur	42	5 "
m	Moffett Sadie—†	13	housewife	45	here
n	Donovan John W	13	laborer	44	"
o	Donovan Josephine—†	13	housewife	44	"
p	Cowan Marjorie—† ·	14	"	38	
r	Cowan Martin J	14	welder	46	"
s	Russell Maureen—†	14	technician	21	New Jersey
u	Strano Manuel	15	welder	25	here ·
v	Strano Rose—†	15	housewife	26	"
w	Lydon Edward	15	longshoreman	33	"
x	Lydon Mary A—†	15	cleaner	32	"
y	Maye William	15	longshoreman	63	"
z	Hartnett John	15	laborer	65	"
	1117				
a	Crowell Esther G—†	16	housewife	34	"
b	Crowell Wesley S	16	shipfitter	33	"
c	Morse Alice V—†	16	biller	37	
d	Morse Francis X	16	U S A	24	"
e	Morse Frank F	16	drawtender	65	"
f	Morse Helen M—†	16	housewife	64	"
g	Helmboldt Rose C—†	17	housekeeper	58	"
h	Smart James	17	clerk	54	"
k	Leveroni Elizabeth—†	17	housewife	53	"
l	Leveroni John	17	inspector	50	"
	Paulding Agnes M—†	17	housewife	61	"
	Mullett Helen J—†	18	"	32	
	Mullett Stanley J—†	18	chauffeur	31	"
m n	Driscoll Anna R—†	18	stenographer	22	"

Page.	Letter.	FULL NAME.	Residence, Jan. 1, 1944.	Occupation.	Supposed Age.	Reported Residence, Jan. 1, 1943. Street and Number.

Mystic Street—Continued

	R	Driscoll Catherine M—†	18	housewife	55	here
	S	Driscoll John J	18	tavernkeeper	31	"
	T	Driscoll Nicholas J	18	U S N	26	"
	U	Driscoll Patrick J	18	tavernkeeper	55	"
	V	Driscoll Rita N—†	18	printer	24	"
	W	Fowler Margaret V—†	18	housewife	28	"
	X	Fowler William T	18	electrician	26	"
	Y	Smet Gerard	18	bartender	56	"

1118

	A	Saul Dorothy—†	19	housewife	25	"
	B	Fitzpatrick James	19	U S A	23	
	C	Fitzpatrick Louise—†	19	housekeeper	25	"
	D	Fitzpatrick Winifred—†	19	welder	21	"
	E	Mansfield Michael	20	houseman	61	"
	F	Mansfield Nellie—†	20	domestic	61	"
	G	Ambrose Christine—†	20	"	50	"
	H	Ambrose Eugene	20	laborer	49	"
	K	Ambrose William	20	houseman	57	"
	L	McKay John	20	longshoreman	38	"
	M	McKay Margaret—†	20	housewife	38	"
	N	Flynn John J	21	counterman	34	"
	O	Flynn Josephine—†	21	housewife	38	"
	P	Masterson Emily J—†	21	supervisor	36	"
	R	Masterson John J	21	longshoreman	30	"
	S	Mahan Catherine—†	22	housewife	55	11 Hillside pl
	T	O'Brien Rita—†	22	"	27	Medford
	U	Flynn Lester J	22	clerk	43	here
	V	Gearin John J	22	"	51	"
	W	Gearin Mary F—†	22	housewife	50	"
	Y	Hall Harland M	23	U S A	20	
	Z	Hall Mary A—†	23	housewife	48	"

1119

	A	Hall Mary N—†	23	saleswoman	20	"
	B	Pepper Elizabeth—†	23	housewife	36	"
	C	Pepper Frederick	23	salesman	38	"
	E	McGonagle Catherine—†	24	housewife	55	3 Simpson ct
	F*	McGonagle James J	24	retired	64	3 "
	G	McGonagle James J, jr	24	U S N	24	3 "
	H	McGonagle Robert L	24	laborer	20	3 "
	K*	Harper Delia T—†	24	housewife	63	here
	L	Harper John M	24	U S A	31	"

12

M *Harper Walter C	24	packer	64	here
N *Harper Walter M	24	R A F	32	"
O *Maher Mary—†	24	housewife	79	"
R Eldridge Mildred—†	25	"	40	"
S Eldridge Walter	25	foreman	41	"
U Crowell Charles M	26	porter	34	
V Heath Alice—†	26	housewife	28	"
W *Vernon Elizabeth—†	26	"	62	"
X Gargaro Margaret—†	26	stitcher	24	"
Y *Gargaro Prospero	26	laborer	58	"

1120

A Walsh Edward	27	"	46	
B Walsh Margaret—†	27	housewife	46	"
C Hall Anna—†	27	"	48	
D Shea Catherine—†	27	tel operator	30	"
E Goen Celia—†	27	housewife	42	"
G Delaney Henry B	28	painter	37	"
H Walsh Anna M—†	28	housewife	65	"
K Walsh Martin	28	laborer	60	"
b Butts Elizabeth R—†	30	housewife	23	88 Warren
R Butts George K	30	U S A	24	88 "
S LaTerz Margaret F—†	30	waitress	21	37 Mystic
T O'Connor John J	30	pipefitter	45	37 "
U O'Connor Mary E—†	30	housewife	43	37 "
V Sullivan Stephen	30	retired	75	37 "
W Vanderhoff Hazel—†	30	operator	24	37 "
X Kane Adeline—†	31	housewife	30	here
Y Hoban Catherine—†	31	"	66	"
Z Hoban Helen—†	31	packer	32	"

1121

A Hoban Margaret—†	31	operator	30	"
B Landry Francis	31	motorman	35	"
C Landry Mary—†	31	housewife	34	"
D Kelly Mary—†	32	"	32	Medford
E Kelly Phillip	32	U S A	32	"
F Sullivan Florence J	32	fireman	33	here
G Sullivan Mary I—†	32	housewife	30	"
H Martin Mary—†	32	"	23	"
K Martin William	32	electrician	27	"
M Gillis Helen—†	33	housewife	30	"
N Gillis Neil A	33	steamfitter	32	"

13

Mystic Street—Continued

o	Lane Alice—†	33	operator	24	454 Medford
p	Lane Helen—†	33	housewife	40	454 · "
R	Lane John	33	laborer	45	454 "
s	Everett Edward J	34	fireman	28	here
T	Everett Marie E—†	34	housewife	26	"
U	Breen Elizabeth E—†	34	"	27	"
v	Breen John J	34	U S A	28	
w	O'Connor John E	34	metalworker	29	"
x	O'Connor Nora T—†	34	housewife	25	"
Y	O'Brien James H	35	welder	37	89 Polk
z	O'Brien Mary—†	35	housewife	33	89 "
	1122				
A	Colclough Albert E	35	printer	32	here
B	Colclough Grace H—†	35	housewife	35	"
c	Kelly Albert J	35	U S N	30	"
D	Kelly Hugh	35	retired	65	"
E	Kelly Sarah—†	35	housewife	66	"
F	*Lawless Nora—†	36	"	75	
G	*Lawless Patrick	36	retired	75	
H	Twomey Hugh	36	longshoreman	21	"
K	Twomey Jeremiah	36	"	54	
L	Twomey Jeremiah P	36	U S N	24	
M	Twomey Nellie—†,	36	housewife	49	"
N	McCarron Edward J	37	longshoreman	26	37 Haverhill
o	McCarron Jane J—†	37	housewife	61	37 "
P	McCarron Theresa M—†	37	WAVE	22	37 "
R	McCarron William	37	foreman	31	37 "
s	Orpen Henry	37	longshoreman	27	40 Corey
T	Orpen Jeanie—†	· 37	housewife	23	40 "
U	Kane Francis	37	retired	71	here
v	Kane Luke	37	U S A	20	"
w	Kane Mark	37	longshoreman	20	"
x	Wall Ellen L—†	38	housewife	66	1 McNulty ct
Y	Wall Patrick F	38	retired	70	1 "
z	O'Reilly Elizabeth—†	38	housewife	65	here
	1123				
A	Murray John H	38	laborer	57	
B	Murray Margaret F—†	38	housewife	67	"
c	Collins Eva—†	39	"	21	11 Sackville
D	Collins Fredrick	39	laborer	22	18 "
E	Gallo Joseph	39	"	55	here

14

Mystic Street—Continued

		Res.	Occupation	Age	Residence
F	Gallo Mary—†	39	housewife	47	here
G	Aylward Eileen M—†	40	"	37	"
H	Aylward James	40	operator	37	"
K	Sullivan Mary E—†	40	clerk	39	"
L	Sullivan Mary T—†	40	housewife	74	"
M	*McDonald Annie—†	41	"	66	
N	*McDonald John	41	carpenter	66	"
O	Connolly Anna M—†	41	welder	25	"
P	Connolly Ellen—†	41	factoryhand	23	"
R	Connolly Michael	41	longshoreman	55	"
T	Fox Alice—†	42	housewife	21	"
U	Fox John	42	freighthandler	20	"
V	Dundon Helen T—†	42	housewife	69	"
W	Flynn James J	42	U S A	24	
X	Twohig Mary—†	42	clerk	40	
Y	Dowling Annie E—†	43	housewife	58	"
Z	Dowling James	43	machinist	26	"
	1124				
A	Boudoux Annie—†	43	housewife	75	"
B	Wallace Ellen F—†	43	"	42	
C	Wallace Ernest S	43	seaman	37	"
D	McKay Frank	43	tender	63	54 Mystic
E	McKay Mabel—†	43	housewife	64	54 "
F	Jenks Grace—†	44	"	33	here
G	Jenks Leo M	44	plumber	40	"
L	Dolan May—†	45	housewife	46	"
M	Hart Henry	45	electrician	22	"
O	Corbett Margaret—†	46	housewife	67	"
P	Doherty Ethel E—†	46	"	52	2 Lincoln pl
R	Doherty William T	46	nickelplater	55	2 "
T	DiMauro Grace—†	47	housewife	42	here
U	DiMauro Jennie—†	47	stitcher	21	"
V	DiMauro Joseph	47	blacksmith	47	"
W	DiMauro Vincent	47	U S A	23	
Y	Smith Andrew G	48	photographer	29	"
Z	Smith Sally M—†	48	housewife	28	"
	1125				
A	Gallagher Edith J—†	48	"	27	97 Bunker Hill
B	Gallagher Richard G	48	chauffeur	44	97 "
C	Fee Edward F	50	U S A	30	here
D	Fee Eleanor A—†	50	secretary	21	"

15

Page.	Letter.	Full Name.	Residence, Jan. 1, 1944.	Occupation.	Suppressed Age.	Reported Residence, Jan. 1, 1943. Street and Number.

Mystic Street—Continued

	E	Fee John J	50	longshoreman	55	here
	F	Fee John J, jr	50	U S A	23	"
	G	Fee Regina—†	50	housewife	52	"
	H	Passalacqua Claire—†	50	"	21	"
	K	Passalacqua Santo J	50	U S A	22	"
	O	Donnelly Anne M—†	54	housewife	29	"
	P	Donnelly John T	54	clerk	39	
	R	LaPointe Margaret P—†	54	housewife	45	"
	S	Campagna Josephine—†	56	"	43	
	T	Campagna Salvatore	56	janitor	51	
	U	Collins Mary—†	56	nurse	58	
	V	McPartland Ellen E—†	58	housewife	43	"
	W	McPartland Frederick P	58	warehouse	43	"
	X	Cain Mary F—†	58	stenographer	45	"

1126　Pearl Street

	A	Ward Anne T—†	59	secretary	37	here
	B	Ward Catherine—†	59	at home	74	"
	C	Ward Mary E—†	59	supervisor	43	"
	D	Sullivan Helen F—†	61	clerk	32	
	E	Sullivan James P	61	retired	59	
	G	Edwards John F	63	blacksmith	67	"
	H	Edwards Julia—†	63	at home	60	"
	K	Edwards Lawrence F	63	shipper	27	
	L	Edwards Margaret A—†	63	housewife	23	"
	M	Edwards Michael J	63	oiler	37	"
	N	McGonagle Charles A	65	letter carrier	49	"
	O	McGonagle Estelle J—†	65	at home	37	"
	P	Fall Lilla—†	67	"	65	
	R	Woods Arthur T	69	U S A	25	
	T	Woods Imelda B—†	69	at home	57	"
	S	Woods Leo H	69	U S A	23	
	U	Woods Paul J	69	painter	61	"
	V	Kelly Bernard F	69	clerk	51	
	W	Kelly Helen F—†	69	at home	49	"
	X	O'Leary John F	71	U S A	32	
	Y	O'Leary John J	71	chauffeur	61	"
	Z	O'Leary Mary F—†	71	at home	62	"
		1127				
	A	Curtis Anna C—†	73	"	32	

16

B	Curtis Arthur G	73	driller	33	here
C	Keane Anne—†	73	bookkeeper	44	"
D	Stanton Helen C—†	75	at home	38	"
E	Stanton Robert E	75	drawtender	46	"
G	Lewis Octava—†	77	at home	21	"
H	Lewis Simeon C	77	U S N	29	
K	Martin Bradley W	77	laborer	45	"
L	Martin Esther E—†	77	at home	40	"
M	Martin Mary P—†	77	clerk	21	
O	Furlong Basil J	79	shipfitter	50	"
P	Furlong Francis	79	U S A	22	
R	Furlong Helen R—†	79	tel operator	26	"
S	Hawes Mary C—†	79	at home	59	"
T	McCarthy Catherine T—†	79	"	25	"
U	McCarthy Dennis J	79	watchman	65	"
V	Magner Joseph	81	clerk	34	Somerville
W	Sullivan James P, jr	81	maintenance	30	61 Pearl
X	Sullivan Margaret M—†	81	at home	29	61 "
Y	Kelly Annie L—†	83	"	80	here
Z	Furlong Bridget—†	85	"	61	"

1128

A	Furlong James E	85	U S N	22	··
B	Furlong John P	85	freighthandler	27	"
C	Furlong Marion E—†	85	clerk	34	
D	Furlong Nicholas F	85	"	37	
E	Furlong Thomas	85	cook	67	
F	Keenan Anna M—†	85	WAC	39	
G	Keenan Charles F	85	U S N	39	
H	Davis Earl F	89	longshoreman	28	"
K	Davis Elizabeth G—†	89	at home	61	"
L	Davis Evelyn R—†	89	"	27	
M	Lee Albert J	89	machinist	27	"
N	Lee Marion E—†	89	at home	23	"
O	Carroll Charlotte—†	91	"	77	
P	Fisher Elsie M—†	91	"	62	
R	Boyce Roland L	91	shipfitter	49	"
S	McGonagle Ethel M—†	91	at home	51	"
T	McGonagle Helen F—†	91	stenographer	24	"
U	Jennings Mary T—†	93	at home	53	"
V	Sullivan Charles E	93	U S A	27	
W	Sullivan Lawrence W	93	electrician	22	"

2—11   17

Page.	Letter.	FULL NAME.	Residence, Jan. 1, 1944.	Occupation.	Supposed Age.	Reported Residence, Jan. 1, 1943. Street and Number.

Pearl Street—Continued

x	Sullivan Mary V—†	93	at home	49	here
y	Sullivan Paul F	93	U S N	20	"
z	Magner Veronica M—†	93	welder	23	"
	1129				
A	McGonagle Mary—†	95	at home	52	"
B	Pigott Maurice P	95	porter	46	
C	Calabrese Domenic	95	laborer	51	
D	Calabrese Tina—†	95	at home	38	"
E	Ward Alice M—†	97	"	23	
F	Ward Jane B—†	97	saleswoman	26	"
G	Ward Joseph	97	manager	60	"
H	Ward Loretta M—†	97	at home	59	"
K	Gilmartin Mary F—†	97	"	45	

Polk Street

L	Donovan John J	16	chauffeur	50	here
M	Donovan Stella M—†	16	housewife	52	"
N	O'Brien Martin A	16	mason	47	"
O	O'Brien Mary—†	16	matron	44	"
P	Green Francis J	16	retired	37	26 Elm
R	Jackson Catherine E—†	16	operator	61	26 "
S	Norton Helen G—†	16	tester	24	26 "
T	O'Leary Albina F—†	16	clerk	38	26 "
U	Fitzgerald Agnes E—†	16½	"	25	here
V	Fitzgerald Joseph P	16½	chauffeur	50	"
W	Fitzgerald Joseph P, jr	16½	U S A	27	"
X	Fitzgerald Leo W	16½	"	21	
Y	Fitzgerald Marion—†	16½	housewife	46	"
	1130				
A	Wilson Dorothy E—†	17	at home	31	"
B	McGrath Catherine R—†	17	housewife	35	"
C	McGrath Edward J	17	painter	36	"
D	Murray Margaret A—†	17	at home	65	"
E	Steele Frances T—†	17	nurse	25	"
F	Steele Robert	17	U S A	31	Milton
G	Wheeler Mary A—†	17	housewife	33	here
H	Wheeler Ralph H	17	laborer	32	"
K	Beir Charles D	17	U S N	26	"
L	Beir Velaska—†	17	housewife	24	New Jersey
M	Ryan Marion T—†	17	"	30	here

18

N	Ryan Thomas J	17	shipper	29	here
O	White Anna—†	17	housewife	27	"
P	White Robert M	17	U S N	27	"
R	Coyle Veronica—†	17	housewife	48	"
S	Burke Anna—†	17	at home	47	"
T	Foley Mary A—†	17	housewife	33	"
U	Foley Peter J	17	rigger	42	"
V	Ramsey Catherine—†	17	clerk	27	37 Walker
W	Ramsey William R	17	"	34	37 "
X	Hickey Dennis T	18	U S A	22	here
Y	Hickey Edward L	18	laborer	27	"
Z	Hickey James J	18	"	52	"
	1131				
A	Hickey John P	18	"	26	
B	Hickey Josephine M—†	18	housewife	52	"
C	Hickey Matthew L	18	laborer	25	"
D	McIntosh Helen C—†	20	shipfitter	21	"
E	McIntosh Nellie C—†	20	housewife	44	"
F	McIntosh William H	20	policeman	45	"
G	McNulty Catherine E—†	25	housewife	64	"
H	McNulty George J	25	retired	66	
K	McNulty Joseph P	25	U S A	28	"
L	McNulty Thomas F	25	laborer	34	"
M	Johnson Agnès E—†	25	housewife	29	82 Walford way
N	Johnson Carl W	25	guard	27	82 "
O	Leahy Helen—†	25	housewife	26	43 Mystic
P	Howell Emily A—†	25	"	29	here
R	Howell John B	25	clerk	28	"
S	Burke John	25	U S N	26	"
T	Burke Marguerite—†	25	housewife	24	"
U	Lowney Joseph	25	laborer	31	"
V	Lowney Susan—†	25	housewife	28	"
X	Burke Anna M—†	33	"	37	
Y	Burke Robert W	33	operator	42	"
Z	Johnson Emil J	33	retired	73	
	1132				
A	Johnson Mary L—†	33	housewife	72	"
B	Hess Elizabeth—†	33	clerk	22	
C	Hess Robert	33	U S N	22	
E	Auffrey Eva—†	33	housewife	30	"
F	Auffrey Victor J	33	welder	33	

1

19

Polk Street—Continued

G	Oksomitis Anne A—†	33	waitress	35	here
H	Callahan Elizabeth B—†	33	housewife	65	"
K	Callahan Martin J	33	retired	75	"
L	Turner Gertrude—†	33	housewife	25	83 Polk
M	Turner William	33	electrician	30	83 "
O	Blanchard Erma—†	33	housewife	48	here
P	Blanchard Wilbur W	33	U S N	21	"
R	Cash Elizabeth M—†	33	waitress	26	"
S	Oelgart Harry	33	rigger	38	Canada
T	*Oelgart Margaret F—†	33	housewife	26	"
U	McGloin George	33	chauffeur	41	21 Lincoln
V	McGloin Theresa—†	33	housewife	40	21 "
W	Marques Jeannette—†	41	operator	30	here
X	Farley Anne—†	41	housewife	39	"
Y	Farley Hugh F	41	shipper	38	"
Z	McGee Daniel	41	boilermaker	51	"
	1133				
A	McGee Rose—†	41	housewife	49	"
C	Pierce Agnes M—†	41	"	38	
D	Rounbehler Beatrice R—†	41	"	28	
E	Rounbehler Charles P	41	pipefitter	34	"
F	Ellsworth Edward F	41	chauffeur	42	"
G	Ellsworth Margaret—†	41	housewife	36	"
H	Beckwith Dorothy—†	41	"	27	"
K	Beckwith Elmer	41	policeman	28	"
L	Marshall Edward S	41	painter	40	
M	Marshall Mildred M—†	41	housewife	35	"
N	Brough Margaret—†	42	"	65	
O	Houghton Daniel	42	laborer	63	"
P	Grace Elizabeth A—†	42	housewife	32	384 Amory
R	Connell Francis	42	chauffeur	41	here
S	Connell Mary—†	42	housewife	39	"
U	Lane James	44	chauffeur	46	"
V	Swales Alice J—†	44	housewife	52	"
W	Swales George W	44	chauffeur	52	"
X	Swales Mildred L—†	44	manager	23	"
Y	Sullivan Agnes—†	46	housewife	37	"
Z	Sullivan Leo F	46	laborer	36	
	1134				
A	Connelly Gertrude—†	46	housekeeper	34	"
B	Connelly William F	46	orderly	22	"

c	Connelly William M	46	laborer	47	here
d	*Urquhart John	46	"	60	"
e	Urquhart Margaret—†	46	housewife	63	"
f	Perry Anna—†	48	"	47	
g	Perry Fred	48	baker	52	
h	Desmond Isabelle—†	48	housewife	28	"
k	Desmond Michael J	48	longshoreman	34	"
l	Desmond Thomas V	48	U S A	23	··
m	Hurley James	49	laborer	37	"
n	Hurley Josephine—†	49	housewife	35	"
o	Hartnett Julia—†	49	"	41	"
p	Hartnett Lawrence	49	milkman	42	"
r	Harrington John	49	laborer	40	"
s	Harrington Mary—†	49	housewife	38	"
t	Judge Florence—†	49	clerk	23	3 Hancock
u	Judge Helen—†	49	"	22	3 "
v	Judge James	49	longshoreman	28	3 "
w	Judge Margaret—†	49	housewife	56	3 "
x	Swirbalus Joseph	49	shipfitter	39	41 Polk
y	Swirbalus Josephine—†	49	housewife	36	41 "
z	Shoop Arley	49	electrician	33	Lynn

1135

a	Shoop Evelyn—†	49	housewife	28	"
b	Burgess Jean—†	57	"	34	here
c	Burgess William	57	motorman	40	"
d	Vita Frank	57	salesman	38	"
e	Vita Mildred—†	57	housewife	30	"
f	Burhoe Arthur	57	chauffeur	26	"
g	Burhoe Helen—†	57	housewife	26	"
h	Steinbrecher Joseph	57	welder	38	49 Union av
k	McPhee Ethel—†	57	housewife	41	here
l	McPhee Joseph	57	U S N	41	"
m	O'Rourke Eleanor—†	57	at home	20	"
n	O'Rourke Jeremiah	57	U S A	23	
o	Tucker Catherine—†	57	housewife	37	"
p	Tucker Henry	57	manager	38	"
r	Sutherland David G	57	salesman	31	"
s	Sutherland Martha E—†	57	housewife	30	"
t	Kennedy Catherine M—†	57	"	32	
u	Kennedy Edward J	57	clerk	34	
v	Bindman Albert	57	pharmacist	47	"

21

Page.	Letter.	FULL NAME.	Residence, Jan. 1, 1944.	Occupation.	Supposed Age.	Reported Residence, Jan. 1, 1943. Street and Number.

Polk Street—Continued

	w	Bindman Jennle—†	57	housewife	44	here
	x	Andrea Michael L	65	laborer	26	121 Bunker Hill
	y	Andrea Ruth C—†	65	housewife	25	121 "
	z	McDonough John F	65	longshoreman	30	here
1136						
	A	McDonough Mabel R—†	65	housewife	25	"
	B	Frost Anna—†	65	"	29	
	c	Frost Leslie	65	laborer	27	"
	D	Haley Eleanor—†	65	housewife	32	10 St Martin
	E	Haley John	65	plumber	31	10 "
	F	Small Mary—†	65	housewife	24	370 Bunker Hill
	G	Small William	65	operator	26	370 "
	H	Cullen Albert	65	U S N	33	58 Pearl
	K	Cullen Alice—†	65	housewife	29	58 "
	L	Caples James	65	clerk	30	here
	M	Caples Mary—†	65	housewife	28	"
	N	Galvin Catherine F—†	65	"	54	"
	o	Galvin James F	65	custodian	21	"
	P	McNeff Ann—†	65	housewife	38	"
	R	Palmer Edward F	73	laborer	46	46 Fisher av
	s	Palmer Gertrude M—†	73	housewife	43	46 "
	T	Devlin James C	73	laborer	41	here
	U	Devlin Rose—†	73	housewife	45	"
	v	McKee James J	73	bartender	31	"
	w	McKee Mildred J—†	73	housewife	27	"
	x	Barlow Edith—†	73	"	31	
	Y	Barlow Leo	73	operator	38	"
	z	Greenwood Charles	73	U S A	21	
1137						
	A	O'Leary John	73	machinist	34	"
	B	O'Leary Mildred—†	73	housewife	30	"
	c	O'Leary Alice F—†	73	"	30	
	D	O'Leary John N	73	operator	35	"
	E	Phillips John R	81	U S N	35	
	F	Phillips Mary L—†	81	housewife	27	"
	G	Linehan Agatha M—†	81	"	31	Somerville
	H	Linehan Raymond J	81	driller	31	"
	K	Comeau Margaret—†	81	housewife	47	here
	L	Rowell Elsie R—†	81	"	37	"
	M	Rowell William F	81	guard	38	"
	N	Getz Mary E—†	81	housewife	24	79 Lamartine

o	Getz William C	81	U S N	23	79 Lamartine
p	Spellman Charles F	81	chauffeur	60	here
r	Spellman Mary F—†	81	housewife	56	"
s	Karg Helen A—†	81	"	34	"
t	Karg William P	81	retired	44	"
u	O'Brien Margaret Y—†	81	housewife	25	Medford
v	O'Brien Walter F	81	welder	27	"
w	Shackford Frances M—†	81	housewife	35	here
x	Shackford Henry D	81	laborer	39	"
y	Sweeney Elizabeth—†	89	housewife	34	"
z	Sweeney William A	89	operator	37	"

1138

a	Cook Albert J	89	guard	37	66 Decatur
b	Cook Antoinette—†	89	housewife	25	66 "
c	Byrne Alice J—†	89	operator	27	54 Tremont
d	Flynn Catherine A—†	89	housewife	46	64 Walker
e	Flynn Catherine P—†	89	at home	20	64 "
f	O'Neil Helen—†	89	housewife	37	here
g	O'Neil Leonard	89	electrician	40	"
h	Patras Catherine—†	89	housewife	43	"
k	Patras Constantine	89	retired	48	
l	Cottier Frances M—†	89	housewife	28	"
m	Cottier Joseph	89	chauffeur	30	"
n	Sargent Harry J	97	"	42	
o	Sargent Lillian R—†	97	housewife	40	"
p	Quilty Anna A—†	97	"	49	..
r	Quilty Michael	97	laborer	57	"
s	Sullivan Daniel J	97	U S A	39	65 Polk
t	Sullivan Rose E—†	97	housewife	35	65 "
u	Wilkinson Catherine B—†	97	"	29	Somerville
v	Wilkinson William H	97	U S N	29	"
w	Mahoney Mary—†	97	operator	43	here
x	Steen Catherine—†	97	housewife	32	31 Colonial av
y	Steen Raymond T	97	U S N	38	31 "
z	Stafford Antoinette M—†	97	housewife	28	9 Corey

1139

a	Stafford William W	97	fireman	31	9 "
b	Katis Frances T—†	97	brazier	39	here
c	Katis Virginia E—†	97	at home	20	"
d	McLellan Alan R	97	salesman	39	"
e	McLellan Alma M—†	97	housewife	41	"

1

Ward 2–Precinct 12

CITY OF BOSTON

LIST OF RESIDENTS
20 YEARS OF AGE AND OVER

(NON-CITIZENS INDICATED BY ASTERISK)
(FEMALES INDICATED BY DAGGER)

AS OF

JANUARY 1, 1944

THOMAS F. SULLIVAN, *Chairman*
FREDERIC E. DOWLING, *Secretary*
WILLIAM A. MOTLEY, JR.
FRANCIS B. McKINNEY
EVERETT R. PROUT

Listing Board.

CITY OF BOSTON PRINTING DEPARTMENT

1200
Allston Street

A	Doherty Catherine—†	3	at home	32	here
B	Gately Charles	3	contractor	39	"
C	Fone Anna—†	3	housewife	45	"
D	O'Brien Louise—†	3	operator	27	"
E	O'Brien William	3	U S N	28	
F	O'Connor John	5	retired	73	
G	O'Connor Mary E—†	5	matron	47	
H	Kennedy Gladys—†	5	housewife	35	"
K	Readdy Mary P—†	7	at home	55	"
L	Dailey Fannie—†	7	housewife	79	"
M	Early Sadie—†	7	stenographer	50	"
N	Harrington Catherine T—†	9	housewife	52	"
O	Harrington John	9	laborer	57	
P	O'Connor Margaret—†	11	housewife	45	"
R	O'Connor Patrick	11	machinist	45	"
S	Sheehan Mary G—†	11	housewife	33	"
T	Sheehan William	11	laborer	41	
V	Devine John A	13	shipper	39	
W	Devine Nellie—†	13	at home-	66	"
X	Devine Mary A—†	13	milliner	57	"
Y	Landman Doris—†	15	housewife	25	Vermont
Z	Landman Winfred	15	carpenter	29	"

1201

B	Walsh William F	15	salesman	57	here
C	Delaney Rita—†	17	housewife	27	"
D	Sullivan Ellen T—†	17	"	70	"
E	Sullivan Ellen T—†	17	tel operator	39	"
F	Sullivan Joanna—†	17	at home	35	"
G	Sullivan Mary—†	17	tel operator	34	"
H	Sullivan Michael	17	retired	66	"
K	Twiss Arthur	17	machinist	40	Brookline
L	Twiss Catherine—†	17	housewife	32	"
N	Casey Elizabeth—†	19	"	45	here
O	Casey John	19	blacksmith	46	"
P	Hourihan John	19	fireman	39	35 Mead
R	Traisi Catherine B—†	19	housewife	42	here
S	Traisi Charles F	19	guard	50	"
T	Desmond Agnes—†	21	housewife	28	86 High
U	Desmond John B	21	printer	33	86 "
V	Doherty John J	21	laborer	56	here

Letter.	Full Name.	Residence, Jan. 1, 1944.	Occupation.	Supposed Age.	Reported Residence, Jan. 1, 1943. Street and Number.

Allston Street—Continued

w	Doherty Nora—†	21	housewife	52	here
x	Wagner Charles	23	laborer	35	"
y	Wagner Eileen—†	23	housewife	34	"
	1202				
a	Allen Annie—†	25	"	75	
b	Russell James A	25	clerk	58	
c	Russell Nellie G—†	25	operator	54	"
d	Clark Walter E	25	laborer	65	
e	Welch Lillian—†	27	housewife	44	"
f	Welch Michael	27	laborer	53	"
g	Welch Mildred—†	27	clerk	21	
h	Ward James	29	electrician	32	"
k	Ward Michael	29	U S A	27	"
l	Ward Rose—†	29	housewife	58	"
m	Cushing Dorothy—†	31	machinist	20	"
n	Cushing Mary G—†	31	housewife	45	"
o	Cushing William F	31	watchman	47	"
p	O'Brien John B	33	U S A	24	
r	O'Brien Margaret F—†	33	housewife	47	"
s	O'Brien Margaret M—†	33	clerk	22	
t	O'Brien William E	33	U S A	26	
u	O'Brien William T	33	electrician	47	"
v	Desmond Catherine—†	35	housewife	32	"
w	Desmond Francis X	35	printer	35	
x	Desmond Gerald A	35	U S N	28	"
y	Desmond Matthew	35	printer	31	"
z	Desmond Nellie F—†	35	housewife	70	"
	1203				
a	Desmond Richard P	35	U S A	22	
b	Kelly Patrick H	37	janitor	65	"
c	Sullivan Catherine—†	37	supervisor	41	"
d	Herrick Catherine—†	39	housewife	23	"
e	Herrick Roy	39	chauffeur	26	"
f	Graney Florence—†	39	inspector	30	"
g	Graney Mary L—†	39	housewife	60	"
h	Graney Peter	39	laborer	66	
k	Power Mary—†	39	clerk	28	
l	Graney Julia—†	43	metalworker	21	"
m	Graney Martin F	43	U S N	20	
n	Kane Mary—†	45	laborer	46	
o	Cronin Annie—†	47	typist	25	

Page.	Letter.	FULL NAME.	Residence, Jan. 1, 1944.	Occupation.	Supposed Age.	Reported Residence Jan. 1, 1943. Street and Number.

Allston Street—Continued

P	Cronin Elizabeth—†	47	at home	37	here
R	Cronin Ellen—†	47	housewife	66	"
S	Cronin John L	47	salesman	65	"
T	Braman A Wilhelmina—†	49	secretary	50	"
U	Braman Carolina—†	49	clerk	48	"
V	Braman Edith W—†	49	supervisor	46	"
W	Braman Robert F	49	contractor	52	"
X	Donovan Catherine—†	49	housewife	41	"
Y	Donovan J Paul	49	laborer	22	
Z	Logue John A	51	"	54	

1204

A	Logue Rose—†	51	housewife	78	"
B	Sullivan Agnes R—†	51	"	43	
C	Sullivan William P	51	plumber	54	"
D	Russell Joseph A	51	machinist	33	"
E	Russell Margaret—†	51	housewife	31	"

Avon Place

F	McCusker Charles A	1	U S A	28	here
G	McCusker Ellen E—†	1	housewife	29	"
H	Boyle Sarah J—†	2	clerk	65	"
K	Harrington Agnes—†	2	at home	88	"
L	Shea Catherine M—†	3	housewife	47	"
M	Shea Elizabeth M—†	3	clerk	21	
N	Shea William P	3	laborer	49	
O	Shea William P	3	U S N	20	
R	Bulzomi Joseph	6	carpenter	50	"
S	*Bulzomi Mary—†	6	housewife	42	"
T	Brown Martha V—†	7	operator	43	"
U	Creedon Anne C—†	7	at home	28	"
V	Creedon John J	7	U S A	28	
W	De St Croix Charles H	7	"	25	
X	De St Croix Mary A—†	7	housewife	59	"
Y	Nicoli Catherine G—†	7	operator	37	"
Z	Ray Lila W—†	8	clerk	44	

1205   Bartlett Street

A	Ryan John	54	retired	80	here
B	Ryan Margaret—†	54	housewife	65	"

Bartlett Street—Continued

	Full Name.	Residence, Jan. 1, 1944.	Occupation.	Supposed Age.	Reported Residence Jan. 1, 1943. Street and Number.
c	Cameron Margaret E—†	54	housewife	34	here
d	Cameron William J	54	policeman	35	"
	Monahan Catherine V—†	54	housewife	54	"
e	Monahan Catherine R—†	54	clerk	21	
g	Monahan Frederick O	54	laborer	55	"
h	Murphy Mary T—†	56	housewife	69	58 Pearl
k	Ferguson Audrea M—†	56	bookkeeper	20	here
l	Ferguson Francis J	56	U S A	23	"
m	Ferguson Mary A—†	56	housewife	42	"
n	Murphy Henry L	56	supervisor	58	"
o	Fitzpatrick Helen M—†	56	housewife	41	"
p	Fitzpatrick William J	56	welder	40	
r	Neville Nicholas	57	retired	71	
s	McShane Virginia—†	57	housewife	40	"
t	Wormell Avard	57	machinist	65	"
u	Wormell Luetta—†	57	housewife	61	"
v	George Patricia M—†	57	shipfitter	36	6 Holden row
w	Hamilton Orpha—†	57	housewife	39	here
x	Hamilton Ross	57	laborer	39	"
y	Hamilton Rufus	57	U S N	21	"
z	Wilson Edward H	57	U S A	21	6 Holden row

1206

	Full Name.	Residence, Jan. 1, 1944.	Occupation.	Supposed Age.	Reported Residence Jan. 1, 1943. Street and Number.
a	Wilson Melinda M—†	57	housewife	62	6 "
b	Smith Casilda—†	58	"	42	here
c	Fallon Joseph J	58	laborer	38	"
d	Fallon Mildred G—†	58	housewife	39	"
e	Sullivan Elizabeth—†	58	"	38	
f	Sullivan William	58	baker	37	
g	*Madruga Mary—†	63	housewife	47	"
h	Auld Helen—†	63	"	27	283 Main
k	Kuschensky Adam	63	U S A	24	283 "
l	Kuschensky Agnes—†	63	woodworker	20	283 "
m	Kuschensky Rose—†	63	assembler	22	283 "
n	Connolly Anna—†	63	housewife	29	Chelsea
o	Connolly John	63	laborer	28	"
r	Coughlin Francis R	67	painter	38	19 Mystic
s	Coughlin Margaret I—†	67	housewife	34	19 "
u	Kelly Joseph	73	storekeeper	52	here
v	Motherway Annie—†	75	housewife	53	"
w	Motherway John	75	laborer	61	"
x	Motherway John P	75	U S A	21	

Bartlett Street—Continued

	Y	Motherway William J	75	U S A	26	here
	z	Motherway William P	75	foreman	28	"
1207						
	A	Garvin Catherine—†	77	housewife	63	"
	B	Garvin Francis J	77	welder	29	
	C	Garvin Mary M—†	77	typist	25	
	D	Garvin Patrick	77	laborer	69	
	E	Whitlock Catherine A—†	79	housewife	40	"
	F	Whitlock Charles J	79	laborer	51	
	G	Doherty Ann G—†	79	housewife	70	"
	H	Doherty Catherine A—†	79	maid	30	
	K	Doherty Fráncis X	79	U S N	27	
	L	Doherty Patrick J	79	fireman	70	,,
	M	Farrell Mary J—†	79	librarian	39	"
	O	Clafferty Bridget—†	82	housewife	47	"
	P	Clafferty Edward	82	teamster	53	"
	R	Clafferty Edward	82	welder	20	
	S	Clafferty Ellen—†	82	at home	23	"
	T	Clafferty Margaret—†	82	"	25	
	U	Clafferty Mary—†	82	WAC	24	
	w*	DiStasis George	rear 83	laborer	51	
	x*	DiStasis Grace—†	" 83	housewife	31	"
	Y	Riley Frank H	84	clerk	37	"
	z	Riley Sarah M—†	84	housewife	32	"
1208						
	A	Doyle Frank F	85	retired	77	
	B	Murray Ernest B	85	agent	63	
	C	Murray George A	85	retired	65	
	D	Sullivan Ernest	85	welder	30	
	E	Sullivan Georgiana—†	85	housewife	25	"
	F	Heffernan Elizabeth A—†	86	clerk	22	
	G	Heffernan James V	86	U S N	25	"
	H	Carroll Catherine L—†	86	housewife	52	"
	K	Carroll Edward A	86	U S C G	22	"
	L	Carroll Ralph R	86	U S M C	23	"
	M	Carroll William R	86	cooper	58	
	N	Heffernan James J	86	clerk	59	
	O	Collins Mary M—†	87	housewife	81	"
	P	McDonald Michael	87	laborer	40	106 High
	R	McDonald Sarah M—†	87	housewife	36	106 "
	S	Ducette Irene—†	87	"	54	here

Bartlett Street—Continued

T	Ducette Joseph	87	storekeeper	56	here
U	Ducette Lawrence	87	U S N	30	"
V	McLaughlin Catherine E–†	88	housewife	56	"
W	McLaughlin John L	88	B F D	58	
X	McLaughlin John L, jr	88	U S A	24	
Y	Bixley Ambrose W	88	shipfitter	27	"
Z	Collins James P	88	drawtender	56	"

1209

A	Collins James P	88	U S C G	22	"
B	Collins Mary A—†	88	housewife	60	"
C	Grady Alice N—†	88½	"	44	
D	Grady Patrick J	88½	clerk	44	"
E	Mahoney Catherine—†	88½	stenographer	23	"
F	*Munden John T	89	laborer	52	"
G	*Munden Mary M—†	89	housewife	71	"
H	Page Alice—†	89	tel operator	45	"
K	Stephens James A	89	cook	66	
L	Stephens Sarah—†	89	housewife	59	"
N	Sweatt Esther—†	92	"	44	
O	Sweatt Shirley—†	92	blacksmith	49	"
P	*Parks Florence—†	94	waitress	44	"
R	Parks Lyman	94	painter	45	"
S	Parks Rose R—†	94	houseworker	20	"
T	Smith Clifford	94	pipefitter	27	Vermont

1

Blaban Place

U	Leary Edward A	1	laborer	42	here
V	Leary Rose M—†	1	at home	47	"
W	Townes Sarah—†	2	"	75	"
X	Gabryk Eugenia—†	3	ropemaker	23	"
Y	Gabryk Mary—†	3	at home	48	"
Z	*Gabryk Treff	3	laborer	48	"

1210   ## Bunker Hill Street

A	Carpenter Edward M	212	longshoreman	39	23 Allston
B	Carpenter Loretta C—†	212	housewife	33	23 "
C	Calhoun Frederick R	212	electrician	32	here

Bunker Hill Street—Continued

	D	Calhoun Mildred L—†	212	housewife	32	here
	F	LaPage Florence L—†	218	"	46	2 Mystic
	G	LaPage Joseph	218	laborer	47	2 "
	H	LaPage Kenneth	218	U S A	23	here
	K	Doherty Catherine R—†	218	at home	22	"
	L	McCarthy Annie C—†	218	housewife	47	"
	M	McCarthy John J	218	longshoreman	49	"
	N	McCarthy Joseph F	218	"	25	
	O	O'Doherty Margaret—†	220	housewife	68	"
	P	O'Doherty Michael	220	operator	62	"
	R	Hill Chever A	220	chauffeur	35	"
	S	Hill Mildred—†	220	housewife	28	"
	T	Staples Mary E—†	220	"	58	
	W	Nelson George A .	224	retired	59	

1211

	B	Kent Daniel F	234	U S N	24	
	C	Kent James J	234	longshoreman	56	"
	D	Kent John J	234	U S N	25	
	E	Kent Margaret—†	234	housewife	56	"
	F	Kent Margaret M—†	234	clerk	23	
	G	Rooney Anna J—†	234	housewife	69	"
	H	Rooney Catherine E—†	234	"	26	
	K	Rooney James H	234	ropemaker	28	"
	L	Canty Julia J—†	234	housewife	67	"
	M	Canty William M	234	watchman	67	"
	O	Taylor Gertrude—†	236	at home	42	"
	R	Costello Doris A—†	236	housewife	31	"
	S	Costello Michael F	236	U S N	37	"
	V	Clements Frances M—†	239	housewife	47	"
	W	Clements Fred W.	239	chauffeur	52	"
	X	Clements Fred W, jr	239	U S A	26	
	Y	Keefe Elizabeth A—†	239	bookbinder	48	"

1212

	A	Welch Elizabeth—†	241	housewife	53	"
	B	Welch Leo J	241	machinist	61	"
	E	Griffin Ellen F—†	243	housewife	49	"
	F	Griffin John C	243	fireman	52	
	G	Griffin John J	243	U S N	29	
	H	Kelley Catherine—†	244	packer	28	
	K	Kelley Daniel	244	laborer	61	
	L	Kelley George P	244	U S A	21	"

Bunker Hill Street—Continued

M	Kelley John M	244	U S A	23	here
N	Kelley Joseph P	244	realtor	29	"
O	Kelley Michael O	244	retired	65	"
P	Kelley Timothy	244	U S A	22	
S	Green Catherine M—†	247A	housewife	33	"
T	Green Edward M	247A	ropemaker	44	"
X	Donovan Edward F	248½	shipper	28	"
Y	Donovan Rita—†	248½	housewife	26	"
Z	Barnard Helen B—†	250	"	23	

1213

A	Doherty John A	250	laborer	47	"
B	Donovan Ellen T—†	250	housewife	51	"
C	Donovan Joseph D	250	supervisor	54	"
D	Donovan Robert G	250	U S A	21	
E	Jewett Blanche M—†	250	at home	26	"
F	Finn Catherine—†	252	"	63	
G	Finn John F	252	shipfitter	42	"
H	Finn Mary A—†	252	at home	34	"
K	Grider James W	252	U S A	26	
L	Grider Josephine C—†	252	housewife	31	"
M	Keyes James E	252	retired	73	
N	Keyes Lillian E—†	252	housewife	70	"
O	Michaud Ellen G—†	254	"	43	333 Bunker Hill
P	Quigley Josephine V—†	254	"	71	Somerville
R	McKenna Daniel F	256	chauffeur	41	272 Bunker Hill
S	McKenna Mary V—†	256	housewife	37	272 "
T	Reardon Catherine V—†	256	"	31	here
U	Reardon Edward T	256	laborer	38	"

Coral Place

W	Perry Eileen—†	1	at home	30	7 Webster av
X	Perry Joaquin P	1	electrician	37	7 "
Y	Alexander Frederick C	2	chauffeur	34	here
Z	Alexander Lucy A—†	2	at home	73	"

1214

A	Alexander William J	2	clerk	33	
B	Fraher Emily V—†	2	housewife	28	"
C	Fraher Harold F	2	U S A	25	
D	McColgan Agnes—†	3	at home	56	"

9

Elm Street

E	Murray Alice I—†	16	housewife	34	here
F	Murray James I	16	laborer	35	"
G	Coyne Bartholomew J	16	custodian	51	"
H	Coyne Catherine F—†	16	housewife	39	"
K	Coyne John M	16	clerk ·	40	
L	Hurley John J	16	U S A	44	
M	Potter Catherine A—†	18	housewife	27	"
N	Potter William T	18	operator	29	"
O	Kenneally Daniel	18	laborer	62	
P	Kenneally James	18	U S N	21	
R	Kenneally Margaret—†	18	housekeeper	59	"
S	Kenneally Walter	18	U S N	24	
T	Stearns Ruth M—†	22	housewife	25	"
U	Stearns William	22	foreman	28	"
V	Clark Emma—†	22	housewife	58	"
W	Clark James H	22	fireman	62	"
X	Clark James H, jr	22	salesman	40	"
Y	Clark William J	22	longshoreman	31	"
Z	Porter Rose E—†	22	clerk	32	

1215

	Sullivan Dora—†	24	housewife	60	"
A	Sullivan Mary E—†	24	at home	74	"
C	Dowdell Elizabeth M—†	26	housewife	58	195 Bunker Hill
D	Dowdell Willard F	26	foreman	69	195 "
E	McDonald James F	28	clerk	58	here
F	Toomey Caroline L—†	28	housewife	72	"
G	Toomey William H	28	retired	74	"
H	Whelton Helen L—†	28	clerk	42	
K	Donahue Helen T—†	30	"	39	
L	Donahue Nora M—†	30	secretary	33	"
M	Donahue Nora T—†	30	housekeeper	69	"
N	Flagg Alta H—†	30	housewife	57	"
O	Flagg Howard H	30	physician	59	"
P	Fitzpatrick Beatrice—†	34	housewife	55	"
R	Fitzpatrick Edward F	34	retired	55	
S	Hollmaier Leo	34	chauffeur	49	"
T	Flaherty Mary—†	36	housewife	62	"
U	Sheehan Bartholomew F	36	shipfitter	35	"
V	Sheehan Mary E—†	36	housewife	32	"
W	Burke Edward J	36	chauffeur	29	"
X	Burke Evelyn L—†	36	housewife	26	"

Page.	Letter.	FULL NAME.	Residence, Jan. 1, 1944.	Occupation.	Supposed Age.	Reported Residence, Jan. 1, 1943. Street and Number.

Elm Street—Continued

	z	Ahern Elizabeth A—†	40	inspector	52	here
1216						
	A	Ahern Jennie—†	40	clerk	40	
	B	Ahern Joseph	40	welder	50	
	c	Doherty Alice E—†	40	clerk	21	
	D	Doherty Joseph	40	welder	24	"
	E	Doherty Margaret—†	40	clerk	26	"
	F	Doherty Martha—†	40	housewife	50	"
	G	Murphy Mary—†	40	stenographer	30	"
	K	McKenney Catherine—†	42	packer	45	"
	L	McKenney Mary—†	42	housewife	65	"
	M	McKenney Mary A—†	42	packer	36	"
	N	Cassidy Rose—†	42	secretary	43	"
	o	McGrale Amy O—†	44	cook	63	..
	P	Oesting Amy E—†	44	stitcher	34	"
	R	Sprague Charles H	44	retired	73	
	s	Sprague Harriet N—†	44	housewife	65	"
	T	Broderick Catherine M–†	50	"	82	
	U	Broderick Catherine M–†	50	instructor	40	"
	v	Brogi Adelaide J—†	50	operator	26	"
	w	Brogi Elizabeth C—†	50	clerk	48	
	x	Williams Margaret M—†	52	at home	68	"
	Y	Herne Mary E—†	52	housewife	61	"
	z	Murphy Annie F—†	52	at home	74	25 Elm
1217						
	A	Finan Annie C—†	54	housekeeper	73	here
	B	Finan John J	54	retired	76	"
	c	Finan John M	54	guard	41	"
	D	Finan Paul M	54	U S A	37	"
	E	Sweeney Lillian—†	54	housewife	38	"
	F	Fitzgerald Emily A—†	56	housekeeper	67	"
	G	Fitzgerald Helen L—†	56	clerk	32	..
	H	Fitzgerald Walter L	56	shipper	22	
	K	McCormack Elizabeth—†	56	housewife	23	"
	L	McCormack John J	56	pipefitter	25	"
	M	Hackett Mary—†	58	housewife	44	"
	N	Hackett Matthew	58	machinist	42	"
	o	Canney Anna—†	58	housewife	40	"
	P	Canney Owen	58	longshoreman	42	"
	R	Finan Annie G—†	60	at home	70	"
	s	Finan Mary J—†	60	"	73	"

11

Elm Street—Continued

T	Williams Mary—†	62	housewife	31	here
U	Williams Richard J	62	electrician	33	"
V	Boyle Anne M—†	64	housewife	25	"
W	Boyle Edward J	64	U S N	26	
X	McGonagle Charles G	64	clerk	33	"
Y	McGonagle Helen F—†	64	housewife	33	"
Z	Callahan John J	66	supt	36	
	1218				
A	Callahan Lillian V—†	66	housewife	35	"
B	O'Neill Dennis	68	guard	60	
C	O'Neill Ellen—†	68	housewife	52	"
D	Carey Nicholas	68	laborer	41	"
E	Hutt James P	68	electrician	24	"
F	Hutt Norah—†	68	housewife	40	"
G	Hutt William H	68	clerk	49	"
H	Lyman Mary T—†	70	housewife	32	"
K	Lyman Sylvester P	70	pipefitter	39	"
L	Fennell Catherine B—†	72	housewife	30	"
M	Fennell Thomas F	72	stevedore	39	"
N	Welsh Alice E—†	72	clerk	22	
O	Welsh Arthur R	72	chauffeur	53	"
P	Welsh Ellen M—†	72	housewife	47	"
S	Weeks Anna—†	74	operator	68	"
T	Askew Alice—†	74	packer	22	
U	Askew William T	74	U S A	23	

Exeter Court

V	Nickerson John C	1	U S A	25	here
W	Nickerson John N	1	watchman	57	"
X	Nickerson Joseph S	1	U S A	20	"
Y	Nickerson Margaret M—†	1	housewife	52	"
Z	Nickerson Robert M	1	U S A	23	
	1219				
A	Cowin Cornelius	1	plater	61	Nahant
B	McDermott James J	1	longshoreman	45	"
C	McDermott Mary E—†	1	housewife	30	"
D	Cowin Catherine—†	1	"	55	32 Pleasant
E	Cowin Frederick	1	U S A	22	32 "
F	Cowin Joseph	1	"	24	32 "

High Street

H	O'Donnell Edward J	81	machinist	40	here
K	O'Donnell Gladys—†	81	housewife	38	"
L	Sturm Julius J	81	machinist	47	"
M	Dennis Ethel A—†	83	clerk	33	
N	Dennis Mary E—†	83	housekeeper	66	"
O	Pingree Abbie F—†	83½	"	71	
P	Whouley Grace F—†	83½	"	37	"
R	Whouley Joseph T	83½	longshoreman	40	"
S	Murphy George L	83½	laborer	28	
T	Murphy Susan A—†	83½	housekeeper	63	"
U	Drinkwater Minnie—†	85	"	66	"
V	Penta Anthony J	85½	U S A	33	"
W	Penta Daniel G	85½	painter	23	
X	Penta Margaret—†	85½	housewife	55	"
Y	Penta Mark	85½	baker	56	
Z	Wall Mary A—†	85½	housewife	29	"
	1220				
A	Wall Samuel G	85½	sailmaker	37	"
B	Heelen David	87	rigger	58	
C	Heelen James H	87	U S A	20	
D	Heelen Julia M—†	87	clerk	26	"
E	Heelen Nellie E—†	87	housewife	58	"
F	Heelen David F	87½	fireman	28	"
G	Heelen Mary R—†	87½	housewife	26	"
H	Ezekiel Anne—†	87½	"	57	
K	Ezekiel Mary—†	87½	operator	20	"
L	Ezekiel Peter	87½	U S A	28	
M	Ezekiel William	87½	"	22	"
N	Kuchinski Elizebeth E—†	91	housewife	38	23 Elm
O	Kuchinski Joseph	91	machinist	45	23 "
P	Doherty Catherine—†	91	clerk	22	here
R	Doherty Elizabeth—†	91	housewife	51	"
S	Doherty James	91	U S A	25	"
T	Doherty Patrick	91	cook	53	
U	Doherty Rose—†	91	clerk	20	
V	O'Neil Mary E—†	91	housekeeper	72	"
W	Scalli James V	91	rigger	31	"
X	Scalli Mary A—†	91	housewife	30	"
Y	Kennedy George E	93	contractor	33	15 Lexington
Z	Kennedy Glenna A—†	93	housewife	30	here

13

1221
High Street—Continued

	Letter	Full Name	Residence	Occupation	Age	Reported Residence
	A	Dumas William A	93	electrician	24	Louisiana
	B	McConologue Mary F—†	93	housewife	46	here
	C	McConologue Thomas R	93	retired	64	"
	D	Purcell Andrew	93	U S A	34	739 E Fifth
	E	Purcell Martha—†	93	housewife	29	739 "
	F	Addison Beatrice V—†	97	"	39	here
	G	Addison Thomas J	97	longshoreman	41	"
	H	Dall Rita—†	97	housewife	20	California
	K	Stevens Henrietta F—†	97	housekeeper	51	10 Tufts
	L	Sullivan Dorothy V—†	97	typist	26	here
	M	Sullivan Elizabeth E—†	97	housewife	63	"
	N	Sullivan Ida C—†	97	clerk	23	"
	O	Sullivan William P	97	laborer	34	
	P	Cassettari Angelo	99	clerk	63	
	R	Cassettari Italia—†	99	housewife	49	"
	T	Doherty Gertrude B—†	103	"	47	
	U	Doherty Jacqueline M—†	103	clerk	22	
	V	Lange Henrietta—†	103	U S M C	26	"
	W	Lange Mary—†	103	housewife	65	"
	X	Lange Walter L	103	painter	67	
	Y	Lange Walter L	103	U S M C	24	"
	Z	Baldwin Joseph M	103	instructor	25	"

1222

	Letter	Full Name	Residence	Occupation	Age	Reported Residence
	A	Baldwin Ruth M—†	103	housewife	24	"
	B	Wolf Frank J	103A	storekeeper	75	"
	C	Connors Lillian T—†	103½	housewife	39	"
	D	Connors Timothy F	103½	ropemaker	43	"
	E	Smith Eleanor M—†	103½	typist	20	
	F	Smith Elizabeth L—†	103½	housewife	·56	"
	G	Smith Elizabeth L—†	103½	typist	27	
	H	Smith Joseph G	103½	fireman	56	
	K	Smith Joseph G, jr	103½	U S N	25	
	L	Murray John T	103½	technician	33	"
	M	Murray Mary E—†	103½	housewife	56	"
	N	Murray Thomas	103½	longshoreman	51	"
	O	Murray Winifred—†	103½	housewife	29	"

Holden Row

	Letter	Full Name	Residence	Occupation	Age	Reported Residence
	P	Heatley Albert F	1	chauffeur	25	here
	R	Heatley Alice M—†	1	housewife	25	"

14

s	Beauregard Mary A—†	1	housewife	41	here
t	Beauregard William E	1	ropemaker	44	"
u	McCloud Carmille—†	2	housewife	37	"
v	Harrington Dennis R	2	U S A	23	
w	Harrington Jeremiah J	2	fireman	55	"
x	Harrington Margaret M—†	2	housewife	44	"
y	Harrington Mary—†	2	secretary	20	"

1223

a	Hickey Elizabeth L—†		housewife	38	"
b	Hickey George T	3	seaman	43	"
d	Mahoney Frances G—†	4	housewife	39	"
e	Veazie Mary T—†	5	"	29	
f	Veazie Warren T	5	chauffeur	34	"
g	Connors James L	5	U S A	28	
h	Connors John J	5	retired	65	
k	Connors John J, jr	5	welder	26	
l	Connors Margaret T—†	5	stenographer	22	"
m	Connors Minnie C—†	5	housewife	61	"
n	McCarthy Mary A—†	5	"	24	"
o	Keith Elmina—†	6	"	35	Windsor
p	Keith Reginald	6	seaman	35	"
r	Nutter Nellie—†	6	housekeeper	60	5 Crossin pl
s	Cheverie Annie M—†	7	housewife	39	here
t	Cheverie William J	7	shipwright	39	"
v	*Hughes Catherine—†	7	housewife	70	148 Bunker Hill
w	*Hughes Peter P	7	retired	75	148 "

1224   **Mason Court**

a	Carvalho Gertrude V—†	1	housewife	48	here
b	Carvalho Joseph S	1	clerk	55	"
c	Bonetti Anna—†	2	housewife	47	"
d	Bonetti Joseph	2	laborer	55	"
e	Courtney Clarence	3	"	55	

Pearl Street

f	Colclough Anna A—†	3	manager	48	here
g	Sablock Edward T	3	U S A	31	"
h	Sablock John R	3	electrician	34	"
k	Sablock Mary G—†	3	housewife	31	"
l	O'Laughlin Elizabeth A—†	3	"	44	

Page.	Letter.	FULL NAME.	Residence, Jan. 1, 1944.	Occupation.	Supposed Age.	Reported Residence, Jan. 1, 1943. Street and Number.

Pearl Street—Continued

	M	O'Laughlin Thomas	3	carpenter	48	here
	N	Kane Michael J	5	foreman	43	"
	O	Kane Thomas J	5	paperhanger	52	"
	P	Leahy Annette T—†	5	housewife	45	"
	R	Leahy William J	5	salesman	50	"
	S	Brigandi Basil P	7	U S N	24	Somerville
	T	McGowan James F	7	U S A	23	21 Wall
	U	McGowan Mary—†	7	housewife	22	21 "
	V	O'Connor Mary M—†	7	clerk	45	Somerville
	W	O'Connor Timothy M	7	U S A	20	"
	X	Maloney Grace—†	12	housewife	28	here
	Y	Maloney Joseph P	12	clerk	31	"
	Z	O'Leary Agnes J—†	12	housewife	50	23 Pearl
		1225				
	A	O'Leary Dennis F	12	clerk	26	23 "
	B	Harrington Alice G—†	12	housewife	40	27 Walker
	C	Harrington Francis	12	operator	43	27 "
	D	O'Connell Alice A—†	14	housewife	40	here
	E	O'Connell Charles L	14	laborer	39	"
	F	Dionne Catherine E—†	14	matron	62	"
	G	Doherty James E	14	U S A	33	
	H	White John T	14	seaman	50	
	K	White Mary G—†	14	laundress	49	"
	L	Walsh Edward J	16	longshoreman	47	"
	M	Walsh Mary—†	16	housewife	45	"
	N	Addison John T	16	laborer	68	
	O	Addison Mary—†	16	housewife	63	"
	P	LaRoque Arthur	16	U S N	29	
	R	LaRoque Gertrude—†	16	housewife	24	"
	S	Sinclair George	18	brakeman	30	"
	T	Sinclair Helen—†	18	housewife	28	"
	U	Doherty Alice P—†	18	"	25	
	V	Doherty Stephen J	18	laborer	27	
	W	Norton William E	18	printer	48	
	X	Dion Catherine I—†	18	housewife	36	"
	Y	Dion Leroy J	18	inspector	40	"
	Z	McConologue James	22	chauffeur	70	5 Athens
		1226				
	A	McConologue Margaret–†	22	housewife	60	5 "
	C	O'Donnell Anna E—†	23	machinist	24	22 Pearl
	D	O'Donnell Joseph J	23	U S N	21	22 "

Pearl Street—Continued

E	O'Donnell Mary A—†	23	housewife	52	22 Pearl
F	O'Neil John F	23	clerk	47	here
G	O'Neil John F, jr	23	U S A	24	"
H	O'Neil Margaret T—†	23	housewife	46	"
K	Wachter Margaret—†	23	at home	56	"
M	Collins John	24	molder	34	"
N	Collins Mildred—†	24	housewife	35	"
O	Reilly Edward J	25	operator	67	24 Pearl
P	Reilly Edward F	25	longshoreman	33	24 "
R	Reilly Isabella F—†	25	housewife	59	24 "
S	Reilly William J	25	freighthandler	26	24 "
T	Kinsella Annie E—†	25	sorter	48	here
U	Kinsella Francis W	25	longshoreman	25	"
V	Kinsella Lawrence	25	operator	52	"
W	Leverone Agnes—†	26	clerk	26	
X	Leverone Catherine—†	26	secretary	24	"
Y	Leverone Francis J	26	operator	29	Walpole
Z	Leverone Frank J	26	blacksmith	56	Wilmington
	1227				
A	Leverone Joseph	26	U S N	20	here
B	Leverone Marguerite—†	26	defense wkr	22	"
C	Leverone Martin	26	electrician	23	"
D	Leverone Mary—†	26	housewife	54	"
E	Carr Daniel	27	U S A	24	"
F	Carr Francis W	27	"	28	"
G	Carr James P	27	"	30	"
H	Carr James W	27	laborer	57	"
K	Carr John J	27	U S A	23	
L	Carr Louise M—†	27	housewife	52	"
M	Kearns John F	30	chauffeur	33	"
N	Kearns Louise—†	30	storekeeper	30	"
O	Keddie Alexander C	30	boxmaker	58	"
P	Keddie Alexander J	30	U S A	24	
R	Keddie Jessie C—†	30	packer	28	"
S	Keddie Louise T—†	30	housewife	57	"
T	O'Brien John D	31	clerk	39	"
U	O'Brien Julia M—†	31	housewife	59	"
V	O'Brien Richard S	31	meter reader	64	"
W	Eldredge Lillian—†	32	housewife	34	"
X	Eldredge Paul	32	electrician	34	"
Y	O'Brien Francis X	33	fireman	23	"

Page:	Letter.	Full Name:	Residence, Jan. 1, 1944.	Occupation:	Supposed Age.	Reported Residence, Jan. 1, 1943. Street and Number:

Pearl Street—Continued

	z	O'Brien James V	33	U S A	27	here
		1228				
	A	O'Brien John J	33	"	32	
	B	O'Brien Mary E—†	33	housewife	56	"
	C	O'Brien Mary T—†	33	bookkeeper	26	"
	E	O'Brien Alice E—†	35	housewife	23	84 Baldwin
	F	O'Brien Richard F, jr	35	U S N	23	84 "
	G	Robbins Alice F—†	35	housewife	50	here
	H	Robbins Florence R—†	35	defense wkr	20	"
	K	Robbins George A	35	laborer	50	"
	L	Robbins George A, jr	35	U S N	21	"
	M	Duffy Edward T	36	foreman	54	"
	N	Duffy Mary E—†	36	housewife	56	"
	O	Walsh James	37	seaman	34	
	P	Walsh John A	37	drawtender	42	"
	R	Walsh Joseph F	37	clerk	30	
	S	Walsh Mary J—†	37	housewife	28	"
	T	Walsh Stephen J	37	U S N	27	
	U	Pierce Lida A—†	39	housewife	66	"
	V	Butler Anna M—†	39	"	23	
	W	Butler Francis J	39	U S N	23	
	X	Doe Eugene J	39	chauffeur	29	"
	Y	Doe Rose M—†	39	housewife	26	"
	Z	Shanahan Alice—†	40	"	45	
		1229				
	A	Shanahan Thomas	40	U S A	38	
	B	Flavin Dorothy—†	40	housewife	27	"
	C	Veazie Warren	40	laborer	59	
	F	Duffy Bernard T	41	clerk	52	"
	G	Duffy Bridget A—†	41	at home	74	"
	H	Duffy Francis C	41	supervisor	37	"
	K	Duffy James J	41	laborer	49	
	L	Duffy Leo L	41	"	46	
	M	Duffy Mary—†	41	clerk	50	
	N	Duffy William J	41	laborer	40	
	O	Dillon Catherine—†	42	matron	53	
	P	Blackstone Elizabeth B—†	43	housewife	54	"
	R	Blackstone Margaret B—†	43	operator	24	"
	S	Timoney Nora—†	43	housewife	39	"
	T	Timoney Peter	43	watchman	40	"
	U	Ferretti Albert	44	B F D	26	

Pearl Street—Continued

v	Ferretti Madeline F—†	44	housewife	21	here
w	Donohue Eileen—†	45	"	24	"
x	Donohue Michael	45	rigger	34	"
y	Sullivan Florence G—†	45	housewife	54	"
z	Sullivan John J	45	U S Customs	60	"
	1230				
a	Sullivan Paul B	45	U S N	27	"
b	Juliano John	46	laborer	46	"
c	Juliano Lillian—†	46	housewife	46	"
d	Randall Gertrude H—†	47	"	64	
e	*Sullivan Esther—†	47	"	79	
f	Sullivan John J	47	U S A	37	
g	Sullivan Joseph A	47	electrician	41	"
h	Sullivan Mary R—†	47	at home	53	"
m	Foster Edgar	48	shipfitter	26	Connecticut
n	Foster Rita—†	48	housewife	28	"
o	O'Hara Estelle—†	48	"	32	here
p	Ahearn Helen—†	49	"	23	"
r	Ahearn William	49	electrician	25	"
s	Hegarty Catherine—†	49	housewife	64	"
t	Hegarty Dorothy A—†	49	clerk	20	"
u	Hegarty Joseph J	49	U S M C	27	"
v	Hegarty Stephen	49	laborer	65	"
w	Quinn Rita A—†	49	clerk	26	
x	Wholley Michael	49	U S C G	42	"
y	Landry Eugene	50	boilermaker	49	"
z	Landry Florence—†	50	housewife	40	"
	1231				
a	Sennett Audrey—†	50	waitress	30	"
e	Harris George W	58	painter	69	10 Chestnut
f	Harris Mary E—†	58	housewife	64	10 "
g	Kenefick Edwina M—†	58	clerk	29	here
h	Kenefick Katherine—†	58	housewife	53	"
k	Kenefick Marguerite L-†	58	operator	27	"
l	Kenefick Thomas W	58	U S A	22	
m	Connor Alfred W	60	chauffeur	43	"
n	Donovan Charles B	60	clerk	30	"
o	Donovan Mary C—†	60	operator	42	"
p	Burke Dorothy—†	60	housewife	26	"
r	Burke Wlliam G	60	longshoreman	29	"
s	Sullivan Eleanor—†	62	teacher	33	"

Pearl Street—Continued

	T	Sullivan Ella—†	62	housewife	56	here
	U	Sullivan Philip J	62	U S A	29	"
	V	Enos John J	64	plumber	48	"
	W	Enos Mary V—†	64	housewife	44	"
	Y	McCallum George H	68	longshoreman	36	"
	Z	McCallum Margaret—†	68	housewife	37	"
		1232				
	A	Donohue William M	70	retired	75	
	B	Connolly Alexander I	70	U S M C	29	"
	C	Connolly Flora N—†	70	housewife	55	"
	D	Connolly James P	70	operator	59	"
	E	Connolly John J	70	U S A	32	"
	F	McLaughlin James	70	laborer	56	
	G	Dolan Frances—†	72	housewife	55	"
	H	Dolan Joseph L	72	welder	27	
	K	Sullivan John J	74	U S A	27	
	L	Sullivan Mary—†	74	housewife	50	"
	M	Sullivan Mary C—†	74	operator	29	"
	N	Sullivan Neil W	74	U S A	28	
	O	Collins Charlotte—†	74	housewife	64	"
	P	Collins Edward C	74	laborer	34	
	R	Collins Edward M	74	machinist	64	"
	S	Collins John H	74	electrician	29	"
	T	Blood Eleanor—†	74	housewife	75	"
	V	Hughes Joseph	76	inspector	46	"
	W	Hughes Josephine—†	76	housewife	39	"
		1233				
	A	Harrington Daniel H	80	electrician	37	"
	B	Harrington Eileen P—†	80	housewife	32	"
	C	Furey Hilary	80	laborer	45	"
	D	Wall James	80	chauffeur	23	"
	E	Geagan Marie—†	80	housewife	63	"
	F	Geagan Michael	80	U S N	37	Virginia
	G	Kavanagh Anna—†	80	housewife	25	here
	H	Kavanagh John	80	warehouse	28	"
	K	O'Neil Edward	82	metalworker	38	"
	L	O'Neil Margaret—†	82	housewife	32	"
	M	Hefferman Catherine—†	82	operator	34	"
	N	Hefferman Margaret—†	82	housewife	67	"
	O	Hefferman Margaret—†	82	operator	31	"

Page.	Letter.	FULL NAME.	Residence, Jan. 1, 1944.	Occupation.	Supposed Age.	Reported Residence, Jan. 1, 1943. Street and Number.

Pearl Street—Continued

	P	Hyde Bridget—†	82	housewife	34	here
	R	Hyde Martin	82	laborer	59	"
	T	Kime Annie—†	86	housewife	43	"
	U	Kime Mary—†	86	bookbinder	20	"
	V	Kime Myrtle—†	86	at home	21	"
	W	Kime Robert	86	painter	47	
	Y	Doherty Anna A—†	90	housekeeper	37	"
	Z	Doherty John E	90	electrician	33	"
1234						
	A	Doherty John J	90	retired	87	
	B	Doherty Hazel M—†	90	estimator	40	"
	C	Ferry Catherine—†	92	housewife	74	"
	D	Ferry Frank J	92	laborer	36	
	E	Campbell Laurence D	100	U S A	23	
	F	Campbell Mary A—†	100	housewife	21	"
	G	Brown George E	100	guard	51	
	H	Brown George E	100	U S A	23	
	K	Brown John F	100	laborer	29	
	L	Brown Mary J—†	100	housewife	51	"
	M	Charbonier Mary—†	102	"	29	
	N	Charbonier William	102	chauffeur	28	"
	O	Copithorn Mary—†	102	housewife	67	"
	P	Wickham Marion—†	102	"	36	
	R	Wickham Michael	102	shipfitter	43	"

Pearl Street Place

	S	Leary Mary A—†	1	housewife	65	here
	T	Leary Michael J	1	mechanic	65	"
	U	Randlett Mildred M—†	1	housewife	29	"
	V	Randlett Vernon P	1	conductor	29	"
	W	Truskey Joseph E	2	chef	35	
	X	Truskey Irene M—†	2	housewife	34	"
	Y	Heath Gertrude—†	3	"	64	
	Z	Heath Harry O	3	plumber	66	"
1235						
	A	Webster Helen—†	3	housewife	38	"
	B	Roach John D	4	laborer	41	
	C	Roach Mary M—†	4	at home	31	"
	D	Roach Regina T—†	4	housewife	31	"

Russell Street

E	Osley Iris—†	1	housewife	48	here
F	Shaw Margaret M—†	1	"	41	"
G	Shaw Phillip F, jr	1	chauffeur	41	"
H	Shaw Anna G—†	1½	housewife	41	"
K	Shaw Louise M—†	1½	housekeeper	41	"
L	Shaw Phillip F	1½	retired	71	"
M	Shaw Thomas F	1½	guard	44	
N	Drew Edwin E	3	operator	61	"
O	Drew Mary E—†	3	housewife	59	"
P	Harrington Daniel F	5	foreman	52	"
R	Harrington Daniel F, jr	5	U S N	22	
S	Harrington Mary A—†	5	housewife	52	"
T	Harrington Rose M—†	5	secretary	27	"
U	Helmund Anna J—†	6	housewife	32	"
V	Helmund Joseph C	6	supt	32	
W	Riordan Eugene J	6	watchman	53	"
X	Riordan Nellie T—†	6	laundress	52	"
Y	Carlin Hannah—†	7	housewife	73	85 Bartlett
Z	Carlin James P	7	electrician	31	29 Soley
	1236					
A	Carlin Margaret E—†	7	housewife	30	29 "
B	Gill Anna T—†	8	"	31	here
C	Gill Michael	8	longshoreman	39	"
D	Connors Ellen M—†	9	housewife	38	"
E	Connors John J	9	roofer	41	
F	Shea James T	9	retired	78	
G	Collins Rita I—†	10	operator	26	"
H	Collins William J	10	U S A	26	3 Payson pl
K	Lynch Catherine V—†	10	housewife	57	here
L	Lynch John A	10	drawtender	57	"
M	Lynch John J	10	U S N	36	"
N	Ellgner Joseph T	11	driller	38	
O	Ellgner Margaret E—†	11	housewife	38	"
P	Fallon Michael J	11	retired	68	
R	Russell Julia A—†	11	housewife	43	"
S	Violante Antonio	11	laborer	56	
T	Violante Concetta—†	11	housewife	47	"
U	McPartland Hugh	1	laborer	39	
W	Bishop Charles J	1	mechanic	28	"
X	Bishop Evelyn R—†	13	bookbinder	45	"
Y	*Bursey Amos	16	longshoreman	60	"

22

z	Warford Ambrose	16	longshoreman	60	here
	1237				
A	Warford David J	16	"	22	
B	Warford Mary B—†	16	housewife	55	"
C	Warford Mary L—†	16	secretary	26	"

School Street

D	*Brown Albert J	31	laborer	61	here
E	Brown John J	31	"	21	"
F	Brown Mary E—†	31	housewife	41	"
G	Kenney Eugene L	31	cobbler	60	"
H	Kenney Mary M—†	31	housewife	60	"
K	Cross Frank	31	retired	75	
L	Wiley Susan E—†	31	housewife	61	"
M	Ahern William J	33	shipper	50	"
N	Brennan Catherine F—†	33	housewife	37	"
O	Brennan Charles B	33	chauffeur	36	"
P	Murphy Claire R—†	33	housewife	33	"
R	Murphy William J	33	rigger	43	
S	Magner Ella V—†	37	housewife	48	"
T	Magner William J	37	clerk	28	
V	Costello Elizabeth—†	38	at home	69	"
W	Corkhill John T	39	retired	51	"
X	Corkhill Mary E—†	39	housewife	51	"
Y	Doherty Cornelius	39	boilermaker	40	48 Baldwin
Z	Doherty Delia—†	39	housewife	30	48 "
	1238				
A	Barclay Gilbert	43	expressman	53	here
B	Barclay Josephine D—†	43	housewife	55	"
C	Barclay Robert	43	U S A	20	"
D	Barclay Wilfred	43	"	27	"
E	Devlin Grace—†	47	maid	40	14 Trenton
F	Doherty Michael	47	repairman	47	14 "
G	Greatorex Harold J	49	clerk	29	here
H	Greatorex Mary—†	49	housewife	28	"
L	Wilde Albert E	51	inspector	40	"
M	Wilde Margaret—†	51	housewife	40	"
N	Pumyea Gordon	51	shipper	39	"
O	Pumyea Robertina—†	51	housewife	40	"
P	Brown Lena M—†	53	housekeeper	57	"

1

Page.	Letter.	Full Name.	Residence, Jan. 1, 1944.	Occupation.	Supposed Age.	Reported Residence, Jan. 1, 1943. Street and Number.

School Street—Continued

	R	Jeffries Louise C—†	53	housewife	43	here
	S	Jeffries Monta L	53	U S N	45	"
	T	Ward Maria—†	56	at home	76	"
	Z	Titcomb Albert E	60	shipfitter	39	"
1239						
	A	Titcomb Jennie L—†	60	at home	38	"
	C	Hurley Charles J	64	chipper	32	Wilmington
	D	Hurley Mary J—†	64	at home	32	"
	E	Hurley Helen M—†	64	"	31	here
	F	Hurley John J	64	chipper	36	"
	G	Taylor Mary—†	64	at home	53	"
	H	Taylor Stanley	64	seaman	27	"
	K	Arving Emma G—†	65	toolkeeper	51	58 Tremont
	L	Arving Florence E—†	65	assembler	21	58 "
	M	Griffin Anna V—†	65	housewife	33	here
	N	Griffin Joseph L	65	U S C G	44	"
	O	Lyons Annie B—†	65	housewife	55	"
	P	Lyons John J	65	U S A	25	
	R	Lyons William D	65	floorman	31	"
	S	Connolly Margaret M—†	66	at home	21	"
	T	Crane Hugh F	66	retired	69	
	U	Doherty Isabelle J—†	66	at home	45	"
	V	Doherty Michael H	66	chauffeur	48	"
	W	Hawkins John	67	laborer	35	
	X	Hawkins Mary—†	67	housewife	62	"
	Y	Hawkins Rita—†	67	waitress	22	"
	Z	Hawkins Samuel, jr	67	U S A	30	
1240						
	A	Hawkins Samuel	67	dairyman	67	"
	B	Hawkins William J	67	U S A	25	"
	C	McCarthy Francis P	68	machinist	33	"
	D	McCarthy Mary F—†	68	at home	30	"
	G	Edson Harry L	70	longshoreman	72	"
	H	Howland Ellery C	70	retired	70	"
	K	McIsaac Mary—†	71	housewife	24	60 School
	L	McIsaac Peter	71	U S N	30	Everett
	M	Upton Melvin	71	longshoreman	23	89 School
	N	Upton Theresa—†	71	housewife	22	89 "
	O	Chase Helen—†	71	"	29	here
	P	Chase Walter	71	longshoreman	32	"
	R	Bowden Anna—†	71	housewife	24	127 High

School Street—Continued

s	Bowden Edward	71	laborer	34	127 High
u	Evers Eunice—†	72	at home	35	here
v	Evers Henry J	72	supervisor	36	"
w	McGovern Bessie—†	73	housewife	59	"
x	McGovern Owen	73	laborer	60	
z	Natolo Pasquale	74	molder	23	

1241

A	Natolo Virginia—†	74	student	21	"
B	Lenzi Joseph	74	shipfitter	48	"
c	Lenzi Lucy—†	74	at home	40	"
D	Higgins Margaret—†	76	"	39	
E	Higgins Thomas	76	chauffeur	41	"
F	O'Malley George F	76	shipfitter	32	"
G	O'Malley Mary—†	76	at home	60	"
H	Hinds Jerome	77	U S N	37	27½ McLean
K	Hinds Kathryn—†	77	housewife	31	27½ "
L	Martini Jane C—†	77	"	21	Virginia
M	Martini William	77	U S N	27	"
N	Lundy Allen W	77	laborer	29	6 Neal ct
o	Lundy Marie J—†	77	housewife	29	6 "
P	McComiskey Sidney	77	U S A	28	Georgetown
R	McComiskey Helen R—†	77	waitress	26	here
s	Ward James J	77	laborer	20	"
T	Ward Mary F—†	77	domestic	56	"
v	Tracy Alice R—†	79	housewife	31	"
w	Tracy Frederick	79	rigger	42	
Y	Innis William A	81	chauffeur	58	"
z	McCormick Phyllis G—†	81	cashier	44	

1242

A	Lifrieri John J	82	machinist	32	"
B	Lifrieri Mary J—†	82	at home	29	"
c	Green Ellen—†	84	"	97	"
D	Green Matthew J	84	retired	60	
E	Green Matthew J, jr	84	U S C G	26	"
F	Crowley John A	84	storekeeper	36	"
G	Crowley Margaret—†	84	at home	37	"
H	McLaughlin Helen—†	84	clerk	22	
K	Clancy Michael	84	retired	71	
L	Stack Annie—†	84	at home	59	"
M	Stack Thomas	84	manager	59	"
N	Blackstone Alexander	85	contractor	30	35 Mystic

School Street—Continued

o	Blackstone Mary—†	85	housewife	35	35 Mystic
p	Picone Elizabeth—†	85	"	25	here
r	Walsh Mary—†	85	"	59	"
s	Walsh Robert	85	baggageman	60	"
t	Walsh Robert T	85	"	22	
v	Otis Burt L	86	clerk	66	
w	Otis Frances G—†	86	at home	63	"
x	Otis John O	86	chauffeur	35	"
y	Otis William J	86	electrician	24	"
z	Bailey William	87	retired	68	

1243

c	Otis Albert P	89	chauffeur	39	74 Elm
d	Otis Sarah R—†	89	housewife	39	74 "
f	Whooley Anna L—†	90	at home	72	here
g	Connolly Ellen T—†	90	"	58	5 Clarken ct
h	Cunningham William H	91	chauffeur	54	here
k	Murdock Anna M—†	91	operator	30	"
l	Murdock Annie G—†	91	housewife	62	"

Sullivan Street

s	Sullivan Joseph X	43	laborer	29	here
t	Sullivan Mary—†	43	housewife	23	"
u	Martin Theresa—†	43	housekeeper	34	"
w	Marquis Cecelia—†	45	housewife	28	Maine
x	Marquis Evangeline—†	45	clerk	21	"
y	Marquis Fernand	45	electrician	29	"
z	Tracey Frank E	45	clerk	26	here

1244

a	Tracey Mabelle A—†	45	housewife	53	"
b	Tracey Thomas	45	policeman	32	"
c	Burke Mary—†	45	at home	69	"
d	*Graham Bridget—†	45	housewife	38	"
e	Young Agnes C—†	47	at home	22	"
f	Young Catherine F—†	47	operator	57	"
g	Lawson Delbert E	47	laborer	34	
h	Lawson Mary R—†	47	housewife	34	"
k	Corti Alphonse	47	sculptor	39	"
l	Corti Elsie—†	47	housewife	39	"
m	Pellegrino Bonugli	47	sculptor	39	"
n	Cunneen Helen—†	51	housewife	24	18 Frothingham av

o	Cunneen James F	51	machinist	26	18 Frothingham av
p	Lincoln Alice A—†	51	housewife	29	here
r	Lincoln Grace M—†	51	at home	53	"
s	Lincoln James W	51	chauffeur	33	"
t	*Dever Nora—†	51	housewife	37	"
u	Dever Patrick	51	freighthandler	37	"
v	Grows Marietta—†	57	at home	66	"
w	Hileman Bernice E—†	59	housewife	21	"
x	Hileman John E	59	U S A	27	Maine
z	Thompson Alice—†	59	at home	80	here

1245

a	Olin Amelia—†	59	clerk	40	
b	Olin Gustaf A	59	mechanic	40	"
e	Booker Elizabeth A—†	63	housewife	69	"
f	Booker William W	63	retired	73	"
g	Stanford Hannah F—†	65	housewife	66	8 Salem
h	Stanford William J	65	metalworker	32	8 "
k	Valeriani Angelo	65	U S A	29	here
l	Valeriani Nickolas	65	"	20	"
m	*Valeriani Palmira—†	65	housewife	56	"
n	Valeriani Paul	65	painter	61	"
p	Sweeney Mary—†	67	housewife	63	"
s	Blackstone Annie—†	67	"	20	85 Bartlett
t	Blackstone William J	67	U S A	32	85 "
x	Welcome Edward A	73	laborer	22	here
y	Welcome Mary—†	73	housewife	48	"

Summer Street

z	Meagher Anna—†	7	housewife	55	here

1246

a	Meagher Irene M—†	7	clerk	27	
b	Meagher James H	7	glazier	20	
c	Meagher James P	7	checker	55	"
d	Meagher Marjorie—†	7	clerk	22	
e	Meagher Walter P	7	longshoreman	24	"
g	Higgins Mae E—†	10	clerk	42	
h	Higgins Robert L	10	U S A	21	
k	Orr Anna E—†	10	housewife	61	"
l	Orr John M	10	retired	65	

Summer Street—Continued

N Benenoti Joseph J	11	U S A	20	here
o Benenoti Mary—†	11	packer	39	"
P Benenoti Melchiore	11	candymaker	47	"
R Fabiano Mario J	11	metalworker	30	"
s Fabiano Rose M—†	11	housewife	25	"
T Bowdren Catherine G—†	12	at home	25	"
u Bowdren Frederick G	12	U S A	22	
v Bowdren Medouph V	12	machinist	63	"
w Giordano Carmen	12	shipfitter	43	"
x Giordano Catherine R—†	12	housewife	29	"
Y Giordano Joseph C	12	U S A	20	"
z Coyne John	12	salesman	55	"

1247

A Finnegan Josephine—†	14	housewife	43	"
B Finnegan Luke	14	laborer	50	
c Hanley Margaret G—†	14	housewife	40	"
D Hanley William J	14	electrician	40	"
E Nadeau Fidell J	14	retired	78	
F Tobin Elizabeth A—†	15	housewife	61	"
G Tobin John J	15	laborer	58	"
H Ferrante Annette A—†	.16	housewife	27	"
K Ferrante Joseph E	16	laborer	29	
L Scales Catherine—†	16	housekeeper	65	"
M Scales Elizabeth G—†	16	operator	58	"
N Scales Francis L	16	laborer	55	
o Scales Joanna A—†	16	housekeeper	63	"
P Jenner Agnes L—†	32	housewife	33	"
R Jenner Charles W	32	welder	34	
s Green Dorothy M—†	32	housewife	37	"
T Green James H	32	mechanic	46	"
u McCullough James F	32	chauffeur	39	"
v McCullough Marion E—†	32	housewife	39	"
w Whelton Jennie E—†	34	"	25	7 Trenton
x Whelton John W	34	U S A	28	7 "
Y Jarasitis Alexander J	34	ice dealer	36	here
z Jarasitis Dorothy M—†	34	housewife	33	"

1248

A Hazelton Charles	34	laborer	37	
B Hazelton Ethel M—†	34	housewife	31	"
c Whelton Beatrice L—†	36	"	42	
D Whelton William J	36	storekeeper	42	"

Wesley Street

E	Bennett Donald G	11	U S A	25	here
F	Bennett Esther G—†	11	housekeeper	49	"
G	Downing Perley A	11	engineer	61	"

Wistar Place

H	Hern Florence—†	1	housewife	42	here
K	Scannell Jessie—†	2	"	49	"
L	Scannell Joseph F	2	laborer	57	"

1

1

13

14

15

16

17

Ward 2–Precinct 13

CITY OF BOSTON

LIST OF RESIDENTS
20 YEARS OF AGE AND OVER

(NON-CITIZENS INDICATED BY ASTERISK)
(FEMALES INDICATED BY DAGGER)

AS OF

JANUARY 1, 1944

THOMAS F. SULLIVAN, *Chairman*
FREDERIC E. DOWLING, *Secretary*
WILLIAM A. MOTLEY, JR.
FRANCIS B. McKINNEY
EVERETT R. PROUT

Listing Board.

CITY OF BOSTON PRINTING DEPARTMENT

1300

Allston Street

A	Begley James L	8	brazier	42	here
B	*Begley Mary—†	8	housekeeper	73	"
C	Begley Mary E—†	8	bookkeeper	45	"
D	Byrne George P	8	shipfitter	21	"
E	Byrne Katherine F—†	8	housewife	47	"
F	Byrne Patrick J	8	foreman	48	"
G	Byrne William P	8	U S N	22	
H	Doherty Ellen G—†	10	housekeeper	73	"
K	Coughlin Mary—†	10	maid	62	"
L	Herlihy Ella—†	10	housewife	46	"
M	Herlihy Irene—†	10	inspector	28	"
N	Herlihy James J	10	U S A	20	"
O	Herlihy Rita—†	10	clerk	23	
P	Smith Melvin	10	longshoreman	39	"
R	O'Brien Catherine M—†	12	clerk	33	
S	O'Brien David J	12	laborer	44	
T	O'Brien Joseph J	12	cashier	38	
U	O'Brien Margaret M—†	12	housekeeper	73	"
V	O'Brien Mary C—†	12	"	27	
W	O'Brien Thomas F	12	clerk	42	
X	Gill Annie—†	14	housewife	59	"
Y	Gill Francis M	14	U S A	22	
Z	Gill James J	14	plater	35	

1301

A	Gill Margaret M—†	14	packer	38	
B	Gill Michael	14	watchman	72	"
C	Gill Michael J	14	longshoreman	30	"
D	Clark Della—†	16	housewife	36	"
E	Clark John	16	longshoreman	41	"
F	Burk Lambert	16	retired	75	"
G	Gill Abbie F—†	16	housekeeper	66	"
H	Gill Catherine V—†	16	bookkeeper	56	"
K	McGonagle Henry J	18	fireman	59	"
L	McGonagle Lillian E—†	18	housewife	55	"
M	Murphy Josephine—†	18	clerk	50	
N	McGonagle Henry J	18	painter	35	"
O	McGonagle Margaret E-†	18	housewife	35	"
P	Barry Daniel J	20	laborer	59	
R	Barry Margaret T—†	20	housewife	59	"
S	McGrath James J	20	U S N	41	

Allston Street—Continued

T	Nelson Catherine—†	20	housewife	29	here
U	Nelson Charles	20	U S A	28	"
V	Schneider Charles W	22	retired	69	"
W	Jones Catherine—†	22	housekeeper	48	"
X	Jones Thomas	22	U S C G	23	"
Y	Ferretti Alfred J	24	polisher	47	"
Z	Ferretti Mabel G—†	24	housewife	38	"
	1302				
A	Campbell John J	24	longshoreman	29	"
B	Campbell Winifred—†	24	housewife	25	"
C	Mantine Annie—†	24	housekeeper	80	"
D	Cullen Ann V—†	26	housewife	42	"
E	*Cullen Patrick H	26	steamfitter	46	"
F	Marshall Kenneth P	26	seaman	20	"
G	McGeouch Ella M—†	26	housewife	68	"
H	McGeouch Leonard	26	guard	68	
K	Payne Martha—†	26	housewife	51	"
P	Payne Raymond	26	painter	52	"
M	Murphy Anna E—†	30	housewife	36	"
N	Murphy Harry W	30	fireman	38	"
O	MacLoon Dorothy C—†	34	clerk	27	
P	MacLoon Marion L—†	34	housekeeper	54	"
R	MacLoon William G	34	U S A	22	"
S	Pratt Andrew C	34	U S N	24	
T	Pratt Charles H	34	laborer	48	"
U	Pratt Florence M—†	34	U S M C	22	"
V	Pratt Laura—†	34	housewife	47	"
W	Fitzgerald Annie—†	38	"	52	
X	Fitzgerald Edward F	38	checker	63	"
Y	Fitzgerald William M	38	U S A	23	"
Z	Connolly Bridie—†	38	housewife	40	"
	1303				
A	Connolly Stephen	38	longshoreman	47	"
B	Randall Florence—†	38	housewife	35	"
C	Randall George	38	fireman	34	"
D	Sherwood Emery W	40	operator	43	"
E	Boice Mary A—†	40	housekeeper	70	33 Bunker Hill
F	Murphy Irene A—†	40	welder	20	33 "
G	Murphy Irene J—†	40	housewife	43	33 "
H	Murphy William A	40	mechanic	47	33 "
K	Colman Arline—†	40	instructor	32	36 Concord

3

Page.	Letter.	FULL NAME.	Residence, Jan. 1, 1944.	Occupation.	Supposed Age.	Reported Residence, Jan. 1, 1943. Street and Number.

Allston Street—Continued

L	Mellino Alfred J	44	boilermaker	46	here
M	Mellino Charlotte—†	44	housewife	42	"
N	Fehlan Gertrude—†	44	housekeeper	64	"
O	Fehlan Louis	44	longshoreman	33	"
P	McLaughlin Arthur L	46	guard	54	
R	McLaughlin Frances—†	46	housewife	51	"
S	McLaughlin Frederick J	46	stockboy	22	"
T	McLaughlin John E	46	collector	30	"
U	Regan Francis M	48	chauffeur	27	"
V	Regan John J	48	"	52	
W	Regan Nellie M—†	48	housewife	56	"
X	Regan Robert	48	U S A	20	
Y	Regan Thomas J	48	U S N	24	

1304   Belmont Street

A	Chase Clinton	7	printer	39	here
B	Chase Mary—†	7	packer	36	"
C	Kinsella Helene E—†	7	housewife	27	"
D	Kinsella Michael F	7	salesman	47	"
E	Aylward George F	8	U S N	21	
F	Aylward Mary E—†	8	tel operator	23	"
G	Aylward Mary S—†	8	housewife	54	"
H	Aylward Michael J	8	B F D	54	
K	Aylward Thomas J	8	U S N	25	
M	Buckley Esther M—†	10	inspector	27	"
N	Buckley Lillian R—†	10	secretary	22	"
O	Buckley Mary A—†	10	housewife	58	"
P	Buckley Michael F	10	engineer	63	"
R	Noyes Margaret I—†	10	saleswoman	33	"
V	Fardig Harold A	12	shipper	40	..
W	Fardig Margaret M—†	12	housewife	45	"
X	Shepard Catherine R—†	12	secretary	40	"
Y	Shepard Mary V—†	12	bookkeeper	43	"
	1305					
C	Hickey Mary A—†	14	waitress	35	"
D	Hickey Patrick J	14	welder	38	
E	Lawn Edward P	14	U S A	22	
F	Leahy Daniel F	15	"	27	
G	Leahy Ellen—†	15	housewife	63	"
H	Leahy James J	15	longshoreman	35	"

Belmont Street—Continued

K	Leahy Patrick L	15	U S A	21	here
L	Leahy Rita T—†	15	welder	20	"
M	Leahy Thomas P	15	U S A	30	"
N	Leahy William P	15	longshoreman	37	"
O	Sullivan Margaret M—†	15	housewife	30	"
P	Sullivan Robert L	15	U S N	32	"
R	Aylward Catherine—†	16	at home	80	"
S	Aylward Mary C—†	16	librarian	40	"
T	Shepard Anna—†	18	housewife	38	"
U	Shepard John P	18	clerk	39	
Y	Stone Clara—†	26	housekeeper	59	"
	1306				
A	Hart Jeremiah	28	chauffeur	37	"
B	Hart Lucille—†	28	housewife	38	"
C	McCarthy Charles J	28	laborer	65	"
D	McCarthy Florence—†	28	clerk	67	
E	McCarthy John	28	laborer	60	"
F	McCarthy Mary A—†	28	bookbinder	50	"
G	Bratton Catherine—†	28	waitress	32	"
H	Bratton Edward A	28	shipfitter	37	"
K	Hickey Margaret J—†	29	tel operator	22	"
L	Hickey Robert J	29	laborer	29	"
M	Hickey Thomas M	29	U S A	33	
N	Hickey William C	29	U S N	25	
O	Connors Catherine B—†	30	housewife	33	"
P	McGrath John C	30	laborer	47	"
R	Owens Enola B—†	31	housewife	34	"
S	Owens Ward R	31	U S C G	40	"
U	Black Margaret M—†	33	housewife	44	"
V	Prendeville Margaret E–†	33	"	24	
W	Prendeville Ronald J	33	U S A	24	
X	Bratton Catherine A—†	33	housewife	38	"
Y	Bratton Philip F	33	riveter	40	"
	1307				
A	O'Brien Edna C—†	rear 33	housewife	23	"
B	O'Brien Edward J	" 33	longshoreman	25	"
E	McEleney Anna L—†	37	housewife	46	"
F	McEleney Edward R	37	U S N	20	
G	McEleney Hugh	37	operator	53	"
H	Lifrieri Milio	38	cook	54	
K	Saccardo Guy	38	pipefitter	36	"

Belmont Street—Continued

L	Saccardo Silda—†	38	housewife	30	here
M	Alves Joseph F	38	welder	31	"
N	Alves Rita F—†	38	housewife	28	"
O	Shea Francis L	39	longshoreman	36	"
P	Shea Helen J—†	39	housewife	33	"
R	Gans Louise—†	43	at home	75	"
S	McEmery Marion—†	43	stenographer	35	"
U	Scottron Pearl—†	45	housekeeper	45	"
V	Shea Elizabeth J—†	46	housewife	67	"
W	Shea John J	46	longshoreman	39	"
Z	Waters Catherine G—†	52	housewife	54	"

1308

A	Waters John J	52	waiter	55	
B	Stewart Dorothy E—†	56	housewife	26	"
C	Stewart William F	56	seaman	30	
D	Kirby Catherine H—†	56	waitress	21	"
E	Kirby William F	56	U S A	33	
F	Miller Sadie A—†	56	housewife	62	"
G	Lanou Georgie—†	rear 56	housekeeper	63	"
H	Wells Hugh	" 56	pedler	70	..

Bunker Hill Court

K	Boyle Helen F—†	1	housewife	33	here
L	Boyle Vincent J	1	laborer	34	"
M	O'Donnell Agnes G—†	2	tester	36	"
N	O'Donnell Mary F—†	2	storekeeper	44	"
O	Reagan Mary —†	3	at home	62	"
P	Lewis Amelia A—†	4	typist	30	
R	Lewis Joseph T	4	laborer	39	..
S	Lewis Mary J—†	4	clerk	25	
T	Lewis Philomena—†	4	typist	29	
U	Lewis Phylomena P—†	4	housewife	60	"
V	McGonagle Michael	6	shipfitter	39	"
W	McGonagle Veronica—†	6	housewife	33	"
X	Fleming Annie T—†	7	at home	58	"

Bunker Hill Street

Y	Baldwin Anne E—†	249	housewife	25	here
Z	Baldwin Leo T	249	U S A	28	"

1309
Bunker Hill Street—Continued

A	Condon Dennis M	249	U S A	20	here
B	Condon Nora E—†	249	housewife	60	"
C	McCarthy Lucy E—†	249	"	28	"
D	McCarthy William J	249	U S N	33	"
E	Sullivan Margaret M—†	249	secretary	32	"
F	Pace Michael	251	laborer	44	"
G	Pace Vincent	251	U S N	20	
H	Kelley John V	251	electrician	35	"
K	Kelley Josephine—†	251	housewife	35	"
L	Neary John J	251	policeman	44	"
M	*Alves John	251	seaman	62	
N	*Alves Mary—†	251	housewife	58	"
O	Alves Mary—†	251	factoryhand	23	"
P	*Soares Rose—†	251	at home	71	"
R	Bradley Frank	255	painter	36	
S	Bradley Helen—†	255	housewife	34	"
T	Danahy Anna—†	255	"	39	
U	Danahy Frank	255	retired	53	"
V	Nearin John	255	U S A	22	
W	Wheeler Dorothy—†	257	housewife	39	"
X	Wheeler Frank	257	guard	37	"
Z	Glennon Helen—†	261	housewife	23	Malden

1310

A	Glennon Leo	261	operator	29	"
B	Dean Gladys G—†	261	housewife	45	here
C	Dean Lawrence J	261	laborer	20	"
D	Dean William L	261	U S A	23	"
E	Jones George	261	longshoreman	43	"
F	Jones Josephine E—†	261	housewife	36	"
G	O'Keefe Annie—†	265	matron	69	"
H	O'Keefe John J	265	U S N	30	"
K	O'Keefe Michael C	265	retired	39	
L	Dowd Nora F—†	265	housewife	36	"
M	Dowd William E	265	clerk	39	" .
N	*Cooperman Anna—†	267	housewife	53	"
O	Cooperman Philip	267	merchant	54	"
P	Murphy Mary A—†	267	housewife	55	9 Carney ct
R	Murphy William J	267	clerk	51	9 "
S	Murphy William J, jr	267	U S N	27	9 "
T	Murphy William R	267	chauffeur	42	73 Lawrence

Bunker Hill Street—Continued

U	Moynihan Mary O—†	269	tailor	65	here
V	Murphy Anna G—†	269	operator	46	"
W	Murphy John J	269	retired	73	"
X	Murphy Mary R—†	269	housewife	41	"
Y	Clark Eileen—†	270	"	42	
Z	Clark Mary B—†	270	clerk	21	

1311

A	Clark Peter	270	U S A	22	
C	Reese June L—†	270	housewife	32	"
D	Reese Raymond T	270	operator	43	"
E	Dever James	271	B F D	28	
F	Dever Mildred—†	271	at home	28	"
G	Harrington Daniel G	271	B F D	53	"
H	DeMinico Joseph M	272	clerk	29	306 Bunker Hill
K	DeMinico May E—†	272	housewife	29	306 "
L	O'Malley Eunice G—†	272	"	43	306 "
M	O'Malley John F	272	brazier	25	306 '
N	O'Malley John J	272	clerk	49	306 '
O	O'Malley Thomas F	272	"	46	306 "
R	Freedman Pauline—†	273	teacher	35	Malden
S	Tolman Alice G—†	273	clerk	42	here
T	Blake Maud M—†	273	housewife	67	"
U	Finnan Martin T	273	seaman	34	"
V	Finnan Virginia M—†	273	clerk	26	
W	Gosnell Margaret A—†	273	teacher	53	
X	Soccardo Antonina—†	274	housewife	62	"
Y	Soccardo Caroline—†	274	cigarmaker	31	"
Z	Soccardo Christine—†	274	housekeeper	33	"

1312

A	Soccardo Leo	274	U S M C	38	"
B	Soccardo Sadie—†	274	packer	29	
C	Soccardo Salvatore	274	U S A	27	
D	Soccardo Steve	274	barber	40	"
E	Carberry Ellen—†	274	matron	51	42 Elm
G	Keliher Louise—†	275	housewife	30	here
H	Keliher Michael C	275	machinist	35	"
K	O'Brien Claire—†	275	clerk	40	"
L	O'Brien Elizabeth—†	275	housewife	58	"
M	O'Brien James	275	guard	45	
N	Leary Catherine—†	276	packer	31	
O	Leary Leo F	276	U S A	29	

8

Bunker Hill Street—Continued

	Letter.	FULL NAME.	Residence, Jan. 1, 1944.	Occupation.	Supposed Age.	Reported Residence
	P	Leary Margaret—†	276	housewife	68	here
	R	Leary Margaret A—†	276	packer	35	"
	S	Leary Mary—†	276	"	33	"
	T	Cleary David M	276	retired	42	
	U	Cleary Gladys E—†	276	housewife	42	"
	V	Jewett Margaret K—†	276	attendant	67	Peabody
	W	McLaughlin John A	276	operator	42	here
	X	Curneil James	276	electrician	48	"
	Y	Curneil Mary T—†	276	housewife	49	"
	Z	Loughman Honora G—†	278	"	64	
		1313				
	A	Burke Catherine—†	278	"	60	90 Elm
	B	Burke Dorothy—†	278	packer	24	90 "
	C	Burke Margaret—†	278	at home	28	90 "
	D	Burke Mary C—†	278	boxmaker	33	90 "
	E	Loughman Eleanor T—†	278	housewife	24	here
	F	Loughman Michael G	278	U S N	28	"
	H	Brennan Bernard J	282	clerk	58	"
	K	Brennan Esther E—†	282	housewife	48	"
	L	Brennan John A	282	lawyer	51	
	M	Donovan Ellen T—†	282	at home	65	"
	N	O'Brien Edward F	282	inspector	38	"
	O	O'Brien Eleanor M—†	282	housewife	37	"
	P	O'Brien Ellen A—†	282	"	67	
	R	O'Brien Florence R—†	282	clerk	22	
	S	O'Brien James J	282	retired	72	
	T	O'Brien Margaret J—†	282	clerk	36	
	U	O'Brien Mary E—†	282	"	40	"
	V	O'Brien Rose R—†	282	packer	35	"
	W	O'Brien William H	282	U S N	28	
	X	Murphy Catherine B—†	284	at home	54	"
	Y	Murphy Helen G—†	284	"	58	
	Z	Murphy Margaret F—†	284	"	56	"
		1314				
	A	Malone Lillian L	284	housewife	32	"
	B	Malone William H	284	foreman	36	"
	C	Brock John B	284	U S A	35	
	D	Brock Madeline M—†	284	housewife	30	"
	E	Brock Nellie J—†	284	bookkeeper	40	"
	F	Brock Owen F	284	U S N	26	"
	G	McGrady Marion—†	285	housewife	35	"

9

Bunker Hill Street—Continued

H	McGrady Paul	285	mechanic	33	here
K	Brennan Mary—†	285	housewife	60	"
L	Foley Elizabeth E—†	285	boxmaker	33	"
M	Marshall Anna—†	285	welder	26	
N	Marshall Bessie—†	285	housewife	62	"
O	Marshall Bessie B—†	285	boxmaker	22	"
P	Marshall Catherine A—†	285	baker	27	"
R	Marshall Edward W	285	fireman	31	"
S	Marshall Helen J—†	285	baker	30	
T	Marshall John	285	engineer	66	"
U	Brennick Katherine—†	286	housewife	67	"
V	Brennick Robert	286	attendant	65	"
W	Brennick Thomas	286	laborer	29	
X	Trainor Joseph F	286	U S N	27	
Y	Trainor Mary A—†	286	housewife	63	"
Z	Trainor Rita C—†.	286	social worker	29	"
	1315				
A	Cushing Annie—†	286	housewife	58	2 Sackville
B	Cushing Mildred—†	286	clerk	28	2 "
C	Felleter Johanna—†	287	housewife	63	here
D	Felleter Mary—†	287	clerk	30	"
E	Felleter Nicholas	287	retired	67	"
G	O'Brien Catherine—†	287	clerk	35	
H	Anderson Agnes—†	288	teacher	48	"
K	Kirkpatrick Catherine G—†	289	housewife	35	"
L	Kirpatrick Francis J	289	collector	46	"
M	Whiteman John L	289	retired	55	"
N	Whiteman Marion E—†	289	housewife	38	"
O	Long Christine—†	289	teacher	40	
P	Delay Jennie E—†	291	housewife	73	"
R	Delay John J	291	court officer	50	"
S	Delay Joseph E	291	executive	39	"
T	Delay Mary E—†	291	secretary	47	"
U	Delay Patrick J	291	retired	75	"
V	*Arnone Charda—†	292	housewife	82	"
W	Arnone Gaetano	292	machinist	55	"
X	*Arnone Julia—†	292	housewife	52	"
Y	Lifrieri Angelina—†	292	"	41	
Z	Lifrieri Saverio	292	glazer	61	
	1316				
A	Reid Lawrence	292	rigger	47	

Bunker Hill Street—Continued

B	*Reid Mary A—†	292	housewife	47	here	
C	Finn John	293	longshoreman	41	34 Bartlett	
D	Finn Mary—†	293	housewife	48	34 "	
E	Hanlon James E	293	longshoreman	41	here	
F	Hanlon Veronica F—†	293	housewife	40	"	
G	Goff John F	294	registrar	43	"	
H	Goff Mary A—†	294	housewife	42	"	
K	Hickson Annie J—†	294	"	57		
L	Hickson John J	294	U S A	23		
M	Hickson Louis R	294	retired	57		
N	Hickson Louis R, jr	294	seaman	30		
O	Doherty Anna—†	295	clerk	27		
P	Doherty Helen—†	295	housewife	53	"	
R	Doherty James	295	U S N	28		
S	Doherty Joseph	295	longshoreman	30	"	
T	Doherty Sarah—†	295	clerk	25		
U	Glavin Helen A—†	295	housewife	32	"	
V	Glavin Walter	295	machinist	34	"	
W	Murphy Agnes—†	296	housewife	65	"	
X	Murphy Francis D	296	U S A	27	"	
Y	Murphy Helen A—†	296	secretary	36	"	
Z	Murphy Kathryn M—†	296	housewife	28	"	

1317

A	Murphy Rita M—†	296	bookkeeper	30	"	
B	Murphy Theresa M—†	296	manager	38	"	
C	Murphy Veronica R—†	296	teacher	34		
D	Murphy William	296	retired	70		
E	Winnett Catherine—†	296	housewife	65	"	
F	Winnett Francis A	296	florist	37	Medford	
G	Bailey Catherine—†	297	at home	55	here	
H	Trainor Catherine—†	297	matron	55	"	
K	Sharkey Catherine—†	297	housewife	56	"	
L	Sharkey Edward	297	plumber	60	"	
M	Sharkey Sarah—†	297	clerk	54		
N	Hoban Catherine—†	298	housewife	32	"	
O	Hoban Edwin	298	longshoreman	34	"	
P	Ahern Arthur	298A	policeman	36	"	
R	Ahern Gertrude—†	298A	housewife	37	"	
S	McNerlin Frances—†	298A	"	48	"	
T	McNerlin William L	298A	foreman	57	"	
U	Whitman Catherine E-†	299	housewife	72	"	

11

Bunker Hill Street—Continued

Page.	Letter.	FULL NAME.	Residence, Jan. 1, 1944.	Occupation:	Supposed Age.	Reported Residence, Jan. 1, 1943. Street and Number:
	v	Whitman John L	299	merchant	70	here
	w	Russell Edmund F	299	laborer	70	"
	x	Russell Julia F—†	299	housewife	53	"
	y	Doyle Catherine—†	300	"	40	
	z	Doyle Richard A	300	chauffeur	40	"
1318						
	A	Norris Helen M—†	300A	housewife	31	431 Bunker Hill
	B	Duffy Elmer E	300A	foreman	43	10 St Martin
	D	Hunt Loretta—†	300A	clerk	39	10 "
	c	Hunt Manuel	300A	shipper	39	17 McNulty ct
	E	O'Callahan Albert T	301	salesman	68	here
	F	O'Callahan Martha A—†	301	housekeeper	73	"
	G	O'Callahan Theresa E—†	301	teacher	71	"
	H	Corcoran Dorothy J—†	302	mechanic	29	"
	K	Corcoran Leo F	302	welder	23	
	L	Corcoran Mary J—†	302	housewife	63	"
	M	Corcoran William H	302	retired	72	
	N	Broderick George F	302A	laborer	47	''
	o*	Broderick Marion—†	302A	housewife	46	"
	P	O'Brien Charles F	302A	custodian	60	1 Bunker Hill ct
	R	O'Brien Nettie M—†	302A	housewife	54	1 "
	s*	Burns Celia—†	303	domestic	38	here
	T*	Burns Nellie—†	303	"	39	"
	u	Conlon James L	303	clergyman	40	"
	v*	Houlihan Bridget—†	303	cook	70	
	w	McMamon John J	303	clergyman	27	"
	x	Quirback Conrad J	303	"	56	Greenwood
	y	Robinson Joseph A	303	"	46	here
1319						
	A	Doherty Edward J	304A	U S A	26	
	B	Doherty Gertrude—†	304A	secretary	30	"
	D	Doherty James F	304A	electrician	27	"
	c	Doherty James J	304A	engineer	71	"
	E	Doherty Mildred—†	304A	clerk	24	
	F	Carlin James J	304A	repairman	63	"
	G	Carlin Margaret T—†	304A	housewife	56	"
	H	Gallagher Catherine E-†	306	at home	74	"
	K	Gallagher Frances C—†	306	housewife	40	"
	L	Gallagher Patrick J	306	shipper	44	"
	M	Carr Bridget M—†	306	housewife	84	"
	N	Doherty Charles J	306	checker	56	"

12

Bunker Hill Street—Continued

o	Doherty Nora C—†	306	housewife	47	here
R	Connors Joseph F	308	policeman	43	"
s	McCarthy Louise G—†	308	typist	50	"
T	Pendergast Helen M—†	308	at home	35	"
u	McCarthy Ellen T—†	308	housewife	53	"
v	McCarthy Florance	308	packer	53	
w	McCarthy Florance	308	U S N	21	"
x	Vanderpot Margaret—†	308	housewife	29	13 Trenton
y	Vanderpot William P	308	welder	29	13 "
z	Godsell James E	310	collector	34	here

1320

A	Godsell Susan—†	310	housewife	33	"
B	Tague Margaret E—†	310	"	55	
c	Tague Philip A	310	retired	70	"
D	White Eleanor F—†	310	housewife	53	"
E	White Eleanor F—†	310	secretary	27	"
F	White George E	310	retired	55	"
G	White Mary E—†	310	clerk	26	
H	Powers Grace—† rear	310	housewife	24	"
K	Powers John W "	310	packer	24	
L	Gillen Sarah A—† "	310	housewife	52	" ·
M	Gillen Sarah M—† "	310	clerk	21	
N	Flaherty Helene—†	312	housewife	31	"
o	Flaherty Robert	312	manager	36	"
P	Sullivan Catherine—†	312	housewife	62	"
R	Sullivan John	312	retired	73	
s	Sullivan Margaret M—†	312	secretary	29	"
T	Sullivan Mary E—†	312	"	32	"
Y	Connolly Helen—†	312	housewife	24	"
z	Connolly Michael	312	U S C G	22	"
u	Curran Catherine—†	312	housewife	58	"
v	Curran Margaret—†	312	dressmaker	28	"
w	Curran Mary—†	312	nurse	30	"
x	Curran Thomas	312	laborer	60	

1321

A	Montville Hattie—†	314	housewife	61	"
B	Sasso Leona C—†	314	"	41	
c	Sasso Joseph M	314	U S N	38	"
D	Buckley Frank	314	agent	58	
E	Sullivan Agnes—†	314	housewife	52	"
F	Sullivan Edward	314	U S A	25	"

Bunker Hill Street—Continued

G	Sullivan Richard J	314	repairman	54	here
H	Sullivan Richard J, jr	314	fireman	27	"
K	Sullivan William	314	U S A	30	"
L	Caffrey Francis G	314A	"	27	81. Pearl
M	Caffrey Rose D—†	314A	stenographer	34	81 "
N	Hickey Agnes M—†	314A	housewife	32	here
O	Hickey John J	314A	electrician	32	"
R	Mayhew Helen—†	314A	at home	75	"
S	McCarthy Elizabeth L—†	314A	teacher	61	
P	Hennessey Matthew D	314A	U S A `	43	
T	Hennessey Theresa—†	314A	housewife	43	"
U	Enright Charles	318	U S A	22	
V	Enright Thomas	318	builder	24	
X	McInnes Mary—†	318	housewife	49	"
W	McInnes Raymond	318	U S A	39	''
Y	Ferry Julia J—†	318	housewife	44	"
Z	Ferry Michael J	318	U S A	20	
	1322				
A	Ferry Peter P	318	U S M C	43	"
B	Murphy Margaret J—†	322	at home	66	"
C	Sawyer Frederick P	322	bailiff	30	
D	Sawyer Margaret M—†	322	housewife	60	"
F	Flaherty Alice V—† rear	322	packer	27	
G	Flaherty Francis X "	322	U S A	32	
H	Flaherty Mary G—† "	322	housewife	66	"
K	Flaherty Patrick H "	322	clerk	72	
L	Geary Philip D 2d r	322	laborer	63	
M	Geary William L 2d "	322	"	51	
N	McCormack Anne—† 2d	322	housewife	66	"
O	Russell John J	324	laborer	38	
P	Russell Mary E—†	324	housewife	32	"
R	Gore Anna T—†	324	bookkeeper	39	"
S	Gore Richard A	324	retired	71	''
T	Butler Albert	324A	laborer	44	
U	Butler Johanna—†	324A	housewife	38	"
V	Blake Margaret E—†	325	teacher	57	"
W	Butler Frances R—†	325	"	35	"
X	Coleman Carrie A—†	325	"	47	
Y	Coleman Elizabeth H—†	325	"	46	
Z	Collins Agnes—†	325		26	

1323
Bunker Hill Street—Continued

A	Devine Cecelia E—†	325	teacher	52	here
B	Durkin Elizabeth A—†	325	"	52	"
C	Fleming Margaret E—†	325	"	60	"
D	Hart Emily—†	325		71	
E	Keenan Margaret—†	325	"	40	"
F	Lafayette Catherine—†	325	"	37	Cambridge
G	Lynch Agnes—†	325	"	45	here
H	Lynch Mary—†	325	"	48	"
K	Lyons Olive K—†	325	housekeeper	47	"
L	Martin Elizabeth—†	325	teacher	41	W Virginia
M	McHugh Roberta F—†	325	"	44	here
N	McMahon Myrtle—†	325	"	47	"
O	Murphy Alice—†	325	"	29	"
P	Murphy Mary E—†	325	"	34	
R	Punch Loretta—†	325	"	46	"
S	Phelan Alice—†	325	"	53	Wash'n D C
T	Ryle Elenor F—†	325	"	29	here
U	Walsh Agnes M—†	325	"	25	"
W	McNamara Karen—†	326A	cleaner	51	"
X	McEleney Elizabeth M—†	326A	clerk	37	
Y	McEleney Joseph P	326A	U S N	34	
Z	McEleney Margaret—†	326A	housewife	68	"

1324

A	Parker Charlotte—†	328	"	34	
B	Parker George W	328	shipfitter	42	"
C	Hoey Annie—†	328	housewife	47	"
D	Hoey Thomas	328	foreman	51	"
E	Barry John A	328A	retired	83	
F	Kilroy Mary—†	328A	at home	71	"
G	Smith Bernard	329	letter carrier	26	"
H	Smith Mary—†	329	housewife	22	"
K	Evans Ernest W	329	laborer	45	
M	Evans Pauline—†	329	housewife	40	"
L	Evans Leona—†	329	clerk	21	
N	Livingston Margaret—†	330	housewife	76	"
O	Livingston Veronica C—†	330	stenographer	35	"
P	Ducey Thomas W	330	retired	66	"
S	Myles Marion A—†	331	housewife	26	16 Eden
T	Myles Robert E	331	pressman	28	16 "

15

Page.	Letter.	FULL NAME.	Residence, Jan. 1, 1944.	Occupation.	Supposed Age.	Reported Residence, Jan. 1, 1943. Street and Number.

Bunker Hill Street—Continued

U	Boylan Catherine F—†	331	stenographer	21	here
V	Boylan James F	331	U S A	29	"
W	Boylan Margaret A—†	331	housewife	52	"
X	Boylan Margaret T—†	331	factoryhand	23	"
Y	Owens James J	331	brushmaker	62	"
Z	Farrell Edward P	333	U S A	25	

1325

A	Farrell Henry F	333	U S N	27	
B	Farrell Margaret—†	333	housewife	48	"
C	Farrell William J	333	electrician	23	"
D	Garlinghouse Elmer B	333	merchant	49	"
E	Garlinghouse Mary J—†	333	housewife	49	10 N Mead
F	Curwin Erwin	333	longshoreman	31	here
H	Curwin Helen—†	333	at home	33	"
G	Curwin Margaret—†	333	operator	35	"
K	Cavanough Mary—†	335	housewife	56	"
L	Cavanough Peter J	335	laborer	35	
M	Cavanough Rita—†	335	bookkeeper	21	"
N	Harrington Marie—†	335	housewife	25	"
O	Embuley Julia—†	335	"	50	
P	Embuley William P	335	fireman	48	
R	Murray Mary—†	335	at home	93	"
S	Herre Esther—†	335	housewife	27	"
T	Herre Harold	335	chauffeur	28	"
U	Lyons Timothy	335	retired	78	
V	Carolin Alice—†	337	tel operator	33	"
W	Carolin Catherine—†	337	packer	35	
X	Gorman Catherine—†	337	housewife	67	"
Y	O'Brien Charles V—†	337	auditor	34	
Z	O'Brien Ellen A—†	337	housewife	79	"

1326

A	Kelly Annie—†	339	at home	72	"
B	Kelly Ellen—†	339	housewife	60	"
C	Holmes Alfred J	339	retired	74	
D	Holmes Arthur W	339	clerk	38	
E	Wheeler John T	339	pipefitter	43	"
F	Wheeler Mary C—†	339	housewife	42	"
G	Shea Daniel	341	clerk	34	46 Belmont
H	Shea Ellen—†	341	housewife	28	25 Auburn
K	Buckley James	341	seaman	26	here
L	Buckley John J	341	fireman	51	"
M	Buckley Mary—†	341	housewife	55	"

16

Clarken Court

N	McArdle Edward	3	painter	58	here
o	McArdle Edward, jr	3	U S A	27	
P	McArdle Eleanor—†	3	housewife	56	"
R	Connolly Annie—†	4	"	67	65 O'Reilly way
S	Connolly Frank E	4	retired	69	65 "
T	McDougall Margaret—†	5	clerk	47	here
U	Powell Leonora—†	5	housewife	66	"
V	Stone Ethel—†	5	stenographer	28	"

Cook Street

W	Keniston Dorothy—†	4	housewife	21	here
X	Keniston William	4	U S A	24	"
Y	O'Callahan Margaret—†	4	waitress	29	"
Z	Potter Mary—†	4	housewife	47	"
1327						
	Hurley Ellen M—†	4	"	75	
B	Hurley Joseph M	4	inspector	48	"
C	Rush Frank V	4	U S A	34	
D	Rush John J	4	laborer	40	"
E	Rush Mary F—†	4	housewife	63	"
F	Rush Walter L	4	printer	63	"
G	Blake Grace—†	4	housewife	26	14 Hudson
H	Blake Leo F	4	welder	26	14 "
K	Collett Henry F	6	inspector	63	here
L	Collett Katherine A—†	6	housewife	39	"
M	Crowley Charles F	6	retired	62	9 Eden
N	Ahern Gerald R—†	7	policeman	46	here
o	Cass James L	7	retired	72	"
P	Cass Marguerite—†	7	housewife	46	"
R	Cass Catherine M—†	7	"	42	
S	Cass Robert L	7	chauffeur	44	"
T	Kinsella Catherine—†	8	housewife	70	"
U	Gardner Helene G—†	9	"	26	
V	Gardner Joseph P	9	welder	31	
W	Kelle Mary—†	9	housewife	50	"
X	Kelle Mary—†	9	"	21	
Y	Kelle William	9	chauffeur	49	"
Z	Cronan Alice M—†	12	housewife	42	"
1328						
A	Cronan Dennis E	12	manager	79	"
B	Cronan Edward	12	mechanic	42	"

Cook Street—Continued

c	Cronan Edward	12	U S A	21	here
d	Johnston John J	13	checker	25	"
e	Johnston Lillian A—†	13	operator	20	"
f	Johnston Mary K—†	13	housewife	55	"
g	Johnston Patrick	13	laborer	49	
h	Gavin Gertrude M—†	14	housewife	41	"
k	Russell Henry	14	laborer	38	
l	Smith Anna—†	14	housewife	42	"
m	Smith Warren E	14	laborer	44	
n	Rogers John	16	retired	80	
o	Rogers Mary A—†	16	housewife	73	"
p	Tipping Edward J	16	manager	49	"
r	Tipping Edward J, jr	16	clerk	26	
s	Brown Edith C—†	17	housewife	43	"
t	Brown Warren F	17	U S A	37	
u	McCarthy Francis A	17	clerk	23	
v	McCarthy Josephine M—†	17	housewife	62	"
w	McCarthy Marie A—†	17	clerk	21	
x	McCarthy Robert J	17	U S A	32	
y	McCarthy William P	17	retired	69	
z	Rowse Marion—†	18	housewife	29	"

1329

¹A	Rogers Edward J	18	laborer	52	8 Sheafe
A	Rogers Veronica—†	18	housewife	44	8 "
B	Ward George W	18	U S A	23	8 "
c	Ward Helen—†	18	packer	22	8 "
D	Saltonick Anthony P	18	laborer	33	here
E	Saltonick Joseph S	18	"	33	"
G	Mahoney Mary J—†	20	housewife	34	27 Cook
H	Furlong Ann D—†	20	"	32	Somerville
K	Furlong Walter F	20	fisherman	32	"
L	Harney Elizabeth—†	20	housewife	52	here
M	Harney Elizabeth C—†	20	WAVE	21	"
N	Harney John F	20	compositor	53	"
O	Riley Ann L—†	21	housewife	48	"
P	Riley Edward J	21	chauffeur	51	"
R	McGaugh Catherine—†	21	operator	25	"
s	McGaugh Delia—†	21	housewife	65	"
T	McGaugh Edward	21	laborer	23	
u	McGaugh James	21	U S A	30	
v	McGaugh Thomas J	21	bookkeeper	37	"

Page	Letter	Full Name.	Residence, Jan. 1, 1944.	Occupation.	Supposed Age.	Reported Residence, Jan. 1, 1943. Street and Number.

Cook Street—Continued

	W	Myra Ella—†	23	housewife	66	27 Brighton
	X	Myra Robert	23	retired	63	27 "
	Y	Mahoney Alice E—†	23	housewife	34	here
	Z	Mahoney John J	23	laborer	40	"
		1330				
	A	Topalian Mary—†	23	housewife	48	"
	B	Topalian Sarkis	23	laborer	54	"
	C	Whelan Ann—†	23	housewife	22	Cambridge
	D	Whelan Ignatius E	23	U S A	23	"
	E	Barrett Martin	24	laborer	36	19 Decatur
	F	Barrett Rita—†	24	housewife	41	19 "
	H	Donnelly Thomas	25	laborer	51	here
	K	Donnelly William	25	"	52	"
	L	Roche David	26	"	45	"
	M	Roche Julia—†	26	housewife	79	"
	N	McGowan Mary A—†	26	clerk	21	
	O	McGowan Terence	26	"	55	..
	P	Prendergast John	27	watchman	65	"
	R	Prendergast John, jr	27	laborer	28	..
	S	Prendergast Matthew	27	"	30	
	T	Prendergast Michael	27	U S A	23	
	U	Prendergast Thomas	27	"	24	
	V	Roche Hannah—†	27	housewife	56	"
	W	Tallent Edna H—†	27	"	33	Everett
	X	Tallent Frank L, jr	27	laborer	29	"
	Y	Mingo Margaret—†	27	housewife	52	70 Wait
	Z	Dunnion Grace—†	31	clerk	22	here
		1331				
	A	Dunnion Mary—†	31	housewife	50	"
	B	Dunnion Michael	31	chauffeur	59	"
	C	Lee James J	33	U S A	21	
	D	Lee John M	33	laborer	51	
	E	Lee Mary—†	33	housewife	50	"
	F	Rose Mary R—†	33	tel operator	23	"
	G	Wilson Frank	35	painter	61	38 Cook
	H	Lynch John F	35	laborer	37	here
	K	Lynch Louise A—†	35	housewife	35	"
	L	Sullivan John F	35	machinist	65	"
	N	Smith Margaret—†	36	housewife	76	"
	O	Kelly Bertha M—†	36	"	47	
	P	Kelly William A	36	laborer	57	

19

Page.	Letter.	Full Name.	Residence, Jan. 1, 1944.	Occupation.	Supposed Age.	Reported Residence, Jan. 1, 1943. Street and Number.

Cook Street—Continued

	s	Marsden John F	38	brakeman	30	39 Cook
	t	Marsden Mary—†	38	housewife	29	39 "
	u	Gardner Mary—†	39	"	68	38 "
	v	Gardner Patrick	39	retired	70	38 "
	w	Thompson Ernest G	39	U S A	21	here
	x	Thompson Myrtle—†	39	housewife	49	"
	y	Hickey Mary C—†	40	"	39	"
	z	Hickey William C	40	U S A	20	
1332						
	a	Hickey William P	40	laborer	45	"
	b	Colton Ruth—†	41	housewife	24	358 Medford
	c	Dicker Clara E—†	41	"	40	here
	d	Dicker Frank E	41	laborer	44	"
	e	Foley Nora—†	41	packer	48	"
	f	Lucia Edward	41	laborer	61	
	g	Flaherty Irene—†	41	housewife	33	"
	h	O'Flaherty John	41	laborer	63	63 Elm
	k	O'Flaherty Thomas	41	shipper	35	here
	l	Davis Robert W	42	agent	47	"
	m	Royal Ruth M—†	42	housewife	34	"
	n	Morrissey John P	43	laborer	40	
	o	Morrissey Joseph E	43	operator	36	"
	p	Morrissey Margaret—†	43	housewife	36	"

Cook Street Court

	u	Canty Marion—†	6	housewife	41	18 Cook
	v	Canty Simon P	6	laborer	49	18 "
	w	Hickey Edward	7	riveter	42	90 Decatur
	x	Hickey Margaret—†	7	housewife	40	90 "
	y	Mullan Elizabeth M—†	9	"	37	here
	z	Mullan Michael	9	welder	44	"

1333   Grant's Court

	a	Burns Annie—†	1	housewife	70	here
	b	Donohue Ann G—†	1	"	41	"
	c	Donohue Daniel T	1	U S M C	20	"
	d	Donohue Margaret D—†	1	clerk	21	"
	e	Hickey Luke	1	U S A	38	Revere
	f	Hickey Mary—†	1	housewife	25	"

20

Page	Letter	Full Name.	Residence, Jan. 1, 1944.	Occupation.	Supposed Age.	Reported Residence, Jan. 1, 1943. Street and Number.

Grant's Court—Continued

| | H | Newell Mary—† | 9 | housewife | 62 | here |
| | K | Newell Patrick | 9 | blacksmith | 62 | " |

Hill Street

	N	Stearns Annie—†	2	at home	72	here
	O	Stearns Charles N	2	chauffeur	51	"
	P	Stearns Nellie L—†	2	housewife	53	"
	R	St John John	4	retired	73	"
	S	St John Mary—†	4	chemist	41	"
	T	Barnes Mary J—†	4	clerk	53	Everett
	U	Banfield Catherine—†	5	housewife	33	here
	V	Banfield William J	5	chauffeur	35	"
	W	McGovern Helen—†	6	packer	24	"
	X	McGovern Josephine—†	6	"	22	
	Y	McGovern Sarah—†	6	housewife	62	"
	Z	Dunbar John	6	B F D	25	

1334

	A	Dunbar Margaret—†	6	housewife	30	"
	B	Cadigan Catherine—†	7	at home	63	"
	C	Finn Patrick J	7	watchman	68	28 Cordis
	D	Ryan Thomas	7	retired	80	here
	E	Hughes Margaret—†	8	at home	45	"
	F	Hughes William	8	clerk	48	"
	G	Thomas Florence—†	8	bookbinder	21	"
	H	Cadigan Cornelius	9	clerk	33	
	K	Cadigan Frances—†	9	housewife	28	"
	L	McLaughlin Annie—†	10	"	43	
	M	McLaughlin John	10	rigger	44	"
	N	Fillard Ingeborg—†	12	housewife	35	Florida

Kelley Court

	R	Miles George	3	laborer	52	5 Short St ct
	S	O'Rourke John J	3	"	41	5 "
	V	Hillman Robert	7	retired	72	here

Mead Street

| | W | Hebert Allen J | 41 | U S C G | 39 | Texas |
| | X | Hebert Victoria—† | 41 | housewife | 35 | Pennsylvania |

1

Page.	Letter.	FULL NAME.	Residence, Jan. 1, 1944.	Occupation.	Supposed Age.	Reported Residence, Jan. 1, 1943. Street and Number.

Mead Street—Continued

	Y	Malone Margaret M—†	41	housewife	33	here
	Z	Malone Thomas R	41	laborer	34	"
1335						
	A	Malone Edward M	41	"	35	..
	B	Keenan Madeline G—†	43	housewife	23	"
	C	Keenan Thomas F	43	oiler	30	
	D	Sullivan Catherine E—†	43	secretary	22	"
	E	Sullivan Elizabeth B—†	43	housewife	53	"
	F	Sullivan Timothy F	43	welder	24	
	G	Sullivan Timothy L	43	packer	51	"
	H	Gilman Charles	43	mechanic	57	"
	K	Gilman Mary F—†	43	housewife	81	"
	L	Herman Ena—†	47	"	62	
	M	Herman George	47	U S A	22	
	N	Herman Walter	47	"	23	"
	O	Flaherty Florence—†	47	housewife	28	55 Baldwin
	P	Flaherty Thomas	47	shipper	34	55 "
	R	Forrestall Frederick	47	watchman	60	55 "
	S	Griffin Mary E—†	47	clerk	53	here
	T	Griffin Mary E—†	47	"	22	"
	U	Donovan Mary—†	49	housewife	54	"

Medford Street

	W	Gorman John	334	laborer	58	here
1336						
	A	Mahoney Edward J	338	merchant	41	"
	H	Smith Leo H	348	baker	52	
	K	DeVita Giovanni	350	machinist	42	"
	L	DeVita Rose—†	350	at home	29	"
	M	DeVita Adeline—†	352	"	47	
¹M		DeVita Eliza—†	352	dressmaker	20	"
	N	DeVita Peter	352	laborer	48	
	O	DeVita Jessamina—†	354	packer	27	
	P	DeVita Luigi	354	retired	71	"
	R	DeVita Luigina—†	354	at home	54	"
	S	DeVita William P	354	carpenter	31	"
	U	Staffieri Pauline—†	358	at home	53	"
	V	Jose Henry M	358	watchman	75	"
	W	Maxwell Mabel—†	358	at home	49	"

Medford Street—Continued

x	Rand Madeline—†	370	at home	70	here
y	Carr Dorothy—†	370	"	31	"
z	Daly Bridget A—†	370	cook	44	"
1337					
a	Daly Margaret A—†	370	at home	61	"
c	Stevens Barbara A—†	372	shipper	25	"
d	Stevens Dorothea C—†	372	at home	59	"
e	Stevens Irene C—†	372	tel operator	20	"
f	Stevens William W	372	retired	65	"
g	Murphy Francis E	372	repairman	40	"
h	Murphy Mary C—†	372	at home	41	"
k	Ryan Thomas P	372	retired	75	
l	Butler Anna—†	374	at home	42	"
m	Butler Francis	374	laborer	45	"
n	Keane Frances—†	374	at home	40	"
o	Keane Thomas F	374	seaman	23	"
p	Keane William S	374	U S A	20	

Mystic Place

x	Joy Joseph A	1	carpenter	30	here
y	Tucker Margaret E—†	1	at home	34	"
z	Rowe Elizabeth—†	2	"	66	"
1338					
a	Rowe William G	2	retired	66	"
b	McLaughlin Daniel	3	"	64	
c	McLaughlin Mary—†	3	at home	66	"
f	Fitzpatrick Edward J	6	chauffeur	44	"
g	Fitzpatrick Helen W—†	6	housewife	38	"
h	Manning William J	6	inspector	68	"
k	Monagle James	7	laborer	49	"
l	Monagle Mary—†	7	housewife	47	"
m	Mento Samuel	8	laborer	36	"

North Mead Street

p	McDonough Mary E—†	6	stenographer	57	here
r	Owens Margaret T—†	6	housewife	55	"
s	Owens William P	6	operator	57	"
t	Spencer Eleanor—†	6	matron	50	
u	Spencer John	6	U S A	22	

North Mead Street—Continued

v	Spencer Robert	6	foreman	51	here
w	Spencer William	6	U S A	21	"
x	Harrington Ann M—†	8	stenographer	21	"
y	Harrington James R	8	U S N	23	,,
z	Harrington John R	8	B F D	50	"

1339

a	Harrington Mary E—†	8	housewife	49	"
b	Lombard Elizabeth—†	10	housekeeper	75	Somerville
c	Zanstuck Anna—†	10	housewife	25	here
d	Zanstuck John	10	operator	27	"
e	Jennings Mary—†	19	housewife	77	"
f	Maher Ellen—†	19	"	64	"
g	Maher James J	19	U S N	31	
h	Maher Josephine A—†	19	tel operator	27	"
k	Maher Margaret M—†	19	"	33	
l	Maher William	19	U S A	25	"
m	Ciccarelli Catherine R—†	22	housewife	37	"
n	Ciccarelli Francis	22	machinist	38	"
o	Lynch Eugene B	24	letter carrier	51	"
p	Lynch Margaret—†	24	housewife	43	"

North Mead Street Court

r	O'Rourke Cecelia K—†	1	housewife	42	here
s	O'Rourke John J	1	U S A	20	"
t	O'Rourke Owen	1	weigher	53	"
u	Quinn Edmund F	2	U S A	30	
v	Quinn Francis E	2	U S N	20	
w	Quinn John T, jr	2	U S A	26	
x	Quinn Lydia—†	2	housewife	53	"
y	Quinn Mildred T—†	2	waitress	27	"
z	Bamberg Allen J	3	U S N	25	

1340

a	Harrington Mary J—†	3	waitress	47	"
b	Headle Philomina—†	4	housewife	39	"
c	Headle Wayne C	4	supervisor	35	"
d.	Boyden Anna V—†	5	housewife	49	"
e	Boyden Anna V—†	5	stenographer	23	"
f	Boyden James R	5	letter carrier	51	"
g	Logue Agnes—†	5	seamstress	47	"
h	Logue Helen T—†	5	cleaner	53	

Russell Street

K	Dugas Frances M—†	51	housewife	46	here
L	Canty Julia P—†	51	manager	30	"
M	Canty Mary—†	51	housewife	73	"
N	Canty Mary A—†	51	secretary	40	"
O	Canty William J	51	U S A	46	
P	Coughlin Julia M—†	53	housekeeper	72	"
R	Forrest Frank	53	U S C G	27	"
S	Forrest Laura—†	53	housewife	56	"
T	Durham Helen E—†	55	"	21	
U	Durham Paul J	55	longshoreman	24	"
V	Hogan Alice P—†	55	at home	36	"
W	Hogan Madeline G—†	55	typist	39	
X	Hogan Preston T	55	policeman	47	"
Z	Sheedy Alice E—†	59	operator	32	"
	1341				
A	Sheedy Mary—†	59	housewife	65	"
B	Farrell James A	63	shipper	50	
C	Farrell Margaret C—†	63	saleswoman	41	"
D	Fleming Thomas	65	retired	72	
E	Harrington Catherine A—†	67	typist	21	
F	Harrington Edward F	67	U S A	22	"
G	Harrington Margaret M—†	67	housewife	60	"
H	Doherty Mary—†	67	"	40	
K	Doherty Owen	67	laborer	47	"
M	Dennehy Catherine—†	75	housewife	43	"
N	Mulvehill Alice L—†	75	"	45	"
O	Mulvehill John T	75	letter carrier	46	"
P	Record Elizabeth S—†	77	housewife	43	"
R	Record Kathleen—†	77	operator	22	"
S	Record Scott E	77	fireman	56	
T	Leary Margaret—†	79	housewife	82	"
U	Melanson Mary A—†	81	"	62	
V	Melanson Otis A	81	attendant	61	"
W	Nystrom Edgar	81	metal wkr	26	"
X	Harding Jennie W—†	83	housewife	68	"
Y	Morris Fred J	83	bartender	60	"
Z	Keefe Jane E—†	85	operator	47	"
	1342				
A	Bennett James M	87	retired	71	
B	Frayher Arthur	87	policeman	38	"
C	Frayher Esther—†	87	housewife	37	"

Russell Street—Continued

D	French Arthur	87	rigger	38	here
E	French Evelyn M—†	87	housewife	33	"
F	Porter Catherine—†	89	"	57	"
G	Porter Helen—†	89	"	22	
H	Porter James	89	retired	72	
K	Porter John J	89	U S A	36	
L	Porter Philip	89	U S N	28	
M	Porter Stephen	89	shipfitter	22	"
N	Porter Thomas	89	electrician	20	"
O	Belle John J	91	retired	71	
P	Belle Margaret M—†	91	stenographer	27	"
R	Drew Ann M—†	91	housewife	24	"
S	Broadley Marion—†	91½	dietitian	35	125 Parker Hill av
T	Enright Helen—†	91½	clerk	49	here
U	Fitzgerald Mary A—†	91½	nurse	48	"

Sackville Street

V	Curran Marion—†	2	housewife	65	here
W	Curran William	2	retired	74	"
	1343				
B	Gervino Ernesto	6	laborer	60	
C	Gervino Joseph	6	U S A	21	
D	Gervino Michael	6	laborer	32	..
E	Gervino Ralph	6	U S A	28	"
F	Stewart George V	8	"	37	"
G	Stewart Susan—†	8	housewife	41	"
H	Prato Concetta J—†	8	"	21	"
K	Prato Nicholas	8	U S A	24	
L	Prato Rose—†	8	housewife	47	"
M	Prato Samuel	8	laborer	51	
N	Faletra Julia C—†	8	housewife	30	"
O	Faletra Rocco J	8	laborer	29	
P	Cunio Augustus	10	machinist	37	"
R	Cunio Helena—†	10	housewife	35	"
S	Beninati Joseph	10	laborer	56	
T	Beninati Nancy—†	10	stitcher	24	"
U	Beninati Vincenzina—†	10	housewife	47	"
V	Patterson Joseph	12	U S N	28	
W	Patterson Mary—†	12	housewife	26	"
X	Cushing Mary E—†	12	"	51	

Sackville Street—Continued

Y	Cushing Michael J	12	steamfitter	55	here
z	Devery Oscar	14	foreman	62	"
	1344				
A	Devery Sarah—†	14	housewife	61	"
B	Murphy Catherine—†	14	packer	26	"
C	Murphy Elizabeth—†	14	housewife	60	"
D	Murphy Eugene	14	U S A	20	
E	Murphy George	14	"	22	"
F	Murphy Grace A—†	14	clerk	20	271 Bunker Hill
G	Murphy Henry	14	U S N	24	here
H	Murphy John	14	operator	60	"
K	Murphy John	14	laborer	38	"
L	Murphy Ruth—†	14	operator	29	"
M	Carter Catherine—†	16	clerk	39	
N	Kingston Florence A—†	16	at home	41	"
o	Kingston Frank A	16	shipper	57	"
P	Kingston Joseph L	16	chauffeur	47	"
R	Kingston Samuel J	16	contractor	52	"
s	Collins Edward M	'17	rigger	34	
T	Collins Margaret—†	17	housewife	27	"
U	Collins Annie—†	17	"	53	
V	Collins Frederick	17	laborer	54	
W	Collins Mildred—†	17	packer	20	
X	Lifriere Albina	18	housewife	31	"
Y	Lifriere Frank	18	painter	43	"
z	Robinson Edward R	18	clerk	20	84 Green
	1345				
A	Sears Fannie E—†	18	laundress	59	84 "
B	Whalen Eileen—†	20	housewife	31	here
C	Whalen Walter T	20	clerk	30	"
D	Broderick Anna—†	20	housewife	54	"
E	Broderick John J	20	merchant	43	"
F	Broderick Thomas	20	boilermaker	57	"
G	Whelton John J	21	U S A	26	
H	Whelton Kathleen—†	21	bookbinder	24	"
K	Whelton Margaret—†	21	operator	27	"
L	Whelton Michael	21	machinist	23	"
M	Whelton William	21	U S A	28	
N	Jackson Elizabeth—†	23	housewife	68	"
o	Jackson John G	23	laborer	64	
R	Kelley Ellen—†	23	at home	59	"

Page.	Letter.	FULL NAME.	Residence, Jan. 1, 1944.	Occupation.	Supposed Age.	Reported Residence, Jan. 1, 1943. Street and Number.

Sackville Street—Continued

s	Downes Catherine—†	25	operator	47	here
т	Downes John	25	rigger	48	"
u	Maguire Bartholomew	27	retired	71	"
v	Maguire Margaret M—†	27	housewife	66	"
w	Maguire Sarah—†	27	operator	39	"
x	Campbell Elizabeth—†	31	housewife	34	"
y	Campbell John	31	laborer	35	
z	Canavan Robert	31	"	44	

1346

a	McSweeney John	31	retired	73	"
b	McSweeney Nora A—†	31	housewife	57	"
c	Riley Joseph	31	longshoreman	33	"
d	Riley Margaret—†	31	packer	31	"
e	Gately Peter	33	retired	76	
f	Gibbons Mary E—†	33	housewife	42	"
g	Gibbons Philip J	33	guard	52	
h	Sweeney Annie—†	34	housewife	71	"
k	Sweeney John	34	retired	82	
l	Sweeney Rita—†	34	clerk	29	
m	Sweeney William	34	attorney	39	"
n	Ahern Sarah—†	35	at home	76	"
o	Cella Margaret—†	35	housewife	37	"
p	Cella Paul	35	shipfitter	36	"
r	Seager Donald J	36	laborer	47	..
s	Seager Helen—†	36	housewife	41	"
t	Seager John J	36	U S N	20	"
u	Hogan Helen—†	37	packer	43	29 Mystic
v	Wightman Amy E—†	37	housewife	70	here
w	Wightman Henry L	37	retired	75	"

Sheafe Street

x	Prodan Stephanie—†	2	housewife	39	here
y	Prodan Stephen B	2	carpenter	43	"
z	Mullen Luke	3	longshoreman	54	"

1347

a	Mullen Luke A	3	U S A	20	
b	Mullen Mary K—†	3	housewife	43	"
c	Nigrelli Carnelo	4	operator	55	75 Endicott
d	Merrill Harry E	4	laborer	61	45 Pleasant
e	Robinson Lucille—†	4	operator	46	here

28

Page.	Letter.	FULL NAME.	Residence, Jan. 1, 1944.	Occupation.	Supposed Age.	Reported Residence, Jan. 1, 1943. Street and Number.

Sheafe Street—Continued

F	Robinson William	4	metalworker	52	here
G	*Cross Donald	4	retired	60	"
H	Cross Margaret—†	4	housekeeper	64	"
K	*Martin Johanna—†	4	at home	62	"
L	Martin William F	4	laborer	32	"
M	Post Elizabeth—†	5	housewife	31	Chelsea
N	Post Joseph	5	operator	35	"
O	Baker Catherine F—†	6	housekeeper	65	here
P	Morris Elizabeth G—†	6	"	65	"
R	Morris George H	6	U S A	35	"
S	Morris Rita E—†	6	operator	26	"
T	Morris Victor L	6	freighthandler	23	"
U	Twohig Catherine V—†	6	bookbinder	35	"
V	Prymak Michael	6	U S A	25	
W	Prymak Tanka—†	6	housekeeper	50	"
X	Prymak Walter	6	boilermaker	48	"
Y	Hoy George A	7	longshoreman	48	6 Sackville
Z	Hoy George A, jr	7	"	21	6 "

1348

A	Cronin Louise—†	7	housekeeper	52	256 Bunker Hill
B	Green James A	7	salesman	46	256 "
C	Sims Mary M—†	8	housekeeper	33	141 High
D	*Dvorak Michael	8	baker	56	here
E	Mendaluk Peter	8	laborer	54	"
F	Mendaluk Sophia—†	8	housewife	47	"
G	Malinowski Richard	8	carpenter	30	"
H	Malinowski Stella—†	8	housewife	27	"
K	Cahill Catherine—†	10	"	30	
L	Cahill Robert	10	laborer	41	
M	Donavan Edward	10	orderly	50	"
N	Nestor Mary—†	10	housewife	58	"
O	Nestor William	10	seaman	58	..
P	Tkachuk Albert	10	laborer	22	"
R	Tkachuk Eileen—†	10	housewife	20	"
S	Harkins Frank G	12	laborer	34	
T	Harkins Mary E—†	12	housewife	32	"
U	Mayaka Rose—†	12	"	61	
V	Mayaka Stephen	12	clerk	30	
W	Mayaka Walter	12	"	27	"
X	Downey Catherine T—†	12	housewife	43	29 Mystic
Y	Downey Edward L	12	laborer	23	29 "

Page.	Letter.	FULL NAME.	Residence, Jan. 1, 1944.	Occupation.	Supposed Age.	Reported Residence, Jan. 1, 1943. Street and Number.

Sheafe Street—Continued

	z	Downey John	12	laborer	44	29 Mystic
1349						
	A	Downey John K	12		21	here
	B	Kane James P	12	"	58	29 Mystic
	c	*Tkachuk Ellen—†	14	housewife	50	here
	D	Tkachuk Felixa—†	14	cleaner	22	"
	E	*Tkachuk John	14	factoryhand	47	"
	F	Tkachuk Joseph	14	brakeman	25	"

Walker Street

	G	McGaffigan Elizabeth—†	58	candyworker	56	here
	H	McGaffigan Mary H—†	58	housekeeper	61	"
	K	McGaffigan Susan G—†	58	clerk	58	"
	L	Stewart Rena—†	60	housewife	35	N Hampshire
	M	Stewart Thomas	60	brakeman	36	"
	N	Wadleigh Henry C	60	retired	73	here
	O	Wadleigh Mildred C—†	60	housewife	60	"
	P	Heffernan George	62	longshoreman	30	45 Mystic
	R	Heffernan Mary C—†	62	housewife	26	45 "
	S	Far Nina—†	62	housekeeper	58	11 St Martin
	T	Jackson Catherine V—†	62	housewife	33	here
	U	Jackson Frank W	62	laborer	38	"
	W	Soriano Angelo	64	metalworker	27	33 Essex
	X	Soriano Blanche—†	64	housewife	25	33 "
	Y	Antonetti Ettose	64	operator	58	here
	z	*Antonetti Marisa—†	64	housewife	43	"
1350						
	B	Conway Ethel P—†	66	"	34	15 Walker
	c	Conway Thomas F	66	chauffeur	36	15 "
	D	Kane Gertrude L—†	66	housewife	32	here

Wall Street

	E	Hayes Francis E	20	electrician	27	73 Sullivan
	F	Hayes John F	20	laborer	35	73 "
	G	Hayes Joseph J	20	U S A	25	73 "
	H	Hayes Margaret E—†	20	housewife	64	73 "
	K	Hayes Theresa S—†	20	"	23	73 "
	L	Catanzaro Joseph L	20	chauffeur	28	here
	M	Catanzaro Viola Y—†	20	housewife	27	"

30

Page.	Letter.	FULL NAME.	Residence, Jan. 1, 1944.	Occupation.	Supposed Age.	Reported Residence, Jan. 1, 1943. Street and Number.

Wall Street—Continued

	N	Ragusa Madeline—†	20	housewife	30	1 Salem
	O	Ragusa Mario	20	chauffeur	31	1 "
	P	McCabe George J	21	fireman	26	89 Baldwin
	R	McCabe Majorie P—†	21	housewife	23	89 "
	S	Denehy Mary—†	21	packer	23	here
	T	Connors Arthur C	21	laborer	46	"
	U	Connors Charles A	21	retired	71	"

Webster Court

	W	Taylor Catherine M—†	4	housewife	40	here
	X	Taylor Melton C	4	mechanic	40	"

Woods Place

	Y	Kelly Alice M—†	2	stenographer	34	here
	Z	Kelly Edward P	2	chauffeur	39	"
		1351				
	A	Kelly Mary A—†	2	housewife	76	"
	B	O'Connor Thomas	2	machinist	41	"
	C	Doherty John E	4	retired	60	
	D	Doherty Mary E—†	4	housewife	59	"
	E	Bamberg Alphonse	6	electrician	39	"
	F	Bamberg Ann T—†	6	packer	38	
	G	Bamberg Grace A—†	6	housewife	71	"
	H	Bamberg Joseph P	6	electrician	40	"

Ward 2—Precinct 14

CITY OF BOSTON

LIST OF RESIDENTS
20 YEARS OF AGE AND OVER

(NON-CITIZENS INDICATED BY ASTERISK)
(FEMALES INDICATED BY DAGGER)

AS OF

JANUARY 1, 1944

THOMAS F. SULLIVAN, *Chairman*
FREDERIC E. DOWLING, *Secretary*
WILLIAM A. MOTLEY, JR.
FRANCIS B. McKINNEY
EVERETT R. PROUT

Listing Board.

CITY OF BOSTON   PRINTING DEPARTMENT

1400
Bartlett Street

A	Nissinen Hilda—†	94A	housewife	65	50 Sullivan	
B	Nissinen Lawrence W	94A	mechanic	64	50 "	
D	Ebert George B	94A	clerk	46	here	
E	Ebert Sophia—†	94A	housewife	45	"	
F	Ebert William J	94A	U S A	21	"	
L	Sawicki John	97	chauffeur	30	"	
M	Sawicki Stella M—†	97	housewife	29	"	
N	Wadleigh Rita M—†	97	typist	21		
O	Wadleigh Sadie T—†	97	housekeeper	42	"	
P	Farren Nellie—†	97	"	52	"	
R	Farren Richard J	97	U S N	31	"	
T	Healy Catherine—†	98	housewife	34	"	
U	Healy Timothy	98	clerk	37		
W	McCarthy Mary—†	99	housekeeper	78	"	
X	Sullivan Jeremiah J	99	clerk	59		
Y	Fama Louise—†	99	"	26	"	
Z	Kelly Arthur	99	laborer	30	31 Oak	

1401

A	Kelly Dorothy M—†	99	clerk	24	here	
B	Kelly Susan—†	99	housewife	63	"	
¹B	Kelly Wilfred L	99	chauffeur	38	"	
C	VanWart Helen S—†	99	clerk	24		
E	Walsh John F	100	custodian	29	"	
F	Walsh Mary—†	100	clerk	25	12 Franklin	
G	Walsh Annie—†	100	housewife	67	here	
H	Walsh Maurice	100	sexton	66	"	
K	Walsh Thomas J	100	salesman	35	"	
L	Dudley Mary—†	101	housewife	53	"	
M	Dudley William W	101	rigger	55	"	
N	Robinson Jennie W—†	101	at home	66	N Hampshire	
P	Lydon Thomas E	102	court officer	43	here	
R	Lydon Winifred C—†	102	clerk	40	"	
S	*Quinn Mary T—†	102	housewife	64	"	
T	Connolly Mary G—†	103	"	40		
U	Connolly William J	103	laborer	42		
V	Carney James J	103	"	46		
W	Carney Madeline B—†	103	housewife	41	"	
X	Venezia Alfred	104	metalworker	24	"	
Y	Venezia Michael	104	laborer	55		
Z	Venezia Orlando	104	U S A	20		

1402
Bartlett Street—Continued

	A	Venezia Rose—†	104	housewife	50	here
	B	Brown James A	105	B F D	55	"
	C	Brown Margaret T—†	105	housewife	55	"
	D	Sweeney Alice M—†	105	"	30	267 Bunker Hill
	E	Sweeney Edward J	105	clerk	35	267 "
	F	Sweeney George P	105	retired	73	267 "
	G	Fleming James G	105	"	63	here
	H	Fleming John J	105	U S A	28	"
	K	Hoey Helen—†	105	clerk	21	"
	L	Hoey Joseph	105	U S A	22	8 Sackville
	M	Jesson Arthur M	105	"	26	here
	N	Jesson Dorothy—†	105	housewife	25	"
	O	Mahoney Francis	105	U S A	24	33 Russell
	P	Mahoney Mary—†	105	housewife	22	here
	R	Prendergast William	105	clerk	58	"
	S	Flynn John	106	machinist	55	"
	T	Flynn John F	106	U S A	21	
	U	Flynn Mary A—†	106	housewife	49	"
	V	Dewey Lawrence A	107	glazier	27	"
	W	Dewey Mary A—†	107	housewife	23	"
	X	Riordan Abigail T—†	107	"	41	"
	Y	Riordan Mary T—†	107	nurse	21	"
	Z	Riordan William H	107	chauffeur	43	"

1403

	A	Monagle Cecelia M—†	108	housewife	35	"
	B	Monagle John	108	foreman	43	"
	C	Smith Albert W	108	clerk	26	117 Bartlett
	D	Smith Anna V—†	108	housewife	24	117 "
	E	MacNeil Marie A—†	109	"	64	here
	F	MacNeil Neil	109	pipefitter	69	"
	G	Patterson Margaret T—†	109	housekeeper	57	"
	H	Patterson William J	109	fireman	55	
	L	Kral Geraldine M—†	110	housewife	26	"
	M	Kral Joseph	110	U S A	26	
	N	Collins Grace K—†	111	housewife	37	"
	O	Collins Jeremiah R	111	electrician	42	"
	P	Canfield Elizabeth—†	111	forewoman	50	"
	R	Canfield James N	111	chauffeur	60	"
	S	Waugh William	111	guard	48	
	T	*Monahan Agnes—†	111	at home	75	"

3

Page.	Letter.	FULL NAME.	Residence, Jan. 1, 1944.	Occupation.	Supposed Age.	Reported Residence, Jan. 1, 1943. Street and Number.

Bartlett Street—Continued

u	*Monahan Annie—†	111	at home	75	here
v	Kane Isabelle—†	112	housewife	40	"
w	Kane Joseph H	112	laborer	50	"
x	Kane Joseph H, jr	112	U S C G	21	"
y	Blackstone Marguerite–†	113	housewife	30	"
z	Blackstone Wesley	113	laborer	39	"

1404

a	Cassettari Aladino	113	shipper	22	
b	Cassettari Ruth—†	113	housewife	23	"
c	*McDonnell Helen—†	113	"	56	"
d	McDonnell Yvonne—†	113	waitress	27	"
e	Michan Elmer E	114	shipfitter	48	"
f	Michan Elmer E	114	U S N	24	
g	Michan Kenneth A	114	U S A	21	
h	Michan Margaret L—†	114	housewife	45	"
k	Michan Sarah J—†	114	at home	77	"
l	Carbone James J	115	chauffeur	35	"
m	Carbone Mary V—†	115	housewife	33	"
n	Brennan John F	115	laborer	20	"
o	Brennan Lillian H—†	115	housewife	62	"
p	McCarthy Sarah T—†	115	maid	63	
r	Dunlea Catherine—†	116	housewife	50	"
s	Dunlea Jeremiah	116	clerk	58	
t	Dunlea Kathleen—†	116	"	23	
u	Dunlea Mary C—†	116	secretary	25	"
v	Harrigan Mary—†	117	housewife	40	11 Thompson
w	Helphinstine Lena—†	117	"	42	here
x	Helphinstine Paul	117	machinist	39	"
y	Follins William	117	guard	52	12 Johnson av
z	McGowan Frank J	117	checker	28	here

1405

a	McGowan Mary—†	117	waitress	32	"
b	White Robert W	118	U S A	21	
c	White Roseanna T—†	118	housewife	54	"
d	White Thomas C	118	U S N	26	
e	Grace Anthony	119	"	26	
f	Grace Nora M—†	119	housewife	27	"
g	Hurley Margaret M—†	119	at home	62	"
h	Hurley Martin	119	retired	70	"
k	Hogan Annette C—†	120	packer	59	"
l	Hogan Josephine C—†	120	at home	56	"

Bartlett Street—Continued

M	Hogan Lillian M—†	120	candymaker		52	here
N	Garrity Anna T—†	120	clerk		57	"
O	Garrity John A	120	"		58	"
P	Garrity Laura M—†	120	housewife		70	"
R	LeClair Emil	121	machinist		26	71 Austin
S	LeClair Lillian I—†	121	housewife		25	71 "
U	Harris Fred B	122	pressman		64	here
V	Harris Louise A—†	122	housewife		63	"
W	Calla Florence—†	122	operator		20	"
X	Calla Lena—†	123	housewife		54	"
Y	Martine Jeannette—†	123	egg candler		22	"
Z	Martine John	123	U S A		26	

1406

A	Fitzpatrick Theresa—†	125	at home		73	"
B	McCarthy Mary E—†	125	"		59	
C	Ryan Elizabeth—†	125	housekeeper		68	"
D	Ryan Mary E—†	125	stitcher		35	"
E	Ryan Philip A	125	U S A		38	··

Bolton Place

H	Hume Francis D	4	metalworker		36	here
K	Kenefick Joseph T	4	electrician		23	"
L	Kenefick Mary A—†	4	housewife		56	"
M	Hickey Augustus R	5	U S N		33	"
N	Hickey Dennis J	5	receiver		38	"
*O	Hickey Josephine B—†	5	housewife		34	"
P	Blake Patrick J	6	operator		26	"
R	*Murphy Mary—†	6	housewife		63	"
S	Murphy Michael J	6	guard		53	"
T	Price Richard A	7	chauffeur		31	5 Albion pl
U	Price Ruth M—†	7	housewife		27	5 "
V	Noone Elizabeth G—†	8	"		34	here
W	Noone Wilbur J	8	shipfitter		33	"
Y	Curtin Earl E	10	shipper		23	"
Z	Rice Earl	10	"		58	

1407

A	Anderson Albert M	11	machinist		24	"
B	Anderson Irene N—†	11	at home		27	"
C	Anderson John	11	machinist		26	"
D	*Anderson Sarah E—†	11	housewife		58	"

Page.	Letter.	Full Name.	Residence, Jan. 1, 1944.	Occupation.	Supposed Age.	Reported Residence, Jan. 1, 1943. Street and Number.

Bolton Place—Continued

	E	Campano Andrew G	12	operator	27	here
	F	Campano Bertha A—†	12	housewife	25	"
	G	Doherty James M	13	carpenter	59	"
	H	Doherty Winifred A—†	13	housewife	56	"
	K	Libby Bessie—†	14	"	48	9 Bolton pl
	L	Libby Charles E	14	laborer	53	9 "
	M	Libby Dyer E	14	U S A	20	9 "
	N	Libby Elmer L	14	"	27	9 "
	O	Kane Joseph	16	chauffeur	38	here
	P	Kane Theresa G—†	16	housewife	36	"

Carey Place

	R	Rivers George	2	retired	49	here
	S	Rivers George	2	machinist	21	"
	T	Rivers Mary—†	2	housewife	47	"
	U	Kerrigan Anthony A	3	machinist	33	"
	V	Kerrigan Rita A—†	3	housewife	27	"

Eden Street

	X	Bruno Michael L	3	manager	46	here
	Y	Stubbs Goodwin O	3	shipper	40	"
	Z	Stubbs Mildred L—†	3	housewife	38	"
1408						
	A	Wright Eva M—†	3	"	57	
	B	Wright Harry T	3	manager	63	"
	C	Lynch George	7	laborer	75	"
	D	Patterson Fannie—†	7	housewife	67	"
	E	Patterson James	7	engineer	34	"
	F	Somerville John	7	"	53	"
	G	Crafin Benjamin	9	merchant	55	"
	H	Crafin Lillian—†	9	housewife	23	"
	K	Crafin S Isadore	9	watchmaker	27	"
	L	McClellan Catherine—†	9	housewife	30	97 High
	M	McClellan Frank H	9	manager	32	97 "
	N	McClellan James F	9	painter	63	97 "
	O	Burke Edward F	11	shipper	41	here
	P	Burke Pauline—†	11	housewife	31	"
	R	Lyons Bernard J	11	retired	65	"
	S	Lyons Catherine T—†	11	housekeeper	75	"

Eden Street—Continued

	T	Lyons James A	11	clerk	43	here
	U	Power Margaret J—†	13	secretary	27	"
	V	Ruane Michael J	13	laborer	68	"
	W	Ruane Rose—†	13	housewife	63	"
	X	Feiss Chester	13	U S N	38	
	Y	Feiss Mary C—†	13	clerk	32	
	Z	Ford Helen B—†	13	"	28	
1409						
	A	Ford Nellie—†	13	housewife	64	"
	B	Gordon Sarah—†	13	packer	59	362 Main
	C	Smith Dorothy—†	15	housewife	24	Medford
	D	Smith James B	15	U S A	25	"
	E	Cherry James	15	U S N	31	Florida
	F	Cherry Ruth E—†	15	housewife	23	"
	H	Landucci Marina A—†	31	nurse	33	Brookline
	K	*Vinci Levia—†	31	at home	74	here
	L	Zana Angelo	31	bartender	50	"
	M	Zana Doris M—†	31	welder	21	"
	N	Zana Lillian P—†	31	operator	20	"
	O	Zana Mary—†	31	housewife	43	"
	P	Skeffington John R	37	B F D	42	"
	R	*Skeffington Theresa—†	37	housewife	36	"
	S	Noyes Catherine M—†	37	"	34	16 Eden
	T	Noyes Theodore E	37	longshoreman	35	16 "
	U	Cronin James F	37	policeman	41	58 Trenton
	V	Doe Isabelle H—†	37	housewife	27	here
	W	Donovan Florence J—†	37	"	40	"
	X	Donovan John F	37	B F D	44	"
	Y	Hanley Gertrude—†	39	waitress	32	"
	Z	Hewson Lillian T—†	39	at home	30	Wilmington
1410						
	A	O'Brien Jessie H—†	39	housewife	57	here
	B	O'Brien John J	39	laborer	23	"
	C	Waterhouse William W	39	U S A	35	"
	D	Johnson Mary E—†	39	housewife	40	"
	E	Conlon Delia M—†	39	"	46	
	F	Conlon James P	39	baker	44	"
	H	Connolly John F	41	laborer	40	7 Kenton rd
	K	Connolly Patricia—†	41	housewife	32	7 "
	¹K	Gibbons Michael	41	laborer	44	here
	L	Gibbons Sadie J—†	41	housewife	39	"

Page	Letter	Full Name.	Residence, Jan. 1, 1944.	Occupation.	Supposed Age.	Reported Residence, Jan. 1, 1943. Street and Number.

Eden Street—Continued

	M	*Walsh Elizabeth—†	43	housewife	36	here
	N	*Walsh Michael	43	laborer	42	"
	O	Corbett Bernard·	43	"	58	"
	P	Corbett Nicholas	43	U S A	24	
	R	Corbett Philip	43	mechanic	25	"

Franklin Street

	S	McCormick Catherine—†	1	housewife	51	here
	T	McCormick Mary A—†	1	waitress	22	"
	U	*McCormick Thomas	1	laborer	53	"
	V	McCormick Thomas F	1	U S A	26	"
	W	Tucker Charles E	2	chauffeur	47	"
	X	Tucker Charles H	2	U S A	22	
	Y	Tucker Edna M—†	2	housewife	43	"
	Z	Tucker George E	2	U S A	21	"
		1411				
	B	Chapman Emily—†	4	housewife	65	"
	C	Chapman Harry	4	retired	73	
	D	Nadeau Loretta M—†	6	housewife	23	"
	E	Nadeau Theodore D	6	pipefitter	28	"
	H	Tompkins Mary A—†	8	housewife	59	"
	K	Tompkins Pearle A—†	8	merchant	66	"
	L	Freker Albert E	8	U S N	29	9 Franklin
	M	Freker Charlene M—†	8	housewife	28	9 "
	N	Fulton Edythe—†	8	tel operator	29	Maine
	O	James Lawrence	8	machinist	50	here
	P	James Mary—†	8	clerk	48	"
	R	James Roy	8	salesman	29	"
	S	Burrows Samuel	9	"	47	
	T	Leventon Abraham	9	bartender	60	"
	U	Leventon Lena—†	9	housewife	59	"
	V	Donahue Agnes V—†	9	"	60	17 Franklin
	W	Donahue Daniel W	9	clerk	64	17 "
	X	Donahue Leo J	9	U S A	21	17 "
	Y	Matthews Beatrice—†	9	secretary	28	here
	Z	Matthews Bessie—†	9	housewife	53	"
		1412				
	A	Matthews Charles B	9	checker	59	"
	B	Matthews Irving T	9	U S A	29	

Page.	Letter.	Full Name.	Residence, Jan. 1, 1944.	Occupation.	Supposed Age.	Reported Residence, Jan. 1, 1943. Street and Number.

Franklin Street—Continued

	c	Matthews Robert J	9	U S N	24	here
	d	Frederickson Paul E	11	chauffeur	32	"
	e	Frederickson Rita C—†	11	housewife	28	"
	f	Jones Anna L—†	11	"	39	"
	g	Jones George H	11	shipfitter	36	"
	h	Kearns Mary L—†	11	mechanic	28	"
	k	Selig Annie L—†	11	housewife	65	"
	l	Selig Henry J	11	U S A	26	"
	m	Selig James B	11	U S N	23	
	n	Manning Cornelius	11	retired	67	
	o	Manning Cornelius J	11	U S A	28	
	p	Manning Mary A—†	11	clerk	29	"
	r	Manning Mary T—†	11	housewife	66	"
	s	Fraser James D	12	retired	69	"
	w	Servent Beatrice M—†	16	housewife	30	15 Chappie
	x	Servent John P	16	cleaner	37	15 "
	y	Noonan Anna M—†	16	housewife	32	here
	z	Noonan Daniel J	16	U S A	36	"
1413						
	a*	Knowles Evelyn—†	16	laundress	37	Malden
	b	Murphy Catherine—†	17	housewife	37	30 Chestnut
	c	Murphy Michael	17	freighthandler	41	30 "
	d*	Harrington Mary E—†	17	domestic	25	30 "
	g	White Austin P	20	mechanic	50	Cohasset
	h	King Anna C—†	20	housewife	28	9 Forster's ct
	k	King William T	20	seaman	29	9 "
	l	Lucia Agnes V—†	20	housewife	34	here

High Street

	n	Halpin James	104	teamster	77	here
	o	Halpin Julia—†	104	housewife	67	"
	p	Williams Margaret E—†	104	cleaner	73	"
	r	Shea Florence—†	104	at home	37	"
	s	Shea Mary—†	104	housewife	55	"
	u	Carey Catherine—†	106	matron	57	60 Harvard
	v	Scanlan Elizabeth—†	106	clerk	24	here
	w	Scanlan Margaret—†	106	housewife	65	"
	x	Scanlan Richard	106	seaman	25	"
	y	Scanlan Rita—†	106	clerk	20	

Page.	Letter.	FULL NAME.	Residence, Jan. 1, 1944.	Occupation.	Supposed Age.	Reported Residence Jan. 1, 1943. Street and Number.

High Street—Continued

z	Scanlan Samuel	106	janitor	66	here
	1414				
A	Scanlan Samuel	106	U S A	26	
B	King John J	106	chipper	36	
c	King Mary H—†	106	housewife	31	"
E	Dwyer Catherine—†	108	"	68	
F	Dwyer John	108	laborer	37	
G	Dwyer William	108	"	40	
H	*Yarmanian Tervis—†	108	at home	79	"
K	Sullivan Charles H	108	U S A	25	
L	Sullivan Gertrude—†	108	housewife	23	"
M	Walsh Edna—†	108	clerk	29	Everett
N	Finnigan Irene—†	108	housewife	42	here
o	Finnegan John	108	laborer	46	"
P	Reardon Charles	108	"	61	"
R	Reardon Mary—†	108	housewife	75	"
s	Feeney Helen—†	109	"	31	
T	Greatorex Frederick	109	U S N	21	"
U	Cavanaugh Elizabeth—†	111	housewife	75	"
v	Cavanaugh James	111	retired	75	
w	Cavanaugh James L	111	rigger	36	
x	Cavanaugh Morris	111	U S A	23	"
Y	Ringer Mary B—†	112	waitress	23	4 Harvard pl
z	Frances Gladys—†	112	housewife	30	23 Russell
	1415				
A	Frances Leo C	112	laborer	35	23 "
B	Long Josephine—†	113	housewife	20	here
c	Thompson Elizabeth—†	113	"	70	"
D	Thompson Eugene A	113	U S A	33	"
E	Crowley James	113	U S N	24	
F	Crowley Laura—†	113	housewife	21	"
G	Ison Kelio	113	U S N	42	
H	Ison Marie—†	113	housewife	39	"
L	Devlin Owen	114	laborer	66	
M	Devlin Susan—†	114	housewife	66	"
N	Gentile Frederick	114A	chemist	63	"
o	Gentile Margaret—†	114A	housewife	50	"
P	Gentile Vincent	114A	laborer	34	"
R	Shea Albert	115	"	23	20 Bartlett
s	Shea Anna—†	115	housewife	22	20 "
T	Freeman Frances—†	115	factoryhand	34	here

Page.	Letter.	Full Name.	Residence, Jan. 1, 1944.	Occupation.	Supposed Age.	Reported Residence, Jan. 1, 1943. Street and Number.

High Street—Continued

	u	Mannix Jeannette—†	115	housewife	38	here
	v	Mannix Patrick	115	U S N	39	"
	y	Vibert Margaret—†	116A	housewife	49	"
	z	Hulme Henry	117	retired	79	"

1416

	a	O'Brien Catherine J—†	117	housewife	52	"
	b	O'Brien Michael	117	manager	53	"
	c	Sheehan John	117	laborer	37	"
	d	Welsh Joseph	117	longshoreman	36	11 Wall
	e	McGonagle Mary E—†	118	housewife	34	here
	f	McGonagle Patrick J	118	foreman	41	"
	g	Merrick James J	118	U S A	22	"
	h	Merrick Mary A—†	118	housewife	60	"
	k	Pugh Grace E—†	118	"	24	
	l	Williams Julia—†	118A	"	35	
	m	Doherty George F	119	laborer	63	"
	n	Munson Myron J	119	carpenter	55	"
	o	Price John	119	laborer	57	"
	p	Pyne Catherine—†	119	housewife	56	"
	r	Pyne John	119	watchman	61	"
	s	Smith Mazie—†	119	laundress	44	4 Winthrop
	t	Crowley Helen—†	120	housewife	38	here
	u	Crowley John J	120	boilermaker	43	"
	v	Creamer Annie—†	120	housewife	35	"
	w	Creamer John	120	laborer	39	"
	x	Kiley Evelyn—†	121	housewife	37	"
	y	Kiley Thomas	121	metalworker	37	"
	z	Sands Charles W, jr	121	U S N	29	

1417

	a	Sands George W	121	"	25	"
	b	Sands Mary E—†	121	at home	87	"
	c	Sands Mary E—†	121	housewife	62	"
	d	Hennessey Nora—†	121	"	53	
	e	Hennessey William C	121	laborer	54	"
	f	Biggi Jean—†	126	at home	28	"
	g	McHugh Joseph H	126	electrician	32	"
	h	McHugh Ruth M—†	126	housewife	33	"
	k	Freeman Douglas	127	machinist	22	"
	l	Freeman Nora—†	127	housewife	52	"
	m	Freeman Singley	127	checker	50	"
	n	Mohr Henry	127	machinist	28	Alabama

1

High Street—Continued

o	Mohr Margaret—†	127	housewife	26	here
p	Pynn Helen—†	127	"	21	366 Mass av
r	Pynn Thomas	127	laborer	38	366 "
s	Chisholm Catherine—†	128	housewife	67	here
t	Chisholm Edward	128	chauffeur	43	"
u	Harvey Marion—†	128	domestic	42	"
v	Howard Catherine—†	129	housewife	66	"
w	Howard Lawrence	129	carpenter	76	"
x	Howard William F	129	motorman	29	"
z	Blackmore Alvina—†	133	housewife	59	"

1418

a	Blackmore George L	133	porter	59	
b	Blackmore Walter	133	laborer	26	"
c	Fraser Mary A—†	134	housewife	59	"
d	Fraser Thomas	134	retired	70	
e	Perron Arthur	134	pressman	57	"
f	Perron Julia—†	134	housewife	60	"
g	Whalen Josephine—†	134	"	60	
h	Whalen Patrick	134	laborer	63	
k	Roberts John	135	"	45	
l	Roberts Maude—†	135	housewife	45	"
m	Monihan Frank	136	laborer	45	20 Franklin
n	Fitzpatrick Eleanor—†	136	housewife	26	here
o	Fitzpatrick John	136	mechanic	26	"
r	Little Howard	137	U S A	20	7 Bolton pl
s	Little Lillian—†	137	housewife	53	7 "
t	Little William B	137	janitor	54	7 "
u	Blackmore Catherine M—†137		housewife	29	here
v	Blackmore George W	137	chauffeur	31	"
w	Mainey Francis J	137	clerk	33	"
x	Mainey Mildred T—†	137	housewife	30	"
y	Connors Charles	138	retired	75	5 Wall
z	Connors James	138	laborer	37	5 "

1419

a	Thompson Helen H—†	138	domestic	28	18 Sullivan
b	Thompson Mary E—†	138	housewife	60	18 "
c	Urquahart Grace A—†	138	"	25	20 "
d	Urquahart William R	138	U S A	30	20 "
e	Moulaison Ada—†	138	housewife	44	here
f	Moulaison Leander	138	chauffeur	52	"
g	Coughlin James	138	U S A	24	"

High Street—Continued

H	Coughlin May—†	139	housewife	22	here
K	Twomey Irene—†	139	"	21	"
L	Twomey Mathews	139	metalworker	25	"
M	Boyce Albert	139	molder	26	
N	Boyce Dorothy—†	139	housewife	20	"
O	Murray John F	140	shipper	47	..
P	Murray Josephine A—†	140	housewife	47	"
R	King Frank	140	manager	54	"
S	King Rita—†	140	housewife	46	"
T	King Sarah—†	140	clerk	20	"
U	Carr Arlene—†	141	housewife	27	92 Bunker Hill
V	Carr Roland	141	boatbuilder	34	92 "
W	Kilduff Margaret—†	141	housewife	29	here
X	Kilduff William	141	bartender	37	"
Y	Connolly Irene T—†	141	housewife	28	"
Z	Connolly Michael	141	retired	68	

1420

A	Connolly Walter	141	laborer	35	"
B	Martin Ruth A—†	142	housewife	30	"
C	Lynch Anna—†	142	"	33	..
D	Lynch William F	142	longshoreman	37	"
F	Catanzaro Eugene	143	chauffeur	36	"
G	Catanzaro Frances—†	143	housewife	35	"
H	Deldatto Alfred	143	painter	36	
K	Deldatto Mary E—†	143	housewife	33	"
L	Dowd Cristopher	143	laborer	35	
M	*Dowd Marie—†	143	housewife	33	"

Main Street

N	Zucciardi Settimi	273	merchant	67	here
S	Murphy William J	279	"	64	"
T	Nolan Ellen T—†	279	at home	57	"
U	Nolan Frank	279	pipefitter	62	"
V	Nolan George J	279	U S A	25	
W	Nolan Joseph W	279	"	21	
X	Brotherston James F	279	laborer	64	..
T	Brotherston Mary E—†	279	housewife	63	"

1421

B	Connolly Eva—†	281½	"	58	
C	Connolly William H	281½	molder	60	

Page.	Letter.	FULL NAME.	Residence, Jan. 1, 1944.	Occupation.	Supposed Age.	Reported Residence, Jan. 1, 1943. Street and Number.

Main Street—Continued

D	Connolly William H	281½	laborer	31	Everett
G	Wilson Francis B	283	machinist	20	16 Frothingham av
H	Wilson Frank J	283	custodian	41	16 "
K	Wilson Madelyn—†	283	housewife	39	16 "
P	Laudato Anna—†	291	"	45	here
R	Laudato Gaetano	291	tailor	53	"
S	Laudato Rose	291	stitcher	23	"
T	Thompson Alice G—†	293	housewife	40	"
U	Thompson Leo F	293	machinist	42	"

1422

A	McElaney Elizabeth—†	309	housewife	56	"
B	McElaney Margaret—†	309	clerk	20	
C	McElaney Mary—†	309	"	26	
D	McElaney William	309	laborer	58	
E	McElaney William T	309	U S A	23	
H	Russell Albert V	rear 313	U S N	22	
K	Russell Bridget—†	" 313	housewife	60	"
L	Russell George P	" 313	laborer	27	
M	Arzoomanian Estelle—†	315	pharmacist	35	"
N	Arzoomanian Sarah—†	315	housewife	28	"
O	Arzoomanian Sarkis	315	surveyor	22	"
P	O'Brien Catherine—†	317½	housewife	32	"
R	O'Brien Frederick	317½	paver	45	
S	Smith Austin R	317½	watchman	69	"
T	Smith Eva—†	317½	housewife	69	"
U	McLean John	319	laborer	58	39 Bartlett
V	McLean Mary A—†	319	housewife	65	39 "
W	Blankhorn Bertha E—†	321	"	38	here
X	Blankhorn Brenton A—†	321	welder	45	"

1423

B	Myers David M	327	U S N	22	
C	Myers Mary—†	327	housewife	50	"
E	Powers Margaret—†	337	at home	26	Wellington
F	Woods Josephine—†	337	housewife	46	here
G	Woods Robert L	337	U S A	22	"
H	Woods Walter L	337	merchant	46	"

Pearl Street

M	King Mabel E—†	2	shipfitter	36	43 Auburn
N	Rex Donald B	2	electrician	39	43 "

Pearl Street—Continued

o	McGuire Charles G	2	laborer	47	here
p	McGuire Mary—†	2	housewife	77	"
r	McGuire Ruth—†	2	at home	43	"
s	Scott Margaret—†	2	housewife	37	Billerica
t	Scott Norman	2	machinist	37	"
u	Johnson Harry J	2	watchman	58	here
v	Johnson John H	2	chauffeur	23	"
w	Johnson Mary F—†	2	housewife	55	"
x	Barry John	2	manager	51	"
y	Lyons John L	2	chauffeur	55	"
z	Lyons Mary N—†	2	housewife	52	"

1424

a	Burke Joseph	2	laborer	40	
b	Burke Mary—†	2	housewife	47	"
c	Fitzpatrick Dorothy—†	2	tel operator	34	"
d	Marston Annie—†	2	matron	52	
e	McCullough Francis—†	2	housewife	65	"
f	McCullough George	2	glazier	21	
g	Tasker Ella M—†	2	clerk	47	"
h	Tasker Everett H	2	photographer	28	"
k	Yeranian Anna M—†	2	housewife	32	"
l	Yeranian Joseph H	2	clerk	41	
m	Nelson Mary—†	2	at home	70	"
n	Stearns Catherine—†	2	housewife	42	"
o	Carvalho Jesse	2	mechanic	43	"
p	Carvalho Madeline H—†	2	housewife	34	"
r	McKenna Catherine—†	2	at home	69	"
s	Stevens Robert	2	clerk	37	"
t	Stevens Susan—†	2	housewife	72	"
u	Ryan Thomas	2	supervisor	52	Medford
v	Skinner Emeline—†	2	housewife	42	"
w	Lyman Lillian	2	"	34	17 Franklin
x	Lyman Ralph P	2	laborer	38	17 "
y	Roche Catherine—†	2	at home	65	97 Condor
z	Roche Charles A	2	laborer	25	97 "

1425   Russell Street

b	Ferri George	17	seaman	44	here
c	Ferri George	17	U S N	20	"
d	Ferri Rose—†	17	candymaker	43	"

15

Russell Street—Continued

E	McDonall Frederick C	17	cook	41	here
F	McDonall Helen—†	17	housewife	39	"
G	Brooks Theresa M—†	17	cleaner	50	"
H	Brooks Virginia—†	17	packer	23	
K	Nelson Edward L	17	guard	43	"
L	Galloway Elizabeth—†	19	clerk	25	"
M	Galloway James	19	chauffeur	56	"
N	Galloway Margaret—†	19	clerk	21	
O	Galloway Rose—†	19	housewife	51	"
P	Forbes Gloda L—†	20	"	30	"
T	Higgins Nellie—†	21	"	60	20 Sullivan
U	McCarthy James F	22	longshoreman	47	here
V	McCarthy Margaret—†	22	housewife	43	"
Y	Murray Mary E—†	24	"	39	"
Z	Murray Michael H	24	janitor	48	

1426

A	Dolan Hanora J—†	25	housewife	62	"
B	Dolan Philip J	25	laborer	65	
C	Burke James G	26	foreman	53	"
D	Burke Michael	26	laborer	27	
E	Burke Winifred—†	26	housewife	52	"
F	Powers Mary—†	26	"	24	
G	Eaton George	27	custodian	66	"
H	Eaton Isabelle G—†	27	housewife	70	"
K	Enos Grace P—†	27	clerk	46	
L	Igo Bernard	28	watchman	65	"
M	Murphy Agnes B—†	28	housewife	52	"
N	Murphy John R	28	U S A	24	
O	Murphy Timothy B	28	watchman	55	"
P	Murphy Timothy M	28	locksmith	26	"
R	Clark Charles F	29	laborer	76	
S	Robinson Charles	29	printer	30	"
T	Robinson Gladys—†	29	housekeeper	60	"
U	Boyd Elizabeth F—†	30	clerk	41	"
V	Boyd James H	30	U S A	44	
W	Boyd Mary—†	30	housewife	76	"
X	Boyd Patrick	30	retired	81	
Y	Herlihy Margaret—†	31	housewife	74	"
Z	Herlihy Mary—†	31	"	42	

1427

A	Herlihy Patrick	31	freighthandler	76	"

Russell Street—Continued

B	Quinn Julia—†	31	bookbinder	44	here
D	DeGrenier Leo	33	U S A	28	764 Columbia rd
E	DeGrenier Margaret—†	33	housewife	27	here
F	Mahoney Joseph	33	operator	22	"
G	Mahoney Margaret M—†	33	housewife	53	"
H	Mahoney Michael J	33	coremaker	57	"
K	Richardson Eleanor—†	33	housewife	26	"
L	Richardson Kenneth S	33	U S N	27	"
M	Noonan James	34	retired	81	
N	Noonan Mary—†	34	housewife	49	"
O	Noonan Michael	34	laborer	55	
P	Doherty Bridget V—†	35	proofreader	29	"
R	Doherty Ellen—†	35	housewife	57	"
S	Doherty Jane M.—†	35	tel operator	27	"
T	Doherty Margaret M—†	35	"	20	"
U	Doherty Neil	35	freighthandler	67	"
V	Doherty Owen J	35	electrician	24	"
Y	Galaso Angelo	37	rubberworker	35	Chelsea
Z	Galaso Florence—†	37	housewife	33	"
	1428				
A	Glenn Etta—†	37	merchant	54	here
B	Glenn Harry	37	"	56	"
C	Glenn Helen A—†	37	bookkeeper	21	"
D	Clark Frank F	38	retired	57	"
E	Fultz Elizabeth—†	38	housekeeper	82	"
G	Gravelle Charles	39	baker	50	33 Winthrop
H	Gravelle Emma—†	39	housewife	45	33 "
K	Gravelle Eugene J	39	U S A	23	33 "
L	Gravelle Leo J	39	U S N	20	33 "
M	*Elles Lillian N—†	40	housewife	34	10 Lawrence
N	Elles Robert	40	fireman	35	10 "
O	Gauthier Leslie J	40	metalworker	35	here
P	Gauthier Mary G—†	40	housewife	33	"
R	Gauthier Mary H—†	41	"	30	"
S	MacDonald John F	41	U S N	20	"
T	MacDonald John H	41	carpenter	57	"
U	MacDonald Marie—†	41	housewife	53	"
V	Sullivan Edward F	42	electrician	39	"
W	Sullivan Mary E—†	42	housewife	34	"
X	Fraser Armand A	43	laborer	32	108 Bartlett
Y	Fraser Gladys—†	43	housewife	29	108 "

Russell Street—Continued

z	Audrey Mabel—†	43	musician	54	here
	1429				
A	Denvir George H	43	laborer	56	"
B	Denvir Marie E—†	43	dietitian	60	"
C	Lally James	43	merchant	45	"
D	Blaikie Clarence W	44	U S A	30	"
E	Blaikie Laura A—†	44	housewife	50	"
F	Blaikie William E	44	meatcutter	50	"
G	York Alice G—†	45	clerk	56	100 Bartlett
H	York Chester A	45	sprayer	51	100 "
K	Monbouquette Annie—†	45	housewife	70	here
L	Monbouquette George	45	longshoreman	38	"
M	Monbouquette Margaret-†	45	laundress	32	"
N	*Doherty Margaret—†	46	housewife	53	"
O	Doherty Mary V—†	46	housekeeper	21	"
P	Doherty Michael	46	U S N	20	
R	*Doherty Patrick	46	laborer	58	
S	Doherty Patrick J	46	U S N	22	
T	Ketch Florence D—†	47	cook	40	
U	Ketch Mary J—†	47	housekeeper	68	"
V	Peters Margaret—†	47	housewife	34	"
W	Peters Warren	47	trainman	34	"
X	Shaw Laura—†	47	housekeeper	45	"
Z	Bryson Anna M—†	48	operator	20	"
Y	Bryson Margaret—†	48	housewife	55	"
	1430				
A	Bryson Theobald	48	pipecoverer	50	"
B	Cavanaugh Mary—†	48	housekeeper	55	"
C	Tennyson Daniel	48	laborer	43	"
U	Cronin Catherine—†	58	defense wkr	21	"
V	Cronin Charles	58	U S N	24	
W	Cronin John	58	U S A	27	
X	Cronin Mary—†	58	housewife	49	"
Y	Cronin Mary—†	58	clerk	23	
Z	Cronin Thomas	58	printer	29	
	1431				
A	Cullen John F	60	electrician	23	"
B	Cullen Michael J	60	U S A	25	"
C	O'Rourke Harriet M—†	60	housekeeper	55	"
D	Shields Owen S	60	seaman	66	..
F	Kearns Frank	66	printer	42	

18

Page.	Letter.	FULL NAME.	Residence, Jan. 1, 1944.	Occupation.	Supposed Age.	Reported Residence, Jan. 1, 1943. Street and Number.

Russell Street—Continued

	H	Everett Frank J	68	laborer	48	109 Bartlett
	K	Everett William H	68	"	51	109 "
[1]	K	Rea Ellen P—†	68	clerk	42	here
	L	Rea John J	68	constable	47	"
	M	Cassidy Anna—†	68	housekeeper	40	"
	N	Bodisch Arpod	70	U S N	23	28 Joiner
	O	Bodisch Lillian M—†	70	housewife	21	28 "
	R	Selig Eleanor—†	70	"	37	here
	S	Selig Warren	70	U S N	39	"

Salem Street

	T	Mederos Marie—†	2	housewife	60	here
	U	Bradbury Marie—†	2	"	58	"
	V	Bradbury William	2	electrician	60	"
	W	Hurley James	2	laborer	55	6 St Martin
	X	Brannon Edward J	4	"	42	here
	Y	Brannon Elizabeth G—†	4	housewife	44	"
	Z	Brannon Richard W	4	electrician	48	"
1432						
	A	Miarra Theodore	8	chauffeur	31	Medford
	B	*Olsen Lars	8	laborer	50	49 Tremont
	C	Stanford Anna M—†	8	housewife	66	here
	D	Stanford William J	8	metalworker	32	"
	E	Fields Walter S	10	steamfitter	43	"
	F	Poole Edith—†	10	seamstress	39	"
	G	Richardson Edna—†	10	factoryhand	33	"

Salem Street Avenue

	H	Gray Edith M—†	2	housewife	66	here
	K	Gray James E	2	fireman	39	"
	L	Gray Pearl I—†	2	housewife	38	"
	N	German William	4	laborer	50	
	O	Phillips Gertrude—†	4	housewife	40	"
	P	Flynn Edward J	6	laborer	52	"
	R	Gill Daniel	6	U S N	25	
	S	Gill Eleanor—†	6	packer	22	
	T	Kelley Anna—†	6	housewife	45	"
	U	Kelley Lester A	6	retired	43	
	V	Kelley Thomas E	6	U S N	20	

Salem Street Avenue—Continued

w	Hennessey Mary—†	6A	housekeeper	38	here
x	Cregg Benjamin J	8	laborer	57	"
y	*McEleney William	8	"	45	"
z	Chambers Joseph	10	"	39	

1433

a	Ciampa Blanche—†′	10	housewife	43	"
b	Ciampa Charles A	10	laborer	47	
c	Ciampa Robert J	10	U S A	20	"
e	Galvin Anna E—†	11	housewife	45	"
f	Galvin Anna L—†	11	clerk	22	
g	Galvin James J	11	laborer	45	
h	Galvin Maurice J	11	retired	70	"
l	Cordero Dorothy—†	12	housewife	26	39 Harvard sq
m	LaRosa Joseph	12	fisherman	36	here
n	*LaRosa Mary—†	12	housewife	40	"

Sullivan Street

o	Noonan Mildred—†	3	housewife	39	here
r	*Elliott Blanche—†	4	"	49	"
s	Elliott Harry	4	merchant	53	"
t	Justice David E	9	foreman	43	"
u	Justice Emily M—†	9	housewife	42	"
v	Brooks Alonzo P	9	U S C G	43	"
w	Brooks Beatrice J—†	9	housewife	39	"
x	Brooks Eva H—†	9	clerk	23	"
y	Cofram Emily E—†	9	secretary	21	7 Auburn
z	Cofram Robert M	9	U S A	23	7 "

1434

c	Caddigan William	13	clerk	40	here
d	McCarthy Eugene	13	laborer	60	"
e	Moloney Helen A—†	13	housekeeper	54	"
f	O'Connell Richard	13	retired	75	"
h	Murdock Lela C—†	15	at home	76	"
k	Wight Arthur W	15	retired	72	
l	Wight Nina L—†	15	at home	72	"
m	Gregoire Conrad	16	chipper	35	"
n	Gregoire Florence—†	16	housewife	31	"
o	Heffron Edward D	16	U S M C	23	"
p	Heffron Eli	16	merchant	70	"
r	Heffron Ida—†	16	"	60	

Sullivan Street—Continued

s	Carey Walter	16	laborer	60	here
T	Dellorfano Armanda	18	packer	25	Medford
U	Dellorfano Marie—†	18	housewife	25	"
w	Kavanaugh Edward	18	laborer	43	25 Jefferson av
x*Kavanaugh Mary—†		18	housewife	34	25 "
Y	Passalacqua Helen A—†	19	"	29	here
z	Passalacqua Mario	19	rigger	28	"
	1435				
A	Chiampa Albert E	19	printer	31	
B	Chiampa Anna C—†	19	housewife	26	"
c	Passalacqua Leo	19	laborer	55	
D	Passalacqua Marianne—†	19	housewife	56	"
E	Beckerer Clarence	20	U S N	34	Illinois
F	Beckerer Helen—†	20	housewife	30	"
G	Cullity Eugene	20	laborer	58	20 Brighton
H	Donegan John M	20	guard	55	Woburn
K	Forbes George	20	laborer	65	258 Main
L	Garrison Arthur	20	guard	53	175 Rutherford av
M	Garrison Mary—†	20	housewife	40	175 "
N	Mansolilli Emily—†	20	waitress	23	Chelsea
o	McDevitt John	20	laborer	27	34 Medford
P	O'Connell John	20	"	35	here
R	Yandle Lulu M—†	21	at home	50	"
s	McDonough Catherine—†	21	housewife	26	"
T	McDonough Thomas	21	laborer	27	
U	Nihan John	22	"	58	··
v	Nihan Leo	22	foreman	43	"
w	Nihan Mary—†	22	housewife	74	"
X	Nihan Mary E—†	22	clerk	46	"
Y	Nihan Richard	22	electrician	50	"
z	White Daniel D	23	mechanic	49	"
	1436				
A	White Edna M—†	23	clerk	20	
B	White Elizabeth M—†	23	housewife	49	"
c	White Mary E—†	23	clerk	24	
D	Connolly Ellen—†	23	"	51	
E	Biagiotti Abele	23	manager	45	"
F	Biagiotti Adele—†	23	housewife	59	"
G	Biagiotti Delia—†	23	clerk	23	··
L	Caughey Mabel A—† ·	25	housewife	56	"
M	Darragh Helen V—†	25	hostess	32	"

Sullivan Street—Continued

N	Marcella William H	25	U S A	30	here
P	Brotherstone James	26	fireman	53	"
R	Brotherstone Mary E—†	26	housewife	45	"
s	*Flynn John	26	laborer	65	
T	Greenleaf Ernest	26	"	53	
U	Perkins Elizabeth—†	26	housekeeper	60	"
v	Creamer Harry	34	boilermaker	36	"
w	Creamer Louise J—†	34	housewife	33.	"
x	Crowley Patrick	34	laborer	58	
Y	Keyes Elizabeth—†	34	housekeeper	55	"
z	Sullivan Francis X	34	U S C G	30	"
	1437				
A	Sullivan Frank J	34	retired	70	
B	Coyne Elizabeth—†	36	housewife	80	"
c	Fitzgerald William J	36	painter	42	21 Harvard
D	Hallam William	36	retired	54	here
E	Provencher Louis E	36	laborer	54	"
F	Tyrell George	36	"	40	"
G	Smith Jeanne—†	38	housewife	55	"
H	Smith Joseph P	38	U S A	28	
K	Smith William J	38	clerk	60	
L	Micheli Bruna—†	39	housewife	33	"
M	Micheli Gabriel	39	carpenter	50	"
N	Hennessey Bella M—†	39	housewife	21	"
o	Hennessey Eugene J	39	laborer	·27	"
P	Doherty Helen—†	39	housekeeper	39	"
R	Doherty Margaret—†	39	cook	43	"
T	Campbell Blanche—†	40	housekeeper	60	"
U	Connolly James	40	retired	71	5 Clarken ct
v	Harrington Gertrude—†	40	domestic	59	here
w	Harrington John A	40	laborer	37	"
x	Roy Edwin L	40	"	34	52 Waltham
Y	Roy Honora V—†	40	housewife	32	52 "
z	Tinsley John	42	laborer	45	here
	1438				
A	Gillis Alton M	44	U S A	21	
B	Gillis Joseph F	44	laborer	58	
c	Gillis Mary E—†	44	cleaner	42	
E	Tully Paul R	48	chauffeur	45	"
K	Rose Elizabeth M—†	52	housekeeper	26	"
L	Rose George D	52	electrician	58	"

Sullivan Street—Continued

	M	Rose Margaret T—†	52	housekeeper	24	here
	N	Rose Richard C	52	inspector	21	"
	O	Dionne Marie—†	52	housekeeper	67	25 Charles St pl
	P	Dionne William M	52	U S N	35	25 "
	S	Brodie Ethel B—†	58	waitress	54	here
	T	Brooks Earl R	58	U S N	20	60 Sullivan
	U	Brooks George F	58	U S C G	21	here
	V	Brooks Grace E—	58	packer	23	60 Sullivan
	W	Schofield Edith F—†	58	at home	66	here
	X	Stillman Elizabeth S—†	58	housekeeper	78	"
	Y	Smith Annie B—†	58	housewife	79	387 Main
	Z	Spinney Elvin M	58	U S N	26	here
1439						
	A	Spinney Howard	58	fireman	67	387 Main
	B	Spinney Rita M—†	58	housewife	48	387 "
	C	Bates Florence E—†	60	clerk	78	here
	D	Bates Gardner	60	realtor	77	"
	E	Brooks Grace—†	60	housewife	23	"
	F	Dicenzo Frank	62	mason	42	
	G	Dicenzo Mary—†	62	housewife	29	"
	H	Cacicio Augustino	62	laborer	37	
	K	Cacicio Eileen—†	62	housewife	34	"
	M	Christoforo Anthony	64	welder	25	
	N	*Christoforo Daniel	64	laborer	61	
	O	*Christoforo Madeline—†	64	housewife	58	"
	P	Turner Cornelius J	64	laborer	67	58 Sullivan
	R	Turner Gladys B—†	64	housekeeper	39	58 "
	S	Day Irene M—†	64	clerk	28	here
	T	Day Margaret C—†	64	operator	27	"
	U	Day Thomas J	64	chauffeur	50	"
	V	Mile Joseph	66	laborer	58	"
	W	Mile Sarah M—†	66	housewife	58	"
	X	O'Donnell Daniel J	68	operator	48	"
	Y	O'Donnell Matthew J	68	mechanic	37	"
	Z	Burns Joseph	70	laborer	43	"
1440						
	A	Vinezia Agnes—†	70	housewife	29	"
	B	Vinezia Raffaele	70	welder	30	
	C	Richardson Marjorie—†	72	housewife	26	"
	D	Richardson Woodrow	72	dispatcher	29	"
	E	Peterson Hazel E—†	72	packer	22	

Sullivan Street—Continued

F	Power John J	72	bartender	33	here	
G	Power Maurice—†	72	"	35	"	
H	Power Ruth B—†	72	housewife	28	"	
K	Barry Helen—·†	72	"	29		
L	*Barry Patrick J	72	cook	33	"	
M	*Dunphy Sarah—†	72	housewife	66	408 Bennington	

Walker Avenue

N	O'Halloran Annie M—†	20	housewife	70	here	
O	O'Halloran John	20	retired	75	"	

Walker Street

Z	Lucey Christopher A	7	longshoreman	42	75 Main	

1441

A	Lucey Daniel J	7	U S A	38	75 '	
B	Lucey Dennis	7	foreman	44	75 "	
C	Lucey Mary E—†	7	operator	34	75 "	
D	Day Anna C—†	9	housewife	45	here	
E	Day John E	9	clerk	47	"	
F	*Driscoll Mary T—†	9	housewife	71	"	
G	Hughes Edward S	9	U S C G	31	"	
H	Hughes Katherine—†	9	housewife	76	"	
K	O'Leary Arthur J	11	laborer	37		
L	O'Leary Margaret F—†	11	operator	35	"	
M	Wilson Joseph A	11	shipfitter	41	"	
N	Wilson Mary A—†	11	housewife	40	"	
P	Dagle Alfred W	13	electrician	42	"	
	Dagle Anna M—†	13	housewife	40	"	
R	Burke Charles L	13	foreman	26		
S	Burke Henrietta A—†	13	housewife	21	Malden	
T	Burke Mary F—†	13	"	54	here	
U	Dagle Michael J	13	retired	78	"	
W	Campbell Jeanette—†	17	at home	26	"	
X	*Campbell Jennie—†	17	housewife	63	"	
Y	Campbell Joseph	17	laborer	21		
Z	Gile John	19	stagehand	55	"	

1442

A	Trafton Dexter L	19	shipper	56		
B	Trafton James A	19	retired	66		

Walker Street—Continued

c	Woods Catherine B—†	19	housewife	54	here
d	Woods John P	19	U S A	21	"
e	Woods Thomas J	19	"	20	"
f	Fritze Carl	21	cabinetmaker	52	"
g	Fritze Elsie—†	21	housewife	42	"
h	Humphrey George W	21	retired	69	"
k	Humphrey Herbert C	21	U S N	21	
l	Humphrey Isaiah H	21	manager	42	"
m	Humphrey Winifred M–†	21	housewife	68	"
n	Watson Daniel J	21	manager	45	"
o	Watson Gladys E—†	21	housewife	47	"
r	Nagle Dorothy E—†	27	"	29	
s	Nagle Walter T	27	chauffeur	32	"
t	Burlock Matilda J—†	27	housewife	34	"
u	Bridge James A	31	retired	79	
v	Dineen Thomas	31	"	67	
w	Marden Ellen W—†	31	clerk	53	"
z	Regan Adrene—†	37	housewife	34	48 Allston

1443

A	Regan John	37	chauffeur	25	48 "
B	Waite Myrtle B—†	37	housewife	73	here
C	Cadell Cora—†	37	"	49	5 Frothingham av
D	Cadell William C	37	laborer	53	5 "
E	Costa Clementine—†	46	housewife	30	477 Summer
F	Fernandes Frank	46	shipfitter	22	here
G	Fernandes Mary C—†	46	housewife	58	"
N	Doherty Anna—†	53	"	28	"
O	Rynkiewicz Mary—†	53	"	49	"
P	Rynkiewicz Paul	53	merchant	58	"

Wall Street

s	Kiley Bridget—†	1	housewife	62	here
t	Kiley James J	1	attorney	32	"
u	Kiley Thomas F	1	retired	72	"
v	Kiley William	1	"	29	
w	Martinelli John	2	U S N	38	
x	Russell Herbert E	3	rigger	53	
y	Russell Mary A—†	3	housewife	47	"
z	Russell William H	3	U S N	24	

2—14   25

1444
Wall Street—Continued

A	Callahan Patrick J	3	retired	81	here
B	Callahan Timothy J	3	"	84	"
C	Manone Angelo	4	U S M C	20	"
D	Manone Joseph	4	finisher	47	
E	Manone Rose—†	4	housewife	42	"
F	Anderson Ethel K—†	5	"	50	
G	Anderson Stephen J	5	seaman	50	"
H	Curran Arthur L	5	supt	49	Rhode Island
K	Curran Florence M—†	5	housewife	40	"
L	McLaughlin Arthur T	5	longshoreman	28	48 Mystic
M	McLaughlin Josephine—†	5	housewife	20	48 "
N	Novackis Peter	6	laborer	22	here
O	Novackis Theresa T—†	6	housewife	22	"
P	Gallagher Patrick	6	retired	79	"
R	Gallagher Sarah—†	6	at home	61	736 Cambridge
S	Cole Ann—†	6	housewife	31	7 Wall
T	Cole Walter	6	shipper	42	9 Cordis
U	Lawler Annie T—†	7	housewife	52	here
V	Lawler Eleanor P—†	7	clerk	21	"
W	Lawler Ruth—†	7	housewife	40	"
X	Lawler Thomas P	7	pressman	55	"
Y	Mannone Catherine—†	8	housewife	48	"
Z	Mannone Jasper J	8	U S A	21	

1445

A	Mannone Joseph	8	laborer	49	
B	Mannone Vincenza M—†	8	stenographer	24	"
C	O'Neil Bernard F	9	electrician	33	23 Green
D	O'Neil Mary G—†	9	housewife	29	23 "
E	Scanlon Joseph T	9	timekeeper	39	here
F	Scanlon Mary A—†	9	housewife	62	"
G	Lake Bridget M—†	10	"	43	"
H	Lake John J	10	janitor	49	
K	Lake Patrick J	10	U S A	22	
L	Welch John E	11	B F D	36	
M	Welch Michael P	11	drawtender	34	"
N	Welch Nicholas J	11	merchant	36	"
O	Welch William N	11	clerk	26	
P	Stanton James	12	laborer	66	
R	Stanton Maggie—†	12	housewife	66	"
S	DeAngelo James	13	laborer	46	

26

Wall Street—Continued

T	DeAngelo Jennie—†	13	clerk	21	here
U	DeAngelo Josephine—†	13	housewife	42	"
V	Ciaramataro Clara C—†	14	"	33	"
W	Ciaramataro Vincent B	14	U S N	34	"
X	Woods John L	14	laborer	29	69 Pearl
Y	Woods Ruth—†	14	housewife	22	69 "
Z	Kane Daniel C	15	molder	65	here
	1446				
A	Kane Margaret P—†	15	packer	27	
B	Kane Mary V—†	15	housewife	49	"
C	Palermo Elretta—†	16	at home	25	"
D	Palermo Paulina—†	16	housekeeper	62	"
E	Junta Louis J	17	fireman	26	
F	Junta Matilda M—†	17	housewife	25	"
G	Higginbotham Helen C—†	17	"	38	"
H	Higginbotham Thomas H	17	longshoreman	45	"
K	Banfield Michael A	18	laborer	33	
L	Ketch Hazel—†	18	housewife	44	"
M	Mulcahy Catherine—†	18	housekeeper	75	"
N	Griffin Joseph	19	U S A	23	
O	Griffin Mary A—†	19	cleaner	44	
P	Griffin Rita J—†	19	stenographer	20	"
R	Moran Cecelia M—†	19	housewife	28	5 Short St ct
S	Moran Francis J	19	laborer	36	5 "

15

16

17

Ward 2–Precinct 15

CITY OF BOSTON

LIST OF RESIDENTS
20 YEARS OF AGE AND OVER

(NON-CITIZENS INDICATED BY ASTERISK)
(FEMALES INDICATED BY DAGGER)

AS OF

JANUARY 1, 1944

THOMAS F. SULLIVAN, *Chairman*
FREDERIC E. DOWLING, *Secretary*
WILLIAM A. MOTLEY, Jr.
FRANCIS B. McKINNEY
EVERETT R. PROUT

Listing Board.

CITY OF BOSTON PRINTING DEPARTMENT

1500

Auburn Place

	B	Ferry Annie—†	1	at home	80	here
	c	Berry Charles	1	painter	52	"
	D	*Howard Mary—†	1	houseworker	52	"
	E	Conway Mary—†	1	matron	60	

Auburn Street

	L	Casey Thomas J	1	U S A	30	here
	M	Casey Timothy L	1	retired	70	"
	N	Casey Winifred—†	1	clerk	32	"
	o	Derrick Mary E—†	1	at home	45	"
	P	Foster Catherine—†	3	housewife	68	"
	s	McMahon Arthur	5	laborer	67	"
	u	Leahy Edward L	5	U S A	22	
	v	Leahy Francis	5	"	23	
	w	Leahy Margaret A—†	5	clerk	21	"
	x	Leahy Nora A—†	5	housewife	48	"
	Y	Leahy Thomas H	5	laborer	48	
	z	Dignan Agnes M—†	7	housewife	67	"

1501

	A	Jennings Jennie M—†	7	boxmaker	63	"
	B	Babcock David	9	retired	73	
	c	Babcock Isabel—†	9	at home	70	"
	D	Swiney Elizabeth M—†	9	housewife	65	"
	E	Swiney Grace E—†	9	operator	34	"
	G	Ployer Dorothy—†	11	chauffeur	30	"
	H	Ployer John	11	stockman	35	"
	K	Ployer Mary E—†	11	housewife	71	"
	M	Kiley Francis	13	painter	38	
	N	Kiley Margaret—†	13	housewife	21	"
	o	Dunleavy Caroline—†	13	"	21	
	P	Dunleavy Mathew J	13	checker	37	"
	R	Myers Frederick	15	clerk	46	
	s	Hengstler Eugene	15	retired	80	
	T	Green Ethel V—†	17	clerk	23	
	u	McDonnell John E	17	porter	61	
	v	McDonnell Joseph D	17	U S A	25	
	w	McDonnell Margaret—†	17	housewife	57	"
	x	McDonnell Peter A	17	janitor	59	
	Y	McDonnell Rita A—†	17	nurse	21	

Auburn Street—Continued

z	Tessaro Mary L—†	17	at home	27	California
	1502				
A	Donovan Mary E—†	19	"	48	here
B	Friend Alice F—†	19	clerk	42	"
C	Friend Catherine—†	19	housewife	77	"
D	Stickney Francis	21	carpenter	28	"
E	Stickney John	21	laborer	25	
F	*Woodburn Catherine—†	21	housewife	76	"
G	Woodburn James	21	baker	52	
H	*Woodburn Robert	21	carpenter	87	"
K	Lefley Edward C	23	retired	67	"
L	Bowen Frances T—†	23	clerk	39	
M	Little Lucy—†	25	housewife	28	"
N	Little William T	25	machinist	29	"
O	Bowdren Catherine—†	25A	housewife	68	"
P	Bowdren Charles	25A	electrician	26	"
R	Bowdren John	25A	watchman	71	"
S	Bowdren Mary—†	25A	operator	39	"
T	Bowdren Patrick	25A	U S N	40	
U	O'Donnell John L	27	driller	36	
V	O'Donnell Richard	27	clerk	69	
W	O'Donnell Richard	27	chauffeur	36	"
X	Devlin Elizabeth J—†	27	housewife	64	"
Y	Devlin John F	27	retired	80	
z	Devlin Joseph A	27	U S N	23	
	1503				
A	Corbett Edith—†	27	operator	25	"
B	Corbett Laurie	27	freighthandler	55	"
C	Corbett Mary—†	27	housewife	50	"
D	Leary Eleanor L—†	29	at home	71	"
E	Shute Jessie—†	29	maid	53	"
F	Shute Mona—†	29	secretary	40	"
G	Britton Herbert L	35	chauffeur	29	"
H	Britton Josephine—†	35	housewife	25	"
K	Smith Catherine—†	35	"	55	15 Salem
L	Smith Warren H	35	guard	46	15 "
M	McArdle John	35	chauffeur	28	here
N	McArdle Rita—†	35	housewife	29	"
O	Parsons Foster D	37	U S A	27	"
P	Parsons Helen—†	37	housewife	24	"
R	Carroll Lena—†	37	"	53	

Auburn Street—Continued

s	Carroll Margaret—†	37	bookkeeper	22	here
t	Carroll Vance A	37	watchman	57	"
u	Devlin Catherine—†	39	housewife	21	Somerville
v	Devlin James	39	cutter	31	"
w	Devlin Owen	39	electrician	33	here
x	Devlin Ruth—†	39	housewife	29	"
y	Kroon Mary—†	39	"	37	"
z	Linehan Catherine—†	39	at home	62	"
	1504				
a	Linehan Helen—†	39	clerk	26	"
c	Burke Catherine—†	43	housewife	27	32 Mead
d	Burke James J	43	pipefitter	29	32 "
e	Sullivan John F	43	U S A	25	32 "
f	Sullivan Mary T—†	43	at home	62	32 "
g	Gilson Herbert E	45	machinist	32	here
h	Gilson Mary—†	45	housewife	33	"
k	Clinton Bernard	47	retired	74	"
l	Clinton Bernard W	47·	clerk	41	
m	Clinton Catherine D—†	47	operator	45	"
n	Clinton Francis C	47	printer	38	
o	Clinton James J	47	laborer	43	
p	Clinton Mary E—†	47	housewife	70	"
r	Clinton Michael R	47	U S A	29	

Bunker Hill Street

s	Glufflin Arthur	332	U S C G	26	here
t	McGeough Catherine—†	332	housewife	48	"
u	McGeough George	332	U S A	22	"
v	McGeough John	332	"	21	
w	McGeough Mary—†	332	bookkeeper	28	"
x	Doe Leo A	332	U S A	25	"
y	Doe Mary E—†	332	housekeeper	63	"
z	Doe Walter A	332	chauffeur	32	"
	1505				
a	Doe Walter C	332	storekeeper	58	"
b	Melville Frank J	332	boilermaker	43	"
c	Melville Frank J, jr	332	U S A	22	
d	Melville Irene M—†	332	storekeeper	40	"
e	Lynch Helen C—†	334	housewife	32	"

Page.	Letter.	Full Name.	Residence, Jan. 1, 1944.	Occupation.	Supposed Age.	Reported Residence, Jan. 1, 1943. Street and Number.

Bunker Hill Street—Continued

F	Lynch John P	334	chauffeur	44	here
G	Preston Leroy W	334	mechanic	52	"
K	Coughlin Nellie T—†	356	housekeeper	62	"
L	Harrigan Francis W	356	shipper	47	"
M	Harrigan Jeremiah F	356	retired	84	
N	Harrigan Nora T—†	356	housewife	50	"
O	Donovan Mary E—†	356	stenographer	55	"
P	Donovan Mary R—†	356	at home	27	"
R	Power Mabel H—†	358	housewife	27	"
S	Power Michael F	358	B F D	32	
T	Hatton Catherine J—†	358	U S A	28	
U	Hatton Margaret E—†	358	housewife	65	"
V	Hatton Mary M—†	358	W A V E	30	"
W	Healey Johanna—†	358	housewife	72	"
X	Scribner Ralph G	360	repairman	54	"
Y	Scribner Rose S—†	360	housewife	49	"
Z	Hayes Catherine M—†	360	"	64	
	1506				
A	Hayes Catherine R—†	360	packer	24	
B	Hayes Timothy F	360	warehouse	23	"
C	Hayes Timothy J	360	retired	63	
D	*Donovan Jeremiah J	360	"	56	
E	Lynch Joseph D	360	"	51	"
F	McGowan Francis T	360	clerk	25	
G	O'Connor Hannah M—†	360	at home	79	"
H	Crowley Alma—†	362	housewife	30	"
K	Crowley Timothy J	362	clerk	33	
L	Jollimore Helen R—†	362	defense wkr	23	"
M	Martin Loretta V—†	362	housewife	55	"
N	Martin Louis H	362	printer	57	"
O	Martin Louis H, jr	362	U S N	20	
P	Martin Walter E	362	U S A	25	"
R	Katoff Anna—†	364	housewife	28	20 Wall
S	Katoff Murray	364	longshoreman	34	20 "
T	Mahoney James	364	diestamper	43	here
U	Mahoney Sarah—†	364	housewife	38	"
V	McLaughlin Patrick	364	retired	70	"
W	Mahoney Elizabeth—†	364	housewife	72	"
X	Mahoney John J	364	retired	72	
Y	Mahoney John J, jr	364	custodian	34	"

Bunker Hill Street—Continued

z	Autonelli Angelo	366	warehouse	40	here	
1507						
A	Antonelli Theresa—†	366	housewife	38	"	
B	Doherty Elizabeth M—†	366	"	59		
c	Doherty John J	366	glazier	61	"	

Crystal Place

D	Chandler Alvah S	1	retired	75	here	
E	Colbert Margaret—†	1	shoeworker	45	"	
F	Campbell Martha—†	2	housewife	52	"	
G	Campbell Walter	2	chauffeur	48	"	
H	Stella Albert	3	trackman	45	"	
K	Stella Mary C—†	3	housewife	35	"	
L	Doherty John	4	motorman	51	"	
M	Driscoll Ida—†	4	housewife	41	"	
N	Driscoll William	4	checker	52	"	

Eden Street

o	Carlson Edith—†	4	housewife	41	here	
P	Carlson Svante	4	U S A	47	"	
R	Gilmore Clarence H	4	mechanic	50	"	
s	Gilmore Ruth T—†	4	housewife	53	"	
T	Hill Naomi—†	4	at home	68	"	
1508						
A	Shea Dorothy M—†	4	housewife	20	"	
B	Shea Robert J	4	U S N	22		
c	Harvey Lawrence J	16	longshoreman	28	"	
D	Harvey Marion A—†	16	housewife	53	"	
E	Quinn Eileen B—†	16	clerk	21		
F	Quinn John P	16	U S A	21		
G	Noyes Isabella—†	16A	housewife	61	"	
H	Ringer Alice—†	16A	teacher	50		
K	Harty Anna F—†	18	housewife	40	"	
L	Harty Nicholas J	18	clerk	42		
M	O'Brien Susan A—†	18	at home	75	"	
N	Fitzpatrick Catherine A-†	20	housewife	26	"	
o	Fitzpatrick James M	20	welder	26		
P	Kenney John P	20	freighthandler	29	"	
R	Kenney Kieran F	20	laborer	67		

Page.	Letter.	FULL NAME.	Residence, Jan. 1, 1944.	Occupation.	Supposed Age.	Reported Residence, Jan. 1, 1943. Street and Number.

Eden Street—Continued

s	Kenney Kieran F, jr	20	electrician	25	here
t	Kenney Mary A—†	20	housewife	58	"
u	Kenney Mary B—†	20	social worker	30	"
x	Doherty Helen M—†	22	bookkeeper	31	"
v	Paul Claude F	22	seaman	60	New York
w	Paul Nellie—†	22	housewife	54	here
y	Doris Alice E—†	24	"	34	"
z	Doris John E	24	policeman	38	"
	1509				
a	Doucette Helen—†	24	welder	34	
b	Ahern Mary—†	26	at home	70	"
c	Carroll Elizabeth R—†	26	housewife	25	"
d	Carroll Frank	26	U S N	25	
e	Davis Fred	26	mechanic	50	"
f	Davis Helen—†	26	housewife	40	"
g	Desmond Daniel S	26	janitor	64	
h	Desmond Elizabeth V—†	26	housewife	65	"
k	Healey Edith—†	26	clerk	38	
l	Healey James	26	drawtender	40	"
m	Babcock Alexander A	30	chauffeur	30	"
n	Babcock Bernadette T—†	30	housewife	27	"
o	O'Connell Madeline—†	30	bookkeeper	38	"
p	Seibolt Edward J	30	policeman	49	"
r	Seibolt Edward J	30	U S A	20	
s	Seibolt Kathleen F—†	30	housewife	48	"

Essex Street

t	Brandon Ann—†	2	housewife	38	here
u	Brandon Wilmer	2	checker	40	"
v	Kepple Edward	2	laborer	66	"
w	Kepple George	2	U S A	31	
x	Kepple John E	2	retired	67	
y	Kepple Margaret—†	2	at home	55	"
z	Kepple William	2	U S A	29	
	1510				
a	Sanborn George V	4	retired	71	
b	Sherrick Alva M—†	6	housewife	48	"
c	Sherrick Alva M—†	6	companion	26	"
d	Sherrick Frank	6	operator	51	"
e	Sherrick Frank, jr	6	U S A	25	

Essex Street—Continued

	Letter	FULL NAME	Residence	Occupation	Age	Reported Residence
	F	Sherrick Howard A	6	U S A	22	here
	G	Grace Charles H	7	mechanic	49	"
	H	Grace James J	7	U S N	27	"
	K	Grace Palmeda—†	7	housewife	44	"
	L	Grace William S	7	U S N	22	"
	M	Gonzalo Frederick F	8	retired	69	4 Mill
	N	Gonzalo Isabella L—†	8	at home	64	4 "
	O	Gonzalo Thomas B	8	U S A	37	4 "
	P	Hoey George F	8	grinder	39	4 '
	R	Hoey Isabelle C—†	8	housewife	36	4 "
	S	Bailey Doris—†	9	"	40	here
	T	Bailey Doris—†	9	clerk	20	"
	U	Bailey Harold	9	machinist	41	"
	V	Doherty John	9	laborer	50	
	W	Loud Agnes F—†	10	supervisor	36	"
	X	Loud Ellen T—†	10	housewife	58	"
	Y	Loud Helen T—†	10	floorwoman	30	"
	Z	Loud Helena M—†	10	clerk	32	"
		1511				
	A	Loud Regina M—†	10	boxmaker	20	"
	B	Loud William B	10	machinist	58	"
	C	McLaughlin Daniel	11	retired	73	
	D	McLaughlin John P	11	bartender	44	"
	E	McLaughlin Margaret—†	11	housewife	72	"
	F	Wheeler George E	11	U S A	22	
	G	Furlong Helen L—†	12	housewife	54	"
	K	Familetto Dominic	14	shipper	50	
	L	Littlefield Ralph B	14	machinist	60	"
	M	Mehagan Eugene	14	laborer	60	
	N	Spratt Florence L—†	14	housewife	58	"
	O	Hausherr Catherine T—†	16	assembler	44	"
	P	Hausherr Sylvester J	16	machinist	24	"
	R	McElroy Isabella M—†	16	housewife	65	"
	S	McElroy Thomas J	16	messenger	67	"
	T	Clivio Ernest	17	manager	32	"
	U	Clivio Vera—†	17	housewife	32	"
	V	Miller Catherine—†	17	matron	68	
	W	Clivio Mario	17	U S M C	24	"
	X	Clivio Mary—†	17	housewife	51	"
	Y	Harvey Catherine—†	18	"	63	Wilmington
	Z	Harvey Una B—†	18	at home	43	"

1512
Essex Street—Continued

A	McCarthy Michael	18	operator	40	here
B	Recor Arthur H	18	laborer	62	"
C	Recor Elizabeth—†	18	housewife	59	"
D	Murphy Dorothy A—†	19	bookkeeper	34	"
E	Murphy Frances C—†	,19	housewife	65	"
F	Murphy John E	19	U S A	30	
G	Leydon Bessie—†	20	housewife	64	"
H	Leydon John J	20	foreman	68	"
K	Hopper Katie—†	21	housewife	70	"
M	Kelly Lillian E—†	22	at home	24	31 Essex
N	Maguire Frank G	22	checker	49	here
O	Maguire Mary A—†	22	housewife	48	"
P	Maguire Rose M—†	22	operator	21	"
R	McLaughlin John J	22	U S A	30	
S	McLaughlin Ruth C—†	22	housewife	25	"
W	Irving Sarah A—†	24	"	66	"
X	Prendergrace Robert J	24	foreman	60	Medford
Y	Cadigan Frank	26	roofer	51	here
Z	Colton Hattie—†	26	housewife	74	"

1513

A	Colton John	26	U S A	26	
B	Oxner Gladys—†	26	operator	36	"
D	Ballam John L	28	"	44	
E	Ballam Rose V—†	28	housewife	42	"
F	Kirby Elizabeth P—†	28	"	21	
G	Kirby Joseph F	28	U S N	26	
L	O'Leary James H	30	laborer	63	
M	Wittig Robert	30	"	65	"
N	Harris Edith—†	31	housewife	25	8 Mill
O	Harris Howard	31	laborer	25	8 "
P	Walsh Agnes—†	31	housewife	53	here
R	Walsh George	31	laborer	58	"
S	McInerney Catherine F–†	32	bookkeeper	30	"
T	McInerney Francis P	32	U S N	30	Somerville
U	White Anna R—†	32	at home	28	here
V	White Catherine A—†	32	housewife	63	"
W	White James J	32	U S N	25	"
X	White Jeremiah J	32	retired	60	
Y	White John F	32	checker	23	"
Z	*Fiori Adele—†	33	housewife	58	"

9

1514

Essex Street—Continued

A	Fiori Anna—†	33	operator	24	here
B	Fiori Domenic	33	finisher	59	"
C	Fiori Ivo	33	electrician	27	"
D	Fiori John	33	U S A	22	
E	*Ceccarelli Elisa—†	33	housewife	60	"
F	*Ceccarelli Emilio	33	laborer	62	
G	Biagotti Leo	33	"	48	
H	Notini Caesare	33	salesman	60	"
K	Doyle Mary—†	35	at home	47	"
L	Rogers Mary—†	37	inspector	45	"
M	Smith James J	37	clerk	40	
N	Smith Mary—†	37	housewife	39	"
O	Milani Maurice	39	electroplater	38	"
P	Milani Rita—†	39	housewife	28	"
R	Rigale Alfred L	41	U S A	22	"
S	Rigale Humbert J	41	manager	58	"
T	Rigale Louise—†	41	housewife	45	"
U	Calonico Ida—†	43	waitress	43	"
V	Marchetti Ida—†	43	housewife	45	"
W	Marchetti Leo	43	U S A	20	
X	Marchetti Mario	43	"	24	
Y	Marchetti Peter	43	painter	56	
Z	*Lucarotti Adolfo	45	finisher	62	

1515

A	Lucarotti Alfred	45	metalworker	32	"
B	Lucarotti Arsinoe—†	45	housewife	56	"
C	Murphy Margaret—†	47	stenographer	25	"
D	Slater Alice V—†	47	teacher	27	"
E	Slater Dennis	47	janitor	53	
F	Slater Thomas B	47	U S A	22	
K	Corrieri Adele—†	51	housewife	50	"
L	Corrieri Amedio	51	finisher	63	
M	Corrieri Amelia—†	51	housewife	61	"
N	Gabrielli Frank	51	milliner	58	"

Forest Place

O	Wells Mary L—†	1	at home	76	here
P	DePauw Clorice E—†	2	clerk	22	"
R	DePauw Jennie J—†	2	housewife	53	"

Forest Place—Continued

s	Nadeau Charles J	3	buffer	43	here
T	Nadeau Viola M—†	3	housewife	· 37	"
U	Gallagher Edward H	4	sorter	61	"
V	Gallagher Edward H, jr	4	longshoreman	25	"
W	Gallagher Margaret E—†	4	housewife	56	"
X	Gallagher Raymond J	4	U S A	23	
Y	Gallagher Robert T	4	U S N	20	
Z	McKinley Alexander A	5	shoeworker	52	"
	1516				
A	McKinley Louise F—†	5	housewife	50	"
B	McKinley Nettie M—†	5	tester	22	
c	McKinley William D	5	U S A	24	
D	Desmond James J	6	longshoreman	39	"
E	Desmond Marjorie M—†	6	housewife	27	"

Frothingham Avenue

F	Alongi Charles L	2	U S A	20	here
G	Alongi Rosario	2	plasterer	45	"
H	Alongi Salvatrice—†	2	at home	39	"
K	Alongi Sebastian R	2	U S A	23	"
L	Mazzola Anna C—†	2	at home	25	7 Drake pl
M	Mazzola Anthony	2	chauffeur	23	7 "
s	Cusack Frederick T	8	longshoreman	44	here
T	Cusack John R	8	pipefitter	42	"
U	Cusack Stephen J	8	retired	46	"
V	Valle Rosetta—†	8	clerk	33	"
W	Colman Florence V—†	8A	at home	33	256 Main
X	Colman Rita—†	8A	"	24	50 Sullivan
Y	Colman Theodore V	8A	clerk	42	256 Main
Z	Parent Catherine M—†	8A	housewife	39	24 Lincoln
	1517				
A	Parent William H	8A	U S N	20	here
B	Parent William L	8A	janitor	43	24 Lincoln
C	Guittarr Mary F—†	10	at home	23	here
D	Murray James J	10	custodian	62	328 Main
E	Ridings Alfred	10	agent	43	here
F	Ridings Alfred L	10	U S A	21	"
G	Ridings Frances E—†	10	housewife	42	"
H	Owens Leola—†	12	"	38	
K	Owens Patrick	12	painter	42	

Frothingham Avenue—Continued

L	Dineen John J	14	retired	66	here
M	Fleming Georgianna—†	14	housekeeper	56	"
N	Sullivan Helen—†	14	housewife	28	Malden
O	Sullivan John	14	U S N	30	"
P	Smith Edward	14	rigger	26	here
R	Smith Marion—†	14	housewife	24	"
S	Downey Mary A—†	16	at home	77	"
T	Carroll Patricia—†	16	housewife	36	"
U	Carroll Richard J	16	U S A	37	

1518

B	Martell Sadie—†	24	housewife	56	"
C	Martell Theodore	24	shipfitter	60	"
E	Bradley Carl	26	U S A	23	"
F	Bradley Diana—†	26	housewife	21	"
G	*Caruso Lucy—†	26	"	54	
H	*Caruso William	26	laborer	57	

Lincoln Street

M	Sanseverino Alice—†	2	housewife	48	here
N	Sanseverino Dorothy A—†	2	clerk	21	"
O	Sanseverino Frank M	2	U S A	29	"
P	Sanseverino Michael	2	barber	57	
T	Florentino Elsie—†	4	laundress	38	"
U	Florentino Ernest	4	coppersmith	43	"
V	Florentino John J	4	mechanic	50	"
W	*Florentino Mary—†	4	housewife	74	"
X	Brooks Joseph E	6	guard	47	
Y	Blake Clement	6	leathercutter	33	"
Z	Blake Helen—†	6	housewife	31	"

1519

A	Ouelette Esther—†	6	"	39	
B	Ouelette Joseph O	6	checker	38	"
C	*Henningan Margaret A—†	8	housewife	31	6 Concord av
D	Henningan Patrick F	8	trackman	32	6 "
E	Hennigan Catherine—†	8	cleaner	34	here
F	Hennigan Thomas	8	repairman	39	"
G	White Anna—†	8	housewife	21	"
H	White Austin	8	pipefitter	28	"
P	Saunders Chester J	11	U S N	34	"
R	Saunders Helena C—†	11	housewife	33	"

Lincoln Street—Continued

s	Sutton Mary—†	11	housewife	51	here
T	Defina Helen—†	11	operator	35	"
U	Defina Vincent	11	U S A	31	"
V	Nugent Annie—†	11	housewife	64	"
W	Costa Eliza—†	12	"	40	"
X	Costa Joseph	12	laborer	46	
Y	Brougham Eileen—†	12	clerk	25	
Z	Brougham Ellen S—†	12	housewife	65	"
	1520				
A	Brougham John	12	clerk	68	
B	Bassett Charles R	13	machinist	35	"
C	Bassett Palma E—†	13	housewife	31	"
D	Hegarty Agnes—†	13	clerk	23	
E	Hegarty Helen—†	13	operator	30	"
F	Hegarty Jennie—†	13	housewife	61	"
G	Hegarty Jeremiah	13	inspector	60	"
H	Hegarty Jeremiah, jr	13	U S A	31	
K	Hegarty Margaret—†	13	operator	21	"
L	Hegarty Mary—†	13	clerk	27	
O	Calderone Nicanto	15	laborer	76	
P	Calderone Philomena—†	15	housewife	80	"
R	DiNovo Elizabeth—†	15	machinist	30	66 Walker
S	Fitzgerald Lillian—†	15	housewife	21	12 Salem St av
T	Flynn Helen J	16	"	43	here
U	Flynn John J	16	U S A	22	"
V	Flynn Joseph F	16	"	21	"
W	Seward Elizabeth—†	16	housewife	52	"
X	Seward John	16	freighthandler	25	"
Y	Elliott Mildred—†	17	housewife	50	"
Z	Connors Alfred	17	chauffeur	39	"
	1521				
A	Connors Nellie J—†	17	housewife	69	"
B	Connors Paul H	17	U S A	34	
C	Connors Richard	17	"	28	
D	Ryan Catherine—†	19	housewife	29	"
E	Ryan Joseph F	19	chauffeur	31	"
F	Ryan Joseph L	19	retired	55	
G	Hennigan Dennis M	19	foreman	65	"
H	Hennigan Dennis M, jr	19	U S A	31	
K	Hennigan Mary M—†	19	housewife	63	"
L	Reardon Mary J—†	19	"	36	

13

Page.	Letter.	FULL NAME.	Residence, Jan. 1, 1944.	Occupation.	Supposed Age.	Reported Residence, Jan. 1, 1943. Street and Number.

Lincoln Street—Continued

	M	Reardon Roger F	19	painter	45	here
	N	Keating Delia A—†	20	housewife	56	15 Lincoln
	O	Keating George J	20	laborer	60	15 "
	R	Kinsman Mary—†	20	housewife	54	here
	S	Mellen Edna—†	20	laundress	31	"
	T	DuBois Ellen—†	21	housewife	52	"
	U	Drohan Elizabeth—†	21	"	76	20 Lincoln
	V	Drohan Ellen—†	21	"	34	20 "
	W	Drohan Stephen	21	plumber	35	20 "
	X	Blankenburg Arthur W	21	janitor	63	32 Russell
	Y	Ambrose John	22	painter	53	27 Lincoln
	Z	Ambrose John, jr	22	U S A	22	27 "
		1522				
	A	Ambrose Pauline—†	22	housewife	46	27 "
	B	Ambrose William E	22	U S C G	21	27 "
	D	Costello Charles	22½	U S A	21	here
	E	Costello James P	22½	laborer	28	"
	F	Costello Lawrence	22½	seaman	24	"
	G	Costello Margaret—†	22½	defense wkr	25	"
	H	Costello Margaret E—†	22½	housewife	58	"
	K	Costello Michael	22½	U S N	26	
	L	Costello Thomas F	22½	fireman	65	"
	M	Zyirek Mary—†	22½	waitress	30	19 Parker
	N	Colton Emma L—†	22½	housewife	56	here
	O	Colton John H	22½	U S A	29	"
	P	Colton Richard C	22½	U S N	27	"
	R	Colton Robert F	22½	U S M C	20	"
	S	Colton Thomas E	22½	chauffeur	25	358 Medford
	T*	McMahon Elizabeth—†	23	housewife	30	1 Exeter ct
	U	McMahon John	23	shipwright	34	1 "
	V	Auch Joseph B	23	rigger	36	here
	W*	Auch Mary E—†	23	housewife	36	"
	X	Boudreau Sarah—†	23	waitress	29	"
	Y	Leahy James	24	laborer	38	
	Z	Leahy Margaret—†	24	housewife	38	"
		1523				
	A	Ready Arthur	24	retired	75	24½ Lincoln
	B	Ready Howard	24	laborer	43	24½ "
	C	Ready Ida—†	24	housewife	62	24½ "
	D	Steckling Edward	24	U S C G	36	24½ "
	E	Steckling Mildred—†	24	housewife	33	24½ "

14

Page.	Letter.	FULL NAME.	Residence, Jan. 1, 1944.	Occupation.	Supposed Age.	Reported Residence, Jan. 1, 1943. Street and Number.

Lincoln Street—Continued

F	Carroll Josephine—†	24½	housewife	37	1 Pleasant
G	Carroll Maurice	24½	operator	45	1 "
H	Fitzgerald Francis X	25	U S A	30	here
K	Fitzgerald Sarah—†	25	housekeeper	53	"
M	Venesky Leona—†	25	operator	39	"
N	Venesky Sigmund	25	boilermaker	52	"
O	Pickett Frank	26	longshoreman	33	4 Alleghany
P	Pickett Helen—†	26	housewife	33	4 "
R	Callahan Anna M—†	26½	"	40	here
S	Callahan Philip G	26½	shipper	43	"
T	Costello Mary—†	26½	housewife	24	"
U	McDevitt James J	26½	machinist	56	"
V	Tully John	27	laborer	63	"
W	Leach Helen J—†	27	housewife	33	28 Lincoln
X	Leach Leo A	27	U S A	20	28 "
Y	Leach Raymond C	27	agent	44	28 "
Z	Ross Eleanor—†	27	housewife	27	Somerville
	1524				
A	Ross William J	27	chauffeur	28	"
B	Ford Rubie	28	laborer	58	Malden
C	Stillman Lillian—†	28	housewife	39	62 Walker
D	Stillman Melvin	28	chauffeur	44	62 "
E	Stillman Melvin, jr	28	"	21	62 "
F	Cheever Albert	28½	"	52	here
G	Cheever Eva—†	28½	housewife	36	"
H	Fitzpatrick Eleanor—†	29	"	25	136 High
K	Fitzgerald John	29	freighthandler	30	136 "
N	Ford Daniel	30	laborer	63	here
O	Ford Daniel, jr	30	U S A	30	"
P	Ford Jane—†	30	housewife	63	"
R	Ford John J	30	clerk	36	
S	Ford Matthew B	30	U S A	28	
T	Coyne John M	30	manager	30	"
U	Coyne Julia A—†	30	housewife	68	"
V	Coyne Martin J	30	retired	71	
W	Coyne Mary C—†	30	secretary	27	"
X	Coyne Sarah A—†	30	electrician	33	"
Y	Coyne Thomas P	30	U S A	24	
	1525				
A	Whitten Elizabeth—†	31	housekeeper	69	"
B	Howell Clyde A	31	machinist	52	"

15

Page.	Letter.	FULL NAME.	Residence, Jan. 1, 1944.	Occupation.	Supposed Age.	Reported Residence, Jan. 1, 1943. Street and Number.

Lincoln Street—Continued

	c	Howell Helen L—†	31	clerk	22	here
	d	Howell Rose A—†	31	housewife	51	"
	e	Lawson Alice M—†	31	"	66	"
	f	Lawson William M	31	hostler	66	
	g	Grimes Edward F	32	storekeeper	54	"
	h	Grimes Florence A—†	32	marker	24	"
	k	Grimes Helen—†	32	"	22	
	l	Grimes Mina—†	32	housewife	52	"
	n	Rexford Ernest	32	retired	64	
	s	Gallagher Margaret—†	36	operator	24	"
	t	Terwilliger Harold	36	painter	43	"
	u	Terwilliger Mary—†	36	housewife	30	"
	v	Dunning Mary J—†	38	"	47	
	w	Dunning Ray H	38	foundryman	48	"
	y	Geary Helen—†	40	housewife	38	"
	z	McCarthy Catherine T—†	40	"	45	397 Main
		1526				
	a	McCarthy Charles F	40	laborer	54	397 "
	b	McCarthy Charles F, jr	40	longshoreman	23	397 "
	c	McCarthy William J	40	U S A	24	397 "
	d	Barnett Emmett H	40	chauffeur	34	here
	e	Barnett Mary—†	40	housewife	33.	"

Ludlow Street

	f	Brackett Ellen J—†	1	housewife	43	here
	g	Brackett Stanley M	1	engineer	44	"
	h	Guinee Timothy	2	retired	57	"
	k	Guinee William	2	U S N	63	
	l	Russell Edward J	2	B F D	43	
	m	Russell Katherine M—†	2	housewife	40	"
	n	Wilson Sarah—†	3	"	68	"
	o	Wilson William	3	watchmaker	71	"
	p	McDonald Donald G	4	chauffeur	23	"
	r	McDonald Helen—†	4	housewife	45	"
	s	McDonald John J	4	pipefitter	46	"
	t	Connolly Edward	5	bookkeeper	47	"
	u	Nugent Delia E—†	5	at home	80	"
	v	Kaliher Annie T—†	6	housewife	70	"
	w	Kaliher James D	6	retired	77	

Ludlow Street—Continued

	Letter	FULL NAME	Residence	Occupation	Age	Reported Residence
	x	Hitchcock Alice C—†	7	housewife	54	here
	y	Hitchcock James T	7	U S N	22	"
	z	Hitchcock John F	7	U S A	25	"
1527						
	a	Hitchcock Mary T—†	7	mechanic	24	"
	b	Hitchcock William F	7	packer	22	
	c	Hughes Charles E	8	electrician	58	"
	d	Hughes Margaret E—†	8	housewife	47	"
	e	Hughes Margaret E—†	8	secretary	22	"
	f	Kirkpatrick Alice—†	9	housewife	40	"
	g	Kirkpatrick Charles	9	glasscutter	43	"
	h	Barrett Robert	10	carpenter	50	"
	k	Maraghy Aloysius	10	clerk	45	
	l	Maraghy Helen A—†	10	stenographer	24	"
	m	Maraghy Irene—†	10	housewife	46	"
	n	Maraghy Walter	10	U S N	28	"
	o	Prendergast Elinor—†	11	housewife	67	"
	p	Prendergast John B	11	janitor	69	"
	r	Prendergast Marie B—†	11	packer	31	"
	s	O'Connor Nora—†	12	at home	63	"
	t	Vachon Mary V—†	12	operator	53	"

Lyndeboro' Street

	Letter	FULL NAME	Residence	Occupation	Age	Reported Residence
	u	McSweeney Mary E—†	1	housewife	69	here
	v	Palmer Catherine—†	1	"	61	"
	w	Palmer Robert C	1	clerk	22	"
	x	Palmer William A	1	watchman	58	"
	y	Howard Arthur	3	U S A	22	"
	z	Howard Marie—†	3	housewife	21	"
1528						
	a	Snell Benjamin	3	retired	53	
	b	Snell Helen—†	3	housewife	47	"
	c	Christensen Edna M—†	5	"	52	"
	d	Schoffield Ruth—†	5	manager	21	7 Trenton
	e	Burke John F	7	chauffeur	34	here
	f	Waugh Cora M—†	7	housewife	45	"
	g	Myers John W	9	accountant	39	"
	h	Tarrant Margaret M—†	9	operator	20	"
	k	Tarrant Mary H—†	9	housewife	47	"

Lyndeboro' Street—Continued

L	Tarrant Samuel J	9	clerk	51	here
M	Tarrant Thomas J	9	U S A	24	"
N	Headle Evan	18	manager	55	"
O	Headle Molly—†	18	housewife	53	"
P*	Harris Mary F—†	20	"	43	
R*	Harris Wilmot W	20	brakeman	54	"
S	Mullen William F	20	repairman	35	"
T	Salerno Alphonse	22	electrician	28	"
U	Salerno Anthony	22	U SA	30	..
V	Salerno George	22	"	26	
W	Salerno Joseph	22	machinist	32	"
X	Salerno Lucy—†	22	housewife	58	"
Y	Salerno Paul	22	shoeworker	68	"
Z	Salerno Pearl—†	22	clerk	21	
	1529				
A	Graham Edward J	24	bartender	39	"
B	Graham Jessie V—†	24	housekeeper	60	"
C	Iula Anna—†	24	housewife	41	"
D	Iula Joseph	24	cooper	43	
E	Smith Carrie—†	25	housewife	80	"
F	Michaud Clara—†	25	"	47	
G*	Michaud Louis	25	carpenter	57	"
H	Michaud Pauline—†	25·	clerk	22	
L	Corbin Lucy—†	26	"	22	
M	Corbin Mary—†	26	housewife	49	"

Main Street

S	O'Donnell Anna—†	314	housewife	32	here
T	O'Donnell John F	314	electrician	38	"
U	Lockhart Catherine—†	314	housewife	26	"
V	Lockhart Cornelius	314	mechanic	28	"
Y	McCann Anna—†	320	housewife	46	"
Z	McCann Daniel	320	gardener	46	"
	1530				
A	Ryan Florence—†	320	housewife	20	"
B	Ryan William	320	cleaner	20	"
C	Mitchell Helen C—†	322	housewife	24	5 Walker
D	Mitchell Joseph F	322	chauffeur	27	5 "

Main Street—Continued

E	Mitchell Lillian—†	322	housewife	48	5 Walker
F	Young George	322	laborer	35	233 Main
G	Young Laura—†	322	housewife	42	233 "
L	Davidson Harry	345	laborer	45	here
M	DeStCroix John	345	electrician	23	"
N	DeStCroix Rose—†	345	housewife	23	"
O	Driscoll Charles	345	laborer	50	"
P	Ford John	345	retired	66	
R	Drew John	347	fireman	42	..
S	Larsen Peter	347	foreman	55	"
T	Peabody Mabel—†	347	at home	72	"
U	Powers Mary B—†	347	bookkeeper	27	"
V	Powers Mary J—†	347	housewife	72	"
W	Stanton Joseph F	347	chauffeur	45	"
X	Donovan Ellen—†	349	matron	53	116 High
Y	Donovan Frank	349	U S N	25	116 "
Z	Donovan George	349	laborer	55	116 "
	1531				
A	Donovan John	349	U S N	26	116 '
B	Sharkey John L	349	fireman	54	116 '
C	Sharkey Mary L—†	349	hygienist	51	116 "
D	Logan Catherine—†	353	housewife	25	here
E	Logan Joseph J	353	seaman	43	"
F	Poulin Laura—†	353	housewife	61	"
G	Poulin William	353	boilermaker	58	"
K	Hardy George F, jr	357	accountant	30	"
L	Hardy Herbert L	357	laborer	28	..
M	Hardy Ida M—†	357	housewife	57	"
N	MacPhee Norman J	357	baker	63	"
O	Gallorelli Emily—†	357	housewife	22	"
P	Gallorelli James	357	laborer	56	"
R	Gallorelli James, jr	357	U S A	26	
S	Gallorelli John	357	upholsterer	30	"
T	*Gallorelli Josephine—†	357	housewife	51	"
Y	Larrabee Jean M—†	362	"	42	
Z	Larrabee Orris B	362	retired	79	
	1532				
A	Larrabee Orris B, jr	362	welder	45	
B	Syria Albert	362	machinist	26	"
C	Syria Myrtle—†	362	housewife	23	"

Page.	Letter.	FULL NAME.	Residence, Jan. 1, 1944.	Occupation.	Supposed Age.	Reported Residence, Jan. 1, 1943. Street and Number.

Main Street—Continued

	D	Thistle Barbara—†	362	housekeeper	21	here
	E	Thistle Gordon C	362	clerk	21	Everett
	G	Wilson Charles	366	machinist	44	here
	H	Wilson Mary—†	366	housewife	38	"
	K	McHugh Edward	368	pressman	39	"
	L	McHugh Kathleen—†	368	housekeeper	53	"
	M	Morgan Celia—†	368	housewife	58	"
	N	Morgan Edward	368	painter	60	
	O	Riley Margaret—†	368	housekeeper	69	"
	P	Ahern Gerald F	370	U S N	21	"
	R	Ahern Helena—†	370	housewife	49	"
	S	Ahern John J	370	U S N	30	
	T	Ahern Joseph B	370	U S A	25	
	U	Ahern Mary—†	370	operator	20	"
	V	Ahern William J	370	laborer	54	
	W	Donovan Alice—†	372	housewife	50	"
	X	Donovan Joseph	372	chauffeur	40	"
	Y	Roundtree Joseph	372	U S A	31	
	Z	Roundtree Mary—†	372	housewife	57	"

1533

	A	Roundtree Michael	372	retired	60	"
	B	Enokian Florence—†	374	housewife	36	20 Belmont
	C	Enokian Kahan	374	shipfitter	51	20 "
	E	Curran John F	376	chauffeur	52	here
	F	Curran John J	376	retired	74	"
	G	Curran Michael	376	chauffeur	51	"
	H	Nicholson Mildred F—†	377	housewife	45	"
	K	Nicholson Nancy F—†	377	"	42	
	L	Smith Raymond A	377	rigger	43	
	M	Daly William	377	clerk	44	
	N	Joyce Gertrude—†	377	housekeeper	20	"
	O	Joyce Nancy—†	377	housewife	42	"
	P	Joyce Thomas	377	chauffeur	57	"
	R	Cunio Augustus	378	retired	68	
	S	Cunio Joseph E	378	mechanic	35	"
	T	Cunio Leona V—†	378	housewife	34	"
	U	McGrath Elsie—†	379	"	36	
	V	McGrath George	379	foreman	35	"
	W	Considine Dorothy—†	379	housewife	27	"
	X	Considine Lawrence	379	clerk	37	
	Z	Reeves Anastasia—†	380	housewife	64	"

1534
Main Street—Continued

A	Stapleton Mary L—†	380	waitress	32	here
B	Stapleton Thomas	380	laborer	34	"
C	Babcock Winifred—†	381	housewife	37	"
D	Kennedy Albert L	381	guard	47	
E	Kennedy Sarah C—†	381	housewife	38	"
G	Barnes Marland	384	waiter	63	"
H	Costello James	384	retired	65	
K	MacPhee Edward	384	waiter	63	
L	Martell William	384	retired	66	
M	Moran John	384	welder	67	
N	O'Keefe Cornelius	384	laborer	57	
O	Phillips Flora A—†	384	housewife	57	"
P	Phillips James H	384	watchman	57	"
R	Nolan Margaret A—†	385	housewife	86	"
S	Nolan Rose M—†	385	agent	46	"
T	Cameron John	386	laborer	50	6 Lawnwood pl
U	Carmody Mabel—†	386	at home	45	here
V	Downes Vincent	386	laborer	39	"
W	Holmes Edward	386	"	52	18 Parker
X	Johnson George	386	paperhanger	48	Somerville
Y	Mahoney Jeremiah	386	laborer	61	here
Z	Middleton James	386	clerk	64	Chelsea

1535

A	Murphy Mary E—†	386	housekeeper	71	here
B	Robertson William	386	laborer	50	"
C	Smith John F	386	U S N	51	"
D	Sullivan Patrick	386	laborer	33	405 Main
G	*Keady John	388	"	63	here
H	Maguire James	388	"	52	"
K	Maguire Mary—†	388	housewife	52	"
L	McCoy Evelyn—†	388	"	34	"
M	Diamond Molly—†	389	"	40	
N	Diamond Norman	389	U S A	20	
O	Diamond Samuel	389	storekeeper	46	"
P	*Camuso Angelina—†	389	housewife	63	"
R	Camuso Antonio	389	laborer	34	
S	Camuso Pasquale	389	"	64	"
T	Crisafulli Elena—†	389	housewife	24	"
U	Crisafulli Vincenzo	389	welder	27	
V	Sullivan Alice—†	390	operator	20	"

Main Street—Continued

w	Sullivan Eugene	390	U S A	23	here
x	Sullivan Mary—†	390	inspector	53	"
y	Sullivan William J	390	laborer	25	"
z	Taylor George	390	U S A	26	

1536

b	Williams Alice—†	392	housewife	36	"
c	Williams James	392	mechanic	40	"
d	Clune Joseph A	393	U S N	50	
e	Clune Mary S—†	393	housewife	44	"
f	Hines Helen—†	394	"	42	
g	Hines Mary H—†	394	clerk	20	··
h	DeDonato Angelina—†	394	housewife	36	"
k	DeDonato Michael	394	barber	53	
n	McNulty Alice—†	399	housewife	50	"
o	McNulty Charles J	399	attorney	58	"
p	McNulty Ruth E—†	399	student	21	"

Mead Street

u	Fallon Patrick J	16	policeman	51	here
v	Fallon Rose A—†	16	housewife	53	"
w	McDonald Marie—†	25	"	43	"
x	McDonald Peter, jr	25	clerk	45	
y	McDonald Thomas J	25	U S A	20	
z	McElaney Daniel J	27	fireman	36	··

1537

a	McElaney James F	27	chauffeur	33	"
b	McElaney Neal	27	retired	75	
c	Hayes Frances S—†	28	housewife	37	"
d	Hayes Peter A	28	mechanic	46	"
e	Barringer Anna J—†	28	clerk	44	"
f	Barringer George	28	longshoreman	45	"
g	Barringer Mildred—†	28	clerk	26	
h	Kearns James A	29	"	28	
k	Lane Mary F—†	29	housewife	41	"
l	Lane William P	29	chauffeur	42	"
m	Stronach Helen—†	30	housewife	37	"
n	Stronach Raymond	30	laborer	38	
o	Tipping Mary A—†	30	housewife	50	"
p	Tipping Thomas W	30	guard	57	

Mead Street—Continued

T	McCarthy Margaret—†	32	housewife	38	here
U	McCarthy Walter A	32	shipfitter	40	"
W	Jewett Joseph F	32	U S A	25	"
X	McNamara Elizabeth M-†	32	housewife	45	"
Y	McNamara Hugh	32	guard	58	"
Z	Burns Catherine—†	33	clerk	26	Malden
	1538				
A	Dee Christina—†	33	"	35	here
B	Dee Jeanette F—†	33	housekeeper	70	"
C	Haley Kenneth T	33	chauffeur	38	"
D	Harvey Hugh	33	painter	67	12 School
E	Williams Christina—†	34	at home	77	here
F	Mahoney Catherine—†	34	housewife	65	"
G	Mahoney John	34	laborer	33	"
H	O'Leary Dennis	34	longshoreman	59	"
L	Devlin Charlotte E—†	35	housewife	31	"
M	Devlin Richard F	35	fireman	29	
N	McLaughlin Ann—†	35	housewife	33	"
O	McLaughlin James H	35	clerk	36	"
R	Crockett Dorothy C—†	37	housewife	36	" .
S	Crockett Douglas A	37	laborer	35	
T	Driscoll Elizabeth—†	37	at home	65	"
U	McElaney Virginia L—†	37	housewife	22	"
V	Morley Helen V—†	37	attendant	50	"
W	Campbell Amanda M—†	38	housewife	52	"
X	Gould Everett C	38	U S A	35	Hamilton
Y	Gould Helen L—†	38	stitcher	30	"
Z	Joslyn Mildred—†	38	at home	67	here
	1539				
A	Murphy Cornelius	39	longshoreman	26	"
B	Murphy Mary—†	39	housewife	22	78 Russell
C	Kane Francis M	39	laborer	26	43 School
D	Kane Helen M—†	39	operator	23	43 "
E	Hynes Mary A—†	40	housewife	25	here
F	Meehan Catherine E—†	40	"	47	"
G	Meehan Catherine E—†	40	clerk	24	" .
H	Meehan Helen G—†	40	typist	22	
K	Meehan Robert E	40	machinist	46	"
L	Meehan Robert E, jr	40	U S N	21	
M	Donovan Mary—†	44	housewife	56	" .
N	Donovan Robert	44	ropemaker	59	"

Mead Street Court

o	Wenhold Josephine A—†	1	at home	42	here
p	Hurley Grace—†	2	"	45	"
R	Greatorox John	3	chauffeur	33	"
s	Greatorox Mabel—†	3	housewife	24	"

Middlesex Street

u	Luti Anna M—†	24	bookkeeper	29	here
v	Luti Elda B—†	24	housewife	28	"
w	Luti Guido A	24	manufacturer	34	"
x	Luti Joseph E	24	laborer	72	
y	Luti Mary T—†	24	housewife	70	"
z	Luti Waldo J	24	metalworker	42	"

1540   Mill Street

A	Marks Catherine—†	2	housewife	48	Virginia
B	Marks Walter E	2	inspector	59	"
c*	Campbell John L	2	chauffeur	35	here
D	Campbell Mary M—†	2	housewife	34	"
E	Dugan Marie E—†	2	"	34	"
F	Dugan William	2	fireman	40	85 School
G	Garrigan Elizabeth M—†	4	domestic	44	2 Mill
H	Garrigan James E	4	freighthandler	44	2 "
K	Hayes Catherine E—†	4	housewife	27	34 Lincoln
L	Hayes Edmund J	4	U S N	27	34 "
M	Tatten George D	4	builder	46	here
N	Tatten Mary E—†	4	at home	85	"
o	Morrison Pauline G—†	4	waitress	50	"
P	Cosgrove Catherine—†	6	housewife	69	"
R	Cosgrove John	6	laborer	55	
s	McClair James W	6	longshoreman	38	"
T	McClair Margaret A—†	6	housewife	35	"
u	Dineen Jerome J	6	checker	43	"
v	Dineen Margaret A—†	6	housewife	43	"
w	Dineen Marguerite M—†	6	SPAR	21	
x	Dowd Margaret M—†	6	at home	75	"
y	Fitzgerald Mary E—†	6	housewife	23	"
z	Brown Joseph W	8	chauffeur	35	"
	1541					
A	Brown Mary G—†	8	housewife	35	"

Page.	Letter.	FULL NAME.	Residence, Jan. 1, 1944.	Occupation.	Supposed Age.	Reported Residence, Jan. 1, 1943. Street and Number.

Mill Street—Continued

	B	McAuliffe John	8	retired	68	here
	C	Hart Diana—†	8	domestic	40	"
	D	Hart William J	8	U S A	20	" ·
	E	Reardon Mary L—†	8	housewife	22	"
	F	Reardon Walter F	8	U S A	28	
	G	Vergeron Napoleon	8	retired	63	"
	H	Nordyke Mary C—†	8	housewife	36	31 Carney ct
	K	Lacey Elvie L—†	9	"	24	here
	L	Lacey George F	9	laborer	23	"
	M	Lacey Herbert F	9	"	29	"
	N	Lacey Michael T	9	"	65	
	O	Lacey Zelma M—†	9	housewife	26	"
	P	Hynes Frederick	10	guard	56	
	R	Hynes Jennie E—†	10	packer	48	··
	S	Bassett Catherine F—†	10	operator	39	"
	T	Bassett Joseph E	10	pipefitter	49	"
	U	Brett James E	10	chipper	42	··
	V	Brett Mary A—†	10	housewife	41	"
	W	Cronin Walter L	10	B F D	44	
	X	Conway Abbie—†	12	housekeeper	78	" .
	Y	Florentino Albert F	12	glazier	40	" ·
	Z	Florentino Rose A—†	12	housewife	38	"
		1542				
	A	McCall Edwin H	14	clerk	35	
	B	McCall Grace E—†	14	housewife	35	"
	C	Merullo Dorothy M—†	14	"	28	··
	D	Merullo Victor E	14	shipper	28	"
	F	Brewster Albert J	23	stevedore	42	"
	G	Brewster Catherine L—†	23	housewife	38	"
	K	Harrington Charles J	25	retired	76	8 Essex
	L	McCool Joseph T	25	U S A	30	here
	M	McCool Lillian A—†	25	housewife	30	"

Oak Street

	P	Robinson Edward	1	laborer	38	42 St Martin
	R	Robinson Margaret—†	1	operator	32	42 "
	T	Breen Grace A—†	3	housewife	41	here
	U	Breen Kenneth J	3	manager	41	"
	V	McDonough Annie E—†	3	housewife	72	"
	W	McDonough Helen F—†	3	clerk	41	··

Page.	Letter.	FULL NAME.	Residence, Jan. 1, 1944.	Occupation.	Supposed Age.	Reported Residence, Jan. 1, 1943. Street and Number.

Oak Street—Continued

x	Campbell Alexander	4	laborer	32	here
y	Campbell Lillian—†	4	housewife	24	"
z	Leighton Edwin C	4	guard	54	"

1543

A	Leighton Jennie M—†	4	housewife	51	"
c*	Heanue Bessie T—†	7	"	43	
D	Heanue Michael J	7	distiller	52	
F	Kelly George W·	9	guard	38	
G	Kelly Monica A—†	9	clerk	33	
H	Rielly Albert F	9	policeman .	36	"
K	Rielly Mary J—†	9	clerk	43	
L	Rielly Mary V—†	9	housewife	72	"
M	Rielly Rita B—†	9	"	28	
N	Rielly Thomas A	9	retired	77	
o	Grows Perley A	11	manager	56	"
P	Dullea Dennis	15	laborer	48	
R	Glynn Estella—†	15	housewife	48	"
s	Larocque Helen A—†	15	operator	24	"
T	McCree James A	15	chauffeur	52	"
U	McCree Martha—†	15	housewife	49	"
V	Weir James D	15	guard	73	Brookline
w	Weir James D, jr	15	mechanic	40	here
Y	Price Sarah—†	16	housewife	60	"
z	Price Thomas H	16	laborer	61	"

1544

A	Dowgos Anthony I	17	machinist	30	25 Pleasant
B	Dowgos Mary I—†	17	housewife	26	25 "
c	Dever Elmer F	17	U S N	30	184 Fisher av
D	Dever Helena R—†	17	housewife	23	184 "
E	Mahoney Daniel L	17	foreman	53	172 Chelsea
F	Mahoney Margaret V—†	17	clerk	21	172 "
G	Brooks Frank B	18	retired	74	here
H	Brooks Katherine T—†	18	at home	77	"
K	MacIntyre Sarah A—†	18	housekeeper	64	"
L	Hirtle Lynwood L	20	clerk	34	..
M	Hirtle Olive M—†	20	housewife	34	"
N	Libby Inez—†	20	operator	30	"
o	McCutcheon Annie M—†	20	housewife	60	"
P	McCutcheon George O	20	laborer	62	
R	McCormack Mary—†	21	at home	71	"
s	Smith John T	21	retired	77	

Oak Street—Continued

T	Russell Frederick	21	B F D	50	here
U	Russell Margaret I—†	21	housewife	43	"
W	Driscoll Andrew J	23	retired	66	"
X	McCarthy Arthur J	23	U S N	34	
Y	McCarthy Leo C	23	"	33	.
Z	McCarthy Mary G—†	23	operator	28	"
	1545				
A	McCarthy Mary L—†	23	housewife	66	"
B	McCarthy Timothy F	23	inspector	65	"
C	Lordan Nora T—†	24	housewife	73	"
D	Lordan Timothy	24	retired	73	
E	White Georgietta—†	24	at home	94	"
F	Fleming Julia V—†	25	housewife	43	"
G	Fleming Patrick E	25	retired	51	
H	Carney James J	26	salesman	48	"
K	Carney Margaret V—†	26	housewife	44	"
L	Doherty Dennis F	26	laborer	49	
M	Doherty Frederick V	26	"	34	"
N	Doherty John J	26	"	47	
O	Doherty Walter J	26	clerk	39	
P	Caruso Elaine—†	28	"	26	
R	Donovan Daniel F	28	"	38	
S	Donovan Greta C—†	28	housewife	38	"
T	Donovan Daniel D	28	manager	66	"
U	Donovan Helen G—†	28	clerk	35	
V	Donovan John J	28	"	30	
W	Donovan Margaret M—†	28	"	36	"
X	Griffin Elizabeth B—†	28	housewife	33	Medford
Y	Griffin John J	28	U S N	33	"
Z	Hartigan Joseph P	28	U S A	29	here
	1546				
	Hartigan Mary T—†	28	housewife	26	"
A	Brennan Christina B—†	30	"	41	
D	Brennan Joseph O	30	electrician	44	"
E	Brennan Joseph O, jr	30	U S N	21	"
F	Cobb Herbert C	30	machinist	43	"
G	Cobb Margaret F—†	30	housewife	43	"
H	Kelleher Frank J	30	clerk	50	"
K	Redden Alice N—†	31	saleswoman	63	107 Russell
L	Kirk Joseph G	31	inspector	38	here
M	Kirk Mildred D—†	31	housewife	36	"

Page.	Letter.	FULL NAME.	Residence, Jan. 1, 1944.	Occupation.	Supposed Age.	Reported Residence, Jan. 1, 1943. Street and Number:

Oak Street—Continued

	N	Whelan Mary J—†	32	housewife	35	here
	o	Whelan Thomas C	32	clerk	36	"
	P	Whelan Joseph E	32	"	47	"
	R	Whelan Laura M—†	32	housewife	49	"

Russell Street

	s	Hallett Anna—†	74	at home	73	here
	T	Campbell Charles W	74	mechanic	57	Wilmington
	u	Campbell Laura—†	74	housewife	56	"
	v	Campbell Phyllis L—†	74	student	20	"
	w	Wheeler Herbert F	74	carpenter	74	here
	x	Barker Charlotte M—†	76	housewife	55	"
	Y	Barker William G	76	laborer	55	"
	z	Lasky Florence A—†	76	inspector	51	"
1547						
	A	McGowan Isabel—†	78	housewife	50	Medford
	B	McGowan Margaret—†	78	baker	20	"
	c	Mercer Mary—†	78	housewife	27	"
	E	Lane Daniel	80	longshoreman	39	here
	F	Lane Mary—†	80	housewife	37	"
	G	Connors Eugene P	82	foreman	34	"
	H	Connors Florence H—†	82	housewife	30	"
	K	Scott Catherine A—†	82	"	20	Somerville
	L	Scott Thomas J	82	laborer	22	"
	M	Olsen Andrew	84	painter	36	here
	N	Olsen Stella—†	84	housewife	37	"
	o	Andrews Edith H—†	86	"	36	"
	P	Andrews Edward W	86	U S A	36	
	R	Keefe Charles	86	splicer	40	
	s	Keefe Doris—†	86	housekeeper	25	"
	T	Shea Margaret M—†	86	housewife	41	33 Mystic
	u	Shea Robert J	86	laborer	44	33 "
	v	McCarthy Daniel	88	U S N	40	here
	w	McCarthy Frances—†	88	housewife	40	"
	x	Burke Dennis F	88	U S A	21	26 Russell
	Y	Burke Margaret—†	88	housewife	20	here
	z	Ryle Mary—†	88	"	46	"
1548						
	A	Ryle William	88	guard	47	
	B	Nearen Dorothy—†	88	WAVE	21	"

28

Russell Street—Continued

c	Nearen Edward	88	longshoreman	24	here
D	Nearen John	88	U S A	25	"
E	Nearen Mary—†	88	dietitian	48	"
F	Nearen William	88	clerk	26	"
G	Marsh Victoria—†	92	domestic	58	"
H	Ruby Katherine—†	93	housewife	43	"
K	Ruby Samuel A	93	presser	48	"
L	Winslow Lillian A—†	95	housewife	41	"
M	Winslow Percy E, jr	95	milkman	21	"
O	McFee Barbara—†	103	housewife	84	"
P	Wilson Charles R	103	U S A	24	
R	Wilson Grace I—†	103	housewife	25	"
S	Wilson John M	103	longshoreman	28	"
T	Wilson Marion P—†	103	housewife	57	"
U	Wilson Walter P, jr	103	U S N	31	
V	Wilson William	103	clerk	35	"
X	Colby Alfred	107	packer	30	7 Phipps
Y	Colby Marion—†	107	housewife	26	7 "
Z	Fitzgerald James	107	pipefitter	24	here
	1549				
A	Shea Dorothy—†	109	housewife	26	3 Short
B	Shea William	109	chauffeur	30	3 "
C	Tagen Frederick.	109	laborer	47	here
D	Tagen Margaret—†	109	WAC	22	"
E	Tagen Sarah—†	109	housewife	48	"
F	Robinson Patrick J	111	retired	70	"
G	Robinson William F	111	U S N	38	
H	Golding Frederick	111	carpenter	37	"
K	Golding Mary—†	111	housewife	35	"
L	Fisher Maisey D—†	113	at home	81	"
M	Lee Frank E	115	retired	75	
N	Lee Frank E, jr	115	laborer	44	
O	Lee Helen—†	115	housewife	75	"
P	Lee James H	115	longshoreman	42	"
R	Lee Warren J	115	seaman	34	"
S	Moran Catherine—†	115	housewife	39	62 Wash'n

Ward 2–Precinct 16

CITY OF BOSTON

LIST OF RESIDENTS
20 YEARS OF AGE AND OVER

(NON-CITIZENS INDICATED BY ASTERISK)
(FEMALES INDICATED BY DAGGER)

AS OF

JANUARY 1, 1944

THOMAS F. SULLIVAN, *Chairman*
FREDERIC E. DOWLING, *Secretary*
WILLIAM A. MOTLEY, JR.
FRANCIS B. McKINNEY
EVERETT R. PROUT

Listing Board.

CITY OF BOSTON PRINTING DEPARTMENT

1600

Albion Place

A	Campin William J	1	retired	74	here	
B	Doherty Mary—†	1	waitress	36	13 Belmont	
C	Goossens Marian H—†	1	tailor	40	13 "	
D	Kane Hazel S—†	1	housewife	55	here	
E	Kane Helen M—†	1	moulder	20	"	
F	Kane James J	1	engraver	28	"	
G	Kane William E—†	1	U S A	30	"	
H	MacDonald Alexander	1	U S N	23	445 Main	
K	MacDonald Alice—†	1	housewife	24	445 "	
L	Graves Lydia M—†	3	"	30	here	
M	Graves Percy F	3	chauffeur	36	"	
N	*Campbell Daniel E	4	"	33	32 Albion pl	
O	Campbell Maude M—†	4	operator	29	32 "	
P	Davidson Florence—†	4	at home	63	32 "	
R	Lyons Anna—†	5	machinist	25	4 Seaver	
S	Lyons Edward	5	U S N	22	4 "	
T	Lyons James F	5	constable	35	4 "	
U	Lyons Mary L—†	5	housewife	58	4 "	
V	Belyea Gertrude T—†	5	"	51	here	
W	Belyea Paul V	5	U S N	27	"	
X	Belyea William F	5	U S A	24	"	
Y	Maag Bertha L—†	5	clerk	49		
Z	Maag Mary E—†	5	at home	85	"	

1601

C	Finnigan Dennis	8	retired	66		
D	Gravel Lillian A—†	8	metalworker	23	"	
E	Toomey Lillian F—†	8	housewife	44	"	
F	McManus Charlotte M—†	9	stitcher	43	13 Perkins	
G	McManus John F	9	metalworker	51	13 "	
H	Bragan Mary R—†	10	housewife	32	104 Baldwin	
K	Bragan William J	10	drawtender	50	104 "	
L	Harrington John	10A	foreman	40	here	
M	McCree Helen—†	10A	housewife	47	"	
T	McFadden Allan B	19	U S N	22	"	
U	McFadden Charles J	19	machinist	52	"	
V	McFadden Margaret—†	19	housewife	52	"	
W	McFadden Rita M—†	19	stenographer	23	"	
X	Fay Anna M—†	20	clerk	20	..	
Y	Fay Helen E—†	20	stenographer	22	"	
Z	Fay Mary—†	20	housewife	53	"	

1602
Albion Place—Continued

	Letter.	Full Name.	Residence, Jan. 1, 1944.	Occupation.	Supposed Age.	Reported Residence, Jan. 1, 1943. Street and Number.
	A	Fay Mary F—†	20	waitress	23	here
	B	Fay Peter J	20	laborer	52	"
	C	Fay Peter J, jr	20	electrician	26	"
	D	Dirring Johan C	20	pipefitter	26	473 Main
	E	Dirring Nora H—†	20	housewife	29	473 "
	F	Horgan James F	20	laborer	36	473 "
	G	Rinaldi Concetta—†	rear 20	housewife	42	here
	H	Rinaldi Joseph W	" 20	U S A	23	"
	K	Rinaldi Onorato	" 20	cook	50	"
	L	Powers John J	21	laborer	52	"
	M	Powers John J	21	U S N	22	
	N	Powers Mary F—†	21	housewife	49	"
	O	Powers Ruth M—†	21	trimmer	20	"
	P	Rossetti Margaret—†	21	housewife	24	"
	R	Rossetti Stephen O	21	U S A	25	
	S	Coffey Edward J	22	U S N	25	..
	T	Coffey Jeremiah C	22	U S A	21	
	U	Coffey Mary—†	22	housewife	61	"
	V	Coffey Timothy	22	packer	61	
	W	Dennehy Marian A—†	22	at home	38	"
	X	Dennehy Mary E—†	22	housewife	62	"
	Y	Dennehy Michael J	22	retired	70	"
	Z	Dennehy Richard J	22	U S N	29	"

1603

	Letter.	Full Name.	Residence, Jan. 1, 1944.	Occupation.	Supposed Age.	Reported Residence, Jan. 1, 1943. Street and Number.
	A	Mansfield Catherine A—†	22	housewife	33	Wash'n D C
	B	Mansfield Thomas F	22	printer	39	"
	C	Boles Charles A	23	retired	67	here
	D	Boles Theresa—†	23	housewife	60	"
	E	Farren Eugene A	23	court officer	59	"
	F	Sommers Charles M	24	machinist	35	26 Albion pl
	G	Sommers Grace—†	24	housewife	37	26 "
	H	Doherty Aloysius L	25	U S A	23	here
	K	Doherty Charles	25	laborer	53	"
	L	Doherty Helen T—†	25	S P A R	27	"
	M	Doherty Joseph I	25	U S A	25	"
	N	Doherty Mary A—†	25	housewife	50	"
	O	Doherty Mary F—†	25	pipefitter	20	"
	P	Brown Gertrude K—†	26	saleswoman	23	Maine
	R	Norton George J	26	rigger	44	42½ St Martin
	S	Thompson Gertrude M-†	26	housewife	66	Maine

Albion Place—Continued

T	Hughes Dennis	26	laborer	40	322 Main
U	Hughes Jennie—†	26	housewife	21	322 "
V	Towle Ellen G—†	27	at home	60	here
W	Goodwin Mary A—†	28	housewife	34	2994 Wash'n
X	Goodwin Walter L	28	retired	50	2994
Y	Dunleavy Annie E—†	29	at home	67	here
Z	Dunleavy Francis J	29	U S A	34	"

1604

A	Dunleavy Joseph T	29	electrician	36	"
B	Dunleavy Theresa C—†	29	housewife	28	"
C	Murphy Frederick W	29	U S A	25	"
D	Desmarinas Gaetano S	30	chef	40	1 Phipps
E	McCusker John J	30	manager	45	here
F	Evelyn Daniel	30	chauffeur	30	"
G	Evelyn Helen—†	30	housewife	22	"

Armory Street

M	Reardon Mary B—†	2	housewife	64	here
N	Reardon Theodore B	2	U S A	34	"
O	Reardon Timothy J	2	retired	62	"
P	McNally Cecelia—†	3	housekeeper	27	74 Decatur
R	McNally Warren E	3	U S N	26	here
S	Cameron John S	3	retired	75	"
T	Sweeney Margaret E—†	3	clerk	20	"
U	Sweeney Mary C—†·	3	housewife	52	"
V	Sweeney Patrick	3	letter carrier	49	"
W	McMakin Frank H	4	retired	77	
X	Romeo Edna R—†	4	housewife	61	"
Z	Irvine Abigail—†	5	"	22	

1605

A	Irvine Gerald C		seaman	26	
B	Tobin Marie M—†		housewife	37	"
C	Tobin William		storekeeper	40	"
D	McLaughlin Albert	½	B F D	29	"
E	McLaughlin Rita B—†	½	housewife	30	"
F	Harrington Catherine—†		"	54	
G	Harrington Dennis	6	watchman	70	"
H	Serafini Flaviano	7	U S A	30	
K	Serafini Margaret—†	7	housewife	36	"
L	Eagan Johanna B—†	8	clerk	28	

Page.	Letter.	Full Name.	Residence, Jan. 1, 1944.	Occupation.	Supposed Age.	Reported Residence, Jan. 1, 1943. Street and Number.

Armory Street—Continued

	M	Murray Catherine M—†	8	clerk	20	here
	N	Murray Ellen—†	8	housewife	57	"
	O	Murray Mary P—†	8	instructor	25	"
	P	Murray Thomas J	8	U S A	26	
	R	Dowd Florence M—†	9	housewife	26	"
	S	Dowd James H	9	chauffeur	37	"
	T	Dowd William H	9	laborer	39	"

Auburn Square

	W	Schiavo Gabriel M	2	electrician	30	30 Oak
	X	Schiavo Mary—†	2	housewife	26	30 "
	Y	French Florence L—†	2	"	35	here
	Z	French Gerald N	2	machinist	37	"
1606						
	A	Marsh Arthur	3	U S N	26	92 Russell
	B	Marsh Mary—†	3	housewife	22	here
	C	Potocki Daniel J	3	machinist	45	"
	D	Potocki Miranda—†	3	housewife	35	" .
	E	Driscoll James	4	retired	72	
	F	Driscoll James	4	seaman	25	"
	G	Driscoll Margaret—†	4	packer	30	
	H	Driscoll Mary—†	4	housekeeper	66	"
	L	Murphy John W	5	electrician	56	"
	M	McAlevey Madeline—†	5	housewife	38	"

Auburn Street

	O	Mahoney Cecelia F—†	8	housewife	38	here
	P	Mahoney Daniel F	8	chauffeur	44	"
	R	Mahoney Mary E—†	8	housewife	34	"
	S	Mahoney Timothy W	8	laborer	41	"
	T	Flanagan Catherine—†	10	binder	65	
	U	Flanagan Daniel	10	U S N	62	
	V	Ryle Leo B	10	operator	38	"
	W	Ryle Mary T—†	10	housewife	70	"
	X	Lynch Joseph T	12	laborer	44	"
	Y	Miller Catherine—†	12	housewife	32	"
	Z	Miller Gerald	12	U S A	38	
1607						
	A	Shea Elizabeth M—†	12	inspector	36	"

5

Page.	Letter.	Full Name.	Residence, Jan. 1, 1944.	Occupation.	Supposed Age.	Reported Residence, Jan. 1, 1943. Street and Number.

Auburn Street—Continued

	B	Ployer Alice L—†	12	clerk	21	here
	c	Ployer Helen F—†	12	housewife	38	"
	D	Ployer Paul J	12	inspector	44	"
	E	Canney John	14	accountant	45	"
	F	Canney Margaret—†	14	housewife	45	"
	G	Canney Mary—†	14	"	65	
	H	Tobin Mary A—†	16	housekeeper	47	"
	K	Tobin Thomas	16	laborer	35	··
	L	Flaherty Catherine H—†	20	housewife	47	"
	M	Flaherty Francis E	20	supervisor	47	"
	N	Flaherty Francis E, jr	20	U S A	21	
	O	Shea Bridget—†	20	housekeeper	83	"
	P	Donohue John J	20	electrician	52	"
	R	Donohue Mary S—†	20	housewife	50	"
	S	Shea Margaret M—†	20	"	52	
	T	Shea Matthew P	20	chauffeur	52	"
	U	Silva Anna B—†	22	housewife	33	"
	V	Silva George T	22	U S N	35	
	X	Keough Peter J	24	drawtender	39	"
	Y	Keough Veronica M—†	24	housewife	40	"
	Z	McNally Martin	24	candyworker	38	"
		1608				
	A	McNally Anna J—†	24	housewife	72	"
	B	McNally John J	24	U S N	35	
	C	McNally Katherine A—†	24	housewife	31	"
	D	Duggan Mary—†	26	"	37	
	E	McDonald Joseph N	26	supervisor	33	"
	F	McDonald Margaret—†	26	housewife	67	"
	G	McDonald Richard	26	finisher	31	5 Auburn
	H	Shields Anna—†	28	housewife	59	here
	K	Shields Mary A—†	28	clerk	35	"
	L	Shields Michael	28	laborer	66	"
	M	Shields Rita M—†	28	clerk	22	
	N	Shields Robert F	28	machinist	38	"
	O	Shields Teresa—†	28	housewife	32	"
	P	McCarthy Eileen—†	30	stenographer	40	"
	R	McCarthy Charles F	30	fireman	49	··
	S	McCarthy Eleanor B—†	30	housewife	49	"
	T	O'Brien Cornelius F	32	policeman	45	"
	U	O'Brien Margaret E—†	32	housewife	45	"
	V	Whelan Daniel L	32	clerk	49	

6

Page.	Letter.	Full Name.	Residence, Jan. 1, 1944.	Occupation.	Supposed Age.	Reported Residence, Jan. 1, 1943. Street and Number.

Auburn Street—Continued

w	Whelan Isabelle—†	32	at home	72	here
x	Whelan John H	32	retired	81	"
y	Whelan Leslie P	32	letter carrier	42	"
	1609				
a	Burnham Rose L—†	36	housekeeper	66	"
b	Sargent Abbie S—†	36	"	70	"
c	Sargent Alice E—†	36	"	72	··
d	Werner Ferdinand	38	retired	72	
e	White Clayton F	38	fireman	42	"
f	White Mary E—†	38	housewife	41	"
·h	Barker Catherine—†	40	"	24	"
k	Barker Ernest	40	U S A	27	
l	Shaw Frank W	40	guard	43	
m	Shaw Ruby F—†	40	housekeeper	80	"
n	Maheigan John A	42	shipfitter	46	"
o	Maheigan Mary E—†	42	housewife	36	"

Baldwin Street

p	Fitzgerald James L	41	inspector	38	here
r	Sheehan Annie E—†	41	housewife	55	Somerville
s	Sheehan Charles J	41	laborer	32	here
t	Sheehan John J	41	U S N	21	"
u	Sheehan Mildred F—†	41	clerk	22	Somerville
v	Sheehan Patrick W	41	machinist	33	"
w	Frawley Alice N—†	43	housewife	67	here
x	Frawley Helen M—†	43	stenographer	36	"
y	Frawley Michael J	43	shipper	70	"
z	Wilkinson Christopher	45	metalworker	51	"
	1610				
a	Wilkinson Edith—†	45	housewife	49	"
b	Barry Emma B—†	45	"	32	"
c	Barry John P	45	laborer	37	"
e	Thompson Helen E—†	46	housewife	30	"
f	Thompson Norman W	46	machinist	27	"
g	Murphy Ellen—†	46	housewife	72	"
h	Murphy Helen E—†	46	clerk	36	
k	Murphy John	46	fireman	75	"
l	Sullivan Eugene C	47	U S A	24	
m	Sullivan Helen—†	47	operator	20	"
n	Sullivan John C	47	U S A	26	"

7

1

Page.	Letter.	Full Name.	Residence, Jan. 1, 1944.	Occupation.	Supposed Age.	Reported Residence, Jan. 1, 1943. Street and Number.

Baldwin Street—Continued

	o	Sullivan Nora A—†	47	housewife	52	here
	p	Foley Patrick	47	retired	75	"
	R	Tomkewicz Charles J	48	U S N	24	497 Main
	s	Tomkewicz Dorothy M—†	48	housewife	23	497 "
	T	Quinlan Daniel C	48	salesman	42	here
	U	Quinlan Helen P—†	48	housewife	45	"
	v	Mullen Helena W—†	49	"	42	"
	w	Mullen Thomas L	49	salesman	43	"
	x	Mullen Bridget E—†	49	housekeeper	76	"
	y	Mullen William	49	retired	78	"
	z	Cullen Anna A—†	50	housewife	29	"

1611

	A	Cullen John H	50	U S N	29	
	B	Lordan Dennis M	50	maintenance	71	"
	c	Lordan Henry F	50	boilermaker	35	"
	D	Lordan Jennie—†	50	housewife	69	"
	E	Lordan John J	50	U S A	37	
	F	Lordan Margaret F—†	50	housewife	32	"
	G	Hammond Emma E—†	51	"	62	
	H	Murphy John J	51	clerk	64	
	K	Murphy Margaret D—†	51	at home	49	"
	L	McNelley Eugene C	52	electrician	28	96 Elm
	M	McNelley Mary E—†	52	housewife	57	here
	N	McNelley Mary T—†	52.	"	26	96 Elm
	o	Murphy Edna—†	52	"	22	here
	P	Murphy Walter B	52	U S A	26	"
	R	Murphy William E	52	laborer	54	"
	s	Connors Elizabeth G—†	53	candymaker	48	"
	T	Connors John J	53	laborer	53	"
	U	Connors Mary F—†	53	housewife	84	"
	v	Connors Mary L—†	53	at home	55	"
	w	Zermani Alice M—†	53	housewife	25	"
	x	Zermani Arthur E	53	metalworker	28	"
	y	Hally Rita M—†	54	housewife	29	"
	z	Hally William H	54	rigger	32	

1612

	A	Carbone Angelo	54	retired	60	
	B	Carbone Emma—†	54	housekeeper	33	"
	c	Carbone George	54	machinist	23	"
	D	Carbone Herbert	54	metalworker	21	"
	E	Quinlan Julia—†	55	housewife	48	"

Baldwin Street—Continued

F	Lee Ellen M—†	55	housewife	29	here
G	Lee Francis A	55	fireman	29	"
H	Carven Agnes M—†	56	housewife	65	"
K	Carven Agnes M—†	56	teacher	43	"
L	Carven Rupert S	56	retired	74	
M	Keizer Dorothy A—†	57	housewife	25	"
N	Sullivan Herbert F	57	pipefitter	29	"
O	Sullivan Mary E—†	57	housewife	51	"
P	Young Theresa G—†	57	"	80	
R	Morrissey Catherine—†	58	"	82	
S	Morrissey Catherine B—†	58	teacher	50	"
T	Morrissey Gertrude A—†	58	stenographer	38	"
U	Conway James J	59	retired	73	
V	Graham John J	59	chauffeur	48	"
W	Graham Mary L—†	59	housewife	45	"
Y	Scannell Dennis F	60	welder	30	
Z	Scannell Mary—†	60	housewife	30	"
	1613				
A	DiVola Angelina—†	60	"	33	
B	DiVola James	60	U S A	23	
C	DiVola Pasquale	60	operator	49	"
D	Ferrante Anthony	60	retired	76	
E	Fernandez Joseph	60	barber	64	
F	Porter Mary J—†	60	housewife	63	"
G	Shaw Gertrude M—†	60	"	39	
H	White Ira F	61	shipfitter	30	"
K	White Jeannette M—†	61	housewife	27	"
L	Cunniff Helen T—†	61	at home	37	"
M	Cunniff Lawrence E	61	electrician	45	"
N	Cunniff Luke F	61	painter	51	"
O	Cunniff William E	61	electrician	39	"
P	Pierce Elizabeth A—†	61	hairdresser	41	"
R	Duggan John F	61	pipefitter	46	"
S	Duggan Mary E—†	61	housewife	50	"
T	Giroux Howard E	63	dairyman	35	"
U	Giroux Mary E—†	63	housewife	38	"
V	Jesson Agnes—†	63	"	38	
W	Jesson George	63	laborer	36	"
X	Bird Charles E	63	"	23	2 Auburn sq
Y	Bird Weltha L—†	63	housewife	23	2 "
Z	Lightizer Mildred L—†	65	"	43	here

1

1614
Baldwin Street—Continued

A	Lightizer William A	65	chauffeur	45	here
B	Driscoll Albert L	65	laborer	46	"
C	Driscoll Catherine T—†	65	housewife	71	"
D	Osburn Jennie—†	67	"	58	260 Medford
E	Osburn Joseph F	67	chauffeur	33	260 "
F	Walsh John F	67	"	42	here
G	Walsh Mary—†	67	housewife	42	"
H	Morris Cecelia M—†	67	"	25	"
K	Morris Lester L	67	U S N	26	
L	Sprague Agnes L—†	67	inspector	20	"
M	Sprague Kathleen R—†	67	packer	22	"
N	Sprague Margaret E—†	67	housewife	54	"
O	Sprague Willis B	67	U S N	30	Somerville
P	Drew James F	69	chauffeur	30	here
R	Drew Marian C—†	69	housewife	35	"
S	Wilbur Louis T	69	repairman	60	"
T	Connell Harold V	69	laborer	43	1 Short Street ct
U	Connell Mary C—†	69	housewife	38	1 "
v*	Davidson Margaret C—†	69	"	33	here
W	Davidson Robert J	69	chauffeur	33	"
X	Bailey Edward E	71	machinist	60	"
Y	Bailey Maude B—†	71	housewife	61	"
Z	Page Annie C—†	71	"	64	

1615

A	Page George W	71	mechanic	60	"
B	Tobin Etta R—†	71	housewife	39	27 Cook
C	Tobin Thomas W	71	laborer	60	27 "
D	Strickland Mary T—†	73	housewife	26	here
E	Strickland William F	73	rigger	26	"
F	Leahy Charles E	87	retired	70	"
G	Leahy Ellen M—†	87	housekeeper	73	"
H	Leahy Katherine A—†	87	at home	71	"
K	Devine John F	89	U S A	35	
L	Devine Mary—†	89	housewife	31	"
M	Doherty Ann C—†	89	stenographer	25	"
N	Doherty Charles	89	operator	61	"
O	Doherty Nellie—†	89	housewife	59	"
P	Doherty Phillip P	89	U S A	29	
R	Leahy Katherine C—†	91	housekeeper	81	"
S	Henchey Eugene E	91	retired	70	

Baldwin Street—Continued

T	Henchey Jennie A—†	91	accountant	65	here
U	Driscoll Jeremiah J	93	chauffeur	36	118 Medford
V	Driscoll Theresa L—†	93	housewife	38	118 "
W	Norris C Marie—†	93	"	30	here
X	Norris Thomas F	93	chauffeur	31	"
Y	Powers Gertrude R—†	95	housewife	38	"
Z	Powers John J	95	painter	38	"

1616

A	Fay Lawrence F	97	shoeworker	47	"
B	Fay Susan M—†	97	housewife	47	"
C	Furlong Catherine L—†	97	"	42	
D	Furlong Joseph R	97	selector	40	"
E	Leary Edward J	99	clerk	40	"
F	Leary Mary J—†	99	housewife	40	"
G	Dix Mary R—†	101	"	21	
H	Geagan Grace E—†	101	"	25	
K	Geagan Thomas E	101	U S N	27	
L	Hammond Ruth R—†	101	secretary	24	"
M	Riley Frank J	101	supervisor	61	"
N	Riley Margaret F—†	101	housewife	54	"
O	Doherty Mary—†	103	"	36	
P	McLaughlin Edward	103	laborer	28	"
R	Gibbons Anne—†	105	housekeeper	83	"
S	Gibbons Daniel	105	pipefitter	44	"
T	Goulding Mary T—†	107	housewife	55	"
U	Goulding Patrick J	107	laborer	55	"
V	Flynn Helen F—†	109	housewife	48	"
W	Flynn James F	109	U S A	23	
X	Flynn John J	109	"	20	
Y	Flynn Mary T—†	109	stenographer	20	"
Z	Flynn Michael J	109	laborer	50	"

1617

A	Grail Elaine G—†	109	teacher	34	Newton
B	Johnson Thomas T	109	U S A	44	here
C	Mahoney Susan H—†	111	secretary	47	"
D	Tillson Augustus J	111	salesman	65	"
E	Tillson Josephine L—†	111	bookkeeper	51	"
F	McNamee Margaret G-†	115	housewife	58	"
G	McNamee Michael J	115	inspector	54	"
H	Green Bridget C—†	117	at home	66	"
K	Green James I	117	inspector	55	"

11

1

Baldwin Street—Continued

l	Green Joseph G	117	agent	45	here
m	Green Katherine M—†	117	stenographer	50	"
n	Green Mary L—†	117	at home	47	"
o	Green Olive—†	117	housewife	38	"
p	Green Thomas H	117	executive	60	"

Bellows Place

r	Maraccia Salvatore	4	retired	71	here

Bunker Hill Street

s	McCarthy Daniel	370	clerk	22	397 Main
t	McCarthy Irene—†	370	housewife	20	21 Tremont
u	Cullity Bartholomew	370	mechanic	53	41 Auburn
v	Cullity Bartholomew V, jr	370	U S A	24	41 "
w	Cullity James M	370	laborer	20	41 "
x	Cullity John F	370	U S A	30	41 "
y	Cullity Joseph E	370	storekeeper	28	41 "
z	Cullity Leo	370	laborer	22	41 "

1618

a	Cullity Mary E—†	370	housewife	49	41 "
b	Cullity Thomas P	370	U S A	26	41 "
c	Semonian James	372	machinist	31	36 "
d	Semonian Marian F—†	372	housewife	29	36 "
e	Parker Anna—†	372	tiemaker	35	here
f	*Parker Catherine—†	372	housewife	70	"
g	Parker Mary—†	372	packer	33	"
h	*Parker Richard	372	retired	71	"
k	Doherty James L	372	salesman	33	10 St Martin
l	Doherty Jessie R—†	372	welder	28	10 "
m	Sullivan Joseph F	375	machinist	40	9 Lincoln
n	Connolly Stephen	375	laborer	27	here
o	Mulkern Ann—†	375	housewife	73	"
p	Mulkern Mark	375	clerk	39	"
r	Mulkern Patrick	375	U S A	31	117 High
s	Jesson James	377	checker	31	here
t	Jesson Margaret—†	377	housewife	30	"
u	Smith Daniel	377	laborer	27	"
v	Dowd Mary—†	377	housewife	35	"
w	Dowd Stephen	377	checker	38	"

Page.	Letter.	FULL NAME.	Residence, Jan. 1, 1944.	Occupation.	Supposed Age.	Reported Residence, Jan. 1, 1943. Street and Number.

Bunker Hill Street—Continued

x	Conlon Ann—†	379	housewife	60	here
y	Conlon Mildred—†	379	stenographer	23	"
z	Powers Daniel	379	clerk	39	"
	1619				
A	Powers William	379	salesman	49	"
B	Quinlan Nellie—†	379	housekeeper	72	"
C	Leary Dennis	379	retired	70	"
D	Leary Mary—†	379	housewife	72	"
F	Lafayette Elizabeth—†	381	"	78	
M	Rock John F	389	miller	56	
N	Rock John F, jr	389	electrician	31	"
O	Rock Margaret—†	389	housewife	25	"
P	Rock William T	389	attendant	27	"
R	Ryan Mary E—†	389	cleaner	54	"
S	Ryan Michael J	389	retired	75	"
T	Smith Mary A—†	389	housewife	70	Somerville
U	Powers Helen A—†	389	machinist	35	here
V	Powers Margaret C—†	389	bookkeeper	38	"
W	Powers Nellie—†	389	housewife	72	"
X	Carroll John L	391	electrician	47	"
Y	Carroll Katherine—†	391	housewife	41	"
Z	Moynihan Bartholomew	391	rigger	45	
	1620				
A	Moynihan Elizabeth—†	391	housewife	45	"
B	Belisle Harley	391	electrician	58	"
C	Belisle Rose—†	391	housewife	53	"
D	Young Sarah J—†	391	at home	57	"
E	Burns Helen F—†	393	housewife	35	286 Bunker Hill
F	Burns John J	393	boilermker	34	286 "
G	Stearns Mary T—†	393	defense wkr	61	here
H	Tierney Carrie—†	393	waitress	56	"
K	Tierney John	393	foreman	66	"
L	Manning John	393	clerk	50	
M	Manning John, jr	393	chauffeur	25	"
N	Manning Julia—†	393	housewife	50	"
O	Manning Robert	393	U S A	27	
P	Freeto Elizabeth A—†	395	teacher	63	"
R	Kiley Alice V—†	395	"	55	
S	Kiley Irene E—†	395	"	45	
T	Kiley Mary G—†	395	"	61	
U	Chambers Margaret F—†	399	stenographer	33	"

1

Page.	Letter.	FULL NAME.	Residence, Jan. 1, 1944.	Occupation.	Supposed Age.	Reported Residence, Jan. 1, 1943. Street and Number.

Bunker Hill Street—Continued

v	Flaherty Marian C—†	399	housewife	43	here
w	Flaherty Thomas A	399	commissioner	45	"
x	Hegarty Jeremiah J	399	bookkeeper	44	"
y	Hegarty Marie P—†	399	clerk	41	"
z	O'Brien Katherine T—†	399	"	53	

1621

A	Malone Katherine—†	401	housewife	64	"
B	Malone Mary T—†	401	clerk	31	
C	O'Connell Regina P—†	401	collector	25	"
E	Tobin Ann—†	404	housewife	74	"
F	Tobin Edward P	404	retired	76	
G	Cella John J	404	longshoreman	24	"
H	Cella Margaret R—†	404	housewife	23	"
K	Kenney George E	404	U S M C	22	417 Main
L	Kenney Mary—†	404	housewife	22	370 Bunker Hill
M	Welch Lillian—†	406	"	29	375 "
N	Welch Walter F	406	chauffeur	36	375 "
O	Breslin Frank H	406	agent	55	here
P	Breslin Thomas P	406	laborer	58	"

Chappie Street

s	Hagen Anthony P	2	chauffeur	28	here
t	Hagen Mary E—†	2	housewife	35	"
u	O'Connell Patrick J	2	chauffeur	38	"
v	Whalen Anna J—†	2	housewife	42	"
w	Whalen Francis C	2	chauffeur	41	"
y	Maloney Mary E—†	14	at home	66	"
z	Lindsay Annie S—†	14	housewife	65	"

1622

A	Lindsay James A	14	guard	69	
B	Kurowski Anne L—†	15	housewife	35	"
C	Kurowski Chester	15	laborer	31	
D	Scannell Catherine—†	15	housewife	67	"
E	Quinn John	15	retired	67	528 Medford
F	Quinn Nora—†	15	housewife	67	528 "
G	Arigo Joseph A	17	mechanic	28	here
H	Arigo Louise A—†	17	housewife	31	"
K	O'Hehir Genevieve E—†	17	"	27	Medford
L	O'Hehir Martin M	17	meter reader	34	"

Chappie Street—Continued

M	O'Hehir Mary E—†	17	at home	74	Medford
N	Durham John J	17	retired	65	here
O	Durham Madeline G—†	17	cutter	35	"
P	Durham Mary E—†	17	clerk	25	"
R	O'Leary Daniel F	18	retired	72	
S	O'Leary David	18	laborer	70	"
U	Yasi Martha J—†	19	housewife	38	93 Decatur
V	Yasi William C	19	U S A	48	93 "
W	Michalski Katherine A—†	19	housewife	35	here
X	Swett Etta B—†	19	housekeeper	71	"
Y	Barry Catherine M—†	20	saleswoman	30	"
Z	Barry Julia A—†	20	housekeeper	70	"

1623

A	Broderick Rose T—†	21	at home	70	395 Main
B	Sheehan Catherine T—†	21	housekeeper	65	here
C	Sheehan Elizabeth T—†	21	housewife	34	"
D	Sheehan John P	21	machinist	31	"
E	Coyle Edward E	23	shipfitter	61	"
F	Coyle Elizabeth D—†	23	housewife	60	"
G	Coyle Elizabeth D—†	23	welder	21	..
H	Coyle Mary J—†	23	clerk	26	"
K	Terrio Beatrice A—†	23	housewife	23	172 Heath
L	Terrio John J	23	U S N	25	172 "
M	Bellino Lillian I—†	25	housewife	20	Medford
N	Bellino Samuel L	25	U S A	21	"
O	Collins Patrick J	25	longshoreman	36	here
P	Collins Rita E—†	25	housewife	33	"
R	Collins Francis	25	electrician	30	"
S	Francis Rita M—†.	25	housewife	27	"
V	Parsons Dorothy E—†	39	clerk	23	..
W	*Parsons Rebecca—†	39	at home	61	..
X	Woods Flora M—†	39	housewife	26	"
Y	Woods Paul	39	U S N	30	
Z	Songailo Agata K—†	39	housewife	60	"

1624

A	*Songailo John P	39	retired	70	
B	Songailo William J	39	U S A	33	
C	Saccardo Anna M—†	39	housewife	26	"
D	Saccardo Roger G	39	letter carrier	29	"
G	Serino Angelo J	44	laborer	60	"

15

1

Page;	Letter.	Full Name.	Residence, Jan. 1, 1944.	Occupation.	Supposed Age.	Reported Residence, Jan. 1, 1943. Street and Number.

Chappie Street—Continued

K	Keating Susanna A—†	47	housewife	45	here
L	Keating William F	47	longshoreman	49	"
M	Caldwell Ralph H	47	roofer	38	"
N	Caldwell Theresa F—†	47	housewife	36	"
P	De Lacy Albert O	50	longshoreman	38	"
R	De Lacy Mary E—†	50	housewife	41	"
T	Downey Caroline—†	51	housekeeper	63	"
V	McCarthy John A	51	policeman	30	"
w*	McCarthy Vivian M—†	51	housewife	25	"
Y	DeRosa Joseph A	55	chauffeur	41	1 Albion pl
z	DeRosa Mary L—†	55	housewife	37	1 "

1625

A	Jesson George F	55	retired	65	here
B	Prendible Charles E	55	laborer	31	"
C	Prendible Margaret E—†	55	housewife	29	"
D	McLaughlin Charles J	57	bartender	37	"
E	Riordan Helen A—†	58	housewife	33	"
F	Riordan Joseph R	58	laborer	43	"
G	Muchlada Peter	58	"	55	73 Reading
H	Roulind Anna S—†	58	packer	33	here
K	Roulind Walter	58	chauffeur	34	"
L	Tomkiewicz Gertrude M-†	58	WAC	22	"
M*	Tomkiewicz Sophie—†	58	housewife	50	"
N	Riley Catherine—†	58	packer	45	"
O	Hubert Alma L—† rear	58	housewife	46	California
P	Lyman James W	59	operator	47	Lowell
R	McCabe Edward A	59	laborer	60	here
S	McCabe Marietta E—†	59	housewife	43	"
T	Callahan Josephine B—†	59	housekeeper	78	"
U	Mason Irene A—†	59	stenographer	23	"
V	Mason Ruth M—†	59	"	25	"
w*	Yarasitis Elizabeth T—†	61	housewife	32	"
X	Yarasitis Francis J	61	bartender	33	"
Y	Waitte Charles	61	seaman	34	
z	Waitte Frank B	61	shipper	32	

1626

A	Waitte Mary F—†	61	housewife	27	"
B	Griffin Ethel M—†	63	"	37	
C	Griffin Martin F	63	laborer	38	
E*	Belat Joseph	65	"	59	
F	Muchlada William	65	"	50	

Page.	Letter.	Full Name.	Residence, Jan. 1, 1944.	Occupation.	Supposed Age.	Reported Residence, Jan. 1, 1943. Street and Number.

Chappie Street—Continued

	G	Dame Margaret M—†	66	at home	65	here
	H	Siebert John F	66	baker	50	"
	K	Siebert John F, jr	66	U S A	23	"
	L	Siebert Mary M—†	66	housewife	30	"
	M	Zingarella Henry E	66	welder	23	
	N	Zingarella Madeline V—†	66	checker	22	"
	O	Zingarella Victoria H—†	66	housewife	40	"

Charles Street

	P	Litchfield George	3	boilermaker	51	Michigan
	R	Litchfield Jeannette—†	3	housewife	38	"
	S	McGinley John J	3	electrician	50	295 W Second
	T	Muri Giuseppa—†	3	at home	66	51 Cambridge
	U	*Muri Salvatore	3	retired	66	51 "

Charles Street Place

	V	Johnson Mary J—†	7	at home	46	here
	W	Gifford Emily F—†	9	housekeeper	51	"
	X	Gifford Waldo H	9	custodian	51	"
	Y	Panneton Joseph W	9	carpenter	48	"
	Z	Connolly George	21	clerk	35	37 Rockford av
		1627				
	A	Sullivan Francis	21	"	35	37 "
	B	Concannon John	21	laborer	39	459 Main
	C	Thompson Lucy A—†	21	housewife	55	459 "

Hayes' Block

	E	Murphy William E	1	painter	55	here
	F	Melnick Phillip	1	laborer	57	"
	G	Healey Catherine—†	1	at home	80	"
	K	Gill Blanche E—†	2	"	63	
	L	Sawin Julius C	2	painter	59	"

Kelly's Block

	R	Devine Margaret—†	4	at home	88	here
	S	Levesque Sarah—†	4	maid	45	"
	T	Jordan Isabella—†	6	at home	56	"

2—16   17

1

Page.	Letter.	Full Name.	Residence, Jan. 1, 1944.	Occupation.	Supposed Age.	Reported Residence, Jan. 1, 1943. Street and Number.

Kelly's Block—Continued

u	Jordan Maurice	6	plumber	30	here
v	Jordan William J	6	retired	62	"
w	Shappie Edith E—†	8	at home	34	"
x	Shappie Henry F	8	retired	41	

Main Street

y	Arnaud Augustus	401	laborer	55	here
z	Mills Jane—†	401	at home	26	"
	1628					
a	Williams Edward	401	plumber	43	"
b	Williams Mary—†	401	housewife	38	"
c	Carr Gwendolyn—†	403	"	36	10 Sullivan
d	Carr Kenneth	403	U S A	34	10 "
e	Currus Garland L	403	machinist	34	39 Mead
f	Currus Mildred N—†	403	housewife	26	39 "
g	Stivers John	403	manager	23	Medford
h	Stivers Marian—†	403	housewife	23	"
k	Donovan John	405	laborer	55	here
l	Guy Delia—†	405	housewife	53	"
m	Guy George	405	longshoreman	71	"
n	Houlihan John	405	"	50	Somerville
o	Leonard John	405	laborer	60	here
p	McDonald Robert	405	"	67	65 Main
r	Sullivan Cornelius	405	longshoreman	42	here
s	Sullivan James	405	"	44	"
t	*O'Connell Catherine—†	407	housewife	60	"
u	O'Connell Daniel	407	laborer	37	
v	O'Connell Dennis	407	retired	67	
w	O'Connell Margaret—†	407	supervisor	40	"
x	O'Connell Mary—†	407	clerk	38	
y	O'Connell Nora—†	407	tel operator	35	"
	1629					
a	Curley Peter	409	laborer	40	Lynn
b	Demmerritt Winslow	409	retired	67	here
c	Fitzgerald John	409	cook	45	"
d	Gardner Michael	409	laborer	59	8 E Brookline
e	Hogan John	409	retired	74	16 Sever
f	McKenna Peter	409	"	49	34 Sullivan
g	Murray Thomas	409	"	49	here
h	Roach Annie—†	409	housewife	59	"
k	Roach Harry	409	watchman	60	"

Main Street—Continued

L	Roach Henry	409	laborer	28	here
M	Roach John	409	U S N	22	"
N	Roach Thomas	409	clerk	31	"
O	Aldrich Frank	411	seaman	21	Connecticut
P	Connolly Thomas	411	retired	59	here
R	Daley John J	411	laborer	31	"
S	Doherty Robert F	411	welder	49	"
T	Elms Mary G—†	411	housekeeper	65	"
U	Esterbrook William B	411	retired	68	"
V	Farrasy John	411	laborer	56	"
W	*Morris Ellsworth J	411	retired	67	
X	Lally Mary—†	417	housewife	42	"
Y	Leahy Margaret—†	417	"	49	
Z	Leahy Mary—†	417	packer	24	
	1630				
A	Duffy Daniel F	417	U S N	26	
B	Duffy Frederick G	417	U S A	28	
C	Roust Margaret F—†	417	housewife	52	"
D	Roust Thomas F	417	laborer	47	"
E	Leahy John	419	fireman	69	" .
F	Leahy Margaret—†	419	housewife	70	"
G	Leahy Thomas M	419	U S N	27	
H	Martis Frank C	419	policeman	48	"
K	Martis Josephine M—†	419	housewife	29	"
L	Eldridge Catherine—†	420	housekeeper	41	"
M	MacAdams Frances F–†	420	housewife	45	"
N	MacAdams Harold	420	laborer	49	"
O	Gould Nettie—†	420	housewife	47	"
P	Cummings Anna J—†	421	clerk	27	
R	Cummings William J	421	U S N	28	"
S	Quinlan Dennis F	421	clerk	70	
T	Stack Daniel P	421	yardmaster	56	"
U	Stack Edward T	421	machinist	22	"
V	Stack Florence C—†	421	housewife	48	"
W	Bartlett Annie—†	422	"	75	44 Wash'n
X	Brown Dorothy T—†	422	stenographer	23	here
Y	Brown Marian—†	422	housewife	46	"
Z	Curran Agnes V—†	422	"	45	"
	1631				
A	Curran Coleman	422	longshoreman	50	"
C	Heffron Elizabeth—†	423	housewife	39	"
D	Heffron Francis	423	retired	47	

19

1

Page.	Letter.	FULL NAME.	Residence, Jan. 1, 1944.	Occupation.	Supposed Age.	Reported Residence, Jan. 1, 1943. Street and Number.

Main Street—Continued

E	Heffron Helen—†	423	packer	22	here
F	Heffron Robert	423	U S N	21	"
O	Kepple Catherine G—†	427	housewife	28	"
P	Kepple Joseph K	427	operator	30	"
R	Smith Anderson	427	cleaner	54	
S	Smith Viola F—†	427	housewife	46	"
T	Quinn Mark	427	welder	26	
U	Quinn Rita—†	427	housewife	25	"
	1632				
C	Dowd Beatrice—†	431	"	46	85 School
D	Dowd Peter J	431	U S A	21	85 "
E	Dowd Stephen T	431	"	20	85 "
F	Cavanaugh Alice—†	431	housewife	23	Everett
G	Cavanaugh Robert H	431	U S A	25	"
N	Semonian Goldie—†	435½	housewife	33	here
O	Semonian Harry	435½	laborer	34	"
P	Semonian Mary—†	435½	housewife	65	"
R	Semonian Nazareth—†	435½	storekeeper	72	"
S	Semonian Rose—†	435½	factoryhand	41	"
X	Shea Edward T	441	U S A	32	
Y	Shea Helen V—†	441	housekeeper	34	"
Z	Shea John P	441	retired	69	..
	1633				
A	Shea Richard F	441	U S A	27	
B	Shea William H	441	"	38	
C	Treiber Catherine—†	441	stenographer	29	"
D	Charbonnier Julius P	443	laborer	46	
E	Charbonnier Mary O—†	443	housewife	47	"
F	Harrold Anne—†	443	"	38	
G	Harrold Richard C	443	longshoreman	37	"
H	Charbonnier August P	443	laborer	66	
K	Charbonnier Augustus P	443	clerk	36	
L	Charbonnier Helen—†	443	housewife	23	"
M	Charbonnier Leo F	443	U S A	22	
O	Creaser Anne—†	445	housewife	53	"
P	Creaser Frank	445	machinist	53	"
R	McDonald Donald	445	chauffeur	39	"
S	McDonald Genevieve—†	445	housewife	26	"
T	Kallen Jennie—†	453	"	35	
U	Kallen Peter	453	storekeeper	40	"
V	Polishuk Jennie—†	453	housewife	32	"
W	Polishuk Kuzma	453	contractor	46	"

1634
Main Street—Continued

B	Case Mary—†	457A	housewife	51	here
C	Case Walter	457A	laborer	55	"
F	Ward Delmont	459A	retired	58	"
H	Knott Frank	459A	laborer	46	12 Chappie
L	Sharon Arthur	459A	"	50	here
M	McGowan Edward	459A	retired	71	8 Essex
N	*Clements William	461	laborer	69	Everett
O	Dukeshire Myra E—†	461	housewife	63	5 Sheafe
P	Dukeshire Walter E	461	chauffeur	38	5 "
S	Cameron Catherine—†	463	at home	75	here
V	O'Connor James M	465	U S N	24	"
W	O'Connor Mary E—†	465	housewife	24	"

1635

D	Bonner Catherine—†	475	"	65	"
E	Bonner Patrick	475	watchman	55	"
G	Meilus Stephen	479	laborer	47	"
H	Wolansky John	479	retired	79	

Marshall Block

	Millard Albert	7	machinist	30	here
K	Millard Charles	7	chauffeur	26	"
M	Puleo Stella—†	7	at home	21	"
N	Severino Maria—†	7	"	56	

Marshall Place

P	Serino Annetta—†	2	at home	49	here
R	Serino John	2	custodian	57	"
S	Morang Mary—†	3	at home	58	"
T	Daley Catherine—†	4	"	85	
U	Lappin Elizabeth—†	4	"	70	

Medford Street

W	Curran Elizabeth—†	460	at home	75	here
X	Curran Michael J	460	retired	78	"
Y	D'Alelio Angelina—†	462	at home	30	"
Z	D'Alelio Arthur H	462	U S N	27	

1636

A	D'Alelio Enrico	462	barber	61	"

1

Medford Street—Continued

B	D'Alelio Maria—†	462	at home	62	here
C	Johnston Charles	464	stockman	60	"
D	Johnson Jessie—†	464	at home	60	"
E	Walter Elizabeth—†	464	"	34	
F	Mulkern Mary M—†	466	"	32	..
G	Mulkern Stephen J	466	laborer.	37	
H	Reed Bridget C—†	468	at home	46	"
K	Reed Frank G	468	laborer	48	
L	*Temoshuk Mary—†	468	at home	53	"
M	*Temoshuk Sava	468	laborer	52	
O	Mayberry Frederick W	470	retired	68	
P	Paradis Marie R—†	470	at home	69	"
R	Jerome William	470	laborer	35	
S	Conlon Alice L—†	472	at home	58	"
T	Conlon Michael J	472	retired	71	"
U	Breen Charles	474	laborer	40	55 Chappie
V	Breen Mary—†	474	at home	38	55 "
W	Kosolowski Joseph	474	carpenter	55	here
X	Mellerick James	474	longshoreman	57	"
Y	Mellerick Margaret—†	474	at home	52	"

1637

A	Cavossa Catherine—†	488	"	31	7 Thacher ct
B	Kane Margaret—†	488	"	22	39 Ferrin
C	Morency Adolph	488	retired	70	here
D	Morency Annie M—†	488	at home	67	"
E	Gill Bernard	488	laborer	28	"
F	Gill Margaret—†	488	at home	24	"
G	*Heeney Martin	490	laborer	54	426 Medford
H	Sullivan Mary—†	490	at home	65	426 "
K	Clough James W	490	laborer	43	here
L	Clough Josephine H—†	490	at home	44	"
N	O'Hara Annie E—†	492	"	71	"
O	Hayes Margaret—†	492	"	30	"
P	Canty Florence M—†	492	"	24	38 St Martin
R	Canty James F	492	clerk	24	38 "

North Quincy Place

S	Flanagan Bernard	1	retired	82	here
T	Norton Rose E—†	1	housekeeper	45	"

Page.	Letter.	Full Name.	Residence, Jan. 1, 1944.	Occupation.	Supposed Age.	Reported Residence, Jan. 1, 1943.
						Street and Number.

Saint Martin Street

o	Kelliher Nora—†	2	housewife	48	here	
p	Walsh Joseph	2	U S A	22	"	
r	Walsh Mary—†	2	housewife	20	"	
s	McInnes George	4	shipfitter	43	"	
t	McInnes Helen—†	4	housewife	34	"	
u	Nolette Nola R—†	6	· "	30	"	
v	Nolette Victor	6	metalworker	33	"	
w	Lawler Helen J—†	6	housewife	28	"	
x	Lawler Joseph G	6	supt	24		
y	Leahy John J	6	U S A	21		
z	Leahy Julia T—†	6	operator	26	"	
	1639					
a	Leahy Margaret—†	6	housewife	60	"	
b	Leahy Margaret M—†	6	brazier	25	"	
c	Leahy Michael J	6	guard	54		
d	Leahy Nellie—†	6	at home	67	"	
e	Leahy William P	6	U S A	23		
f	Doherty Catherine—†	8	housewife	39	"	
g	Doherty Dennis F	8	clerk	44	"	
h	Lord George W	8	machinist	31	"	
k	Lord Mary—†	8	housewife	30	"	
l	Conroy Mary L—†	8	"	40		
m	Conroy Patrick J	8	laborer	40	"	
o	Padanon Clara—†	10	welder	36	32 Chestnut	
p	Padanon Flavino	10	U S N	43	32 "	
r	Mayhew George	10	laborer	21	14 Franklin	
s	Mayhew Minnie F—†	10	cashier	56	14 "	
t	Taylor Howard	10	chauffeur	54	14 "	
u	Doherty Gertrude M—†	12	housewife	44	here	
v	Doherty Josephine—†	12	clerk	20	"	
w	Doherty Arthur D	12	U S A	37	"	
x	Doherty Margaret M—†	12	saleswoman	39	"	
y	McCool John	12	retired	65	"	
z	Reilly Anna K—†	12	operator	21	"	
	1640					
a	Reilly Anna M—†	12	housewife	46	"	
b	Reilly William J	12	clerk	51		
c	Keane Mary—†	14	operator	29	"	
d	Keane Nellie A—†	14	clerk	60		
e	Keane William	14	laborer	39	"	

1

Saint Martin Street—Continued

F	Bowen Helen—†	14A	clerk	29	here
G	Bowen Katherine—†	14A	housewife	50	"
H	Bowen Walter	14A	U S N	21	"
K	Murphy Louise—†	14A	clerk	27	
L	Murphy Timothy	14A	U S A	·27	
M	Jacobs Alice—†	14A	housewife	60	"
N	Jacobs Patrick	14A	retired	68	
O	Nash Ellen—†	14A	clerk	30	"
P	Small Annie M—†	16	packer	21	"
R	Small Margaret M—†	16	housewife	56	"
S	Small William J	16	laborer	54	
T	Chardavayne Albert	18	U S A	22	
U	Chardavayne Nora—†	18	housewife	23	"
V	Madden John J	18	steamfitter	51	"
W	Madden Sarah—†	18	housewife	49	"
X	Madden Thomas J	18	longshoreman	29	"
Y	Joyce Blanche–† 2d rear	18	housewife	34	"
Z	Joyce William J 2d "	18	shipfitter	44	"

1641

A	Smith Alexander	28	tester	33	
B	Smith Dorothy M—†	28	housewife	31	"
C	Barringer Helen B—†	28	"	31	
D	Barringer Walter E	28	guard	38	
E	Silva Antonio	28	inspector	66	"
F	Silva Marian F—†	28	attendant	38	"
G	Babcock Mary—†	34	housekeeper	62	"
H	Harrington Josephine L-†	36	accountant	65	"
K	Harrington Thomas F	36	retired	71	"
L	Millerick Eleanor—†	38	housewife	24	82 Walford way
M	Millerick William	38	B F D	26	82 "
O	Galvin Eileen—†	42	housewife	39	458 Medford
P	Galvin Francis	42	laborer	42	458 "
S	Schiavo Joseph A	42	retired	59	here
T	Schiavo Maria—†	42	housewife	38	"
U	Schiavo Silvanio	42	chauffeur	26	"
V	Schiavo Marie A—†	42	housewife	22	"
W	Schiavo Samuel	42	chauffeur	28	"

Wellington Place

Y	Katkin James	6	chauffeur	45	here
Z	Katkin Mary—†	6	housewife	45	"

1

Ward 2–Precinct 17

CITY OF BOSTON

LIST OF RESIDENTS
20 YEARS OF AGE AND OVER

(NON-CITIZENS INDICATED BY ASTERISK)
(FEMALES INDICATED BY DAGGER)

AS OF

JANUARY 1, 1944

THOMAS F. SULLIVAN, *Chairman*
FREDERIC E. DOWLING, *Secretary*
WILLIAM A. MOTLEY, Jr.
FRANCIS B. McKINNEY
EVERETT R. PROUT

Listing Board.

CITY OF BOSTON ⬤ PRINTING DEPARTMENT

1700
Arlington Avenue

H	Horan Jane—†	80	housewife	50	here
K	Horan Thomas	80	laborer	53	"
L	Flynn Mary—†	80	housekeeper	42	"
P	Harrigan Margaret J—†	88	"	70	"
R	Clifford Irene—†	88	student	20	"
S	Clifford Margaret M—†	88	matron	43	

Baldwin Street

X	Motherway Helen N—†	84	housekeeper	41	here
Y	Shea Thomas T	84	electrician	35	"
Z	Connolly Anna C—†	86	marker	24	"

1701

A	Donahue Anna E—†	86	operator	32	"
B	Donahue Helen A—†	86	housewife	48	"
C	Donahue John J	86	chauffeur	51	"
D	Donahue John J, jr	86	U S N	20	"
E	Savage Lawrence H	86	laborer	43	29 Mt Vernon
F	Savage Patrick J	86	inspector	45	here
G	Sheehan David J	86	policeman	47	"
H	Sheehan Sarah J—†	86	housewife	48	"
K	Skane Edward D	86	U S M C	22	"
L	Skane Edward J	86	laborer	48	
M	Brown Margaret M—†	88	teacher	33	
N	Brown Thomas F	88	retired	79	
O	O'Brien Catherine F—†	90	housewife	38	"
P	O'Brien Leo F	90	U S C G	44	"
R	Malone John J	90	teacher	34	
S	O'Brien Catherine B—†	90	housewife	34	"
T	Kilfoyle Mary—†	92	at home	71	"
U	Kilfoyle Sarah—†	92	housekeeper	65	"
V	Kiely Bartholomew	94	U S C G	38	"
W	Kiely Gertrude—†	94	housewife	38	"
X	D'Arolio Dominick	94	welder	25	"
Y	D'Arolio Elizabeth—†	94	housewife	24	"
Z	Murphy Anna—†	96	"	46	

1702

A	Murphy Thomas	96	laborer	48	"
B	Connolly Hannah—†	96	housekeeper	61	"
C	Crowley Jeremiah J	98	clerk	47	"
D	Crowley Mary J—†	98	housewife	42	"

2

Baldwin Street—Continued

E	Gallagher Mary E—†	98	bookbinder	66	57 Decatur
F	Ducey Catherine A—†	100	clerk	25	here
G	Ducey Leo E	100	salesman	53	"
H	Ducey Leo E, jr	100	U S A	23	"
K	Ducey Mary C—†	100	housewife	50	"
L	Boland Mary —† rear	100	"	70	
M	Boland William H "	100	retired	74	
N	Elliot Edward T "	100	policeman	39	"
O	Elliot Mary G—† "	100	housewife	42	"
P	Queenan Gertrude M-† "	100	packer	22	
R	Long Alice—†	102	housewife	36	"
S	Long Daniel	102	letter carrier	38	"
T	Long John	102	U S A	26	
U	Nelson Helen—†	102	housewife	37	"
V	Nelson Howard	102	shipper	46	..
W	Salmon May—†	102	housewife	39	"
X	Bandy Helen—†	104	"	20	
Y	Bandy Owen L	104	U S N	25	
Z	McMakin Francis J	104	"	22	

1703

A	McMakin Frank	104	retired	51	
B	McMakin Margaret E-†	104	housewife	49	"
D	Mainey Dennis	106	U S A	23	
E	Mainey Frank	106	retired	55	"
F	Mainey Mary—†	106	housewife	54	"
G	Mainey Thomas	106	U S N	21	
H	Mainey William	106	laborer	31	
K	McColgan Dennis	106	retired	78	
L	Mulkern Ann—†	106	packer	29	
M	Mulkern Patrick	106	U S A	31	
N	Thompson Caroline—†	106	inspector	22	"
R	Riordon Mary—†	110	housewife	72	"
S	McCarthy Catherine B-†	112	"	45	
T	Bailey Margaret N—†	112	"	41	
U	Burke Alexander P	114	U S A	21	
V	Burke Mary—†	114	housewife	49	"

Beach Street

Z	*Marafsky Alexander	13	mechanic	50	here

1704

A	*Sadolsky Domenic	13	laborer	55	

Beach Street—Continued

B	*Kanofsky Helen—†	13	housewife	60	here	
c	Kanofsky John	13	laborer	24	"	
D	Kanofsky Joseph	13	"	28	"	
E	Kanofsky Phillip	13	chauffeur	37	"	
F	Furdeck Helen—†	13	housewife	32	"	
G	Furdeck William	13	butcher	34	"	
H	*Sargelis Alexander	15	retired	57		
K	*Rahrickey Catherine—†	15	housewife	63	"	
L	*Rahrickey Joseph	15	retired	64	"	
M	*Rodack Harry	15	laborer	46		
P	*Dabelsky Michael	17	retired	70		
R	Shilzewick Anthony	17	U S A	31		
s	*Shilzewick Charles	17	stableman	70	"	
T	Shilzewick Francis	17	U S A	27		
U	*Shilzewick Mary—†	17	housewife	60	"	
v	Shilzewick Mary—†	17	at home	23	"	
w	*Szweda Alexander	17	retired	59		

1705

A	Sadofsky Frances—†	19	packer	21		
B	*Sadofsky Sophia—†	19	housewife	51	"	
c	*Trochuk Trofin	19	laborer	60		
D	McCarthy Ann—†	20	operator	26	"	
E	*Dykon Harry	20	laborer	61	"	
F	Tyminski Annette—†	20	housewife	30	New York	
G	Tyminski Anthony	20	chauffeur	28	"	
H	*Grenda Bernard	20	retired	65	here	
L	Hutchins Harold	21	U S A	30	"	
M	Hutchins Isabelle—†	21	housewife	27	"	
N	Milley Harold	21	laborer	25		
O	Milley Helen—†	21	housewife	23	"	
R	Foss Catherine—†	22	"	27	17 Beach	
s	Foss Chandler	22	laborer	35	17 "	
T	Blakely Helen—†	22	packer	27	here	
U	*Blakely Mary—†	22	housewife	57	"	
w	Poleatewich Mary—†	23	"	35	"	
x	*Koslosky Anne—†	23	"	35		
Y	Koslosky Victoria—†	23	packer	25		
z	*Mack William	24	junk dealer	50	"	

1706

A	*Skavinki Nellie—†	24	housekeeper	53	"	
B	*Smith Julia—†	24	housewife	50	"	

Beach Street—Continued

c	*Smith Michael	24	baker	49	here
d	Chitrofsky Francis	24	laborer	28	"
e	*Chitrofsky James	24	"	65	"
f	*Chitrofsky Sophia—†	24	housewife	60	"

Brighton Street

h	Siggins Margaret—†	4	housekeeper	82	here
k	Tanner Henry	4	policeman	45	"
l	Tanner Mary—†	4	housewife	47	"
m	Burke Catherine—†	4	housekeeper	72	"
n	Burke Mary—†	4	social worker	36	"
o	McCabe Mary—†	4	housekeeper	60	"
p	McCabe Myles	4	U S A	30	..
r	Leet Jane—†	6	housekeeper	72	"
s	Trayers Alice M—†	6	housewife	31	11 Coniston rd
t	Trayers Anna B—†	6	"	70	here
u	Trayers Farrell B	6	U S A	33	11 Coniston rd
w	McNeely John J	8	engineer	63	here
x	McNeely Mary F—†	8	housewife	54	"
y	Sullivan Anna F—†	8	operator	31	" .
z	Sullivan Daniel	8	U S A	27	

1707

a	Sullivan Julia T—†	8	clerk	36	
b	Sullivan Margaret M—†	8	housewife	66	"
c	Sullivan Mildred R—†	8	"	24	
e	Crowley Daniel J	10	laborer	37	
f	Crowley Marion S—†	10	housewife	36	"
g	Ryan Alice M—†	10	"	33	
h	Ryan James H	10	pipefitter	49	"
k	Elio Anna—†	11	operator	24	"
l	Elio Antonette—†	11	housewife	56	"
m	Elio Josephine—†	11	operator	24	"
n	Elio Carmen	11	chauffeur	34	"
o	Elio Helen M—†	11	housewife	33	"
p	Smedberg Earl	11	fireman	26	
r	Smedberg Grace—†	11	housewife	27	"
t	Fitzgerald Cecilia—†	12	"	66	
u	Carter Doris—†	13	"	25	
v	Carter John J	13	mechanic	30	"
w	Nolan Alice K—†	13	housewife	44	"

Brighton Street—Continued

x	Nolan Grace A—†	13	electrician	22	here
y	Nolan Joseph H	13	chauffeur	47	"
z	Nolan Joseph H, jr	13	U S A	21	"
	1708				
a	Nolan Margaret J—†	13	operator	23	"
b	Benkert Arthur	13	guard	38	
c	Benkert Helen—†	13	housewife	34	"
d	Gould Anna—†	14	housekeeper	62	"
e	Pyne Edward	14	bartender	41	"
f	Pyne Mary—†	14	housewife	35	"
g	*Cadigan Josephine—†	15	"	31	76 Tremont
h	Cadigan Timothy	15	rigger	35	76 "
k	Hogan Frank B	15	painter	60	here
l	Hogan Harriet M—†	15	housewife	54	"
m	Meara Catherine—†	15	housekeeper	44	"
n	Ahern Jeremiah E	16	rigger	52	,,
o	Ahern Joseph E	16	U S N	24	"
p	Ahern William F	16	painter	61	
r	Maguire Francis E	16	U S N	30	
s	Maguire Helen E—†	16	housewife	26	"
t	Costello John J	16	U S A	25	
u	Costello Margaret—†	16	housewife	67	"
v	Costello Martin F	16	electrician	33	"
w	Shea John F	16	chauffeur	41	"
x	Shea Mary M—†	16	housewife	-35	"
y	Fontaine George	17	machinist	44	"
z	Fontaine Pearl—†	17	clerk	22	
	1709				
a	Beals Arthur W	17	chauffeur	34	35 Chelsea
b	Beals Lillian L—†	17	housewife	32	35 "
c	Rochefort Mary—†	19	"	32	here
d	Rochefort Walter H	19	chauffeur	32	"
f	McGlinchey William	20	laborer	50	Medford
g	Quigley Harry	20	machinist	65	"
h	Brush Carroll	20	clerk	23	here
k	Brush Julia—†	20	housewife	50	"
m	Strasser Charles	21	U S N	21	"
n	Strasser Frederick	21	engineer	55	"
o	Strasser Frederick	21	seaman	26	
p	Strasser Herbert	21	U S A	22	
r	Strasser Paul	21	seaman	25	

Page.	Letter.	FULL NAME.	Residence, Jan. 1, 1944.	Occupation.	Supposed Age.	Reported Residence, Jan. 1, 1943. Street and Number.

Brighton Street—Continued

	s	Strasser Rita—†	21	housewife	55	here
	t	Meehan Catherine—†	22	"	59	"
	u	Meehan Elizabeth—†	22	nurse	24	"
	v	Meehan James M	22	U S N	26	
	w	Meehan John	22	"	28	
	x	Meehan Marjorie—†	22	housewife	28	"
	y	Riley Charles	22	machinist	59	"
	z	Cullity Barbara—†	23	housewife	37	"
1710						
	a	Cullity Daniel F	23	shipfitter	33	"
	b	Cullity Marie E—†	23	teacher	36	"
	c	Cullity Nora—†	23	housekeeper	64	"
	d	Burns Lawrence E	24	retired	68	"
	e	Burns Mary F—†	24	housewife	70	"
	f	Sammon Catherine M—†	25	"	40	
	g	Sammon John F	25	chauffeur	41	"
	m	Grimes Delia—†	28	housewife	66	"
	n	Grimes Margaret B—†	28	clerk	32	
	o	Grimes Patrick	28	fireman	66	"
	r	Hallihan Mabel T—†	29	clerk	27	"
	s	Hallihan Sadie E—†	29	"	21	
	t	Hallihan Thomas	29	U S A	22	
	u	Price Margaret M—†	29	at home	32	"
	v	Comeau William A	31	carpenter	53	"
	w	Sullivan Charles F	31	mechanic	44	"
	x	*Sullivan Mary E—†	31	housewife	49	"
	y	*Jodrey Nellie—†	31	"	52	
	z	Jodrey William C	31	laborer	26	"
1711						
	a	Butler Elizabeth M—†	33	housewife	53	"
	b	Butler John J	33	chauffeur	25	"
	c	Butler Oliver, jr	33	laborer	57	
	e	Lordan D Joseph	35	teller	40	
	f	Lordan Edna J—†	35	housewife	38	"
	g	Shea John W	35	printer	39	
	h	Ford John P	37	electrician	36	"
	k	Ford Marion E—†	37	housewife	32	"
	l	Ford John J	37	retired	70	
	m	Leavitt Frederick	39	painter	46	
	n	Leavitt Hester—†	39	clerk	20	
	o	Leavitt Lillian M—†	39	housewife	47	"

Page.	Letter.	FULL NAME.	Residence, Jan. 1, 1944.	Occupation.	Supposed Age.	Reported Residence, Jan. 1, 1943. Street and Number.

Brighton Street—Continued

	P	Young Charles N	41	carpenter	51	here
	R	Young Grace E—†	41	housewife	44	"
	S	Murphy Catherine—†	43	housekeeper	63	"
	T	Murphy Edward F	43	chauffeur	26	"
	U	Murphy Eileen M—†	43	accountant	40	"
	V	Murphy Katherine A—†	43	clerk	32	
	W	Murphy Patricia B—†	43	"	23	"
	X	Sullivan Cecelia A—†	43	housewife	29	Somerville
	Y	Hardy Florence M—†	71	at home	63	here
	Z	Stearns Lillian E—†	71	"	62	"
		1712				
	A	Lansil Minnie G—†	71	housekeeper	61	"

Bunker Hill Street

	B	Murphy Mary E—†	411	housewife	41	here
	C	Murphy Richard J	411	estimator	44	"
	E	Collins James T	413	accountant	61	"
	F	Fitzgerald Edward T	413	clerk	42	
	G	Waters John A	413	salesman	61	"
	H	McGonagle John	413	plumber	28	"
	K	McGonagle Rita—†	413	housewife	27	"
	L	Sullivan John M	413	retired	67	
	M	Sullivan Julia A—†	413	housewife	63	"
	N	Sullivan Julia T—†	413	bookkeeper	33	"
	O	Crowley Margaret F—†	415	housewife	66	"
	P	Hurley Catherine F—†	415	stenographer	29	"
	R	Hurley Jerome	415	retired	69	"
	S	Hurley Margaret M—†	415	stenographer	26	"
	T	Hurley Mary A—†	415	"	28	"
	U	Flanigan Katherine L—†	417	at home	51	"
	V	Flanigan Loretta G—†	417	secretary	56	"
	W	Flanigan Mary E—†	417	musician	58	"
	Y	McGuinness Eleanor P-†	423	clerk	22	
	Z	McGuinness John P	423	foreman	51	"
		1713				
	A	McGuinness Louise P—†	423	wrapper	27	"
	B	McGuinness Mary L—†	423	housewife	46	"
	C	Colgan Thomas B	423	retired	70	
	D	McElhinney Josephine A—†	423	housewife	44	"

Bunker Hill Street—Continued

E	Driscoll Margaret M—†	423	housekeeper	64	here
F	Driscoll Mary E—†	423	"	54	"
G	Smith Louise A—†	423	housewife	60	"
H	Walsh Frederick C	425	guard	28	
K	Walsh Margaret—†	425	housewife	26	"
L	Gordon Annie—†	425	"	52	"
M	Gordon Sarah J—†	425	clerk	22	"
N	Gordon William J	425	operator	56	"
O	Dolan John T	426	shipfitter	27	"
P	Dolan Mary J—†	426	housewife	30	"
R	O'Leary Ella M—†	426	teacher	35	"
S	O'Leary Jeremiah J	426	retired	66	
T	O'Leary Margaret A—†	426	teacher	28	"
U	Apel Frederick W	427	repairman	41	"
V	Apel Mary E—†	427	housewife	41	"
W	O'Connor Charles	427	laborer	24	
X	O'Connor Jennie—†	427	boxmaker	25	"
Y	O'Connor Nora—†	427	housekeeper	42	"

1714

A	Summerhayes Estelle—†	428	"	63	"
B	Welch Ethel—†	428	housewife	59	"
C	Welch William F	428	gatetender	75	"
E	Ellis Delia—†	429	housewife	48	"
F	*Ellis William	429	laborer	48	"
G	Caddigan Bridget E—†	429	housewife	71	"
H	Caddigan George H	429	ropemaker	45	"
K	Caddigan John F	429	inspector	40	"
L	O'Brien Mary M—†	429	housewife	37	"
M	O'Brien Timothy J	429	shipfitter	41	"
N	Cotter Elizabeth K—†	429	housewife	35	"
O	Cotter James P	429	kitchenman	37	"
P	Holland Rose—†	430	housewife	74	11 Allston
R	*Dowd Francis J	430	laborer	46	4 Avon pl
S	*Dowd Hannah—†	430	housewife	45	4 "
T	*Dowd Mary E—†	430	clerk	22	4 "
U	Dowd Stephen J	430	U S A	20	4 "
V	Coveney Edward	431	painter	33	here
W	Coveney Matthew	431	laborer	76	433 Bunker Hill
X	Norris John M	431	inspector	34	here
Y	Norris Marion A—†	431	housewife	34	"

Bunker Hill Street—Continued

z	Norris Edward	431	coppersmith	25	here
	1715				
A	Norris James	431	clerk	39	
B	Norris Mary—†	431	housewife	69	"
C	Norris Michael	431	retired	77	"
D	Norris William P	431	blueprints	41	"
E	Monahan Margaret—†	432	housekeeper	69	"
G	Doherty Bernard	433	chauffeur	39	"
H	Doherty Catherine—†	433	housewife	40	"
K	Smith Anastasia—†	433	"	62	
L	Smith Annie—†	433	clerk	37	"
M	*Smith John	433	storekeeper	74	"
N	Fama Frank	433	barber	55	
O	Fama Genevieve—†	433	candy packer	21	"
P	Fama Margaret—†	433	housewife	49	"
R	Fama Maurice	433	laborer	30	
S	Fama Frances—†	433	shoeworker	24	"
T	Fama Joseph	433	U S A	26	
U	Crowley Julia M—†	434	housekeeper	60	"
V	Crowley Maria T—†	434	housewife	69	"
W	Crowley Nellie J—†	434	storekeeper	51	"
X	Crowley Nora T—†	434	"	53	"
Y	Crowley Patrick	434	retired	72	
Z	McCarthy Francis P	436	mechanic	33	"
	1716				
A	McCarthy Margaret J-†	436	housekeeper	70	"
B	Needham Eileen M—†	436	stenographer	36	"
C	McGeouch Elizabeth F-†	438	housewife	85	"
D	McGeough Robert C	438	U S C G	47	"
E	Upton Harriet I—†	438	housewife	24	"
F	Upton John F	438	U S A	30	
H	Quill Catherine—†	441	housekeeper	69	"
K	Quill Margaret—†	441	"	64	"
L	Jordan Elizabeth—†	441	clerk	43	
M	Jennings Hazel F—†	441	housewife	43	"
N	Jennings Mary R—†	441	housekeeper	24	"
O	Jennings William J	441	clerk	50	"
P	O'Brien James J	441	shipfitter	47	"
R	Finn Catherine C—†	443	housewife	35	"
S	Finn Leo T	443	B F D	32	"
T	Hewitt Ellen—†	443	housewife	70	503 Main

Bunker Hill Street—Continued

u	Hewitt Richard J	443	retired	68	503 Main
v	Reilly Mary V—†	443	housekeeper	42	here
y	Carron Daniel M	447	laborer	64	"
w	Kumbatovic Catherine—†	447	housewife	44	"
x	Kumbatovic Nicholas	447	laborer	54	..
z	Olson Elmer	458	shoeworker	32	"

1717

a	Olson Mary—†	458	housewife	29	"
b	Sprague Catherine—†	458	"	28	
c	Sprague Francis	458	welder	28	"
d	Veino Catherine—†	458	housewife	46	"
e	Veino Earl E	458	welder	46	
f	Veino Edward E	458	U S A	21	
g	Chamberlain Benjamin R	458	retired	70	
h	Chamberlain Florence M—†	458	housewife	60	"
k	Monahan James	458	guard	53	
l	Monahan Josephine—†	458	dietitian	50	"
m	Sullivan John F	458	welder	34	
n	Sullivan Margaret—†	458	housewife	39	"

Caldwell Street

o	Dempsey Raymond	1	waiter	41	here
p	Laduc Flora—†	1	waitress	35	"
r	Laduc Thomas	1	foreman	43	"
s	Marchand Lillian—†	1	waitress	26	"
v	Sullivan Elizabeth—†	3	at home	75	"
w	Durkin Catherine—†	3	housewife	42	"
x	*Durkin Joseph	3	machinist	42	"
y	MacDonald Catherine—†	3	housewife	52	"
z	MacDonald Julia—†	3	operator	20	"

1718

b	Ramsay George	4	U S A	37	
c	Ramsay Lillian—†	4	housewife	30	"
d	Belyea Arthur	5	printer	55	
e	Belyea Edith—†	5	housewife	50	"
f	Corkum Muriel—†	5	"	39	
g	Harkins John	5	longshoreman	28	"
h	Harkins Rita—†	5.	housewife	28	"
k	Avallone Carolyn—†	6	clerk	20	
l	Avallone Mary—†	6	housewife	55	"

Page.	Letter.	FULL NAME.	Residence, Jan. 1, 1944.	Occupation.	Supposed Age.	Reported Residence, Jan. 1, 1943. Street and Number.

Caldwell Street—Continued

M	*Kravitz Minnie—†	7	housekeeper	36	here
N	*Shutti Andrew	7	laborer	64	"
O	Cole Florence—†	7	housewife	24	"
P	Cole Jesse	7	clerk	25	
R	Baressi Agrippino	7	"	26	
S	Baressi Angelina—†	7	housewife	25	"
T	O'Donnell Hugh	7½	cook	49	94 Queensberry
U	O'Donnell Rose—†	7½	housewife	56	94 "
W	Banks Mary—†	7½	"	53	here
X	Banks Michael G	7½	laborer	25	"
Y	Banks Samuel	7½	mechanic	31	"
Z	Banks William	7½	U S M C	21	"

1719

A	Phillips Blanche—†	13	housewife	36	"
B	Phillips Matthew	13	barber	39	
D	Goodwin Margaret—†	23	defense wkr	48	"
E	Goodwin Ruth—†	23	"	20	
F	DeRoche Florence—†	23	at home	69	"
G	Langille Wellman	23	retired	60	
H	Poirier Ida—†	23	at home	65	"
K	Mahoney Catherine—†	25	housewife	58	"
L	Mahoney Daniel	25	laborer	63	

Cambridge Street

P	Maffa Paul	33	barber	51	here
R	Maffa Pauline—†	33	stitcher	21	"
S	Maffa Rose—†	33	housewife	44	"
T	Sutton Frank A	35	laborer	65	
U	Sutton Richard	35	U S N	21	"
V	Ford Daniel	35	shipfitter	38	Somerville
W	French Elsie—†	35	housewife	31	"
X	French William	35	seaman	33	"
Y	Moore Mary—†	35	housewife	51	here
Z	Moore Mary M—†	35	packer	20	"

1720

A	Darling Henry A	37	shipper	41	
B	Darling Mary—†	37	housewife	35	"
C	Salvato Antoinette M—†	37	"	44	
D	Salvato Domenic	37	laborer	57	"
E	Salvato Candeloro	37	U S A	21	

Cambridge Street—Continued

F	Salvato Francis J	37	U S A	24	here
H	O'Leary Ellen—†	39	housewife	62	6 Kingston
K	O'Leary John F	39	retired	72	6 "
L	O'Leary Margaret—†	39	clerk	23	here
M	*Maffa Pauline—†	39	at home	73	"
N	Ruggieri Mary—†	39	housewife	33	"
O	Ruggieri Michael	39	clerk	38	"
P	Sanseverino James	41	operator	26	7 Holden row
R	Sanseverino Mary—†	41	housewife	27	7 "
S	Libby Alma—†	41	"	28	58 Polk
T	Libby Edward	41	machinist	29	58 "
U	Gillis Anne—†	41	housewife	60	here
V	Denehy John W	43	watchman	60	"
W	Sullivan Mary T—†	43	packer	50	"
X	Carolan Catherine V—†	43	tel operator	48	"
Y	Denehy John F	43	U S N	26	
Z	Denehy Ruth T—†	43	stenographer	30	"

1721

A	Sullivan Ellen M—†	43	at home	52	"
C	O'Neil Charles	47	longshoreman	49	"
D	O'Neil Ruby F—†	47	housewife	45	"
E	St Claire Harold A	47	U S A	26	
F	St Claire Rose M—†	47	housewife	24	"
G	Sullivan William F	47	laborer	26	
H	Peritzian Dorice A—†	47	at home	20	"
K	Peritzian Estelle—†	47	housewife	49	"
L	Peritzian John	47	machinist	47	"
M	Salvato Anna—†	47	housewife	40	"
N	Salvato Nunziato	47	machinist	45	"
O	Guilfoyle Frank W	47	longshoreman	37	"
P	Guilfoyle Margaret—†	47	housewife	36	"
T	*Kalosky Elizabeth—†	49	"	66	
U	Kalosky Leo	49	laborer	30	
V	Kalosky Thomas	49	shipper	30	
W	Kalosky William	49	laborer	59	
X	Kalosky William	49	U S A	34	"
Z	Gilman Arlene—†	51	housewife	31	7 Holden row

1722

A	Gilman Charles T	51	laborer	41	7 "
C	Gehan Charles	83	"	40	here
D	Gehan Louise—†	83	housewife	40	"

Cambridge Street—Continued

E	Harrington Nora—†	83	housewife	35	here
F	Harrington Patrick	83	clerk	36	"
G	Whalen Margaret M—†	83	housewife	55	"
H	Whalen Parrick J	83	foreman	55	"
K	Whalen Thomas E	83	U S A	27	
M	Duddy Helen—†	85	waitress	35	"
N	Duddy John	85	U S A	45	"
O	Byrnes Harold	85	machinist	45	Somerville
P	Byrnes Hester—†	85	housewife	30	"
S	Brady Catherine M—†	87	"	66	here
T	Brady Francis J	87	welder	38	"
U	Brady Henry L	87	salesman	31	"
V	Denehy Anna R—†	87	clerk	34	
Z	Bonanno Joseph	109	proprietor	60	"
	1723				
A	Bonanno Joseph, jr	109	U S A	21	"
B	Morris Gertrude—†	109	housewife	36	"
C	Morris Walter	109	chauffeur	38	"
G	Watson Alexander	115	millwright	32	"
H	Watson Eva—†	115	housewife	31	"
L	Vocino Gertrude—†	117	"	32	78 Wash'n
R	McCann Mary—†	135	"	26	here
S	McCann William F	135	U S A	26	"
T	Ogden Beatrice—†	135	housewife	32	Somerville
U	Ogden Jesse	135	dyesetter	37	"

Carter Street

X	McDonald Waldo E	2	laborer	51	here
Y	Reale Pasquale	2	manager	54	"
Z	Sweeney Charlotte—†	2	housekeeper	79	"
	1724				
A	Blute Dorothy M—†	9	waitress	31	"
B	Durante Louis	9	laborer	38	Medford
C	Galego Manuel	9	"	44	Somerville
D	Haranak John	9	carpenter	34	here
E	Hinde Albert	9	retired	70	"
F	Witchel Fred	9	laborer	23	Somerville
G	Crowley Gladys—†	11	clerk	38	"
H	Wilmot Annie—†	11	housekeeper	57	"
K	Hyland Frank J	13	shipper	56	here
L	Hyland Hazel M—†	13	matron	44	"

Page.	Letter.	FULL NAME.	Residence, Jan. 1, 1944.	Occupation.	Supposed Age.	Reported Residence Jan. 1, 1943. Street and Number.

Charles Street

	o	Laughlin Gertrude—†	14	hostess	50	here
	p	Lynch Charles	14	U S N	32	"
	r	Shannon Alice—†	14	housekeeper	58	"
	s	Sodergren Ada—†	16	housewife	48	"

Clinton Place

	t	Banfield Mary J—†	5	housekeeper	59	here
	u	Richards Anna A—†	6	mechanic	22	"
	v	Richards Dorothy A—†	6	supervisor	26	"
	w	Richards James E	6	chauffeur	24	"
	x	Richards Mary C—†	6	housewife	54	"
	y	Richards Shirley I	6	laborer	54	..
	z	Haggerty Margaret—†	8	secretary	24	"
		1725				
	a	Killoran Helen P—†	8	clerk	22	
	b	Whelan Delia—†	8	housewife	47	"
	c	Whelan Joseph P	8	U S A	21	
	d	Whelan Thomas J	8	porter	53	
	e	Whelan Thomas J	8	U S N	23	"

Crescent Street

	f	Micco Albert E	11	chauffeur	29	133 Cambridge
	g	Micco Marie C—†	11	housewife	24	133 "
	h	Nardone Benedict F	11	U S A	23	here
	k	Nardone Frank B	11	janitor	51	"
	l	Nardone Mary G—†	11	housewife	46	"
	m	Duddy Arthur	35	U S A	22	
	n	Duddy Elizabeth J—†	35	housewife	41	"
	o	Duddy William J	35	pipefitter	48	"
	p	Champion Andrew	43	U S N	37	"
	r	Champion Dora—†	43	housewife	32	N Hampshire
	s	Costello John	43	salesman	34	here
	t	Hughes Rose H—†	43	housewife	42	Somerville
	u	Platt Robert E	43	U S A	23	Pennsylvania

Dorrance Street

	v	Barris Walter J	8	lumber dealer	65	here
	y	*Collins Amanda—†	14	housewife	82	"
	z	*Collins Samuel	14	retired	74	"

15

1726
Dorrance Street—Continued

A	McKenna Mary—†	14	waitress	28	here
B	Gillis Anna T—†	14A	housewife	21	Somerville
C	Gillis Neil W	14A	U S C G	25	"
H	Larrabee Ernest J	30	stripper	24	here
K	Larrabee Estella—†	30	housewife	65	"
L	Krichmar Marcus	30	proprietor	44	"
M	*Krichmar Pauline—†	30	housewife	42	"

Gardner Street

S	Allie Jeffrey F	1	chauffeur	49	here
T	Allie Mary R—†	1	housewife	52	"
U	Corwin Charlotte E—†	5	"	28	"
V	Corwin Marcy	5	B F D	29	"
W	Bassett Alice—†	5	housewife	50	Cambridge
X	Bassett Chester	5	conductor	49	"

1727 Haverhill Street

A	Harrington Charles J	1	U S N	35	here
B	Harrington Margaret—†	1	housekeeper	68	"
C	Murphy Hannah—†	1	housewife	41	"
D	Murphy Patrick	1	laborer	42	
H	Coffey Miller	3	"	22	
K	Lehan Thomas	3	"	60	
L	McGill David J	3	"	65	
M	McGill Josephine—†	3	housewife	70	"
N	Whittier Joseph C	3	laborer	44	"
P	Flynn Elizabeth—†	5	housewife	31	7 Haverhill
R	Flynn Gertrude—†	5	operator	35	7 "
S	Flynn James	5	clerk	32	7 "
T	Flynn Joseph	5	"	38	7 '
U	Flynn Mary—†	5	housekeeper	42	7 "
V	Appleby George L	5	metalworker	41	here
W	Appleby Ira M	5	baker	61	"

1728

A	Collings Mary—†	7	housewife	74	447 Main
B	DeCarlos Catherine—†	7	"	34	here
C	DeCarlos John C	7	inspector	43	"
D	Colman Helen—†	7	housewife	27	"

16

Haverhill Street—Continued

E	Colman Joseph A	7	operator	31	here
G	O'Connell John E	8	U S A	21	"
H	O'Connell Margaret E—†	8	weaver	22	"
K	O'Connell Michael J	8	laborer	50	
L	Connolly Catherine—†	9	housewife	43	"
M	Connolly Eleanor—†	9	WAVE	20	..
N	Connolly William D	9	U S A	23	"
O	McCune Herbert M	9	laborer	35	Honolulu
P	Finn John T	10	checker	34	here
R	Finn Veronica B—†	10	housewife	31	"
S	Crawford Anna M—†	12	operator	21	"
T	Crawford James A	12	chauffeur	52	"
U	Crawford Margaret M—†	12	housewife	50	"
Y	Gilmartin John J	14	drawtender	52	"
Z	Walker John J	14	laborer	48	

1729

A	Walker Mary M—†	14	housekeeper	45	"
B	Coffey James	16	retired	71	..
C	Dolan Catherine S—†	16	housewife	52	"
D	Dolan Frederick	16	U S A	36	
E	Dolan Thomas F	16	U S C G	59	"
F	Hood Andrew	16	retired	70	
G	O'Donnell Bernard T	16	chauffeur	42	"
H	O'Donnell Bernard T, jr	16	U S A	21	
K	O'Donnell Hugh R	16	U S C G	20	"
L	O'Donnell Margaret—†	16	housewife	41	"
M	Mulvey James H	18	electrician	35	"
N	Mulvey John F	18	salesman	39	"
O	Mulvey Thomas B	18	U S A	29	
P	Collins Cornelius J	20	U S N	30	"
R	Collins Patrick J	20	janitor	62	
S	Fehiley Annie T—†	20	housewife	55	"
T	Fehiley Hannah H—†	20	waitress	58	"
V	Smith David	24	janitor	56	
W	Smith Eliza—†	24	housewife	55	"
X	Smith Josephine E—†	24	teller	25	
Y	Smith Lillian—†	24	stenographer	24	"
Z	O'Brien Charles	26	janitor	46	"

1730

A	O'Brien Mary—†	26	housewife	37	"
C	Delorey Ellen A—†	30	housekeeper	59	"

2—17

Haverhill Street—Continued

D	Kelly Anastasia—†	30	cleaner	56	here
F	Stella Jesse	32	chauffeur	41	Everett
G	Wakely Helen—†	32	waitress	43	"
H	Hanson Jessie—†	32	housewife	75	here
K	Hanson William	32	retired	89	"
M	Mehigan Helen C—†	34	housewife	32	"
N	Mehigan Patrick	34	operator	39	"
P	Devine Mary—†	34	housewife	48	"
R	Devine William	34	paperhanger	52	"
S	Martin Mary—†	36	housewife	71	"
T	Martin William S	36	retired	76	
U	Collins Lillian M—†	36	housekeeper	35	"
V	Lanagan Arthur	36	U S A	25	..
W	Lanagan Francis J	36	"	28	
X	Lanagan Herbert H	36	"	38	
Y	Lanagan Joseph F	36	laborer	40	
Z	Lanagan Rita G—†	36	textileworker	23	"

1731

B	Williams Charles F	38	pipefitter	50	"
C	Williams Sarah G—†	38	housewife	48	"
D	Brennan Mary E—†	38	"	44	
F	Coghlan Sarah—†	40	housekeeper	68	"
G	Greeley Edna H—†	40	bookkeeper	34	"
H	McNeely Edward N	40	metalworker	30	"
K	McNeely James	40	retired	70	
L	McNeely Mary E—†	40	bookkeeper	36	"

Hillside Place

M	Crummet Walter	1	engineer	63	here
N	MacInnis Margaret—†	1	matron	66	"
O	Regan Catherine—†	1	housekeeper	71	"
P	Regan Daniel	1	laborer	33	"
R	Harkins Delia—†	2	housekeeper	65	90 School
S	McLaughlin Ellen—†	2	housewife	66	here
T	McLaughlin John	2	retired	66	"
U	Lowe Allison	2	laborer	55	"
V	McGovern Annie—†	3	housekeeper	69	"
W	McNamara Charlotte—†	3	housewife	64	"
X	McNamara Elizabeth—†	3	clerk	24	
Y	McNamara Thomas F	3	laborer	64	

18

Hillside Place—Continued

	Z	Johnson John F	3	retired	72	490 Medford
1732						
	A	Bower Dorothy—†	4	housewife	33	here
	B	Bower Harold J	4	agent	38	"
	C	Breen Bridget—†	4	maid	41	"
	D	McKay Margaret—†	4	housekeeper	72	"
	E	Dionne Alfred	5	checker	39	"
	F	Dionne Martha—†	5	housewife	39	"
	G	Stull Sadie—†	5	messenger	64	"
	H	Pike Lillian—†	5	cashier	49	"

Kingston Place

	K	Donahue Irene—†	1	operator	40	here
	L	Donahue James F	1	welder	39	"
	M	Regan Frank C	1	bartender	50	"
	N	Sullivan Daniel	2	U S A	28	
	O	Sullivan John F	2	"	25	
	P	Todd Archie W	2	guard	60	"
	R	Todd Francis T	2	U S A	22	"
	S	Todd John J	2	"	20	"
	T	Todd Margaret—†	2	housewife	55	"
	U	Todd William	2	U S A	31	

Kingston Street

	V	Boyle Irving	2	laborer	22	here
	W	Boyle Susan—†	2	at home	54	"
	X	Farrell William	2	laborer	57	Somerville
	Y	Rondeau Nellie—†	4	at home	55	here
	Z	Dolber Celia—†	4	housewife	46	"
1733						
	A	Dolber John G	4	U S A	22	
	B	McManus Philip	4	baker	44	"
	C	Green Elizabeth—†	6	laundress	56	47 Perkins
	D	Green Myron	6	laborer	31	47 "
	F	Lundy Francis	8	"	50	here
	G	Lundy Mary—†	8	housewife	50	"
	H	*Flaherty Barbara—†	8	"	37	"
	K	Flaherty John J	8	laborer	40	"
	L	Noyes Sadie—†	10	housewife	47	"

Kingston Street—Continued

M	Dow Charles	10	timekeeper	30		39 Cambridge
N	Dow Doris—†	10	housewife	28		39 "
O	Barry Mary—†	11	"	80		here
P	Milleravage John J	11	student	22		"
R	Sparks Paul V	11	U S A	22		"
S	Richards Georgianna—†	12	housewife	30		"
T	Richards John J	12	laborer	30		"
U	Callahan John	12	conductor	50		"
V	Callahan Mary—†	12	at home	86		"
W	Kilcourse Margaret—†	12	housewife	52		"
X	Junta Agnes E—†	13	"	43		
Y	Junta John A	13	U S A	22		
Z	Junta Josephine A—†	13	packer	20		"
	1734					
A	Junta Samuel	13	laborer	55		"
B	Ames Frank	14	"	65		Maine
C	Ames Jeanette M—†	14	waitress	65		"
D	Ducharme Alfred F	14	molder	39		here
E	*Ducharme Marie—†	14	housewife	39		"
F	Sullivan Nora E—†	15	"	36		"
G	Sullivan Patrick J	15	laborer	46		"
H	O'Connell John	15	welder	30		51 Cambridge
K	O'Connell Mary—†	15	packer	21		51 "
L	O'Connell Patrick	15	machinist	53		51 "
M	Tierney Joseph H	16	policeman	42		here
N	Tierney Mary—†	16	housewife	38		"
O	Cullity Daniel	17	clerk	45		"
P	Cullity Marion—†	17	housewife	43		"
R	McGahey Anna—†	18	"	57		
S	McGahey Matilda—†	18	clerk	48		
T	McGahey Robert	18	floorlayer	53		"
U	McGahey William	18	laborer	55		
V	Constantine Mary A—†	19	housewife	37		"
W	Constantine William J	19	foreman	37		"
X	Conway Daniel D	19	fireman	65		
Y	Conway Daniel J	19	U S A	33		
Z	Conway Veronica R—†	19	clerk	22		
	1735					
A	Callahan Michael	21	retired	73		Somerville
B	Carlson Albert	21	carpenter	33		here
C	Carlson Mary—†	21	housewife	34		"

Kingston Street—Continued

D	Gannon Catherine—†	21	housewife	70	here
E	Kenefick Michael	21	retired	68	"
F	Mahoney Jeremiah	21	laborer	65	Everett
G	White Michael	21	retired	78	here
K	Dever George E	26	laborer	21	"
L	Dever Hugh	26	"	62	"
M	Dever Mary—†	26	housewife	52	"
H	Doherty Alice—†	26	at home	55	"
N	Shea Daniel	26	retired	75	
O	Shea Mary—†	26	at home	77	"
P	DeGrasse Charles	28	U S N	20	3 Haverhill
R	DeGrasse Mildred—†	28	housewife	43	3 "
S	Doherty Catherine—†	28	waitress	22	48 Lincoln
T	McCarthy Beatrice—†	28	packer	43	48 "

Main Street

U	Lynch Mary M—†	474	at home	32	79 Pearl
V	Lynch Owen G	474	laundrywkr	27	79 "
W	Cassell Catherine E—†	474	housewife	48	here
X	Cassell Frederick J	474	chauffeur	45	"
Y	Gerry Catherine A—†	474	at home	38	"
Z	McIntosh John J	474	retired	42	

1736

A	McIntosh Sarah A—†	474	at home	68	"
B	Couture Bertha M—†	474	"	50	
C	Couture Louis	474	laborer	37	
D	Connors Edward L	474	welder	47	
E	Kelty Julia A—†	480	at home	59	"
F	McLaughlin Helen—†	480	stenographer	22	"
G	McLaughlin Margaret—†	480	U S A	24	New Mexico
H	Carton John	480	blacksmith	65	here
K	Carton Mary E—†	480	housewife	65	"
L	McGrath James L	482	U S A	21	"
M	McGrath Margaret M—†	482	housewife	51	"
N	McGrath William J	482	retired	54	
O	Daly John T	482	driller	52	
P	Daly Lola M—†	482	housewife	40	"
R	Daly Lola M—†	482	WAC	21	
S	Upton Etta—†	482	clerk	50	
U	Tolan Bridget—†	487	housewife	63	"

Main Street—Continued

v	Tolan John J	487	U S A	30	here
w	Tolan Martin	487	laborer	62	"
x	Tolan Mary—†	487	defense wkr	25	"
z	Scales George P	488	seaman	23	

1737

A	Scales John T	488	laborer	67	
B	Scales John T, jr	488	U S A	36	"
c	Scales Leo J	488	laborer	32	
D	Scales Mildred M—†	488	housewife	66	"
E	Charbonnier Francis	488	machinist	30	"
F	Charbonnier Margaret—†	488	housewife	67	"
G	Charbonnier Mildred—†	488	at home	24	"
H	Charbonnier Phillip F	488	retired	77	
K	Murphy Hugh F	488A	chauffeur	44	"
L	Murphy Mary—†	488A	housewife	41	"
M	Murphy Peter J	488A	B F D	46	
N	Myers Frances T—†	488A	packer	22	"
O	Noonan Annie—†	488A	housewife	47	"
P	Noonan John F	488A	U S N	23	
R	Noonan Joseph T	488A	electrician	22	"
s	Newell Catherine A—†	489	housewife	72	"
T	Newell Chauncy P	489	dairyman	64	"

1738

B	Cleveland Lillian—†	496	housewife	27	"
c	DeFelice Frank	496	laborer	48	
D	DeFelice Helen—†	496	housewife	45	"
E	Kelly Margaret A—†	496	at home	46	"
F	Beechin Gertrude E—†	496	clerk	22	
G	Beechin Mary—†	496	housewife	45	"
H	Beechin Willis R	496	longshoreman	51	"
L	DeCoste Helen—†	496	at home	38	Everett
M	Mack Delia—†	496	"	55	here
N	Bolts Richard	496	laborer	65	"
R	Ferguson Charles	496	"	42	"
s	Ferguson Ethel—†	496	housewife	40	"
T	Nugent Joseph	496	chauffeur	45	"
U	O'Malley Florence—†	496	housewife	37	39 Cambridge
v	O'Malley Walter	496	laborer	20	39 "
Y	Andrew William	497	rubberworker	43	3 Charles
z	McKinnon Ethel C—†	497	housewife	45	3 "

1739

A	McKinnon William	497	sandblaster	47	3 "

Main Street—Continued

B	Leonard Patricia—†	497	housewife	41	401 Main
C	Leonard William	497	bartender	45	401 "
D	O'Leary John W	497	chauffeur	27	here
E	O'Leary Robert E	497	"	20	"
F	O'Leary Ruth A—†	497	waitress	47	"
G	O'Leary Ruth A—†	497	"	21	"
H	Andrea Anthony J	497	electrician	28	"
K	Andrea Gertrude M—†	497	housewife	25	"
L	Meyer Ruth G—†	497	machinist	27	"
M	Small Josephine—†	497	housekeeper	62	"
N	Pike Charles W	497	milkman	25	"
O	Pike Mary H—†	497	housewife	22	"
T	Bodoin Catherine A—†	503	"	57	
U*	Bodoin Robert A	503	chauffeur	58	"
V	Murray George	503	mechanic	49	"
W	Murray Mabel E—†	503	housewife	37	"
X	Smith Grace—†	503	"	45	47 Russell
Y	Smith Howard	503	shipper	50	47 "
Z	Ropple Catherine E—†	503	housewife	60	here
	1740				
A	Ropple Florence L—†	503	packer	31	
B	Ropple Joseph L	503	retired	77	
C	Ropple Marie G—†	503	tel operator	33	"
D	McDaniel George H	503	shipwright	59	"
E	McDaniel George H, jr	503	welder	22	"
F	McDaniel Margaret E—†	503	operator	26	"
G	McDaniel Sarah E—†	503	housewife	58	"
H	Macauley Frank D	503	carpenter	46	"
K	Macauley Hattie E—†	503	housewife	45	"
L	Macauley Metta L—†	503	clerk	20	
Y	Studley Frederick B	516A	laborer	58	
Z	Studley Mary H—†	516A	housewife	56	"
	1741				
A	Studley Rita F—†	516A	at home	24	"
D	Macomber Catherine—†	522	housewife	54	"
E	Macomber Edward	522	laborer	50	
F	Macomber Irene—†	522	at home	22	"
	1742				
P	Mackesey Edward	653	U S A	27	
R	Mackesey Margaret—†	653	nurse	24	
S	Sheehan Catherine J—†	653	housewife	59	"
T	Sheehan Gertrude—†	653	packer	21	"

23

Main Street—Continued

U	Sheehan James F	653	U S A	27	here
V	Sheehan Leo J	653	"	27	"
W	Sheehan Thomas J	653	laborer	59	"
X	Flavin Joseph T	655	"	39	
Y	Young Louis	655	retired	75	
Z	Ezrow Daisy—†	655	housewife	55	"
1743					
A	Ezrow Philip	655	cleaner	55	
G	Ragusa Gabriel	662	chauffeur	35	"

Medford Street

W	Shea Mathilda—†	502	at home	60	here
X	Joyce Agnes V—†	504	stenographer	48	"
Y	Joyce Raymond S	504	laborer	57	"
Z	Meehan Matilda—†	506	at home	62	"
1744					
A	Guittarr Eleanor F—†	508	"	35	
B	Guittarr William E	508	salesman	35	"
c*Walsh Leo J		510	laborer	40	"
D	Walsh Margaret—†	510	at home	38	"
E	Murray Margaret—†	512	clerk	55	
F	Haggie Mary C—†	514	packer	21	
G	Haggie Mary J—†	514	housewife	51	"
H	Haggie William W	514	laborer	50	
K	Dillon Anastasia—†	516	at home	69	"
L	Sullivan Alice M—†	516	"	27	
M	Sullivan William H	516	U S N	28	
o*Sullivan Catherine—†		528	at home	33	"
P	Sullivan Dennis	528	baker	41	
R	Lutton Violet M—†	528	at home	48	"
S	O'Neal Harold E	528	laborer	49	58 Chappie
T	O'Neal Ruth M—†	528	at home	43	58 "
U	Fitzpatrick Mary—†	530	bookkeeper	42	here
V	Fitzpatrick William	530	auditor	50	"
Y	Andrews Dorothy M—†	537	at home	31	4 Marcella
Z	Andrews Edward A	537	inspector	21	here
1745					
a*Andrews Helen M—†		537	at home	57	"
B	Andrews John J	537	U S A	30	

Medford Street—Continued

c	Andrews Paul L	537	laborer	34	4 Marcella
D	Thomas John	537	U S A	27	here
E	Thomas Lucy—†	537	at home	25	"
F	Pentowski Anthony J	539	laborer	24	"
G	Pentowski Eva M—†	539	at home	55	"
H	Pentowski Mary E—†	539	clerk	21	"
K	Pentowski Stanley S	539	electrician	28	"
L	Pentowski Stephen S	539	retired	55	
M	Jenolis John	539	laborer	54	
N	Burke Julia—†	541	clerk	45	
O	Callahan Julia—†	541	at home	62	"
P	Shea Roger	541	U S A	26	
R	McGowan James P	541	laborer	39	
S	McGowan Peter	541	U S A	44	
T	Flint George H	543	laborer	34	
U	Flint Sophie T—†	543	at home	29	"
X	Berkowitch Dora—†	545	"	54	
Y	Berkowitch Joseph	545	blacksmith	65	"
z*	Jerasitis Blanche—†	545	at home	57	"
	1746				
A	Jarasitis William	545	laborer	59	
C	Bowman Elizabeth—†	547	at home	50	"
D	Bowman John	547	laborer	21	
E	Bowman Marion—†	547	at home	23	"
F	Bowman Walter	547	welder	61	
G	Juliano James J	548½	coppersmith	44	"
H	Juliano Lucy B—†	548½	at home	45	"
K	Juliano Mary—†	548½	"	78	
L	Rudilosso Letterio	548½	laborer	55	

Neal Court

O	McLaughlin Andrew	1	warehouse	38	here
P	McLaughlin B Theresa—†	1	housewife	48	"
R	James Margaret F—†	6	"	42	Somerville
S	James Wilfred G	6	laborer	48	"
T	Pasanio Margaret—†	6	housewife	23	Connecticut
U	Kloman Conrad	7	waiter	52	6 Kingston
V	Sherman Rita—†	7	at home	45	6 "
X	Dow Agnes—†	9	housewife	60	13 Charles St pl

25

Page.	Letter.	Full Name.	Residence, Jan. 1, 1944.	Occupation.	Supposed Age.	Reported Residence, Jan. 1, 1943. Street and Number.

Neal Court—Continued

	Y	Dow Joseph J	9	U S A	33	13 Charles St pl
	Z	Dow Paul J	9	U S N	23	13 "
1747						
	A	Walsh Eileen—†	9	waitress	29	13 "

North Short Street Place

	E	Liogier Peter	3	waiter	64	here
	G	Catania Annie—†	6	housewife	55	"
	H	Catania Guido	6	U S A	22	"

Parker Street

	L	Hall John M	2	retired	74	here
	M	Hall Sarah A—†	2	housewife	63	"
	N	Myers Patrick J	2	retired	70	"
	O	Roberts Louis	2	machinist	66	"
	P	Parkes George	3	boilermaker	63	"
	R	Parkes Martha—†	3	housewife	69	"
	S	Herra Harry J	5	inspector	65	"
	T	Herra Mary M—†	5	housewife	63	"
	U	Herra William E	5	U S A	30	"
	V	Leary John J	5	fireman	53	..
	W	Pierce Elizabeth—†	6	factoryhand	58	"
	X	Pierce William G	6	U S A	28	
	Y	Roust Edward D	6	"	23	"
	Z	Roust John J	6	"	21	"
1748						
	A	Roust Richard J	6	operator	57	"
	B	Roust William J	6	U S A	27	
	C	Rogers Benjamin	7	laborer	49	
	D	Rogers Sophia—†	7	housewife	44	"
	E	McIntire Etta M—†	7	"	59	"
	F	Bryson Gertrude—†	8	welder	21	Somerville
	G	Bryson Leo	8	chauffeur	35	"
	H	Curtin Daniel	8	U S A	20	here
	K	Curtin Edna—†	8	housewife	57	Somerville
	L	Curtin Thomas, jr	8	U S A	24	"
	M	Jones George W	8	operator	58	"
	N	Ployer Bertha G—†	8	housewife	45	here
	O	Ployer Walter	8	laborer	48	"

Parker Street—Continued

P	Skillings Margaret A—†	8	housewife	63	Somerville
R	*Kelly Agnes G—†	9	"	33	here
S	*Kelly John F	9	salesman	38	"
T	Martineau Eugene	9	laborer	60	7 Parker
U	Martineau Marie—†	9	housewife	57	7 "
W	Snow Alfred J	10	foreman	43	here
X	Snow Evelyn D—†	10	housewife	45	"
Y	Bonin Amelia—†	10	at home	78	"
Z	Murray Ella—†	11	housewife	63	"

1749

A	Murray James	11	U S A	25	
B	Murray Joseph	11	"	23	
C	Murray William	11	laborer	27	
D	DiDonato Pasquale	12	barber	46	
E	DiDonato Teresa—†	12	housewife	36	"
F	DiDonato Florenzo	12	laborer	45	"
G	DiDonato Venerando—†	12	housewife	35	"
H	Whitney Alice M—†	13	"	50	
K	Whitney Catherine—†	13	SPAR	22	
L	Whitney Claire—†	13	"	24	"
M	Whitney Clarence	13	engineer	50	"
N	Whitney Francis I	13	seaman	25	"
R	Cronin Catherine F—†	15	beautician	24	"
S	Cronin Margaret T—†	15	at home	71	"
T	Dowd Mary E—†	15	metalworker	33	Dedham
U	Mason Arthur J	15	chauffeur	32	here
V	Mason Eleanor L—†	15	nurse	29	"
W	Mason John J	15	metalworker	63	"
X	Mason John J, jr	15	U S A	28	
Y	Mason Mary C—†	15	housewife	58	"
Z	Mason Robert F	15	U S A	34	"

1750

A	McDermott Frederick H	16	B F D	57	"
B	McDermott Mary—†	16	housewife	50	"
C	Stokes Lester W	16	seaman	31	"
D	Stokes Veronica R—†	16	housewife	29	Somerville
E	Redmond Bridget M—†	17	"	60	here
F	Redmond John J	17	rigger	50	"
G	Lyons Annie—†	17	housewife	58	"
H	Lyons Jeremiah	17	engineer	60	"
K	Daley Frank J	18	cooper	74	7 Chapman

Parker Street—Continued

	L	Daley Margaret—†	18	at home	29	7 Chapman
	M	Daley William C	18	laborer	32	7 "
	S	Flynn John F	20	retired	61	here
	T	Flynn John F	20	clerk	27	"
	U	Flynn Margaret G—†	20	housewife	54	"
	V	Donegan Thomas	20	storekeeper	60	"
	W	O'Leary Daniel	20	metalworker	27	"
	X	O'Leary Jeremiah	20	electrician	24	"
	Y	O'Leary Mary—†	20	housewife	57	"
	Z	Johnson Enfred	21	chauffeur	48	"

1751

	A	Kolifrath Albert C	21	welder	40	
	B	Kolifrath Margaret M—†	21	housewife	38	"
	C	Hegarty William	22	clerk	50	Somerville
	D	Costello Patrick	22	longshoreman	40	Milton
	E	*Reardon Helen—†	22	housewife	38	37 Walker
	F	Reardon Jeremiah	22	longshoreman	42	37 "
	G	Calandra Joseph	22	U S N	34	New Jersey
	H	Calandra Mary—†	22	housewife	29	here
	K	Morris Alfred F	23	guard	44	"
	L	Morris Alice M—†	23	clerk	37	"
	M	Morris Mary—†	23	housewife	68	"
	N	Connell Thomas	24	machinist	42	New York
	O	Murray Francis L	24	"	44	here
	P	*Murray Mary E—†	24	housewife	72	"
	R	Wayts Francis	24	guard	46	Salem
	S	St Louis Albertine—†	26	housewife	35	here
	T	St Louis Rudolph	26	tester	34	"
	U	McCarthy Johanna—†	27	housekeeper	29	"
	V	Whooley John	27	laborer	44	"
	W	Whooley Mary B—†	27	housewife	33	"
	X	O'Brien Catherine—†	27	"	47	"
	Y	O'Brien John F	27	machinist	25	"
	Z	Harrington James	' 27	checker	38	"

1752

	A	St Louis Irene—†	28	housewife	26	Lawrence
	B	St Louis Rene J	28	metalworker	32	"
	C	Rudge John H	28	electrician	65	here
	D	Hennessy Thomas	29	retired	79	"
	E	Maisey Bertram G	29	manager	43	"
	F	Maisey Mary E—†	29	housewife	43	"

Parker Street—Continued

G	Gile Albert T	30	retired	71	15 Brighton
H	Reynolds Austin H	30	cook	64	15 "
K	Waters Christina—†	30	housewife	40	here
L	Brennick Charles F	31	pedler	31	"
M	Brennick Josephine E—†	31	nurse	28	"
N	Aylesbury Flora M—†	32	housewife	67	"
O	Cushman Roderick J	32	operator	55	"
P	*Collins Elizabeth—†	32	housewife	35	"
R	*Collins Timothy A	32	molder	47	
W	McGlinchey Charles H	33	mechanic	39	"
X	McGlinchey Margaret M–†	33	housewife	37	"
Y	McGlinchey Isabel—†	36	maid	59	
Z	Smith Charles	36	clerk	56	"

1753

A	Farrell Ella—†	36	packer	39	..
B	Farrell George	36	U S A	24	
C	Malone Edward	36	shipper	39	"
D	Malone Samantha—†	36	housewife	49	"
E	Kiley James	37	fireman	72	"
F	Kiley John T	37	chauffeur	41	"
G	Ryan Anna R—†	37	at home	28	"
H	Ryan Helen B—†	37	housewife	30	"
K	Ryan James J	37	U S A	25	
L	Ryan William L	37	chauffeur	32	"
M	Lehan James	38	chef	49	
N	Lehan Mary A—†	38	housewife	34	"
O	Chapman Alice—†	39	folder	22	Somerville
P	Chapman Charles H	39	chauffeur	50	"
R	Chapman Margaret V—†	39	housewife	51	"
S	King Margaret—†	39	packer	24	"
T	McGrath Helen—†	39	housewife	27	117 Cambridge
U	McGrath Neil	39	laborer	29	117 "
V	*Lynch Ida—†	40	housewife	46	here
[W	Lynch John J	40	rubberworker	55	"
X	Munroe Elizabeth—†	40	housewife	68	"

Perkins Street

Y	Rochford Charles F	13	electrician	23	254 Medford
Z	Rochford Edward T	13	tinsmith	43	254 "

1754

Perkins Street—Continued

A	Rochford Irene—†	13	housewife	45	254 Medford
B	Rochford John J	13	shoeworker	54	254 "
C	Rochford William S	13	U S A	25	254 "
D	Connolly Patrick M	13	laborer	52	Somerville
E	Folan Nora—†	13	housekeeper	53	here
F	Mishniewicz Claire H—†	13	housewife	22	"
G	Mishniewicz Joseph	13	machinist	22	"
L	Baker John J	19	woodworker	60	"
M	Conway Joseph	19	longshoreman	48	"
N	O'Leary John	19	painter	30	"
O	Reed William	19	"	46	
V	Schofield Charles D	40	U S A	36	
W	Schofield Frances A—†	40	housewife	36	"
X	Nault Maretta—†	40	manager	32	"
Y	Taylor Bradlee M	42	shipper	28	
Z	Taylor Olive M—†	42	housewife	29	"

1755

B	Richards Clarence A	47	carpenter	53	"
c*	Richards Daisy R—†	47	housewife	34	"
D	Smith Marjorie—†	47	clerk	47	
E	Richards Howard D	49	chauffeur	42	"
f*	Richards Louise—†	49	housewife	36	"
G	Thomas Etta M—†	49	"	42	
H	Thomas Sidney B	49	roofer	54	
M	Hegarty Helen—†	62	housewife	28	"
N	Hegarty Joseph	62	welder	33	
O	Toomey James F	64	clerk	34	
P	Toomey Ruth—†	64	housewife	35	"
R	Fisher Esther—†	71	housekeeper	60	"
S	Lozier Blanche—†	71	"	50	"
T	O'Brien Anna—†	71	waitress	27	"
U	O'Brien Walter	71	chauffeur	32	"
V	Griffith Hilda—†	71	housewife	24	"
W	Griffith Robert	71	clerk	24	"
X	Welte Lea—†	71	typist	20	Missouri
Y	Welte Lloyd	71	U S A	20	Illinois
Z	Raye Joseph	71	clerk	26	here

1756

A	Raye Mary—†	71	waitress	24	"
B	Winam Roger	71	mechanic	42	"

Perkins Street—Continued

c	Glidden Gertrude—†	71	waitress	36	here
d	Wright Leona—†	71	seamstress	55	"
e	Corcoran Michael	71	retired	73	"
f	Shea Walter	71	longshoreman	34	"
g	Wormell Elmer	71	chauffeur	36	"
h	Rogers Lawrence	71	engineer	34	New York
k	Munson Fred	71	musician	58	Somerville
l	Thompson Frank	71	chauffeur	42	here
m	Burke Helena W—†	72	housewife	55	"
n	Burke John	72	attorney	59	"
o	Keane Margaret—†	72	maid	51	Somerville

1757   Sever Street

x	Driscoll Jeremiah	4	welder	35	here
y	Driscoll Margaret—†	4	housewife	37	"
z	Clifford James J	4	U S A	26	Somerville

1758

a	Clifford Mary J—†	4	housewife	22	"
b	Douglas Antoinette—†	4	"	21	"
e	Collins Francis P	6	rigger	28	here
f	Collins Helen C—†	6	housewife	27	"
g	Hookailo Florence I—†	8	"	25	"
h	Riley Ernest F	8	chauffeur	44	"
k	Riley Lavina M—†	8	housewife	43	"
l	Conway Christine—†	10	"	27	651 Main
m	Krajewski Frank	10	molder	36	here
n	Krajewski Mary—†	10	housewife	33	"
o	Givern Altrua	12	counterman	35	Texas
p	Leary John F	12	plumber	58	here
r	*McKernan Patrick	12	retired	61	"
s	O'Neil John F	12	clerk	54	"
t	Whitney Elma R—†	12	housewife	84	"
u	Belcher Edward J	16	chauffeur	28	"
v	Kelley Bertha M—†	16	housewife	47	"
w	Kelley Joseph F	16	U S C G	22	"
x	Kelley Joseph P	16	drawtender	48	"
y	Neville Pauline—†	16	housewife	80	"
z	Cronin Nellie—†	16	at home	70	"

1759

a	Long Ellen—†	16	housewife	68	"

Sever Street—Continued

B	Meckle Edward J	16	laborer	65	Cambridge
C	Kerrigan Margaret A—†	16	waitress	28	here
D	Kerrigan Mary—†	16	housewife	47	"
F	Frank Robert R	20	U S N	25	Newfoundland
G	Stone Amos R	20	U S A	22	380 Main
H	Stone Anna T—†	20	housewife	21	380 "
L	McMahon Beatrice D—†	22	nurse	31	here
M	McMahon Leo R	22	chauffeur	31	"
N	Glover Florence—†	22	housewife	40	Wakefield
O	Glover Fred A	22	laborer	44	"
P	Cain Francis E	24	metalworker	46	Somerville
R	Catano Ann—†	24	clerk	30	here
S	Keenan Bessie J—†	24	housewife	46	"
T	Keenan Frederick	24	U S A	25	"
U	Keenan Michael M	24	ironworker	55	"
V	Litchfield Henrietta—†	24	at home	75	"
W	Styles Naaman	24	laborer	59	
X	Allen Fred	26	engineer	57	"
Y	Callahan Phillip	26	shipper	44	"
Z	Harrington Daniel	26	laborer	40	47 Sever
	1760				
A	McNerland Henry	26	retired	48	411 Main
B	O'Keefe Peter	26	warehouse	39	here
C	Quinn John	26	milkman	53	Quincy
D	*Romkey Arthur	26	laborer	58	here
E	*Romkey Helen—†	26	housewife	53	"
F	Young Alfred	26	chef	64	"
G	Carter Frances E—†	28	housewife	23	"
H	Lacey Arthur	28	chauffeur	38	"
K	Lacey Eileen—†	28	housewife	34	"
L	Murray Agnes G—†	28	"	49	
M	Murray Evelyn M—†	28	clerk	24	
N	Murray Francis W	28	carpenter	51	"
O	Carney John	30	chauffeur	52	"
P	Fletcher George	30	laborer	45	45 Sever
R	Lally Patrick	30	lumberman	71	Somerville
S	McMillan John	30	trainman	63	32 Sever
T	Mills Frederick J	30	retired	74	here
U	Shea Timothy	30	operator	49	Somerville
V	Smart Ernest	30	U S N	21	New York
X	Twomey Francis J	30	chauffeur	49	here

Sever Street—Continued

w	Twomey Gertrude M—†	30	housewife	48	here
y	Bourke Ernest L	32	brakeman	59	Somerville
z	Eskey Michael	32	storekeeper	49	here
	1761				
A	Gledell Phyllis—†	32	housekeeper	35	"
B	Perry Gerald S	32	glazier	60	"
c	Poole Harold	32	laborer	37	N Hampshire
D	Daly Charles	34	proprietor	43	here
E	Davison Charles	34	metalworker	74	"
F	Feeney Michael	34	laborer	40	"
G	Grant William	34	watchman	68	32 Sever
H	Hanneberry Martin	34	laborer	40	Newton
K	McSweeney Dennis	34	retired	71	here
L	McSweeney Mary—†	34	housekeeper	73	"
M	Pickett Richard	34	rigger	68	38 Sever
N	O'Brien Annie T—†	36	housewife	54	here
o	O'Brien Margaret C—†	36	secretary	24	"
P	O'Brien Mary A—†	36	clerk	20	"
R	O'Brien Timothy J	36	foreman	55	"
s	Hickey Mary L—†	37	housewife	69	"
T	LaVecta Albert	38	chef	43	New Bedford
U	Rock William	38	chauffeur	64	Somerville
v	Scanlon James F	38	laborer	29	here
w	Scanlon Margaret M—†	38	housewife	67	"
x	Flynn Esther A—†	41	"	25	"
y	Flynn Thomas J	41	welder	26	
z	Flynn Thomas R	41	proprietor	47	"
	1762				
A	Lynch Leo D	41	chauffeur	28	"
B	Lynch Marie E—†	41	housewife	28	"
c	Cannon John G	43	clerk	63	
D	Sheehan Francis M—†	43	housewife	49	"
E	Sheehan John J	43	U S A	20	
F	McGlinchey Catherine A—†	43	housewife	56	"
G	McGlinchey John J	43	clerk	57	
H	Charlson Katherine A—†	45	at home	73	"
K	Corwin Alice E—†	45	"	73	
L	Corwin Francis H	45	B F D	32	
M	Corwin Mark C	45	clerk	46	
N	Corwin Mary E—†	45	housewife	51	"
o	Corwin Walter W	45	B F D	52	

Page.	Letter.	FULL NAME.	Residence, Jan. 1, 1944.	Occupation.	Supposed Age.	Reported Residence, Jan. 1, 1943. Street and Number.

Sever Street—Continued

	P	Corwin Walter W, jr	45	U S A	21	here
	R	Newell George A	45	mariner	29	"
	S	Newell Norma E—†	45	housewife	24	"
	T	Hanley Bridget A—†	46	"	79	
	U	Hanley Joseph M	46	garageman	54	"
	V	Newell Francis R	47	mariner	30	"
	W	Newell Joy L—†	47	housewife	26	"
	X	Ropple Mary E—†	47	"	36	88 Ferrin
	Y	Ropple William T	47	watchman	46	88 "
	Z	Ropple William T, jr	47	U S A	21	88 "

1763

	A	Noonan Jeremiah	48	retired	73	here
	B	Noonan John E	48	pilot	27	"
	C	Noonan Margaret E—†	48	stenographer	30	"
	D	Noonan Mary A—†	48	housewife	68	"
	E	Noonan Mary E—†	48	supervisor	28	"
	F	Galvin Edward L	49	U S A	39	"
	G	Galvin Helen C—†	49	supervisor	39	"
	H	Riley Margaret C—†	52	housewife	52	"
	K	Riley Owen R	52	fireman	60	"

Sherman Square

	L	Arnold Walter A	2	retired	77	here
	M	Bassett Annie—†	2	housewife	70	"
	N	Bassett Charles B	2	chauffeur	37	"
	O	Stockton Ella—†	2	at home	72	"
	P	Waite Nellie—†	3	"	76	
	R	Littlefield Elizabeth—†	3	"	70	
	V	Bradbury Charles H	5	U S A	28	
	W	Bradbury Harry	5	machinist	68	"
	X	Bradbury Louise—†	5	stenographer	27	"
	Y	Bradbury Susanna—†	5	housewife	63	"
	Z	O'Keefe Grace—†	6	"	33	

1764

	A	O'Keefe James	6	expressman	33	"
	B	Ripley Alice M—†	6	clerk	39	"
	C	Corrigan Nora—†	7	at home	58	"
	D	Galvin Catherine—†	7	packer	23	
	E	Kinsella Eileen—†	7	at home	25	"
	O	Kennealy Margaret—†	11	"	76	"

Sherman Square—Continued

s	Barry Catherine M—†	12	at home	74	here	
u	Smith Flora F—†	12A	dressmaker	50	"	
v	Smith Mary L—†	12A	"	48	"	

1765 Short Street

c	Shea Catherine M—†	8	factoryhand	23	here
d	Shea Rita A—†	8	operator	21	"
e	Smicer Esther J—†	10	bookkeeper	47	"
f	Smicer William B	10	metalworker	45	"
g	Jaworski Antonia—†	12	housewife	67	"
h	*Jaworski Fukash	12	laborer	75	

Short Street Court

k	Welch Elizabeth F—†	1	housewife	51	here
l	Welch Frederick T	1	laborer	61	"
m	Hannon Elinor F—†	1	housewife	40	"
n	Hannon Henry J	1	laborer	41	
o	Coakley Dennis E	1	"	53	
p	Connell Harold V	1	"	43	
r	Connell Mary C—†	1	housewife	38	"
s	Ford Henrietta—†	2	"	53	
t	Ford Irving D	2	rigger	54	
u	*Callahan John	3	laborer	35	
v	Johnson William E	3	retired	76	
x	Moran Cecilia M—†	5	housewife	28	"
y	Moran Francis J	5	laborer	35	
z	O'Rourke Anna M—†	5	housewife	47	"

1766

a	O'Rourke Edward P	5	laborer	47	"
b	Kiley Ella F—†	6	housekeeper	52	"

Lightning Source UK Ltd.
Milton Keynes UK
UKHW010402271118
332995UK00013B/1249/P